SOUNDINGS

Music in the Twentieth Century

SOUNDINGS

Music in the Twentieth Century

GLENN WATKINS

SCHIRMER BOOKS
A Division of Macmillan, Inc.
NEW YORK

COLLIER MACMILLAN PUBLISHERS
LONDON

Schirmer Books
A Division of Macmillan, Inc.
866 Third Avenue, New York, N.Y. 10022

Collier Macmillan Canada, Inc.

Library of Congress Catalog Card Number: 87-13115

Printed in the United States of America

printing number
1   2   3   4   5   6   7   8   9   10

Library of Congress Cataloging-in-Publication Data

Watkins, Glenn, 1927–
Soundings : music in the twentieth century.
   1. Music—20th century—History and criticism.
I. Title.
 ML197.W44   1987   780'.904   87-13115
 ISBN 0-02-873290-1

For Janey
with whom I first discovered music as a child

CONTENTS

vii

PART 5: EMERGING NATIONAL ASPIRATIONS: 1910–1945

*PART 7: POSTWAR SERIALISM AND
THE RISE OF AN INTERNATIONAL AVANT-GARDE*

PART 8: THE QUEST FOR NEW SOUNDS

PREFACE

It is a fairly tall order to talk about a century of music—any century. But when the terminus of the period in question purports to take into account last night's review (or next year's premiere), then the task is one obviously suited to fools. I would propose, however, that the difficulty is not limited to sensing the state of affairs in the 1980s but that, indeed, a determination of the enduring values of the late 1960s and 1970s still awaits the consensus that only time can provide. We know this from our memory of the early 1950s, when claims for total serialism as the only wave of the future were being forwarded, a claim that was soon drowned out by a chorus of alternative makers.

The story is thus much more readily told and interpreted through the period until World War II, less readily so for the fascinating time that followed, when stylistic and aesthetic options compounded almost yearly. For the period since 1950 we must frequently be content to report and to connect. In fact there is much to report, and this is in itself a very large task.

The idea, however, that history is based upon empirically testable data which provide the ingredients for interpretation through the search for context (or multiple contexts) should not diguise the fact that synthesis, at whatever distance, is largely an illusion. Evidence and its assessment do not inevitably lead to inescapable conclusions, and the reader of histories should be as aware as the historian that the telling of history is generally only an attempt to create a consistent fiction. In an attempt to balance the evidence and its exegesis, the author has sought to promote the former in the guise of a good story and to subsume the latter through the choice of materials and their organization. Thus the personalities and repertoires that are presented already involve an interpretation which says more about our current view of the matters at hand than any lengthy critique. In addition, however, further interpretation of a highly provocative nature is continually provided through the citation of numerous composers' opinions of their own work and its perceived relation to others. No period in musical history has been so rich in the recorded testimony of its composers as the twentieth century, and the periodic assemblage and juxtaposition of such views throughout the book makes not so much for a controversy which demands resolution by the historian as an indispensible confrontation of which the reader-listener must be made aware. If the issues have been well chosen and the conflict of attendant philosophies reasonably clearly expounded, then the main task will have been accomplished. History rarely provides answers, only good questions which are relevant to the age.

The present volume is intended, therefore, not as a comprehensive history of music over the past century, but as a delineation, through representative examples, of some of the most important paths that have been struck. The reader who is unaware of this premise may be wary of the seemingly protracted attention given to Mahler and Debussy in the opening sections and judge it to be out of scale with the book as a whole. It will soon be discovered, however, that the approach is not rigorously monographic. Suggestions along the way concerning Mahler's relevance to composers today, such as Berio, Foss, and Crumb; the immediately following appraisal of Schoenberg and Webern to the Mahler tradition; and the more lengthy consideration of Berg's relationship to all three may be used as a fair test of the success or failure of the method and aims that have been attempted throughout. That all of these figures will reappear in later discussions and in different contexts is intended to suggest the variety of issues upon which their careers impinge (e.g., Berg in relation to Mahler, Schoenberg, Ravel, Gershwin, Baudelaire, Neoclassicism, Expressionism, Decadence, folksong, jazz, serialism, rhythmic organization, and *Klangfarbenmelodie*).

In an organizational gambit that seeks to face aesthetic issues and at the same time retain a reasonable chronological order, I have not parried the temptation to invoke the various "isms." Though the idea of studying history through recourse to such labels has been frequently condemned in the past, I have decided not only to employ them without apology, but to attempt to indicate their genesis and the ramifications of such designations through reference to the other arts. This has seemed prudent because the expressions are typically not the confection of the historian but rather a reflection of the artist's credo in an age when the manifesto, the broadsheet, or the journal typically announced the intentions of the avant-garde. These intentions can and must be checked against the work of art, to be sure, and variances between announced aim and result noted. But any judgment of the latter without a knowledge of the former can be a risky business. Ultimately the ism will, properly, fade away as stylistic investigation leads to the discussion of specific pieces whose personalities confirm an increasing independence from any spawning aesthetic. Indeed, throughout history, as soon as the ism has achieved currency, need for the term has diminished and its use has frequently been condemned by its most famous practitioners.

In 1970, Carl Dahlhaus noted that "the idea that aesthetic access to a work is gained through understanding of technique has become a ruling maxim" and judged it "as questionable as many of the pedagogical consequences."[1] Yet the musicologist, recognizing the need to bring the best of the theorist's thinking into the argument, has been beset with problems of how to achieve a homogenous union. A decade later, Dahlhaus, reviewing the Romantics' promotion of the cult of genius, spoke of their view of composition as "fragments of biography".[2] Yet some of the most recent and telling researches into the musical world of Alban Berg, for example, have paid notable attention to the biographical component and have even argued its fundamental importance for an appreciation of his music. From such a personal microcosm the historian can move to the *Zeitgeist* and try to sense the trends of the time, only to be finally stranded with the largest question of all, the philosophical inquiry that aims to address the question of "meaning": not who, what, where, but why and for whom. The notion has understandably been increasingly put forward that the time when a comprehensive overview of a large historical period was possible has now passed, and that, henceforth, discrete studies, currently surfacing at a vigorous rate, will offer the only meaningful discourse, promote further insights, and increasingly mitigate against the possibility of a synthesis of the best available information.

Of necessity in the present attempt at such a synthesis, the portion devoted to biographical detail, cultural context, and artistic interchange varies from section to section as widely as the attention given to general formal questions and, occasionally, more detailed analytical observation. Obviously there is no magic formula for the proportion, and the final choice has frequently been determined by a personal preference based to a large extent on experience in the classroom. The options for enlargement by the reader in one direction or another are, of course, endless. The luxury of the contemporary analytical techniques course that may take up only two or three acknowledged masterworks in an entire semester is denied the presentation at hand; the opportunities offered for seeking out developments and relationships of a wider range, however, are enlarged.

The astronomer is fond of reminding us that to look out into space is to look back in time. It is a much less commonly expressed but equally valid opinion with respect to the perception of works of art. Such a temporal relationship is not only inherent in the meaning of history but in our approach to all creative musical experience: Criticism of even the most recent repertoires is already a report on the past. Thus the task before us, in bringing the story of twentieth-century music up to date, is not only to portray the current status of the art work, whether in the eyes of the connoisseur or the public concertgoer, but to appreciate the conditions that attended its birth. This bifocal view is complex, and current judgment is always colored by the accretion of opinion over the years. The enduring favor accorded a so-called masterwork is, in retrospect, no absolute guide to its value, except as a public commodity. Contrarily, without some sign of currency in the performer's repertoire, the protestations of the specialist-apologist mean little.

The apologists for many of the twentieth-century music surveys of past decades tended to identify a Big Five or Six (Schoenberg, Webern, Berg, Stravinsky, Bartók, Hindemith) and to elevate them to cult status, with all other composers placed in orbit around them. This has for some time now proven to be too narrow a focus. Indeed, these six, who tended to form two orbits of three, only reinforced the idea of a singular Schoenberg-Stravinsky dichotomy, and promoted the notion that the principal choices in the first half of the century revolved only around the aesthetic viewpoints of these two men. Not surprisingly, as apologists for the Big Six diminished, a growing number busied themselves promoting some of the more interesting "lesser" figures. Satie, Ives, and Varèse are good examples of composers who have been enjoined in the rewriting of music history as told by an earlier standard.[3] And for the recent past, partisanship appears to splinter at a seasonal rate so rapid that to report on it is to risk journalism more than criticism.

This volume, then, consists of a set of mutually related studies whose complementary nature should reveal a reasonably complete picture of the most vital movements and figures of twentieth-century music: periodic "soundings," if you will, rather than an excavation of every inch of soil. Such soundings, however, will rarely be able to treat a given work from every angle, so that frequently the aim will be to open windows of recognition which hopefully will be useful for later attempts at increased familiarity. Some readers will note the omission of a rigorous treatment of the vernacular or jazz traditions that in recent decades has increasingly vied for the attention of the musical historian. Partial redress is offered, however, in the repeated consideration of such popular repertoires for the composer of art music. From the world of the cabaret at the turn of the century to the "art of the everyday" defined by *Les Six* to the ragtime revival of the 1960s, its force is noted and its effect judged.

Even among those repertoires that fall within the purview of the present volume, a given person's particular favorite may not be discussed, and in the section that covers the music of the period 1950–1985 the hazards are particularly obvious. The absence or cursory treatment of such significant composers as Adler and Andriessen, Baird and Berry, Cardew and Cooper, Gerhard and Goehr, Hodkinson and Hovhaness, Nono and Nielsen, Orff and Oliveros, Pijper and Powell, Rouse and Rzewski, Spies and Shapey, Tippett and Takemitsu or Weber and Westergaard is something of which I am all too keenly aware. The only rationale for the omission of so many figures of such importance is that the book was written primarily for my students (some of whom are composers) and the literate concertgoer rather than for my many composer friends (who may rightfully feel a twinge of neglect in discovering the absence of their names in the Index). Consequently, this book's most important objective is that the reader be challenged to listen further, to make a personal judgment, and ultimately to expand upon what is presented here. Fortunately, the wide availability of recordings of virtually all the principal works discussed, as well as numerous others of similar merit, makes the challenge a legitimate one. The lengthy, though admittedly highly selective, repertoire and reading lists at the end of each chapter are intended to serve as a guide for further exploration. The numerous titles of works written in the last two decades in particular must be viewed merely as samples drawn from a constantly expanding roster. Its currency I am constantly obliged to check with the composer network whose access to a seemingly limitless underground of scores and tapes is a modern wonder. The age of photocopying and the audiocassette has brought new dimensions to the idea of *publica*tion.

The reader should note that all English translations of foreign language texts are those of the author unless otherwise noted. Quotations from E. W. White, *Stravinsky* and I. Stravinsky and R. Craft, *Conversations. Expositions and Developments. Memories and Commentaries* and *Dialogues and a Diary* are reprinted by permission of the University of California Press and Faber and Faber Ltd.; those from Boulez, *Orientations* by permission of Harvard University Press and Faber and Faber Ltd.

I also wish to express my gratitude to Maribeth Anderson Payne, senior editor at Schirmer, who provided repeated encouragement with respect to the labyrinthine details regarding permissions and other editorial matters, to Glenn Kurtz, editorial assistant, and to Elyse Dubin, managing editor, whose watchful eyes kept the manuscript on course during its production.

Finally, I am pleased to acknowledge the capable assistance of Scott Messing, Susan Cook, Nancy Perloff, Cathy Gordon, Randy Neighbarger, and Brent Fegley, who at various stages of the manuscript were sent in search of numerous details and always returned with more than was requested. To the students in my graduate seminars from whom I continue to learn and to the patient classes who allowed me to try out various repertoires and organizational plans, I can only register my thanks and hope that some of them, recognizing many of the ingredients, will find this version useful.

SOUNDINGS
Music in the Twentieth Century

PART I

VIENNA: 1885–1915

"The twentieth century could not wait fifteen years for a round number; it was born, yelling, in 1885."

Roger Shattuck, *The Banquet Years* (1955)

CHAPTER 1

THE GERMAN ROMANTIC LEGACY

The Path to the New Music, as Webern phrased it, is inevitably marked by signposts from the past. Ingredients that point to the future, however telling and remarkable, are typically appliquéd onto or integrated into a traditional language that provides the foundational voice. As we move into the final years of the twentieth century, it becomes increasingly obvious how fundamental the Romantic legacy has been both to the formation of Modern music in its first blush and to its final flowering. A sense of the continuity of tradition persistently outweighs any sense of the iconoclastic.

This is not to say that there have not been notable changes, only that what at one point may have seemed irrational and incomprehensible may now frequently be seen in a totally different perspective. In this regard it is comforting to remember how those most prominently associated with the seeming destruction of an old order were often the first to deny that they were revolutionaries.

In tracing lines of continuity, musicians have tended to emphasize the role of Claude Debussy (1862–1918) not only as a link between Berlioz (d. 1869) and the new music, but as a principal avenue to events of the early years of the twentieth century. On the other hand, the works of Richard Strauss (1864–1949) and Gustav Mahler (1860–1911) during the same period have typically been seen as post-Wagnerian remnants without the same clarifying potential. The role of their production in the period following Wagner's death in 1883 to about 1910 is, however, indispensible to any comprehension of the events that followed. Moreover, a consideration of the most prominent themes of fin-de-siècle Vienna in particular, both literary and musical, can help to provide a bridge across the seemingly unfathomable abyss of 1909. Schoenberg, Berg, and Webern would have been the first to insist upon the debt.

RICHARD STRAUSS (1864–1949): TONE POEM AND SONG

The revival of the music of Gustav Mahler in the post-World War II period has somewhat obscured the fact that at the turn of the century Richard Strauss was a composer whose prestige could not seriously have been challenged by any living composer other than Claude Debussy. Though Strauss's career was centered in Munich, Berlin, and only for a time in Vienna, his devotion to the idea of Wagner's *Zukunftmusik* (music of the future), Nietzsche's *Also sprach Zarathustra* (1896), and his infatuation with the autobiographical and the concept of the artist as hero (*Ein Heldenleben*, 1898) place him, in many respects, close to the aesthetic of Mahler. Furthermore, the pantheistic note of even so late a work as Strauss's *Alpine Symphony* (1911–1915) is clearly descendant from Mahler's Third (1895–96).

Yet for all of Strauss's belief that "new ideas must search for new forms—this basic principle of Liszt's symphonic works, in which the poetic idea was really the formative element,"[1]—the net result of his extraordinary early tone poems was highly dramatic and effective program music served up in the traditional forms, however freely employed, of sonata (*Tod und Verklärung*, 1889), rondo (*Till Eulenspiegel*, 1895), and variation (*Ein Heldenleben*, 1898). In this, Strauss stood firmly against the critical point of view expressed by Eduard Hanslick (1825–1904) in his *On the Beautiful in Music* (1854). Hanslick, a believer in the abstract formalizations of Brahms, retaliated with some of his most vitriolic pronouncements, charging that Strauss had substituted poetic content for musical content, had become a translator, indeed one of those who "translate badly, unintelligibly, tastelessly, with exaggeration."[2]

Yet Strauss's merging of classic formal principles with narrative proved to be not just an extension of the Romantic predeliction for program music from Beethoven, Berlioz, and Liszt, but also an important ally of Mahler and, though infrequently noted, of Arnold Schoenberg (e.g., *Verklärte Nacht, Pelleas und Melisande, String Quartets No. 1* and 2)[3] and, of course, Schoenberg's pupil, Alban Berg. Also in Strauss's periodic excursions into bitonality (e.g., the B major/C major confrontation, unresolved even at the close of *Zarathustra*; or the modulation from G minor to D minor over a G♭ major pedal chord in the love music of *Ein Heldenleben*); in his continuing Romantic preoccupation with cyclic formal considerations (as in the casting of his *Symphonia domestica*, 1902–3, as a symphony in one movement with four sections); and in his search for plasticity and a chamber music scoring even when dealing with an enormously swollen orchestral apparatus, he reflected or prefigured contemporary attitudes of both Mahler and Schoenberg. For all of Strauss's purported discomfort with the dialectic of sonata form, his sense of proportion and love of clarity was incontestable and allied to his love of Mozart, whose influence (along with Wagner) can be seen from his first to last works. Indeed, the roots of the Neoclassic movement at the turn of the century, as well as its development in the second through fourth decades, can hardly be accurately perceived without Strauss's example.

Strauss's career as a supreme composer of songs was also launched during the period of his first tone poems, and works such as *Zueignung* and *Allerseelen* (1885), *Ruhe, meine Seele* and *Morgen* (1894) confirm his lyric genius and Romantic inclination from the beginning. Not until the advent of *Salome* (1903–5) and *Elektra* (1906–8), however, was there evidence of a composer apparently eager to reject the status quo. Strauss took the musical world to the edge of the precipice with these two operas, and in a startling volte-face followed it with *Der Rosenkavalier* (1909–10). His place in the history books faded, if it did not disappear, with that chapter, but through these works he must be regarded as a seminal figure in the birth of modern music. If after that time he was no longer at the front of the avant-garde, his tangential relation to several prominent aesthetic movements, amongst them Expressionism and Neoclassicism (see p. 312), is unusually clear. The enormous influence of *Salome* above all of his scores, on composers of the early twentieth century demands an extended consideration of this work in a separate context (see pp. 135–49).

GUSTAV MAHLER: SONG AND SYMPHONY

In the tone poems of the 1890s, Strauss had employed a mixture of Teutonic legend, Nietzschian philosophy, and folk hero, and his emphasis on the program aspect of his works had helped to create a controversy. Gustav Mahler (1860–1911), who espoused the symphony and rejected the tone poem, was nevertheless as involved in the problem of the program as his competitor. In a letter to a friend in 1897, Mahler tried to make a distinction between their two approaches.

> You have defined my aims, as distinct from those of Strauss quite accurately. You are right in saying that 'my music *generates* a programme as a final imaginative elucidation, whereas with Strauss the programme is a set task.' . . . Whenever I plan a large musical structure, I always come to a point where I have to resort to 'the word' as a vehicle for my musical idea.—It must have been pretty much the same for Beethoven in his Ninth.[4]

Mahler's invocation of Beethoven follows in the mold of Wagner's essay on the Ninth Symphony, and confirms the necessity of maintaining the Beethoven Succession (which by this time must be spelled Beethoven-Wagner).[5]

A consideration of Mahler's infatuation with certain textual sources should thus help us to understand the song composer as well as the symphonist, and by extension the inclination of a slightly younger group of Viennese composers. For if Claude Debussy prepared the Parisian soil in which Stravinsky was to thrive, it is fair to claim that Mahler, as much or more than Strauss, set the tone in Vienna for many of the attitudes that were to appeal to Schoenberg and his circle. Schoenberg's dedication of his *Harmonielehre* (1911) and his essay, *Gustav Mahler: In Memoriam* (1912), encourage us to emphasize the connection.

DES KNABEN WUNDERHORN.   The appearance of the anthology of old "folk-poetry," *Des Knaben Wunderhorn* (The Youth's Magic Horn), published by Achim von Arnim and Clemens Brentano between 1805 and 1808, signaled a new and important motif in the developing Romantic consciousness. An enormous three-volume compilation of 1,250 pages, the anthology was significantly subtitled "Alte deutsche Lieder." The contention that it was an assemblage of folk-poetry is, however, specious: Only a third of its contents even purports to stem from an oral tradition, while the remainder comes from sixteenth- and seventeenth-century German "art poetry" which conformed to the spirit of the *Wunderhorn* collection. The aim of the anthology was to tap the German consciousness and was openly popular and national in tone, giving in to the Romantic need to search for collective roots in a remote past. The anthology was addressed to and approved by Goethe, who was ecstatic and sensed its potential appeal to the musician. This appeal is first apparent in the works of Weber (1786–1826), extends to Webern (1883–1945), and includes Mendelssohn, Schumann, Franz, Brahms, Wolf, Mahler, Humperdinck ("Abends wenn ich schlafen geh'" from *Hänsel und Gretel*, 1890–93), R. Strauss, and Schoenberg along the way.

In Arnim and Brentano's liberal adaptation of early German sources, they wished to suggest that in the *Wunderhorn* they had collected a folk treasury long lost and now rediscovered. Mahler and Schoenberg, however, approached the *Wunderhorn* collection not out of any affinity with folk art, but through its appeal to a sense of alienation found in so many of its poems, which stressed the irony, uncertainty, and brevity of life. Mahler's settings, in particular, are more notable for the hint of sophistication that mirrors Arnim's transformations than for any sense of artless naiveté matched to a genuine folk poetry. At the same time, it was not the literary quality of these poems, but rather the simplicity and the musicality inherent in them that triggered the new wave of enthusiasm, which quickly became a vogue. The folksong quality and disarming sincerity of the lyrics offered Mahler the possibility of inventing a new childlike song, essentially diatonic and direct, and supported by an orchestra that was similarly shorn of excess, operating in an economical, even chamberlike, fashion. All of these qualities, paradoxically antithetical to the popular view of Mahler as the composer of the "Symphony of a Thousand" (No. 8), were to prove fundamental to musical developments of the early twentieth century.

Mahler's thoroughgoing discovery of the *Wunderhorn* anthology is manifest in twelve songs taken from that source and composed principally between 1892 and 1896. The themes of the texts are varied, but in many instances they foreshadow motifs taken up by the Viennese circle of the early twentieth century: The various soldier songs (*Serenade of the Sentry, Reveille, The Drummer-Boy*) belong to the world of Schoenberg's *The Lost Brigade*, op. 12 (1907, see p. 26) and the barracks of Berg's *Wozzeck* (1915–21), reflecting a world of abandoned hopes, of neglected, downtrodden, and suffering creatures. There is also an attendant ghostliness in the contrasting mood of march and lyric song in the dialogue of *Serenade of the Sentry* and its lingering, unresolved dominant at the end (initially with added 6th and 7th before thinning out to a single 5th scale degree) that prefigures the spectral note of the Expressionists (see pp. 6, 26); and the military march music that introduces the third stanza of *Reveille* anticipates both mood and melody of the drum-major's music in Berg's *Wozzeck*, Act I, scene 3 (see 361–63). As a child, Mahler lived near a military barracks and often played in the shadow of nearby marching soldiers. His infatuation with march rhythms found expression not only in the numerous soldier songs of the *Wunderhorn* group but throughout his career as a symphonist.

In works such as "St. Anthony of Padua's Sermon to the Fish" ("Des Antonius von Padua Fischpredigt") and "In Praise of Wisdom" ("Lob des hohen Verstands") another note is struck, one that is jocular and potentially moralistic. The capacity for the transformation of such messages into the sardonic and ultimately the tragic is one that Mahler was to explore in the scherzi of his Second and Third Symphonies (see p. 10).

There are numerous folk tunes associated with *Wunderhorn* texts, and Mahler occasionally modeled his own melodies on them. Quotation of Ländler rhythms and melodies by Schubert as well as mottos from Beethoven have likewise been spotted in the *Wunderhorn* settings, the composite of such references alluding strongly to folk and Viennese elements.

Des Knaben Wunderhorn

DER SCHILDWACHE NACHTLIED

Ich kann und mag nicht fröhlich sein!
Wenn all Leute schlafen,
so muss ich wachen, ja, wachen!
Muss traurig sein!

Lieb' Knabe, du musst nicht traurig sein!
Will deiner warten
im Rosengarten,
im grünen Klee.

Zum grünen Klee geh ich nicht!
Zum Waffengarten
voll Helleparten
bin ich gestellt!

Stehst du im Feld, so helf' dir Gott!
An Gottes Segen
ist alles gelegen!
Wer's glauben tut!

Wer's glauben tut, ist weit davon.
Er ist ein König!
Er ist ein Kaiser!
Er fuhrt den Krieg!
Halt! Wer da! Rund!
Bleib' mir vom Leib!

Wer sang es hier? Wer sang zur Stund?
Verlorne Feldwacht
sang es um Mitternacht!
Mitternacht! Mitternacht! Feldwacht!

THE SENTINEL'S SERENADE

I can and may not be merry!
When all people are asleep
then must I be on guard, yes, keep watch!
I must be sad.

Dear boy, you need not be sad!
I will wait for you
in the rose garden,
in the green clover.

I am not going to the green clover!
In the garden of weapons
full of halberds
am I stationed!

Standing in the field, may God help you!
On God's blessing
is everything dependent!
For those who believe it!

Whoever believes it is far off.
He is a king!
He is an emperor!
He is waging war!
Halt! Who goes there! Speak up!
Keep off!

Who was singing here? Who sang just now?
A forlorn sentry
was singing at midnight!
Midnight! Midnight! Sentry!

DES ANTONIUS VON PADUA FISCHPREDIGT

Antonius zur Predigt
die Kirche find't ledig.
Er geht zu den Flüssen
und predigt den Fischen!
Sie schlag'n mit den Schwänzen,
im Sonnenschein glänzen.

Die Karpfen mit Rogen
sind all hierherzogen;
hab'n d'Mäuler aufrissen,
sich Zuhör'n's beflissen.
Kein Predigt niemalen
den Fischen so g'fallen!

Spitzgoschete Hechte,
die immerzu fechten,
sind eilends herschwommen,
zu hören den Frommen!
Auch jene Phantasten,
die immerzu fasten:
die Stockfisch ich meine,
zur Predigt erscheinen.
Kein Predigt niemalen
den Stockfisch so g'fallen.

ST. ANTONY'S SERMON TO THE FISH

St. Antony for his sermon
finds the church empty.
He goes to the rivers
and preaches to the fish!
They clap with their tails,
glistening in the sunshine.

The carp together with their spawn
have all assembled here;
have mouths wide open,
intent upon listening.
Never has a sermon
so pleased the fish.

The pointed nose pike,
who are always fighting,
have hastily swum here
in order to hear this godly man!
Also those dreamers,
who are always fasting,
the cod, I mean,
appear for the sermon.
Never has a sermon
so pleased the fish.

Gut Aale und Hausen,
die vornehme schmausen,
die selbst sich bequemen,
die Predigt vernehmen!
Auch Krebse, Schildkroten,
sonst langsame Boten,
steigen eilig vom Grund,
zu hören diesen Mund!
Kein Predigt niemalen
den Krebsen so g'fallen!

Fisch' grosse, Fisch' kleine,
vornehm' und gemeine,
erheben die Köpfe
wie verständ'ge Geschöpfe,
auf Gottes Begehren
die Predigt anhören.

Die Predigt geendet,
ein Jeder sich wendet
Die Hecht bleiben Diebe,
die Aale viel lieben;
die Predigt hat g'fallen,
sie bleiben wie Allen!

Die Krebs' geh'n zurücke,
die Stockfisch bleib'n dicke,
die Karpfen viel fressen,
die Predigt vergessen!
Die Predigt hat g'fallen,
sie bleiben wie Allen!

Even the elegant eels and sturgeon,
who feast so fashionably,
are contented
listening to the sermon.
The crabs, too, and the turtles,
normally slow movers,
rise quickly from the bottom
to hear this oracle!
Never has a sermon
so pleased the fish.

Fish, both large and small,
genteel and ordinary,
raising their heads
like intelligent creatures,
at God's command
listen to the sermon.

When the sermon is ended,
everyone of them turns round.
The pike remain thieves,
the eels make a lot of love,
the sermon has pleased them,
they remain like everybody else!

The crabs move backwards,
the cod remain fat,
the carp eat a great deal,
the sermon is forgotten.
The sermon has pleased,
they remain like everybody else!

REVELGE

Des Morgens zwischen drei'n und vieren,
da mussen wir Soldaten marschieren
das Gasslein auf und ab,
trallali, tralleley, trallalera,
mein Schatzel sieht herab!

"Ach, Brüder, jetzt bin ich geschossen,
die Kugel hat mich schwere getroffen,
trag' mich in mein Quartier,
trallali, tralleley, trallalera,
es ist nicht weit von hier!"

"Ach, Brüder, ach, Brüder,
ich kann dich nicht tragen,
die Feinde haben uns geschlagen,
helf' dir der liebe Gott!
Trallali, trallaley, trallalera,
ich muss marschieren bis in Tod!"

"Ach, Brüder, ach, Brüder,
ihr geht ja mir vorüber,
als war's mit mir schon vorbei!
Trallali, trallaley, trallalera,
ihr tretet mir zu nah!"

"Trallali, trallaley, trallali, trallaley,
Ich muss meine Trommel wohl rühren,
trallali, trallaley, trallali, trallaley,

REVEILLE

In the morning between three and four
then must we soldiers march
up and down the street.
Trallali, trallaley, trallalera,
my sweetheart is looking down.

"Ah, brother, now I am shot,
the bullet has severely wounded me.
Carry me to my quarters,
trallali, trallaley, trallalera,
it is not far from here!"

"Ah, brother, ah, brother,
I cannot carry you,
the enemy has beat us,
may the dear Lord help you!
Trallali, trallaley, trallalera,
I must march until I meet death."

"Ah, brothers, ah, brothers,
you are moving on past me
as though it were already over for me!
Trallali, trallaley, trallalera,
you step too close to me!"

"Trallali, trallaley, trallali, trallaley,
I must beat my drum,
trallali, trallaley, trallali, trallaley,

sonst werd' ich mich verlieren. Die Brüder, dick gesä't, sie liegen wie gemäht."	else I will become lost. My brothers, thickly piled, are lying as though mown down."
Er schlägt die Trommel auf und nieder, er wecket seine stillen Brüder, Trallali, trallaley, trallali, trallaley, sie schlagen und sie schlagen ihren Feind, trallali, trallaley, trallalerallala, ein Schrecken schlagt den Feind!	He beats the drum up and down, he wakes his silent brothers. Trallali, trallaley, trallali, trallaley They strike and defeat their enemy, trallali, trallaley, trallalerallala, a scream of terror strikes the foe.

Er schlagt die Trommel auf und nieder,
da sind sie vor dem Nachtquartier schon
  wieder,
trallali, trallaley, trallali, trallaley,
in's Gässlein hell hinaus, hell hinaus!
Sie zieh'n vor Schatzlein's Haus.
Trallali, trallaley, trallali, trallaley, trallalera,
sie ziehen vor Schatzelein's Haus, trallali.
	He beats the drum up and down,
	there they are before their night quarters
	  already,
	trallali, trallaley, trallali, trallaley,
	right out into the street, right out!
	They draw up to his sweetheart's house.
	Trallali, trallaley, trallali, trallaley, trallalera,
	they draw up to his sweetheart's house, trallali.

Des Morgens stehen da die Gebeine in Reih' und Glied, sie steh'n wie Leichensteine in Reih', in Reih' und Glied. Die Trommel steht voran, dass sie ihn sehen kann, trallali, trallali, trallalera, dass sie ihn sehen kann!	In the morning there stand the bones in rank and file, they stand like tombstones in rank, in rank and file. The drum stands at the front, so that she can see him, trallali, trallali, trallalera, so that she can see him!

THE *WUNDERHORN* SYMPHONIES.   Many of the messages of the Romantic Age placed an emphasis on pathos, world-weariness (*Weltschmerz*), and a cult of suffering that found refuge in·the notion of redemption. Whenever music takes on such a task of expression, it is obliged to find new technical means beyond the time-honored classical constructions. In the nineteenth-century chromatic harmonies, cyclical forms that promoted a sense of narrative, and ultimately the cojoining of text with music in a formal context previously reserved for abstract musical messages (symphony, string quartet, sonata) all served in the exploration. The "Eroica" (No. 3) and "Pastoral" (No. 6) symphonies; the Piano Sonata, op. 81a ("Les Adieu"); the "Heiligen Dankgesang" movement of the string quartet op. 132; and especially the Ninth Symphony ("Choral") reflect the extent to which this Romantic predilection was already forecast in the works of Beethoven. Its intensification in the works of Berlioz, the tone poems of Liszt, and a new type of opera dubbed "music drama" by Wagner are symptomatic of the varied means by which composers searched for new expressive values not totally independent of but decidedly in reaction to the classical formal values preached by the aesthetician Hanslick (1854) and exemplified in the works of Brahms.

While the pursuit of similar aims in the work of Mahler suggests that his contribution belongs to the final stages of the Romantic Age, his music inspired in the work of the succeeding generation a point of view that, if initially it did not run totally counter to Romantic ideals, promoted new attitudes which were to be the mark of a new modernism.

The role of the song in Mahler's symphonies is fundamental: The Second, Third, and Fourth Symphonies include settings from the *Wunderhorn* anthology, and the Eighth Symphony and *Das Lied von der Erde* rely on a Latin hymn,

Goethe, and poems from the Chinese. Even Mahler's early *Songs of a Wayfarer* provide the foundation for his First Symphony, whose "Funeral March" also quotes the well-known *Frère Jacques* (known in Germany as *Bruder Martin*) cast in a somber setting in the minor mode. As to the inclusion and treatment of this well-known song, Mahler himself clarified his reason by stating that even as a child the melody struck him as being deeply tragic in nature rather than gay. This corresponds closely with an interpretation Mahler also made concerning another folksong of his youth. At 50 years of age in a psychoanalytic session with Freud, he confessed that after a particularly violent quarrel he had witnessed between his parents as a child, he ran into the streets and was confronted with a barrel organ intoning "Ach, du lieber Augustin." Mahler felt that the incident was of fundamental importance and helped to explain why in moments of creative ecstasy he would frequently hear the strains of a popular streetsong. Such intrusions he felt were the source of much of the bittersweet quality that characterizes his music.

The legacy of such a point of view is clear. The momentary flickering of a waltz tune or a Ländler melody is also a feature that can be spotted on occasion in the music of Schoenberg, including the quotation of "Ach, du lieber Augustin" in the second movement of his *String Quartet No. 2* and the folk-like "Ännchen von Tharau" in his *Suite,* op. 29. It appears with even greater poignance in the work of Alban Berg, where the barrel-organ music and "Lautenlied" in *Lulu* (see p. 379), the Carinthian folksong in the *Violin Concerto* (see p. 376), or the musical response to folksong verses in *Wozzeck* (see pp. 358–59) create a stylistic dichotomy with powerful psychological overtones.

Symphony No. 2.   Though an early work, the Second Symphony epitomizes in many ways Mahler's approach to the genre. It is in five movements, of which the first three for orchestra alone prepare for the concluding two movements with text. Both the number of movements and the programmatic nature of the symphony, as well as the use of texts projected by soloists and chorus, could not help but promote the notion that Mahler was already self-consciously involved in contributing to the Beethoven Succession.

Mahler referred to the first movement as "Funeral Rite" (*Totenfeier*), a dirge wherein the hero of his First Symphony is borne to the grave.[6] It parallels not only the third movement of his First Symphony, but belongs to a lineage that includes the second movement of Beethoven's "Eroica" and Siegfried's "Funeral March" in *Die Götterdämmerung.* The march was to reappear prominently in Mahler's Third, Sixth, and Ninth Symphonies, and must be recognized as one of the notable signposts of his style—one that would later be emulated by Berg, Hindemith, Britten, Shostakovich, and others. The subtitle, *Totenfeier,* comes from a German translation of the Polish Mickiewicz's *Dziady* (published in 1823–33) by Mahler's friend Siegfried Lipiner. Published in 1887, it served as a direct inspiration for Mahler's composition of 1888–94. The hero of parts two and four of the poem is named Gustav who suffers increasing madness over a hopeless love affair for a young girl who marries another man. The impasse, which drove the poet to the brink of suicide, was mirrored in Mahler's morbid visions of death over his desparate emotional involvement with Marion Mathilde von Weber, who was similarly married to another man. The two interpretations linking musical tradition with personal biography are far from being at odds with each other; indeed, they reinforce the central thesis of the Artist as suffering Hero which dominates virtually all of Mahler's works. Similarly, the incorporation of a "Dies irae" motif in the first movement has a lengthy ancestry in Romantic music, and the notion of the Hero struggling with fate and destiny suggests an infatuation with Beethoven's Third and Fifth. Finally, citation of the music announcing Hunding's entrance in the first act of *Die Walküre* in Mahler's first movement can be no more accidental than the *notatim* recall of the instrumental coda to "Das ist ein Flöten und Geigen" from Schumann's *Dichterliebe* in the final measures of the third movement. Schumann's text, which speaks of flutes and fiddles joined by the trumpets blare and the sobbing of angels as the poet views his beloved dancing at her wedding,[7] forces a further consideration of Mahler's program for the Second Symphony.

Mahler classified the second movement as a sunny and idyllic intermezzo, while the atmosphere and thematic material of the third movement (scherzo) is taken directly from one of his *Wunderhorn* songs, "St. Anthony's Sermon to the Fishes." Although Mahler devised several variant programs for the Second Symphony, after the premiere of the work in December 1895 Mahler described the third movement thus:

> When you awaken from this melancholy dream [2nd mvt.] and must return to life's confusion, . . . the meaningless bustle of life seems to you unreal, like dancing forms in a brightly lit ballroom: you watch them from the darkness and from a distance, so that you cannot hear the accompanying music! And so life seems without meaning, a fearful nightmare from which you awaken with a cry of horror.[8]

While the citation from the *Dichterliebe* is clear in this context, the recognition of two virtually complete quotations of the *Wunderhorn* song "St. Anthony's Sermon to the Fishes" in Mahler's scherzo forces the listener to consider the relevance of the *Wunderhorn* text to Mahler's descriptive statement. Their very different programs, the change of mood from the jocular (song) to the ironic and tragic (symphony)—serves only to confirm our knowledge of Mahler's indebtedness to Nietzsche, who was to serve him textually in his Third Symphony. Nietzsche's concept of tragedy as part of a larger cosmic principle, which is neither happy nor sad and which spawns an ineffable humor that can only be mocked with affection, finds a counterpart in Mahler's music. The serious is counterbalanced by the sardonic in an attempt to elucidate the fundamental quality of the tragedy of life. In St. Anthony's song there is an ominous change of mood at the end of the third stanza, and similarly at the end of the "Fischpredigt" scherzo of the symphony there is a sudden turn reflecting the hero's cry of despair. Far from picturing a pointless and loquacious sermon, the symphonic scherzo now points to man's restlessness in his ceaseless struggle to comprehend human existence. This dual interpretation helps to explain the wild swings in mood in Mahler's music which were so disquieting to first audiences but which were also considered to be prophetic by later commentators such as Adorno, Krenek and Stockhausen, who have heralded its modernism.

Mahler's scherzo leads to the hauntingly beautiful fourth movement, "Urlicht," also a *Wunderhorn* text newly composed for the symphony. This simple song of faith serves as a preparation to the visions of the Last Judgment in the final movement, whose text gives the title "Resurrection" to the symphony. It is based on an ode by Klopstock, but only the opening five lines are by him, and in the manner of *The Songs of a Wayfarer* Mahler composed his own text for the conclusion. The use of the solo voice and chorus in the finale suggests that Beethoven's Ninth Symphony, which had cast a shadow across the entire nineteenth century, was still very much in Mahler's mind.

Though the formal outlines of Mahler's individual movements are clearly related to the symphonic prototypes of sonata (1st mvt.) and song and trio (2nd and 3rd mvts.), and the more sprawlingly formless finale rationalized by cyclic recalls from the first, third, and fourth movements, the modulatory schemes within the movements and the expanded orchestral resource (10 horns, 8 trumpets) provide a new richness. Even more interesting is the tonal frame of the Second Symphony, which begins in C minor and concludes in Eb major. Though the relationship is classic, its positioning is as unusual as it is symbolic (Death-Resurrection). It is an attitude that Mahler was to pursue with a similar purpose in the Fourth Symphony, where the progression from G major to E major during the course of the work reflects a movement from Earthly Life to Paradise. The emphasis on the third relationship may owe something to Beethoven, but the assertion of different levels at the beginning and end of a work in the service of a tonal dialectic with philosophical as well as narrative implications was Wagnerian in conception and of fundamental consequence, not only for the Viennese atonalists but for such an essentially tonal composer as Hindemith (see the discussion of *Mathis der Maler*, pp. 347–48).

Gustav Mahler, *Symphony No. 2 in C minor* ("Resurrection")

4th Movement

O Röschen roth	O rosebud red
Der Mensch liegt in grösster Noth!	Man lies in greatest need!
Der Mensch liegt in grösster Pein!	Man lies in greatest woe!
Lieber möcht' ich in Himmel sein.	I would rather be in Heaven.
Da kam ich auf einem breiten Weg;	Then I came upon a broad path
Da kam ein Engelein und wollt' mich abweisen;	Whence came an angel who wished to send me away.
Ach nein! Ich liess mich nicht abweisen.	But no, I would not be rejected.
Ich bin von Gott und will wieder zu Gott!	I am of God and will return to God.
Der liebe Gott wird mir ein Lichtchen geben,	My beloved God will give me a candle
Wird leuchten mir bis in das ewig selig Leben!	And will light the path toward an eternal, happy life.

Des Knaben Wunderhorn

5th Movement

Aufersteh'n, ja aufersteh'n wirst du, mein Staub, nach kurzer Ruh!	Rise again, indeed, you will rise again, my dust, after a short rest!
Unsterblich Leben! Unsterblich Leben wird der dich rief dir geben.	Immortal life! Immortal life will he grant who called out.
Wieder aufzublüh'n wirst du gesät!	The seed sown will bloom once more;
Der Herr der Ernte geht und sammelt Garben	The Lord of harvests goes forth
Uns ein, die starben.	To bind the sheaves of those who died.
O glaube, mein Herz, O glaube: es geht dir nichts verloren!	O believe, my heart, believe: you have lost nothing.
Dein ist, dein, ja dein, was du gesehnt!	It is yours, yours, yes yours, all that you longed for.
Dein, was du geliebt, was du gestritten!	Yours, what you loved, what you struggled for.

O glaube: du wardst nicht umsonst geboren!
Hast nicht umsonst gelebt, gelitten!
Was enstanden ist, das muss vergehen!
Was vergangen, aufersteh'n!
Hör auf zu beben!
Bereite dich zu leben!
O Schmerz! Du Alldurchdringer!
Dir bin ich entrungen,
O Tod! Du Allbezwinger!
Nun bist du bezwungen!
Mit Flügeln die ich mir errungen,
In Liebesstreben werd' ich entschweben
Zum Licht zu dem kein Aug' gedrungen!
Sterben werd' ich um zu leben!
Aufersteh'n, ja aufersteh'n wirst du, mein
   Herz, in einem Nu!
Was du geschlagen
Zu Gott wird es dich tragen!

O believe that you were not born in vain.
You have not lived and suffered in vain.
What has been now must pass.
What has passed will rise again.
Cease trembling.
Prepare to live.
O Pain, all-penetrating one,
I have escaped you.
O Death, all-conquering one,
Now you are conquered.
With wings I have won for myself,
In aspiring love I shall soar
To the Light unseen which no eye hath
   penetrated. I shall die to live.
Rise again, yes, you will rise again, my heart,
   in an instant!
And all that has befallen will now be
   transported to God.

Beethoven and the Viennese Secession. The specter of Beethoven continues to be reflected in Mahler's Fourth Symphony (1892, 1899–1900) in its cyclic procedures as well as in the classic purity of the music it quotes. The delicate grace-note figuration reminiscent of the second movement of Beethoven's Eighth Symphony at the opening of Mahler's first movement is matched by the redolent glow of *Fidelio*'s "Mir ist so wunderbar" (Ex. 1.1) at the opening of Mahler's third movement (Ex. 1.2).

Example 1.1. Beethoven, *Fidelio*, Act I, s. 4, "Mir ist so wunderbar" (Introduction), mm. 1–5.

Example 1.2. Mahler, *Symphony No. 4*, Mvt. 3, mm. 1–4.

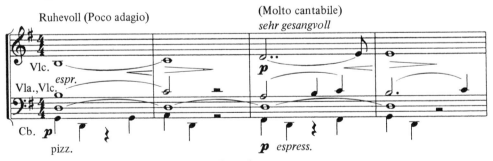

At about the same time, the view of Mahler as Artist-Hero and Beethoven successor was captured and dramatically projected by Gustav Klimt (1862–1918), renowned painter and leader of the Viennese Secession movement dedicated to the overthrow of conservative Viennese taste. Although they were not personal friends before 1902, Klimt's and Mahler's overlapping social and intellectual circles had brought them in contact as early as 1897. In April 1902, Klimt was commissioned to execute an enormous Beethoven frieze for the Secession exhibition in Vienna (Figure 1.1). At the inaugural concert before a large statue of Beethoven by Max Klinger (Figure 1.2), Mahler conducted the final movement of the Beethoven Ninth Symphony in his own arrangement for winds. Klimt's knight, whose profile recalls Mahler, may be compared to Rodin's bust of the composer made in 1909 (Figure 1.3), and their apparent connection can be sealed with the knowledge that for a collection of tributes gathered by Paul Stefan (Mahler's first biographer) in 1910, Klimt offered this very figure. Klimt's frieze, a highly philosophical interpretation of Schiller's *Ode to Joy*, not only speaks of Beethoven, but in the incorporation of a portrait of Mahler as a nobly armoured knight pointedly underscores Mahler's references to both the Beethoven "Eroica" and Wagner's *Parsifal* in the finale of his

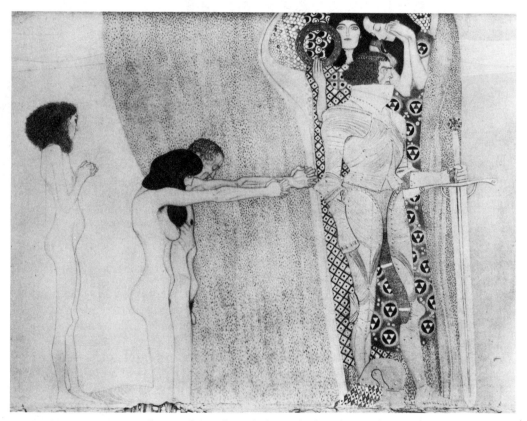

Figure 1.1. Gustav Klimt, *Sehnsuch nach dem Glück* ("Longing for Happiness"). A section of the Beethoven frieze commissioned for the Secession exhibition in Vienna, April 1902, showing Mahler's likeness as an armored knight.

Galerie Welz, Salzburg.

Figure 1.2. Max Klinger, statue of Ludwig van Beethoven (1886–1902). Originally exhibited in 1902 at the Secession headquarters, Vienna, before which Mahler conducted the final movement of Beethoven's Ninth Symphony in an arrangement for winds.
Museum der Bildenden Künste, Leipzig.

Third Symphony (1895–6). Just as Wagner had decreed a new beginning with Beethoven's setting of the *Ode to Joy*, so Mahler stressed his origins in his arrangement of that work and in the citation of works by his spiritual predecessors.

We know from Alma Mahler that Mahler often claimed that, except for Wagner's Beethoven essay, only Schopenhauer's *World as Will and Idea* had said anything of value about the essence of music. Wagner's Beethoven essay is, in fact, an interpretation of the Bayreuth master's view of Schopenhauer.[9] He believed that musical creation sprang from the subconscious activated through the will, and that through man's inner self he was related to the whole of Nature; his reliance upon Nietzsche's distinction between the Apollonian and Dionysian elements led him to suggest that too great an emphasis had

Figure 1.3. August Rodin, bust of Mahler (1909). Musée August Rodin, Paris, S. 812. Bronze, 34″ × 24″ × 22″.
Photo by Bruno Jarrett. © VAGA, New York, 1986.

been placed on reason, and that only through the introduction of emotion could a proper balance be achieved in musical creation. Wagner also held that the emphasis upon reason was a foreign importation from France; that Beethoven had overcome the rigid bonds of rationalism and restored music to its true realm of feeling; and that through him a new German music was destined to lead the way to a general cultural rebirth. Beethoven, Schopenhauer, Nietzsche, and Wagner together provide the foundation for an appreciation of Mahler's view of creativity and the roles of reason and emotion.

Nothing could better indicate Mahler's faith in this instinctive metaphysical approach than a statement he made to Natalie Bauer-Lechner:

> Have you noticed that with me the melody always proceeds from the word, which, so to speak, creates it for itself, never the reverse? It is that way with Beethoven and Wagner. And . . . only in this way is there created what one would like to describe as the identity of word and tone.[10]

Not only was Arnold Schoenberg to be a firm believer in the destiny of German music ("I have made a discovery [in the method of composing with twelve tones] thanks to which the supremacy of German music is ensured for the next hundred years"),[11] but in his article, "The Relationship to the Text," which appeared in the almanac, *Der Blaue Reiter* (1912), he propounded in even more extreme terms than Mahler his belief in the role of intuition in fashioning an identity between word and tone.[12] Such a point of view is demonstrable not only in Mahler's early song cycles, or the *Wunderhorn* symphonies, but also in his later *Rückert-lieder* (1901–02), the *Kindertotenlieder* (1901–04), his *Eighth Symphony* ("Symphony of a Thousand," 1906) and *Das Lied von der Erde* (1908–09).

In addition to the textual element, Mahler's attention to the idea of the symphony as opposed to the tone poem was also obviously inspired by Beethoven. In his continuation of the formal revolution within the genre Boulez has judged Mahler's contribution as comparable to Wagner's destruction of the artificial order of the opera.[13] In his solutions which involved the exploration of tonal relationships, five- and six-movement formats (e.g., Symphonies No. 2 and 3), cyclic thematic connections between movements, autobiographical backgrounds, and rhythmic motifs frequently attached to motives of Fate and Death, Mahler in turn left a legacy that was to be tapped by numerous later composers. This was true not only in the obvious case of Alban Berg (see pp. 55–60) but of a host of composers from 1960 on, following a genuine Mahler revival, which continues to the present day. With Lukas Foss's return to Nietzsche's *Mitternachtlied* of Mahler's *Third Symphony* (1893–96) in his *Time Cycle* of 1960, as well as in Luciano Berio's extended critique of Mahler's "Fischpredigt" scherzo in the third movement of his *Sinfonia* of 1968 (see p. 000), it was apparent that for many composers of their generation (as with Berg) the idea of a Beethoven-Wagner-Mahler succession was inescapable. The note of *Weltschmerz* which rings from Nietzsche's lines was sufficiently proximate that its transfer to the young Berg's "Warm die Lüfte," op. 2, no. 4 (see p. 46) of 1910 was readily achieved, and its preoccupation with eternity ("Ewigkeit") proved to be a quality which Berg would remember to the end of his career (see p. 20). The attraction of such values of composers like Foss and Berio (see p. 648) in the 1960s, however, involved not so much revival as reinterpretation in a post-war world fraught with a sense of history and its almost unbearable weight for the creative spirit.

Mahler, *Symphony No. 3*, 4th movement

O Mensch! Gib Acht!	Oh man, pay heed.
Was spricht die tiefe Mitternacht?	What does deep midnight say?
Ich schlief!	I slept!
Aus tiefem Traum bin ich erwacht!	From a deep dream I have wakened.
Die Welt ist tief!	The world is deep,
Und tiefer als der Tag gedacht!	And deeper than the day imagined!
Tief ist ihr Weh!	Deep is its grief!
Lust tiefer noch als Herzeleid!	Joy deeper still than the heart's suffering!
Weh spricht: Vergeh!	Grief speaks: Away!
Doch alle Lust will Ewigkeit!	But all joy seeks eternity,
Will tiefe, tiefe Ewigkeit!	Seeks deep, deep eternity!

Nietzsche

DAS LIED VON DER ERDE.   If the discovery of the *Wunderhorn* lyrics was in part reflective of national aspirations for both the nineteenth century and the early twentieth, equally important was the revival and translation of numerous poems from Oriental sources. Goethe once again had been instrumental in sensing their appeal, and his *Chinesische Jahres- und Tageszeiten* of 1830 was an important attempt to marry the sensibilities of the East and West. This appeal was further strengthened by Hans Bethge (1876–1946), who in his *Chinesische Flöte* (1907) performed an act of translation dear to the heart of Goethe, whose concept of *Weltliteratur* aimed through translation and criticism to advance civilization through understanding and respect.

Bethge's translations, which were in truth highly liberal paraphrases from English, French, and German sources, must be seen as stylizations with only a hint of the originals. They nonetheless proved to be irresistible to Mahler as the primary textual source for his *Das Lied von der Erde* (1908–09), to which he made alterations and additions himself. Mahler was attracted to Li-Tai-Po and the Chinese poets for the same reasons as Goethe, whom he also revered, and the appeal of the message was in its universality as projected through the multiple themes of World Sorrow and the forces of Nature: alienation, loneliness, momentary release through intoxication, and resolution through death. The fervor that spills from many of Mahler's texts, from his Second Symphony to his Eighth and *Das Lied von der Erde*, can be seen alternately as the product of his fiery Catholicism or as the heir to Goethe's and Spinoza's cosmic mysticism, which approaches pantheism.

The specific appeal of the Chinese element, however, cannot be denied. The Viennese Secession formed in 1902 was a revolt against the conservative and academic taste of the city, and it was natural, if not inevitable, that the French art nouveau, which had been spawned under similar circumstances, should have appealed to the principal proponents in the formation of their *Jugendstil.* Though the roots of both movements can be seen in part in the Pre-Raphaelite painters of the 1850s and the Aesthetic Movement of the 1880s in England, the emphasis on a mythologized Middle Ages (e.g., Wagner's *Wunderhorn*-based *Tannhäuser*, 1843–45) and the rejection of the Renaissance image of man set the stage for a study of textures and forms drawn from Nature, whose relation to Man was rendered increasingly mysterious. The lyrics of the Chinese and Japanese, as well as the patterns of their prints, enjoyed an overwhelming vogue in fin-de-siècle Vienna and served the new cult of Nature admirably. The use to which such themes were put range from the brocaded patterns of Klimt, which reflect the enormous sway that things Oriental held over feminine fashion of the time, to Mahler's Chinese-Nature symphony (*Das Lied von der Erde*). The more ascetic interpretation of the Japanese house by the contemporary Viennese architect Adolf Loos was to lead away from the curvilinear ornamentation of the *Jugendstil* and point the way toward the Bauhaus and the formation of the international style of the 1920s. Yet, for all its purity, one of the most familiar objects of the Bauhaus—Mies van der Rohe's renowned Barcelona chair of 1929—still retains something of its origins in the lyric curves of its profile.

In the first movement of Mahler's *Das Lied von der Erde*, "Drinking Song of the Sorrow of the Earth," as well as the "Drunkard in Spring," movement five, the poet speaks not of a drunkard's stupor but of his perceptions induced by wine, which lead both to ecstasy and to sorrow. The appeal of Li-Tai-Po's texts for Mahler parallels the appeal of Baudelaire's wine songs for Berg twenty years later, and in its emphasis on the mysteriousness of existence and a pre-

Example 1.3. Mahler, *Das Lied von der Erde*, Mvt. 1, m. 385.

Dun - kel ist das Le - ben, ist der Tod!

vailing sense of pity, epitomized in the first movement's refrain "Dunkel is das Leben, ist der Tod," it complements the contemporary sensibility of Maeterlinck's symbolist tableaux.

<table>
<tr><td>

1. DAS TRINKLIED VOM JAMMER DER ERDE

Schon winkt der Wein im gold'nen
   Pokale,
Doch trinkt noch nicht, erst sing' ich euch ein
   Lied!
Das Lied vom Kummer
Soll auflachend in die Seele euch klingen.
Wenn der Kummer naht,
Liegen wust die Gärten der Seele,
Welkt hin und stirbt die Freude, der Gesang.
Dunkel is das Leben, ist der Tod.

Herr dieses Hauses!
Dein Keller birgt die Fülle des goldenen
   Weins!
Hier, diese Laute nenn' ich mein!
Die Laute schlagen und die Gläser leeren,
Das sind die Dinge, die zusammen passen,
Ein voller Becher Weins zur rechten Zeit
Ist Mehr wert, als alle Reiche dieser Erde!
Dunkel ist das Leben, ist der Tod.

Das Firmament blaut ewig, und die Erde
Wird lange feststeh'n und aufblüh'n im Lenz.
Du aber, Mensch, wie lang lebst denn du?
Nicht hundert Jahre darfst du dich ergötzen
An all dem morschen Tande dieser Erde!

Seht dort hinab! Im Mondschein auf den
   Gräbern
Hockt eine wild-gespenstische Gestalt!
Ein Aff ist's! Hört ihr, wie sein Heulen
Hinausgellt in den süssen Duft des Lebens!

Jetzt nehmt den Wein! Jetzt ist es Zeit,
   Genossen!
Leert eure gold'nen Becher zu Grund!
Dunkel ist das Leben, ist der Tod!

</td><td>

1. THE DRINKING SONG OF THE SORROW OF THE EARTH (after Li-Tai-Po)

Already the wine beckons from the golden
   goblet,
But drink not yet, first I will sing you a
   song!
The song of sorrow
Shall burst out laughing in your soul.
When sorrow nears,
The gardens of the soul lie fallow,
Both joy and song wither and die.
Dark is life, and so is death.

Master of this house!
Your cellar conceals a treasure of golden
   wine!
Here, this lute I name my own!
To play the lute and empty the glass,
These are the things which harmonize together.
A full cup of wine at the right time
Is worth more than all the riches of the earth!
Dark is life, and so is death.

Heaven is forever blue, and the earth
Will long remain and blossom in the spring.
But you, o Man, how long do you live?
Not even for a hundred years may you enjoy
The decaying trifles of this earth!

Look down there! In the moonlight on the
   tombstone
Crouches a wild and ghostly figure!
It's an ape! Listen, how his howling
Pierces life's sweet fragrance.

Now take up the wine! The time has come,
   comrades,
Empty your golden beakers to the bottom!
Dark is life, and so is death!

</td></tr>
</table>

Although there are six movements to Mahler's symphony, the two drinking poems, movements one and five, provide a frame for the main body of the work, not only with respect to their text but also their tonality, the keys of the several movements being as follows: a-d-B♭-G-A-c/C. Reminders of the early

Wunderhorn composer are numerous, and include the horn fanfares of the opening movement and the grotesquerie of the march-scherzo that attends the third and fourth verses of the fourth movement. Even a reference to Wagner's *Parsifal* returns in the fourth verse of the fifth song: Having drunk his gullet and soul to the full, the poet falls asleep but is awakened by a bird chirping. "Yes! Spring is here, it came overnight!" The text "Der Lenz ist da" ("Spring is here") is a modification of Bethge's original German in order to conform exactly to Gurnemanz's narrative and music at the opening of Act III.[14]

Example 1.4. Wagner, *Parsifal*, Act III, s. 1.

Example 1.5. Mahler, *Das Lied von der Erde*, Mvt. 5.

The last movement, "The Farewell," breaks the concentric tonal plan of the first five and must be seen as a thing apart. A song of resignation almost as long as all of the earlier movements combined, it joins two preexistent poems to which Mahler makes his own emendations and additions. The initial oboe figuration, which appears throughout the movement, and the ominous use of the tam-tam may hint at an awareness of Eastern musical values, but Mahler's fundamental language for the most part eschews the brand of musical exoticism practised by French composers at the turn of the century. Yet the pentatonicism in which the whole symphony is submerged suggests in figurations such as those found in the third and fourth movements a genuine concession on Mahler's part to a directly perceivable Oriental symbolism (Exs. 1.6 and 1.7).

Its less superficial and more fundamental application, which lends a motivic and harmonic unity to the entire work, can be witnessed in the minor pentatonic refrain of the first movement (Ex. 1.3) as well as in the final cadence chord of the concluding movement, where to a major triad is added a sixth (clarinet) and a disappearing ninth (voice) on the final utterance of the word "Ewig." It is a sonority that Berg would remember and use as a personal state-

Example 1.6. Mahler, *Das Lied von der Erde*, Mvt. 3, m. 3.

Example 1.7. Mahler, *Das Lied von der Erde*, Mvt. 4, m. 7.

ment of farewell in his last two works: (a) In the Violin Concerto, whose last section is a set of variations on the chorale, "O Ewigkeit, du Donnerwort," Berg adds a C and G above the foundational B♭ major triad; (b) in the closing bars of *Lulu*, to the pedal A-E Berg adds a B and an F as a coda to the Countess Geschwitz's concluding words "in Ewigkeit."

6. DER ABSCHIED [After Mong-Koo-Jen]

Die Sonne scheidet hinter dem Gebirge.
In alle Täler steigt der Abend nieder
Mit seinen Schatten, die voll Kühlung
   sind.
O sieh! Wie eine Silberbarke schwebt
Der Mond am blauen Himmelsee herauf.
Ich spüre eines feinen Windes Weh'n
Hinter den dunklen Fichten!

Der Bach singt voller Wohllaut durch das
   Dunkel.
Die Blumen blassen im Dämmerschein.
Die Erde atmet voll von Ruh' und
   Schlaf;
Alle Sehnsucht will nun träumen.
Die müden Menschen geh'n heimwärts,
Und im Schlaf vergess'nes Glück
Und Jugend neu zu lernen.
Die Vögel hocken still in ihren Zweigen.
Die Welt schläfft ein!

Es wehet kühl im Schatten meiner
   Fichten.
Ich stehe hier und harre meines Freundes;
Ich harre sein zum letzten Lebewohl.
Ich sehne mich, O Freund, an deiner Seite
Die Schönheit dieses Abends zu geniessen.
Wo bleibst du! Du lässt mich lang allein!
Ich wandle auf und nieder mit meiner Laute
Auf Wegen, die von weichem Grase schwellen.
O Schönheit! O ewigen Liebens-,
   Lebens-trunk'ne Welt!

[After Wang-Sei]

Er stieg vom Pferd und reichte ihm
Den Trunk des Abschieds dar.

6. THE FAREWELL [After Mong-Koo-Jen]

The sun sets behind the mountains.
In every valley evening descends
With its shadows filled with refreshing
   coolness.
O look! Like a silver barque
Soars the moon on the heaven's sea of blue.
I feel a soft breeze stirring
Behind the dark pine-trees!

The brook sings a pleasant melody through
   the darkness.
The flowers grow pale in the twilight glow.
The earth breaths quietly, full of peace and
   slumber,
All our longings wish now to dream.
Weary men turn homeward,
So that in sleep forgotten joy
And youth may once again be found!
The birds perch quietly on the branches.
The world falls asleep.

The air stirs with coolness in the shade of my
   pine-trees.
I stand here and wait for my friend.
I wait for him to bid a last farewell.
I long, o friend, to share
The beauty of this evening at your side.
Where art thou! You leave me so long alone!
I wander up and down with my lute
Over paths swollen with soft grass.
O beauty! O world, eternally intoxicated by
   love and life!

(After Wang-Sei)

He alighted from his horse and offered him
The drink of farewell;

Er fragte ihn, wohin er führe	He asked him whither he headed
Und auch warum es müsste sein.	And also why it must be so.
Er sprach, seine Stimme war umflort:	He spoke, his voice was veiled:
Du, mein Freund,	You, my friend,
Mir war auf dieser Welt das Glück nicht hold!	In this world fortune was not kind!
Wohin ich geh'? Ich geh', ich wand're in die Berge.	Where do I go? I go, I wander in the mountains.
Ich suche Ruhe für mein einsam Herz!	I seek peace for my lonely heart.
Ich wandle nach der Heimat, meiner Stätte.	I wander to my homeland, my abode.
Ich werde niemals in die Ferne schweifen.	I shall no longer roam in distant lands.
Still is mein Herz und harret seiner Stunde!	My heart is still and awaits its hour!
Die liebe Erde allüberall	The lovely earth everywhere
Blüht auf im Lenz und grünt aufs neu!	Blossoms into spring and turns green anew!
Allüberall und ewig blauen licht die Fernen!	Everywhere and forever the horizon shines blue!
Ewig . . . Ewig . . .	Forever . . . forever . . .

Source: Hans Bethge, Die chinesische Flöte (1907).

Mahler's funeral took place on May 21, 1911, and the wreath that Schoenberg and his pupils placed on his grave bore the inscription: "This rich man through whom we have come to know the deepest sorrow—the loss of the saintly Gustav Mahler—has left us, for life, a model we cannot lose: his work and his works." The last of Schoenberg's *Six Little Piano Pieces*, op. 19, whose static chords sound like tolling bells, is said to have been sketched out immediately after Schoenberg returned home from Mahler's funeral, and a painting depicting the mourners at graveside followed (Figure 1.4). The pilgrimage to the posthumous first performance of *Das Lied von der Erde* (conducted by Bruno Walter) in Munich the following November included the most important musical personalities from Vienna (Schoenberg, Berg, Webern, Zemlinsky), and together with Mahler's Ninth Symphony, which premiered a few months later, helped to seal the idea of a great man who had been neglected as a composer in his time. Boulez correctly observed that such devotion was later frequently mistrusted as a "narrow, local sentimental attachment" for "their link with this music was not at first sight obvious, whereas the contrasts between it and theirs was patent."[15]

The ultimate redress, however, was not long in coming, not only in an outpouring of essays, among which Schoenberg's lengthy tributes are especially notable, but in the veneration that numerous composers were to demonstrate in their own music. Mahler, together with Strauss, not only paved the way for the experience of Expressionism, but also spawned musical values of a wider and more enduring appeal. Indeed, a reinterpretation of Mahler's sonorities, nocturnal pedals, melodic figurations, rhythmic symbols, and textual themes were to reappear in such diverse works as Schoenberg's *Pierrot lunaire* (1912), Berg's *Three Pieces for Orchestra* (1914) and *Wozzeck* (1917–22), Zemlinsky's *Lyric Symphony* (1922), Krenek's *Symphonies 1–3* (1919–22), Weill's *Violin Concerto* (1924), Berg's *Der Wein* (1929) and *Violin Concerto* (1934), Shostakovich's *Symphony No. 4* (1935–36) and *Symphony No. 14* (1969), Foss's *Time Cycle* (1960), Berio's *Sinfonia* (1968), Crumb's *Ancient Voices of Children* (1970), Rochberg's *String Quartet No. 3* (1971–72), and Leif Segerstam's *String Quartet No. 6* (1974). It is likely that Mahler's shadow is destined to fall on works yet unwritten.

Figure 1.4. Arnold Schoenberg, *Gustav Mahler's Funeral* (1911).
Courtesy of Lisa Aronson. Photo by Robert Galbraith.

REPERTOIRE

Mahler, *Des Knaben Wunderhorn*
   "Der Schildwache Nachtlied" (1892)
   "Des Antonius von Padua Fischpredigt" (1893)
   "Revelge" (1899)
Mahler, *Symphony No. 2* ("Resurrection") (1888–94, rev. 1903)
   Scherzo, 3rd mvt. (based on "Des Antonius von Padua Fischpredigt")
   "Urlicht", 4th mvt. (*Des Knaben Wunderhorn*)
   "Aufersteh'n, ja aufersteh'n wirst du," 5th mvt. (Klopstock)
Mahler, *Symphony No. 3* (1893–96, rev. 1906), A solo, women's vv, boys' vv, orch
   "O Mensch! Gib Acht!", 4th mvt. (Nietzsche)
   "Es sungen drei Engel" (*Des Knaben Wunderhorn*)
Mahler, *Das Lied von der Erde* (1908–09), T, A/Bar, orch

Foss, *Time Cycle* (1960), S, orch
   "O Mensch! Gib Acht!" (Nietzsche)
Berio, *Sinfonia* (1968)
   Section III (based on Mahler, *Symphony No. 2*, scherzo)

READING

Arnold Schoenberg, "Gustav Mahler: In Memoriam," (1912) and "Gustav Mahler" (1912, rev. 1945) in *Style and Idea*, ed. Leonard Stein (New York, 1975), 447, 449.

Benjamin Britten, "On Behalf of Gustav Mahler," *Tempo*, ii (1942).

Hans Tischler, "Mahler's 'Das Lied von der Erde'," *Music Review*, x (1949), 111.

J. Diether, "Mahler and Atonality," *Music Review*, xvii.2 (May 1956).

Henry-Louis de La Grange, *Mahler* (Garden City, New York, 1973).

Eric Sams, "Notes on a Magic Horn," *The Musical Times*, cxv (1974), 556–7.

Donald Mitchell, *Gustav Mahler: The Wunderhorn Years* (London, 1975).

Arthur Wenk, "The Composer as Poet in *Das Lied von der Erde*" in *19th Century Music*, i (1977), 33.

Dika Newlin, *Bruckner, Mahler, Schoenberg* (New York, 1947, rev. 1978).

Donald Mitchell, "Mahler: 'Wunderhorn Works'," in *The New Grove Dictionary of Music and Musicians* (London, 1980), vol. 11, 515–18.

Carl Schorske, *Fin-de-siècle Vienna* (New York, 1980), Chapter V, "Gustav Klimt: Painting and the Crisis of the Liberal Ego."

Pierre Boulez, "Gustav Mahler: Why Biography?" Preface to *Mahler*, vol. I, by Henry-Louis de LaGrange (Paris, 1979). English translation in *Orientations* (Cambridge, Mass., 1986), 292–94.

Pierre Boulez, "Gustav Mahler: Our Contemporary?" Preface to *Gustav Mahler et Vienne* by Bruno Walter (Paris, 1979). English translation in *Orientations* (Cambridge, Mass., 1986), 295–303.

CHAPTER 2

SCHOENBERG TO 1909: EXTENDING TRADITIONS

The disparity between the acknowledged importance of the music of Arnold Schoenberg (1874–1951) and the minimal attention given to it in the concert hall focuses on one of the most interesting parodoxes of contemporary music. Schoenberg's name is typically linked with cacophonous and psychically disturbed messages that seemingly contain little to endear themselves to a mass audience. As the father of "atonality" and the inventor of a method of composing with 12-tones, he has been blamed for much, praised by some, and championed by few. Yet his name looms large to all who would claim to be conversant with music in the twentieth century as one of the seminal minds and most original creative figures of our age. This paradox poses a challenge—namely, to search for a clarification of his artistic roots in the hope of formulating a sound basis for an appreciation.

The view of Schoenberg as a dissident revolutionary intent on the destruction of a venerable tradition runs counter to his own opinion concerning his development. In a retrospective statement made in 1931, Schoenberg judged that his foundations lay in the great German models: Bach (counterpoint), Mozart (thematic relationships), Beethoven (development), Wagner (harmonic expression), and Brahms (phraseology).[1] To these names he adds Schubert, Mahler, Strauss, Reger, and Zemlinsky,[2] preserving the national bias of his list and accounting for the following extraordinary assessment of Debussy:

> Here is a remarkable fact, as yet unnoticed: Debussy's summons to the Latin and Slav peoples, to do battle against Wagner, was indeed successful; but to free *himself* from Wagner—that was beyond him. His most interesting discoveries can still only be used within the form and the way of giving shape to music that Wagner created. Here it must not be overlooked that much of his harmony was also discovered independently of him, in Germany. No wonder; after all, these were logical consequences of Wagner's harmony, further steps along the path the latter had pointed out.
>
> It is a remarkable thing, as yet unnoticed by anyone—although a thousand facts point to it, and although the battle against German music during the war was primarily a battle against my own music; . . . remarkably, nobody has yet appreciated that my music, produced on German soil, *without foreign influences* (author's italics), is a living example of an art able most effectively to oppose Latin and Slav hopes of hegemony and derived through and through from traditions of German music.[3]

EARLY WORKS

Schoenberg's beginnings are thus securely anchored in fin-de-siècle Vienna, and the traditions of Wagner, Strauss, and Mahler are betrayed in many of his earliest compositions. His string sextet, op. 4, of 1899 carries the title *Verklärte Nacht* ("Transfigured Night") and a program based on a poem of Richard Dehmel that is as explicit as anything Mahler or Strauss ever claimed for any of their works. The same may be said for his *Pelleas and Melisande*, op. 5, of 1902, an orchestral piece predictably and firmly based on the principles of sonata form and leitmotif thoroughly expounded in the tone poems of Liszt and Strauss. It was Strauss, in fact, who suggested the project to Schoenberg initially. The published analysis by his pupil Alban Berg and the composer's discussion near the end of his life of its intricate system of leitmotifs makes a specific association between musical figure and form, and character, idea and mood, legitimizing his claim that the 45-minute work unfolds Maeterlinck's drama in a logical and coherent fashion.

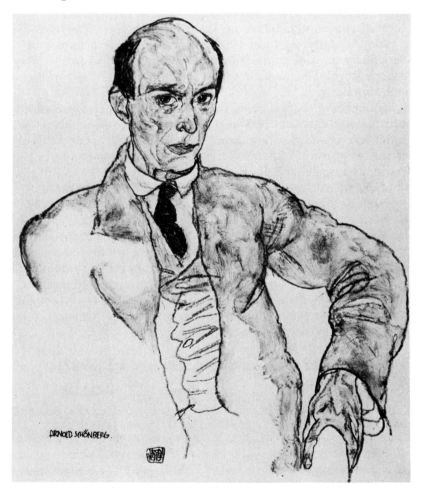

Figure 2.1. Egon Schiele, *Arnold Schoenberg* (1917). Watercolor. Private collection, Austria.

Photo from The Galerie St. Étienne, New York. Reproduced by permission of Dr. Rainer Handl, Vienna.

In Schoenberg's *Gurrelieder*, which dates from the same period, the listener is drawn into a world of Teutonic myth and legend that can hardly fail to recall Wagner's panoramic landscapes. The study of the heroic Gothic past, particularly as expressed in pre-Christian mythology, was undertaken by many northern European artists of the nineteenth century with the object of raising the moral tone of society, and the accompanying motifs of purification and redemption can be noted from *Faust* to the *Niebelungenlied*. It persists as well in Jens Peter Jacobsen's (1847–85) *Songs of Gurre*, a retelling of a twelfth-century legend dating from the late 1860s. Jacobsen was known for his pioneering activity as a natural scientist and translator of Darwin into Danish, and in his poem of Gurre, narrative and action have been replaced by psychological themes of Man in Nature. Of the two sections that comprise the final part, "The Wild Hunt" and "The Wild Hunt of the Summer Wind," the first is notable for its six-part male *Sprechstimme* (cf. p. 185) chorus and the latter for the extended melodrama for speaker and orchestra that extols the beauties of Nature. The conclusion in its full-blown Romanticism is awesome, and parallels the orchestral and vocal forces as well as the redemptive note sounded by Mahler in his contemporaneous Eighth Symphony ("Symphony of a Thousand") of 1906. Actually begun in 1900 and finished in short score by the next year, Schoenberg did not complete the orchestration until 1911. His breathtaking stylistic development during that period made the task of orchestration particularly taxing.

Schoenberg also reflected something of Mahler's approach to the *Wunderhorn* texts as early as 1903 in the opening song of his op. 3, "Wie Georg von Frundsberg von sich selber sang." And in "Das Wappenschild" of 1903–04, the setting of stormy *Wunderhorn* verses as an orchestral song looks beyond Mahler as a model and draws on both the harmonies and full-throated orchestra of Wagner. "Der verlorene Haufen" from his *Two Ballades*, op. 12, of 1907, although on a poem of Viktor Klemperer also rests squarely in the tradition of the *Wunderhorn*, which addresses the false glorification of a soldier's life and the specter of war later caught with a different accent in Berg's *Wozzeck* (p. 465). Though the tonal language is only slightly more ambiguous than Mahler's (beginning and cadencing in D minor but introducing the voice with an ascending octave on Db at m.3), the vocal style marginally enlarged upon, and the piano writing (including an extended coda) thoroughly traditional, Schoenberg near the end of his life pointed to the *Ballades* as "a decisive step forward" together with his piano pieces, op. 11.[4]

Arnold Schoenberg, *Two Ballades*, op. 12 (1907)

DER VERLORENE HAUFEN

Trinkt aus, ihr zechtet zum letzten Mal,
Nun gilt es Sturm zu laufen;
Wir stehen zuvorderst aus freier Wahl,
Wir sind der verlorne Haufen.

Wer länger nicht mehr wandern mag,
Wes Füsse schwer geworden,
Wem zu grell das Licht, wem zu laut
    der Tag,
Der tritt in unsern Orden.

THE LOST BRIGADE

Drink up, you've caroused for the last time,
Now the assault is to begin.
We stand at the front out of free choice.
We are the lost brigade.

Those who no longer want to roam,
Who have become weary of foot,
For whom the light is too bright and the day
    too loud,
They join our ranks.

Trinkt aus, schon färbt sich der Osten fahl,	Drink up, the east is already turning pale,
Gleich werden die Büchsen singen,	Presently the rifles will be singing.
Und blinkt der erste Morgenstrahl,	And when the first ray of morning gleams,
So will ich mein Fähnlein schwingen.	I will be swinging the banner.
Und Wenn die Sonne im Mittag steht,	And when the sun stands at midday
So wird die Bresche gelegt sein;	The breach will have been made;
Und wenn die Sonne zur Rüste geht,	And when the sun sinks,
Wird die Mauer vom Boden gefegt sein.	The wall will be swept to the ground.
Und wenn die Nacht sich niedersenkt,	And when night falls
Sie raffe den Schleier zusammen,	Let her draw the veil together,
Dass sich kein Funke drin verfängt	So that no spark is caught in it
Von den lodernden Siegesflammen!	By the glowing flames of victory!
Nun vollendet der Mond den stillen Lauf,	Now the moon completes her silent course,
Wir sehn ihn nicht verbleichen.	Yet we do not watch her fade.
Kühl zieht ein neuer Morgen herauf—	A fresh, new morning approaches—
Dann sammein sie unsere Leichen.	And they are coming to collect our corpses.

Viktor Klemperer. Used by Permission of Belmont Music Publishers.

TWO STRING QUARTETS AND A SYMPHONY, OP. 7, 9, 10

As a young composer, Schoenberg, like so many at the turn of the century, was infatuated with the integrating potential of the leitmotif and cyclic patterning: the *First String Quartet*, op. 7 (1905) and the *Chamber Symphony*, op. 9 (1906) are both single-movement structures that combine qualities of the multimovement symphony with the interior characteristics of the single-movement sonata form. Thus, in a thematic and formal analysis published in 1913, Berg argued that Schoenberg's *Kammersymphonie* could be viewed as (a) sonata exposition, scherzo, development of exposition, adagio, finale (recapitulation and coda) as in the several movements of a symphony; or as (b) the first movement of a sonata with scherzo and adagio as interpolations. Behind this lay a powerful tradition beginning with the tendency toward cyclicism in Beethoven's op. 101 and the integration of the three- or four-movement sonata idea into a single movement in Schubert's *Wanderer-Fantasie*. Numerous composers throughout the nineteenth century were attracted to one or both of these propositions: The idée fixe of Berlioz, the leitmotif of Wagner, the thematic interrelationships of Schumann's *Fourth Symphony* (originally entitled *Symphonische Phantasie*), the sonatas and tone poems of Liszt, and the cyclic predelictions of Franck and d'Indy all promoted the Beethoven-Schubert Succession with respect to this formal issue. The endorsement of the cyclic principle in Mahler's symphonies merely provides the confirmation of a legacy. It should come as no surprise, therefore, to observe such principles at work in the early compositions of Schoenberg.

The paring of the color component to a chamber symphony of fifteen solo instruments (fl/pic, ob, eng hn, 3 cl, bn, cbn, 2 hn, str qt, db) can also be seen as a logical consequence of Mahler's tendency to highlight smaller groups within the larger orchestral ensemble. Beyond the coloristic and the cyclic, multifunctional formalisms of the *Kammersymphonie*, op. 9, Schoenberg also manifests an interest in exploring whole-tone scalar formations (Ex. 2.1) and harmonic and melodic ideas built on fourths (Exs. 2.2 and 2.3), which at the time left Webern thunderstruck.

Example 2.1. Schoenberg, *Kammersymphonie,* op. 9, mm. 9–12.

Vlc.

Example 2.2. Schoenberg, *Kammersymphonie,* op. 9, m. 2.

Example 2.3. Schoenberg, *Kammersymphonie,* op. 9, mm. 5–7.

Very fast (♩ = ca. 104)
Horn (actual sound)

Both of these ideas were to be discussed a few years later in the final chapter of Schoenberg's *Harmonielehre* (1911). The opening chord of the symphony (Ex. 2.2), although seemingly a pile of perfect fourths, can be interpreted through its ensuing resolution to an F major triad as a collection of appogiature. Yet the immediate announcement of this series of fourths (Ex. 2.3) as a heraldic horn fanfare worthy of Richard Strauss confirms the independence of the idea. It is a fanfare that will return at the end of the symphony, but in forwarding a sense of recapitulation of the introduction as coda, Schoenberg constructs a symmetrical arch through the presentation of the figure in its inverted form.

The E-major signature (Ex. 2.1) that is affixed following the F-major resolution of the Introduction (Ex. 2.2) is allowed to triumph at the end of the work, but the final memory of the piece is not one of harmonic entanglements or formal complexities. It is, as William Austin has properly noted, the unprecedented instrumentation, which in spite of its reduced means, operates not only at a high dynamic level throughout most of the piece, but in high tessituras with octave doublings that create a laser-like shrillness. Individual parts are written at a virtuoso level, balances are difficult to achieve, and sadly the piece is little heard in live performance.

The *Second String Quartet* (1907–08) endorses the cyclicism of the *First* and the *Chamber Symphony,* although now in a traditional four-movement guise. In the introduction to the printed score, Schoenberg took great pains to point out the thematic interrelationships of the several movements. A comparison of the opening of the first and third movements is a good place to test the audibility of his claims. It is a constructive posture that Schoenberg would maintain to the end, and, as we shall see, is not unrelated to his insistence in later years that a single 12-note set should serve as the total resource for multimovement compositions.[5]

Example 2.4. Schoenberg, *String Quartet No. 2*, Mvt. 1, mm. 1–2; Mvt. 3, mm. 1–3.

Used by permission of Belmont Music Publishers.

More novel is the employment of the solo voice for the final two movements of the quartet, although this is clearly within the Beethoven-Mahler tradition of mixing literary and musical values, of cojoining the voice with an essentially abstract instrumental form. The consequences of such an alliance are extended here, and the large vocal leap on "Liebe" (love) near the end of the third movement (Ex. 10.2) suggests something of the Expressionist vocabulary that was to emerge in the setting of "Hilfe!" (help!) at the climax of *Erwartung* (Ex. 10.3) written shortly thereafter in 1909. A reading of the texts readily reveals not only the renowned breeze from other planets at the opening of the fourth movement but also the pervading philosophical mood of world sorrow upon which both are based ("Tief ist die Trauer," p. 31) and their relation to the world of Mahler ("Die Welt is tief, und tiefer als der Tag gedacht," p. 16) and Berg ("Das macht die Welt so tief schön," p. 46). But there is a spiritual note that is also strongly in evidence, and it ultimately prevails in the final lines: "I am only a sparkle of the holy fire, I am only a roaring of the holy voice."

The keys of the opening three movements are F♯ minor, D minor, and E minor respectively, but the prophetic text that opens the final movement ("I feel a breeze from other planets") appears to have led Schoenberg to a new style marked by increasing tonal instability. Yet, while the instrumental introduction is marked by a sequential though somewhat disorienting use of the total chromatic which reflects the absence of a key signature (Ex. 2.5), the movement is characterized by sections that periodically articulate tonal goals (Ex. 2.6), and in its final measure cadences firmly in F♯, the key of the first movement.

The entrances of the four instruments on G♯, D♯, B♭ and F at the beginning of the last movement endorse a classic tonal relationship. More dramatic is the tendency of the figure to establish F♯ as a tonal base. The intervalically identical 32nd-note pattern played by each of the instruments is divisible into two four-note patterns, both finishing with an appogiatura-like, downward semitonal resolution. The first four-note groups in cello and viola end on F♯ and C♯, as do the concluding four-note groups in the violins (marked * in Ex. 2.5). The importance Schoenberg attributed to melody as an expression of

Example 2.5. Schoenberg, *String Quartet No. 2*, Mvt. 4, opening.

Used by permission of Belmont Music Publishers.

Example 2.6. Schoenberg, *String Quartet No. 2*, Mvt. 4, vocal opening.

Used by permission of Belmont Music Publishers.

inner necessity placed in the service of a formal plan has traditionally been forwarded here as an explanation for the composer's "atonal" inclination. As if to protest that this was not due to a lack of traditional technique, Schoenberg demonstrated his mastery in the manipulation of tonal harmonic complexes in his contemporaneous *Harmonielehre* of 1911. Despite the discussion of 4th-chords and whole-tone segments near the end of the treatise, however, Schoenberg failed to provide a new set of laws for harmony, hoping only to demonstrate the basis of his craft. In his own music Schoenberg intuitively had begun to place in action a set of guidelines that tended to be reducible to the following:[6] a) avoid octaves (melodic and harmonic) and undiluted references to major and minor triads or dominant sevenths; b) emphasize melodic phrases exceeding an octave in range, and in so doing do not duplicate the same pitch in both octaves. Both the prescriptive and proscriptive qualities of such an attitude would continue to thrive in his formulation of a Method of Composing With Twelve Tones ten years later.

Little by little, as the erosion of a tonal base for his music became apparent, his choice of texts helped to indicate his expressive intentions. The George texts for the final two movements of Schoenberg's *Quartet No. 2* (1907–08) as well as for the song-cycle *The Book of the Hanging Gardens* (1908–09) proved to be catalytic for the developments that lay ahead.

Schoenberg, *String Quartet No. 2*

Mvt. 3: LITANEI

Tief ist die trauer die mich umdüstert,
Ein tret ich wieder, Herr! in dein haus.
Lang war die reise, matt sind die glieder,
Leer sind die schreine, voll nur die qual.
Durstende zunge darbt nach dem weine.
Hart war gestritten, starr ist mein arm.
Gönne die ruhe schwankenden schritten,
Hungrigem gaume bröckle dein brot!
Schwach ist mein atem refend dem traume,
Hohl sind die hände, fiebernd der mund.
Leih deine kühle, lösche die brände,
Tilge das hoffen, sende das licht!
Gluten im herzen lodern noch offen,
Innerst im grunde wacht noch ein schrei.
Töte das sehnen, schliesse die wunde!
Nimm mir die liebe, gib mir dein glück!

LITANY

Deep is the sadness that overclouds me,
once more I enter, Lord! in thy house.
Long was the journey, weak is my body,
bare are the coffers, full but my pain.
Thirsting, the tongue craves wine to refresh it,
hard was the fighting, stiff is my arm.
Grant thou a rest to feet that are falt'ring
nourish the hungry, break him thy bread!
Faint is my breath, recalling the vision,
empty my hands, and fev'rish my mouth.
Lend me thy coolness, quench thou the blazes,
let hope be perished, send forth thy light!
Fires are still burning open within me,
down in the depth still wakens a cry.
Kill ev'ry longing, close my heart's wound,
take from me love, and give me thy peace!

Mvt. 4: ENTRÜCKUNG

Ich fühle luft von anderem planeten.
Mir blassen durch das dunkel die gesichter
Die freundlich eben noch sich zu mir drehten.
Und bäum und wege die ich liebte fahlen
Dass ich sie kaum mehr kenne und du lichter
Geliebter schatten—rufer meiner qualen—
Bist nun erloschen ganz in tiefern gluten
Um nach dem taumel streitenden getobes
Mit einem frommen schauer anzumuten.
Ich löse mich in tönen, kreisend, webend,
Ungründigen danks und unbenamten lobes

TRANSPORT

I feel the air of another planet
the friendly faces that were turned toward me
but lately, now are fading into darkness.
The trees and paths I knew and loved so well
are barely visible, and you beloved
and radiant specter—cause of all my anguish—
You are wholly dimmed within a deeper glow,
whence, now that strife and tumult cease, there
comes the soothing tremor of a sacred awe.
I am dissolved in swirling sound, am weaving
unfathomed thanks with unnamed praise, and

Dem grossen atem wunschlos mich ergebend.	wishless I yield myself into the mighty breath.
Mich überfährt ein ungestümes wehen	A wild gust grips me suddenly, and I can
Im rausch der weihe wo inbrünstige schreie	hear the fervent cries and prayers of women
In staub geworfner beterinnen flehen:	prone in the dust and seized in pious rapture:
Dann seh ich wie sich duftige nebel lüpfen	And then I see the hazy vapors lifting
In einer sonnerfüllten klaren freie	above a sunlit, vast and clear expanse
Die nur umfängt auf fernsten bergesschlüpfen.	that stretches far below the mountain crags.
Der boden schüffert weiss und weich wie molke.	Beneath my feet a flooring soft and milky,
Ich steige über schluchten ungeheuer.	or endless chasms that I cross with ease.
Ich fühle wie ich über letzter wolke	Carried aloft beyond the highest cloud,
In einen, meer kristallnen glanzes schwimme—	I am afloat upon a sea of crystal splendor,
Ich bin ein funke nur vom heiligen feuer	I am only a sparkle of the holy fire,
Ich bin ein dröhnen nur der heiligen stimme.	I am only a roaring of the holy voice.

Stefan George
(As a typographical mannerism, Stefan George consistently avoided capitalizing the first letter of nouns, typical of standard German.)

English translation by Carl Engel, used by permission of Belmont Music Publishers.

THREE PIECES FOR PIANO, op. 11, and FIVE PIECES FOR ORCHESTRA, op. 16.

In 1909, a crucial year in Schoenberg's career, three works marked a stylistic change of fundamental importance: *Three Pieces for Piano*, op. 11; *Five Pieces for Orchestra*, op. 16; and *Erwartung*, op. 17. The piano pieces were Schoenberg's first works to suppress the key signature throughout, but motivic work in the first piece and an underlying ostinato in the second that emphasizes f-d-f provide the requisite anchors for orientation. In the third of the set, however, both tendencies are virtually abandoned in a discourse whose connective tissue resembles nothing so much as a literary stream of consciousness in spite of a lingering but faded motivic content.

The first piece of the set, op. 11, no. 1, has become the veritable symbol of a burgeoning atonality. Webern discussed it in his *The Path to Twelve-Note Composition* (1932) and tried to explain how the composition came to end on E flat, noting that the pitch fails to make an appearance until bar 12. The use of various analytical tools to show the stabilizing influence of particular pitch sets as well as their transformative capacity has spawned a literature like no other in the twentieth century, and indeed the question of pitch and motivic work is fascinating, even for fledgling analysts. In spite of rhythmic differences, the modest intervallic expansion between motif a' (minor 3rd–minor 2nd) and a" (major 3rd–minor 2nd) confirms their relationship in fusing a larger phraseological idea, A (Ex. 2.7). Moreover, harmonies clearly derived from the vertical alignment of a' can be noted at measure 3 and in the presentation of B and C materials, whose nonchanging pitch material is compensated for by a constant temporal shifting between them. Ultimately, the ear finds very little difficulty in following the music's course, though there are flickering interruptions that provide a memorable contrast (mm. 12–14), as well as new sonorities such as the piano harmonics (mm. 14–16), where the silently pressed notes of the right hand resonate in sympathetic vibration with the left hand in what sounds like a refracted recollection of "Paganini" from Schumann's *Carnaval*.

The orchestral pieces, op. 16, were an even more radical source for what was to come, not only with respect to a musical vocabulary that increasingly

Example 2.7. Schoenberg, *Three Pieces for Piano*, op. 11, mm. 1–16.

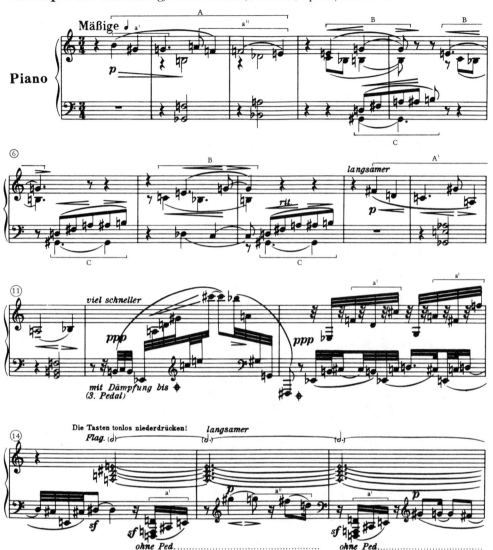

Used by permission of Belmont Music Publishers.

courted atonality and a syntax that encouraged free association, but with respect to a new psychological and form-giving color component. This is not to say that all the vestiges of an old order are abandoned as a new foundation is firmly secured for future works. In the first piece (see Ex. 2.8), a pedal chord (a), motivic work (b), and ostinato (c) act as a substitute life-support system for a waning tonality,[7] and the various sectional repetitions, both local and large-scale, of the second and fourth pieces neatly counterbalance the virtual suppression of these tendencies in the fifth.

The *Klangfarben* ("sound-color") idea of the third piece, however, is not only technically innovative but psychologically innervating. Although a five-note chord is continually recolored (note the simultaneous color change of

Example 2.8. Schoenberg, *Five Pieces for Orchestra*, op. 16, no. 1: a, b, c.

Used by permission of Belmont Music Publishers.

each pitch on the second half of m. 1, Ex. 2.9a) and subjected to semitonal modulation via a three-note canonic motif (note the black notes in Exs. 2.9a, c),[8] which accelerates precipitously at mm. 28–9 (Ex. 2.9b), the principal events are neither harmonic, melodic, nor rhythmic. The pulsating colors seep as if by osmosis through an essentially static landscape and induce a feverish stupor.

A brief article, *Anton Webern: Klangfarbenmelodie*, written by Schoenberg only four months before his death in 1951, is informative with respect to the composer's view of the term and his claims to originality.

> But as far as *Klangfarbenmelodien* are concerned it is above all untrue that I invented this expression after hearing Webern's *Klangfarben*-compositions. Particularly, anyone can see that I had thought of progressions of tone-colours equalling harmonic progression in terms of inner logic. These I called melodies, because, like melodies, they would need to be given form, and to the same extent— but according to laws of their own, in keeping with their nature . . . For progressions of tone-colours would certainly demand constructions different from those required by progressions of tones, or of harmonies. For they were all that, and specific tone-colours as well.[9]

Years before, with the composition of op. 16 just behind him, Schoenberg had been prompted to similar remarks in his *Harmonielehre* of 1911:

> The distinction between tone color and pitch, as it is usually expressed, I cannot accept without reservations. I think the tone becomes perceptible by virtue of tone color, of which one dimension is pitch. Tone color is, thus, the main topic, pitch a subdivision. Pitch is nothing else but tone color measured in one direction. Now, if it is possible to create patterns out of tone colors . . . then it must also be possible to make such progressions out of the tone colors . . . progressions whose relations with one another work with a kind of logic entirely equivalent to that logic which satisfies us in the melody of pitches.[10]

Example 2.9. Schoenberg, *Five Pieces for Orchestra*, op. 16, no. 3; harmonic reduction.

(a)

fl/eng hn
fl/tpt
cl/bn

bn/Fr hn
va/db

(b)

(c)

Used by permission of Belmont Music Publishers.

While the titles to the five movements were affixed at the request of the publisher, Schoenberg's agony over them and eventual capitulation to their use is not unlike Mahler's lifelong dilemma concerning programs for his symphonies. An entry in Schoenberg's diary of January 27, 1912 reads in part[11]:

> Now, the titles which I may provide give nothing away, because some of them are very obscure and others highly technical. To wit:
>
> I. Premonitions (everybody has those)
> II. The Past (everybody has that, too)
> III. Chord-Colours (technical)
> IV. Peripetia (general enough, I think)
> V. The Obligato (perhaps better than 'fully-developed' or the 'endless') Recitative.
>
> However, there should be a note that these titles were added for technical reasons of publication and not to give a 'poetic' content.

In spite of Schoenberg's disclaimer of their importance, it will be noted that the titles for I, II, and IV have a pronounced psychological undertone; also, from a technical standpoint, the pervasiveness of "liberating" forces in the *Five Pieces* is ultimately uncontestable. Their fitness for a new assignment in *Die glückliche Hand* and *Erwartung* as companions to literary texts with a highly developed Expressionist content was to prove patently providential.

REPERTOIRE

Verklärte Nacht, op. 4 (1899), str sxt
Pelléas und Mélisande, op. 5 (1902–03), orch
Gurrelieder (1900–01; orch. 1901–03, 1910–11), solo vv, choruses, orch
Orchesterlieder, op. 8 (1903–05), S, orch
       "Sehnsucht" (1905) (*Des Knaben Wunderhorn*)
Kammersymphonie No. 1, op. 9 (1906), fl/pic, ob, eng hn, 3 cl, bn, cbn, 2 hn, str qnt
String Quartet No. 2, op. 10 (1907–08)
"Der verlorene Haufen" from *Two Ballads*, op. 12 (1907), Bar, pf
Drei Klavierstücke, op. 11 (1909), pf
Fünf Orchesterstücke, op. 16 (1909), orch

READING

Arnold Schoenberg, *Harmonielehre* (1911), Eng. trans. Roy Carter (Berkeley, 1978).
Arnold Schoenberg, "Franz Liszt's Work and Being" (1911); "Gustav Mahler: In Memoriam" (1912) in *Style and Idea*, ed. Leonard Stein (New York, 1975).
Alban Berg, thematic analyses of Schoenberg's *Gurrelieder* (1913), *Pelleas und Melisande*, op. 5 (1920), and *Kammersymphonie*, op. 9 (1921).
Philip Friedheim, "Rhythmic Structure in Schoenberg's Atonal Compositions," *Journal of the American Musicological Society*, xix (1966), 59–72.
Benjamin Boretz and Edward Cone, eds., *Perspectives on Schoenberg and Stravinsky* (Princeton, 1968).
Robert Craft, "Schoenberg's Five Pieces for Orchestra," *Perspectives on Schoenberg and Stravinsky* (1968), 3–24.
Reinhold Brinkmann, *Arnold Schönberg: Drei Klavierstücke Op. 11* (Wiesbaden, 1969).
Erich Doflein, Peter Förtig, Josef Rufer, "Schoenberg's Op. 16," *Melos*, xxxvi (1969), 203, 206, 209, 366.
Ursula von Rauchhaupt, ed., *Schoenberg, Berg, Webern: the String Quartets, a Documentary Study* (Munich, 1971).
Willi Reich, *Schoenberg: a critical biography*, trans. Leo Black (London, 1971), 1–52.

Charles Rosen, *Arnold Schoenberg* (New York, 1975).

Allen Forte, "Schoenberg's Creative Evolution: The Path to Atonality," *Musical Quarterly*, 64 (1978).

Glenn Watkins, "Schoenberg Re-Cycled" in *Essays on Music for Charles Warren Fox* (Eastman School of Music Press, 1979), 72.

Dika Newlin, *Schoenberg Remembered* (New York, 1980).

Allen Forte, "The Magical Kaleidoscope: Schoenberg's First Atonal Masterwork, Opus 11, No. 1," *Journal of the Arnold Schoenberg Institute*, ii (1981), 127.

Will Ogdon, "How Tonality Functions in Schoenberg's Opus 11, No. 1," *Journal of the Arnold Schoenberg Institute*, ii (1981), 169.

CHAPTER 3

WEBERN: OPUS 1 TO OPUS 12

BACKGROUNDS AND EARLY WORKS: NATURE AND THE *WUNDERHORN*

Anton Webern (1883–1945), the Sphinx of twentieth century music, immutable, inimitable, and enigmatic, was born in Vienna in the year of Wagner's death. His parents had a sufficiently cultivated taste for music that he was rewarded with a trip to the Bayreuth Festival in 1902 upon his graduation from the Gymnasium. His reaction to the performance of *Parsifal* that he heard there was stereotypical for the time: "In the face of such magnificence, one can only sink to one's knees and pray in silent devotion."[1] A similar reaction to Beethoven's Ninth Symphony, which he heard in 1903, was equally predictable: "O, divine Beethoven! It was the most sacred hour of my life up till now."[2] In the Fall of 1902 he enrolled at the University of Vienna, where he studied musicology with the eminent scholar Guido Adler. His introduction to the mysteries of Medieval and Renaissance mensural notation coincided with his increasing knowledge of and admiration for the music of Strauss, Liszt, Mahler, Wagner, and Beethoven.

Having written a ballad for voice and full orchestra entitled *Siegfried's Sword* in the Fall of 1903, Webern's studies at the university introduced him to a series of topics and figures including Kant, Schopenhauer, Nietzsche, Goethe, Schiller, and their relation to music, as well as a continuing course on "Analysis and Evaluation of Art Works." He had also heard a performance of Schoenberg's *Verklärte Nacht* in the 1903–04 concert season and had seen a score of *Pelleas und Melisande*. He later wrote Schoenberg (1907) that

> . . . the thing never let go of me after that. I could not stop wondering what this music might be like. I still remember how, during the following summer, I was almost exclusively possessed by this thought.[3]

In the summer of 1904, Webern wrote the orchestral idyll *Im Sommerwind*, which had a literary base in a poem by Bruno Wille and carried an echo from Schoenberg's *Gurrelieder* ("The Wild Hunt of the Summer Wind"). Its voice, although traditional, is securely proportioned and scored. The sounds of the forest murmurs of *Siegfried* are not far distant, but the dynamic prescription for the final cadence "bis zu gänzlicher Unhörbarkeit" ("down to total inaudibility") is prescient in light of his future development.

Together with Alban Berg he became a private composition student of
Schoenberg in the Fall of 1904. It should be underscored that Schoenberg's own
musical language at this time was thoroughly traditional, and the crucial developments that lay just ahead would be made in full view of Schoenberg's two
talented students who, it must be added, participated in the ferment with individual compositions of their own. Webern reflected about the importance of
these years in a 1932 lecture entitled *The Path to the New Music:*

> With all these things we approach the catastrophe: 1906, Schoenberg's *Chamber
> Symphony* (fourth-chords!); 1908, music by Schoenberg that's no longer in any key
> . . . In 1906 Schoenberg came back from a stay in the country, bringing the
> *Chamber Symphony.* It made a colossal impression. I'd been his pupil for three
> years, and immediately felt "You must write something like that, too!" . . . Under
> the influence of the work I wrote a sonata movement the very next day. In that
> movement I reached the farthest limits of tonality.[4]

Webern goes on to illustrate the dissolution of tonality in Schoenberg's
Three Piano Pieces, op. 11, and the *Georgelieder,* op. 15, noting the logic of
several final cadences that are neither triadic or in significant relation to the
pitch levels of the beginning. Webern might also have recalled that his own
path had been swiftly and decisively traversed. Although his *Passacaglia,* op. 1,
contains a D minor theme suggestive of the finale to Beethoven's "Eroica" in its
preponderance of rests, the further extension of tonal boundaries was soon
clearly perceivable in his *Entflieht auf leichten Kähnen,* op. 2 (1908), for unaccompanied mixed chorus, the Five Songs for voice and piano, op. 3 (1907–08),
and the Five Songs, op. 4 (1908–09), all on texts of Stefan George.

While the abolition of tonality appeared to be the principal aim of some of
these pieces, Schoenberg and his pupils insisted that it was the result of an
inner necessity rather than a predetermined goal. As Webern remarked in 1912
concerning Schoenberg's early music:

> The experiences of his heart become music. Schoenberg's relation to art is rooted
> entirely in the need for expression. His emotions are of burning fire: they create
> completely new values of expression, and so they need new means of expression.
> Content and form cannot be separated.[5]

Such sentiments are almost a direct mirror of contemporaneous statements
made by Kandinsky in his essay "On the Question of Form" and Schoenberg's
"The Relationship to the Text," both of which appeared in the almanac *Der Blaue
Reiter* (1912). But they are also rooted, especially with Webern, in an abiding
devotion to Goethe's *Farbenlehre* ("Theory of Color," 1805–10) and *Die Meta-
morphose der Pflanzen* ("The Metamorphosis of Plants," 1790) and the belief
that musical composition reflects the more general principles of nature. The
initial lecture of his "The Path to the New Music" (1932) is almost totally given
over to a discussion of Goethe and Webern's dependent view that musical
questions deal of necessity not with *aesthetic* issues but with principles of
natural law. Nature's coherent premise—"always the same, always different"—
provides the basis for all expression. That this is a point of view that will
underlie his later adoption of the method of composing with 12 notes should be
kept in mind.

Webern's lifelong intoxication with Nature can be noted in his original
poetry written as early as 1904, as well as in his choice of Bruno Wille's paean to

nature, "Im Sommerwind," as the textual inspiration for his symphonic idyll of the same year. Corroborations of this almost consuming orientation, and especially of his love for the high mountain regions, can be seen in the following excerpt from a letter of 1910:

> I will ascend the Triglav, a very high and rather difficult peak. Perhaps you find it ridiculous that I do something like this, but what attracts me is the unique atmosphere on the heights of the mountains, its delicate and pure quality.[6]

In turn we are reminded of the line from the final movement of Mahler's *Das Lied von der Erde:* "Where am I going? I go wandering in the mountains. I seek peace from my lonely heart."

In spite of the stylistic gulf that seems to separate the world of Webern and Mahler, it is intriguing to note a common sensibility in their choice of texts. The simple charm of Goethe's scientifically enlightened gem, "Gleich und Gleich," set earlier by Wolf, appears in Webern's *Four Songs,* op. 12, alongside the *Volkslied,* "Der Tag ist vergangen,"[7] a poem of Strindberg and another from *Des Knaben Wunderhorn.* Similarly, poems by Karl Kraus and George Trakl frame two selections from Bethge's *Chinesische Flöte* in his op. 13 set. Many of the songs of op. 15–18, which date from 1917–25, continue to emphasize in their textual choices the simplicity of a number of the folk-religious poems of the Arnim and Brentano anthology, particularly on themes of the Virgin Mary. While there is a general absence of folk-like melodies in Webern's world, texture and dimension are typically pared to the bone and are in total harmony with the texts they project. Occasionally, Webern will adopt the four-square phraseology of the texts, promoting a feeling for the antecedent and consequent phraseology typical of folksong, as in "Der Tag ist vergangen," which also courts F major in the vocal line (see Ex. 3.1).

Webern, *Two Songs* from op. 12

GLEICH UND GLEICH

Ein Blumenglöckchen vom Boden hervor war früh gesprosset in lieblichem Flor; da kam ein Bienchen und naschte fein: Die müssen wohl beide für einander sein. *Goethe*	A flowerbell from the soil blossomed early in a lovely bloom; a little bee came and nibbled delicately: They must have been meant for each other.

DER TAG IST VERGANGEN

Der Tag ist vergangen, die Nacht is schon hier, gute Nacht, o Maria, bleib ewig bei mir.	Day is done night is already here, good night, O Maria, remain always with me.
Der Tag ist vergangen, die Nacht kommt herzu, gib auch den Verstorbnen die ewige Ruh. *Volkslied*	Day is done, night approaches, give also to the deceased eternal rest. *Folksong*

Elsewhere, however, as in "Dormi Jesu," a later *Wunderhorn* setting of 1924, Webern used the folk-text tradition as a springboard for a highly individual art

Example 3.1. Webern, "Der Tag ist vergangen," from *Vier Lieder*, op. 12, no. 1.

characterized by an even more exaggerated intervallic content that favors tritones, sevenths, and ninths (see Ex. 18.2).

ORCHESTRAL WORKS, OP. 6 AND 10

The reduction of the orchestra to a group of 13 instruments in Webern's op. 13 songs of 1914–18 is reflective not only of his chamber approach to the orchestra in his *Six Pieces* for large orchestra, op. 6, (1909) and the *Five Pieces*, op. 10 (1911–13), but also Schoenberg's ground-breaking *Kammersymphonie*, op. 9 (1906), and beyond that the world of Mahler. The *Klangfarben* idea applied to linear ideas, as in the opening of Webern's op. 6, no. 1,

Example 3.2. Webern, *Six Pieces for Orchestra*, Op. 6 (original 1909 version), no. 1, mm. 1–2.

or in a harmonic progression, as in the opening chord sequence of the fourth movement from the same set (*alla marcia funebre*),

Example 3.3. Webern, *Six Pieces for Orchestra* (original 1909 version), op. 6, no. 4, 3 chords from Rehearsal No. 2.

2 Fl.   4 Hr.   4 Trp.
2 Clar.   (con sord.) (con sord.)

clearly point to Schoenberg's op. 16, no. 3 as model. But the delicate use of harmonium, celesta, mandoline, guitar, and harp in the opening of Webern's op. 10, no. 3 (Ex. 3.4), colored by bells of indefinite pitch and carrying the direction "hardly audible—fading away," evokes the sound of distant cowbells high in the mountains of his native Mittersill, and can also be heard as a reflection of a similar imagery in the final movement of Mahler's Sixth Symphony. Webern's veneration of the Viennese master seals the palpability of such a relationship. The extreme brevity of many of the movements of the op. 10 set (they are 12, 14, 11, 6, and 32 bars long, respectively), together with many other of his works of the period (the three cello pieces, op. 11, for example, are 9, 13, and 10 bars in length), may have been suggested by Schoenberg's *Six Little Piano Pieces*, op. 19 (1911). But what for his teacher was a singular essay became for Webern a dimension of his personality and a measure of the concision of his thought.

In an introduction to the equally brief *Bagatelles for String Quartet*, op. 9 (1913), for their initial printing in 1924, Schoenberg wrote in part:

> Though the brevity of these pieces is a persuasive advocate for them: on the other hand this very brevity needs an advocate. One has to realize what restraint it needs to express oneself with such brevity. Every glance can be expanded into a poem, every sigh into a novel. But to express a novel in a single gesture, joy in a single breath: such concentration can only be found where self-pity is lacking in equal measure.

Example 3.4. Webern, Five Pieces for Orchestra, op. 10, no. 3, mm. 1–4.

These pieces can only be understood by those who believe that sound can say things which can only be expressed through sound.

They stand up to criticism as little as beliefs of any kind.[7]

REPERTOIRE

Im Sommerwind (1904), orch
Passacaglia, op. 1 (1908), orch
Entflieht auf leichten Kähnen, op. 2 (1908), chorus
Five Movements for String Quartet, op. 5 (1909)

Six Pieces for Orchestra, op. 6 (1909)
Six Bagatelles for String Quartet, op. 9 (1913)
Five Pieces for Orchestra, op. 10 (1911–13)
Three Little Pieces for Cello and Piano, op. 11 (1914)
Four Songs, op. 12 (1915)
    "Der Tag ist vergangen" (Volkslied)
    "Gleich und Gleich" (Goethe)

READING

Anton Webern, *The Path to the New Music*, ed. Willi Reich (Eng. trans. Bryn Mawr, Pa., 1963).

Arnold Elston and others, "Some Views of Webern's Op. 6, no. 1," *Perspectives of New Music*, vi.1 (1967), 63.

Walter Kolneder, *Anton Webern* (Berkeley, 1968).

Hans Moldenhauer, *Anton von Webern* (New York, 1979).

Paul Griffiths, "Anton Webern", *The New Grove Dictionary of Music and Musicians* (1980), vol. 20, 271–3, sec. 2, 3.

Edward Reilly, *Gustav Mahler and Guido Adler* (New York: Cambridge Univ. Press, 1982).

Nancy Perloff, "Klee and Webern: Speculations on Modernist Theories of Composition," *Musical Quarterly*, lxix.2 (1983), 180.

CHAPTER 4

ALBAN BERG
BEFORE *WOZZECK*

As we have seen, Alban Berg (1885–1935) joined the composition class of Schoenberg in 1904 at the same time as Webern. In spite of the differences in the musical personalities of these three composers, the following excerpt from a letter written by Berg to his wife on his way to Munich for the first performance of Mahler's *Das Lied von der Erde* with Bruno Walter as conductor indicates with unusual clarity the degree to which he shared their common spiritual affinity for the world of nature.[1]

On the train to Munich
20 November 1911

. . . Anyhow, an hour has gone as I sit in this compartment, my sadness for you mixed with expectations of the concert, and all the time magnificent scenery gliding past: dark forests in the horizon; closer up, the purple-brown strips of woodland with bare leafless trees; and right in the foreground vast frosty meadows; a pale-blue sky above, almost white, with a rare magical radiance. New valleys continually emerging, the mountains receding, till at last the immense plain lies before me . . . You will understand what I mean, Helene, since God has bestowed on you the gift of appreciating and praising his Creations, a solitary tree, a book of Strindberg, a symphony by Mahler, or anywhere His mysteries can be perceived behind the blemishes . . . This is our Song of the Earth, scoffed at and misunderstood by the materialists, who know nothing of life or death being twilight, for whom everything on earth has its clear-cut, scientific explanation.

Mahler had died on May 18, leaving this work as part of his legacy. The reference to "life or death being twilight" clearly refers to the refrain "Dunkel ist das Leben, ist der Tod" in the first song of Mahler's symphony and indicates that Berg had received notice of the texts in advance.

"WARM DIE LÜFTE," OP. 2, NO. 4

Such reflections help to tune the reader to the poetry of Berg's early songs where we note a familiar ring in the final line of the Mombert song, op. 2, no. 4 ("Das macht die Welt so tief schön"), which recalls Nietzsche's "Die Welt ist tief und tiefer als der Tag gedacht" (see p. 16) used by Mahler in the *Third Symphony.*

45

Warm die Lüfte, es spriesst Gras auf sonnigen Wiesen,	In the warm breezes, grass sprouts from sunny meadows.
Horch! Horch es flötet die Nachtigall.	Listen! Listen, the nightingale pipes away.
Ich will singen:	I wish to sing:
Droben hoch im düstern Bergforst es schmilzt und glitzert kalte Schnee,	High in the dark mountain forest, cold snow melts and glitters,
Ein Mädchen in grauen Kleide lehnt an feuchten Eichstamm,	A maiden clad in grey leans against the damp trunk of an oak tree.
Krank sind ihre zarten Wangen,	Sick are her tender cheeks,
Die grauen Augen fiebern durch Düsterriesenstämme.	Her grey eyes feverish through the sombre giant tree trunks.
"Er kommt noch nicht. Er lässt mich warten."	"He still does not come! He leaves me waiting."
Stirb! Der Eine stirbt, daneben der Andre lebt:	Die! The one dies, the other lives:
Das macht die Welt so tiefschön.	From such stems the world's profound splendor.
Mombert	

Berg's first published work was a *Piano Sonata* of 1908, but almost simultaneously he returned to writing a set of songs—about 70 earlier examples survive—that was to become his op. 2. The last of these, "Warm die Lüfte," miraculously captures in microcosm numerous traits that were to appear in Berg's late style: (a) the contrary motion white-note/black-note glissando at m. 15 (climaxing at the end of the following text: "A girl dressed in grey leans against the moist bole of an oak; Sickness is in her tender cheeks; The grey eyes febrile through the sombre forest giants") prefigures similar juxtapositions not only in *Der Wein* (1929), mm. 196–7, and *Lulu*, Act III, s. 1 (mm. 560–3, where the Groom exchanges clothes with the sick Lulu in order to evade the police), but other black-white hexachordal collections in the late serial style; and (b) the prominence of ascending parallel fifths a tritone apart at mm. 11–12 ("cold snow melts and glitters") is an almost uncanny foretelling of the music that immediately follows the 12-note chord that announces the death of Lulu at the hands of Jack the Ripper in Act III, scene 2.

Example 4.1. Berg, "Warm die Lüfte," op. 2, no. 4, m. 11.

*) *Der Vorschlag ruhig und langsam zu nehmen!*

Reprinted by permission of the original publisher Robert Lienau, Berlin.

Example 4.2. Berg, *Lulu*, Act III, s. 2, mm. 1294–5.

In addition to the prominent use of French sixths in the second song, which suggests a familiarity with Debussy's *Pelléas* (see p. 79), and the augmented-triad/whole-tone formations in the third, the last song of the set approaches its final cadence with a series of progressions composed of quartal structures in the right hand (previously utilized in the first song of the set) now descending chromatically over rising fourths in the bass voice (Ex. 4.6). While its genesis in a passage such as the following from Brahms (Ex. 4.3) is convincing in light of nationalist legacies, given Schoenberg's predeliction for quartal structures and whole-tone patterns from the time of his *Kammersymphonie* (Ex. 2.2) as well as his discussion of them in the final chapters of his *Harmonielehre* (including a citation of Ex. 4.6, m. 22), it would be logical to assume that whatever we find of these two issues in the music of Berg at this time would have come to him

Example 4.3. Brahms, "Intermezzo," op. 116, no. 2, m. 63.

directly via the music of his teacher. But it is also known that in his early studies, Berg had been attracted to the music of the French Impressionists, a music largely unknown to Schoenberg by his own admission. While it is unlikely that Berg would have known Satie's quartal prelude *Le fils des étoiles* at this date (Ex. 4.4; later orchestrated by Ravel in 1914), he undoubtedly knew Ravel's excursions into this harmonic terrain, particularly "La valée des cloches," the final piece of his *Miroirs* of 1905 (Ex. 4.5).

Example 4.4. Satie, *Le fils des étoiles* (opening) (1891).

Example 4.5. Ravel, *Miroirs*: "La valée des cloches," mm. 4–5.

While Ravel's example may be seen as a harmonic embellishment (added sixth and ninth) of an E major triad—a rather more airborne version of Schoenberg's appoggiature 4th-chord at the opening of his *Kammersymphonie*—the independence of his fourths is dramatized in the final cadence sonority. In light

Example 4.6. Berg, 'Warm die Lüfte," op. 2, no. 4, mm. 18–25.

Reprinted by permission of the original publisher Robert Lienau, Berlin.

of Berg's professed admiration for the music of Debussy and Ravel at this time, it is intriguing to juxtapose the finale of the last Mombert song, op. 2 (Ex. 4.6), completed in 1910, with the passage in Ravel's "Le gibet" from *Gaspard de la nuit* (Ex. 4.7) finished in the summer of 1908.

Example 4.7. Ravel, *Gaspard de la nuit:* "Le gibet," mm. 24–25.

The downward rush from Berg's climax comes to rest on a B♭(Ex. 4.6, m. 18), which is treated to a tolling repetition directly referrable to the pedal-note of Ravel's entire composition (see Ex. 6.2, p. 109). This is followed by a chord progression at the same pitch level on which it occurs in "Le gibet". The appropriateness of such an allusion is compounded by the juxtaposition of the two attending texts, Ravel's hanging corpse (see p. 106) and Berg's words "Der Eine stirbt" (see p. 46).[2]

Before pressing the possibility of a connection between Ravel and the youthful Berg, it is helpful to recall that the Viennese Secession had gotten underway at the turn of the century with headquarters in the same building in which Berg was raised as a boy. The importance of the French art nouveau movement for progressive Viennese taste of the time is especially obvious in Berg's own highly stylized lettering for the title pages of both his *Piano Sonata,* op. 1 and his *Four Songs,* op. 2 (Figure 4.1). Here, Berg dramatically betrays in nonmusical terms his allegiance to the art nouveau-based *Jugendstil* of Klimt, and by extension reflects his awareness of contemporary French musical values, especially those of Ravel, whose music he followed assiduously at the time. His lingering taste not only for Ravel but for *Gaspard de la nuit* in particular is reflected in the appearance of the latter work in one of the "propaganda evenings" of Schoenberg's Society for Private Musical Performances, May 20, 1919, which also included Berg's *Piano Sonata,* op. 1.[3] The work was to resurface under the same auspices the next year on October 23, 1920, with Ravel in attendance (see p. 193).

In addition to an ameliorating French influence and the direct guidance of his teacher Schoenberg, the figure of Gustav Mahler was to prove fundamental for Berg to the end of his career. The directness—even simplicity of approach without any hint of spareness that was so typical of the works of Mahler—was to be the key to the appeal. Not only precision and reduction (which were the mark of so much of the work of Loos, Webern, and Schoenberg at this time), but especially the use of forcefully recognizable ingredients of a more directly appealing language, is the common denominator that joins Klimt, Mahler, and Berg. It is the musician, Mahler, who was naturally best able to suggest to Berg the basis of such an appeal through recourse to the thoroughly German traditions of the Ländler, the march and folksong—ingredients that appear only sporadically and more covertly in the works of Schoenberg. We shall see how this tendency quickly develops once Berg is no longer a student of Schoenberg, even as the pupil will protest to the end of his days his undying devotion to his master. The sense of struggle that was present in preserving this loyalty is also

ALBAN·BERG
VIER·LIEDER
FÜR·EINE·SINGSTIME
MIT·KLAVIER·OPUS·2
NACH·GEDICHTEN·VON
HEBBEL·UND·MOMBERT

Figure 4.1. Berg's own *Jugendstil* lettering, which appears on the title pages of his *Piano Sonata,* op. 1, and the *Four songs,* op. 2, reflects the influence of *art nouveau* on *Secession* taste.

Reprinted by permission of the original publisher Robert Lienau Musikverlag, Berlin.

one of the keys to an appreciation of the ultimate posture of Berg as a mature artist.

THE *ALTENBERGLIEDER*, OP. 4

In the *Altenberglieder*, op. 4 (1912), the pervasive influence of Schoenberg is naturally present. But there are other forces as well. The idea of the song, so congenial to the early composer, now takes a decisive step through the introduction of the orchestra. Mahler's orchestral songs are the clear progenitors, although Schoenberg's orchestral songs, op. 8, had already appeared in 1904. The spiritual ancestry of Berg's opus is underscored in the program that saw the premiere of two of the songs in March 1913, where they were performed together with Mahler's *Kindertotenlieder* and Zemlinsky's *Four Maeterlinck Songs* as well as Webern's orchestral pieces, op. 6, and Schoenberg's *Kammersymphonie*, op. 9. Although formal lessons with Schoenberg had come to an end, Berg still visited Schoenberg regularly, as he stated, ". . . twice a week at his house . . . when to each lesson I bring the continuation of the *Gurrelieder* work, see his new paintings, and look at songs by Mahler."[4]

The original idea for the *Altenberglieder* was a large work with voices on the order of the Mahler symphonies. What he wrote instead suggests how Berg achieved a distillation of Mahler's world and the newer trends of his teacher:

1. The idea of the orchestral song was clearly Mahlerian.

2. The opening orchestral introduction may be compared directly through ostinato figure and texture with the orchestral prelude to Schoenberg's *Gurrelieder*, a work with which Berg had been involved as an editorial assistant. Berg was responsible for the proofreading of the parts for the first performance of Schoenberg's *Gurrelieder* on February 23, 1913, and also in part for the preparation of the chorus. His original guide to the work, published in 1913, was a large analytical work of over 100 pages. A shortened version appeared in the next year. In the orchestral introduction to the first song, Berg introduces as many as six independent ostinati, the most prominent of which is a five-note idea (g"-e"-f'-b'-a') heard in the piccolo, clarinet, glockenspiel/xylophone, violins, and violas. Beginning in measure 5, Berg transposes the figure sequentially, with the initial note appearing on G, A♭, B♭, C♯, and E, pitches that will reappear at the opening of his Passacaglia, the last song of the set (see Ex. 4.8). The urge to incorporate cyclic details, familiar from works by both Mahler and Schoenberg, is apparent.

3. The entrance of the voice following the introduction of the first song is on three levels of audibility: lips closed, lips half closed, and finally a full-voiced intonation of the opening word "Seele." While the *Sprechstimme* clearly marked with crossed stems in the third song of the set (at "plötzlich ist alles aus") more clearly reflects Berg's awareness of Schoenberg's prior concern for vocal refinements and extensions in *Gurrelieder, Die glückliche Hand* and *Pierrot lunaire*, the entrance of the voice in the first piece marks not only Berg's initiation into the arena of expanded vocal means, but prefigures a concern that was to persist to the end of his career. The Prologue to *Lulu*, for example, is a virtual catalogue of such practices, ranging from spoken voice through *Sprechstimme* to normal singing style.

Example 4.8. Berg, *Altenberglieder*, op. 4, no. 5, piano vocal score, 11 mm. from the Introduction, Rehearsal no. 1, to the beginning of Rehearsal no. 2.

4. The use of the orchestra in a manner that emphasizes subtle chamber groupings, while stemming from Mahler, reflects directly on his familiarity with Schoenberg's orchestral pieces, op. 9 and 16: The colorations of the opening 12-note chord of the third song, for example, in which each tone is played by a different solo instrument—phasing out to a single tone and mirroring the process in reverse with strings and celesta at the end—suggests that Schoenberg's *Klangfarben* technique of op. 16, no. 3, was clearly in Berg's mind.

5. The subtle instrumental details at the close of the first song (harmonium, celesta) recall not only Schoenberg's orchestral pieces, particularly op. 16, no. 2, but his evocative *Herzgewächse* (voice, harmonium, celesta, harp) which, we note with interest, had been published together with Berg's Mombert song, op. 2, no. 4 (see pp. 45–51), in *Der Blaue Reiter*, a journal edited by Kandinsky

and Marc in 1912. The piece concludes with a violin glissando marked by a wavy line which ascends to a note of indeterminate pitch. It was perhaps details such as this which prompted Schoenberg to charge Berg with "novelties" in this work.

6. Finally, the last song (Ex. 4.8), and the most Romantic of the set, is a passacaglia that addresses the prevalent concern at the time for the potentially disastrous formal consequences of a loosening tonal structure, evidenced by Schoenberg's introduction of a freely fashioned passacaglia in *Pierrot lunaire* only shortly before. Following the basic five-note motif (x), Berg employs a wedge-like 12-note countersubject (y), which reinforces the evidence of the third song with respect to Berg's systematic exploration of the total chromatic. About halfway through this countersubject, Berg introduces two chains of rising fourths (z). The cojoining of chromatic sopranos with functional-looking basses had not only appeared earlier (Ex. 4.6) but was a feature that Berg would retain into his maturity.

Berg's admiration for Peter Altenberg (1859–1919) found a special creative outlet in his set of *Five Orchestral Songs*. That Altenberg's poetry caught the spirit of the composer's infatuation with Nature we sense from the first song, wherein he speaks of snowstorms of the soul. The gradually gathering fury of the snowstorm portrayed in its orchestral introduction is counterbalanced by the conclusion of the final song, wherein decaying strokes of the tam-tam mirror its dissolution: "Here snow drops gently into pools of water . . ." A friend of Berg, as well as Karl Kraus, Adolf Loos, and Oskar Kokoschka, Altenberg was an eccentric with a special talent for the prose aphorism. Not given to the treatment of universals but rather the fleeting quality of existence, he had a keen eye and ear that could extract essences from the trivia of daily life and deliver them in what he called the "telegram-style of the soul." His spareness betrayed no hint of "decadence" and was in harmony with Loos's architectural approach, which idealized the purity of the Japanese house; with Kraus's crusade to bring the German language to a new level of precision and economy; and only marginally with the tortured mind of Kokoschka, whose portraits of Altenberg (1909) and Webern (1914) show him moving directly into the maelstrom of Expressionism.

The historic nature of the first performance of these songs was not only in the artistic association (Berg, Webern, Schoenberg, Zemlinsky) but in the event itself, which was rocked by scandal when Berg's cycle was broken off after the second song. A critic wrote in the *Musical Courier* for April 23, 1913, the following account:

> If the concert was intended to be a memorable occasion, it surely succeeded for it occasioned the greatest uproar which has occurred in a Vienna concert hall in the memory of the oldest critics writing. Laughter, hisses, applause continued throughout a great deal of the actual performance . . . After the Berg songs the dispute became almost a riot . . . Finally, the president of the Society came and boxed the ears of a man who had insulted him . . .

While the songs were destined to remain unperformed complete in Berg's lifetime and unpublished in full score until 1966, they have become increasingly well known and admired by concertgoers since their first performance in 1954.

In addition to being the composer's first work for orchestra, the *Altenberglieder* was a remarkable essay on the relation of the voice to an instrumental ensemble. In this work and the *Three Pieces for Orchestra*, op. 6, of the next year, Berg secured the technical prowess and expressive vocabulary that were to serve in the composition of *Wozzeck*.

Five Orchestral Songs, op. 4, to words written on picture postcards by Peter Altenberg

I.
Seele, wie bist du schöner, tiefer, nach
   Schneestürmen
Auch du hast sie, gleich der Natur.
Und über beiden liegt noch ein trüber Hauch,
   eh das Gewölk sich verzog!

II.
Sahst du noch dem Gewitterregen den
   Wald?!?!
Alles rastet, blinkt und ist schöner als zuvor.
Siehe, Frau, auch du brauchst Gewitterregen!

III.
Über die Grenzen des All blicktest du sin-
   nend hinaus;
Hattest nie Sorge um Hof und Haus!
Leben und Traum vom Leben plötzlich ist
   alles aus.
Über die Grenzen des All blickst du noch
   sinnend hinaus!

IV.
Nichts ist gekommen, nichts wird kommen
   für meine Seele.
Ich habe gewartet, gewartet, oh, gewartet!
Die Tage werden dahinschleichen,
   und umsonst wehen meine aschblonden,
   seidenen Haare um mein bleiches Antlitz!

V.
Hier ist Friede. Hier weine ich mich aus über
   alles!
Hier löst sich mein unfassbares, unermess-
   liches Leid das mir die Seele verbrennt . . .
Siehe, hier sind keine Menschen, keine
   Antsiedlungen . . .
Hier ist Friede! Hier tropft Schnee leise in
   Wasserlachen.

Peter Altenberg—Fünf Texte für Alban Bergs FÜNF ORCHESTERLIEDER. By permission of S. Fisher Verlag GmbH. Frankfurt am Main.

I.
Soul, how much more beautiful, more
   profound you are after snowstorms
You, too, have them as Nature does.
And over both still lies a troubled breath,
Before the clouds disperse themselves!

II.
Have you seen the forest after a
   thunderstorm?!?!
Everything rests, sparkles and is more
   beautiful than before.
See, lady, you too need thunderstorms!

III.
Beyond the boundaries of the universe
   you ponderingly looked out;
You have never had worries about house
   and home!
Life and dream of life are suddenly gone.
Beyond the boundaries of the universe
   you still ponderingly look out!

IV.
Nothing has come, nothing will come for
   my soul.
I have waited, waited, oh, waited!
The days shall slip away, and in vain
   flutters my ash-blond, silken hair around
   my pale face!

V.
Here is peace. Here I weep about
   everything!
Here is released my incomprehensible, ·
   immeasurable sorrow, which consumes
   my soul . . .
See! Here are no people, no compromises . . .
Here is peace!
Here snow drops gently into pools of
   water . . .

English translation by Mark Hall and Glenn Watkins.

THREE PIECES FOR ORCHESTRA, OP. 6

Berg's lifelong infatuation with the music of Gustav Mahler has been amply detailed by the biographers. As a youth of 16 he heard the premiere of the Fourth Symphony in Vienna (January 1902) and was so overcome by the experience that he managed to appropriate Mahler's baton, which he kept for the rest of his life as one of his most cherished mementos. He was part of the crowd that

Figure 4.2. Alban Berg and Anton von Webern (Spring 1912).
Courtesy of Universal Editions A.G. Archive.

saw the maestro off at the train station when he left to assume a conducting
post in New York in 1907; he was among the mourners at Mahler's funeral in
May 1911; and he made a special trip by train to hear the first performance of
Das Lied von der Erde conducted by Bruno Walter in Munich in November
1911.

Berg's intimate connection with the Schoenberg circle and as a member of a
triumvirate that included Webern has provided the primary orientation for any
assessment of him as an artist. But while the association with his mentor
Schoenberg was of incalculable importance, the nourishment he continued to
find in the works of Mahler to the end of his career is undeniable. In testing
such a relationship, Mahler's potential significance for other composers of the
twentieth century can also be underscored.

By the time of Berg's *Three Pieces for Orchestra,* op. 6, Berg's apprentice
days are clearly over. He is a man approaching 30 years of age, and the details
that characterize the whole must now be seen as conscious choices of the
composer and less as youthful imitation in search of a personal style. In light of
the complete date for the set (August 1914), it is only natural that the orchestral
pieces by Schoenberg, op. 16 (1909), and Webern, op. 6 (1909), should come to
mind. But in spite of Berg's incorporation of the markings H (for "Hauptstimme"

= principal voice) and N (for "Nebenstimme" = secondary voice) first used by Schoenberg in his op. 16, no. 5, the allegiance to Mahler with respect to his use of the orchestra, the role of rhythm, and the working out of large-scale formal issues is even more clearly manifest in these works than in the preceding ones. Biographers have noted that during this period, Berg had a falling out with Schoenberg, who had admonished his pupil for the incorporation of "novelties" in his op. 4 songs and in the pieces for clarinet and piano, op. 5, and Berg noted in his correspondence to Webern that Schoenberg had been unduly harsh with him. In spite of its dedication to Schoenberg ("To my teacher and friend in boundless gratitude and love"), the orchestra of the *Three Pieces* does not move on from the consequences of the orchestra of the *Altenberglieder*, but strikes a closer affinity with the world of Mahler.

The first performance of Mahler's Ninth Symphony took place under the baton of Bruno Walter in Vienna in June 1912. That Fall, in a letter to his wife, Berg wrote:

> I have once more played through Mahler's Ninth. The first movement is the most glorious he ever wrote. It expresses an extraordinary love of this earth, for Nature; the longing to live on it in peace, to enjoy it completely, to the very heart of one's being, before death comes, as irresistibly it does. The whole movement is based on a premonition of death, which is constantly recurring . . . death in armour. Against that there is no resistance left, and I see what follows as a sort of resignation. Always, though with thought of 'the other side', which we can see in the *misterioso*, as if in the pure air above the mountains, in the ether itself.[5]

The following July, Berg was in Trahütten busy at work on the *Orchestral Pieces*, op. 6, and the direct influence of Mahler's Ninth has been repeatedly noted in the rhythmic figure of the *Präludium*.

Example 4.9. Mahler, *Symphony No. 9*, Mvt. 1, mm. 1–2.

Example 4.10. Berg, *Three Pieces for Orchestra*, op. 6: "Präludium," mm. 9–10.

Especially memorable are the percussion episodes that open and close the first piece (accelerating at the opening, progressively slowing down at the close)—of which the percussion diminuendo-ritardando is clearly forecast in Mahler's

Third Symphony (1st mvt., 8 bars before 13). Less from the standpoint of the complexity of the percussive detail than from its function as a frame, we are also reminded of the use of the snare drum at the opening and closing of *Tamboursg'sell* (1901), Mahler's final approach to the *Wunderhorn* anthology. The infatuation with symmetries (which the last example suggests) is one that prevails with an ever-increasing intensity throughout Berg's career. Finally, the gentleness of the percussion sonorities in the opening and closing measures reminds us of Berg's fascination for the "magnificent mountain atmosphere and cowbells" of Mahler's Sixth, a factor that undoubtedly also contributed to the creation of Webern's op. 6, no. 4, and his op. 10, no. 3 (see Ex. 3.4).

More obviously indebted to Mahler than either of the two opening movements is the finale, the March. The relationship is due not only to the cyclic transformation of material from the first movement in the third, pointed out by Perle[6]; to thematic similarities with Mahler's Sixth Symphony (Ex. 4.11–12),

Example 4.11. Mahler, *Symphony No. 6,* Mvt. 1, m. 270.

Example 4.12. Berg, *Three Pieces for Orchestra,* op. 6. "Marsch," mm. 110–112.

pointed out by DeVoto[7]; or to the march-like quality of the music, an obsessive trait in the works of Mahler, but also because of the derivation of Berg's rhythmic figure from the motive that dominates the first and last movements of Mahler's Sixth. That the latter was one of Berg's favorites is indicated in a letter to his wife where he remarked that in spite of Beethoven's *Pastorale,* "there is still only one 6th." The Symphony had been dubbed "The Tragic" by Mahler himself, and the rhythmic motif that dominates the work was seen by him as the expression of Fate.[8]

Mahler, Symphony No. 6, mvts. 1 & 4:

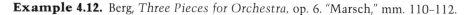

Berg, *Three Pieces*, op. 6, no. 3:

It is possible to see in it the consequence of Mahler's infatuation with Bee-thoven's Fate motive of the Fifth Symphony, which he performed frequently, and the rehearsal of which often turned around the correct tempo and articulation of the initial motif.

The palpability of a relationship between Berg's *Hauptrhythmus* and Mahler's Fate motive is sealed by three hammer blows, in direct reference to Mahler's invention in the finale of his Sixth Symphony, at the climax of the piece (m. 126). The significance of such rhythmic gestures is not confined to the *Three Pieces*, however. While its first highly audible incorporation may have surfaced there, the concept of the *Hauptrhythmus* (or principal rhythm) was to remain of central importance in all of the major works of Berg's maturity. So that there would be no mistaking its assignment, he ultimately confected the sign RH for inclusion in his scores. It is essential to stress in this regard that the presence of such rhythms invariably has important implications beyond its structural function, and Redlich[9] was one of the first to suggest a link between them and the fateful "death rhythms" of Mahler's Sixth and Ninth Symphonies.

The truth of this premise can be audibly tested in those instances where Berg was working with a story or where he has supplied us with a program. Thus the first use of an organized rhythm on a large scale is to be found in *Wozzeck*, and its association with the death of Marie at the conclusion of the imme-diately preceding scene haunts the motive in its subsequent appearances and transformation in the Tavern Scene:

Wozzeck, Act III, scene 2–3:

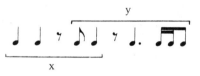

Similarly in *Lulu*, a rhythmic cell, not unrelated to the one heard in *Wozzeck* and by extension to the head-motif of Mahler's Sixth, opens and closes each act and accompanies every pivotal action throughout the course of the opera:

Lulu:

The familial relationship between the *Lulu* theme to the world of Mahler can be even further extended through the observation that the rhythmic opening of Mahler's Ninth Symphony (Ex. 4.9: long-short-long) is ultimately extended in the first movement to a long-short-long-long pattern. Here it is heralded by unison fortissimo brasses at two climactic points, a pattern whose force recalls the *Lulu* rhythmic motif and whose pattern is its retrograde.

The "Marsch" of Berg's op. 6 was written in the period immediately following the assassination at Sarajevo that triggered World War I, and George Perle has sensed in this work a feeling of catastrophe and impending doom:

> Fragmentary rhythmic and melodic figures typical of an orthodox military march repeatedly coalesce into polyphonic episodes of incredible density that surge to frenzied climaxes, then fall apart. It is not a march, but music *about* a march, or rather about *the* march, just as Ravel's *La Valse* is music in which *the* waltz is similarly reduced to its minimum characteristic elements. In spite of the fundamental differences in their respective musical idioms, the emotional climate of Berg's pre-war "march macabre" is very similar to that of Ravel's post-war "valse macabre."[10]

That these pieces were also prescient of Berg's later career was correctly suggested by Stravinsky in 1959:

> . . . [Berg] is the only one to have achieved large-scale development forms without a suggestion of "neoclassic" dissimulation . . . Berg's forms are thematic (in which respect, as in most others, he is Webern's opposite); the essence of his work and the thematic structure are responsible for the immediacy of one form. However complex, however "mathematical" the latter are, they are always "free" thematic forms born of "pure feeling" and "expression." The perfect work in which to study this and, I think, the essential work, with *Wozzeck*, for the study of all of his music—is the *Three Pieces for Orchestra*, op. 6.[11]

A more comprehensive examination of *Wozzeck*, one of the most powerful expressions of the modern theater, will be undertaken in a chronologically more appropriate position (Chapter 17). It will be necessary at that point to keep in mind the importance of the foundations discussed earlier with respect to rhythm, binding thematics, and other figurations—and not only for *Wozzeck* (where the rising chromatics of the drowning scene may be traced back through Berg's "Marsch," beginning at m. 162, to the concluding measures of Schoenberg's *Erwartung*), but for his final creations, *Der Wein, Lulu*, and the *Violin Concerto* as well.

REPERTOIRE

Seven Early Songs (1905–08), v, pf
Piano Sonata, op. 1 (1908)
Four Songs, op. 2 (1910), v, pf
String Quartet, op. 3 (1910)
Altenberglieder, op. 4 (1912), v, orch
Four Pieces, op. 5 (1913), cl, pf
Three Pieces, op. 6 (1914–15), orch

READING

Alan Berg, "Why is Schoenberg's Music so Difficult to Understand?" (1924) in Willi Reich, *Alban Berg* (1965).
Hans Redlich, *Alban Berg: the Man and his Music* (London, 1957).
Willi Reich, *Alban Berg* (Zurich, 1963; Eng. trans., 1965).
Helene Berg, ed., *Alban Berg, Letters to his Wife* (Munich, 1965; Eng. trans. edited and annotated by Bernard Grun, 1971).

H. H. Stuckenschmidt, "Debussy or Berg? The Mystery of a Chord Progression," *Musical Quarterly*, li (1965), 453–59.

Mark DeVoto, "Some Notes on the Unknown Altenberg Lieder," *Perspectives of New Music*, v.1 (1966), 37–74.

Bruce Archibald, "The Harmony of Berg's 'Reigen'," *Perspectives of New Music*, vi.2 (1968), 73.

Klaus Schweizer, *Die Sonatensatzform im Schaffen Alban Bergs* (Stuttgart, 1970).

Douglas Jarman, *The Music of Alban Berg* (London, 1979).

George Perle, "Alban Berg," *The New Grove Dictionary of Music and Musicians* (London, 1980), vol. 2, 524–8.

George Perle, "From the Early Songs to *Wozzeck*" in *The Operas of Alban Berg*, vol. 1: *Wozzeck* (Berkeley, Calif., 1980), 1–21.

Mark DeVoto, "Alban Berg's 'Marche Macabre'," *Perspectives of New Music*, xxii.1–2 (1983–84), 386–447.

PARIS: 1885–1915

"What has been called Symbolism can be quite simply summarized as the desire common to several familiar poets . . . to take back from music what they had given it. The secret of this movement is nothing other than this . . . We were nourished on music and our literary minds only dreamt of extracting from language virtually the same effects that music caused on our nervous system."

—Paul Valéry, Preface to *La Connaissance de la Déesse* by Lucien Fabre (1920).

CHAPTER 5

DEBUSSY: IMPRESSIONISM AND SYMBOLISM

In his insightful monograph on twentieth-century music, William Austin has rightfully cautioned against the "many dubious catchwords of modern music" and their potential to deceive as well as to enlighten. By this he refers principally to the "isms" that are commonly bandied about, typically without definition or precision. Impressionism, Symbolism, Pointillism, Cubism, Futurism, Neoclassicism, Exoticism, Primitivism, Expressionism, Dadaism, Surrealism, Minimalism—a longer list than he considers—are to an extent, however, mirrors of our age. And though the isms can never explain the artist, a collection of artists can illuminate the need for considering the ism. Such aesthetic canopies can aid in sensing the relationship of creative figures with similar aims and help avoid the dangers of treating each artist in isolation.

That the twentieth century has been a century of isms is corroborated not only by the currency of the expressions themselves, but by the numerous manifestos and tracts that have appeared suggesting the intention of an artist or group of artists to react against the status quo in a particular way. Furthermore, it is significant that most of these designations are not ex post facto confections of the historians.

All of this must be said as a prelude to any consideration of Claude Debussy (1862–1918), *musicien français* and supreme innovator of early twentieth-century music, whose international influence has undoubtedly been more far-reaching than any other figure of the period under discussion. Most musicians, as well as amateurs, will suffer no anxiety in describing him as an Impressionist, but it is a designation that Debussy disliked. The term was first used in 1874 by a critic after viewing Monet's picture entitled "Impression: soleil levant" (Impression: Sun Rising). Later, it was widely applied to a group of artists, including Manet, Cézanne, and Renoir, who attempted to record their first impressions of nature by refracting light into its primary components and juxtaposing them onto the canvas, where they were later to be reassembled by the viewer. Form tended to be obscured and a dream-like atmosphere was pervasive. In the world of music, many of these same tendencies were endorsed through a mosaic-like approach to color; a freedom of formal inquiry that eschewed strongly contrasting thematic material or an emphasis upon the dialectic of development; and a loosening of the rhythmic component to the extent that a sense of pulse or undulation tended to replace the organizing properties of the bar line.

A sense of color based upon fluctuating light, indefinite outlines, and anti-monumentality are all qualities of the Impressionists that were even thought by some to be observable in the "Forest Murmurs" of Wagner's *Siegfried;* in this vein the term might well have been applied later to Schoenberg's introduction to *Gurrelieder* or Webern's *Im Sommerwind.* But eventually, though the aesthetic was principally codified by Germans, the term came to refer to the French and Debussy in particular. The Académie des Beaux Arts had already used the adjective in a pejorative fashion with respect to Debussy's second entry for the Prix de Rome in 1887, and by 1905 the term was in common parlance in music circles as indicative of a new anti-Romantic point of view.

The later contention that the term Symbolism offered a more reasonable parallel with music was based on the premise that painting, the main arena of the Impressionists, was not only static but visual, while literature, the initial provenance of Symbolism, unfolded in a time space with a syntax based on a movement that was sonic. Furthermore, Debussy's friend Paul Dukas stated candidly that "The strongest influence to which Debussy submitted was that of the littérateurs, not that of the musicians."[1]

In their interest in the sonic mysteries of language, the Symbolist poets tended naturally to emphasize not only the dream-like image, so dear to the Impressionists, but also the musicality inherent in the inventive arrangement of words. Traditional syntax was obscured and precision of meaning was compromised. The poet was content to seduce and to suggest.

BAUDELAIRE AND WAGNER

The birth of Symbolism was attended by a manifesto written by Jean Moréas in 1886, with the movement flourishing for the next decade in the work of a group of writers who considered themselves disciples of Verlaine (1844–1896) and Mallarmé (1842–1898). It must be quickly added, however, that the foundation was always seen to rest firmly on the art of Baudelaire (1821–1867). The mystery of existence that it was their announced goal to express found the perfect resonator in Baudelaire's theory of "correspondences" and his sonnet of the same name written as early as 1845.

BAUDELAIRE, *Correspondances*

La Nature est un temple óu de vivants piliers
Laissent parfois sortir de confuses paroles;
L'homme y passe à travers des forèts de symboles
Qui l'observent avec des regards familiers.

Comme de longs échos qui de loin se confondent
Dans une ténébreuse et profonde unité,
Vaste comme la nuit et comme la clarté,
Les parfums, les couleurs et les sons se répondent.

Il est des parfums frais comme des chairs d'enfants,
Doux comme les hautbois, verts comme les prairies,
—Et d'autres, corrumpus, riches et triomphants,

Ayant l'èxpansion des choses infinies,
Comme l'ambre, le musc, le benjoin et l'encens,
Qui chantent les transports de l'esprit et des sens.

Correspondences

Nature is a temple where living pillars
Sometimes unleash a confusion of words;
Man traverses it through forests of symbols
Which observe him with knowing glances.

Like extended echoes which mingle far away
In a mysterious and profound unity,
Vast as the night and as light,
Perfumes, colors and sounds answer each other.

There are perfumes fresh as children's bodies,
Fragrant as oboes, green as meadows,
And others which are corrupt, rich and triumphant.

Having the expansion of infinite things,
Such as ambre, musk, benjamin and incense,
Which sing of the ecstasies of the mind and senses.

The Symbolists, who unanimously professed their belief in a correspondence between the senses and Goethe's claim of the "oneness" of nature, were equally devoted to the similar but more explicit equations of Rimbaud's "Voyelles" (see p. 155), the sonic "tintinnabulations" of Edgar Allan Poe (1809–49), and the idealized synthesis of the arts as preached by Richard Wagner. As it turned out, Baudelaire's theory of correspondence was to be responsible for a protracted misunderstanding of Wagner among the French. An important art critic as well as poet, Baudelaire's enthusiasm for the Wagner Paris concerts of 1860 and the 1861 production of *Tannhäuser* led him to his only musical statement. His ardor was as genuine as it was misguided in attempting to explain Wagner's *Gesamtkunstwerk* as a transference of ideas "by reciprocal analogy" between sound, color, and word rather than a simultaneous alliance of the arts.

The *Fleurs du mal*, Baudelaire's principal though constantly changing anthology of poems, first appeared in print in 1857, though a number of the more erotic poems were quickly excised by French law, which deemed them obscene. Henri Duparc (1848–1933) was one of the first composers to set the verses of Baudelaire to music, and although he wrote only 17 songs all before he was 36 years old, they include some of the most memorable ones in the French language. His musical speech, which characteristically engages a rich Wagnerian harmonic palette softened by static pedal figures, is a natural for Baudelaire's dream world. The note of Orientalism, the reveries steeped in drugs, and the imaginary voyage of the mind that appealed to so many Romantics was captured with a new accent by Duparc in his setting of Baudelaire's *L'invitation au voyage* (1870)[2] and with a new vision by Matisse in his painting of 1905 entitled "Luxe, calme et volupté," the poem's insistent refrain. Many of these qualities are even more pronounced in Baudelaire's prose poem of the same time and name, a poem that was to serve as a model for Tristan Klingsor in a somewhat more decadent "Asie" set by Ravel in his *Shéhérezade* (see pp. 124–25) of 1903.

Debussy tapped Baudelaire for his cycle of 1887–89 and never again. The music reflects the stylistic ambiguities that many French composers had not yet resolved at this time, and underscores the intensity of the Wagner cult in France in the 1880s, both in literary and musical circles. Articles by Huysmans on the overture to *Tannhäuser*, by Swinburne on Wagner's death, and six sonnets in praise of the master of Bayreuth, including poems by Verlaine and Mallarmé, all appeared in the *Revue wagnerienne*, a monthly journal published between 1885 and 1888. Just as Wagner's *Gesamtkunstwerk* held a vague appeal for the followers of Baudelaire's *correspondences* in search of a new and mystical alliance between poetry and the art of music, numerous French composers openly and directly adopted elements of Wagner's harmonic vocabulary and system of leitmotifs. Examples of this inclination are to be found in Duparc's *Extase* (1874) written in imitation of Wagner's *Wesendoncklieder*, Chabrier's *Gwendoline* (1886), d'Indy's *Fervaal* (begun in 1881), and Debussy's *La damoiselle élue* (1887–89).

In light of Debussy's pilgrimages to Bayreuth in 1888 and 1889 at the time he was composing his *Cinq poèmes de Charles Baudelaire* (1887–89), it is not surprising to find traces of Wagnerian harmonies in "Le balcon" in addition to the consistent use of a whole-tone chord to announce the refrain in "Le jet d'eau." But while elsewhere in the cycle the synesthetic overtones of "Harmonie du soir" seem to suggest the way to the future,[3] Debussy's interest in Wagner was not about to dissolve as admiration continued to be coupled with the struggle for independence. Recent claims have been made for the prominent role of *Parsifal* and *Tristan* with respect to both sensibility and thematics in works ranging from *Pelleas and Melisande* (1893–1902) to *Jeux* (1912–13), and the judgment has been forwarded that while Debussy is no traditional heir to Wagner, his "possession and transformation of Wagner gives him substantiality, signification, and depth."[4] The reader will be reminded at this point of Schoenberg's less positive observations regarding the Debussy-Wagner relationship cited earlier (see p. 24).

ARIETTES OUBLIÉES AND VERLAINE

Verlaine's art, like all later products of the Symbolists, emphasized the lyric nature of the French language and sought to discover in its sounds a new musicality that transcended classical syntax and the cliché. The nuances of human feeling are suggested through illusion, understatement, and a vagueness that prizes sonority above all. The first line of Verlaine's *Art poétique*, "De la musique avant toute chose" ("Music above all"), explains the appeal of his verses to so many composers, including Fauré, Chabrier, Charpentier, and Chausson, as well as Stravinsky in the first blush of his French residency. But it is especially in the art of Claude Debussy, in his *Fêtes galantes*, which evokes the figures of the *commedia dell'arte* and the world of Watteau and Fragonard, as well as in the *Ariettes oubliées* that we witness the perfect alliance of poet and musician.

Debussy's *Ariettes oubliées* (1885–88) on texts of Verlaine were supplied with various changes for their initial publication in 1903. Dedicated to Mary Garden, "incomparable Melisande," the musical language of the set explores alternatives to Wagnerian chromaticism, such as the modality of "Il pleure dans mon coeur" or the gliding parallel chords that decorate and prolong a dominant-9th chord at the beginning of "C'est l'extase."

Example 5.1. Debussy, *Ariettes oubliées*: "C'est 'extase," m. 1–10.

C'est l'extase langoureuse,
C'est la fatigue amoureuse,
C'est tous les frisson des bois
Parmi l'étreinte des brises,
C'est, vers les ramure grises,
Le coeur des petites voix.

This is langourous ecstasy,
This is amorous fatigue,
It is all the fluttering of the woods
Among the embrace of the breezes.
It is, amongst the grey branches,
The chorus of little voices.

O le frêle e frais murmure! O the fragile yet fresh murmuring
Cela gazouille et susurre. That whispers and twitters
Cela ressemble au cri doux Resembling the soft cry
Que l'herbe agitée expire . . . Which stirring grass exhales . . .
Tu dirais, sous l'eau qui vire, You speak, under the turning water,
Le roulis sourd des cailloux. Through the muted rolling of the pebbles.

Cette âme qui se lamente This soul which sighs
En cette plainte dormante, In this sleeping plaint
C'est la nôtre, n'est-ce pas? Is ours, is it not?
La mienne, dis, et la tienne, Mine, say it, and yours,
Dont s'exhale l'humble antienne Whose humble hymn breathes
Par ce tiède soir, tout bas? In the balmy evening, quite softly?

Verlaine

Here we realize how far Debussy has travelled from the world of Massenet, which tints his setting of "Beau soir" (c. 1883), or of Fauré's "C'est l'extase" (1870), and in such exquisitely stifled utterances as "C'est la nôtre, n'est-ce pas?" in the final stanza, the accents of *Pelléas* seem securely prepared.

In spite of an essentially syllabic style that promotes textual clarity, all is not recitative in Debussy's fin-de-siècle songs, and the extended lyric gesture enveloped by enriched harmonies frequently emerges at the moment when monotony threatens. In spite of Debussy's professed disdain for the piano, his keen ear for its potential is already evident in the accompaniments to the *Ariettes oubliées*, which easily surpass the piano writing of the *Deux ara-besques* (1888–91), his earliest forays of note into the solo piano literature.

POUR LE PIANO AND SATIE

Two piano cycles of the time, however, forecast to some degree Debussy's inventions for the instrument which were to be written after the turn of the century. The *Suite bergamasque* (1890, rev. 1905), with its Prélude, Menuet, and Passepied, belongs to the lengthy preparation by the French for the appearance of Neoclassicism around 1920, though it is only the movement entitled "Clair de lune" that has endured as a concert piece. The Prélude, Sarabande, and Toc-cata of the suite *Pour le piano* (1894–1901) conjure up more than the ghost of Rameau and Couperin, however, especially in the elegant Sarabande (1894).

If here the spell of Wagner seems to have been completely broken, another wind now blows gently from Montmartre, where Satie was writing some of his earliest works. In the parallelisms of the opening chords (Ex. 5.2) and the brief allusion to modal plainchant (m. 5), it is possible to detect more than the shadow of Satie, whom Debussy met in 1891 and with whom he was to maintain a lifelong friendship. In the 1880s and 1890s, Satie had designated himself as the first musical Impressionist, purportedly basing his techniques directly on the work of contemporary French painters such as Monet, Cézanne, and Toulouse-Lautrec. In later years Satie reflected:

> In several of his works Debussy's aesthetics are related to symbolism; his work as a whole is impressionistic. Forgive me for mentioning it, but am I not to some extent the cause of this? People say so . . . When I first met Debussy . . . I was writing my *Fils des étoiles* . . . and I explained to Debussy how we French needed to break away from the Wagnerian adventure, which did not correspond with our natural

Example 5.2. Debussy, *Pour le piano:* "Sarabande" (1894), mm. 1–8.

aspirations. And I told him that I was not at all anti-Wagnerian, but that we needed a music of our own—preferably without sauerkraut.

Why not use the representational methods demonstrated by Claude Monet, Cézanne, Toulouse-Lautrec and so on . . . ? Why not make a musical transposition of these methods? Nothing more simple. Are they not expressions?

This was a profitable starting point for experiments abounding in tentative—and even fruitful—results . . . Who could show him examples? reveal to him lucky finds? point out the ground to be explored? give him the benefit of experience? . . . Who?

I shall not reply: that interests me no more.[5] (*Vanity Fair*, 1923.)

Taking Satie at his invitation, one need not resist comparing features of the first of Satie's Sarabandes with Debussy's similarly named piece. Beyond the details noted in the initial measures, a comparison of two interior passages discloses an affinity between the enharmonically equivalent opening (A♭/G♯) and close (E♭/D♯) as well as in the eighth-note chordal anticipation at the cadence where Debussy's series of tenuto markings seem to reflect Satie's placement of the eighth-note on the downbeat.

Example 5.3. Satie, *Premiere Sarabande* (1887), mm. 17–25.

Copyright Editions Salabert. Used by permission of G. Schirmer.

Example 5.4. Debussy, *Pour le piano*: "Sarabande" (1894), mm. 50–60.

Copyright 1896 Sociètè des Editions Jobert. Used by permission of the publisher. Theodore Presser Company, sole representative U.S.A.

While no formula was given for the transference of Impressionist painterly qualities to the world of sound, Satie's reference to *Fils des étoiles* (see p. 48) pointed to the style he had in mind. There, and in the slightly earlier *Ogives* (1886), *Sarabandes*, and *Gymnopédies* (both of 1887), Satie, in spite of his disclaimer, offered as much a declaration of war against Wagner as a set of alternatives. In retrospect, these works, which forward static parallelisms as an ideal, must be considered avant-garde as much for their nihilism as for their newness.[6] In this, Satie struck an attitude that was to resound periodically throughout the twentieth century whenever the trend setters placed more of a premium on the destruction of tradition than on its continuation and development.

Debussy, who was eager to leave the world of Wagner behind, took the bait and quickly outstripped Satie's original offerings. Satie, all too keenly aware of this following the highly successful premiere of *Pelléas* in 1902, abandoned ship, expressing no future interest in such an idiom. "There is nothing more to do in this direction," he remarked. "I'll have to look for something else or I am lost."[7] That Satie was a precursor of Debussy's so-called Impressionism was repeatedly stated over the next 15 years; and, indeed, with the assertion that his presence was catalytic there can be no argument. In taking leave of Wagner's realm—a more difficult proposition than Debussy could ever have imagined—Debussy remarked in 1903:

> Wagner ... was a beautiful sunset mistaken for a dawn. There will always be periods of imitation or influence whose duration and nationality one cannot foretell—a simple truth and a law of evolution. These periods are necessary to those who love well-traveled and tranquil paths. They permit others to go much further.[8]

PRELUDE À L'APRÈS-MIDI D'UN FAUNE

In spite of his liberating force on French literature, Verlaine was generally out of sympathy with the younger Symbolists who used his art as the basis for further licenses of form or the abandonment of rhyme. Yet no poetry is more reflective of the sonic tendencies so prized by Verlaine than that of Mallarmé, whose seductive arias would frequently seem to be textless vocalises, where the syntax is so obscure, the relationship of words so tenuous, that they appear to be shed of meaning beyond their sound. It is a quality many composers were to contemplate throughout the twentieth century.

Mallarmé's "L'après-midi d'un faune" is, next to "Hérodiade," his longest poem. Its fame is in no small part attributable to its association with the other arts. Its earliest version comes from 1865 and, like "Hérodiade," was initially considered as a stage piece. In spite of the dialogue that is present in both of them, it soon became apparent that their destiny lay elsewhere. The definitive version of "The Faune" appeared in 1876, handsomely illustrated by Manet (Figure 5.1), an act of homage that was to be repeated by Matisse as late as 1932.

Figure 5.1. Édouard Manet, illustration for the first edition of Mallarmé's *L'après-midi d'un faune* (1876).

MALLARMÉ, *L'après-midi d'un faune*

Ces nymphes, je les veux perpétuer.	These nymphs, I desire to perpetuate them.
Si clair,	So bright
leur incarnat léger, qu'il voltige dans l'air Assoupi de sommeils touffus.	their rosy flesh color that it hovers in the air drowsy with tufted sleepiness.
Aimai-je un rêve?	Did I love a dream?

Huysmans had made note of the elegance of the 1876 edition in his novel, *A rebours* (1884), and by the time Debussy was preparing his orchestral score, *Prelude à "L'aprés-midi d'un faune"* between 1892 and 1894, Mallarmé's fame was already established.

Numerous commentators have attempted an exegesis of Debussy's score as a direct parallel to Mallarmé's poem, but the composer stated his intentions with reasonable clarity in a letter of 1895, two years after the work's premiere:

> The *Prélude à "L'après-midi d'un faune,"* dear Sir, might it be what remains of the dream at the tip of the faun's flute? More precisely, it is a general impression of the poem, for if music were to follow more closely it would run out of breath, like a dray horse competing for the Grand Prize with a thoroughbred . . . Now still, all of it does follow the rising movement of the poem . . . The end is the last line prolonged: 'Couple, goodbye! To see the shadow you become, I go.'[9]

Yet, while the theme of the flute is omnipresent in the first half of Mallarmé's poem, only to disappear for good, Debussy's opening flute solo resounds throughout the work and provides the source material for the entire piece. In spite of the discovery that the number of lines of Mallarmé's poem is identical to the number of measures in Debussy's score, Arthur Wenk in his detailed comparison of the two works was forced to conclude with Debussy that his *Prelude* is not a word-by-word translation, but rather a companion to its "rising movement."[10]

The overall form of the piece has, as a consequence of such questions, been subjected to periodic scrutiny. General consensus suggests that the piece is cast in an ABA' form. Whether the B section begins with the D♭ section at m. 55, as Austin proposes, or at m. 37 as others have argued, the relationship of all this material to the opening flute solo reveals that the work is a gradually unfolding transformation of a single idea. Wenk's juxtapositions (Ex. 5.5) are especially compelling.

Leonard Bernstein, in the fourth of his Charles Eliot Norton Lectures (*The Unanswered Question,* 1973) entitled "The Delights and Dangers of Ambiguity," considered the opening statement as a reflection of Mallarmé's poetry at length. Not only the instability of the opening melodic tritone (C♯-G) but the harmonies implicit in measure 3 (E major), which are compromised in measure 4 and juxtaposed against another tritone relationship (B♭) in measure 5, are held to be analogous to Mallarmé's method. Ambiguity, momentary resolution, followed by ambiguity in a continuing stream that nonetheless periodically endorses symmetry and finally offers resolution (the piece ends in E major) mirror the syntactical license of the poet. This is reinforced on the level of rhythm and phraseology where an undulating pulse replaces the tyranny of the bar line: The movement in measures 56-7 (Ex. 5.5, BII) sounds not so much like

Example 5.5. Debussy, *Prélude à "L'après-midi d'un faune,"* mm. 1–5, 37–38, 55–58.

syncopation as a momentary fluctuation away from triple simple into duple compound meter, supported by an underlying wave motion that is one of the magical moments of the piece. About these very qualities Debussy spoke directly in a conversation with his teacher Ernest Guiraud (1837–92):

> [I have] no faith in the supremacy of the C major scale. The tonal scale must be enriched by other scales. Nor am I misled by equal temperament. Rhythms are stifling. Rhythms cannot be contained within bars. It is nonsense to speak of "simple" and "compound" time. There should be an interminable flow of both. Relative keys are nonsense, too. Music is neither major nor minor. Minor thirds and major thirds should be combined, modulation thus becoming more flexible. The mode is that which one happens to choose at the moment. It is inconstant. There must be a balance between musical demands and thematic evocation. Themes suggest their orchestral coloring.[11]

In a remark possibly intended as a program note and claimed in the Eulenberg score as belonging to the original edition, the composer speaks of the music as a free illustration of the poem, a succession of scenes expressing "the desires and dreams of the faun in the heat of the afternoon." Finally, weary of his pursuit of the nymphs, the faun "succumbs to intoxicating sleep, in which he can finally realize his dreams of possession in universal Nature."[12]

Boulez's judgement that

> just as modern poetry surely took root in certain of Baudelaire's poems, so one is justified in saying that modern music was awakened by *L'après-midi d'un faune*[13]

is as perplexing as it may be unarguable. For just as Debussy translated the image of the flute directly at the beginning of the work, he also presented it unaccompanied. In this he helped to establish one of his characteristic habits—namely, of formulaic openings that frequently begin monophonically or with modal chord patterns (Pelléas, Ex. 5.6a). In such gestures, "whose purpose is to move from silence to a world of motion,"[14] Debussy not only relied on syntactical models from Liszt to Massenet, but also signaled that the "four-square, periodic phrase was under attack."[15] It was also obviously in harmony with the world of Mallarmé, whose own reaction to Debussy's music he relayed to the composer in a letter stating that the music

> introduces no dissonance with my text, except to explore further, indeed, the nostalgia and the luminosity, with finesse, with malaise, with richness.[16]

PELLÉAS AND MÉLISANDE

Debussy's achievement in *Pelléas* (1893–1902) has seemed so singular to many as to defy articulation. The use of the Wagnerian system of leitmotifs, the occasional reliance on his orchestra (especially in the interludes), the parlando techniques associated with French opera since the eighteenth century—all help to provide the requisite anchor for understanding. Yet his magical combination of tonal evasion, his avoidance of major-minor tonality in favor of a pervasive modality, his deployment of scalar patterns in such a fashion as to have audible formal implications, his color inventions (as opposed to "orchestration clothing," as Boulez puts it),[17] the silences, quiet reserve, and uncanny sense of understatement—all serve to promote Maeterlinck's symbol-laden *drame-statique*. The exact meaning of stagnating pools, of blind men, and people of indefinite origin find their perfect match in Debussy's shifting, evanescent landscape. Maeterlinck's world, which would initially seem to incorporate ingredients of Teutonic myth and to carry with it a deeper message concerning the origins of things and the meaning of life, is ultimately seen to be without issue, lacking point, and leaving us only to wonder about the mystery of existence. Debussy's score is the perfect expression of these values, which are Symbolist to the very core.

It is revealing to note the similarity between the themes of love, jealousy, and revenge in both *Tristan* and *Pelléas*, as well as to recall that in writing *Pelléas*, Debussy stated that he still feared "the ghost of old Klingsor." The extent to which both the parallel sentiments and thematics of *Parsifal* were mined by Debussy may be demonstrated by comparing the orchestral interlude that leads from the forest to the castle between scenes 1 and 2 of Act I (especially the dotted figure of Ex. 5.6b) with Wagner's entrance music into the Castle of the Grail. Similarly, the use of the Tristan chord in Act IV, scene 4, at the words ". . . mais je suis *triste*" underscores Debussy's interest in precise, if fleeting, references to Wagner. In fact, this latter scene, which was the first to be composed and the only one composed out of order, holds numerous parallels with the action of Act II of *Tristan*, and it has been suggested that Debussy's text-determined harmonic design for the scene is Wagnerian in concept. Not only does Debussy associate certain characters with particular key areas (Mélisande with F♯, Pelléas with E♭), but in structuring a movement from C♯/C to F♯/G–C following a tonally ambiguous opening it has been suggested that he shows an awareness of Wagnerian dramatic-harmonic laws.[18]

Debussy was also right to recognize the extent to which the Wagnerian premise still lingered on in the marriage of endless melody with French recitative and in the wholesale adoption of a system of leitmotifs. While Debussy may have objected in print that Wagner's leitmotifs served as a kind of calling card that superfluously announced the arrival of every character, he was not insensitive to the psychological value a system of such motifs could impose. As a device it had long shown its adaptability to both opera and tone poem. Its compatibility with the construction of abstract formal solutions was as congenial a discovery to Strauss and Schoenberg as it was later to be with Berg in *Wozzeck*.

To equate Wagner's leitmotifs with Maeterlinck's symbols is not only to simplify but to run the risk of falsification: The meaning of Wagner's musical figures was meant to be directly perceived, that of the Symbolists only vaguely inferred. Maeterlinck has narrowed his symbolic field to a set of polar opposites: *darkness* (death, night, blindness, danger, deep forest, grotto, winter) and *light* (birth, day, sun, summer), and even the frequent water images (fountain, sea, tears, pools) are relatable to one or the other. These recurring and related symbols, present in every scene of Debussy's libretto, surface and disappear in a fluctuating mosaic that suggests more than it insists. Somewhere between Wagner and Maeterlinck lies the musical symbol as it is utilized by Debussy. His capacity for figural variation is larger than Wagner's, though similar to Schoenberg's; the key to the association between music and text is less easy to find than in either. In the following motifs, for example, 5.6a is first heard in the opening scene in the forest and again in Act II, scene 2, as Golaud describes the old castle and the ancient surrounding woods.

Example 5.6-a. Debussy, *Pelléas et Mélisande:* "Primeval Origins."

But it also appears in the initial scene as Golaud retreats to a tree, promising not to touch Mélisande, and in the final scene of the opera, where Mélisande on her death bed mysteriously queries Golaud as to whether it has been a long time since they have seen each other. Frequently applied labels such as "Forest" and "Ancestral Legend" fail to hint at the symbolic relationship between Golaud and Mélisande—a dimension that the motif persistently attends and which, for all of its allusiveness, is central to the story. The second motif to appear in the opera (Ex. 5.6b), while frequently associated with Golaud's entry or at the mention of his name, also is intoned in the opening measures as Golaud indicates that he has lost his way; in the orchestral interlude, Act I, scene 1–2, discussed earlier; at Pelléas' statement to Mélisande that Golaud has spotted them (III.1); at Mélisande's explanation for her tardiness (IV.4); and with Arkel's pronouncement that Mélisande has passed away (V).

Example 5.6-b. Debussy, *Pelléas et Mélisande:* "Fate" (Golaud).

These multiple associations suggest more of the inexorable destiny of the several principals than with any particular person. Similar observations can be drawn with respect to those labeled with a single name.

Debussy continues to use many of the technical musical devices of the early songs and places them in the service of his drama. The avoidance of the perfect cadence, the prevalent modality (Ex. 5.6a), and the gliding parallel sonorities (Ex. 5.6e) recall the composer of the *Ariettes oubliées.* Whole-tone patterns appear with both formal and psychological overtones. Overall, their association with impending doom is unmistakable, and the way in which Debussy repeat-

Example 5.6-c. *Pelléas,* "Mélisande."

Example 5.6-d. *Pelléas,* "Golaud's Love."

Example 5.6-e. *Pelléas,* "Vengeance."

Example 5.6-f. *Pelléas,* "Arkel."

edly introduces a menacing quality through their employment is masterful: Whole-tone formations appear both in Golaud's "Fate" motif (Ex. 5.6b) and in the "Threat" ("Cavern") motif (Ex. 5.6h). The latter dominates the orchestral part of an entire scene in Act III, scene 2, which takes place in the castle vaults (see libretto). Forecasting the manner of the composer of "Voiles" (see p. 97–98), De-

Example 5.6-g. *Pelléas, "Pelléas."*

Example 5.6-h. *Pelléas, "Threat" (Cavern).*

bussy articulates a tripartite structure in this scene by deploying a whole-tone set on C-natural in the outer sections, while utilizing a transposition to C♯ for the interior section (beginning at "Lean over", p. 87).

Beyond the compatability of the French 6th chord with whole-tone structures, the independence Debussy accords this sonority through its rhythmic placement in Ex. 5.6b from *Pelléas* recalls the debate with his teacher Guiraud:

Guiraud: *(Debussy having played a series of chords on the piano) What's that?*

Debussy: *Incomplete chords, floating. One can travel where one wishes and leave by any door. Greater nuances.*

Guiraud: *But when I play this (a "French sixth" chord on A♭, evidently one of the chords Debussy had played) it has to resolve.*

Debussy: *I don't see that it should. Why?*

It is an attitude with respect to the French 6th chord that Berg was to endorse in a striking fashion in both his early (op. 2, no. 2) and late works (*Der Wein*, final cadence chord). The conversation ended with the following aesthetic rationale.

Guiraud: *Well, do you find this lovely? (He plays a series of parallel triads.)*

Debussy: *Yes, yes, yes!*

Guiraud: *I am not saying that what you do isn't beautiful, but it's theoretically absurd.*

Debussy: *There is no theory. You merely have to listen. Pleasure is the law.*[19]

While because of its length, *Pelléas* is difficult to grasp in all of its details, a study of the score not only secures most of the features associated with Debussy's mature language, but underscores through its textual background the relationship of Symbolist values to the development of a new musical language. The Wagnerisms that infiltrate the orchestral interludes and on rare occasions (the love scene, Act IV, scene 4) push the note of hysteria surprisingly close to Puccini, can come, as in the same example, only moments after the lovers have whispered "Je t'aime"; "Je t'aime aussi" against an orchestra that has fallen silent.

The list of these eight motifs (Exs. 5.6a–h), though partial, is sufficient to sense their function in those sections for which a text is provided: Act I, complete; Act III, scenes 2, 3; Act IV, scene 4. These portions should allow ample opportunity to test the symbolic categories of both text and motif alluded to earlier, the contrast in length of the several scenes, the almost total stasis of some (Act III, scene 2 and 3), and the peripeteia of others (Act IV, scene 4).

Claude Debussy, *Pelléas et Mélisande*, Act I

SCENE 1

A FOREST
(Golaud enters.)

GOLAUD   (a, b, c)*
I shall never get out of this forest. God
knows where that beast has brought me. I
thought I had killed it, and here are traces
of blood. But now I've lost sight of it. I
think I'm lost, too, and my hounds won't
find me. I must retrace my steps.   (b)
I hear someone crying. Oh! Oh! What's
that, there by the water? A girl crying at   (c)
the water's edge? She doesn't hear me. I
can't see her face. Why are you crying?
Don't be frightened. You've nothing to fear. (a)
Why are you crying here, all alone?   (d)

MELISANDE
Don't touch me! Don't touch me!

GOLAUD
Don't be afraid. I won't do you any—Oh,
you're beautiful!   (d)

MELISANDE
Don't touch me. Don't touch me, or I'll
throw myself in the water.

GOLAUD
I won't touch you. Look, I'll stay here, by   (a)
the tree. Don't be afraid. Has someone hurt
you?

MELISANDE
Oh yes, yes, yes.

SCENE 1

UNE FORET
(Entre Golaud.)

GOLAUD
Je ne pourrai plus sortir de cette forêt.
Dieu sait jusqu' où cette bête m'a mené. Je
croyais cependant l'avoir blessée à mort, et
voici des traces de sang. Mais maintenant
je l'ai perdue de vue. Je crois que je me
suis perdu moi-même, et mes chiens ne me
retrouvent plus. Je vais revenir sur mes
pas. J'entends pleurer. Oh! Oh! qu'y a-t-il là
au bord de l'eau? Une petite fille qui pleure
au bord de l'eau? Elle ne m'entend pas. Je
ne vois pas son visage. Pourquoi pleures-
tu? N'ayez pas peur. Vous n'avez rien à
craindre. Pourquoi pleurez-vous ici, toute
seule?

MELISANDE
Ne me touchez pas, ne me touchez
pas!

GOLAUD
N'ayez pas peur. Je ne vous ferai pas . . .
Oh, vous êtes belle!

MELISANDE
Ne me touchez pas. Ne me
touchez pas, ou je me jette à l'eau.

GOLAUD
Je ne vous touche pas. Voyez, je resterai
ici, contre l'arbre. N'ayez pas peur.
Quelqu'un vous a-t-il fait du mal?

MELISANDE
Oh, oui, oui, oui.

*The letters a–h refer to the leitmotifs as they appear in Exs. 5.6 a–h.

GOLAUD
Who has hurt you?

MELISANDE
Everyone! Everyone!

GOLAUD
What have they done to you?

MELISANDE
I don't want to say, I can't say.

GOLAUD
Look, don't cry like that. Where are you from?

MELISANDE
I escaped, fled, ran away.

GOLAUD
Yes, but from where did you run away?

MELISANDE
I am lost, lost! Oh! Oh! lost here! I'm not from here, I wasn't born here.

GOLAUD
Where are you from? Where were you born?

MELISANDE
Oh! Oh! Far from here, a long way.

GOLAUD
What's that, shining under the water?

MELISANDE
Where? Oh, it's the crown he gave me. It fell in when I was crying.

GOLAUD
A crown? Who gave you a crown? I'll try to get it back.

MELISANDE
No, no. I don't want it. I don't want it any more. I would rather die—die now.

GOLAUD
I could easily get it back. The water isn't very deep.

MELISANDE
I don't want it. If you get it back, I'll throw myself in.

GOLAUD
No, no; I'll leave it there. Still, it wouldn't be hard to get it. It looks very beautiful. Is it long since you ran away?

MELISANDE
Yes, yes. Who are you?

GOLAUD
I am Prince Golaud, grandson of Arkel, the old king of Allemonde.

GOLAUD
(d) Qui est-ce qui vous a fait du mal?

MELISANDE
Tous! Tous!

GOLAUD
Quel mal vous a-t-on fait?

MELISANDE
Je ne veux pas le dire, je ne peux pas le dire.

GOLAUD
Voyons, ne pleurez pas ainsi. D'où venez-vous?

MELISANDE
Je me suis enfuie, enfuie, enfuie.

GOLAUD
Oui, mais d'où vous êtes-vous enfuie?

MELISANDE
(d) Je suis perdue, perdue! Oh! Oh! perdue ici! Je ne suis pas d'ici, je ne suis pas née là.

GOLAUD
D'où êtes-vous? Où êtes-vous née?

MELISANDE
(d) Oh, oh! loin d'ici, loin, loin.

GOLAUD
Qu'est-ce qui brille ainsi, au fond de l'eau?

MELISANDE
Où donc? Ah, c'est la couronne qu'il m'a donnée. Elle est tombée en pleurant.

GOLAUD
Une couronne? Qui est-ce qui vous a donné une couronne? Je vais essayer de la prendre.

MELISANDE
(d) Non, non. Je n'en veux plus, je n'en veux plus. Je préfère mourir . . . mourir tout de suite.

GOLAUD
Je pourrais la retirer facilement. L'eau n'est pas très profonde.

MELISANDE
Je n'en veux plus. Si vous la retirez, je me jette à sa place.

GOLAUD
Non, non; je la laisserai là. On pourrait la prendre sans peine, cependant. Elle semble très belle. Y a-t-il longtemps que vous avez fui?

MELISANDE
Oui, oui. Qui êtes-vous?

GOLAUD
(e) Je suis le prince Golaud, le petit-fils
(f) d'Arkel, le vieux roi d' Allemonde.

MELISANDE
Oh, you already have grey hair!

GOLAUD
Yes, some, here at the temples.

MELISANDE
And your beard too. Why do you look at me like that?

GOLAUD
I'm looking at your eyes. Do you never shut them?

MELISANDE
Oh yes, I close them at night.

GOLAUD
Why do you look so astonished?

MELISANDE
You are a giant.

GOLAUD
I am a man, like any other.

MELISANDE
Why did you come here?

GOLAUD
I don't know myself. I was hunting in the forest, chasing a wild boar, and I took the wrong path. You look very young. How old are you?

MELISANDE
I'm beginning to feel cold.

GOLAUD
Will you come with me?

MELISANDE
No, no, I'll stay here.

GOLAUD
You can't stay here all alone. You can't stay all night. What is your name?

MELISANDE
Mélisande.

GOLAUD
You can't stay here, Mélisande. Come with me.

MELISANDE
I'll stay here.

GOLAUD
You'll be frightened, all alone. You don't know what may be here—all night, all alone . . . It's impossible, Mélisande. Come, give me your hand.

MELISANDE
Oh, don't touch me.

GOLAUD
Don't cry. I won't touch you. But come with me. The night will be very dark and cold. Come with me.

MELISANDE
(c) Oh, vous avez déjà les cheveux gris!

GOLAUD
Oui, quelques-uns, ici, près des tempes.

MELISANDE
Et la barbe aussi. Pourquoi me regardez-vous ainsi?

GOLAUD
(d) Je regarde vos yeux. Vous ne fermez jamais les yeux?

MELISANDE
(d) Si, si, je les ferme la nuit.

GOLAUD
Pourquoi avez-vous l'air si étonné?

MELISANDE
Vous êtes un géant.

GOLAUD
Je suis un homme comme les autres.

MELISANDE
Pourquoi êtes-vous venu ici?

GOLAUD
(b) Je n'en sais rien moi-même. Je chassais dans la forêt, je poursuivais un sanglier, je me suis trompé de chemin. Vous avez l'air très jeune. Quel âge avez-vous?

MELISANDE
Je commence à avoir froid.

GOLAUD
Voulez-vous venir avec moi?

MELISANDE
Non, non, je reste ici.

GOLAUD
(d) Vous ne pouvez pas rester ici toute seule. Vous ne pouvez pas rester ici toute la nuit. Comment vous nommez-vous?

MELISANDE
Mélisande.

GOLAUD
Vous ne pouvez pas rester ici, Mélisande. Venez avec moi.

MELISANDE
Je reste ici.

GOLAUD
Vous aurez peur, toute seule. On ne sait pas ce qu'il y a ici—toute la nuit, toute seule . . . Ce n'est pas possible, Mélisande. Venez, donnez-moi la main.

MELISANDE
(c) Oh, ne me touchez pas.

GOLAUD
Ne criez pas. Je ne vous toucherai plus. Mais venez avec moi. La nuit sera très noire et très froide. Venez avec moi.

MELISANDE
Where are you going?

GOLAUD
I don't know. I'm lost too.   **(b)**

                                                     (a, b, c)

SCENE 2

A ROOM IN THE CASTLE

GENEVIEVE
This is what he wrote to his brother
Pelléas: "One evening, I found her, in
tears, at the edge of a spring, in the forest
where I was lost. I don't know her age, or
who she is, or where she is from, and dare
not ask her, because she must have been
terribly shocked and, when asked what
happened, she cries suddenly, like a child,
and sobs so bitterly that it is frightening. I
married her six months ago, and I still
know nothing more about her than on the
day we met.
Meanwhile, dear Pelléas, whom I love
more than a brother, even though we do
not have the same father, meanwhile,
prepare for my return. I know my mother
will forgive me willingly. But I fear Arkel,
despite his kindness. If, however, he
consents to accept her as he would his   **(c)**
own daughter, the third day after you
receive this letter, light a lamp at the top
of the tower overlooking the sea. I will see
it from the bridge of our ship; if not, I
shall travel farther, and never return."   **(c)**
What do you say to that?

ARKEL
I have nothing to say.
This may seem strange to us, because we
only ever see the reverse side of destiny,
the reverse even of our own . . . He always
took my advice until now. I thought it
would make him happy by sending him to
ask for the hand of Princess Ursula.
He could not stay single, and ever since
his wife's death he was saddened by his
solitude: and this marriage was going to
bring an end to long wars and old hatreds.
But he did not want it so. Let it be as he
wishes: I have never stood in the way of
fate; he knows his future better than I.
Perhaps nothing that happens is   **(f)**
meaningless.

GENEVIEVE
He has always been so prudent, so serious
and so dependable. Since his wife's death,

MELISANDE
Où allez-vous?

GOLAUD
Je ne sais pas. Je suis perdu aussi.

SCÈNE 2

UN APPARTEMENT
DANS LE CHATEAU

GENEVIEVE
Voici ce qu'il écrit à son frère Pelléas: "Un
soir, je l'ai trouvée tout en pleurs au bord
d'une fontaine, dans la forêt où je m'étais
perdu. Je ne sais ni son âge, ni qui elle est,
ni d'où elle vient, et je n'ose pas
l'interroger, car elle doit avoir eu une
grande épouvante, et quand on lui
demande ce qui lui est arrivé, elle pleure
tout à coup comme un enfant et sanglote
si profondément qu'on a peur. Il y a
maintenant six mois que je l'ai épousée, et
je n'en sais pas plus que le jour de notre
rencontre. En attendant, mon cher Pelléas,
toi que j'aime plus qu'un frère, bien que
nous ne soyons pas nés du même père, en
attendant, prépare mon retour. Je sais que
ma mère me pardonnera volontiers. Mais
j'ai peur d'Arkel, malgré toute sa bonté. S'il
consent néanmoins à l'accueillir, comme il
accueillerait sa propre fille, le troisième
jour qui suivra cette lettre, allume une
lampe au sommet de la tour qui regarde la
mer. Je l'apercevrai du pont de notre
navire, si non, j'irai plus loin et ne
reviendrai plus."
Qu'en dites-vous?

ARKEL
Je n'en dis rien.
Cela peut nous paraître étrange, parce que
nous ne voyons jamais que l'envers des
destinées, l'envers même de la nôtre . . . Il
avait toujours suivi mes conseils jusqu'ici,
j'avais cru le rendre heureux en l'envoyant
demander la main de la princesse Ursule.
Il ne pouvait pas rester seul, et depuis la
mort de sa femme il était triste d'être seul;
et ce mariage allait mettre fin à de longues
guerres, à de vieilles haines.
Il ne l'a pas voulu ainsi. Qu'il en soit
comme il a voulu: je ne me suis jamais mis
en travers d'une destinée; il sait mieux que
moi son avenir. Il n'arrive peut-être pas
d'événements inutiles.

GENEVIEVE
Il a toujours été si prudent, si grave et si
ferme. Depuis la mort de sa femme il ne

he has lived only for his son, little Yniold. He has forgotten everything else. What shall we do? **(g)**

ARKEL
Who is coming in?

GENEVIEVE
It's Pelléas. He has been crying. **(g)**

ARKEL
Is that you, Pelléas? Come a little closer so I can see you in the light. **(g)**

PELLEAS
Grandfather, I received another letter at the same time as my brother's: it is from my friend Marcellus. He is dying and is asking for me. He says he knows the exact day when death will come. He says I can reach him first, if I want, but there's no time to lose.

ARKEL
You must wait a little longer, though. We don't know what your brother's return has **(h)** in store for us. And besides, isn't your father upstairs perhaps more ill than your friend? Could you choose between father and friend?

GENEVIEVE
Make sure the lamp is lit this evening, Pelléas.

(c, f, b, d)

SCENE 3

IN FRONT OF THE CASTLE

MELISANDE
It's so dark in the gardens. And what forests, what forests all around the palace.

GENEVIEVE
Yes; they amazed me too when I first came here; they amaze everyone. There are places where you never see the sun. But you get used to it so quickly. It's a long time, a long time . . . I've been living here nearly forty years. Look in the other direction and you will have the light from **(c)** the sea.

MELISANDE
I hear a noise down below. **(g)**

GENEVIEVE
Yes; someone's coming up towards us. Ah, **(g)** it's Pelléas . . . he still seems tired after waiting so long for you.

MELISANDE
He hasn't seen us.

vivait plus que pour son fils, le petit Yniold. Il a tout oublié. Qu'allons-nous faire?

ARKEL
Qui est-ce qui entre là?

GENEVIEVE
C'est Pelléas. Il a pleuré.

ARKEL
Est-ce toi, Pelléas? Viens un peu plus près que je te voie dans la lumière.

PELLEAS
Grand-père, j'ai reçu en même temps que la lettre de mon frère une autre lettre: une lettre de mon ami Marcellus. Il va mourir et il m'appelle. Il dit qu'il sait exactement le jour où la mort doit venir. Il me dit que je puis arriver avant elle si je veux, mais qu'il n'y a pas de temps à perdre.

ARKEL
Il faudrait attendre quelque temps cependant. Nous ne savons pas ce que le retour de ton frère nous prépare. Et d'ailleurs ton père n'est-il pas ici, au-dessus de nous, plus malade peut-être que ton ami? Pourrais-tu choisir entre le père et l'ami?

GENEVIEVE
Aie soin d'allumer la lampe dès ce soir, Pelléas.

SCÈNE 3

DEVANT LE CHATEAU

MELISANDE
Il fait sombre dans les jardins. Et quelles forêts, quelles forêts tout autour des palais!

GENEVIEVE
Oui; cela m'étonnait aussi quand je suis arrivée ici, et cela étonne tout le monde. Il y a des endroits où l'on ne voit jamais le soleil. Mais l'on s'y fait si vite. Il y a longtemps, il y a longtemps . . . il y a presque quarante ans que je vis ici. Regardez de l'autre côté, vous aurez la clarté de la mer.

MELISANDE
J'entends du bruit au-dessous de nous.

GENEVIEVE
Oui; c'est quelqu'un qui monte vers nous. Ah, c'est Pelléas . . . il semble encore fatigué de vous avoir attendue si longtemps.

MELISANDE
Il ne nous a pas vues.

GENEVIEVE
I think he has, but he doesn't know what he should do. Pelléas, Pelléas! Is that you?

PELLEAS
Yes! I came up from the sea.

GENEVIEVE
So did we, looking for some light. It's a little brighter here than elsewhere even though the sea is dark.

PELLEAS
We'll have a storm tonight; there have been storms every night for some time, and yet the sea is calm at the moment. You could sail away without realizing it, and never return.

VOICES
Ho! Heave ho! Ho!

MELISANDE
Something is leaving the harbour.

PELLEAS
It must be a big ship; . . .
. . .the lights are very high

VOICES
Ho! Heave ho!

PELLEAS
We will see it in a moment . . .

VOICES
Ho! Heave ho!

PELLEAS
. . . when it enters that patch of light.

GENEVIEVE
I don't know whether we shall see it . . .
. . . there is still some mist on the water.

VOICES
Ho!

PELLEAS
It looks as though the mist is lifting slowly.

MELISANDE
Yes; I can see a small light down there that I couldn't see before.

PELLEAS
That's a lighthouse; there are others that we can't see yet.

MELISANDE
The ship is in the light; it's already quite far off.

PELLEAS
It's moving off under full sail.

MELISANDE
It's the ship that brought me here. It has big sails . . .

(g)

(g)

(b)

(c, b)

GENEVIEVE
Je crois qu'il nous a vues, mais il ne sait ce qu'il doit faire. Pelléas! Pelléas! Est-ce toi?

PELLEAS
Oui! Je venais du côté de la mer.

GENEVIEVE
Nous aussi, nous cherchions la clarté. Ici il fait un peu plus clair qu'ailleurs, et cependant la mer est sombre.

PELLEAS
Nous aurons une tempête cette nuit; il y en a toutes les nuits depuis quelque temps et cependant elle est si calme maintenant. On s'embarquerait sans le savoir et l'on ne reviendrait plus.

VOIX
Hoé! Hisse hoé! Hoé! Hoé!

MELISANDE
Quelque chose sort du port.

PELLEAS
Il faut que ce soit un grand navire; . . .
. . . les lumières sont très hautes.

VOIX
Hoé! Hisse hoé!

PELLEAS
Nous le verrons tout à l'heure . . .

VOIX
Hoé! Hisse hoé!

PELLEAS
. . . quand il entrera dans la bande de clarté.

GENEVIEVE
Je ne sais si nous pourrons le voir . . .
. . . il y a encore une brume sur la mer.

VOIX
Hoé!

PELLEAS
On dirait que la brume s'élève lentement.

MELISANDE
Oui; j'aperçois là-bas une petite lumière que je n'avais pas vue.

PELLEAS
C'est un phare; il y en a d'autres que nous ne voyons pas encore.

MELISANDE
Le navire est dans la lumière; il est déjà bien loin.

PELLEAS
Il s'éloigne à toutes voiles.

MELISANDE
C'est le navire qui m'a menée ici. Il a de grandes voiles . . .

VOICES
Heave ho! Heave ho! Heave ho!

MELISANDE
. . . I recognize it by its sails.

VOICES
Heave ho!

PELLEAS
It will have a rough sea tonight.

(b)

VOICES
Heave ho!

MELISANDE
Why is it going tonight? You can hardly
see it. It could be wrecked!

PELLEAS
Night is falling very . . .
. . . quickly.

VOICES
Ho!

GENEVIEVE
It's time to go in. Pelléas, show Mélisande
the way. I must go and see little Yniold for
a moment.

(b)

(c)

PELLEAS
You can't see anything on the sea.

MELISANDE
I see more lights.

PELLEAS
Those are the other lighthouses. Do you
hear the sea? The wind is rising. Let's go
down this way. Give me your hand.

MELISANDE
But, you see, my hands are full of flowers.

PELLEAS
I'll take your arm; the path is steep and
very dark. I am probably leaving tomorrow.

(c)
(c)

MELISANDE
Oh! Why are you going away?

VOIX
Hisse hoé! Hoé! Hisse hoé! Hisse hoé!

MELISANDE
. . . Je le reconnais à ses voiles.

VOIX
Hisse hoé!

PELLEAS
Il aura mauvaise mer cette nuit.

VOIX
Hisse hoé!

MELISANDE
Pourquoi s'en va-t-il cette nuit? On ne le
voit presque plus. Il fera peut-être naufrage!

PELLEAS
La nuit tombe très . . .
. . . vite.

VOIX
Hoé!

GENEVIEVE
Il est temps de rentrer. Pelléas, montre la
route à Mélisande. Il faut que j'aille voir,
un instant, le petit Yniold.

PELLEAS
On ne voit plus rien sur la mer.

MELISANDE
Je vois d'autres lumières.

PELLEAS
Ce sont les autres phares. Entendez-vous la
mer? C'est le vent qui s'élève. Descendons
par ici. Voulez-vous me donner la main?

MELISANDE
Voyez, voyez, j'ai les mains pleines de
fleurs.

PELLEAS
Je vous soutiendrai par le bras; le chemin
est escarpé et il y fait très sombre.
Je pars peut-être demain.

MELISANDE
Oh! Pourquoi partez-vous?

(b)

Act II

Scene One. Pelléas and Melisande are seen together, close to a fountain in the
park. Melisande is playing with her wedding ring, pitching it high in the air. Pelléas
warns her to be careful. As he does so, the ring eludes her grasp and falls into the
water, where it sinks out of sight to a great depth. Melisande is much distressed
and wonders what she will say to Golaud. Pelléas tells her to speak the truth.

Scene Two. Set in Golaud's sick room with Melisande in dutiful attendance
upon him. His horse ran away at the precise moment Melisande lost the ring and
Golaud was dashed against a tree. Caressing Melisande's hand, he notices the
disappearance of the ring and asks where it is. She says it slipped off her finger
while seeking shells for little Yniold (Golaud's son) in the grotto by the sea. Golaud

says he values the ring above all earthly possessions. She must go to seek for it at once. She is afraid in the dark. He tells her to get Pelléas to help her.

Scene Three. Pelléas and Melisande are in the grotto. As they enter, by a sudden ray of moonlight they see three blind old men, sleeping. Melisande is frightened. Pelléas says the blind men presage misfortune.

Act III

Scene One. Melisande is seen at a window of the tower arranging her long hair for the night. Pelléas enters the walk below and asks her for her hand to kiss before he goes away. She will not let him have it unless he promises to stay and, when he agrees, she leans so far out to let him reach it that her hair runs down over him in a flood and causes an ecstasy of love to bubble up. Both are so entranced that they give no heed to a menacing shadow in the darkness. It is Golaud. He comes upon them suddenly, but treats their alliance as the play of children and leads Pelléas away.

Act III

SCENE 2

THE CASTLE VAULTS

SCÈNE 2

LES SOUTERRAINS DU CHATEAU

GOLAUD
Be careful; this way, this way. Have you never been down into these vaults?

(h) GOLAUD
Prenez garde; par ici, par ici. Vous n'avez jamais pénétré dans ces souterrains?

PELLEAS
Yes, once; some time ago; but it was long ago.

PELLEAS
Si, une fois; dans le temps; mais il y a longtemps.

GOLAUD
Well, here's the stagnant pool I mentioned. Do you smell the scent of death which comes from it? Let's go to the edge of that overhanging rock and lean over a little; the odour will strike you full in the face. Lean over; don't be afraid, I'll hold you. Give me—no, no, not your hand, it could slip—your arm. Do you see the chasm, Pelléas, Pelléas?

(h) GOLAUD
Eh bien, voici l'eau stagnante dont je vous parlais. Sentez-vous l'odeur de mort qui monte? Allons jusqu'au bout de ce rocher qui surplombe et penchez-vous un peu; elle viendra vous frapper au visage.
(h) Penchez-vous; n'ayez pas peur, je vous tiendrai. Donnez-moi—non, non, pas la main, elle pourrait glisser, le bras. Voyez-vous le gouffre, Pelléas, Pelléas?

PELLEAS
Yes, I think I can see to the bottom of it. Is the light flickering? You . . .

PELLEAS
Oui, je crois que je vois le fond du gouffre. Est-ce la lumière qui tremble ainsi? Vous . . .

GOLAUD
Yes, it's the lantern. See, I was swinging it to illuminate the walls.

GOLAUD
Oui, c'est la lanterne. Voyez, je l'agitais pour éclairer les parois.

PELLEAS
I can't breathe here. Let's go out.

PELLEAS
J'étouffe ici. Sortons.

GOLAUD
Yes, let's go out.
(They go silently.)

GOLAUD
Oui, sortons.
(h) (Ils sortent en silence.)

SCENE 3

A TERRACE AT THE ENTRANCE TO THE VAULTS

PELLEAS

Ah! At last I can breathe! I thought, for a moment, that I would be ill in those huge caves; I was on the point of passing out. The air is moist and heavy like a dew of lead down there, with thick shadows like a poisoned paste. And now, all the air from all over the sea!
There's a fresh wind, see, fresh as a leaf that has just opened, with its tiny green blades.
There! They've just watered the flowers along the terrace and the perfume of the greenery and the sprinkled roses reaches up to here. It must be nearly midday; they're already in the shade of the tower. It is midday, I can hear the clocks chiming and the children are going down to the beach to swim.
Look there's our mother and Mélisande by a window in the tower.

GOLAUD

Yes, they're sheltering on the shady side. On the subject of Mélisande, I heard what went on and what was said last night. I know quite well that these are children's games; but it mustn't happen again. She's very delicate, and we must look after her, all the more since she may soon become a mother, and the slightest upset could make her ill. It's not the first time I've noticed that there could be something going on between you . . . You are older than she, and it's enough for me to have spoken to you . . . Avoid her as much as possible; but without making a show of it, of course, without making a show of it.

SCÈNE 3

UNE TERRASSE AU SORTIR DES SOUTERRAINS

PELLEAS

Ah! Je respire enfin! J'ai cru, un instant, que j'allais me trouver mal dans ces énormes grottes; j'ai été sur le point de **(h)** tomber. Il y a là un air humide et lourd comme une rosée de plomb, et des ténèbres épaisses comme une pâte empoisonnée. Et maintenant, tout l'air de toute la mer!
Il y a un vent frais, voyez, frais comme une feuille qui vient de s'ouvrir, sur les petites lames vertes.
(g) Tiens! On vient d'arroser les fleurs au bord de la terrasse et l'odeur de la verdure et des roses mouillées monte jusqu'ici. Il doit être près de midi; elles sont déjà dans l'ombre de la tour. Il est midi, j'entends sonner les cloches et les enfants descendent vers la plage pour se baigner. Tiens, voilà notre mère et Mélisande à une fenêtre de la tour.

GOLAUD

Oui; elles se sont réfugiées du côté de l'ombre. A propos de Mélisande, j'ai entendu ce qui s'est passé et ce qui s'est dit hier au soir. Je le sais bien, ce sont là jeux d'enfants; mais il ne faut pas que cela se répète. Elle est très délicate, et il faut qu'on la ménage, d'autant plus qu'elle sera peut-être bientôt mère, et la moindre émotion pourrait amener un malheur. Ce n'est pas la première fois que je remarque qu'il pourrait y avoir quelque chose entre vous . . . Vous êtes plus âgé qu'elle, il suffira de vous l'avoir dit . . . Evitez-la autant que possible; mais sans affectation, d'ailleurs, sans affectation.

Scene Four. Shows the castle tower and Melisande's window. Golaud questions little Yniold as to the actions of Pelléas and Melisande together. The child endeavors to shield the two. Melisande's window is lighted up and Golaud hoists Yniold so that he may see into the room. The child says that he sees both Pelléas and Melisande there, looking at each other, motionless.

Act IV

Scene One. Shows a passageway of the castle. Pelléas makes a hasty appointment with Melisande to meet him, one last time before he goes away, at the fountain in the park.

Scene Two. Arkel comes in and sympathizes with Melisande's joyless life here, but Golaud, entering, is furious. He hints at danger to her and, growing distraught, seizes her by the hair, bringing her to her knees and dragging her one way and another. She takes it all silently, but Arkel interferes and Golaud desists.

Scene Three. Yniold is lifting a stone to find his golden ball when a runaway flock of sheep is heard, followed by a shepherd. Yniold marvels at their number and that they do not know their way home.

Act IV

SCENE 4

PELLEAS
It's the last night . . . the last night. Everything must end. I've played like a child with something I didn't realize. I have been playing, in a dream, with the strings of fate. Who suddenly brought me to my senses? I shall run away, crying with joy and sadness, like a blind man escaping from a burning house. I'm going to tell her that I'm escaping . . . It's late; she's not coming. I'd do better to leave without seeing her again. I must look carefully at her this time . . . there are things I no longer remember . . . it seems as though I haven't seen her for a hundred years . . . and I've still not looked her full in the eyes. There'll be nothing left for me if I go away like this . . . And all those memories . . . It's as if I were trying to hold water in a muslin bag. I must see her for one last look into the depths of her heart . . . I must tell her all the things I've never said.

MELISANDE (Entering.)
Pelléas!

PELLEAS
Mélisande! Is it you, Mélisande?

MELISANDE
Yes.

PELLEAS
Come here, don't stay on the edge of the moonlight, come here, we have so many things to say to each other . . . Come here into the shadow of the lime-tree.

MELISANDE
Let me stay in the light.

PELLEAS
They might see us from the windows of the tower. Come here; here, we have nothing to fear. Be careful, they might see us!

SCÈNE 4

PELLEAS
C'est le dernier soir . . . le dernier soir. Il faut que tout finisse . . . J'ai joué comme un enfant autour d'une chose que je ne soupçonnais pas. J'ai joué, en rêve, autour des pièges de la destinée. Qui est-ce qui **(g)** m'a réveillé tout à coup? Je vais fuir en criant de joie et de douleur, comme un aveugle qui fuirait l'incendie de sa maison. Je vais lui dire que je vais fuir . . . Il est **(h)** tard; elle ne vient pas. Je ferais mieux de m'en aller sans la revoir. Il faut que je la regarde bien cette fois-ci . . . Il y a des choses que je ne me rappelle plus . . . on dirait par moments qu'il y a cent ans que **(c)** je ne l'ai plus vue . . . Et je n'ai pas encore regardé son regard. Il ne me reste rien si je m'en vais ainsi . . . Et tous ces souvenirs . . . C'est comme si j'emportais un peu **(h)** d'eau dans un sac de mousseline. Il faut que je la voie une dernière fois jusqu'au fond de son coeur . . . Il faut que je lui dise tout ce que je n'ai pas dit.

(Entre Mélisande.)
MELISANDE
Pelléas!

PELLEAS
Mélisande! Est-ce toi Mélisande?

MELISANDE
Oui.

PELLEAS
Viens ici, ne reste pas au bord du clair de lune, viens ici, nous avons tant de choses à nous dire . . . Viens ici dans l'ombre du tilleul.

MELISANDE
Laissez-moi dans la clarté.

PELLEAS
On pourrait nous voir des fenêtres de la tour. Viens ici; ici, nous n'avons rien à craindre. Prends garde, on pourrait nous voir!

MELISANDE

I want to be seen.

PELLEAS

What's the matter? Did you get out
without being seen?

MELISANDE

Yes, your brother was asleep.

PELLEAS

It's late, in an hour they'll shut the gates.
We must be careful. Why are you so late?

MELISANDE

Your brother had a bad dream. Then my
dress got caught on nails in the door. See,
it's torn. I lost all that time and I ran . . .

PELLEAS

My poor Mélisande! I'm almost afraid to
touch you. You're out of breath, like a
hunted bird. Did you do all that for me? I
can hear your heart beating as though it
were my own. Come here, closer to me.

MELISANDE

Why do you laugh?

PELLEAS

I'm not laughing; or rather, I'm laughing for
joy without realizing it . . . I should really
be crying.

MELISANDE

We came here long ago. I remember . . .

PELLEAS

Yes . . . many long months ago. I didn't
know, then. Do you know why I asked you
to come this evening?

MELISANDE

No.

PELLEAS

It's probably the last time I'll see you. I
must go away forever.

MELISANDE

Why do you always say you're going away?

PELLEAS

Must I tell you what you know already!
Don't you know what I'm going to say?

MELISANDE

No, no. I know nothing.

PELLEAS

You don't know why I must leave? You
don't realize that it's because . . . I love you.

MELISANDE

Je veux qu'on me voie.

PELLEAS

Qu'as-tu-donc? Tu as pu sortir sans qu'on
s'en soit aperçu?

MELISANDE

Oui, votre frère dormait.

PELLEAS

(b) Il est tard, dans une heure on fermera les
portes. Il faut prendre garde. Pourquoi est-
tu venue si tard?

MELISANDE

(b) Votre frère avait un mauvais rêve. Et puis
ma robe s'est accrochée aux clous de la
porte. Voyez, elle est déchirée. J'ai perdu
tout ce temps et j'ai couru . . .

PELLEAS

Ma pauvre Mélisande! J'aurais presque
(b) peur de te toucher. Tu es encore hors
d'haleine comme un oiseau pourchassé.
C'est pour moi que tu fais tout cela?
J'entends battre ton coeur comme si c'était
le mien. Viens ici, plus près de moi.

MELISANDE

Pourquoi riez-vous?

PELLEAS

Je ne ris pas; ou bien je ris de joie sans le
savoir . . . Il y aurait plutôt de quoi pleurer.

MELISANDE

Nous sommes venus ici il y a bien
longtemps. Je me rappelle . . .

PELLEAS

Oui . . . il y a de longs mois. Alors, je ne
savais pas. Sais-tu pourquoi je t'ai demandé
de venir ce soir?

MELISANDE

Non.

PELLEAS

C'est peut-être la dernière fois que je te
vois. Il faut que je m'en aille pour toujours.

MELISANDE

Pourquoi dis-tu toujours que tu t'en vas?

PELLEAS

Je dois te dire ce que tu sais déjà! Tu ne
sais pas ce que je vais te dire?

MELISANDE

Mais non, mais non; je ne sais rien.

PELLEAS

Tu ne sais pas pourquoi il faut que je
m'éloigne? Tu ne sais pas que c'est parce
que . . . je t'aime.

MELISANDE

I love you too.

PELLEAS

Oh! What did you say Mélisande! I hardly heard it. The ice has been broken with red-hot irons! You say it in a voice which comes from the ends of the earth! I hardly heard you . . . You love me? You love me too? How long have you loved me?

MELISANDE

Always . . . since I first saw you.

PELLEAS

Your voice sounds as if it had crossed a Spring sea! I have never heard it until now. It's as if rain has fallen on my heart. You said it so openly! Like an angel being questioned . . .
I can't believe it, Mélisande. Why would you love me? Why do you love me? Do you speak truly? You're not deceiving me? It isn't a little lie to make me smile?

MELISANDE

No, I never lie, except to your brother.

(b)

PELLEAS

Oh! How you said that! Your voice! Your voice! It's fresher and purer than water! It's like pure water on my lips . . . like pure water upon my hands . . . Give, give me your hands. Oh! Your hands are so tiny! I didn't realize you were so beautiful! I've never seen anything so lovely before . . . I was restless, searching everywhere in the house, everywhere around the countryside, and could not find beauty . . . And now that I've found you, I've found it . . . I don't believe there can be a more beautiful woman in the world!
Where are you? I can't hear you breathing.

(c)

MELISANDE

Because I am looking at you.

PELLEAS

Why do you look at me so sadly? We are in the shadows. It's too dark beneath this tree. Come into the light. We can't see how happy we are. Come, come; there's so little time left to us.

(g)

MELISANDE

No, no, let's stay here . . . I'm closer to you in the darkness.

MELISANDE

Je t'aime aussi.

PELLEAS

Oh! Qu'as tu dit, Mélisande! Je ne l'ai presque pas entendu. On a brisé la glace avec des fers rougis! Tu dis cela d'une voix qui vient du bout du monde! Je ne t'ai presque pas entendue . . . Tu m'aimes? tu m'aimes aussi? Depuis quand m'aimes-tu?

MELISANDE

Depuis toujours . . . Depuis que je t'ai vu.

PELLEAS

On dirait que ta voix a passé sur la mer au printemps! Je ne l'ai jamais entendue jusqu'ici. On dirait qu'il a plu sur mon coeur. Tu dis cela si franchement! Comme un ange qu'on interroge . . .
Je ne puis pas le croire, Mélisande. Pourquoi m'aimerais-tu? Mais pourquoi m'aimes-tu? Est-ce vrai ce que tu dis? Tu ne me trompes pas? Tu ne mens pas un peu pour me faire sourire?

MELISANDE

Non, je ne mens jamais, je ne mens qu'à ton frère.

PELLEAS

Oh! Comme tu dis cela! Ta voix! Ta voix! Elle est plus fraîche et plus franche que l'eau! On dirait de l'eau pure sur mes lèvres . . . On dirait de l'eau pure sur mes mains . . . Donne-moi, donne-moi tes mains. Oh! tes mains sont petites!
Je ne savais pas que tu étais si belle! Je n'avais jamais rien vu d'aussi beau avant toi . . . J'étais inquiet, je cherchais partout dans la maison . . . Je cherchais partout dans la campagne, et je ne trouvais pas la beauté . . . Et maintenant je t'ai trouvée . . . je l'ai trouvée je ne crois pas qu'il y ait sur la terre une femme plus belle!
Où es-tu? Je ne t'entends plus respirer.

MELISANDE

C'est que je te regarde.

PELLEAS

Pourquoi me regardes-tu si gravement? Nous sommes déjà dans l'ombre. Il fait trop noir sous cet arbre. Viens dans la lumière. Nous ne pouvons pas voir combien nous sommes heureux. Viens, viens; il nous reste si peu de temps.

MELISANDE

Non, non, restons ici . . . Je suis plus près de toi dans l'obscurité.

PELLEAS
Where are your eyes? You won't run away
from me? You aren't thinking of me at this
very moment.

MELISANDE
Yes, I only think of you.

PELLEAS
You were looking somewhere else.

MELISANDE
I was seeing you somewhere else.

PELLEAS
You're uneasy . . . what is it? You don't
seem happy.

MELISANDE
Yes, yes, I'm happy, but I'm sad as well.

PELLEAS
What's that noise? They're shutting the
gates.

MELISANDE
Yes, they've shut them.

PELLEAS
We'll not be able to get in again! Do you
hear the bolts? Listen, listen . . . the heavy
chains! It's too late, too late!

MELISANDE
All the better!

PELLEAS
You? Well, that's it . . . It's no longer what
we might want! All is lost, all is saved! All
is saved this night! Come, come, my heart
is beating madly right up into my throat.
(*They clasp each other.*)
Listen, my heart almost chokes me . . .
Come! . . . Ah! It's so beautiful in the dark!

MELISANDE
There's someone behind us . . .

PELLEAS
I can't see anyone.

MELISANDE
I heard a noise.

PELLEAS
I only hear your heart in the darkness.

MELISANDE
I heard the rustle of dead leaves.

PELLEAS
The wind has suddenly dropped. It stilled
while we kissed.

MELISANDE
How big our shadows are this evening!

PELLEAS
Où sont tes yeux? Tu ne vas pas me fuir?
Tu ne songes pas à moi en ce moment.

MELISANDE
Mais si, je ne songe qu'à toi.

PELLEAS
Tu regardais ailleurs.

MELISANDE
Je te voyais ailleurs.

PELLEAS
Tu es distraite . . . Qu'as-tu donc? Tu ne
me sembles pas heureuse.

(c)   **MELISANDE**
Si, si, je suis heureuse, mais je suis triste.

PELLEAS
Quel est ce bruit? On ferme les portes.

MELISANDE
Oui, on a fermé les portes.

PELLEAS
Nous ne pouvons plus rentrer! Entends-tu
les verroux? Ecoute, écoute . . . les grandes
(e)   chaînes! Il est trop tard, il est trop tard!

MELISANDE
Tant mieux! Tant mieux!

PELLEAS
Tu? Voilà, voilà . . . Ce n'est plus nous qui
le voulons! Tout est perdu, tout est sauvé!
Tout est sauvé ce soir! Viens, viens . . .
mon coeur bat comme un fou jusqu'au
fond de ma gorge. (*Il l'enlace.*)
Ecoute! Mon coeur est sur le point de
m'étrangler . . . Viens! . . . Ah, qu'il fait
(e)   beau dans les ténèbres!

MELISANDE
Il y a quelqu'un derrière nous . . .

PELLEAS
Je ne vois personne.

(e)   **MELISANDE**
J'ai entendu du bruit.

PELLEAS
Je n'entends que ton coeur dans l'obscurité.

(e)   **MELISANDE**
J'ai entendu craquer les feuilles mortes.

PELLEAS
C'est le vent qui s'est tu tout à coup.
Il est tombé pendant que nous nous
embrassions.

MELISANDE
Comme nos ombres sont grandes ce soir!

PELLEAS

They are entwined as far as the end of the garden! Ah! See how they kiss each other far away from us! Look! Look!

MELISANDE

Ah! He is behind a tree! **(e)**

PELLEAS

Who? **(b)**

MELISANDE

Golaud! **(e)**

PELLEAS

Golaud! Where? I can't see anything. **(b)**

MELISANDE

There . . . at the end of our shadows. **(e)**

PELLEAS

Yes, yes; I saw him . . . we mustn't turn suddenly.

MELISANDE

He has his sword.

PELLEAS

I don't have mine.

MELISANDE

He saw us kiss.

PELLEAS

He doesn't know we've seen him. Don't move; don't turn your head. He would run forward. He's watching us. He's still **(b)** standing quite still. Go, go quickly, this way. I'll wait for him and stop him.

MELISANDE

No!

PELLEAS

Go!

MELISANDE

No!

PELLEAS

He's seen everything. He'll kill us!

MELISANDE

All the better!

PELLEAS

He's coming!

MELISANDE

All the better!

PELLEAS

Your mouth! Your mouth!

MELISANDE

Yes! Yes! Yes!

PELLEAS

Oh! Oh! All the stars are falling! **(c)**

MELISANDE

On me, too! On me, too! **(c)**

PELLEAS

Elles s'enlacent jusqu'au fond du jardin! Ah! Qu'elles s'embrassent loin de nous! Regarde! Regarde!

MELISANDE

Ah! Il est derrière un arbre!

PELLEAS

Qui?

MELISANDE

Golaud!

PELLEAS

Golaud? Où donc? Je ne vois rien.

MELISANDE

Là . . . au bout de nos ombres.

PELLEAS

Oui, oui; je l'ai vu . . . Ne nous retournons pas brusquement.

MELISANDE

Il a son épée.

PELLEAS

Je n'ai pas la mienne.

MELISANDE

Il a vu que nous nous embrassions.

PELLEAS

Il ne sait pas que nous l'avons vu. Ne bouge pas; ne tourne pas la tête. Il se précipiterait. Il nous observe. Il est encore immobile. Va-t'en, va-t'en, tout de suite par ici. Je l'attendrai, je l'arrêterai.

MELISANDE

Non!

PELLEAS

Va-t'en!

MELISANDE

Non!

PELLEAS

Il a tout vu. Il nous tuera!

MELISANDE

Tant mieux!

PELLEAS

Il vient!

MELISANDE

Tant mieux!

PELLEAS

Ta bouche! Ta bouche!

MELISANDE

Oui! oui! oui!

PELLEAS

Oh! Oh! Toutes les étoiles tombent!

MELISANDE

Sur moi aussi! sur moi aussi!

PELLEAS		**PELLEAS**
Again! Again! Give me . . .		Encore! Encore! Donne . . .

PELLEAS
Again! Again! Give me . . .

MELISANDE
Everything! . . . Everything, everything! **(b)**

PELLEAS
Give, give . . .

(Golaud runs forward and strikes down
Pelléas with his sword.)

MELISANDE
Oh! Oh! I haven't the courage! I haven't the
courage! Ah!

Translation by Paul Myers, courtesy of CBS Masterworks.

PELLEAS
Encore! Encore! Donne . . .

MELISANDE
Toute! . . .
. . . toute, toute!

PELLEAS
. . . donne, donne . . .

MELISANDE **(e)**
Oh! Oh! Je n'ai pas de courage! Je n'ai pas
de courage! Ah!

Act V

The Fifth Act discloses Golaud, Arkel, and the Physician in the room of Melisande, who is extended on the bed. She partly recovers consciousness after weeks of sickness. Golaud, repentant but still savage and morose, wants her to tell the truth—Did she love Pelléas? Yes. Was it a guilty love? No. Melisande dies.

The synoptic arguments are from the official libretto of the Metropolitan Opera House, New York, with an English version by C. A. Byrne, 1907.

LATER ORCHESTRAL WORKS

Debussy's interest in art, both distant and contemporary, can be noted in the next two works for orchestra. *Nocturnes* of 1897–99 may well reflect his sympathy for James McNeill Whistler, the American artist who was living in Paris at the time and who was a friend of Mallarmé, Huysmans, and Proust. His earlier canvases had frequently carried musical titles—e.g., *Symphony in White, Capriccio, Variation, Harmony in Violet and Yellow*, etc., and in titles such as *Nocturne in Blue and Silver* and *Nocturne in Black and Gold* we are encouraged to recognize that Debussy's spiritual affinity was at least as great for Whistler as for Chopin.[20] Whistler's reliance on memory rather than on perception placed him nearer to Mallarmé than to Degas, and his devotion to the art of the Japanese could also have only appealed to Debussy. Evidence of Debussy's predeliction in this regard is confirmable not only in many musical details, which will be considered later, but in his choice of a Japanese print, *The Great Wave* of Hokusai (1761–1849), for the cover of his first edition of *La mer* (see p. 121).

From the luminosity of the opening of "Nuages" (the figure for which many have traced to Musorgsky's song cycle *Sunless* of 1874) to the bracing movement of "Fêtes" and the subtle seduction of the textless women's chorus of "Sirènes," in his *Nocturnes* Debussy plays with open fifths, pentatonic ideas, Dorian and Phrygian motifs, pure triads, his favored 9th chords, and an occasional explosive array of polyrhythms. Both in "Nuages" and the opening movement of *La mer* (1903–05), his fascination with artificial scales is manifest in themes constructed with a sharp 4 and flat 7 (Ex. 5.7), while the frequent use of augmented triads and the French 6th chord forms a natural alliance with the whole-tone scale. The scale with the sharpened fourth and flattened seventh (in addition to the raised third and sixth) is sometimes identified as the "acoustic scale" because of the approximation of its tones to the harmonic series. It has also recently been identified as one of the Hindu modes, called *Vacaspati,* and one that Debussy probably knew of early in his career.[21] Whatever credit may be given for its genesis, it is a scalar formation that was similarly to appeal to Ravel, Skriabin, and Bartók.

Example 5.7. Debussy, *Nocturnes:* "Nuages," mm. 21–24.

La mer, far from being the formless triptych suggested by the title "Three Symphonic Sketches," moves away from the amorphous outlines of *Prélude à "L'après-midi d'un faune"* and endorses a structural clarity that has been seen to look ahead to his final sonatas: Allegro, Scherzo, and Finale have been described as sonata, free rondo, and concluding fantasy with cyclic recall of the opening two moments. Roy Howat, however, has argued for the presence of a quite different type of formalism, sketching the first movement, "De l'aube à midi sur la mer", as follows: Introduction (mm. 1–30: arch-form ABCBA); First Principal Section (mm. 31–83: idiosyncratic rondo); Second Principal Section (mm.

84–121: strophic); Transition (mm. 122–131: repeated melody over dominant pedal); and Coda (mm. 132–141: extended plagal cadence with thematic returns). Even more tantilizingly, Howat has demonstrated internal divisions in the two principal sections as well as in the movement as a whole, according to the classical division of the Golden Section (.618—i.e., smaller division "b" is to larger division "a" as "a" is to the whole, or b/a = a/a+b). The remaining movements, in addition to many other works of Debussy, are similarly analyzed with respect to such properties. Whether the proportions are the result of a grand plan or a grand instinct, prior charges of formlessness in Debussy's music seem now to have been laid to rest.[22]

The orchestration of *La mer* is more difficult to talk about and is one of its most important components. Here, as in *Pelléas*, Debussy frequently divides his strings into 12 and 15 parts, and the refinement that was involved in such choices is reflected in a statement by Debussy to Victor Ségalen.

> Musicians no longer know how to decompose sound—to give it in all its purity. In *Pélleas* the sixth violin is just as important as the first. I try to employ each *timbre* in its purest form . . . We have been too clever in mixing our *timbres*, and Wagner went very far in this direction, doubling and tripling most of his instruments. Worst of all is Richard Strauss who has made a mess of everything, combining the trombone with the flute . . . I try, on the contrary, to preserve the purity of each *timbre* and to put it in its proper place. Strauss's orchestra . . . is a cocktail orchestra.[23]

In Debussy's final orchestral work, *Jeux* (1912), a ballet commissioned by Diaghilev, we have a rarity and a surprise. The quiet reserve of the score has been noted in Eimert's calculation that of 708 measures, 557 are scored at a level of *piano or pianissimo*, and, speciously or not, the suggestion made that the sound world of Webern is not far distant.[24] But, as even an initial hearing of the work will disclose, the principal newness of the work resides in its formal inquiry. Throughout the period, Debussy's inclinations had run toward part-forms and rondos and had increasingly endorsed the nondevelopmental repetition of ideas presented in pairs. In *Jeux*, Debussy realized the final consequences of such an attitude, where few ideas ever return and where localized repetition tends to provide only a momentary stability.

In a note for a concert performance of *Jeux* on March 1, 1914, however, Debussy provided more than a scenario:

> After a prelude of a few dream-like measures in which a chord composed of notes from the whole-tone scale is heard against a high B minor tonic in the violins, the first theme marked *scherzando* (3/8) is introduced interrupted by the return of the prelude . . . The *scherzando* resumes with a second theme, and the action begins with a tennis ball falling on stage. A young man in tennis clothes and racket held high leaps across the stage and disappears. Then two girls appear, shy and inquisitive. Confiding in each other privately in a corner, they begin their dance but are cut off by the sound of rustling leaves. The young man, who has been watching them through the branches, persuades one of them to dance, even managing to steal a kiss from her. The other girl expresses her jealously in a mocking dance (2/4), and having gained his attention is invited to join in a waltz (3/8) . . . The abandoned, first girl wants to leave, but is held back by the second (3/4, moderate). The three now dance together (3/8), building to a climax which is interrupted by a lost tennis ball falling on stage, causing them all to flee: the chords of the opening prelude return, a few rapid notes slide furtively past, and the piece is done.[25]

The overall form of the work is thus seen to follow the scenario as described by Debussy, and to receive its clearest delineation through changes in movement (tempo and meter). What would seem to be an ever-changing kaleidoscope of motifs subject to brief localized repetition proves to be a network of figures generated by constant division and transformation.

Forgotten after its premiere, the rediscovery of *Jeux* by the post-World War II avant-garde has led to its canonization as a somewhat exaggerated emblem of the crisis of form at the end of the first decade of the century, paralleling the crisis of tonality epitomized by Schoenberg's *Pierrot lunaire* and the crisis of rhythm resounding in the pages of Stravinsky's *The Rite of Spring*.[26] Whatever the later reasons for coupling Debussy's *Jeux* with Webern's *Five Pieces*, op. 10, as emblems of early modernity, there can be little doubt that had it not been for the premiere of Stravinsky's *Rite* two weeks after Debussy's ballet, the latter would have found its audience much sooner.

PRÉLUDES FOR PIANO

Debussy's *Préludes* (1910–13) offer an unusual opportunity to test the Symbolists' ideas of sonority and syntax in more abstract terrain. Yet, though they are for piano alone, the total absence of literary values cannot be claimed. While the two volumes of 12 preludes reflect the legacy of both Bach and Chopin in their number, the appendage of a series of titles to each prelude (although always at the end and in parentheses) not only underscores how much Debussy prized the sonic values of the French language, but also the inherent literary association, which was to be understood but not protested. Just as Debussy had borrowed titles from Verlaine in earlier piano works ("Cortège" and "En bateau," *Petite suite*, 1886–89; "Claire de lune," *Suite bergamasque*, 1890), with "Les sons et les parfums tournent dans l'air du soir" (Book I) we are drawn into the world of Baudelaire and a text, "Harmonie du soir," which he had set before.

The sound of the title and a knowledge of the complete text suggests that Debussy is totally infatuated with the synesthetic overtones and correspondences of the Symbolist master. Beyond such vagaries, whose intentions are supported by a profusion of markings (*de très loin; caressant; coux et rêveur; spiritual et discret*), the *Préludes* are marked by a variety of grammatical licenses that we now hold familiar. Sometimes the use of a whole-tone scalar formation is momentary and utilized in a totally coloristic fashion ("Les sons et les parfums"); elsewhere, recalling *Pelléas*, Act III, scene 2, it can have an overtly formalistic function as in "Voiles," where the outer sections of the work are exclusively fashioned from whole-tone material (Ex. 5.8) and function as a frame to a brief internal episode (Ex. 5.9), which is completely pentatonic.

Other preludes highlight recurring aspects of Debussy's style. "La Cathédrale engloutie," whose opening pentatonicism and use of harmonic fourths and fifths reflects the Symbolist interest in bells (see also Ravel, "La vallée des cloches," Ex. 4.5), also emphasizes through its diatonic parallelisms the French infatuation with linear modality from the time of Satie's *Sarabandes* (1887) and d'Indy's research into Gregorian chant at the Schola Cantorum (Ex. 5.10).

"Feux d'artifice," the brilliant and final prelude to the second book, illustrates the coloristic possibilities of sonorities no more complex than the major triad (note the nonfunctional, tritonally related harmonies in Example 5.11: C–F$\sharp$, E–B$\flat$;

Example 5.8. Debussy, *Préludes*, Book I, "Voiles," mm. 1–5.

Example 5.9. Debussy, *Préludes*, Book I, "Voiles," mm. 42–3.

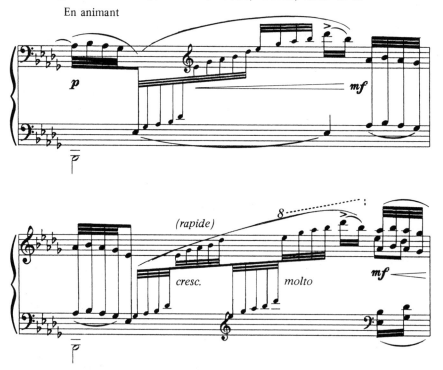

Example 5.10. Debussy, *Préludes*, Book I, "La cathédrale engloutie," mm. 1–7.

Profondément calme (Dans une brume doucement sonore)

Example 5.11. Debussy, *Préludes*, "Feux d'artifice," m. 61.

Rubato

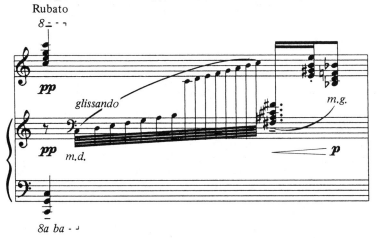

the composer's interest in bitonal clashes (as in the opening measures);

Example 5.12. Debussy, *Préludes*, "Feux d'artifice," m. 1.

the buzzing quasi-atonal figurations that prefigure Bartók (the furious crushed seconds of the following example);

Example 5.13. Debussy, *Préludes*, "Feux d'artifice," mm. 21–22.

and the limited motivic resource that Berg was to decry shortly thereafter:

> In Maeterlinck there is such a hazy mood all the time. It's the same in music: take their hazy harmonies from Debussy, Ravel, Scriabin and the rest, and what is left? (In Debussy's case, two or three five-note motifs). But in Schoenberg's works, particularly where there are rather similar harmonies—whole-tones and fourth-chords—you can also find his unprecedented melodic style, which is not limited to one melodic line but progresses in a continual counterpoint of many beautiful themes.[27]

Indeed, the source for Debussy's entire prelude can be seen as an inflected rising perfect fifth that is subjected to semitonal transposition.

Example 5.14. Debussy, *Préludes*, "Feux d'artifice," mm. 27–30.

At the close of the work, Figure C begins on the same pitch level as Figures A and B—that is, on the pitch C instead of C♯—and therefore ends on D♭, the final key of the piece. The double glissando played simultaneously on the black and white keys summarizes the tonal conflict of the piece that continues in the coda's bitonal and symbolic projection of a strain from the "Marseillaise" in C major against a D♭–A♭ tremolo. The dominant relationship between the opening (F/G♭) and closing (C/D♭) semitonally conflicting pairs (Exs. 5.12, 5.15) recalls Debussy's harmonic plan for Act IV, scene 4 of *Pelléas*.

Example 5.15. Debussy, Pré*ludes*, "Feux d'artifice," mm. 84–98.

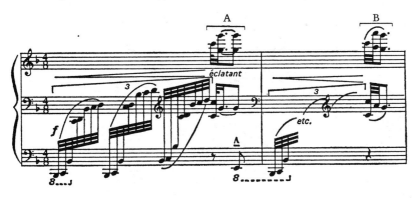

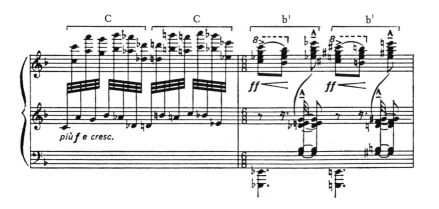

Example 5.15 (Continued)

Ultimately, the vocabulary, which can be described in its details, serves a grander instinct than analysis can suggest. But it is reasonable to claim a hedonistic aspect to the composer's adventure, which seems always to be in search of new and fresh contexts for the projection of sonorities. While the units may be simple or complex, the novelty resides principally in their ordering, which is frequently compromised, judged against the tenets of a former musical language. Through assertion, a new syntax is invented. It is this license that most securely connects the art of Claude Debussy with the premises of Symbolism as well as with future musical developments in the twentieth century.

REPERTOIRE

Duparc, "L'invitation au voyage" (1870), v, pf
Debussy, "Beau soir" (c. 1883), v, pf
Satie, "Ogives" (1886), pf
Debussy, *Ariettes oubliées:* "C'est l'extase" (1887), v, pf

Satie, "Sarabandes" (1887), pf
Debussy, *Pour le piano:* "Sarabande" (1894)
Debussy, *Prelude à "L'après-midi d'un faune"* (1892-94), orch
Debussy, *Nocturnes* (1897-99), orch
Debussy, *Pelléas et Mélisande* (1893-95, 1901-02), opera
Debussy, *La mer* (1903-05), orch
Debussy, *Préludes*, Book I: "Voiles" (1910), pf
Debussy, *Préludes*, Book II: "Feux d'artifice" (1912-13), pf
Debussy, *Jeux* (1912-13), orch

READING

Herbert Eimert, "Debussy's *Jeux*," *Die Reihe*, no. 5 (1959; Eng. trans. 1961), 3.
Edward Lockspeiser, *Debussy, his Life and Mind* (New York, 1962-65).
William Austin, ed., *Prelude to The Afternoon of a Faun* (New York, 1970), with historical and analytical essays.
François Lesure, *Debussy on Music* (Paris, 1971; Eng. trans. New York, 1977).
David Cox, *Debussy's Orchestral Music* (London, 1974).
Stefan Jarocinski, *Debussy: Impressionism and Symbolism* (1966; Eng. trans. Rollo Myers, London, 1976).
Arthur Wenk, *Claude Debussy and the Poets* (Berkeley & Los Angeles, 1976), 148-170.
Laurence Berman, "*Prelude to the Afternoon of a Faun* and *Jeux*: Debussy's Summer Rites," *19th Century Music*, iii.3 (1980), 225-38.
Margaret Cobb, *The Poetic Debussy: A Collection of his Song Texts and Selected Letters* (Boston, 1982).
Carolyn Abbate, "*Tristan* in the composition of *Pelléas*," *19th Century Music*, ii (1981-82), 117-141.
Jan Pasler, "Debussy, *Jeux*: Playing with Time and Form," *19th Century Music*, vi.1 (1982), 60-75.
Roy Howat, *Debussy in Proportion: An Analysis of His Forms* (New York, 1984).
James Hepokoski, "Formulaic Openings in Debussy," *19th Century Music*, viii.1 (1984), 44-59.
Pierre Boulez, "Reflections in *Pelléas et Mélisande*" in *Orientations* (Cambridge, Mass., 1986), 306-17. Originally as "Miroirs pour *Pelléas et Mélisande*" for the 1969 performance at Covent Garden conducted by Boulez. Published with recording on Columbia M3 30119 (1970).
Pierre Boulez, "Debussy: Orchestral Works" in *Orientations* (Cambridge, Mass., 1986), 318-22. Originally for Columbia D 3M-32988.

CHAPTER 6

MAURICE RAVEL TO THE MALLARMÉ SONGS (1913)

It will be unnecessary to restate many of the aesthetic propositions argued in relation to Debussy in considering the early position of Maurice Ravel (1875–1937). Let it be said from the beginning that while they share many characteristics, and Debussy, being 15 years Ravel's senior, is traditionally viewed as the more influential of the two, it would be unfortunate to let the assessment end there. In spite of early charges of "Debussyism," Ravel composed for more than a decade following Debussy's death, and through his contributions of the 1920s can be viewed as a grand participator in the ferment of that decade. It may be fair to claim, therefore, that his scope as a creative artist is broader and more varied than Debussy's, though his historical position may be less fundamental. Details of the first part of this assertion will be discussed periodically in various later chapters.

While Ravel's earliest well known work is his *Pavane pour une infante défunte* of 1899, his first substantial statement was the String Quartet of 1902–03. If we honor his own judgment that the first of these two works labors under the excessive influence of Chabrier's *Dix pièces pittoresques* (1881), it is also reasonable to suggest that the model for the second is the string quartet of Debussy of 1893. The pizzicato opening of the second movement of both quartets has been likened to the sounds of the Javanese gamelan, but the cyclic qualities so apparent in the use of the same material in the first and last movements of both works reflect a century-long preoccupation only recently rekindled in France in the works of Franck and d'Indy.

This cyclic quality was to appear intermittently throughout Ravel's career, from the immediately ensuing *Sonatine* of 1903–05 to the double-function cyclic procedures of Liszt-Strauss-Schoenberg in his *Piano Concerto for the Left Hand* (1929–30). In his *Sonatine*, the Neoclassicism that was to be picked up in his *Tombeau de Couperin* of 1914–17 is evident not only in the formalities but in the texture of the writing. Unlike the expansive gestures that cover the entire compass of the instrument in works like *Jeux d'eau* and *Gaspard de la nuit*, the writing of the *Sonatine* is restricted principally to the center of the keyboard. In the sonatina form of the first movement, as well as in the choice of a minuet for the second (already forecast in his *Menuet antique* of 1895), Ravel parallels Debussy's interest in the nondevelopmental forms and dances of the clavecinists.

Ravel's interest in exotica—Oriental, African, Spanish—is also similar to Debussy's, but his first important brush with a Symbolist literary figure was not in a work for voice but for solo piano.

GASPARD DE LA NUIT

Jacques Louis Napoléon (called Aloysius Bertrand, 1807–1841) is one of those early nineteenth-century writers like George Büchner (1813–1837), the author of *Wozzeck*, whose brief lives and slender output was no obstacle to a fin-de-siècle revival capable of sparking the imagination of the early twentieth century. His major contribution to French literature was the invention of the prose poem, which Baudelaire emulated in his *Spleen de Paris.*

Besides Baudelaire, Bertrand's admirers included Victor Hugo, to whom his *Gaspard de la nuit* is dedicated, but it was not until the end of the century that the Symbolists revived his message and turned him into something of a cult figure. No one was more devoted than Mallarmé, who told his daughter to "Take up Bertrand, where you will find everything." *Gaspard* is subtitled "fantaises à la manière de Rembrandt et de Callot," and various etchings by these two artists as well as others grace the earliest editions. Several artists later undertook to illustrate the collection, and Vollard's edition of 1904 containing wood engravings by Séguin could well have been the immediate inspirational source for Ravel's setting.

Ravel's work carries the subtitle "Trois poèmes de Aloysius Bertrand," and the textual choices are suitably varied. The initial piece, "Ondine," mirrors the Impressionist taste for water images, while the second and third texts carry a decidedly Expressionist overtone. In "Le gibet" we have a perfect reflection of the qualities observable in "Beheading" and "Gallows Song" of Giraud's *Pierrot lunaire,* which was soon to be set to music by Arnold Schoenberg. Bertrand's description of Scarbo as "blue and transparent as the wax of a taper, his face as pale as candle grease" similarly recalls the picture of "The Dandy" before his daily makeup from the same cycle (see p. 190). The distinction between Gallic and Prussian sensibilities is momentarily smudged, and we are reminded that a French poet was the source of inspiration for Schoenberg as well. A reinforcement of this point will be discussed in the section "Ravel and Vienna" (p. 193).

MAURICE RAVEL, *Gaspard de la nuit*

Ondine
. . . . Je croyais entendre
Une vague harmonie enchanter mon sommeil,
Et près de moi sépandre un murmure pareil
Aux chants entrecoupés d'une voix triste et tendre.
Ch. Brugnot, *Les deux génies*

—"Ecoute!—Ecoute!—C'est moi, c'est Ondine qui frôle de ces gouttes d'eau les losanges sonores de ta fenêtre illuminée par les mornes rayons de la lune; et voici, en robe de moire, la dame châtelaine qui contemple à son balcon la belle nuit étoilée et le beau lac endormi.

Listen! Do you know what you hear? A flurry of rain thrown against your window by me, Ondine, spirit of the water. The drops trail down the glass each carrying a point of moonlight in its heart; and there on her castle terrace, her silks rustling like leaves, a woman contemplates the stars in the sky and the resting lake.

Chaque flot est un ondin qui nage dans le courant, chaque courant est un sentier qui serpente vers mon palais, et mon palais est bâti fluide, au fond du lac, dans le triangle du feu, de la terre et de l'air.

The waves are my sisters, swimming the paths which wander towards my palace, the walls of poised water between the triple poles of earth and fire and air.

Ecoute!—Ecoute!—Mon père bat l'eau coassante d'une branche d'aulne verte, et mes soeurs caressent de leurs bras d'écume les fraîches îles d'herbes, de nénuphars et de glaïeuls, ou se moquent du saule caduc et barbu qui pêche à la ligne.

Listen! Do you know what you hear? My father strikes the water with an alderbranch, my sisters clasp the green islands in arms of white foam, lifting the waterlilies, moving the rushes, or tease the ancient willow which casts its line, baited with leaves, in the darting water.

*   *   *

Sa chanson murmurée, elle me supplia de recevoir son anneau à mon doigt, pour être l'époux d'une Ondine, et de visiter avec elle son palais, pour être le roi des lacs.

When she had breathed her song, she begged me, begged me to put her ring on my finger, to be her husband and sink with her down, down to her drowned palace and be king of all the lakes.

Et comme je lui répondais que j'aimais une mortelle, boudeuse et dépitée, elle pleura quelques larmes, poussa un éclat de rire, et s'évanouit en giboulées qui ruiselèrent blanches le long de mes vitraux bleus.

I told her I loved a mortal woman. Abashed and vexed she dissolved in tears and laughter, vanished to the scatter of rain, white streams across the dark night of my window.

Le Gibet

Que vois-je remuer autour de ce Gibet?
Faust

Ah! ce que j'entends, serait-ce la bise nocturne qui glapit, ou le pendu qui pousse un soupir sur la fourche patibulaire?

What is it, this uneasy sound in the dusk? Is it the gasp of the winter wind, or did the hanged man on the gallows let out a sigh?

Serait-ce quelque grillon qui chante tapi dans la mousse et le lierre stérile dont par pitié se chausse le bois?

Was it a frog that croaked down there by the stagnant pond, or the creaking fingers of ivy strangling the tree?

Serait-ce quelque mouche en chasse sonnant du cor autour de ces oreilles sourdes à la fanfare des hallali?

Or the buzz of a fly hunting after raw flesh, knocking against those ears which are deaf to the tolling bell?

Serait-ce quelque escarbot qui cueille en son vol inégal un cheveu sanglant à son crâne chauve?

Or the winged beetle plucking a blood-soaked hair from the skull?

Ou bien serait-ce quelque arraignée qui brode une demi-aune de mousseline pour cravate à ce col étranglé?

Or the swing of the spider knitting a scarf gray as the dust, a shroud for the broken neck?

C'est la cloche qui tinte aux murs d'une ville sous l'horizon, et la carcasse d'un pendu que rougit le soleil couchant.

The clock strikes the hour; the walls of the town harden against the sky; the carcass of a hanged man glows in the dying sunlight.

Scarbo

Il regarda sous le lit, dans le cheminée.
dans le bahut;—personne. Il ne put
comprendre par où il s'était introduit,
par où il s'était évadé.

Hoffmann, *Contes nocturnes*

Oh! que de fois je l'ai entendu et vu, Scarbo,
lorsqu'à minuit la lune brille dans le ciel
comme un écu d'argent sur une bannière
d'azur semée d'abeilles d'or!

I have heard him again and again and seen
him, too. Scarbo, the dwarf, in the dead of
night when the moon was a silver mask on a
dark wall, stars a swarm of bees with piercing
stings of light.

Que de fois j'ai entendu bourdonner son rire
dans 'ombre de mon alcôve, et grincer son
ongle sur la soie des courtines de mon lit!

Heard his laugh in a dark corner and the
grate of his nails on the bed curtain.

Que de fois je l'ai vu descendre du plancher,
pirouetter sur un pied et rouler par la
chambre comme le fuseau tombé de la
quenouille d'une sorcière!

I've seen him drop from the ceiling, twirl on
one foot and roll across the floor like the
spindle of a spinning wheel when a dark
enchantress weaves.

Le croyais-je alors évanoui? le nain grandissait
entre la lune et moi comme le clocher d'une
cathédrale gothique, un grelot d'or en branle à
son bonnet pointu!

Did I think he had vanished? No. He rose up
between me and the moon, as high and
narrow as a Gothic steeple a great bell
swaying in his head.

Mais bientôt son corps bleuissait, diaphane
comme le cire d'une bougie, son visage
blêmissait comme la cire d'un lumignon,—et
soudain il s'éteignait.

But then his body changed, became as blue
and transparent as the wax of a taper, his face
as pale as candle grease, and he guttered out
into darkness.

Aloysius Bertrand

English translation by Christopher Fry, especially for
Mercury Record SR 90391. Copyright © Cefplays Ltd. 1962.
Used by permission of Christopher Fry.

Musically and technically speaking, "Ondine" would seem to mine the consequences of his earlier *Jeux d'eau* (1901, see p. 209) though with a new brilliance. But it is worth emphasizing that while "water music" is also associated with Debussy in such works as "Jardin sous la pluie" (*Estampes*, 1903) and "Reflets dans l'eau" (*Images*, set 1, 1905), Ravel was the first to put the traditions of Liszt's "Les jeux d'eau à la Villa d'Este" to new account. And Debussy's own "Ondine," a spriteful and elegant work but lacking Ravel's flare and sweep, comes from as late as the *Préludes*, Book II (1912–13). Ravel was keenly aware of the historical position of his *Jeux d'eau* in particular, and had occasion in later years to remind musicians of its date when faced with charges of imitation of Debussy.

The accentual spice of the undulating 32nd-note figure that opens "Ondine," where the A-natural occurs on the second, first, and fourth notes of two successive four-note groups (Ex. 6.1), is also mirrored in the use of a pedal B$^{\flat}$ throughout "Le gibet." Here, the pitch component is embued with a "personnage rythmique," to use Messiaen's term (p. 508), consisting of the (1 + 2, 1 + 2 + 2) eighth-note pattern consistently observable in Ex. 6.2. It is ultimately subjected to extensions and contractions, perhaps as a musical response to Bertrand's lines concerning a dying corpse in its final spasm. The incessantly repeated pedal note of "Le gibet" haunts the memory long after the music has stopped, in what must be termed one of Ravel's most magical creations. The tolling B♭ and quartal harmonies (see Ex. 4.7 and discussion, p. 50) bespeak a fascination on the part of Ravel and other of his contemporaries for the bell, not only as sound but as symbol. "Entre cloches" from *Site auriculaires* (1895–97), "La valée des cloches" from *Miroirs* (1905; see Ex. 4.6), and the unfinished opera *La cloche engloutie* (1906–14) based on Hauptmann's play of 1895 all testify to Ravel's engagement in a recurring sonic adventure. But we are also reminded of Debussy's "La cathédrale engloutie" (*Preludes*, Book I) and Rachmaninov's *The Bells* (after Poe's poem of 1849), both of which were completed in 1910, as well as Schreker's *Der ferne Klang* (1912).

While the final movement, "Scarbo," may have had a precedent in Ravel's own *Sérénade grotesque* (c. 1893), both musically and technically it is a new and dazzling creation. The 32nd-notes of the first movement and the tolling reiterations of the second are recalled with a fleeting cyclic function in the opening measures where, following a rising three-note motif, the D♯ is spattered against a symmetrically placed (F^x–G♯/D♯–E) but dissonantly sounding E^7 chord (Ex. 6.3). The repeated notes that the composer had earlier lavished on his "Albarado del gracioso" (*Miroirs*, 1905) are deployed here with a ghoulish touch that ultimately explodes into one of the most technically demanding works of the entire piano repertoire and a mesmerizing reflection of Bertrand's verses.

Example 6.1. Ravel, *Gaspard de la nuit:* "Ondine," mm. 1–4.

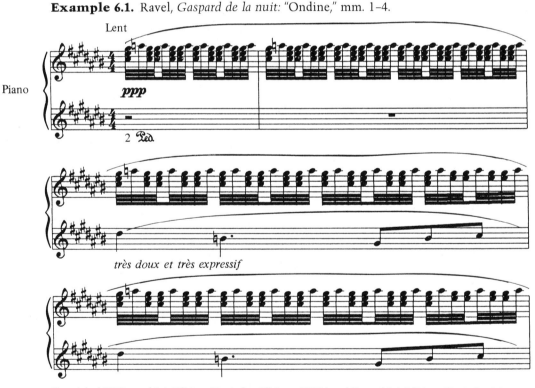

Example 6.2. Ravel, *Gaspard de la nuit:* "Le gibet," mm. 1–7.

Example 6.3. Ravel, *Gaspard de la nuit:* "Scarbo," mm. 1–6.

The repeated notes on D♯ were to be recalled and respelled (E♭ = Es = S) by Berg, undoubtedly with a pointed programmatic intent, in the first movement of his *Chamber Concerto* for piano, violin, and winds of 1923–25, and the climax of the work stands today as a massive outdoor mural on the side of the Schmitt Music Co. in Minneapolis (see Figure 32.1).

TROIS POÈMES DE STÉPHANE MALLARMÉ

Ravel's Mallarmé songs of 1913, the first major work written after the completion of *Daphnis et Chloé* (1909–12), stand at the summit of his early maturity together with the *Piano Trio* of the next year. The instrumental writing is luminous but economical, and the harmony of the set fluctuates from the pentatonic clarity of the opening song to the highly colored final cadence of the third (Ex. 6.7). The vocal writing is mostly syllabic, but carries a rare new expression as in the vocal portamento at the opening of the second song (Ex. 6.4), or as in the ascending augmented octave followed by a falling seventh at "Ni la pastille, ni du rouge, *ni jeux mièvres*" (Ex. 6.5).

Example 6.4. Ravel, *Trois poèmes de Stéphane Mallarmé:* "Placet futile," mm. 5–7.

Example 6.5. Ravel, *Trois poèmes de Stéphane Mallarmé:* "Placet futile," mm. 14–15.

In the final line of the second poem (Ex. 6.6), textual-musical reprise of materials from line 1 (marked 'a') and lines 9 and 12 (marked 'b') is followed by intervals of a diminished octave and a diminished fifth in the melodic line, whose pitches reflect the harmonies of the accompaniment: $\flat7 + \sharp8 + 9 + \sharp11 + 13$. An identical harmonic complex closes the set in the final cadence

Example 6.6. Ravel, *Trois poèmes de Stéphane Mallarmé:* "Placet futile," mm. 25–6.

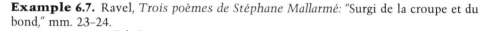

Example 6.7. Ravel, *Trois poèmes de Stéphane Mallarmé:* "Surgi de la croupe et du bond," mm. 23–24.

of the third song, where the C in the bass supports a glistening array of overtones that settles on an A major sonority at the top of the triadic stack.

Ravel's harmonic complexes, especially the 11th and 13th chords with raised fourth and flattened seventh, share an affinity not only with Debussy but even more intimately with the contemporaneous language of Skriabin (p. 166) and Berg (p. 48). The harmonic juxtaposition of triads a semitone apart in Ravel's second Mallarmé song, suggestive of Stravinsky's current manner in *The Rite of Spring* (p. 216), also forces us to recall *Jeux d'eau* and the bitonal cascade of simultaneous C major and F♯ major arpeggios, which antedate *Petrushka* (p. 209). By the same token, Ravel's orientation is always clearly tonal, and analysis consistently favors viewing his most highly colored verticals as appogiatura-laden or extended tertian aggregates.

Although the listener may follow Debussy's and Ravel's musical companions to Mallarmé's poems in a way in which he could never follow the text by itself, it is essential not to bypass Mallarmé's texts altogether (see p. 113) in the name of their incomprehensibility, but rather to face their obscurity directly and with delectation. Ravel stated in his *Autobiographical Sketch*[1] that in these songs he wished to transcribe Mallarmé's poetry into music, especially "Surgi de la croupe et du bon," which he called the strangest and most hermetic of the poet's sonnets. Suggestions that the increasing complexity of the cycle leads in this final song to a brush with genuine atonality are undoubtedly based on the circumstances connecting Ravel with Schoenberg in his choice of an instrumental ensemble (discussed on p. 113), as well as Ravel's acknowledgment of Schoenberg's subliminal presence in the composition of his later Madagascan songs. But Ned Rorem is correct in encouraging analysts to note the root of both of these vocal cycles in an enlarged but, in many ways, traditionally grounded harmonic practice.[2]

Though difficult to read in the original French as well as in English translation, Mallarmé's third song has been interpreted as the verses of a solitary poet, looking down from the ceiling, who contemplates an empty vase that hovers near death because of its inutility. The conclusion hints that the placement of a rose in its opening would have given the vase a reason for existence parallel to the creation of a poem as the rationale for a poet's being.[3]

Similarly, we must remind ourselves that however comfortable we may be in approaching the now familiar language of Ravel and Debussy in these surroundings, they were responsible for developing a musical grammar that took liberties with the vocabulary of the common practice period. Not only their additions to that vocabulary but their redefinition of the rules of syntax paralleled Mallarmé's contribution as central agents in the establishment of new musical values. Such values were ultimately to transcend the aesthetic that spawned them and become the property of all composers.

Ravel's orchestral mastery is frequently conceded to be more brilliant if less integral than Debussy's, and is especially known to concert audiences from the sumptuous scoring of *Daphnis et Chloé*. The lineage for such an achievement is traditionally sought in the Russian presence in French orchestral manners from the time of Rimsky-Korsakov's first appearances in Paris in 1889. Whatever the truth of the matter, Ravel's scrutiny of the function of timbre is unrelenting throughout his life, both in the orchestral realm, from *Daphnis* and *La valse* to *Bolero*, and in the domain of chamber music, from the Mallarmé to the Madagascan songs. However, the unusual circumstances that dictated the instrumental choice of the Mallarmé songs are worth recalling. In the Fall and Winter of 1912, Stravinsky and Ravel were involved in a joint orchestration project for Mussorgsky's *Kovantchina*. In December, Stravinsky was in Berlin and heard a performance of Schoenberg's *Pierrot lunaire* (for *Sprechstimme*, pf, vn, va, vc, fl, pic, cl, b cl), and on returning to Clarens decided to use a chamber ensemble similar to that used by Schoenberg (see p. 185ff) for his *Japanese Lyrics* (see p. 224). Conveying his enthusiasm for the sonority of Schoenberg's *Pierrot* to Ravel, the latter, without ever having heard the Viennese expressionist cycle, adopted an ensemble of piano, string quartet, flute, and clarinet. The three sets are as individual as their composers, but Ravel was fascinated with this historic conjunction and proposed a concert (never realized) in which they would be performed together with Maurice Delage's *Four Hindu Songs* written for a similar ensemble in 1912 (see p. 127).

For all their similarity in instrumentation, the aesthetic distance between these sets of pieces is chasmic. The essentially humorless character in Mahler that is magnified a thousand-fold in Schoenberg's work is summed up in a remark of Paul Klee following a performance of *Pierrot*: "Burst, you stuffed shirt, your knell is ringing." And earlier, Louÿs, author of the *Chansons de Bilitis*, had warned Debussy in a letter of 1899 of the threatening state of affairs following a performance of Strauss's *Zarathustra*: "You must really hurry up and reform music because things really can't go on as they have been for the last fifteen years. We have got to the point where a chord cannot be resolved without pretending to resolve some problem of God himself."[4] It may fairly be claimed that by 1912–13, musical Paris had, indeed, prepared a new alternative and brought it to a point of extraordinary refinement.

Ravel, *Trois Poèmes de Stéphane Mallarmé*

I. SIGH

My soul rises toward your brow where, O
   peaceful sister,
a dappled autumn dreams,
and toward the roving sky of your angelic
   eye,
as in a melancholy garden, faithful,
a white plume of water sighs toward heaven's
   blue!
Toward the compassionate blue of pale and
   pure October
that onto vast pools mirrors infinite indolence

and, over a swamp where the dark death of
   leaves floats in the wind and digs a cold
   furrow
letting the yellow sun draw out into a long
   ray.

I. SOUPIR

Mon âme vers ton front où rêve, ô calme
   soeur,
un automne jonché de taches de rousseur,
et vers le ciel errant de ton oeil angélique
monte, comme dans un jardin mélancolique,
   fidèle,
un blanc jet d'eau soupire vers l'Azur!

Vers l'Azur attendri d'octobre pâle et pur

qui mire aux grands bassins sa langueur
   infinie
et laisse, sur l'eau morte où la fauve agonie
des feuilles erre au vent et creuse un froid
   sillon,
se trainer le soleil jaune d'un long rayon.

II. FUTILE PETITION

Princess! envious of the youthful
   Hebe

(Ex. 6.4)

II. PLACET FUTILE

Princesse! à jalouser le destin d'une
   Hébé

rising up on this cup at the touch of your
  lips,
I spend my ardor, but have only the low rank
  of abbot
and shall never appear even naked on the
  Sèvres.

Since I'm not your whiskered lap-dog,
nor candy, nor rouge, nor   **(Ex. 6.5)**
  sentimental pose,
and since I know your glance on me
  is blind,
O blonde, whose divine hairdressers
  are goldsmiths!

appoint us—you in whose laughter
  so many berries
join a flock of tame lambs
nibbling every vow and bleating with
  joy,

appoint us—so that Eros winged with a
  fan
will paint me upon it, a flute in my fingers to
  lull those sheep,
Princess, appoint us shepherd of your smiles.
                     (Ex. 6.6)

III. RISEN FROM HAUNCH AND SPURT

Risen from haunch and spurt
of ephemeral glassware
without causing the bitter eve to bloom,
the ignored neck is stopped.

I, sylph of this cold ceiling,
do not believe that two mouths—
neither my mother's nor her lover's—
ever drank from the same mad fancy.

The pure vase empty of fluid
which tireless widowhood
slowly kills but does not consent to,
innocent but funereal kiss!
To expend anything announcing
a rose in the dark.   **(Ex. 6.7)**

qui poind sur cette tasse au baiser de vos
  lèvres,
j'use mes feux mais n'ai rang discret que
  d'abbé
et ne figurerai même nu sur le
  Sèvres.

Comme je ne suis pas ton bichon embarbé,
ni la pastille, ni du rouge, ni
  jeux mièvres
et que sur moi je sais ton regard clos
  tombé,
blonde dont les coiffeurs divins sont des
  orfèvres!

Nommez-nous—toi de qui tant de ris
  framboisés
se joignent en troupeaux d'agneaux apprivoisés
chez tous broutant les voeux et bêlant aux
  délires,

Nommez-nous—pour qu'Amour ailé d'un
  éventail
m'y peigne flûte aux doigts endormant ce
  bercail,
Princesse, nommez-nous berger de vos
  sourires.

III. SURGI DE LA CROUPE ET DU BOND

Surgi de la croupe et du bond
d'une verrerie éphémère
sans fleurir la veillée amère
le col ignoré s'interrompt.

Je crois bien que deux bouches n'ont bu,
ni son amant ni ma mère,
jamais à la même chimère
moi, sylphe de ce froid plafond!

Le pur vase d'aucun breuvage
que l'inexhaustible veuvage
agonise mais ne consent,
naïf baiser des plus funèbres!
A rien expirer annoçant
une rose dans les ténèbres.

—Translations by Ned Rorem courtesy of CBS Masterworks

REPERTOIRE

> *Menuet antique* (1895), pf
> *Pavane pour une infante défunte* (1899), pf
> *Jeux d'eau* (1901), pf
> *String Quartet* (1902–03)
> *Sonatine* (1903–05): "Menuet," pf
> *Miroirs* (1904–05): "La valée des cloches," "Alborada del gracioso," pf
> *Gaspard de la nuit* (1908): "Ondine," "Le gibet", "Scarbo," pf
> *Daphnis et Chloé* (1909–12), orch
> *Trois poèmes de Stéphane Mallarmé* (1913), v, pf, str qrt, fl, cl

READING

Arbie Orenstein, *Ravel: Man and Musician* (New York, 1975), 130–181.

Roger Nichols, *Ravel* (London, 1977).

Robert Grouquist, "Ravel's Trois poèmes de Stéphane Mallarmé," *Musical Quarterly*, lxiv.4 (1978), 507.

Pierre Boulez, "Trajectories: Ravel, Stravinsky, Schoenberg" (1949), repr. in *Notes of an Apprenticeship* (New York, 1968), 242.

CHAPTER 7

EXOTICISM: IMPORTATIONS FROM ABROAD

If the Symbolist poets figured prominently in the musician's development in France in the early twentieth century, there were other complementary forces that prompted the exploration of new visions and their attendant sonorities. The notion of Exoticism—the infatuation with foreign cultures—is one that was well defined in the Romantic Age, and as a vivifying factor should be distinguished at the outset from Folklorism, which traditionally speaks of the study and use of one's native musical heritage. Importation is central to the idea of Exoticism and the source of its appeal.

An early such example had been the music of the Janizary, the bodyguard of the Turkish sultans. Known to the courts of Europe from the middle of the eighteenth century, it left the mark of its sonority (bass drum, cymbals, triangle) on Gluck (*Iphigenie en Tauride*, 1775); Mozart (*Entführung aus dem Serail*, 1782); Haydn ("*Military*" *Symphony*, 1794); Beethoven (finale to the *Ninth Symphony*, 1822); Weber (*Abu Hassan*, 1811); and Rossini (*L'italiana in Algeria*, 1813). It was not until the second half of the nineteenth century, however, that the cult of the exotic struck the world of music with its full force.

FRANCE AND RUSSIA: VISIONS OF THE ORIENT, SPAIN, AND AFRICA

Nowhere more than in France did the appeal of remote lands and customs encourage the exploration of new musical motifs, beginning with Felician David's symphonic ode, *Le desert* of 1844. Typically such works were prompted by travels to lands that fired the composer's imagination and the contemporary taste in literature (Gautier, Baudelaire, Flaubert) and painting (Delacroix, Gerricault). The number of works on exotic subjects grew rapidly, and while not always of distinctive quality, included composers such as Gounod (*Reine de Saba*, 1861); Berlioz ("The Dance of the Nubian Slaves," *Les Troyens*, 1862); Massenet (*La roi de Lahore*, 1877, and *Herodiade*, 1881); Bizet (*Djamileh*, 1872); Saint-Saëns (*Samson et Delilah*, 1877); Delibes (*Lakme*, 1883), and d'Indy (*Istar*, 1896). Among these, Saint-Saëns' opera was to achieve the most lasting popularity, and it was his extensive travels to Algeria in particular that prompted an additional series of works with exotic titles (*Suite algerienne*, 1880; *Africa*, 1891). Saint-Saëns pointedly observed in 1879 that "the ancient modes are making a comeback, to be hotly pursued by the scales of the East in all their tremendous variety." He judged that harmony and rhythm were bound to change, too, as a result of such a confrontation, and predicted that a new art would spring from this.

If Napoleon's campaign in Egypt (1798–99) and the conquest of Algeria by France in 1830 opened up an awareness for those areas, the marriage of Napoleon III to Eugenie de Montijo in 1853 stirred an interest in the Iberian peninsula. Manet's painting from the 1860s, Bizet's *Carmen* (1874), Lalo's *Symphonie espagnole* (1873), and Chabrier's *España* (1883) all owe a debt to this influence.

In the 1880s and 1890s, when the cult of Wagner held sway in France, many of these tendencies were momentarily submerged, only to reappear. The Paris World Exhibition of 1889 brought not only the sound of the Javanese gamelan but such scores as Rimsky-Korsakov's *Sheherazade* (1888) and Balakirev's *Islamey* (1869), and this cross-fertilization proved to be fundamental to a generation of composers that included Debussy, Ravel, Dukas, Schmitt, Delage, and Roussel (see the list at the end of this chapter).

In Russia, however, Glinka's role as the founding father of a genuinely Russian music had emphasized much earlier in the century not only the potential use of native Russian materials but the vitalizing capacity of exotic cultures in matters of melody, rhythm, and color. Glinka's incorporation of Oriental melodies in *Ruslan and Lyudmila* extended to the use of Spanish materials following a sojourn to Granada and Madrid from 1845 to 1848, which may owe something to Liszt's Spanish journeys in 1844–45. The reliance on Oriental and Hispanic motifs by other Russian composers can be traced from Glinka through Balakirev, Rimsky-Korsakov, and Glazunov to Stravinsky, as seen in the following list:

Glinka (1804–57)
> *Ruslan and Lyudmila* (1837–42): Oriental dances (Turkish-Arabian-Lezginka)
> *Jota Aragonesa* (Spanish Overture No. 1, 1845)
> *Souvenir d'une nuit d'été à Madrid* (1848–51)
> *Polonaise* for orchestra based on a Spanish bolero theme (1855)

Balakirev (1837–1910)
> *Overture* on a Spanish march theme (1857)
> *Islamey* (Oriental fantasy, 1869)

Rimsky-Korsakov (1844–1908)
> *Spanish capriccio* (1887)
> *Sheherazade* (1888)
> *The Barber of Baghdad* (1895)
> *Sadko* (1894–96)
> *The Golden Cockerel* (1906–07)

Glazunov (1865–1936)
> *Serenade espagnole* (1887–88, cello & orch.)
> *Rêverie orientale* (1888)
> *Oriental Rhapsody* (1889)
> *Oriental Suite* (1895)

Stravinsky (1882–1971)
> *Japanese Lyrics* (1912–13)
> *The Nightingale* (1908–14)
> *Five Easy Pieces:* "Espanola" (1917)
> *Etude for Pianola:* "Madrid" (1917)

The taste for the Orient has already been evident in Mahler's Chinese texts for *Das Lied von der Erde* and the work of other contemporary Viennese artists such as Klimt and Loos, and in Chapter 8 many similarly related works will be discussed as symbols of Decadence—e.g., *Salome*. But central to the movement as it developed in France was its preoccupation with a range of values from the colors of the gamelan (Debussy, Ravel); the trenchant brevity of the haiku (Stravinsky, Delage); tales and fables of pure *chinoiserie* (*Le rossignol*); an infatuation with Spanish (Debussy, Ravel), Indian (Delage, Milhaud, Roussel), and other folk cultures, as well as a lingering taste for the perverse. Delage traveled to India as early as 1912, and Holst's *Japanese Suite* of 1916 includes in the score the dictated Japanese melodies on which it is based. Puccini's *Madame Butterfly* (1904) is an early example of Oriental subject opera outside of France and Russia, but that the exotic appeal persisted well into the 1920s is evident from works like Puccini's *Turandot* of 1926 and Ravel's *Chansons madécasses* of 1927.

In the first two decades of the century in Paris, the public appetite for such works, as a natural extension of nineteenth-century developments, was nowhere more encouraged than by such agencies as the Diaghilev Ballets Russes. Originally undertaken by the great impresario as an export of Russian opera, it soon enlarged its scope of operations to include ballet. The early preference given to Oriental and other exotic subjects can be seen in the following list of works presented by Diaghilev: *Prince Igor* (1909); *Cleopatre* (1909); *Schéhérezade* (1910); *Firebird* (1910); *Les Orientales* (1910); *Sadko* (1911); *Le dieu bleu* (1912); *Le sacre du printemps* (1913); *Salomé* (1913); and *Le coq d'or* (1914). Diaghilev's influence on current fashion and scenic design can be witnessed in the ballet *Le dieu bleu*, adapted by Jean Cocteau and Reynaldo Hahn from Hindu legend and for which Fokine devised a choreography inspired by bas-reliefs of Brahman temples and by Siamese dancers he had seen in St. Petersburg.

DEBUSSY

The foundation for the acceptance of this aspect of Diaghilev's programs had been well laid, however, in fin-di-siècle Paris where the sound of the Javanese gamelan and the sight of Cambodian dancing girls brought by traveling groups had quickly surfaced in the work of numerous artists. In 1900, Debussy once again approached Pierre Louÿs's *Chansons de Bilitis* (1893), selecting 12 poems for which he provided incidental music (two flutes, two harps, celesta, reciter); these in turn served as the source material for his *Six epigraphes antiques* (1914) for piano four-hands. "The Dancing-Girl with Crotales," which appears in both versions (see p. 50, fn. 2), prefigures in literature and music the sound and movement of Rodin's watercolor of 1906 (Figure 7.1).

Example 7.1. Debussy, *Six épigraphe antiques*: "Pour la danseuse aux crotales," mm. 28–30.

La Danseuse aux crotales

Tu attaches à tes mains légères tes crotales retentissants, Myrrihinidion, et à peine nue hors de la robe, tu étires tes membres nerveux.

Tu commences: tes pieds l'un devant l'autre se posent, hésitent, et glissent mollement. Ton corps se plie comme une écharpe.

The Dancing-Girl with Crotales

You attach to your light hands the resounding crotales, Myrrihinidion, and, stepping naked from your robe, extend your nervous limbs.

You begin: your feet, one before the other, pose, hesitate, and glide softly. Your body folds like a scarf.

Tout à coup, tu claques des crotales.	Suddenly you strike the crotales!
Cambre-toi sur tes pieds dressés, et	Arch yourself, erect upon your feet, and
que tes mains pleins de fracas appellent	let the reverberating clamor of your hands
tous les désirs en bande autour	call all the desires in a band about
de ton corps tournoyant.	your turning body.

Pierre Louÿs

In light of the frequent claim that the source of inspiration for Debussy's *La mer* is to be found in the seascapes of Turner, the possibility of an Oriental backdrop for this work seems compromised. But the more contemporary relation to Whistler, another seascape artist and avid Japanophile living in Paris, is an even more striking one. The reproduction of a nineteenth-century Japanese print, "The Hollow of the Wave off Kanagawa" by Hokusai, on the original cover of Debussy's orchestral score seals the connection, especially since we know that Debussy's concern for the decorative aspects of his scores often dominated his correspondence with his publishers (Figures 7.2, 7.3). We know, too, that Debussy's affection for the colors of Japanese prints was responsible for the

Figure 7.1. August Rodin, *Cambodian Dancing Girl* (1908). Watercolor over pencil, $11^{5}/_{16}$″ × 7¾″. An interest in exotic subjects is to be seen in the paintings of Rodin, Matisse, Dufy, and numerous other French artists of the early decades of the twentieth century.

Figure 7.2. Hokusai's *The Wave* was chosen by Debussy for the front cover of the first edition of *La Mer*.

Courtesy of Bibliotheque Nationale, Paris.

precision of his directions in the publication of *Estampes* (1903), which includes "Pagodes." The Japanese print was of fundamental importance in the formation of the *Art nouveau-Jugendstil* aesthetic, and a whole generation of painters from Monet and Degas to Gauguin and Van Gogh received inspiration from it. While Whistler signed his pictures with a logo that looks more like a butterfly than an Oriental ideogram, and those of Debussy and Ravel could be argued as more closely akin to the High Renaissance engraver Albrecht Dürer (1471–1528), Maurice Delage, composer and friend of Ravel, adopted a Kanji-like logo, which was a patent reflection of the extent to which *Japonisme* had caught hold amongst the French in the first decades of the twentieth century (Figure 7.4).

While knowledge that Debussy's "Poissons d'or" was inspired by the contemplation of a piece of Oriental lacquer confirms his visual attraction to Oriental objects, his introduction to Oriental scale patterns is generally conceded to have taken place on a visit to the Paris World Exhibition of 1889, where he heard the gamelans of southeast Asia. The use of pentatonic formations not only in a coloristic way, as in "De l'aube a midi sur la mer" in *La mer*, but as an element of contrast, as in "Voiles" of the first book of *Préludes*,

Figure 7.3. Hokusai's print appears in the background of a photograph of Debussy and Stravinsky taken by Satie in 1910.

suggests that the infatuation had a formal potential as well. But in works like "Pagodes" from *Estampes*, the use of such patterns fleetingly recaptures the sound of the gamelan about which Debussy wrote in a letter to the poet of the *Chansons de Bilitis*, Pierre Louÿs: "Do you not remember the Javanese music able to express every nuance of meaning, even unmentionable shades, and which make our tonic and dominant seem like empty phantoms for the use of unwise infants."[1]

Other cultures similarly made their impact on Debussy's music. During the Paris Exposition he was introduced to the music of Rimsky-Korsakov, and the popularity of folk tunes in the music of numerous composers of the time also suggests that an exotic element was sensed in the music of people much closer to home. This aspect is summed up in Debussy's orchestral *Images*, which blends the taste for Spanish themes (*Iberia*) with an allusion to English folksong (*Gigues*, which quotes "The Keel Row"). In addition to the works of Bizet, Lalo, and Chabrier, the *Capriccio espagnole* (1887) of Rimsky-Korsakov had reinforced the idea of Iberian motifs as exotica, and there can be no doubt that his orchestral brilliance was a powerful ally in similar interpretations by Debussy and Ravel. Ultimately, as we shall see, some of the most important Spanish composers (Albeniz, Falla) would adopt Paris as a second home and develop their Spanish manner under the influence of the French-Russian axis. In piano works

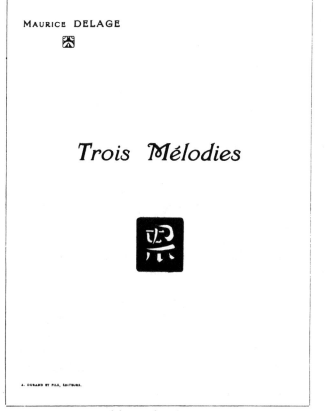

Figure 7.4. Personal logo of Delage.
Courtesy of Durand et Cie.

such as "La sérénade interrompue," where we hear the strumming of the guitar, or "Soirée dans Grenade" (*Estampes*, 1903) and "La puerta del vino" (*Preludes*, Book II, 1913) where the rhythms of the habanera (♫ ♪; ♪♪ ♪♪) invoke visions of the Alhambra, Debussy embellishes on a tradition set earlier by Chabrier (*Habanera*, 1885) and Ravel (*Habanera*, 1895–97) and at the same time demonstrates the function of the ostinato and the pedal as anchors in a harmonic world which, if not tonally threatened, is freely colored.

MAURICE RAVEL: *SHEHERAZADE* AND OTHER WORKS

Ravel's penchant for the exotic is manifest as early as 1898 in *Ouverture de Shéhérazade*, which uses a Persian melody and reflects an obvious spiritual ancestry in Rimsky-Korsakov's *Shéhérazade* of 1888. But in 1903, at a time when he was completing his classically oriented string quartet and beginning his *Sonatine* for piano, he turned again to its title for a cycle of three songs.

Tristan Klingsor, whose Wagnerian nom de plume mirrored the taste of the Symbolists of an earlier decade, provided the magical verses for Ravel's *Shéhérazade* for voice and orchestra. In choosing his name, the poet announces an artistic credo, emphasizing the erotic (Tristan) and the decadent (Klingsor, the eunuch-magician of *Parsifal*). The text, whose Orientalism is witnessed by its title, speaks less of the thousand and one nights and the telling of tales with an Eastern hue, than of the perfection of the setting for the indulgence of perverse tastes, the appetite for luxury, the fascination with death ("Asie"), and concealed personal affinities ("L'indifferent").

The hushed tremolo of the strings, which is joined by the oboe at the beginning of "Asie" quickly establishes the atmosphere of the work. The opening four lines are declaimed syllabically and recitative-like, and we are reminded that *Pelléas*, premiered only the year before, also began in an "enchanted forest", and that Baudelaire's "L'invitation au voyage" was to a fantasy Oriental journey. The grace notes and fluttering strings at the mention of Damascus and Persia and the pentatonicisms that tint the background for "the mandarins paunchy beneath their umbrellas" are only details of a longer poem that is clearly articulated by a series of repetitive incantations beginning "Je voudrais voir . . . " In their obsessive reiteration they prefigure in a similar psychological fashion the decadent refrains of Strauss's *Salome* of 1905 (e.g., Salome's "Du hast einen Eid geschworen, Herodes" and "Ich will den Kopf des Jochannan"). The movement to the climax begins with the invocation of "assassins souriant," and the former periodic appearance of the refrain is accelerated to a three-fold, back-to-back presentation. The final release at "I would like to see them who die for love and them who die for hatred" is one of the most erotic and chilling moments in all Ravel. The piece falls silent and shimmers to a close, exhausted, as the recitative of the opening finishes the tale over a faintly rolling tympani.

Maurice Ravel, *Shéhérazade*

Three Poems by Tristan Klingsor

I. ASIE

Asie, Asie, Asie,
Vieux pays merveilleux des contes de nourrice
Où dort la fantaisie comme une impératrice
En sa forêt tout emplie de mystère.
Asie,
Je voudrais m'en aller avec la goëlette
Qui se berce ce soir dans le port
Mystérieuse et solitaire
Et qui déploie enfin ses voiles violettes
Comme un immense oiseau de nuit
dans le ciel d'or.
Je voudrais m'en aller vers les îles de fleurs
En écoutant chanter la mer perverse
Sur un vieux rythme ensorceleur.
Je voudrais voir Damas
et les villes de Perse
avec les minarets légers dans l'air;
Je voudrais voir de beaux turbans de soie
Sur des visages noirs aux dents claires;
Je voudrais voir des yeux sombres d'amour
Et des prunelles brillantes de joie
En des peaux jaunes comme des oranges;
Je voudrais voir des vêtements de velours
Et des habits à longues franges.

I. ASIA

Asia, Asia, Asia,
marvelous old land of nursery tales
where fantasy sleeps like an empress
in her forest filled with mystery.
Asia,
I would like to disappear with the schooner
that rocks this evening in port
mysterious and solitary
and which will finally unfold its violet sails
like an immense bird of the night
in the golden sky.
I would like to go away to the isles of flowers
listening to the perverse sea sing
in an ancient enchanter's rhythm.
I would like to see Damascus
and the cities of Persia
with their slender minarets in the air;
I would like to see the beautiful turbans of silk
on black faces with bright teeth;
I would like to see the dark eyes of love
and the pupils radiant with joy
in skin yellow as oranges;
I would like to see vestments of velvet
and apparel with long fringes.

Je voudrais voir des calumets entre des bouches	I would like to see long pipes between lips
Tout entourées de barbe blanche;	completely surrounded by white beards;
Je voudrais voir d'apres merchands aux regards louches,	I would like to see sharp merchants with suspicious eyes,
Et des cadis, et des vizirs	and cadis and vizirs
Qui du seul mouvement de leur doigt qui se penche	who with a single movement of their finger, which they bend,
Accorde vie ou mort au gré de leur désir.	grant life or death in accord with their desires.
Je voudrais voir la Perse, et l'Inde et puis la Chine,	I would like to see Persia and India and then China,
Les mandarins ventrus sous les ombrelles,	the mandarins paunchy beneath their umbrellas,
Et les princesses aux mains fines,	and the princesses with slender hands,
Et les lettrés qui se querellent	and the learned ones who argue
Sur la poésie et sur la beauté;	about poetry and about beauty;
Je voudrais m'attarder au palais enchanté	I would like to loiter in the enchanted palace
Et comme un voyageur étranger	and like a foreign traveller
Contempler à loisir des paysages peints	contemplate at leisure landscapes painted
Sur des étoffes en des cadres de sapin	on fabric in frames of fir-wood
Avec un personnage au milieu d'un verger;	with a figure in the middle of an orchard;
Je voudrais voir des assassins souriant	I would like to see assassins smiling
Du bourreau qui coupe un cou d'innocent	as the executioner strikes an innocent neck
Avec son grand sabre courbé d'Orient.	with his great, curved oriental sabre.
Je voudrais voir des pauvres et des reines;	I would like to see paupers and queens;
Je voudrais voir des roses et du sang;	I would like to see roses and blood;
Je voudrais voir mourir d'amour ou bien de haine.	I would like to see those who die for love as well as those who die for hatred.
Et puis m'en revenir plus tard	And then I would return later
Narrer mon aventure	to speak of my adventure
aux curieux de rêves	to those curious about dreams,
En élevant comme Sindbad	raising, like Sinbad,
ma vieille tasse arabe	my old Arabian cup
De temps en temps jusqu'à mes lèvres	from time to time to my lips
Pour interrompre le conte avec art . . .	to interrupt the story artfully . . .

Although *Shéhérazade* is Ravel's first major statement for orchestra, the composer stakes a claim for the future in his mastery of both muted and climactic detail. The colorist of *Daphnis* and *Ma mere l'oye* is already completely in evidence, and Ravel never again wrote with such a combination of ecstasy and restraint for the human voice with the possible exception of "Aoua!", the second of the Madagascan Songs of 1927.

While Ravel's interest in the special flavor of folk tunes of various countries can be seen in his settings of Greek and Hebrew melodies, elsewhere he tended to absorb the essence of exotic climes and without quotation capture the spirit of the region in his own terms. A referential rhythm or scalar design was sufficient, as with Debussy, to establish the atmosphere. Thus in the "Empress of the Pagodas" (*Mother Goose*, 1910) the patterns of the right hand in the original version for piano four-hands are not only pentatonic, but suggest in their quartal grace-notes and secundal alternations a high-pitched percussion instrument in some imaginary Oriental ensemble (Ex. 7.2).

More obscure but equally indebted to Oriental influences was the choice of the title "Pantoum" for the second movement of the Piano Trio of 1914. Of Malaysian origins, the poetic form had been adopted by the French Romantic poets and described in detail by Théodore de Banville in his *Petite traité de*

Example 7.2. Ravel, *Mother Goose:* "Empress of the Pagodas," mm. 19–31
(prima pars).

poésie francaise of 1871. That its interlocking structure, a series of quatrains
that carries lines two and four over to the next stanza as lines one and three, was
freely reflected in Ravel's musical design has been successfully demonstrated.[2]
It may also bespeak a fascination for Schoenberg's response to similar formal
properties in Giraud's *Pierrot lunaire*, which Ravel had been introduced to only
the year before (see p. 113).

Ravel also made several excursions into the Hispanic world, which may
reflect his mother's Basque origins, his admiration for Chabrier, and his friend-
ships with Albeniz and de Falla (though in the latter instance, the influence was

more in the opposite direction). His early *Habanera* (1895–97) was followed by "Alborada del gracioso" (*Miroirs*, 1905), *Rhapsodie espagnole* (1908), and *Bolero* (1928). The infatuation persisted to the end of his career, and in the song cycle *Don Quichotte à Dulcinée* (1933), his opus ultimum, Ravel successively explored the alternating 6/8-3/4 rhythm of the Spanish "quajira" in the first, the quintuple metrics of the Basque "zortzico" in the second, and the rhythm and triple metrics of the "jota" in the concluding drinking song.

MAURICE DELAGE AND LATER ECHOS

Maurice Delage (1897–1961) was a favorite pupil of Ravel and a friend of Stravinsky. The *Four Hindu Songs*, inspired by a trip to India in 1912, recall the sounds of the sitar in the haunting cello glissandi of the second song, while in *Ragamalika* of 1915, both drone and vocalise attain to an even more authentic Indian style. In 1924, he wrote a set of *Sept haikai*, a title later used by Messiaen, for voice and instrumental ensemble (fl, cl, ob, pf, vn, va, vc), which weds the best of Stravinsky's *Japanese Lyrics* with Ravel's *Histoires naturelles*. Even closer in time and concept are the *Seven Haiku* of Roberto Gerhard of 1922 for S/T, fl, ob, cl, bn, pf.

While the heyday of Exoticism was the period prior to World War I, many composers retained knowledge of their discoveries and applied them in nonexotic contexts. The 1920s saw most of its impulse fade as Neoclassicism and Serialism surfaced to serve as stimuli for a new sense of order, and a new interest in jazz and the music hall shifted the spotlight to America (actually a new exotic locale) and everyday life. Enthusiasm for American jazz was also in harmony with a predelection among Western European artistic circles for black culture, both primitive and modern urban, and Jean Cocteau, Jean Wiéner, Blaise Céndrars, and Nancy Cunard are only a few of the names associated with the rise of black themes to a cult status in the early 1920s. Delage's "Les Demoiselles d'Avignon" on a text by René Chalupt after Picasso's renowned painting (Fig. 11.3) and Ravel's *Chansons madécasses*, both of 1927, are examples of this continuing fascination within a nonjazz context.

The second of Ravel's *Madagascan Songs*, "Aoua!", portrays a powerful primitivism dealing with the native's distrust of the white man aided by a new dissonance content and expressive vocal style which the composer said he could not have achieved without the example of Schoenberg. In spite of such claims, however, the memorable exclamation ("Aoua!"), which punctuates the text at beginning, middle, and end (absent in the original poem and added by Ravel himself), can be related directly the peacock's diabolic cry "Léon! Léon!" of *Histoires naturelles* (cf. p. 256). In a word, whatever external forces may have been brought to bear, they simmer beneath the surface of the music: melody, rhythm, and harmony confirm that the underlying personality of the composer is never in question.

While Delage's hushed lament on the death of a samurai (*Une mort de samouri*) of 1951 would seem to have been prompted by the end of World War II, a period that once again provoked a surge of interest in Japan, it provided not a final coda but the impetus for a renewed fascination for the Orient and its music. The work of Colin McPhee and Henry Cowell beginning in the 1930s fed naturally into this postwar phase, which saw reinterpretations of Asian and

African music in particular at the hands of composers like Messiaen, Cage, Stockhausen, and Reich.

Ravel, *Chansons madécasses, no. 2:*

Aoua! Aoua! Méfiez-vous des blancs, habitans du rivage.

Du temps de nos pères, des blancs descendirent dans cette ile;

on leur dit: Voilà des terres; que vos femmes les cultivent.

Soyex justes, soyez bons, et devenez nos frères.

Les blancs promirent, et cependant ils faisaient des retranchements.

Un fort menaçant s'éleva; le tonnerre fut renfermé dans des bouches d'airain;

leurs prêtres voulurent nous donner un Dieu que nous ne connaissons pas;

ils parlèrent enfin d'obéissance et d'esclavage; plûtot la mort!

Le carnage fut long et terrible, mais, malgré la foudre qu'ils vomissaient,

et qui écrasait des armées entières, ils furent tous exterminés.

Aoua! Aoua! Méfiez-vous des blancs!

Nous avons vu de nouveaux tyrans, plus forts et plus nombreux,

planter leur pavillon sur le rivage; le ciel a combattu pour nous;

il a fait tomber sur eux les pluies, les tempêtes et les vents empoisonnés.

Ils ne sont plus, et nous vivons, et nous vivons libres.

Aoua! Aoua! Méfiez-vous des blancs, habitans du rivage.

Evariste Parny

Aoua! Aoua! Do not trust the white man, inhabitants of these shores.

From the time of our fathers, white men descended upon this island;

They said to them: "Here is the soil; have your women cultivate it.

Be just, be kind and become our brothers.

The white men promised, and yet they made entrenchments.

A menacing fort was erected; thunder was stored in mouths of brass;

their priests willed upon us a God we did not know;

they spoke finally of obedience and slavery: sooner death!

The carnage was long and terrible; but, in spite of the lightning which they belched forth,

and which annihilated whole armies, they were all destroyed.

Aoua! Aoua! Do not trust the white man!

We have seen new tyrants, stronger and more numerous,

Stake their tents on the shore; the heavens waged war for us,

Unleashing rains, storms and poisoned winds.

They are no more, yet we live on and live freely.

Aoua! Aoua! Do not trust the white man, inhabitants of these shores.

Delage, *Quatre poèmes hindous, no. 2:*

Un sapin isolé se dresse sur une montagne aride du Nord.

Il sommeille.

La glace et la neige l'environnent d'un manteau blanc.

Il rêve d'un palmier qui là bas dans l'Orient lointain se désole,

solitaire et taciturne, sur la pente de son rocher brûlant.

H. Heine

A solitary pine stands erect on a barren mountain of the North.

It sleeps.

Ice and snow enwrap it in a cloak of white.

It dreams of a palm-tree which younder, in the far-off East, pines away,

Alone and silent on the slope of its scorching craggy rock.

REPERTOIRE

Pagan-Primitive
Stravinsky, *Le sacre du printemps* (1913), orch
Prokofiev, *Ala and Lolly* (arr. *Scythian Suite*) (1914), orch
Ravel, *Chansons madécasses* (1927), S, ens

Japan

Debussy, *La mer* (1903–05), orch
Puccini, *Madame Butterfly* (1904), opera
Stravinsky, *Three Japanese Lyrics* (1913), S, ens
Holst, *Japanese Suite* (1916), orch
Gerhard, *Seven Haiku* (1922), S/T, ens
Delage, *Sept haikai* (1927), S, ens

China

Debussy, *Estampes:* "Pagodes" (1903), pf
Ravel, *Shéhérazade:* "Asie" (1903), S, orch
Ravel, *Ma mere l'oye:* "Laideronette, impératrice des pagodes" (1908–10), pf, 4 hands
Stravinsky, *La rossignol* (1908–09; 1913–14), opera
Busoni, *Turandot* (1917), opera
Bartók, *The Miraculous Mandarin* (1918–19), ballet
Toch, *Die chinesische Flöte* (1921), texts by H. Bethge, S, orch
Puccini, *Turandot* (1924), opera

India

Holst, *Hymns from the Rig Veda* (1908), v, pf
Holst, *Savitri* (1908), opera
Roussel, *Evocations* (1910–11), A, T, Bar, chor, orch
Debussy, *Khamma* (1912)
Delage, *Four Hindu Poems* (1912), S, ens
Carpenter, *Gitanjali* (Tagore, 1913), S, pf
Milhaud, *Poème du "Gitanjali"* (Tagore, 1914), v, pf
Roussel, *Padmâtvi* (1914–18), opera
Delage, *Ragamalika* (1915), S, pf
Milhaud, *Deux poèmes d'amour* (Tagore, 1915), v, pf
L. Boulanger, *Vielle prière bouddhique* (1917), T, chorus, orch
Zemlinsky, *Lyric Symphony* (Tagore, 1921–22), S, Bar, orch

Spain

Debussy, *Estampes:* "La soirée dans Grenade" (1902)
    Images II: "Iberia" (1905–10), orch
    Préludes, Book II: "La puerta del vino" (1912–13), pf
Ravel, *Miroirs* (1905): "Alborada del gracioso", pf
    Rapsodie espagnole (1907), orch
    Bolero (1928), orch
    Don Quichotte à Dulcinée (1932), Bar, pf
Albeniz, *Suite Iberia* (1906–08), pf
Granados, *Goyescas* (1911), pf
Falla, *Pièces espagnoles* (1902–08), pf
    Siete canciones populares espanolas (1914–15), v, pf
    El amor brujo (1915), ballet with songs, orch
    El sombrero de tres picos (1918–19), ballet, orch
    El retablo de maese Pedro (1919–22), puppet opera
    Concerto (1923–26), hpd, fl, ob, cl, vn, vc
Stravinsky, *Etude for Pianola* (1917)

Miscellaneous

Debussy, *Six épigraphes antiques:* "Pour la danseuse aux crotales" (1914), pf 4 hands
Ravel, *Piano Trio* (1914), pf, vn, vc (Malaysian "Pantoum," 2nd mvt.)

READING

Pierre Boulez, "Oriental Music: A Lost Paradise?" in *Orientations* (Cambridge, Mass., 1986), 421–24. Originally as "Musique traditionelle—un paradis perdu?", a trilingual French/English/German text in *The World of Music*, ix (1967).

Takashi Funayama, "*Three Japanese Lyrics* and Japonisme," *Confronting Stravinsky: Man, Musician, and Modernist* (Berkeley, Calif., 1986), 273.

CHAPTER 8

SYMBOLIST REVERBERATIONS ABROAD (I): DECADENT SYMBOLISM

Extending beyond the popular exotic note in France, but clearly related to it, was a strain within the Symbolist movement that may be referred to as Decadence. Its origins are not surprisingly Romantic: Hoffman, Poe, Delacroix had all told of a world inhabited by sphinxes, ghouls, and sirens, and Baudelaire had early sounded an erotic note that had shocked an official France. It was especially the themes of *Fleurs du mal* that were taken over by the movement: satanism, dandyism, exoticism, and especially eroticism—all the things the bourgeoisie regarded as decadent. The central movement, as with Symbolism in general, was defined in France, and by no figure more than the painter Gustave Moreau. But the English aesthetes, and particularly the followers of Oscar Wilde, added a note of perversity that was not lost, and even Nietzsche and the Marxists approved of the term "decadence" to refer to the irrationalism and anxiety that seemed to permeate artistic society.[1]

In the 1880s, the names of Mallarmé and Verlaine were readily associated with this neurotic aspect of Symbolism, an association that Verlaine's intimate personal relationship with Rimbaud did nothing to dispel. Verlaine was explicit: "I love the word 'Decadence,' all gleaming with crimson . . . It is made up of a mixture of carnal spirit and melancholy flesh and all the violent splendors of the Byzantine Empire."[2] To the precision in the use of language and mysterious researches into the formulation of a new syntax, an opulence that bred on luxury and excess was added. Mallarmé's lengthy *Hérodiade*, begun in 1864 but subjected to revision until his death, is ample testimony to this combination and to his fascination with the legend of Salome that had so haunted Gustave Moreau (Figure 8.1).

SALOME

While Mallarmé's lines, which exhude an icy chill and a certain remoteness, were not to serve the musician except in Hindemith's unusual work of 1944, the popularity of the Salome story in the decades of the 1870s and 1880s with

Figure 8.1. Gustave Moreau, *The Apparition* (1876).
Photo courtesy of Musée Nationaux, Paris.

artists, writers, and musicians was without parallel. Among French artists who occupied themselves with the Salome theme were Puvis de Chavannes (1870), Henry Levy (1872), and Odilon Redon (1877). Flaubert's *Hérodiade,* a short story of 1877, inspired Massenet to write his opera of 1881, and his description of Salome's dance, inflamed by memories of Egyptian dancers, cannot but have captured Wilde's imagination. While Massenet's *Hérodiade* has not remained in the repertoire, two arias, "Il est doux, il est bon" and "Vision fugitive," have endured as classics. Similarly, Moreau's paintings of 1876 on the theme would never have achieved their ultimate popularity had it not been for the spotlight placed on them by the hedonist hero, Count des Esseintes, of Huysmans' *A rebours* (1884). Arthur Symons appropriately labeled the novel as "the breviary of the Decadence," and a reading of Chapter V of this work provides the surest route to an understanding of the term.

JORIS-KARL HUYSMANS (1848–1907): A REBOURS, CHAPTER V[3]

Together with the desire to escape from a hateful period of sordid degradation, the longing to see no more pictures of the human form toiling in Paris between four walls or roaming the streets in search of money had taken an increasing hold on him.

Once he had cut himself off from contemporary life, he had resolved to allow nothing to enter his hermitage which might breed repugnance or regret; and so he had set his heart on finding a few pictures of subtle, exquisite refinement, steeped in an atmosphere of ancient fantasy, wrapped in an aura of antique corruption, divorced from modern times and modern society.

For the delectation of his mind and the delight of his eyes, he had decided to seek out evocative works which would transport him to some unfamiliar world, point the way to new possibilities, and shake up his nervous system by means of erudite fancies, complicated nightmares, suave and sinister visions.

Among all the artists he considered, there was one who sent him into raptures of delight, and that was Gustave Moreau. He had bought Moreau's two masterpieces, and night after night he would stand dreaming in front of one of them, the picture of Salome.

This painting showed a throne like the high altar of a cathedral standing beneath a vaulted ceiling—a ceiling crossed by countless arches springing from thick-set, amost Romanesque columns, encased in polychromic brickwork, encrusted with mosaics, set with lapis lazuli and sardonyx—in a palace which resembled a basilica built in both the Moslem and the Byzantine styles.

In the centre of the tabernacle set on the altar, which was approached by a flight of recessed steps in the shape of a semi-circle, the Tetrarch Herod was seated, with a tiara on his head, his legs close together and his hands on his knees.

His face was yellow and parchment-like, furrowed with wrinkles, lined with years; his long beard floated like a white cloud over the jewelled stars that studded the gold-laced robe moulding his breast.

Round about this immobile, statuesque figure, frozen like some Hindu god in a hieratic pose, incense was burning, sending up clouds of vapour through which the fiery gems set in the sides of the throne gleamed like the phosphorescent eyes of wild animals. The clouds rose higher and higher, swirling under the arches of the roof, where the blue smoke mingled with the gold dust of the great beams of sunlight slanting down from the domes.

Amid the heady odour of these perfumes, in the overheated atmosphere of the basilica, Salome slowly glides forward on the points of her toes, her left arm stretched out in a commanding gesture, her right bent back and holding a great lotus-blossom beside her face, while a woman squatting on the floor strums the strings of a guitar.

With a withdrawn, solemn, almost august expression on her face, she begins the lascivious dance which is to rouse the aged Herod's dormant senses; her breasts rise and fall, the nipples hardening at the touch of her whirling necklaces; the strings of diamonds glitter against her moist flesh; her bracelets, her belts, her rings all spit out fiery sparks; and across her triumphal robe, sewn with pearls, patterned with silver, spangled with gold, the jewelled cuirass, of which every chain is a precious stone, seems to be ablaze with little snakes of fire, swarming over the mat flesh, over the tea-rose skin, like gorgeous insects with dazzling shards, mottled with carmine, spotted with pale yellow, speckled with steel blue, striped with peacock green.

Her eyes fixed in the concentrated gaze of a sleepwalker, she sees neither the Tetrarch, who sits there quivering, nor her mother, the ferocious Herodias, who watches her every movement, nor the hermaphrodite or eunuch who stands sabre in hand at the foot of the throne, a terrifying creature, veiled as far as the eyes and with its sexless dugs hanging like gourds under its orange-striped tunic.

The character of Salome, a figure with a haunting fascination for artists and poets, had been an obsession with him for years. Time and again he had opened the old Bible of Pierre Variquet, translated by the Doctors of Theology of the University of Louvain, and read the Gospel of St Matthew which recounts in brief, naïve phrases the beheading of the Precursor; time and again he had mused over these lines:

'But when Herod's birthday was kept, the daughter of Herodias danced before them, and pleased Herod.

'Whereupon, he promised with an oath to give her whatsoever she would ask.

'And she, being before instructed of her mother, said, "Give me here John Baptist's head in a charger."

'And here the king was sorry: nevertheless, for the oath's sake, and them which sat with him at meat, he commanded it to be given her.

'And he sent, and beheaded John in the prison.

'And his head was brought in a charger, and given to the damsel: and she brought it to her mother.'

But neither St Matthew, nor St Mark, nor St Luke, nor any of the other sacred writers had enlarged on the maddening charm and potent depravity of the dancer. She had always remained a dim and distant figure, lost in a mysterious ecstasy far off in the mists of time, beyond the reach of punctilious, pedestrian minds, and accessible only to brains shaken and sharpened and rendered almost clairvoyant by neurosis; she had always repelled the artistic advances of fleshly painters, such as Rubens who travestied her as a Flemish butcher's wife; she had always passed the comprehension of the writing fraternity, who never succeeded in rendering the disquieting delirium of the dancer, the subtle grandeur of the murderess.

In Gustave Moreau's work, which in conception went far beyond the data supplied by the New Testament, Des Esseintes saw realized at long last the weird and superhuman Salome of his dreams. Here she was no longer just the dancing-girl who extorts a cry of lust and lechery from an old man by the lascivious movements of her loins; who saps the morale and breaks the will of a king with the heaving of her breasts, the twitching of her belly, the quivering of her thighs. She had become, as it were, the symbolic incarnation of undying Lust, the Goddess of immortal Hysteria, the accursed Beauty exalted above all other beauties by the catalepsy that hardens her flesh and steels her muscles, the monstrous Beast, indifferent, irresponsible, insensible, poisoning, like the Helen of ancient myth, everything that approaches her, everything that sees her, everything that she touches.

Viewed in this light, she belonged to the theogonies of the Far East; she no longer had her origin in Biblical tradition; she could not even be likened to the living image of Babylon, the royal harlot of Revelations, bedecked like herself with precious stones and purple robes, with paint and perfume, for the whore of Babylon was not thrust by a fateful power, by an irresistible force, into the alluring iniquities of debauch.

Moreover, the painter seemed to have wished to assert his intention of remaining outside the bounds of time, of giving no precise indication of race or country or period, setting as he did his Salome inside this extraordinary palace with its grandiose, heterogeneous architecture, clothing her in sumptuous, fanciful robes, crowning her with a nondescript diadem like Salammbo's, in the shape of a Phoenician tower, and finally putting in her hand the sceptre of Isis, the sacred flower of both Egypt and India, the great lotus-blossom.

Des Esseintes puzzled his brains to find the meaning of this emblem. Had it the phallic significance which the primordial religions of India attributed to it? Did it suggest to the old Tetrarch a sacrifice of virginity, an exchange of blood, an impure embrace asked for and offered on the express condition of a murder? Or did it represent the allegory of fertility, the Hindu myth of life, an existence held between the fingers of woman and clumsily snatched away by the fumbling hands of man, who is maddened by desire, crazed by a fever of the flesh?

Perhaps, too, in arming his enigmatic goddess with the revered lotus-blossom, the painter had been thinking of the dancer, the mortal woman, the soiled vessel, ultimate cause of every sin and every crime; perhaps he had remembered the sepulchral rites of ancient Egypt, the solemn ceremonies of embalmment, when practitioners and priests lay out the dead woman's body on a slab of jasper, then with curved needles extract her brains through the nostrils, her entrails through an opening made in the left side, and finally, before gilding her nails and her teeth, before anointing the corpse with oils and spices, insert into her sexual parts, to purify them, the chaste petals of the divine flower.

Be that as it may, there was some irresistible fascination exerted by this painting; but the water-colour entitled *The Apparition* created perhaps an even more disturbing impression.

In this picture, Herod's palace rose up like some Alhambra on slender columns iridescent with Moresque tiles, which appeared to be bedded in silver mortar and gold cement; arabesques started from lozenges of lapis lazuli to wind their way right across the cupolas, whose mother-of-pearl marquetry gleamed with rainbow lights and flashed with prismatic fires.

The murder had been done; now the executioner stood impassive, his hands resting on the pommel of his long, blood-stained sword.

The Saint's decapitated head had left the charger where it lay on the flagstones and risen into the air, the eyes staring out from the livid face, the colourless lips parted, the crimson neck dripping tears of blood. A mosaic encircled the face, and also a halo of light whose rays darted out under the porticoes, emphasized the awful elevation of the head, and kindled a fire in the glassy eyeballs, which were fixed in what appeared to be agonized concentration on the dancer.

With a gesture of horror, Salome tries to thrust away the terrifying vision which holds her nailed to the spot, balanced on the tips of her toes, her eyes dilated, her right hand clawing convulsively at her throat.

She is almost naked; in the heat of the dance her veils have fallen away and her brocade robes slipped to the floor, so that now she is clad only in wrought metals and translucent gems. A gorgerin grips her waist like a corselet, and like an outsize clasp a wondrous jewel sparkles and flashes in the cleft between her breasts; lower down, a girdle encircles her hips, hiding the upper part of her thighs, against which dangles a gigantic pendant glistening with rubies and emeralds; finally, where the body shows bare between gorgerin and girdle, the belly bulges out, dimpled by a navel which resembles a graven seal of onyx with its milky hues and its rosy finger-nail tints.

Under the brilliant rays emanating from the Precursor's head, every facet of every jewel catches fire; the stones burn brightly, outlining the woman's figure in flaming colours, indicating neck, legs, and arms with points of light, red as burning coals, violet as jets of gas, blue as flaming alcohol, white as moonbeams.

The dreadful head glows eerily, bleeding all the while, so that clots of dark red form at the ends of hair and beard. Visible to Salome alone, it embraces in its sinister gaze neither Herodias, musing over the ultimate satisfaction of her hatred, nor the Tetrarch, who, bending forward a little with his hands on his knees, is still panting with emotion, maddened by the sight and smell of the woman's naked body, steeped in musky scents, anointed with aromatic balms, impregnated with incense and myrrh.

Like the old King, Des Esseintes invariably felt overwhelmed, subjugated, stunned when he looked at this dancing-girl, who was less majestic, less haughty, but more seductive than the Salome of the oil-painting.

In the unfeeling and unpitying statue, in the innocent and deadly idol, the lusts and fears of common humanity had been awakened; the great lotus-blossom had disappeared, the goddess vanished; a hideous nightmare now held in its choking grip an entertainer, intoxicated by the whirling movement of the dance, a courtesan, petrified and hypnotized by terror.

Here she was a true harlot, obedient to her passionate and cruel female temperament; here she came to life, more refined yet more savage, more hateful yet more exquisite than before; here she roused the sleeping senses of the male more powerfully, subjugated his will more surely with her charms—the charms of a great venereal flower, grown in a bed of sacrilege, reared in a hot-house of impiety.

It was Des Esseintes' opinion that never before, in any period, had the art of water-colour produced such brilliant hues; never before had an aquarellist's wretched chemical pigments been able to make paper sparkle so brightly with precious stones, shine so colourfully with sunlight filtered through stained-glass windows, glitter so splendidly with sumptuous garments, glow so warmly with exquisite flesh-tints.

Deep in contemplation, he would try to puzzle out the antecedents of this great artist, this mystical pagan, this illuminee who could shut out the modern world so completely as to behold, in the heart of present-day Paris, the awful visions and magical apotheoses of other ages.

Des Esseintes found it hard to say who had served as his models; here and there, he could detect vague recollections of Mantegna and Jacopo de Barbari; here and there, confused memories of Da Vinci and feverish colouring reminiscent of Delacroix. But on the whole the influence of these masters on his work was imperceptible, the truth being that Gustave Moreau was nobody's pupil. With no real ancestors and no possible descendants, he remained a unique figure in contemporary art. Going back to the beginnings of racial tradition, to the sources of mythologies whose bloody enigmas he compared and unravelled; joining and fusing in one those legends which had originated in the Middle East only to be metamorphosed by the beliefs of other peoples, he could cite these researches to justify his architectonic mixtures, his sumptuous and unexpected combinations of dress materials, and his hieratic allegories whose sinister quality was heightened by the morbid perspicuity of an entirely modern sensibility. He himself remained downcast and sorrowful, haunted by the symbols of superhuman passions and superhuman perversities, of divine debauches perpetrated without enthusiasm and without hope.

His sad and scholarly works breathed a strange magic, an incantatory charm which stirred you to the depths of your being like the sorcery of certain of Baudelaire's poems, so that you were left amazed and pensive, disconcerted by this art which crossed the frontiers of painting to borrow from the writer's art its most subtly evocative suggestions, from the enamellar's art its most wonderfully brilliant effects, from the lapidary's and etcher's art its most exquisitely delicate touches. These two pictures of Salome, for which Des Esseintes' admiration knew no bounds, lived constantly before his eyes, hung as they were on the walls of his study, on panels reserved for them between the bookcases.

WILDE, BEARDSLEY, KLIMT, STRAUSS. Wilde's *Salome* was written in 1891–92, and though he was conversant with the treatment of the legend in the works of Titian, Leonardo Vinci, and Dürer, it was Moreau's pictures and Huysmans' *A rebours* that were the immediate inspiration for his approach to the subject. Like Huysmans and unlike Mallarmé, his Decadent figures are of flesh and blood, and found, not unexpectedly, a personification in the lives of Robert de Montesquiou and Sarah Bernhardt who, like all contributors to the movement, alternately endorsed its taste for death and the occult, the mystical and the erotic. Montesquieu was in fact the model not only for the hero of Huysmans' *A rebours*, the Duc Floressas des Esseintes, but also for Wilde's Dorian Gray and Marcel Proust's Baron de Charlus.

The legendary Bernhardt was initially scheduled to perform Wilde's *Salome* in its original French, though ultimately French officialdom intervened and her performance never came to pass. While she may have likened herself on occasion to Pierrot, Jean Lorrain, who knew her, saw her as the personification of Wilde's heroine:

> Sarah is there, standing before me, with her delicate, irritating profile, and her cold, sparkling eyes, like a pair of precious stones. Seeing her like that, pale and languid beneath the glitter of her metal belt, I reflect that she too belongs to the family of that old King David and that young archangel with the woman's face; yes, the enigmatic Sarah is truly Gustave Moreau's daughter, the sister of the muses carrying decapitated heads, of Orpheus and the slim, blood-thirsty Salomes—the Salome of the famous watercolours praised by Huysmans, the Salome of *The Apparition*, whose triumphant, coruscating costume, incidentally, she wears in *Theodora*.[4]

England banned the production of Wilde's play in 1892 because of its treatment of a Biblical subject, but it was published in French in 1893 and in English translation by Wilde's friend, Lord Alfred Douglas, with illustrations by Aubrey Beardsley in 1894 (Figures 8.2 and 8.3). Wilde's prison sentence began in 1895, and his tragic demise was followed by his death in 1900.

Figure 8.2. Aubrey Beardsley, *Salome: The Dancer's Reward*. Illustration for Oscar Wilde's *Salome* (1894).

Figure 8.3. Aubrey Beardsley, *Salome: The Peacock Skirt*. Illustration for Oscar Wilde's *Salome* (1894).

In 1901, Gustav Klimt, who was just heading up the Secession in Vienna, painted a Judith and Holofernes, whose story was naturally capable of inspiring a similar if not identical iconography. His painting of Judith II in 1909 (Figure 8.4), in the wake of Strauss's operatic success based on Wilde's play, inspired the critics to claim it as Salome. In truth, the anxious facial expression and the menacing hands of this figure have moved far away from the Gibson girl beauty and the untroubled countenance of Judith I (Figure 8.5) and suggest that Klimt is, with Richard Strauss, already on the edge of an Expressionist abyss.

By the time that Richard Strauss had determined on Salome as the subject for an opera, the revival of Herodias' daughter by the Decadents to accompany Melisande and Ophelia as the Symbolist's dream heroines was complete in the public imagination. The premiere of the opera in Dresden in 1905 (in a German translation by Hedwig Lachmann) caused a scandal, and the London and Berlin premieres were delayed until certain objectional details were eliminated. The premiere at New York's Metropolitan Opera in 1907 moved the board of directors to forbid its repetition, a judgment that held until 1934. The atmosphere of Wilde's play is pure Moreau-Huysmans, but in addition to the mood of Decadence, Strauss's opera carried with it a new note reflecting the intervening appearance of Freud's *The Interpretation of Dreams* (1900) and its prevalent

Figure 8.4. Gustav Klimt, *Judith II* (1909).
Photo courtesy of Galerie Welz, Salzburg.

Figure 8.5. Gustav Klimt, *Judith I* (1901).
Photo courtesy of Galerie Welz, Salzburg.

psychosexual orientation. Salome's necrophilia is now seen as a psychosis that demands that we enter her troubled mind, an opportunity Strauss did not fail to pursue in his next opera, *Elektra* (1909). The Freudian components aside, *Salome* is a tale whose appeal, beyond its opulence and color, resides basically in its quality as a story. *Salome* still clearly relates to Saint-Saëns's *Samson and Delilah*, while *Elektra* (1906–08, premiered January 1909) looks ahead to Schoenberg's *Erwartung* (August–September 1909, premiered June 1924). The almost total suppression of the lyric element in *Elektra* and the further clouding of the harmonic and tonal ingredients not only prepares the way for Schoenberg's Expressionist monodrama, but also provokes a crisis in Strauss's art that was to be resolved only in the clarifying reversionism of *Der Rosenkavalier*.

STRAUSS'S *SALOME*.   Strauss's opera is in one act and lasts under 90 minutes. The pacing is calculated and a reflection of Wilde's richly luxurious language. Characterization and psychological mood are clearly delineated with a predictable set of leitmotifs. Two guides were published in 1906/1907 by Lawrence Gilman and Otto Roese, and the following list, though different from either, is based on both of them.

Like Debussy, Strauss took over a preexistent play almost intact, but a comparison of the motivic usage with that found in *Pelléas* reveals that Strauss has constructed a much denser network, as musical figures proliferate and recurr at a dizzying rate. The meaning of the various motifs is also less obscure than in *Pelléas* and betrays a decidedly Wagnerian sensibility. From Salome's "Dance of the Seven Veils" to the end of the opera, the libretto of which is provided, most of the motifs of the entire work return. But several disclose a pronounced kinship to each other (Ex. 8.2, nos. 9, 10, 12, 13) and a developing significance. Others are infrequently employed but with telling effect–e.g., No. 2–associated earlier in the opera with the youthful Narraboth who, enamored of Salome and unable to get her attentions, commits suicide without her taking any notice whatsoever. The single return of the opening figure of his motif comes at Salome's words to the decapitated John: "If thou hadst looked at me thou hadst love me." No. 3 is likewise sparingly used, but its return during Salome's dance and her expectant wait for the head of John the Baptist indicates a calculated placement on the part of the composer.

The form of the motifs in the examples refer to their first appearance. While details of rhythm, melody, harmony, and color are all subject to a considerable metamorphosis during the course of the opera, their initial character (including their instrumentation) is often fundamental to later presentations. Strauss brings his full experience as orchestrator of the tone poems to bear on the score of *Salome*, and his mastery is apparent in the coloristic component of the several motifs: the lower brasses to suggest the majesty of Jokanaan (No. 4); the oriental note of the oboes for Salome's Lust (No. 7) and portions of her Dance; the heinous horns to portray Herodias's willful urgings (No. 12a); or the heraldic use of trumpets to signal Herod's Command (No. 13) at the close of the opera.

The motifs themselves appear and disappear over backgrounds of greater or lesser tonal stability. Salome's vigil for the appearance of the head of John the Baptist, followed by the climactic "Apostrophe to the Head," is illustrative. As she leans over the cistern for the slightest indication that her reward is about to be delivered, an E♭ pedal persists against Salome's exclamations intoned in flashes of several distant tonalities. With the emergence of the black arm of the executioner bearing the head of John on a silver charger, the "atonal" clouds lift and Salome begins her ecstatic finale. Though a note of lyricism that had previously been absent throughout the opera prevails from here to the end, the rate of modulation is swift. In addition, occasional harmonic clusters and polytonal juxtapositions threaten a sense of tonal clarity (see Ex. 8.1), and it is apparent that the earlier explorations of the tone poems have here been pressed to new account. The final instance of such an inclination comes in the orchestra

Example 8.1. Strauss, *Salome*, No. 355.

in the first measure following Salome's concluding words. The willful distortion (No. 6a) is like a chancre, uncurable and synopsizing the moral climate of the opera. Even Herod's order to slay Salome (No. 13) portrayed by a trumpet flourish is no simple arpeggio: The outer fifth (C–G) frames an internal G♭ major triad (C–G♭–B♭–D♭–G) and mirrors the unstableness of Herod's crazed command. Years later in 1942 Strauss openly discussed his use of bitonality as a means of character delineation in *Salome*, though he classified it as a unique experiment and warned against its imitation.[5]

The value of the pedal device in free-tone and appogiatura-laden terrain, as in motif No. 8, is obvious. But Strauss's skill in maneuvering harmonic complexes toward tonal goals (e.g., Nos. 3, 11, 17) suggests a mastery that not only confirms his conquests in the early tone poems, but rivals Schoenberg's contemporaneous demonstrations in his *Harmonielehre* (1911), the tonal harmonization of the 12-note theme of his *Variations for Orchestra* (1931, see p. 000), or the later *Structural Functions of Harmony* (1948). Though the influence of *Salome* on many contemporary composers may be difficult to understand today, Schoenberg, as most composers of the time, was incredulous on its first appearance. Wellesz's recollection helps us to sense its impact, however, and seals the relation of one of the principal opening themes (Ex. 2.1) of Schoenberg's *Kammersymphonie*, op. 9, of 1906 to Strauss's motif No. 5 (Ex. 8.2, No. 5).

It was an afternoon in October 1905. A small, dark room facing the courtyard . . . Arnold Schoenberg with cigarette in hand, his head inclined, pacing ceaselessly up and down. On a chest, a parcel of oversized music paper—the incomplete score of the *Gurrelieder*. On the lectern of the piano, the recently published vocal score of Strauss's *Salome* open at the first page. "Perhaps in twenty years someone will be able to explain these harmonic progressions theoretically," said the composer, who four years later would burst the boundaries of tonality with his *Five Pieces for Orchestra*. That was my first impression of Schoenberg when, during the second year of my studies at the University, I came to his home for lessons in counterpoint.[6]

Example 8.2. Leitmotifs for *Salome*, Final Scene.

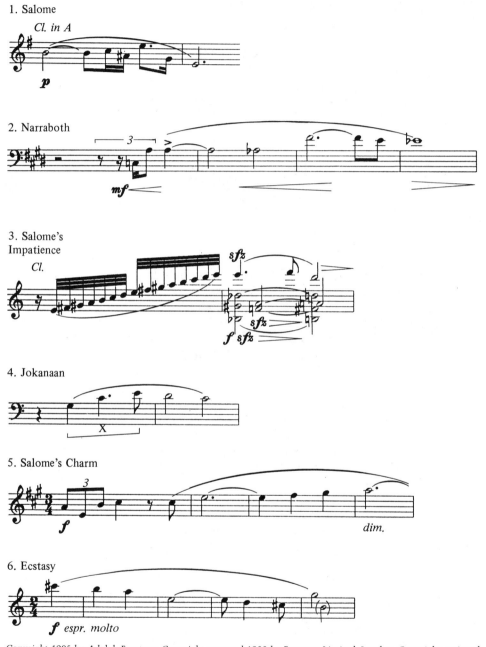

Example 8.2 (Continued)

6a.

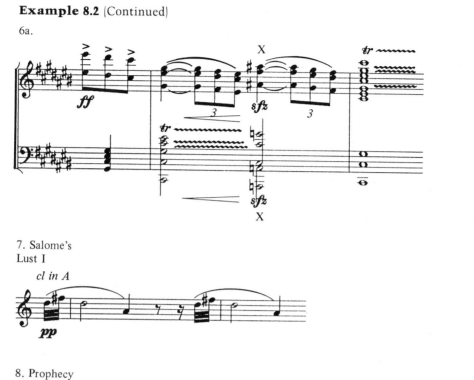

7. Salome's
Lust I

cl in A

8. Prophecy

9. Kiss

Ich will dei-nen Mund küs - sen, Jo - cha - na-an

10. Salome's Revenge:
Jokanaan's Head

Ich will den Kopf _____ des Jo - cha - na - an.

Example 8.2 (Continued)

10a.

11. Herod's Gaze

12. Herodias

12a.

13. Herod's
Command

14. Herod's
Graciousness

15. Salome's Dance I

Example 8.2 (Continued)

16.
Salome's Dance II

p espr.

17. Herod's
Pleading
vc, bss

bcl, bn, hn,
cbn, tb

Richard Strauss, *Salome*, Finale

SALOMES TANZ.

SALOMES DANCE.

15, 1, 7, 9, 3, 5, 16 *

(Die Musikanten beginnen einen wilden Tanz. Salome, suerst noch bewegungslos, richtet sich hoch auf und gibt den Musikanten ein Zeichen, worauf der wilde Rhythmus sofort abgedämpft wird und in eine sanft wiegende Weise überleitet. Salome tanzt sodann den "Tanz der sieben Schleier."

Sie scheint einen Augenblick zu ermatten, jetzt rafft sie sich wie neubeschwingt auf. Sie verweilt einen Augenblick in visionärer Haltung an der Cisterne, in der Jochanaan gefangen gehalten wird; dann stürzt sie vor und zu Herodes' Füssen.)

(The musicians begin with a wild dance. Salome, at first, motionless, draws herself up and gives the musicians a sign upon which the wild rhythm is at once relaxed and a gentle rocking melody takes place. Salome then dances the "Dance of the Seven Veils."

For a moment she seems exhausted, then rouses herself with renewed vigor. She halts an instant in visionary attitude near the cistern where Iokanaan is imprisoned, then falls forward at Herod's feet.)

HERODES

Ah! Herrlich! Wundervoll, wundervoll! (Zu Herodias.) Siehst du, sie hat für mich getanzt, deine Tochter. Komm her, Salome, komm her, du sollst deinen Lohn haben. Ich will dich königlich belohnen. Ich will dir alles geben, was dein Herz begehrt. Was willst du haben? Sprich!

11   HEROD

Ah! wonderful! wonderful! You see that she has danced for me, your daughter. Come near, Salome, come near, that I may give thee thy fee. I will pay thee royally. I will give thee whatsoever thy soul desireth. What wouldst thou have? Speak.

SALOME

(süss.)

Ich möchte, dass sie mir gleich in einer Silberschüssel—

SALOME

(Sweet.)

7,9   I would that they presently bring me in a silver charger—

*The numbers 1–17 refer to the leitmotifs as they appear in Ex. 8.2.

HERODES
(lachend.)
In einer Silberschüssel—gewiss doch—in einer Silberschüssel. Sie ist reizend, nicht? Was ist's, das du in einer Silberschüssel haben möchtest, o süsse, schöne Salome, du, die schöner ist als alle Töchter Judäas? Was sollen sie dir in einer Silberschüssel bringen? Sag es mir! Was es auch sein mag, du sollst es erhalten. Meine Reichtümer gehören dir. Was ist es, das du haben möchtest, Salome?

SALOME
(steht auf, lächelnd.)
Den Kopf des Jochanaan.

HERODES
(fährt auf.)
Nein, nein!

HERODIAS
Ah! Das sagst du gut, meine Tochter. Das sagst du gut!

HERODES
Nein, nein, Salome; das ist es nicht, was du begehrst! Hör' nicht auf die Stimme deiner Mutter. Sie gab dir immer schlechten Rat. Achte nicht auf sie.

SALOME
Ich achte nicht auf die Stimme meiner Mutter. Zu meiner eignen Lust will ich den Kopf des Jochanaan in einer Silberschüssel haben. Du hast einen Eid geschworen, Herodes. Du hast einen Eid geschworen, vergiss das nicht!

HERODES
(hastig.)
Ich weiss, ich habe einen Eid geschworen. Ich weiss es wohl. Bei meinen Göttern habe ich es geschworen. Aber ich beschwöre dich, Salome, verlange etwas andres von mir. Verlange die Hälfte meines Königreichs. Ich will sie dir geben. Aber verlange nicht von mir, was deine Lippen verlangten.

SALOME
(stark.)
Ich verlange von dir den Kopf des Jochanaan!

HERODES
Nein, nein, ich will ihn dir nicht geben.

SALOME
Du hast einen Eid geschworen, Herodes.

HERODIAS
Ja, du hast einen Eid geschworen. Alle haben es gehört.

HERODES
Still, Weib, zu dir spreche ich nicht.

HEROD
(Laughing.)
In a silver charger? Surely yes, in a silver charger. She is charming, is she not? What is it that thou wouldst have in a silver charger, O sweet and fair Salome, thou that are fairer than all the daughters of Judea? What wouldst thou have them bring thee in a silver charger? Tell me. Whatsoever it may be, thou shalt receive it. My treasures belong to thee. What is that thou wouldst have, Salome?

SALOME
(Rising, laughing)
7
10 The head of Iokanaan.

HEROD
(Irritable.)
No, no!

HERODIAS
That is well said, my daughter.

HEROD
No, no, Salome. It is not that thou desirest. Do not listen to thy mother's voice. She is ever giving thee evil counsel. Do not heed her.

SALOME
10 It is not my mother's voice that I heed. It is for mine own pleasure that I ask the head of Iokanaan in a silver charger. You have sworn an oath, Herod. Forget not that you have sworn an oath.

HEROD
(Hasty.)
I know it. I have sworn an oath by my
5 gods. I know it well. But I pray thee, Salome, ask of me something else. Ask of me the half of my kingdom, and I will give it thee. But ask not of me what thy lips have asked.

SALOME
(Strong.)
I ask of you the head of Iokanaan.

HEROD
No, no; I will not give it thee.

SALOME
You have sworn an oath, Herod.

HERODIAS
Yes, you have sworn an oath. Everybody heard you.

HEROD
Peace, woman! It is not to you I speak.

HERODIAS

Meine Tochter hat recht daran getan, den Kopf des Jochanaan zu verlangen. Er hat mich mit Schimpf und Schande bedeckt. Man kann sehn, dass sie ihre Mutter liebt. Gib nicht nach, meine Tochter, gibt nicht nach! Er hat einen Eid geschworen.

HERODES

Still, sprich nicht zu mir! Salome, ich beschwöre dich: Sei nicht trotzig! Sieh, ich habe dich immer lieb gehabt. Kann sein, ich habe dich zu lieb gehabt. Darum verlange das nicht von mir. Der Kopf eines Mannes, der vom Rumpf getrennt ist, ist ein übler Anblick. Hör', was ich sage! Ich habe einen Smaragd. Er ist der schönste Smaragd der ganzen Welt. Den willst du haben, nicht wahr? Verlang' ihn von mir, ich will ihn dir geben, den schönsten Smaragd.

SALOME

Ich fordre den Kopf des Jochanaan!

HERODES

Du hörst nicht zu, du hörst nicht zu. Lass mich zu dir reden, Salome!

SALOME

Den Kopf des Jochanaan.

HERODES

Das sagst du nur, um mich zu quälen, weil ich dich so angeschaut habe. Deine Schönheit hat mich verwirrt. Oh! Oh! Bringt Wein! Mich dürstet! Salome, Salome, lass uns wie Freunde zu einander sein! Bedenk' dich! Ah! Was wollt ich sagen? Was war's? Ah! Ich weiss es wieder! Salome, du kennst meine weissen Pfauen, meine schönen weissen Pfauen, die im Garten zwischen den Myrten wandeln. Ich will sie dir alle, alle geben. In der ganzen Welt lebt kein König, der solche Pfauen hat. Ich habe bloss hundert. Aber alle will ich dir geben.

(Er leert seinen Becher.)

SALOME

Gib mir den Kopf des Jochanaan!

HERODIAS

Gut gesagt, meine Tochter! (Zu Herodes) Und du, du bist lächerlich mit deinen Pfauen.

HERODES

Still, Weib! Du kreischest wie ein Raubvogel. Deine Stimme peinigt mich. Still sag' ich dir! Salome, bedenk, was du tun willst. Es kann sein, dass der Mann von Gott gesandt ist. Er ist ein heil'ger Mann. Der Finger Gottes hat ihn berührt.

HERODIAS

My daughter has done well to ask the head of Iokanaan. He has covered me with insults. One can see that she loves her mother well. Do not yield, my daughter. He has sworn an oath.

HEROD

Peace! Speak not to me! Salome, I pray thee be not stubborn. I have ever been kind toward thee. I have ever loved thee. It may be that I have loved thee too much. **10** Therefore ask not this thing of me. The head of a man that is cut from his body is ill to look upon. Hearken to me. I have an emerald. It is the most beautiful emerald in the whole world. Thou wilt take that, wilt thou not? Ask it of me and I will give it thee.

SALOME

10 I demand the head of Iokanaan.

HEROD

Thou are not listening. Thou art not listening. Let me speak to thee, Salome.

SALOME

10 The head of Iokanaan!

HEROD

Thou sayest that but to trouble me, because that I have looked at thee. Thy **17** beauty has troubled me. Oh! oh! bring wine! I thirst! Salome, Salome, let us be as friends. Bethink thee——— Ah! what **11** would I say? What was't? Ah! I remember it! Salome, thou knowest my white peacocks, my beautiful white peacocks, that walk in the garden between the myrtles. I will give them to thee, all. In the whole world there is no king who possesses such peacocks. I have but a hundred. But I will give them all to thee.

(He empties the cup of wine.)

SALOME

10, 7 Give me the head of Iokanaan.

HERODIAS

Well said my daughter! (to Herodes) As for **12** you, you are ridiculous with your peacocks.

HEROD

Peace! you are always crying out. You cry out like a beast of prey. Your voice wearies **17** me. Peace, I tell you! Salome, think on what thou art doing. It may be that this **4** man comes from God. He is a holy man. The finger of God has touched him. Thou

Du möchtest nicht, dass mich ein Unheil trifft, Salome? Hör' jetzt auf mich!

SALOME
Ich will den Kopf des Jochanaan!

HERODES
(auffahrend.)
Ach! Du willst nicht auf mich hören. Sei runig, Salome. Ich, siehst du, bin ruhig. Höre: (leise und heimlich) Ich habe an diesem Ort Juwelen versteckt, Juwelen, die selbst deine Mutter nie gesehen bat. Ich habe ein Halsband mit vier Reiben Perlen, Topase, gelb wie die Augen der Tiger. Topase, hel-rot wie die Augen der Waldtaube, und grüne Topase, wie Katzenaugen. Ich habe Opale, die immer funkeln, mit einem Feuer, kalt wie Eis. Ich will sie dir alle geben, alle! Ich habe Chrysolithe und Berylle, Chrysoprase und Rubine. Ich habe Sardonyx-und Hyazinthsteine und Steine von Chalcedon.—Ich will sie dir alle geben, alle und noch andere Dinge. Ich habe einen Kristall, in den zu schaun keinem Weibe vergönnt ist. In einem Perlmutterkästchen habe ich drei wunderbare Türkise: Wer sie an seiner stirne trägt, kann Dinge sehn, die nicht wirklich sind. Es sind unbezahlbare Schätze. Was begehrst du sonst noch, Salome? Alles, was du verlangst, will ich dir geben—nur eines nicht: Nur nicht das Leben dieses einen Mannes. Ich will dir den Mantel des Hohenpriesters geben. Ich will dir den Vorhang des Allerheiligsten geben.

DIE JUDEN
Oh, oh, oh!

SALOME
(wild.)
Gib mir den Kopf des Jochanaan!

HERODES
(Herodes sinkt versweifelt auf seinen Sitz zurtick.)
Man soll ihr geben, was sie verlangt! Sie ist in Wahrheit ihrer Mutter Kind! (Herodias zieht dem Tetrarchen den Todesring vom Finger und gibt ihn dem ersten Soldaten, der ihn auf der Stelle dem Henker überbringt.)

HERODES
Wer hat meinen Ring genommen?
  (Der Henker geht in die Cisterne hinab.)
Ich hatte einen Ring an meiner rechten Hand. Wer hat meinen Wein getrunken? Es war Wein in meinem Becher. Er war mit Wein gefüllt. Es hat ihn jemand

17 wouldst not that some evil should befall me, Salome? Listen to me again.

SALOME
10 Give me the head of Iokanaan!

HEROD
(Irritable.)
Ah! thou art not listening to me. Be calm. As for me, am I not calm? Listen. (Soft and secret.) I have jewels hidden in this place—jewels that thy mother even has never seen. I have a collar of pearls, set in four rows. Topazes yellow as are the eyes of tigers, and topazes that are pink as the eyes of a wood-pigeon, and green topazes that are as the eyes of cats. I have opals that burn always, with a flame that is cold as ice. I will give them all to thee, all. I have chrysolites and beryls, and chrysoprases and rubies; I have sardonyx
17 and hyscinth stones, and stones of chalcedony, and I will give them all unto thee, all, and other things will I add to them. I have a crystal, into which it is not lawful for a woman to look. In a coffer of nacre I have three wondrous turquoises. He who wears them on his forehead can imagine things which are not. They are
3 treasures above all price. What desirest thou more than this, Salome? All that thou askest I will give thee, save one thing only, save only the life of one man. I will give thee the mantle of the high priest. I will give thee the veil of the sanctuary.

THE JEWS
Oh! oh! oh!

SALOME
(Wild.)
10 Give me the head of Iokanaan!

HEROD
(Sinking back in his seat.)

11 Let her be given what she asks! Of a truth she is her mother's child! (Herodias draws from the hand of the Tetrarch the ring of death, and gives it to the soldier, who straightway bears it to the executioner.)

13, 12 **HEROD**
13 Who has taken my ring?
(The executioner goes down into the cistern.)
There was a ring on my right hand. Who
4 has drunk my wine? There was wine in my cup. It was full of wine. Some one has

ausgetrunken. (Leise.) Gewiss wird Unheil über einen kommen.

HERODIAS
Meine Tochter hat recht getan!

HERODES
Ich bin sicher, es wird ein Unheil geschehn.

SALOME
   (an der Cisterne lauschend.)
Es ist kein Laut zu vernehmen. Ich höre nichts. Warum schreit er nicht, der Mann? Ah! Wenn einer mich zu töten käme, ich würde schreien, ich würde mich wehren, ich würde es nicht dulden! Schlag zu, schlag zu, Naaman, schlag zu, sag ich dir! Nein, ich höre nichts. (Gedehnt.) Es ist eine schreckliche Stille! Ah! Es ist etwas zu Boden gefallen. Ich hörte etwas fallen. Es war das Schwert des Henkers. Er hat Angst, dieser Sklave. Er hat das Schwert fallen lassen! Er traut sich nicht, ihn zu töten. Er ist eine Memme, dieser Sklave. Schickt Soldaten hin! (Zum Pagen.) Komm hierher, du warst der Freund dieses Toten, nicht? Wohlan, ich sage dir: Es sind noch nicht genug Tote. Geh zu den Soldaten und befiehl ihnen, hinabzusteigen und mir zu holen, was ich verlange, was der Tetrarch mir versprochen hat, was mein ist!
(Der Page weicht zurück, sie wendet sich
   den Soldaten zu.)
Hierher, ihr Soldaten, geht ihr in die Cisterne hinunter und holt mir den Kopf des Mannes! (Schreiend.) Tetrarch, Tetrarch, befiehl deinen Soldaten, dass sie mir den Kopf des Jochanaan holen!

(Ein riesengrosser schwarzer Arm, der Arm des Henkers, streckt sich aus der Cisterne heraus, auf einem silbernen Schild den Kopf des Jochanaan haltend. Salome ergreift ihn. Herodes verhüllt sein Gesicht mit dem Mantel. Herodias fächelt sich zu und lächelt. Die Nazarener sinken in die
   Knie und beginnen zu beten.)

SALOME
Ah! Du wolltest mich nicht deinen Mund küssen lassen, Jochanaan! Wohl, ich werde ihn jetzt küssen! Ich will mit meinen Zähnen hineinbeissen, wie man in eine reife Frucht beissen mag. Ja, ich will ihn jetzt küssen, deinen Mund, Jochanaan. Ich hab' es gesagt. Hab' ich's nicht gesagt? Ja, ich hab' es gesagt. Ah! Ah! Ich will ihn jetzt küssen. Aber warum siehst du mich nicht an, Jochanaan? Deine Augen, die so schrecklich waren, so voller Wut und

drunk it! Oh! surely some evil will befall some one.

HERODIAS
  12 My daughter has done well.

HEROD
  4 I am sure that some misfortune will happen.

SALOME
   (She leans over the cistern and listens.)
There is no sound. I hear nothing. Why **10** does he not cry out, this man? Ah! if any man sought to kill me, I would cry out, I would struggle, I would not suffer. Strike, **10a** strike, Naaman, strike, I tell you! No, I hear nothing. There is a terrible silence. Ah! something has fallen upon the ground. **1** I heard something fall. It was the sword of the executioner. He is afraid, this slave. He has dropped his sword. He dares not kill **13** him. He is a coward, this slave! Let **3** soldiers be sent. (She sees the page of **4** Herodias and addresses him.) Come hither. Thou wert the friend of him who is dead, wert thou not! Well, I tell thee, there are not dead men enough. Go to the soldiers and bid them go down and bring me the thing I ask, the thing the Tetrarch has promised me, the thing that is mine.

(The page recoils. She turns to the
   soldiers.)
15 Hither, ye soldiers. Get ye down into this cistern and bring me the head of this man. Tetrarch, Tetrarch, command your soldiers that they bring me the head of Iokanaan.

(A huge black arm, the arm of the executioner, comes forth from the cistern, bearing on a silver shield the head of Iokanaan. Salome seizes it. Herod hides his face with his cloak. Herodias smiles and fans herself. The Nazarenes fall on their
   knees and begin to pray.)

1 **SALOME**
Ah! thou wouldst not suffer me to kiss thy mouth, Iokanaan. Well! I will kiss it now. I **7, 1** will bite it with my teeth as one bites a ripe fruit. Yes, I will kiss thy mouth, **9, 6** Iokanaan. I said it; did I not say it? I said it. Ah! I will kiss it now. But wherefore dost thou not look at me, Iokanaan? Thine **5, 9** eyes that were so terrible, so full of rage and scorn, are shut now. Wherefore are **5, 7** they shut? Open thine eyes! Lift up thine eyelids, Iokanaan! Wherefore dost thou not

Verachtung, sind jetzt geschlossen.
Warum sind sie geschlossen? Oeffne doch
die Augen, erhebe deine Lider, Jochanaan!
Warum siehst du mich nicht an? Hast du
Angst vor mir, Jochanaan, dass du mich
nicht ansehen willst? Und deine Zunge, sie **14**
spricht kein Wort, Jochanaan, diese
Scharlachnatter, die ihren Geifer gegen
mich spie. Es ist seltsam, nicht? Wie
kommt es, dass diese rote Natter sich
nicht mehr rührt? Du sprachst böse Worte   **5**
gegen mich, gegen mich, Salome, die
Tochter der Herodias, Prinzessin von
Judäa. Nun wohl! Ich lebe noch, aber du   **10a**
bist tot, und dein Kopf, dein Kopf gehört   **4**
mir! Ich kann mit ihm tun, was ich will.
Ich kann ihn den Hunden vorwerfen und
den Vögeln der Luft. Was die Hunde übrig   **1, 5**
lassen, sollen die Vögel der Luft verzehren.
Ah! Ah! Jochanaan, Jochanaan, du warst
schön. Dein Leib war eine Elfenbeinsäule
auf silbernen Füssen. Er war ein Garten
voller Tauben in der Silberlilien Glanz.
Nichts in der Welt war so weiss wie dein   **7**
Leib. Nichts in der Welt war so schwarz
wie dein Haar. In der ganzen Welt war
nichts so rot wie dein Mund. Deine   **6**
Stimme war ein Weihrauchgefäss, und
wenn ich dich ansah, hörte ich
geheimnisvolle Musik.
(In den Anblick von Jochanaans Haupt   **8**
      versunken.)
Ah! Warum hast du mich nicht angesehen,   **7**
Jochanaan? Du legtest über deine Augen   **5**
die Binde eines, der seinen Gott schauen   **4**
wollte. Wohl! Du hast deinen Gott gesehn,
Jochanaan, aber mich, mich hast du nie
gesehn. Hättest du mich gesehn, du hättest   **1, 5**
mich geliebt! Ich dürste nach deiner
Schönheit. Ich hungre nach deinem Leib.   **9**
Nicht Wein noch Aepfel können mein
Verlangen stillen. Was soll ich jetzt tun,
Jochanaan? Nicht die Fluten, noch die
grossen Wasser können dieses brünstige
Begehren löschen. Oh! Warum sahst du   **5**
mich nicht an? Hättest du mich angesehn,   **10, 7**
du hättest mich geliebt. Ich weiss es wohl,   **2, 3**
du hättest mich geliebt. Und das
Geheimnis der Liebe ist grösser als das
Geheimnis des Todes.   **1, 6**
                        7

HERODES
      (leise zu Herodias.)
Sie ist ein Ungeheuer, deine Tochter. Ich   **7, 11**
sage dir, sie ist ein Ungeheuer!

HERODIAS
      (stark.)
Sie hat recht getan. Ich möchte jetzt hier   **11,12**
bleiben.

look at me? Art thou afraid of me,
Iokanaan, that thou wilt not look at me?
And thy tongue, that was like a red snake
darting poison, it moves no more, it speaks
no words, Iokanaan, that scarlet viper that
spat its venom upon me. It is strange, is it
not? How is it that the red viper stirs no
longer? Thou didst speak evil words
against me, to me, Salome, daughter of
Herodias, Princess of Judaea! Well, I still
live, but thou art dead, and thy head
belongs to me. I can do with it what I will.
I can throw it to the dogs and to the birds
of the air. That which the dogs leave, the
birds of the air shall devour. Ah, Iokanaan,
Iokanaan, thou wert beautiful. Thy body
was a column of ivory set upon feet of
silver. It was a garden full of doves and
lilies of silver. There was nothing in the
world so white as thy body. There was
nothing in the world so black as thy hair.
In the whole world there was nothing so
red as thy mouth. Thy voice was a censer
that scattered strange perfumes, and when
I looked on thee I heard a strange music.

(Lost in thought as she gazes upon
      Iokanaan's head.)
Ah! wherefore didst thou not look at me,
Iokanaan! Thou didst put upon thine eyes
the covering of him who would see God.
Well, thou hast seen thy God, Iokanaan,
but me, me, thou didst never see. If thou
hadst seen me thou hadst loved me. I am
athirst for thy beauty; I am hungry for thy
body; and neither wine nor apples can
appease my desire. What shall I do now,
Iokanaan? Neither the floods nor the great
waters can quench my passion. Ah! ah!
wherefore didst thou not look at me? If
thou hadst looked at me thou hadst loved
me. Well I know that thou wouldst have
loved me, and the mystery of Love is
greater than the mystery of Death.

HEROD
      (Softly to Herodias.)
She is monstrous, thy daughter; I tell thee
she is monstrous.

HERODIAS
      (Strong.)
She has done well. And I will stay here
now.

HERODES
(steht auf.)
Ah! Da spricht meines Bruders Weib!
(Schwächer.) Komm, ich will nicht an
diesem Orte bleiben. (Heftig.) Komm, sag'
ich dir! Sicher, es wird Schreckliches
geschehn. Wir wollen uns im Palast **7**
verbergen, Herodias, ich fange an zu **11**
erzittern.
(Der Mond verschwindet.)

(Auffahrend.) Manassah, Issachar, Ozias,
löscht die Fackeln aus. Verbergt den Mond,
verbergt die Sterne! Es wird Schreckliches **11**
geschehn.

(Die Sklaven löschen die Fackeln aus. Die
Sterne verschwinden. Eine grosse Wolke
zieht über den Mond und verhüllt ihn
völlig. Die Bühne wird ganz dunkel. Der
Tetrarch beginnt die Treppe
hinaufzusteigen.)

SALOME **7**
Ah! Ich habe deinen Mund geküsst, **7**
Jochanaan. Ah! Ich habe ihn geküsst
deinen Mund, es war ein bitterer
Geschmack auf deinen Lippen. Hat es **7**
nach Blut geschmeckt? Nein! Doch es
schmeckte vielleicht nach Liebe. Sie sagen, **7, 9**
dass die Liebe bitter schmecke. Allein, was
tut's? Was tut's? Ich habe deinen Mund **9, 6**
geküsst, Jochanaan. Ich habe ihn geküsst,
deinen Mund.
(Der Mond bricht wieder hervor und
beleuchtet Salome.)

HERODES **6a, 7**
(sich umwendend.)
Man töte dieses Weib! **13**
(Die Soldaten stürzen sich auf Salome und
begraben sie unter ihren Schilden.)

(Der Vorhang fällt schnell.) **5**
Ende.

HEROD
(Rising.)
Ah! There speaks my brother's wife! Come!
I will not stay in this place. Come, I tell
thee. Surely some terrible thing will befall.
Let us hide ourselves in our palace,
Herodias. I begin to be afraid.
(The moon disappears.)

(Vehement.) Manasseh, Issachar, Ozias, put
out the torches. Hide the moon! Hide the
stars! Some terrible thing will befall.

(The slaves put out the torches. The stars
disappear. A great cloud crosses the moon
and conceals it completely. The stage
becomes quite dark. The Tetrarch begins
to climb the staircase.)

SALOME
Ah! I have kissed thy mouth, Iokanaan, I
have kissed thy mouth. There was a bitter
taste on thy lips. Was it the taste of blood?
Nay; but perchance it was the taste of
love. They say that love hath a bitter
taste. But what matter? what matter? I have
kissed thy mouth, Iokanaan. I have kissed
thy mouth.

(A ray of moonlight falls on Salome and
illumines her.)

HEROD
(Turning round.)
Kill that woman!
(The soldiers rush forward and crush
beneath their shields Salome.)

Curtain.

FLORENT SCHMITT, *LA TRAGÉDIE DE SALOMÉ*. Winner of the Prix de Rome in
1900, Florent Schmitt (1870–1958) traveled extensively throughout Europe during the following years, capturing some of the local color in a series of instrumental works. In 1902, a group of young artists, who emphasized their rebel-
lious nature by dubbing themselves the Apaches, had formed in Paris, gathering
on Saturday evenings following concerts. Among the group were Ravel, Delage,
Tristan Klingsor, Calvocoressi, the pianist Ricardo Viñes, and the conductor

Inghelbrecht. When he was in Paris, Schmitt joined them and early became a member of their group, which by 1909 also included Stravinsky.

Their common interest in *Pellèas,* which premiered in 1902, provided a starting point for their discussions of avant-garde aesthetic issues and quickly expanded to include an interest in things Russian. Viñes had for years played numerous Russian works that Ravel brought to him, and it has been suggested that his performance of Balakirev's oriental fantasy *Islamey* had inspired Ravel to his own *Jeux d'eau* as early as 1901. Their collective fascination for the Russian mode extended to the adoption of a theme from Borodin's Second Symphony as a secret password, whistled to attract each other's attention or to gain admission to meetings. A gathering of the Apaches with Diaghilev in 1907 centered around their passion for *Boris Godunov* and an attempt to persuade the impresario to produce it the following year in lieu of a projected Tchaikowsky opera.

The fascination for *Pelléas* and *Boris,* for both French and Russian values, and especially those with mysterious or exotic locales, is an attitude that was in harmony with the cult of exoticism currently the rage amongst Parisian artists. As a pupil of Massenet, who had written his own *Hérodiade,* the young Florent Schmitt found the traditions of the Salome legend near at hand. It was not until 1907, however, following the premiere of Strauss's opera, that Schmitt wrote his own Salome ballet. Revised as a symphonic poem in 1910, it discloses a harmonic and instrumental style that alternates between Straussian bellicosity and Debussyan vapors—a not uncommon condition for scores written during the first decade of the twentieth century. If the use of English horn with shimmering strings and a textless women's chorus in the opening sections point to "Nuages" and "Sirènes" of Debussy's *Nocturnes,* respectively, Schmitt's final section, the "Danse de l'éffroi" projects a rhythmic dynamism that appears to forecast Stravinsky's *The Rite of Spring.*

Schmitt, *La tragédie de Salomé,* rhythm, 3 measures before No. 66.

© Durand et fils (Paris, 1912).

The dedication of the score to Stravinsky and the latter's expressions of admiration and promotion of the work with Diaghilev, who mounted it in 1913, encourage a consideration of the potential influence of this portion of the score.[7]

The literary inspiration of Schmitt's *Salomé* was a prose-poem by Robert d'Humières, who in turn provided the elaborate scenario for the ballet. The effusive imagery of the final scenes is typical of the whole.

Danse des eclairs ("Dance of Lightning")

> Total darkness has invaded the scene and the remainder of the drama is seen only imperfectly by flashes of lightning. It is the lascivious dance, the pursuit of Herod, the amorous evasion, Salome possessed, her veils torn away by the hand of Tetrarch . . . She is naked for an instant, but John suddenly appears, advances forward and covers her with his hermit's cloak. Movements of fury by Herod, quickly interpreted by Herodias, from whom a signal delivers John to the execu-

tioner who sweeps him off and soon reappears holding the head on a platter of bronze. Salome, triumphant, seized by her trophy, tries a step, overloaded by her funereal burden. Then, as if touched by a sudden uneasiness, as if the voice of the executed one had murmured in her ear, she runs straight to the edge of the terrace, and from over the battlement throws the platter into the sea. Suddenly it appears the color of blood, and while terror sweeps Herod into a bewildered state and with Herodias and the executioner in·maddened flight, Salome, falling to the ground, looses consciousness.

Salome comes to herself. The head of John appears, stares at her, then disappears. Salome trembles and turns aside, filled with anguish. The head, from another part of the stage, gazes at her anew. Salome wishes to steal away. Heads multiply, rising from all parts.

Terror-stricken, Salome whirls away in order to escape the bloody visions.

Danse de l'effroi ("Dance of Terror")

As she dances, the storm bursts. A furious wind envelops her. Some sulphurous clouds revolve on the precipice; a hurricane rocks the sea. Waterspouts of sand are hurled from the desert solitude. The tall cypresses are tragically twisted, weather-beaten by the tumult. The thunder and lightning burst forth, making the stones of the citadel fly about. Mount Nebo throws off flames and the entire range of Moab is aglow with fire. Everything is humbled and crestfallen on account of the dancer's infernal delirium.

© Durand et fils (Paris, 1912).

The elaborations on the Biblical tale differ in detail from Wilde and indicate the continuing potential for literary as well as musical embellishment. It is interesting to note that further and equally dissimilar transformations of the Salome story have continued to the present in Peter Maxwell Davies's gigantic ballet of 1978, where numerous musical motifs from the early decades of the twentieth century, including a reference to the compulsive horning of Strauss's Herodias motif (No. 18a), spell the persisting fascination for the subject.

Schmitt wrote several later scores on subjects with an exotic flavor, including *Anthony et Cléopâtre* (1920), on a text by Gide after Shakespeare, and *Salammbô* (1925), written for a film of Flaubert's novel. But except for *Dionysiaques*, an energetic piece of primitivism for winds and percussion (1914–25), the large catalogue of his later works failed either to pursue the direction or confirm the promise of his early ballet.

Although Stravinsky's letters to Schmitt preserved in the Bibliothèque Nationale in Paris contain hyperbolic admiration for Schmitt's *Salomé*, Stravinsky later claimed that his promotion of the work with Diaghilev was political in light of Schmitt's power as a critic. The break had come during the World War I years, a time that saw Stravinsky moving closer to Satie, who had no use for Schmitt. When Schmitt was elected to the French Academy over Stravinsky in 1934, Stravinsky's ultimate opinion was sealed.[8] It should be noted, however, that by that time Schmitt had found his own "little classic path," as Cocteau said of Satie, in works entitled *Symphonie concertante* (1928–31) for piano and orchestra and *Sonatine en trio* (1935) for fl, cl, pf/hpd, a trend that was continued in several suites written during the last years of his life.

BLUEBEARD

It may appear difficult to reconcile the fact that Maeterlinck, who gave us the unfathomable Melisande who always seems to be receding into the depths of a medieval landscape, could also give us a play based on Bluebeard, one of the most villainous types in the literature. But it will be remembered that Edgar Allen Poe (1809–1849), master of the tale of horror, had served as one of the most prominent influences on the Symbolists from the inception of the movement. Huysmans praised him in his *A rebours*; Mallarmé included translations of *The Raven* and *Ulalume* in his *Vers et Prose* (1888); Odilon Redon executed a series of lithographs inspired by Poe (1882); Debussy began but never completed both a symphonic poem (1889) and an opera (1904) based on *The Fall of the House of Usher*; and Florent Schmitt's orchestral *La palais hanté* (1904) was based upon a poem recited by the hero in the same tale. Indeed, the note of Decadence that haunts Poe's house similarly permeates Maeterlinck's castle in *Pelléas and Mélisande* and Khnopff's doomed manor of *The Abandoned City*.

MAETERLINCK, DUKAS, AND *ARIANE ET BARBE-BLEUE.*   The stories that treat the legend of Bluebeard are numerous and have been associated with a figure as early as Gilles de Rais (1404–1440), protector of Joan of Arc, master of infanticide, and central character in Huysman's *La bas* (1890). One of the earliest stories about him appears in Perrault's *Mère l'Oye* of 1697, but Maeterlinck's adaptation introduces a new dimension totally in keeping with the predisposition of the Symbolists. The richness of vocabulary as each of the several doors are opened echoes Klingsor and d'Humières; yet the note of uncertainty that persists to the end reminds us of *Pelléas* as past cruelties and possible future ones are placed in parentheses. The note of Decadence is first suggested, enriched, then softened, and in the end we are left, as in Maeterlinck's *Pelléas and Mélisande*, with more questions than answers.

Maeterlinck wrote the play *Ariane et Barbe-bleue* with the express idea in mind that Dukas would set it as an opera. Completed in 1907, it became a cult piece with Maeterlinck's wife in the role of Arianne, a gesture intended to settle an old grudge with Debussy, who in rejecting Maeterlinck's spouse for the role of Mélisande chose Mary Garden. The work, which has fallen from the repertoire but recently revived, is not without charm, though Dukas's highly derivative score has been charged with an excess of whole-tone scales and shallow orchestral effects. For those acquainted with the Bluebeard story in one of its several other versions, Maeterlinck's play appears decidedly tame, highly coloristic but devoid of any genuine mystery or horror. In the end, Ariane is free to leave and does so, though not without attempting to lure Bluebeard's former wives, who decline and remain behind.

BARTOK: *DUKE BLUEBEARD'S CASTLE.*   In a letter written from Paris in 1905 the young Bartók indicated that he had witnessed the decadent side of the city first-hand:

> Then there are other things to see, perhaps not in an artistic sense, but otherwise interesting, such as the Moulin Rouge. . . . I never saw anywhere in a knot so many butterflies of the night with painted faces. . . . A cabaret is called *Le néant.* Here instead of tables there are wooden coffins; the walls of the room are black; the

decorations are human skeletons or parts of skeletons; the waiters serve in clothing of 'pompe funèbre'. The lighting is such that our lips take on the color of
blackberries, our cheeks a waxen yellow, our nails violet (that is, we look like
cadavers) . . .[9]

Bartók turned his attentions in the same letter, however, to the question of
promoting a national Hungarian music. Recognizing the superiority of German
music (Bach, Beethoven, Schubert, Wagner), he introduced the name of Liszt,
whom he noted, however, "seldom writes in Hungarian." These two issues (the
perverse wish for escape from a materialist society so dear to the Decadence
movement; and the potential role of his native language in the pursuit of a
Hungarian manner) were soon to be addressed in Bartók's opera, *Duke Bluebeard's Castle*, based on a libretto fashioned by his friend Béla Balasz. Completed
in 1911 four years after Dukas's play, the subject, as the title suggests, is not
only Bluebeard but his castle as a symbolic locus of unspoken or forbidden acts.
The heroine is no longer Ariane but another symbolic figure, Judith (the inspiration for two of Klimt's most luxurious paintings of 1901 and 1909). The sense
of mystery is all pervasive, and in the end there is no escape.

The vocal style of the opera is characterized by the tonic accent of the
Hungarian language, which places the emphasis on the first syllable of each
word, and by a metric style that Bartók himself labeled "parlando-rubato." Its
basis in peasant music is complemented by an affinity with Debussy. But a
comparison with the recitative style of *Pelléas*, which reveals a profusion of
upbeats in Debussy and their total absence in Bartók, dramatizes the accentual
differences based on language and points up Bartók's claim of the "sharpest
possible contrast to the Schoenbergian treatment of vocal parts.[10]

The various changes of mood that coincide with the opening of each door
are symbolized by the orchestra (e.g., a Salome-type trill for the torture chamber;
horn and string tremolo for the flower garden); and by a use of light and color—a
progression from darkness to light and a return to darkness. The associative
tonal structure of the opera,—beginning and ending on a pentatonic F, and
moving to C major with the shower of light at the opening of the fifth door—
reflects the contemporaneous synesthetic experiments of Kandinsky, Schoenberg, and Skriabin (see pp. 157–168). In addition, Bartók's use of contrasting
pentatonic, folk-like material for Bluebeard and chromatic Romantic music for
Judith suggests a reversal of Stravinsky's formula based on Rimsky-Korsakov's
good-evil/diatonic-chromatic dichotomy (see p. 000). Bartók's interest in symbolic allusion also includes a reference to the St. Matthew Passion in his so-
called "blood motif," a detail that confirms Bartók's interest in Baroque music at
this early date (see pp. 403, 407).

With respect to form, the pitch-color motion of the drama, described earlier,
leads to a palindromic movement that also endorses the rondo, a structural
attitude that Bartók was later to explore in abstract instrumental terrain. To
this extent it could be argued that the residual drama inherent in the opera's
formalization was fundamental for much of Bartók's mature career. *Bluebeard's
Castle* is thus one of Bartók's most important early scores, and although his
devotion to Debussy and Strauss is clearly audible, his musical sensitivity to
the aesthetic and literary issues surrounding the libretto is disarming and suggests an emerging individuality. Failing to win a prize in the competition for

which it was originally submitted, its first production was delayed until 1918, and its general acceptance had to await the composer's death.

The story, when read, would seem to have the same sense of pace we note in *Salome*, but it must be conceded that there is a persistent sameness of mood (if not of detail) in Bartók's score, without Dukas's brilliant flashes or any hint of lyric flight such as we hear in Strauss's final apostrophe to the head. The ultimate effect can only be described as hypnotic, inducing an icy chill rather than a blood-curdling scream. In its treatment of the man–woman relationship, which juxtaposes the natural against the corrupt and provides redemption through love–death at the conclusion, Bartók sounds a note that not only he was to pursue elsewhere (*The Wooden Prince* and *The Miraculous Mandarin*), but one that is familiar to the period in such plays as *Salome* and *Lulu*.

The latter two, along with *Bluebeard's Castle*, may be seen as currents of Decadence that served as transition toward Expressionism, while stopping short of it. In *Pandora's Box* (1895), Frank Wedekind (1864–1918) forwarded a brand of explicit sexuality tinged with violence and the grotesque that captured the attention of Europe in the first years of the twentieth century. But while Berg saw one of the earliest private performances of the work in Vienna in 1905, he would wait another 20 years before returning to a consideration of its message of depravity and nobility of the human spirit (see pp. 000–000).

REPERTOIRE

Moreau, *Apparition* (1876), watercolor
Moreau, *Salomé* (1876), painting
Massenet, *Hérodiade* (1881), opera
Klimt, *Judith* I (1901), painting
Klimt, *Judith* II (1909), painting
Ravel, *Shéhérezade* (1903), S, orch
Strauss, *Salome* (1903–05), opera
Picasso, *Salome* (1905), drawing
von Stuck, *Salome* (1906, three versions), painting
Dukas, *Ariane et Barbe-bleu* (1899–1906), opera
Schmitt, *La tragédie de Salomé* (1907–10), ballet
Bartók, *Duke Bluebeard's Castle* (1911), opera
Berg, *Lulu* (1928–35), opera

READING

Stéphane Mallarmé, *Hérodiade* (1864–71).
Gustave Flaubert, *Hérodiade* (1871).
Joris-Karl Huysmans, *A rebours* (Paris, 1884).
Oscar Wilde, *Salome* (1891–92), illustrated by Aubrey Beardsley (1894).
Frank Wedekind, *Pandora's Box* (1895).
Sir Thomas Beecham, *A Mingled Chime* (London, 1944).
Halsey Stevens, *The Life and Music of Béla Bartók* (Oxford, 1953, rev. 1964).
Norman Del Mar, *Richard Strauss* (London, 1962), vol 1, 239–286.
Philippe Jullian, *Dreamers of Decadence* (Paris, 1969; Eng. trans. R. Baldick, New York, 1971).
Alessandra Comini, *Klimt* (New York, 1975).
Béla Bartók, "Harvard Lectures (No. IV)" (1943) in *Béla Bartók Essays*, ed. Benjamin Suchoff (London, 1976), 386.
Carl Schorske, *Fin-de-siècle Vienna* (New York, 1980).
Jan Pasler, "Stravinsky and the Apaches," *The Musical Times* (1982), 403.

CHAPTER 9

SYMBOLIST REVERBERATIONS ABROAD (II): SYNESTHETIC SYMBOLISM

BAUDELAIRE, RIMBAUD, AND HUYSMANS

In Baudelaire's *Correspondances* (c. 1845), the mysteries of the Symbolists, which thrived on equivocation, illusion, and concealment, flourished naturally in the metaphor. The idea was later pursued by Rimbaud in his widely discussed sonnet, "Voyelles" (c. 1875). Here the metaphor gives way to a new brand of simile that places a high premium on abstraction. "Like" not only flirts with "is," but the elements of the sonic-visual equation are nothing but the vowels themselves and pure color.

RIMBAUD, *Voyelles*

A noir, E blanc, I rouge, U vert, O bleu; voyelles,
Je dirai quelque jour vos naissances latentes:
A, noir corset velu des mouches éclatantes
Qui bombinent autour des puanteurs cruelles,

Golfe᾿ d'ombre; E, candeurs des vapeurs et des
    tentes,
Lances des glaciers fiers, rois blancs, frissons
    d'ombelles;
I, pourpres, sang craché, rire des lèvres belles
Dans la colère ou les ivresses pénitentes;

U, cycles, vibrements divins des mers virides,
Paix des pâtis semés d'animaux, paix des rides
Que l'alchimie imprime aux grands fronts
    studieux;

O, suprême Clairon plein des strideurs
    étranges,
Silences traversés des Mondes et des Anges:
—O l'Oméga, rayon violet de Ses Yeux!

Vowels

A black, E white, I red, U green, O blue; vowels,
I shall speak one day of your secret birth:
A, black hairy corset of sparkling flies
Which swoop around cruel smells,

Bays of shadow; E, candor of vapors and
    tents,
Lances of imperious glaciers, white kings,
    shivers of umbels;
I, purple, spat blood, the smile of beautiful lips
In rage or penitent raptures;

U, cycles, divine vibrations of viridian seas,
The peace of pastures strewn with animals, the
    peace of furrows
Which alchemy prints on large studious brows;

O, supreme trumpet full of strange and strident
    sounds,
Silences traversed by Worlds and by Angels:
—O the Omega, the violet beam of Her Eyes!

The notion of spiritual and material correspondences and intrasensory relationships—ideas directly traceable to Swedenborg's *Arcana coelestia* (1749–56) and Goethe's *Farbenlehre* (1805–10)—were to have fascinating repercussions in the prose works of Huysmans (*A rebours*), the theories of Réné Ghil, the orchestral palette of Rimsky-Korsakov, the sound-color dramas of Kandinsky's *Yellow Sound* (1909), Schoenberg's *Die glückliche Hand* (1910–13), Bartók's *Bluebeard's Castle* (1911), and the synesthetic hermetism of Alexander Skriabin's *Prometheus* (1910). In 1909, the Parisian organist Marcel Dupré also indicated in manuscript charts explicit color correspondences to timbre, key, and vowels.[1]

Once again Count Des Esseintes, the hero of Huysmans' *A rebours* and the archetypal dandy of fin-de-siècle Decadence, provides the perfect introduction to a consideration of the variable mysteries of synesthesia in a "Symphonie des liqueurs." Des Esseintes is both hermitic and hermetic. No excess is untried as he creates a private world that by turns bathes in luxury and perversity, in the beautiful and the grotesque. The exquisite but cruel invention of a jeweled tortoise and the odors of spat blood following a trip to the dentist frame the central episode of Chapter Four excerpted here.[2]

> He shut the window again. This quick change, straight from the torrid heat of the room to the biting cold of midwinter had taken his breath away; and curling up beside the fire again, it occurred to him that a drop of spirits would be the best thing to warm him up.
>
> He made his way to the dining-room, where there was a cupboard built into one of the walls containing a row of little barrels, resting side-by-side on tiny sandalwood stands and each broached at the bottom with a silver spigot.
>
> This collection of liqueur casks he called his mouth organ.
>
> A rod could be connected to all the spigots, enabling them to be turned by one and the same movement, so that once the apparatus was in position it was only necessary to press a button concealed in the wainscoting to open all the conduits simultaneously and so fill with liqueur the minute cups underneath the taps.
>
> The organ was then open. The stops labelled 'flute', 'horn', and 'vox angelica' were pulled out, ready for use. Des Esseintes would drink a drop here, another there, playing internal symphonies to himself, and providing his palate with sensations analogous to those which music dispenses to the ear.
>
> Indeed, each and every liqueur, in his opinion, corresponded in taste with the sound of a particular instrument. Dry curaçao, for instance, was like the clarinet with its piercing, velvety note; kümmel like the oboe with its sonorous, nasal timbre; crème de menthe and anisette like the flute, at once sweet and tart, soft and shrill. Then to complete the orchestra there was kirsch, blowing a wild trumpet blast; gin and whisky raising the roof of the mouth with the blare of their cornets and trombones; marc-brandy matching the tubas with its deafening din; while peals of thunder came from the cymbal and the bass drum, which arak and mastic were banging and beating with all their might.
>
> He considered that this analogy could be pushed still further and that string quartets might play under the palatal arch, with the violin represented by an old brandy, choice and heady, biting and delicate; with the viola simulated by rum, which was stronger, heavier, and quieter; with vespetro as poignant, drawn-out, sad, and tender as a violoncello; and with the double-bass a fine old bitter, full-bodied, solid, and dark. One might even form a quintet, if this were thought desirable, by adding a fifth instrument, the harp, imitated to near perfection by the vibrant savour, the clear, sharp, silvery note of dry cumin.
>
> The similarity did not end there, for the music of liqueurs had its own scheme of interrelated tones; thus, to quote only one example, Benedictine represents, so to

speak, the minor key corresponding to the major key of those alcohols which wine-merchants' scores indicate by the name of green Chartreuse.

Once these principles had been established, and thanks to a series of erudite experiments, he had been able to perform upon his tongue silent melodies and mute funeral marches; to hear inside his mouth crème-de-menthe solos and rum-and-vespetro duets.

He even succeeded in transferring specific pieces of music to his palate, following the composer step by step, rendering his intentions, his effects, his shades of expression, by mixing or contrasting related liqueurs, by subtle approximations and cunning combinations.

At other times he would compose melodies of his own, executing pastorals with the sweet blackcurrant liqueur that filled his throat with the warbling song of a nightingale; or with the delicious cacaochouva that hummed sugary bergerets like the *Romances of Estelle* and the *'Ah! vous dirai-je, maman'* of olden days.

But tonight Des Esseintes had no wish to listen to the taste of music; he confined himself to removing one note from the keyboard of his organ, carrying off a tiny cup which he had filled with genuine Irish whiskey.

He settled down in his armchair again and slowly sipped this fermented spirit of oats and barley, a pungent odour of creosote spreading through his mouth.

If we suspect that such a synesthetic fantasy could only have pleased Baudelaire or Rimbaud, it is interesting to observe the fasionableness which Huysman's exercise had achieved at the turn of the century. Misia Sert, patroness and confidant of the most important Parisian artists, recalled the following visit to the poet of the *Chansons de Bilitis*:

> Pierre Louÿs . . . brought several friends home one day to hear this masterpiece—*Pelléas*—played on an upright piano by Debussy himself, who also sang all the parts. I was the only woman. A servant dressed in a white shirt served us cocktails. I had never drunk in my life. On this occasion they concocted a series of liqueurs—yellow, green, red,—which stayed in layers in the glass. I partook of several, stretched out on a chaise longue, transfixed by a larger-than-life Japanese doll, which was facing me. I hardly listened to the words of Maeterlinck. Distracted, only the playing of Debussy touched my heart, and intoxicated by the colors of the cocktails Mélisande became the Japanese doll: I invented a story that had no connection with the miracles that were taking place in the salon that evening.[3]

KANDINSKY AND *DER BLAUE REITER: THE YELLOW SOUND*

The appeal of intrasensory correspondences, not as a reflection of indulgent appetites but of a creative "inner necessity," surfaces clearly in a group of German and Russian artists of the twentieth-century's first decade. Primary among them is Wassily Kandinsky (1866–1944), Russian painter, writer, and father of Expressionism. Born in Moscow, he had gone to Munich by 1896 where he was introduced to the world of Impressionist color and Art Nouveau form. In the next decade he also made the acquaintance of the Fauvists (Matisse, Vlaminck, Dufy), whose vivid use of pure color and insistence on a direct correspondence between expression and form was consequential to his future development. In a watercolor of 1910 he achieved what is considered to be the first nonobjective painting, and simultaneously proposed a theory of abstract art in his classic essay, "Concerning the Spiritual in Art" (1912).

To his pioneering ventures as painter and essayist must be added his contributions as a playwright. These multiple roles Kandinsky held to be complementary and reliant on the same inner vision and creative intuition. The almanac, *Der Blaue Reiter*, which Kandinsky edited with Franz Marc in 1912, is reflective of a group of artists who shared their aesthetic premises, and is an extraordinary compendium of seemingly unrelated materials. Together, Kandinsky and Marc became the rallying point for the avant-garde. Among the many ideas and issues that were forwarded in the journal, the concept of intrasensory correspondences is dramatically illuminated in Kandinsky's play, *The Yellow Sound*, written in 1909 but published in the journal for the first time.[4]

Even more fundamental was Kandinsky's essay, "Concerning the Question of Form," which preached the emerging Expressionist tenet that form in and of itself was not to be deified; that the ideal formal solution could always be guaranteed if it grew from a truthful, inner necessity; that it could be either abstract or realistic; and that, hence, there was no real problem of form. This search for a spiritual inner vision, which in terms of drama had been lucidly expounded by the Expressionist playwright George Kaiser, was to be dedicated to nothing less than the regeneration of man. Toward this end, Kandinsky adopted ingredients of Symbolist synesthetics and Wagnerian *Gesamtkunstwerk*, marrying intrasensory correspondences to the idea of a collaborative art work.

The Yellow Sound, written in 1909, was a demonstration of the dramatic theory contained in the article, "On Stage Composition," which prefaced its first publication in *Der Blaue Reiter* in 1912. Composed of a Prelude and six Pictures, it is a virtually textless drama with the following cast: five giants, vague creatures, tenor (backstage), a child, a man, people in flowing robes, people in tights, and a chorus (backstage). Seemingly without plot, the stage piece is devoted to a search for spiritual ecstasy in a kind of mystical, theosophical vision. The psychological, sonic, and coloristic interplay can be ascertained from a reading of one of the characteristic pictures.

Thomas Hartmann, who contributed an article, "On Anarchy in Music," to *Der Blaue Reiter*, was commissioned by Kandinsky to write the requisite musical score. Long thought to have been lost, it was recently discovered, and in an orchestration by Gunther Schuller presented for the first time in a New York production in February 1982.

WASSILY KANDINSKY, *The Yellow Sound*,[5] Picture 2

> Gradually the blue haze yields to pure, very intense white light. At the back of the stage, a hill quite round, dazzling green and as large as possible.
> The background is violet, moderately bright.
> The music is shrill, violent with repeated A's and B's and B's and A-flats. These single tones are finally swallowed up by loud stormy sounds. Suddenly everything is silent. A pause. Again A and B whimper sorrowfully but also clearly and sharply. This lasts for some time. Then another pause.
> At this moment the background turns a dirty brown. The hill turns a dirty green. Exactly in the center of the hill a black spot of no particular shape appears, sometimes it is distinct, sometimes blurred. As the spot changes the brilliant white light becomes grayer in abrupt stages. To the left on the hill there appears a *large* yellow flower. From a distance it resembles a large bent cucumber. It steadily becomes more brilliant. The stalk is long and thin. Out of the middle of the stalk grows one small, thorny leaf. It points off to one side. A long pause.
>
> Later, the flower rocks very slowly from right to left, *in complete silence*. Still later the leaf begins to move, not with the flower but independently. Still later they

both rock in an uneven tempo. Then, as before, they move separately. A very thin B sounds when the flower moves—a very deep A when the leaf moves. Then they rock together while both notes accompany their movements. The flower trembles violently and then is quite still. But the notes continue to be heard. Now a number of people enter from the left in long, flowing brightly colored robes (some all in blue, or red, or green, etc. None are in yellow). They carry very large white flowers similar to the one on the hill. They crowd together into a tight group and march up to and past the hill. They come to a halt on the right side of the stage and stand tightly bunched. They speak out in mixed voices:

> The flowers cover everything, cover everything, cover everything.
> Close your eyes! Close your eyes!
> We are looking. We are looking.
> Cover the conception with innocence.
> Open your eyes! Open your eyes!
> It is over. It is over.

First they recite all this in unison, as if in ectasy (very clearly). Then they repeat everything as separate individuals: to each other and to the audience in alto, bass, and soprano voices. B is heard with "We are looking, we are looking." A with "It is over, it is over." Here and there voices become passionate and excited. Here and there someone screams as if possessed. Here and there voices become nasal, sometimes reciting very slowly and sometimes with furious rapidity. In the first case a dull red light suddenly obscures the whole stage. In the second, darkness alternates with a dazzling blue light. In the third, everything suddenly turns a pale gray (all the colors vanish!). However, the yellow flower is brighter than ever.

Gradually the orchestra begins to play and soon the music drowns out the voices. The music then becomes agitated and shifts back and forth from fortissimo to pianissimo. The light brightens somewhat and now the colors of the people can be made out vaguely. Tiny figures move over the hill, from right to left very slowly. They are a dull gray-green. They look straight ahead. The moment the first tiny figure appears the yellow flower shudders convulsively. Suddenly it disappears, and just as suddenly all the white flowers turn yellow.

The crowd now moves as if in a trance to the footlights while gradually dispersing.

The music fades away and the above recitative is heard again. People now stand about half enraptured. They turn around. Suddenly they notice the tiny figures which continue to move in an endless procession over the hill. The people turn away and make several quick steps toward the footlights, stop, turn around and then remain absolutely motionless, transfixed. Finally, they violently free themselves from their paralysis, throw away their flowers which seem to be saturated with blood and run in a tight group to the footlights. Suddenly everything is dark.

SCHOENBERG AND *DER BLAUE REITER*

In the article, "On Stage Composition," which introduces *The Yellow Sound* in *Der Blaue Reiter*, Kandinsky offers a rationale for his play, reflecting a continuing fascination for the Symbolist notion of correspondences and a veneration of the Wagnerian world-idea made manifest in an all-encompassing *Gesamtkunstwerk*. His admiration for Wagner does not prevent him, however, from taking issue with the idea of the leitmotif or from suggesting that Wagner had only hinted at a proposition that was now ripe for refinement and extension.

Many of these points of view were reflected in *Die glückliche Hand* (1910–13) of Arnold Schoenberg, whose intimate connection with Kandinsky's circle is made clear through the inclusion in *Der Blaue Reiter* of his own *Herzgewächse*, op, 20, as well as two songs of his pupils, Berg's "Warm die Lüfte," op. 2, no. 4, and Webern's "Ihr tratet zu dem Herde," op. 4, no. 5. Also included was an article by Schoenberg entitled "The Relationship to the Text," which stresses the need for the composer to move beyond a simple illustration of the text to a more profound vision of the whole wherein a spiritual identity of word and tone takes place.

DIE GLÜCKLICHE HAND.   Composed to a text by the composer, *Die glückliche Hand* includes a chorus of six women, another of six men, a Monster, a Man, a Woman, and a Gentleman. As Egon Wellesz has observed, the work is largely symolic in aim, and it has been suggested that the anonymous Man of the drama may refer not only to the Artist in general but to Schoenberg specifically; that the Monster is the Artist's ego; the seductress Woman, the bitch goddess Success; and the Gentleman, the commercially successful purveyor of Viennese popular music.[6]

The focus on a single character places the libretto in the company of *Erwartung* (written August–September, 1909), both of which antedate the first Expressionist "Ich-Drama" of Sorge written in 1911, where the autobiographical element prevails. Here, in the center of the work, the unidentified Man kindles the wrath of a group of artisans by creating a diadem set with precious stones with a single hammer blow. The identification of the central character with Schoenberg can no more be escaped than the association of the Woman with his wife, who both in real life and in the drama goes away with the Gentleman. In the penultimate scene she returns to crush him with a boulder, and a frame for the work is provided by the six-man, six-woman chorus placed at the beginning and end of the work as commentator in the style of a Greek tragedy. The suffering Artist-Hero, in receiving a goblet from the Woman, recalls *Tristan*, and the use of a bloody sword and the splitting of the anvil in casting his diadem recalls *Siegfried*. The worker's grotto, "somewhere between a mechanic's workshop and a goldsmith shop," also prefigures the symbolic locus of Hindemith's *Cardillac* of 1926.

On a musical level, Schoenberg associates the cello with the Man (Schoenberg himself was a cellist), the Woman with the violin, and the ostinato-like chord of the introduction with the gazes of the chorus members' faces bathed in a greenish light. About a dozen paintings by Schoenberg entitled "Gaze" or "Vision" (see Figure 10.3) and an even more numerous group of self-portraits dating from this period provide a clarifying testimony to the Expressionist symbolism of *Die glückliche Hand*.

The utilization of a small body of thematically perceptible leitmotifs—as in most works of the period buried deep within the texture of the work and yielding themselves only to the most diligent analysis—is in keeping not with an oft-cited nonrepetitive abstraction but with a submerged all-encompassing content which, reflecting Kandinsky's view of the question of form, was only to be intuited. Although musical ideas proliferate continuously throughout the work, Schoenberg's use of the ostinato (brief melodic figures, tremolos, and sustained or repeated chords) is helpful not only in announcing the opening and close of each of the four scenes, but also in providing a periodic stability to the developing maze of musical materials. The oscillating triplets of harp and tympani over the five-note chord of the violas and cellos at the beginning of the work (Ex. 9.1)

Example 9.1. Schoenberg, *Die glückliche Hand*, mm. 1–4.

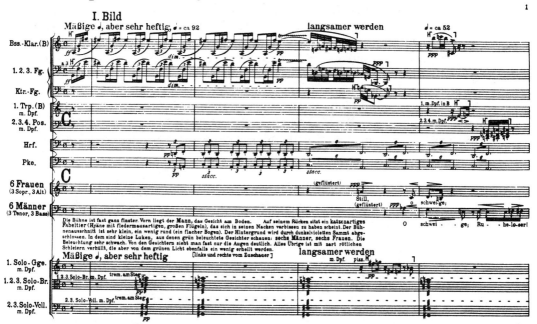

Used by permission of Belmont Music Publishers.

transcend their familiar function in Bruckner's symphonic introductions (or Schoenberg's *Variations for Orchestra*, op. 31) and are sustained throughout the course of the entire first scene, recalling the extended pedal chord of Schoenberg's op. 16, no. 1 (see Ex. 2.8a). The exact return of these opening figures in all parameters (pitch, rhythm, color, and dynamics) at the beginning of the final scene dramatizes their potential as a formal component as well as their clear relationship to the oscillating chords that were later to articulate the opening and close of the several acts of Berg's *Wozzeck*. Finally, the repeated figure of the bass clarinet and bassoons is more than a little reminiscent of the anxiety motifs of Herodias (Ex. 8.2, Nos. 12, 12a) in Strauss's *Salome*.

The common basis that Kandinsky and Schoenberg shared in their exploration of the emancipation of colors, forms, and dissonances, in the dissolution of the portrayed object and tonality, respectively, has been seen as rooted in a

> will to express the primordial, to get past the impediments of artistic tradition in order to discover once more the elemental origin of art. This explains why so many artists were interested in the reduction of artistic means to their smallest components, and the return to primary forms, with a predilection for the archaic, primitive and anarchic.[7]

The specific appeal of primitive art to the *Blaue Reiter* group (see pp. 212–213) corroborates the notion that "Primitivism" was no narrow aesthetic and was in fact detectable in varying degrees throughout a broad creative spectrum which, though sometimes national in tone, was supported by widely divergent creative urges.

Beyond the story, which in some respects must also have been influenced by Kokoschka's *Mörder, Hoffnung der Frauen* of 1907, the meticulous directions for coordination of stage directions and lighting with the musical score is unparalleled in the history of music; the length of these elaborate directions far exceeds the actual spoken text of the libretto. Conceived contemporaneously with Kandinsky's *Yellow Sound* (1909) and Skriabin's *Prometheus* (1908–10), it complements both of them even as it is totally individual and unlike either. The renowned "Wind-Light-Tone Crescendo" following the text "Here is the way to create jewels" is Schoenberg's own version of spiritual exaltation, which he was to pursue in a more mystical and less Expressionist fashion in *Jakobsleiter*.

The Man	Der Mann
"Here is the way to create jewels."	"So schafft man Schmuck."

The workers' gestures become menacing again, then scornful; they counsel together and appear to be planning an attack against the Man. Laughing, the Man throws his jewels to them. They prepare to jump him. He has turned around and does not see them.

He stoops over to pick up his sword. As he touches it with his left hand, the grotto again becomes dark.

Every trace of the workshop disappears behind the dark curtain. As it becomes dark, a wind springs up: at first sighing faintingly, then steadily and threateningly swelling louder (along with the music).

Along with this wind-crescendo is a light-crescendo. It commences with a dim red light (from above) which changes into brown and then to a muddy green. Next it evolves into a dark blue-gray, followed by violet. This splits into an intense dark red which becomes increasingly brighter and more glaring until, after attaining a blood-red, it is mixed more and more with orange and then bright yellow until a glaring yellow light alone remains and is projected from all sides onto the second grotto.

This grotto was already revealed at the beginning of the light-crescendo and (although more weakly than the rest of the stage) both within and without underwent the same range of lighting changes. Now it too streams with yellow light.

The Man has projected this crescendo of light and storm as though both arose from within him. First (the red light) he looks at his hand; it then sinks, visibly exhausted; slowly (muddy green) his eyes become excited. His agitation grows; his limbs tighten convulsively; he stretches out both arms (blood red); his eyes bulge from his head and his mouth opens in terror. When the yellow light appears, his head must appear as though it will explode. The Man does not turn toward the grotto, but stares straight ahead.

When it is totally bright, the storm ceases and the yellow light turns quickly into a delicate blue light.

The grotto is empty for a moment in this lighting. Then with a quick yet easy gait the Woman enters from the left. She is dressed as in the second scene, only the left upper half of her dress is missing so that this portion of her upper body down to her hip is totally naked. When she comes to the middle of the grotto she remains standing and for awhile looks searchingly about. Then she stretches her arms toward the Gentleman, who at precisely that moment becomes visible at the right hand side of the grotto. He has the piece of clothing which was missing in his right hand and beckons her with it.

In the mean time the Man's desperation grows. He bends his fingers into claws, presses his arms to his body, bends his knees, and flexes his upper body backward. As the Gentleman signals with the scrap of clothing, the Man turns about with an impetuous jerk and sinks to his knees, then on his hands, and attempts on all fours to reach the grotto but cannot.

The Man	Der Mann
"You, you, you are mine . . .	"Du, du, du bist mein . . .
you were mine . . .	du warst mein . . .
she was mine . . . "	sie war mein . . ."[8]

Schoenberg's libretto, cast in four scenes entitled *Bild* (picture) like Kandinsky's *The Yellow Sound*, was completed by June 1910, but as the latter work of 1909 was not published until 1912, Schoenberg may not have read it. The contention, however, that the two artists were aware of each other, independently formulating highly similar aesthetic approaches, is sealed by the knowledge that an excerpt of Schoenberg's *Harmonielehre* (1911), which appeared in a journal of 1910, is discussed and praised by Kandinsky in his highly significant "Concerning the Spiritual in Art" of the same year. Kandinsky proposed therein a specific correlation between colors and emotional states and even associative instrumental timbres (e.g., yellow = trumpet fanfares). While endorsing Kandinsky's timbral associations with only a fleeting precision in the work as a whole, Schoenberg's Wind-Light-Sound crescendo is a virtual demonstration of the emotion-color tables in Kandinsky's "The Spiritual in Art," both moving from a state of motionless morbidity (brown, green, violet) through a state of excitement (shades of red) to a climax in orange and yellow (which Kandinsky associated with insanity) and a final repose in a mild bluish vapor (celestial exhaltation). Seen on one level as an expression of jealous feelings about the Woman and the Gentleman, on another it is an ascension through pain to a kind of transcendental release. While the work has rarely been performed and the libretto today appears dated, if not primitively executed, a knowledge of the aesthetic behind it can help tune the listener to a fuller appreciation of residual values and their relationship to other currents of the time.

HERZGEWÄCHSE. Immediately following Kandinsky's play in *Der Blaue Reiter* is a facsimile of Schoenberg's *Herzgewächse*, which was specially commissioned for the almanac. Maeterlinck's "Foliage of the Heart," set by Schoenberg to an extraterrestrial ensemble of harp, harmonium, and celesta, paints a luxuriant picture of entwined plants from which only a single lily escapes upward to the light in mystical prayer. Although the place of the initial publication of this allegory of the human soul would seem to secure its relationship to an emerging Expressionist aesthetic, its visionary-theosophical mood clearly illuminates the angle from which German artists approached a French symbolist text and the consequences of the aesthetic for artists of non-Gallic origins. Structurally the piece is clearly mirrored by the vocal writing, which in the first two stanzas moves recitative-like in the middle and lower ranges. Beginning with the middle of the third stanza, however, broad lines of great lyric beauty begin their ascension, reaching high into the stratosphere (f''' sung *pppp*) at the words "mystiches Gebet." Given the difficulties of the vocal part and of finding a genuine harmonium with the numerous color registers called for by the composer, it is little wonder that this priceless gem is seldom performed.

Arnold Schoenberg, *Herzgewächse,* op. 20

Sous la cloche de cristal bleu	'Neath the azure crystal bell	Meiner müden Sehnsucht blaues Glas
De mes lasses mélancolies,	Of my listless melancholy	deckt den alten unbestimmten Kummer,
Mes vagues douleurs abolies	All my formless sorrows slowly	dessen ich genas,
S'immobilisent peu à peu:	Sink to rest, and all is well;	und der nun erstarrt in seinem Schlummer.
Végétations de symboles,	Symbols all, the plants entwine:	Sinnbildhaft ist seiner Blumen Zier:
Nénufars mornes des plaisirs,	Waterlilies, flowers of pleasure,	Mancher Freuden düstre Wasser-Rose,
Palmes lentes de mes désirs,	Palms desirous, slow with leisure,	Palmen der Begier,
Mousses froides, lianes molles.	Frigid mosses, pliant vine.	weiche Schlinggewächse, kühle Moose,
Seul, un lys érige d'entre eux,	'Mid them all a lily only,	eine Lilie nur in all dem Flor,
Pâle et rigidement débile,	Pale and fragile and unbending,	bleich und starr in ihrer Kränklichkeit,
Son ascension immobile	Imperceptibly ascending	richtet sich empor
Sur les feuillages douloureux,	In that place of leafage lonely	über all dem Blattgeword'nen Leid,
Et dans les lueurs qu'il épanche	Like a moon the prisoned air	licht sind ihre Blätter anzuschauen,
Comme une lune, peu à peu,	Fills with glimmering light wherethro'	weissen Mondesglanz sie um sich sät,
Élève vers le cristal bleu	Rises to the crystal blue,	zum Krystall dem blauen
Sa mystique prière blanche.	White and mystical, its prayer.	sendet sie ihr mystisches Gebet.

—Maurice Maeterlinck
Serres chaudes (1889)

English verse
by Bernard Miall, 1915

German trans. used
by permission of
Belmont Music Publishers.

SKRIABIN AND *DER BLAUE REITER: PROMETHEUS*

Nineteenth-century Russia had seen not only the beginnings of the search for a national music, but in its traditional connections with the West, and France in particular, it had manifested in the last decades of the century an awareness of the most avant-garde artistic modes of expression. This proposition is important in understanding not only how a Stravinsky could emanate from Russian soil, but also the position of an enigmatic figure like Alexander Skriabin (1872–1915).

As the composer of a virtuosic piano literature, an indebtedness to Chopin has been routinely claimed for Skriabin; indeed in many of the figures, both melodic and accompanimental, the relationship is undeniable. Although Skriabin's harmonic style may in part be seen to stem from his devotion to the Polish master as well, it is by common consent the arena in which he defined his personality most vividly.

Overriding everything, however, is a megalomania that is incontestable. The orchestral tone poem *Prometheus* is an expression of his belief in a cataclysmic world event that would lead to the regeneration of humanity. Such a visionary attitude sprang from his philosophical studies, which were reasonably superficial but which included Nietzsche and Wagner, Vladimir Solovyov for his synthetic world-view, and Madame Blavatsky whose mystical theosophy was popular among many artistic intellectuals of the time. An additional catalytic force behind his development was a group of Russian symbolist poets, including Balmont and Ivanov.[9]

The transfigurative notions of a world spinning toward a higher principle beyond materialism common to most of these poets was also at the heart of Solovyov's philosophy, which Skriabin had known earlier. The conjunction of these forces was crucial to his lifelong ambition to create an ultimate masterwork, to be entitled *Mysterium* and to be performed in an Indian temple in a regenerative coming together of all the arts and all the senses. Sound, color, smell, and bodily motion, involving all witnesses (there would be no audience, only participants), would be put in the service of creative synthesis.

While the work remained only partially sketched at his death, Skriabin's *Prometheus* of 1908–1910 is representative of his musical and philosophical orientation rooted in the world of mythology. Through his gift of fire to the earth, the legendary Prometheus had been the savior of the world. But as with all saviors, a price was to be paid, and as the fire had been stolen from Olympus in defiance of Zeus, Prometheus was chained to a rock and his liver torn at daily by an eagle until his ultimate release by Hercules. It does not require much imagination to read Skriabin for Prometheus, his musical creations for the gift of fire (the subtitle of the tone poem is "Poem of Fire"), and his personal punishment and final salvation as analogous to the achievement of Nirvana following cosmic devastation.

The appeal of Skriabin's *Prometheus* to the *Blaue Reiter* group is made clear through the inclusion of an article in their journal of 1912 that provided an exegesis of the work written by Skriabin's friend Sabaneyev. He announces mystical exaltation through a synthesis of the arts as the composition's principal theme and provides crucial information with respect to Skriabin's personal vision of sound–color correspondence.

Skriabin had initially been introduced to the idea of synesthetic relationships between music and color by Rimsky-Korsakov in 1902, but his equations, given below, are his own and are markedly different from the creator of *Sheherazade* and *The Golden Cockerel* except for the common association which they attributed to D and yellow:

C	Red	F-sharp	Bright blue
G	Orange-pink	D-flat	Violet
D	Yellow	A-flat	Purple
A	Green	E-flat	Dark, steely blue
E	Azure	B-flat	Blue-gray
B	Whitish-blue	F	Dark red

The relation to Madame Blavatsky's synesthetic tone-color charts is, however, more direct—Skriabin's color wheel moving in a circle of fifths instead of diatonically stepwise.

In addition, Skriabin's work is founded on a limited pitch content based on an agglomeration of the higher partials of the overtone series (C, C, G, C, E, G, Bb, C, D, E, F#, G, A, Bb, etc.) prominent among which are the flat seventh and augmented fourth. Capable of being spelled horizontally or vertically, its classic harmonic alignment emphasizes a quartal structure and is traditionally referred to as the "mystic chord."

Example 9.2. Skriabin's "Mystic Chord."

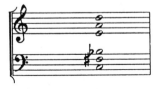

While Sabanayev's fourth-chord overtone theory regarding the genesis of Skriabin's mystic chord lays claim to a powerful locus for its initial presentation, more recent discussions by V. P. Dernova (1968) and Jay Reise (1983) have emphasized its fundamental associations with whole-tone (including French Sixth) and octatonic structures.[10] Related harmonic ideas had been evolving in numerous earlier works by Debussy (see pp. 77, 95), Berg (op. 2, no. 2), and Ravel (see p. 111), and the "mystic chord" itself had already appeared in Skriabin's Fifth Sonata for piano of 1907. There its appearance was incidental; in *Prometheus* it is not only fundamental but all-pervasive.

Various transpositions of the mystic chord account for the changes in color. The root of these transpositions, regardless of the inversion, is indicated in the color-keyboard part (*tastiera per luce*) printed in the score at the top of each system. The composer thus provides a simultaneous color-harmonic analysis of the work's progress. The keyboard, of course, activates no sound but was intended to trigger colors allied to the root color of the momentary version of the "mystic chord." Actually, there are two voices in the *tastiera per luce* part: The faster moving one indicates the root of the "mystic chord," while the slower moving one, which remains static for long periods of time, progresses roughly in a whole-tone scale from F# through C (dividing the octave in half through its tritone and symbolizing earth) to F# (heaven). The piece ends on an F#-major triad (celestial blue), the only triad of the piece. Obviously it is the interplay of the two color voices that determines the color that was to be projected at any given time and that guaranteed the kaleidoscopic range of hues.

While many of the details of Skriabin's work appear fantastic and have rarely if ever found totally satisfactory expression, they are more in tune with the works of other contemporary artists than is generally supposed. The hazy metrics are not too distant from Debussy, and the harmonic stasis is directly relatable to Schoenberg's op. 16, no. 3. Even Stravinsky's *Zvezdoliki* (more properly the "Starry-Faced One" than the French title, "Le roi des étoiles") for male choir and orchestra and written in 1911–12 in the period following the first performance of *Prometheus* in Moscow exhibits a theosophical text by Balmont which is a perfect expression of Delville's cover for the first edition of the latter work (Figure 9.1). And its richly chromatic harmony is more than marginally in tune with Skriabin, a composer whose music, together with that of Debussy, Stravinsky admitted to playing exclusively during the period of its composition.

Figure 9.1. Theosophist Jean Delville's cover for *Prometheus*.
Courtesy of Russischer Musikerverlag, GmbH (Berlin, Moscow).

Skriabin's final completed opus, the five preludes of op. 74, achieve a genuine atonality, and many have speculated on his contributions to music had he lived longer.

Although *The Yellow Sound, Die glückliche Hand*, and *Prometheus* form the most intimate link in both philosophy and time, the subscription to sound-color synesthesia in the visionary-apocolyptic works of Olivier Messiaen and the rejuvenation of the light-sound show in many multimedia works of the 1960s may properly be regarded as a natural legacy. Even in Skriabin's native Russia, the *Prometheus* score has received an updated treatment in Shchedrin's *Poetoria* of 1968. Subtitled a "Concerto for poet accompanied by a woman's voice, mixed chorus and symphony orchestra," the work sets a text by A. Voznesensky. Beginning with a solo contralto intoning the vowels "A" and "O" against the simple accompaniment of a flute, the orchestra makes its entrance on a shimmering twelve-note chord which soon leads to the appearance of a part marked *"Luce"* in the score. Notated in two voices (two solid lines in changing colors) without staff, the work begins with a brilliant blue and proceeds through a spectrum of orange/yellow, blue/orange, violet, green, etc. ending on green/

yellow. Lacking any explanation in the score of a possible association between the designated colors and stipulated pitches, one is obliged, as with *Prometheus*, to divine their true significance elsewhere. Further evidence of interest in the Kandinsky-Schoenberg-Skriabin alliance amongst present-day Soviet composers is provided in the score of Alfred Schnitke's *Der gelbe Klang* of 1973, which interprets Kandinsky's play in a forty-minute work for pantomime, nine musicians, choir (or tape), and light projection. With the appeal of synesthetic equations reaching to such diverse corners—both geographically and philosophically—the concept, for all its subjectivity, must be seen as more fundamental to the creative impulse than its surface description or any body of theory might suggest.

REPERTOIRE

Kandinsky, *Der gelbe Klang (The Yellow Sound)* (1909)
Schoenberg, *Die glückliche Hand* (1910–13)
Skriabin, *Prometheus* (1908–10)
Stravinsky, *Zvezdoliki* (1911–12)
Messiaen, *Couleurs de la cité celeste* (1963)
Shchedrin, *Poetoria* (1968)
Schnitke, *Der gelbe Klang* (1973)

READING

The Blaue Reiter Almanac, ed. by W. Kandinsky and F. Marc (Munich, 1912; English trans. H. Falkenstein, 1974), including:
    Arnold Schoenberg, "The Relationship to the Text," 90–102.
    Thomas von Hartmann, "On Anarchy in Music," 113–118.
    Wassily Kandinsky, "On the Question of Form," 147–187.
    Leonid Sabaneyev, "Skriabin's 'Prometheus'," 127–140.
    Wassily Kandinsky, "The Yellow Sound," 210–224.
Igor Stravinsky and Robert Craft, *Conversations* (Garden City, N.Y., 1959), 54.
Igor Stravinsky and Robert Craft, *Memories and Commentaries* (Garden City, N. Y., 1960), 64, 78.
Varvara P. Dernova, *Garmoniya Scryabina* (Leningrad, 1968).
Fabian Bowers, *Scriabin* (Tokyo, 1969).
Victor Miesel, ed., *Voices of German Expressionism* (Engelwood Cliffs, N. J., 1970): Wassily Kandinsky, "The Problem of Form," 45; *The Yellow Sound*, 137.
Henry-Louis de la Grange, "Prometheus Unbound," *Music and Musicians*, xx.5 (1972), 34.
Fabian Bowers, *The New Scriabin: Enigma and Answers* (New York, 1973).
John C. Crawford, "*Die glückliche Hand*: Schoenberg's Gesamtkunstwerk," *Musical Quarterly*, lx (1974), 583.
Hugh Macdonald, *Skryabin* (London, 1978).
Vera Stravinsky and Robert Craft, *Stravinsky in Pictures and Documents* (New York, 1978), 63.
Malcolm Brown, "Skriabin and Russian 'Mystic' Symbolism," *19th Century Music*, iii.1 (1979), 42–51.
Jelena Hahl-Koch, ed., *Arnold Schoenberg/Wassily Kandinsky: Letters, Pictures and Documents* (1980), Eng. trans. John C. Crawford (London, 1984), 133–70.
Jay Reise, "Late Skriabin: Some Principles Behind the Style, *19th Century Music*, vi.3 (1983), 220–31.
Hannelore Gerlach, ed., *Fünfzig sowjetische Komponisten* (Leipzig, 1984): "Schnittke," 360–371; "Shchedrin," 383–407.
Pierre Boulez, "Kandinsky and Schoenberg" in *Orientations* (Cambridge, Mass., 1986), 344–45. Originally published as "Parallèles" in a special number ("Hommage à Wassily Kandsinky") of *XXe Siècle*, No. 27 (December 1966), 98.

PART 3

EMBLEMS OF CRISIS: 1909–1914

The ambiguities that [*Pierrot lunaire*] contains and Schoenberg's bold ideas about the relation between words and music represent an inexhaustible wellspring for the future.

The *Rite of Spring* serves as a point of reference to all who seek to establish the birth certificate of what is still called 'contemporary' music. A kind of manifesto work, somewhat in the same way and probably for the same reasons as Picasso's *Demoiselles d'Avignon*, it has not ceased to engender, first, polemics, then, praise, and, finally, the necessary clarification . . . In the same way that the name of Schoenberg remains identified primarily with *Pierrot lunaire*, the name of Stravinsky remains attached to the *Rite of Spring*.

—Pierre Boulez, *Orientations* (1983), 337, 362.

CHAPTER 10

EXPRESSIONISM: THE PATH TO *PIERROT*

BACKGROUNDS

In our introductory survey of the musical scene in Vienna and Paris from roughly 1885 to 1915, various aesthetic issues were put forward in the discussion of the principal composers and their development. In retrospect, however, it is inevitable that a limited number of works tend to stand out as emblematic of the more general crisis that seemed to suggest the final overthrow of the Romantic Age. No such event ever took place, of course, but the degree to which the Romantic Agony lingered on is seldom dwelt on in the writing of the history of twentieth-century music. Regardless of one's preferences, it is well to remember that Hanson's *Symphony No. 2* ("Romantic," 1930), Barber's *Adagio for Strings* (1936), Rachmaninov's *Symphonic Dances* (1940), and Richard Strauss's *Four Last Songs* (1948)—all staples of the concert hall—were written at a time, in the fourth and fifth decades of the century, when post-Romanticism was supposedly long since dead.

It is nonetheless traditional and defensible to search for that small cluster of works that can be conveniently seen as a watershed between Romantic and Modern values. World War I is frequently discussed as the temporal point of turning, but though its personal and psychological impact on the arts was enormous, the classic emblems of the musical crisis for the early twentieth century were written just as the war clouds were beginning to gather in the immediately preceding half decade, 1909–1914.

Numerous foreshadowings of a new musical order in German speaking countries have already been considered in the works of Mahler, Strauss, Schoenberg, Berg, and Webern. Indeed, the discussion of Kandinsky, Schoenberg, and the *Blaue Reiter* group has literally taken us to the brink of Expressionism. Let us now consider the term, already invoked on previous occasions, and attempt a clarification in relation to two works of Schoenberg written during the period in question: *Erwartung* (1909) and *Pierrot lunaire* (1912).

As a background to such an inquiry it is well to remember that the subordination of form and nature to emotional and visionary experience, discussed at length in relation to *Die glückliche Hand*, is central to the Expressionist attitude, and has its most direct antecedents in the visual world in the works of Van Gogh and Munch. Though the word *expressionisme* is French and the concept of "self-expression" was initially introduced in the studio of Gustave Moreau followed by his pupil Henri Matisse, the bold use of color by the "Fauvists," while occasionally dubbed Expressionists by the Germans, was too refined for the taste of the *Brücke* and *Blaue Reiter* groups. The first of these, which together are traditionally seen to define the movement, began in Dresden in 1905, in the same city and year that saw the first production of Strauss's *Salome;* the second formed in Munich in 1912.

While the initital definitions of Expressionism tended to be made in the world of painting and literature, it is more than a convenience that a figure like Arnold Schoenberg, whose relation to the *Blaue Reiter* group has already been detailed, was a painter and playwright as well as a composer. The sense of easy access from one mode of creation to another was also increased by the notion of *correspondences* in search of an inner vision. The spiritual bias attendant on all Expressionist urges echoed more than a personal ego, involved collective aspirations that transcended the burgeoning national conscience of the nineteenth century, and sought a union of the people in a higher cosmic awareness. It is a paradox that this essentially Expressionist doctrine was in time taken over by the Nazis, who then ultimately suppressed Expressionist art as degenerate.[1]

If the principal voices of Symbolism were French, then the codifying forces of Expressionism were German. In neither case, however, are the compartments watertight, and the early influence of the Symbolists on the emerging Expressionists is visible in a work such as Kandinsky's *Night: "Melisande"* (1907) (Figure 10.1), where the subject matter is on the edge of being dissolved in an abstraction of dots. Though by 1910 Kandinsky would achieve a totally nonrepresentational art reflective of his "inner visions," it is not only the tendency toward abstraction that identifies the new aesthetic, but also an attendant emotionalism that is nocturnal, by turns visionary or hallucinatory, and

Figure 10.1. Wassiy Kandinsky, *Night: "Melisande"* (1907).
Courtesy Städtische Galerie, Munich, and VAGA, New York © ADAGP, Paris/VAGA, New York, 1985.

marked by distortions that frequently signal not the world of dreams (no matter how exotic) but of nightmares (Munch's *The Scream*, Schoenberg's *Erwartung*) (Figure 10.2). In the preface to his *Dream Play* of 1901, Strindberg stated how he attempted

> to imitate the disconnected but seemingly logical form of the dream. Anything may happen; everything is possible and probable. Time and space do not exist. On an insignificant background of reality, imagination designs and embroiders novel patterns; a medley of memories, experiences, free fancies, absurdities and improvisations. The characters split, double, multiply, vanish, solidify, blur, clarify. But one consciousness reigns above them all—that of the dreamer; and before it there are no secrets, no incongruities, no scruples, no laws. There is neither judgment nor exoneration, but merely narration. And as the dream is mostly painful, rarely pleasant, a note of melancholy and of pity with all living things runs right through the wobbly tale. Sleep, the liberator, plays often a dismal part, but when the pain is at its worst, the awakening comes and reconciles the sufferer with reality, which, however distressing it may be, nevertheless seems happy in comparison with the torments of the dream.[2]

In the projection of the Dream become literature, the Expressionists endorsed a note of subjectivism, which rejected the elements of plausibility and good taste formerly associated with the well-made play. Yet its antecedents in Symbolism and Romanticism are as visible as its kinship with other movements on the international scene such as Cubism, Surrealism, and Futurism, all of

Figure 10.2. Edvard Munch, *The Scream* (1895), woodcut.

which distorted reality in an attempt to extract essential truths. While the movement as a whole lacked a program and had a generally iconoclastic ring, the intensification of German Romantic Naturalism provided an emotional directness that well served the early Expressionist playwrights, painters, and composers in the formation of a new vocabulary. In addition, we note an element of exaggeration with an attendant interest in questions of sexuality, which linked effortlessly with the fin-de-siècle movement of the Decadence. Finally, the myth, populated by types larger than life, served both a waning Wagnerism (*Gurrelieder*) and an emerging Expressionism (Kokoschka's *Mörder, Hoffnung der Frauen*). Yet, if ingredients can be identified that help to promote the idea of a natural stylistic transition, it is fundamental to stress that the distortion so closely identified with Expressionism stems from its proximity to the dream transported well beyond the horrors of Poe or Mary Shelly's *Frankenstein*. And however much the synesthetic equations of Kandinsky's *Yellow Sound* and Schoenberg's *Die glückliche Hand* owe to the French Symbolists, their landscape has now been transformed into the world of the incubus inhabited by giants, monsters, and seductresses. In such a metamorphosis, further pressured by the psychoanalytic explorations of the age of Freud, the world of Expressionism is born.

SCHOENBERG, *ERWARTUNG*

Kokoschka's Mörder, *Hoffnung der Frauen* (Murderer, *The Women's Hope*) was first performed at the Garden Theater of the Vienna Kunstschau on July 4, 1909, and Schoenberg's *Erwartung* was created at white heat later that summer during the seventeen days between August 27 and September 12. It is possible that Schoenberg may have seen Kokoschka's production, and improbable that he would not have at least known about it. But while the two plays have much in common, the social and psychological note that is struck in the works of virtually all Viennese artists of the time rested firmly on a base prepared by Ibsen, Strindberg, Zola, and Baudelaire, just as the appearance of Freud's *The Interpretation of Dreams* of 1900 fixed a point of view much discussed in the immediately preceding decades. The one-act play coupled with anonymity of character, seen earlier in Strindberg and Wedekind, appears simultaneously with Schoenberg's *Erwartung* (1909) and *Die glückliche Hand* (1910–13) in the plays of Kandinsky (*The Yellow Sound*, 1909) and Kokoschka (*The Women's Hope*, 1907).

In spite of these attributes, which it shares with the current Expressionist theater, *Erwartung* can also be seen purely as a psychoanalytic case study of feminine hysteria, a modish reflection of Otto Weininger's study of women's sexuality, *Geschlecht und Charakter*, which had provoked a scandal on its appearance in 1903. Weininger's theories, which forwarded the notion of the creative, rational "masculine" in opposition to the irrational, destructive "feminine," pushed the notion of the *femmes fatales* beyond Klimt's erotic, if deadly, *Judith I* and *Salome*, and promoted a view more in keeping with Wedekind's *Lulu*, a figure who brings the premonition of society's ultimate doom at the mercy of destructive feminine life forces. In a dramatic and troubled exit, Weininger (1880–1903) committed suicide at the age of 23 in the house where Beethoven had died.

Even more directly, Pappenheim's libretto mirrors her firsthand knowledge of psychoanalysis gained not only as a medical student in Vienna but through her relative, Bertha Pappenheim, who was the model for Freud's renowned case-history "Anna O."[3] Just as *Erwartung* carries a symbolic message characteristic of *Die glückliche Hand* and other classic Expressionist pieces, the namelessness of its sole character continues to proclaim a universality beyond time and place.

Tosca (1900) and *Madame Butterfly* (1904), both written in the same decade, seem light years away, and indeed *verismo* has been clearly abandoned for the world of the mind attended by high anxiety and neurosis. If, as some have suggested, Strauss's awareness of *Tosca*'s success had led him to attempt an equally compelling theater in *Salome* (1903–05) and *Elektra* (1906–08; premiered January 25, 1909), the differences not only with respect to musical and dramatic values but especially the psychic terrain that he explored provided a natural preparation for Schoenberg's largely unprecedented accomplishment. As Robert Craft has put it,

> The woman (her namelessness proves that Schoenberg was not interested in her but in an emotional state) is the Isolde of fifty years later and still the type of the *ewig weibliche*, but Isolde has had a nervous breakdown.[4]

The genesis of her cry for help at the climax of the opera can be persuasively traced to Kundry in *Parsifal*,[5] though nearer to hand was Schoenberg's own extravagant vocalism at the close of the third movement of his Second String Quartet, where the agony of the word "Liebe" is directly equatable with "Hilfe." In the latter, however, an expressive legato is exchanged for an atomized

Example 10.1. Wagner, *Parsifal*, Act II, scene 2.

Example 10.2. Schoenberg, *String Quartet No. 2*, Mvt. 3, mm. 64–66.

Used by permission of Belmont Music Publishers.

Example 10.3. Schoenberg, *Erwartung*, mm. 188–193.

Used by permission of Belmont Music Publishers.

reflection of its fragmentary, Expressionist text ("Lord God . . . what is it? . . . Help!"). The preparation for this moment is masterful. The Woman's initial discovery of the body of her lover, "Das ist er!" ("It is he!"), is followed by an

Example 10.4. Schoenberg, *Erwartung*, m. 153.

Used by permission of Belmont Music Publishers.

orchestral shriek worthy of accompanying Munch's disquietingly cadaverous portrait (p. 172). But a new mood of quiet reverie immediately takes over as the Woman wishes the head of her lover away in the wash of the moonlight. In time, her mind returns to the former reality ("It's still there"), and the musical pace begins to quicken, leading to the climactic measures of mm. 188–193 (Ex. 10.3). If there is a touch of Grand Guignol when the Woman stumbles over the dead body of her lover, the attendant cry for help is a blood-curdling scream such as was never heard outside of a dream. The play takes place, therefore, not in a real thicket of trees but in the forest of the mind; what transpires is a nightmare.

Such a shifting psychic landscape is reinforced by a change in tempo marking every three to four measures and by ambiguities in tonality which, together with a refracted color component recently secured in the *Five Pieces*, op. 16, determine the Expressionist vocabulary of the musician. In addition, the profusion of textual ellipses throughout the opera leads to a vocal style that shuns the extended lyric gesture. Building naturally on the Expressionist tendency to substitute the single word for the involved conceptual sentence, a premium is placed on melodic fragmentation and discontinuity. The consequences of this attitude may be viewed in the magnified role given to silence and the pause in the subsequent art of Anton Webern.

The most traditional descriptions of *Erwartung* have suggested that the music follows the text in a stream of consciousness characterized by localized repetition (including the ostinato—e.g., the orchestral interlude between scenes 3 and 4), which shares more than a little with Debussy's method in *Jeux* of only a few years later. Attempts to discuss the work with respect to its motivic content have emphasized the importance of a three-note major-minor third cell. Its appearance in both vocal and accompanimental figurations is clearly visible in Ex. 10.4 ("Das ist er!"), and the prominence accorded its appearance on the pitches D-F-C♯ has been repeatedly noted as evidence of Schoenberg's (as well as Berg's) continuing bias for D minor in many tonal and early atonal works (an early string quartet; the D-A-C♯ pedal chord of op. 16, no. 1; "Der kranke Mond" from *Pierrot lunaire*, op. 21, no. 7; or even the late quasitonal *Variations on a Recitative*, op. 40, for organ). Yet the importance attached to such cellular formations or to the symbolic quotation from an earlier song "Am Wegrand," op. 6, no. 6 (1905), while determinable from a careful scrutiny of the score, provides little by way of orientation to all but the most practised listener, and suggests an internalized formal solution near to that of *Die glückliche Hand.*[6]

Although the sententious rhetoric of both orchestra and voice can hardly fail to impress even the uninitiate, the restrained and telling use of the celesta (e.g., "Oh, der Mond schwankt") and other delicacies of orchestration recall Debussy less than similar expressions in Schoenberg's own op. 16, no. 2, and *Herzgewächse,* and are as important for the establishment of his dream world as the scream of terror. Finally, the chromatically rising augmented triads with which the opera closes were to find echoes in Berg's *Three Pieces for Orchestra,* op. 6, no. 3, from which they were to be quickly transferred to the drowning scene in *Wozzeck.*

Many of Schoenberg's self-portraits and "visions" come from this period (Figure 10.3). Reflecting the Expressionist "Ich-Drama" and other journeys into the subconscious, Schoenberg never painted abstractions. Yet in light of their

Figure 10.3. Arnold Schoenberg, *Vision of Christ* (1910).
Used by permission of the Arnold Schoenberg Institute and Belmont Music Publishers.

character, it is not surprising that they were openly praised by Kandinsky, who saw in Schoenberg's versatility something of the interdisciplinary complementarity he and others prized so highly. The emphasis placed on the gaze, as in *Die glückliche Hand*, and on the eyes as "phosphorous holes," a familiar Expressionist image that casts them as portals to the mind, is reflected in the recurrent use of the word "Augen" throughout the libretto of *Erwartung*. It is a preoccupation that melds nicely with Verlaine's view of Pierrot (p. 184) and Giraud's as well, to whom Schoenberg was soon to turn in fashioning his most notable Expressionist vehicle.

Arnold Schoenberg, *Erwartung* ("Anticipation"), Op. 17

I. SZENE

Am Rande eines Waldes. Mondhelle Strassen und Felder; der Wald hoch und dunkel. Nur die ersten Stämme und der Anfang des breiten Weges noch hell . . . eine Frau kommt.

Hier hinein? Man sieht den Weg nicht . . .
Wie silbern die Stämme schimmern . . . wie Birken!
Oh, unser Garten. Die Blumen für ihn sind sicher verwelkt.
Die Nacht ist so warm.
Ich fürchte mich . . . was für schwere Luft herausschlägt . . .
Wie ein Sturm, der steht . . .
So grauenvoll ruhig und leer . . .
Aber hier ist's wenigstens hell . . .
der Mond war früher so hell . . .
Oh noch immer die Grille . . . mit ihrem Liebeslied . . .
Nicht sprechen . . . es ist so süss bei dir . . .
der Mond ist in der Dämmerung . . .
Feig bist du, willst ihn nicht suchen?
So stirb doch hier.
Wie drohend die Stille ist . . .
der Mond ist voll Entsetzen . . . sieht der hinein?
Ich allein . . . in den dumpfen Schatten.
Ich will singen, dann hört er mich.

II. SZENE

Tiefstes Dunkel, breiter Weg, hohe, dichte Bäume.

Ist das noch der Weg? Hier ist es eben. (*Bückt sich, greift mit den Händen.*)
Was? Lass los!
Eingeklemmt? Nein, es ist etwas gekrochen . . .
Und hier auch . . . Wer rührt mich an?
Fort—Nur weiter . . . um Gotteswillen . . .
So, der Weg ist breit . . .
Es war so still hinter den Mauern des Gartens . . .

SCENE 1.

At the edge of a wood. Streets and fields lit by the moon; the wood tall and dark. Only the first tree-trunks and the beginning of the pathway (through the wood) are also lit by the moon. A woman comes;

Through the wood? . . . I see no pathway . . .
Like silver the trunks are shining . . .
Like birches! . . .
Oh, our garden. The flowers for him Have faded away.
The night is so warm.
I'm frightened . . .
An oppressive air attacks me . . .
Like a storm that waits . . .
So horribly quiet and void . . .
Yet around me still it is bright . . .
The moon just now was so bright . . .
Oh, again the crickets
It is a song of love . . .
Don't speak now . . . it is so sweet with you . . .
The moon is growing fainter now . . .
Cowardly!—would you not seek him? . . .
Then you may die . . .
How baleful the silence is . . .
The moon is full of terror . . . Does it see there? . . .
I'm alone . . . in the gloomy shadows.
If I sing now he'll hear my voice . . .

SCENE 2.

Blackest darkness; broad path; high, thick trees. She gropes forward.

Do I see the way? . . . here it is open.
What? Let go! . . .
Trapped, am I? . . . No—but something was crawling . . .
And here too . . . Who's touching me? . . .
Go—now forward . . . May God be with me . . .
Yes, the path is wide . . .
It was so quiet hidden away in the garden . . .

Keine Sensen mehr . . . kein Rufen und
    Gehn . . .
Und die Stadt im hellen Nebel . . .
so sehnsüchtig schaute ich hinüber . . .
Und der Himmel so unermesslich tief über
    dem Weg,
den du immer zu mir gehst . . .
noch durchsichtiger und ferner . . . die
    Abendfarben . . .
Aber du bist nicht gekommen . . .
Wer weint da?
Ist hier jemand?
Ist hier jemand? Nichts . . .
aber das war doch . . .
Jetzt rauscht es oben . . .
es schlägt von Ast zu Ast . . .
Es kommt auf mich zu . . .
            (Schrei eines Nachtvogels)
Nicht her! . . . lass mich . . .
Herrgott hilf mir . . .
Es war nichts . . .
            (Beginnt zu laufen.)
nur schnell, nur schnell . . .
Oh, oh, was ist das?
Ein Körper . . .
Nein, nur ein Stamm.

III. SZENE

*Weg noch immer im Dunkel. Seitlich vom
    Wege ein breiter heller Streifen.
Das Mondlicht fällt auf eine Baumlichtung.
Die Frau kommt aus dem Dunkel.*

Da kommt ein Licht!
Ach! nur der Mond . . . wie gut . . .
Dort tanzt etwas Schwarzes . . .
hundert Hände . . .
Sei nicht dumm . . . es ist der Schatten.
Oh! wie dein Schatten auf die weissen Wände
    fällt . . .
Aber so bald musst du fort . . .
            (Rauschen)
Rufst du?
Und bis zum Abend ist es so lang . . .
            (leichter Windstoss)
Aber der Schatten kriecht doch!
Gelbe, breite Augen, so vorquellend, wie an
    Stielen . . .
Wie es glotzt . . .
Kein Tier, lieber Gott, kein Tier . . .
Ich habe solche Angst . . .
Liebster, mein Liebster, hilf mir . . .

IV. SZENE

*Mondbeschienene, breite Strasse, rechts aus
dem Walde kommend. Etwas nach links
verliert sich die Strasse wieder im Dunkel
hoher Baumgruppen. Erst ganz links sieht*

All the scything done . . . no calling away,
And the town in shining mist—
With so much love I would look towards
    it . . .
And the heaven so infinitely high over the
    road,
Leading you to my garden . . .
But paler to see and distant . . . the evening
    colours . . .
Ah, but you did not come . . .
Who's weeping? . . .
Is there someone?
Is there someone?
No . . .
But it was something . . . I hear a rustle . . .
It moves from bough to bough . . .
It's over my head!
Not here . . . Leave me . . . God be with
    me! . . .
Nothing there . . .
Be quick, be quick . . .
Oh, oh, what is this? a body . . .
No, just a log.

SCENE 3.

*The path still in darkness. To the side of the
    path, moonlight falls on a clearing,
The woman comes out of the darkness.*

I see a light!
Ah, just the moon . . . how good . . .
There something is dancing . . .
Something black there . . . a hundred hands
Silly fool . . . it's only shadows . . .
Oh! how your shadow falls upon my white
    walls . . .
But you have always to go . . .

Calling?
To wait for evening seems so long . . .

Isn't the shadow moving . . .
Yellow, open eyes
I see rising as on stems . . .
How they stare!
No beast, dear God, no beast!
Oh I feel such a fear . . .
Dearest, my dearest, help me . . .

SCENE 4.

*A broad road, lit up in the moonlight, coming
out of the wood on the right. Meadows and
fields with alternate green and yellow strips.
The road is lost again to the left in the darkness*

man die Strasse freiliegen. Dort mündet auch ein Weg, der von einem Hause herunterführt. Die Frau kommt langsam, erschöpft. Das Gewand ist zerrissen, die Haare verwirrt. Blutige Risse an Gesicht und Händen.

of a group of tall trees. But nearer on the left the road lies open. Into the road comes a path leading down from a house, of which all the windows are closed with black shutters. A white stone balcony. The woman advances slowly, exhausted. Her clothes are torn, her hair dishevelled. Her face and hands have been lacerated and show blood.

Er ist auch nicht da . . .
Auf der ganzen, langen Strasse nichts
   Lebendiges . . .
und kein Laut . . .
Die weiten blassen Felder sind ohne Atem,
   wie erstorben . . .
kein Halm rührt sich.
Noch immer die Stadt . . . und dieser fahle
   Mond . . .
keine Wolke, nicht der Flügelschatten eines
   Nachtvogels am Himmel . . .
diese grenzenlose Totenblässe . . .
ich kann kaum weiter . . .
und dort lässt man mich nicht ein . . .
die fremde Frau wird mich fortjagen!
Wenn er krank ist!
Eine Bank . . . ich muss ausruhn.
Aber so lang hab ich ihn nicht gesehn.
   (Sie stösst mit dem Fuss an etwas.)
Nein, das ist nicht der Schatten der Bank!
Da ist jemand . . .
   (Beugt sich nieder, horcht.)
er atmet nicht . . .
   (Sie tastet hinunter.)
feucht . . . hier fliesst etwas . . .
Es glänzt rot . . .
Ach, meine Hände sind wund gerissen . . .
Nein, es ist noch nass, es ist von dort.
   *Versucht, den Gegenstand
      hervorzuzerren.)*
Ich kann nicht.
   (Bückt sich.)
Das ist er!
Das Mondlicht . . .
nein, dort . . .
das ist der schreckliche Kopf . . . das
   Gespenst . . .
wenn es nur endlich verschwände . . . wie das
   im Wald . . .
Ein Baumschatten . . . ein lächerlicher
   Zweig . . .
Der Mond ist tückisch . . .
weil er blutleer ist . . . malt er rotes Blut . . .
Aber es wird gleich zerfliessen . . .
Nicht hinsehn . . . Nicht drauf achten . . .
Es zergeht sicher . . . wie das im Wald . . .
Ich will fort . . . ich muss ihn finden.
Es muss schon spät sein.
   (Sie wendet sich halb um.)

He isn't here . . .
On this whole long roadway, nothing
   living . . .
And no sound . . .
The broad and pallid fields have nothing
   that's breathing, they are dead fields . . .
No plant stirring
But always the town . . .
And in the paling moon not a cloud,
Not a shadow of a flying bird up in the
   heavens . . .
'Tis an endless and a deathly country . . .
I scarce can walk now . . .
And there they'd not let me in . . . !
That other woman would drive me out.
Is he ill, then?
Here's a bench . . . let me rest here.
But it's so long since I have seen his face.

This is not a shadow I see!
There is someone . . .

I hear no breath . . .

Damp . . . it flows on me . . .
It shines red . . . Ah, both my hands
Have been torn and wounded . . .
No, it is still wet, it comes from there.

I cannot.

It is he!
The moonlight! No, there,
That is the terrible head . . .
'Tis the ghost . . .
Oh if it only would vanish . . .
As in the wood . . . some tree's shadow . . .
Some funny-looking branch . . .
The moon's deceitful . . .
'Tis the bloodless moon seems to paint in
   blood . . .
But I'm sure that it will vanish . . .
I'll not look . . . Take no notice . . .
It will pass over . . . as in the wood . . .
I'll go on . . . I have to find him . . .
It must be late now . . .

Es ist nicht mehr da . . . Ich wusste . . .
    (Sie wendet sich weiter.)
Es ist noch da . . . Hergott im Himmel . . .
Es ist lebendig . . .
Es hat Haut, Augen, Haar . . .
seine Augen . . . es hat seinen Mund.
Du . . . du . . . bist du es . . .
ich habe dich so lang gesucht . . .
im Wald und . . .
Hörst du?
Sprich doch . . . sieh mich an . . .
Herr Gott, was ist . . .
Hilfe! Um Gotteswillen! . . . rasch! hört mich
    denn niemand?
er liegt da . . . Wach auf . . . wach doch
    auf . . .
Nicht tot sein, mein Liebster . . .
Nur nicht tot sein, ich liebe dich so . . .
Unser Zimmer ist halbhell . . .
Alles wartet . . .
Die Blumen duften so stark . . .
Was soll ich tun . . .
Was soll ich nur tun, dass er aufwacht?
    (Sie fasst seine Hand.)
deine liebe Hand . . . so kalt?
Wird sie nicht warm an meiner Brust?
Mein Herz ist so heiss vom Warten . . .
die Nacht ist bald vorbei . . .
du wolltest doch bei mir sein diese Nacht . . .
Oh, es ist heller Tag . . .
Bleibst du am Tage bei mir?
Die Sonne glüht auf uns . . .
deine Hände liegen auf mir . . . deine
    Küsse . . .
mein bist du . . . Du!
Sieh mich doch an, Liebster, ich liege neben
    dir . . .
So sieh mich doch an.
Ah, wie starr, wie fürchterlich deine Augen
    sind . . .
drei Tage warst du nicht bei mir . . .
Aber heute . . . so sicher . . .
der Abend war so voll Frieden . . .
Ich schaute und wartete . . .
Über die Gartenmauer dir entgegen . . .

so niedrig ist sie . . .
Und dann winkten wir beide . . .
Nein, nein, es ist nicht wahr . . .
Wie kannst du tot sein?
Überall lebtest du . . .
Eben noch im Wald . . .
deine Stimme so nah an meinem Ohr,
immer, immer warst du bei mir . . .
dein Hauch auf meiner Wange . . .
deine Hand auf meinem Haar . . .

It's no longer there . . . I knew it . . .
Yes it's still there . . .
Heaven protect me . . .
And it is living . . . with a skin . . .
Eyes, hair . . .
His eyes . . . it has his own mouth.
You . . . you . . . are you this . . .
How long have I been in search of you . . .
The wood and . . .
Can you hear? Speak then . . . look at me . . .
Dear God, what can . . .
Help—me . . .
Oh, help, for God's sake! . . . Quick! . . .
Can no one hear me? . . .
He is there . . .
Wake up . . . waken up! . . .
Not dead now, my darling,
Oh, not dead now . . .
I love you so much . . .
In our room in the half-light . . .
All is ready . . . the flowers' perfume is
    strong . . .
What shall I do . . .
What now shall I do to awake him? . . .
Your darling hand . . .
So cold?
Will it grow warm upon my breast? . . .
My heart is so hot from waiting . . .
The night will soon have gone . . .
You wanted so to be with me tonight . . .
Oh, 'tis the light of day . . .
Will you be mine through the day?
The sun now shines on us . . .
And your hands are resting on me . . .
All your kisses . . . mine you are . . . you!
Look at me now, dearest,
I'm lying here with you . . .
So look at me now—
Ah, they stare . . . how frightening
Are your eyes to me . . .
Three days you did not come to me . . .
But on this day . . . then surely . . .
The evening was sweet and peaceful . . .
I looked out, awaiting you
Over the garden wall I looked towards
    you . . .
So low the wall is . . .
And then we saw each other . . .
No, no—it is not true! . . .
How could you die then?
You the most living thing . . .
Just now in the wood . . .
Your voice was close beside my ear,
Always, always you were with me . . .
Your breath was on my forehead . . .
And your hand was on my hair . . .
Oh yes, it is not true?
Your mouth bent just a moment ago

Nicht wahr . . . es ist nicht wahr?
Dein Mund bog sich doch eben noch unter
    meinen Küssen . . .
Dein Blut tropft noch jetzt mit leisem
    Schlag . . .
Dein Blut ist noch lebendig . . .
Oh, der breite rote Streif . . .
Das Herz haben sie getroffen . . .
Ich will es küssen mit dem letzten Atem . . .
dich nie mehr loslassen . . .
In deine Augen sehen . . .
Alles Licht kam ja aus deinen Augen . . .
mir schwindelte, wenn ich dich ansah . . .
Nun küss ich mich an dir zu Tode.
Aber so seltsam ist dein Auge . . .
Wohin schaust du?
Was suchst du denn?
    (sieht nach dem Hause.)
Steht dort jemand?
Wie war das nur das letzte Mal?
War das damals nicht auch in deinem Blick?

Nein, nur so zerstreut . . . oder . . .
und plötzlich bezwangst du dich . . .
Und drei Tage warst du nicht bei mir . . .

keine Zeit . . .
so oft hast du keine Zeit gehabt in diesen
    letzten Monaten . . .
Nein, das ist doch nicht möglich . . .
das ist doch . . .
Ah, jetzt erinnere ich mich . . .
der Seufzer im Halbschlaf . . . wie ein
    Name . . .
Du hast mir die Frage von den Lippen
    geküsst . . .
Aber warum versprach er mir heute zu
    kommen?
Ich will das nicht . . . nein, ich will nicht . . .
Warum hat man dich getötet? Hier vor dem
    Hause . . .
hat dich jemand eindeckt?
Nein, nein . . .
mein einzig Geliebter . . . das nicht . . .
Oh, der Mond schwankt . . . ich kann nicht
    sehen . . .
Schau mich doch an.
Du siehst wieder dort hin?
Wo ist sie denn, die Hexe, die Dirne . . .
die Frau mit den weissen Armen . . .
Oh, du liebst sie ja, die weissen Arme . . .
wie du sie rot küsst . . .
Oh, du . . . du, du . . . Elender, du
    Lügner . . . du . . .
Wie deine Augen mir ausweichen!
Krümmst du dich vor Scham?
    (Stösst mit dem Fuss gegen ihn)
Hast sie umarmt . . Ja? so zärtlich und
    gierig . . .
und ich wartete . . .

Beneath my kisses . . .
Your blood's flowing still with gentle
    pulse . . .
Your blood is warm and living . . .
Oh, so broad a streak of blood . . .
The heart must itself be bleeding . . .
I want to kiss it till I breathe no longer . . .
And not to part from you . . .
But on your eyes to gaze . . .
All the light came to me from your eyes . . .
I trembled whenever I saw you . . .
I kiss you now and at my dying.
But what a strange look in your eyes . . .
What attracts you?
What do you want?

Is there someone?
How did it seem that last time? . . .
Did I not see it then,
That certain look? . . .
No, but so remote . . . or else . . .
And then you controlled yourself . . .
And three whole days you were not with
    me . . .
You'd no time . . .
So often in all these final months
I found you had no time for me . . .
No, it just couldn't happen . . .
It could not . . .
Ah, now I suddenly recall that sigh
In your sleeping . . . like a name . . .

You stilled all my questioning
By kissing my lips . . .
Oh, but why did he promise me he'd come
    today then? . . .
It must not be . . . No—it must not . . .
Why ever should someone kill you?
Quite near the house, too . . .
Was there someone who knew?
No, no . . . my only beloved . . . not that . . .

Oh, the moon fails . . .
I can see nothing . . .
Please look at me
You look still over there?
Where is she, then, the harlot,
The sorceress, the woman with snow-white
    arms . . .
Oh, you love them—the snow-white arms
Made red by kisses . . .
Oh, you . . . you—you . . . torturer,
You liar . . . you . . .
Oh how your eyes would elude my own!
Cringe and bow for shame!

Did you embrace . . . Yes?
So sweetly and strongly . . .
And I waited . . .
Tell me where she is hidden

Wo ist sie hingelaufen, als du im Blut lagst?

Ich will sie an den weissen Armen
    herschleifen . . .
So . . .
Für mich ist kein Platz da . . .
Oh! nicht einmal die Gnade, mit dir sterben
    zu dürfen . . .
Wie lieb, wie lieb ich dich gehabt hab' . . .
Allen Dingen ferne lebte ich . . . allen fremd.
Ich wusste nichts als dich . . .
dieses ganze Jahr seit du zum ersten Mal
    meine Hand nahmst . . .
Oh, so warm . . . nie früher liebte ich
    jemanden so . . .
Dein Lächeln und dein Reden . . .
Ich hatte dich so lieb . . .
Mein Lieber . . . mein einziger Liebling . . .
hast du sie oft geküsst? . . . während ich vor
    Sehnsucht verging . . .
hast du sie sehr geliebt? Sag nicht: ja . . .
Du lächelst schmerzlich . . .
vielleicht hast du auch gelitten . . .
vielleicht rief dein Herz nach ihr . . .
Was kannst du dafür?
Oh, ich fluchte dir . . .
Aber dein Mitleid machte mich glücklich . . .
Ich glaubte, war im Glück . . .
Liebster, Liebster, der Morgen kommt . . .

Was soll ich allein hier tun?
In diesem endlosen Leben . . .
in diesem Traum ohne Grenzen und
    Farben . . .
denn meine Grenze war der Ort, an dem du
    warst . . .
und alle Farben der Welt brachen aus deinen
    Augen . . .
Das Licht wird für alle kommen . . .
aber ich allein in meiner Nacht?
Der Morgen trennt uns . . . immer der
    Morgen . . .
So schwer küsst du zum Abschied . . .
Wieder ein ewiger Tag des Wartens . . .
oh, du erwachst ja nicht mehr.
Tausend Menschen ziehn vorüber . . .
ich erkenne dich nicht.
Alle leben, ihre Augen flammen . . .
Wo bist du?
Es ist dunkel . . .
dein Kuss wie ein Flammenzeichen in meiner
    Nacht . . .
meine Lippen brennen und leuchten . . . dir
    entgegen . . .
Oh, bist du da . . .
Ich suchte . . .

Now you lie bleeding? . . .
I'd like to take her snow-white arms
And drag her here . . .
So—
For me there's no place here . . .
Oh! Not even the favour of our dying
    together . . .
How dear, how dear you were to me then . . .
Other things were all remote to me . . .
All remote—I knew only you . . .
In this year of ours since first you took my
    hand and held it . . .
Oh, so warm . . . never had I loved anyone
    so . . .
Your laughter and your talking . . .
How dear you were to me . . .
My dearest . . . my only beloved . . .
Did you go much to her?
While I in my longing was faint . . .
Did you love her so much?
Don't say 'Yes' . . . I see you smiling . . .
Perhaps you have also suffered . . .
Your heart may have yearned for her . . .
How can it be helped? . . .
Oh, I cursed you . . . but with your pity
You made me happy . . .
It seemed then I knew joy . . .
Dearest,
Dearest, the morning's near . . .
What shall I do here alone?
In this unending existence . . .
In this long dream with no boundary or
    colours . . .
For my boundary was the place
In which you were . . .
And all the colours on earth
Broke out of your two eyes . . .
The light will still come for others . . .
But for me alone here in my night? . . .
The morning parts us . . .
Always the morning . . .
Such heavy kisses at parting . . .
Once more a life-long day of waiting . . .
Oh you'll awaken no more . . .
Thousands come and pass between us . . .
I can no more see you.
All are living, and their eyes are flaming . . .
Where are you?
It is dark here . . . you kiss like a flaming
    beacon within my night . . .

My lips are burning and shining . . .
They await you . . .
Oh, are you there? . . .
I looked for . . .

*English translation by Arthur Jacobs, 1962. Used by
permission of Belmont Music Publishers.*

SCHOENBERG: *PIERROT LUNAIRE*

BACKGROUNDS.   From their origins in mid-sixteenth century Italy through the age of Watteau (1684–1721), the masked stock characters of the *commedia dell'arte* enjoyed an enduring popularity. Having lost something of its vitality by the early eighteenth century in Italy, the genre continued to flourish in England, where John Rich (c. 1682–1761), actor and founder of Covent Garden Theater, promoted it in the new guise of pantomime. The latter persisted through the nineteenth century in the London music hall satires of the great clown Joseph Grimaldi (1778–1837) and in the French theater, where Pedrolino, recast as Pierrot in white costume and face and dressed in conical hat and loose fitting clothes, was given a new pathos by the mime Jean-Gaspard Debureau (1796–1846). The most famous Pierrot of the day, he was for Baudelaire "le vrai pierrot actuel, le pierrot de l'histoire modern" whom he referred to as "ce personnage pâle comme la lune."

As early as 1881, Claude Debussy had made a vocal setting of Theodore Banville's "Pierrot," whose closing lines are

La blanche lune aux cornes de taureaux   The white moon with horns like a bull
Jette un regard de son oeil en coulisse   casts a glance into the wings
A son ami Jean Gaspard Debureau.   at his friend Jean Gaspard Debureau.

and whose opening lines Debussy matched with a folksong quotation whose opening words are "Au clair de la lune, mon ami Pierrot."

Example 10.5. Debussy, "Pierrot," mm. 1–5.

Supplément musical de numéro special de mai 1926. La Revue musicale.

The Belgian, Albert Giraud, wrote his *Pierrot lunaire,* subtitled "Rondels bergamasques," in 1884, and Debussy began work on his own *Suite bergamasque* in 1890. In this group of piano pieces the age of Watteau is recalled in his Prelude, Menuet, and Passepied, and the moonstruck note of Pierrot from Bergamo is traced in his renowned "Clair de lune."

In Verlaine's *Fêtes galantes* of 1864, whose title was borrowed from Watteau, Pierrot not surprisingly appears among the various characters of the *commedia dell'arte*. Debussy's first set of *Fêtes galantes* (1892) introduces Scaramouche and Pulcinella in the first line of "Fantoches" ("Marionettes"), and in "Clair de lune" he speaks of "charmant masques et bergamasques." Both of these texts he had set a decade before in 1882, the year in which he also introduced Pierrot in a setting of Verlaine's "Pantomime." Even as late as the sonata for cello and piano of 1915, Debussy proposed the subtitle "Pierrot fâché avec la lune" ("Pierrot vexed with the moon").

The new fin-de-siècle stylization of Pierrot as a figure disturbed by a deep melancholy is visible in Leoncavallo's *Pagliacci* (1892). And among the artists themselves, self-stylization as Pierrot became almost epidemic. At the age of 80, after a long absence from the cafés of the Latin Quarter, Verlaine returned virtually unrecognized, prompting a final Pierrot poem that mirrored his personal feelings.

VERLAINE, "Pierrot," from *Jadis et Naguère (1883)*

Ce n'est plus le rêveur lunaire du vieil air	It is no longer the moonstruck dreamer of olden times
Qui riait aux aieux dans les dessus de porte;	Who laughs at his forebears at the top of the entrance;
Sa gaité, comme sa chandelle, hélas! est morte,	His gaiety, like his candle, is gone out,
Et son spectre aujourd'hui nous hante, mince et clair . . .	And his ghost haunts us today, slim and luminous.
Ses yeux sont deux grands trous ou rampe du phosphore	His eyes are two large holes where phosphorus crawls
Et la farine rend plus effroyable encore	And the flour makes more hideous yet
Sa face exsangue au nez pointu de moribond.	His bloodless face with the pointed nose of a dying man.

Not only Verlaine but Sarah Bernhardt thought of herself as Pierrot, as did many an English dandy of the period, and Symons brilliantly captured the new mode of the figure as powdered, moonstruck, and ghostly in his melancholy portrayal of Beardsley:

> Pierrot is passionate; but he does not believe in great passions. He feels himself to be sickening with a fever, or else perilously convalescent; for love is a disease, which he is too weak to resist or endure. . . . He knows that his face is powdered, and if he sobs, it is without tears; and it is hard to distinguish, under the chalk, if the grimace which twists his mouth away is more laughter or mockery. . . . And so he becomes exquisitely false, dreading above all things that 'one touch of nature' which would ruffle his disguise, and leave him defenceless. . . . His mournful contemplation of things becoming a kind of grotesque joy. . . .

The figure of Pierrot was the subject of numerous ballet-pantomimes in the 1880s and 1890s in both Brussels and Paris, and the publication of the cycle of 50 poems entitled *Pierrot lunaire* by Albert Giraud (1860–1929) in 1884 was very much of its time. Giraud summarized both his and an earlier generation's feelings about Pierrot, and at the same time presaged a modern sensibility to its theme. In the free German translation of the collection in 1892, Otto Erich

Hartleben (1864–1905) not only continued to mirror the taste for Baudelairian themes of decadence, but also introduced a note of irony missing in the original. Schoenberg seized the opportunity to take a retrospective glance through formula-bound poetry attached to a familiar literary landscape, qualities missing in both *Erwartung* and *Die glückliche Hand.* The Expressionist *Angst* of these two works is also almost totally missing in *Pierrot,* and the nearest approaches to it involve a "playing at fear" which leads from pretense to unbearable anxiety, then surprise and laughter at the ruse involved.[7]

Lacking a personalized libretto or one with an evident spiritual or ethical base, Schoenberg sought to adapt his Expressionist vocabulary to a special task. In so doing, he chose to eschew musical quotation, a return to tonality, or prefabricated musical forms. But while the anxiety of the two preceding melodramas has now been diffused and distilled, the image of Pierrot as puppet, developed both by Baudelaire and Giraud, is not accorded the sympathy of Stravinsky's contemporary *Petrushka.* Schoenberg's music moves us rather to observe, wistfully at most, and while we may momentarily be dazzled, there is rarely a hint of reality. Even in the potentially touching homecoming of the last piece, Pierrot confesses to "a silly swarm of idle fancies" and befuddled senses. The listener is likely to feel the same, though not without a new conscience pricked by a sensibility won through exposure to Schoenberg's inimitable score.

SCHOENBERG'S OPUS 21.   From Giraud's cycle of fifty poems (1884), Schoenberg chose twenty-one (three times seven) to match the opus number of the work and dressed them in an extraordinarily variegated and original costume. Five performers play eight instruments (fl/picc, vln/vla, clar/bass clar, vc, pf), and while the ad hoc instrumentation was to become increasingly fashionable in the teens and, indeed, a mark of the twentieth century in general, the doubling suggests a certain practical aspect, even an economical solution not unknown to Schoenberg from the cabaret (see p. 286). Each of the twenty-one pieces of the cycle introduces a different combination, with all instruments being utilized only in the final number. At the other end of the scale, the reduction of the accompaniment to a solo flute provides the principal identification, together with a C♯–D–F motif common to *Erwartung* (see p. 175), for "Der Kranke Mond" (No. 7). Failing to suggest any connection with Debussy's *Syrinx* for solo flute written in the same year (1912), in its newly expressive melancholy laced with flashes of delirium it was to become the touchstone for an elaborate and virtuosic literature over the next fifty years.

Neither Stravinsky's *Japanese Lyrics* (p. 224) nor Ravel's Mallarmé songs (pp. 113–14), which share the work's coloristic forces, identify with the one element that creates the principal impression for all who have heard *Pierrot:* the *Sprechstimme.* In his preface to the score, the composer cautioned that "the melody in the speaker's part is *not* meant to be sung," though the rhythm was to be scrupulously observed. With respect to pitch, Schoenberg made the following distinction between *singing tone* and *speaking tone:*

> Singing tone maintains the pitch without modification; speaking tone does, certainly, announce it, only to quit it again immediately, in either a downward or an upward direction.[8]

On the title page of *Pierrot lunaire*, Schoenberg designated the work as a melodrama. The term was used by J. J. Rousseau as early as 1762 in connection with his *Pygmalion*, a work alternating pantomimic gesture and spoken declamation. As a genre it was notably pursued by Georg Benda in works like his *Ariadne auf Naxos* (1775), which interpolated musical interludes with extended monologues. In his *Medea* (1778), music and declamation were occasionally brought together, and later Schubert (*Abschied von der Erde*) and Richard Strauss (*Enoch Arden*, 1897) approached the medium. Yet the precedents for Schoenberg's *Pierrot lunaire* can be found not only in the exaggerated declamation of nineteenth-century melodrama to an instrumental accompaniment, but undoubtedly in the recitations of numerous chanteuses of the music hall and cabaret. Hartleben, translator of Giraud's *Pierrot*, was a German cabaret *littérateur* himself, and like Wedekind was a familiar figure in the recitation of his own verse.

Similarly, in art music, Humperdinck had used a brand of *Sprechstimme* in his children's opera, *Königskinder* of 1897, and Schoenberg had already employed it for brief sections in his *Gurrelieder* (short score, 1901), the choral *Friede auf Erden* (1907), and in his contemporaneous *Die glückliche Hand* (1910–13). Schoenberg's notation in *Pierrot* was explicit with respect to intoning pitch and rhythm, the performance indication for *Sprechstimme* being a cross on the stem. Later, in his opera *Moses and Aron* (1930–32), the cross replaced the notehead itself, while in the *Ode to Napoleon* (1942) and *A Survivor from Warsaw* (1947) the staff was reduced to a single line indicating the middle of the speaking range and notes placed above or below in a manner that suggested approximate interval size but not pitch.

The idea of *Sprechstimme*, then, is a fundamental Schoenbergian concept, and one that was to be adapted with a variety of nuances by later composers from Berg to Boulez, though curiously enough not Webern. It proved to be the perfect invention to underscore the Expressionist qualities residual in Giraud's *Pierrot lunaire*. In the German translation by Hartleben, the grotesquerie so aptly caught by Symons and Verlaine achieves a new level of intensity, which is in no small measure dependent on the obsessively reiterative patterns of the rondeau form utilized (ab--; --ab; ---a), shed of their rhyme for all of the poems. Eschewing exact recall, Nos. 1, 5, and 21 nonetheless use musical ideas from the initial refrain in both of its repetitions; Nos. 3, 4, 8, 9, 17, and 20 bring back material only for the first repetition in stanza two; the remainder ignore the textual formalization of the rondeau. Even in *Nacht* (No. 8), for example, the final memory of the piece hangs more on the recurrent rhythm and textual imagery of "Sinister giant black butterflies" ("Finstre, schwarze Riesenfalter") than on any awareness of Schoenberg's designation of the piece as a Passacaglia—attributable it would seem to a motif of a rising minor third and descending major third that permeates the score (Ex. 10.6).

In persistently atonal surroundings it is not surprising that other pieces also occasionally rely on both pitch and rhythmic motifs for coherency, including the ostinato that is notably exploited in the opening piece. The contrapuntal wizardry of the composer is often proclaimed with respect to the canons in "Parody" and "Moonspot," the latter being a triple canon with retrograde diminution. Not only are these techniques rare in *Pierrot*, but Schoenberg in later years, following his discovery of the twelve-note series as a

Example 10.6. Schoenberg, *Pierrot lunaire:* "Nacht" (No. 8). a) m. 1; b) m. 10.

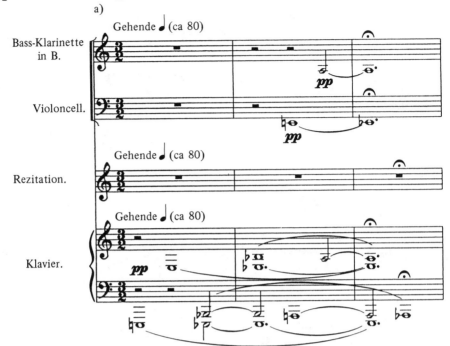

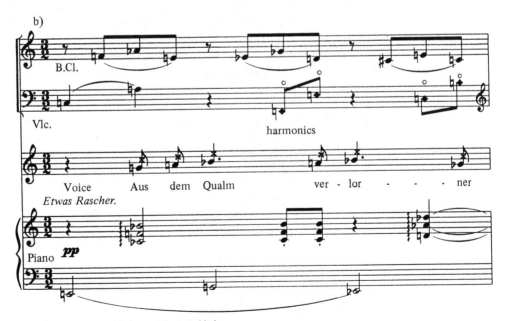

Used by permission of Belmont Music Publishers.

Example 10.6. (Continued)

compositional method, warned against overestimating such constructions in a world without harmonic laws.

The textual imagery is rich, and it is easy to connect various phrases with elements to be met elsewhere in roughly contemporaneous literature: the fascination in virtually all of the pieces with the moon (the opening scene of *Salome*; the death scene in *Wozzeck*); The Dandy's "rouges and oriental greens" (Wilde, Huysmans, and Klingsor); the "scrawny neck" of "Beheading" and "Gallows Song" (Ravel's "Le gibet" in *Gaspard de la nuit*); and the secular anti-Mass of the "Red Mass" (Scriabin's Sonata No. 7, "Messe blanche," 1911; Sonata No. 9, "Messe noir," 1912–13; Huysman's *Là bas*, 1891).

The opening *Moondrunk*'s "wine that only eyes may drink" may encourage the recollection of Baudelaire's wine poems, which were to appeal to Berg in the late 1920s. But one would be nearer the mark in recalling Li-Tai-Po and Mahler's *Das Lied von der Erde* which, like Schoenberg's *Pierrot lunaire*, opens with an Expressionist drinking song on a moonlit night. The conclusion of both works on a note of homeward-bound farewell suggests that Schoenberg may well have chosen and positioned these opening and concluding numbers with referential intent. Actually, the concluding sentiment involves the final two pieces, just as Mahler's final movement was a conflation of two different poems.

The order in which Schoenberg composed the set of twenty-one pieces confirms that the final arrangement imposed on the cycle was not apparent from its inception. Schoenberg's eventual division of the work into three parts has been said to reflect a distinctive mood for each: Pierrot's moonstruck despair followed by his paranoid martrydom and finally nostalgic reflection. The difficulties that some have had in squaring the external figure of Pierrot with the Expressionist need for a personalized world-view as epitomized in the "Ich-Drama" will not hamper the objective ear from noting the use to which Schoenberg has put his recently developed musical vocabulary. If an element of self-parody may be said to exist, there also remains the possibility of viewing *Pierrot* as an allegorical interpretation of the poet's despair and the comfort he seeks in a remembrance of things past (for Schoenberg, canon, passacaglia, sequences, textual forms, a sporadic motivic content, and a hint of tonality in the last number). To the extent that the language discovered in the so-called Expressionist works was to serve as a foundation for the remainder of his career, it will be unnecessary to insist on the "ism" or a mandatory type of textual companion in Schoenberg's later production.

At the premiere performance of the work on October 16, 1912, in Berlin, Schoenberg conducted the musicians placed behind a black Spanish screen, in front of which Albertine Zehme delivered her lines in a Pierrot costume. The accompanying program booklet, which contained the complete text of the poems, was prefaced by a quotation from the German poet Novalis (1772–1801) that should encourage the listener not to struggle too hard for meaning in this fantastic cycle:

> One can imagine tales where there would be no coherence, and yet associations— like dreams; poems that are simply euphonious and full of beautiful words, but with no meaning or coherence whatever—at most, a few comprehensible strophes—like fragments of utterly various things. Such true poesy can have, at most, an allegorical meaning, as a whole, and an indirect effect, like music.[9]

The legacy for Pierrot, as we have noted, is rich. The final effect, however, is individual, even unique, and destined not to be repeated with the same success. While we may become familiar with the work in time, George Perle is probably correct in concluding that "Pierrot . . . is not a work that one ever 'gets use to'."

Arnold Schoenberg, *Pierrot Lunaire*, Op. 21 (1912)

PART I

1. MONDESTRUNKEN

flute, violin, cello, piano

Den Wein, den man mit Augen trinkt,
Gießt Nachts der Mond in Wogen nieder,
Und eine Springflut überschwemmt
Den stillen Horizont.

Gelüste schauerlich und süß,
Durchschwimmen ohne Zahl die Fluten!
Den Wein, den man mit Augen trinkt,
Gießt Nachts der Mond in Wogen nider.

Der Dichter, den die Andacht treibt,
Berauscht sich an dem heilgen Tranke,
Gen Himmel wendet er verzückt
Das Haupt und taumelnd saugt und schlürt er
Den Wein, den man mit Augen trinkt.

1. MOONDRUNK

The wine that only eyes can drink
Pours nighttimes from the moon in waves,
And its springtime tide floods over
The horizon's quiet bowl.

Aching lusts, shocking and sweet,
Float beyond measure in the gushing philter!
The wine that only eyes can drink,
Pours nighttimes from the moon in waves.

The poet, under piety's cover,
Gets fuddled on the holy brew;
Towards Heaven, rapt, tilts back his head
And giddily reeling laps and swills
The wine that only eyes can drink.

3. DER DANDY

piccolo, clarinet in A, piano

Mit einem phantastischen Lichtstrahl
Erleuchtet der Mond die krystallnen Flacons
Auf dem schwarzen, hochheiligen Waschtisch
Des schweigenden Dandys von Bergamo.

3. THE DANDY

With a fantastical ray of light
The moon strikes sparks from the crystal flacons
On that ebony high altar, the washstand
Of the laconic dandy from Bergamo.

In tönender, bronzener Schale
Lacht hell die Fontaine, metallischen Klangs.
Mit einem phantastischen Lichtstrahl
Erleuchtet der Mond die krystallnen Flacons.

Pierrot mit dem wächsernen Antlitz
Steht sinnend und denkt: wie er heute
    sich schminkt?
Fort schiebt er das Rot und des Orients Grün
Und bemalt sein Gesicht in erhabenem Stil
Mit einem phantastischen Mondstrahl.

In the resonant bronze basin
Water spurts noisily with metallic laughter.
With a fantastical ray of light
The moon strikes sparks from the crystal flacons.

He of the waxworks face, Pierrot,
Racks his brain and thinks: How shall I
    make me up today?
Vetoes rouge and Orient green
And paints his phizz in loftier style—
With a fantastical ray of light.

5. VALSE DE CHOPIN

flute, clarinet in A, bass clarinet in B♭, piano

Wie ein blasser Tropfen Bluts
Färbt die Lippen einer Kranken,
Also ruht auf diesen Tönen
Ein vernichtungssüchtger Reiz.

Wilder Lust Accorde stören
Der Verzweiflung eisgen Traum—
Wie ein blasser Tropfen Bluts
Färbt die Lippen einer Kranken.

Heiß und jauchzend, süß und schmachtend,
Melancholisch düstrer Walzer,
Kommst mir nimmer aus den Sinnen!
Haftest mir an den Gedanken,
Wie ein blasser Tropfen Bluts!

5. VALSE DE CHOPIN

Like a spitwatered drop of blood
Rouging the lips of the phthisic sick.
So upon these morbid tones
There lies a soul-destroying spell.

Crimson chords of fierce desire
Splatter despair's white-icy dream—
Like a spitwatered drop of blood
Rouging the lips of the phthisic sick.

Hot exultant, sweetly longing,
Melancholy nightwood waltz
Nagging sleepless at my brain,
Cleaving to my every thought,
Like a spitwatered drop of blood!

7. DER KRANKE MOND

flute

Du nächtig todeskranker Mond
Dort auf des Himmels schwarzem Pfühl,
Dein Blick, so fiebernd übergroß ,
Bannt mich wie fremde Melodie.

An unstillbarem Liebesleid
Stirbst du, an Sehnsucht, tief erstickt,
Du nächtig todeskranker Mond
Dort auf des Himmels schwarzem Pfühl.

Den Liebsten, der im Sinnenrausch
Gedankenlos zur Liebsten schleicht,
Belustigt deiner Strahlen Spiel—
Dein bleiches, qualgebornes Blut,
Du nächtig todeskranker Mond.

7. THE SICK MOON

You darkgloomed lifesick deathbed moon
Splayed white on night-sky's pillow,
Your huge and feverswollen face
Holds me fast, like alien tones.

From stanchless quenchless ache of love
You'll die of yearning, choked and smothered,
You darkgloomed lifesick deathbed moon
Splayed white on night-sky's pillow.

The lovedrunk lover on his way
Thoughtless to his lover's bed
Applauds as charming silver rays
The hueless pain-born blood you spill,
You darkgloomed lifesick deathbed moon.

PART II

8. NACHT (Passacaglia)

bass clarinet in B♭, cello, piano

Finstre, schwarze Riesenfalter
Töteten der Sonne Glanz.
Ein geschlossnes Zauberbuch,
Ruht der Horizont—verschwiegen.

Aus dem Qualm verlorner Tiefen
Streigt ein Duft, Erinnrung mordend!

8. NIGHT (Passacaglia)

Sinister giant black butterflies
Eclipse the blazing disk of sun.
Like a sealed-up book of wizard's spells
Sleeps the horizon—secret silent.

From dank forgotten depths of Lethe
A scent floats up, to murder memory.

Finstre, schwarze Riesenfalter
Töteten der Sonne Glanz.

Und vom Himmel erdenwärts
Senken sich mit schweren Schwingen
Unsichtbar die Ungetüme
Auf die Menschenherzen nieder . . .
Finstre, schwarze Riesenfalter.

Sinister giant black butterflies
Eclipse the blazing disk of sun.

And from heaven downward dropping
To the earth in leaden circles,
Invisible, the monstrous swarm
Descends upon the hearts of men,
Sinister giant black butterflies.

11. ROTE MESSE

11. RED MASS

piccolo, bass clarinet in B♭, viola, cello, piano

Zu grausem Abendmahle,
Beim Blendeglanz des Goldes,
Beim Flackerschein der Kerzen,
Naht dem Altar—Pierrot!

Die Hand, die gottgeweihte,
Zerreißt die Priesterkleider
Zu grausem Abendmahle,
Beim Blendeglanz des Goldes.

Mit segnender Geberde
Zeigt er den bangen Seelen
Die triefend rote Hostie:
Sein Herz—in blutgen Fingern—
Zu grausem Abendmahle!

At the gruesome Eucharist,
In the trumpery golden glare,
In the shuddering candlelight,
To the altar comes—Pierrot!

His hand, by Grace anointed,
Rips open his priestly vestment
At the gruesome Eucharist,
In the trumpery golden glare,

With hand upraised in blessing
He holds aloft to trembling souls
The holy crimson-oozing Host:
His ripped-out heart—in bloody fingers—
At the gruesome Eucharist.

12. GALGENLIED

12. GALLOWS DITTY

piccolo, viola, cello

Die dürre Dirne
Mit langem Halse
Wird seine letzte
Geliebte sein.

In seinem Hirne
Steckt wie ein Nagel
Die dürre Dirne
Mit langem Halse.

Schlank wie die Pinie,
Am Hals ein Zöpfchen—
Wollüstig wird sie
Den Schelm umhalsen,
Die dürre Dirne!

The wood-dry whore
With rope-long neck
Will be the last lover
To hold him tight.

She sticks in his brain
Like a hammered-in nail,
The wood-dry whore
With rope-long neck.

Pinetree-scrawny
With hank of hair,
The lecher, she'll grab
The wretch's neck,
The wood-dry whore!

13. ENTHAUPTUNG

13. BEHEADING

bass clarinet in B , viola, cello, piano

Der Mond, ein blankes Türkenschwert
Auf einem schwarzen Seidenkissen,
Gespenstisch groß —dräut er hinab
Durch schmerzensdunkle Nacht.

Pierrot irrt ohne Rast umher
Und starrt empor in Todesängsten
Zum Mond, dem blanken Türkenschwert
Auf einem schwarzen Seidenkissen.

The moon, a naked scimitar
Upon a black silk cushion.
Ghostly huge hangs threatening down
Through night as dark as woe.

Pierrot, who paces about in panic,
Stares up and feels the clutch of death
At sight of moon, a naked scimitar
Upon a black silk cushion.

Es schlottern unter ihm die Knie,   Knees atremble, quaking, shaking,
Ohnmächtig bricht er jäh zusammen.   He falls into a faint of fright,
Er wähnt: es sause strafend schon   Convinced it's slashing down already
Auf seinen Sünderhals hernieder   On his guilty sinful neck,
Der Mond, das blanke Türkenschwert.   The moon, the naked scimitar.

PART III

19. SERENADE

19. SERENADE

flute, clarinet in A, violin, cello, piano

Mit groteskem Riesenbogen   With grotesquely giant-sized bow
Kratzt Pierrot auf seiner Bratsche,   Pierrot draws cat-squeals from his viola.
Wie der Storch auf einem Beine,   Like a stork, on one leg balanced,
Knipst er trüb ein Pizzicato.   He plucks a doleful pizzicato.

Plötzlich naht Cassander—wütend   Out pops furious Pantaloon
Ob des nächtgen Virtuosen—   Raging at the night-time virtuoso—
Mit groteskem Riesenbogen   With grotesquely giant-sized bow
Kratzt Pierrot auf seiner Bratsche.   Pierrot draws cat-squeals from his viola.

Von sich wirft er jetzt die Bratsche: So the player drops his fiddle;
Mit der delikaten Linken   Delicately, with his skilled left hand,
Faßt den Kahlkopf er am Kragen—   Grabs old baldy by the collar—
Träumend spielt er auf der Glatze   And dreamily plays upon his pate
Mit groteskem Riesenbogen.   With grotesquely giant-sized bow.

20. HEIMFAHRT (Barcarole)

20. HOMEWARD JOURNEY (Barcarole)

flute, clarinet in A, violin, cello, piano

Der Mondstrahl ist das Ruder,   With moonbeam as his rudder,
Seerose dient als Boot;   His boat a water lily,
Drauf fährt Pierrot gen Süden   Pierrot sails softly southward
Mit gutem Reisewind.   Driven onward by the wind.

Der Strom summt tiefe Skalen   The river hums its watery scales
Und wiegt den leichten Kahn.   And gently rocks his skiff,
Der Mondstrahl ist das Ruder,   With moonbeam as his rudder,
Seerose dient als Boot.   His boat a water lily.

Nach Bergamo, zur Heimat,   To Bergamo, his native land,
Kehrt nun Pierrot zurück;   Pierrot is homeward bound.
Schwach dämmert schon im Osten   Pale dawns already in the east
Der grüne Horizont.   The green of morning's rim
—Der Mondstrahl ist das Ruder.   —With moonbeam as his rudder.

21. O ALTER DUFT

21. O SCENT OF FABLED YESTERYEAR

flute, piccolo, clarinet in A, bass clarinet in B♭, violin, viola, cello, piano

O alter Duft aus Märchenzeit,   O scent of fabled yesteryear,
Berauschest wieder meine Sinne;   Befuddling my senses with bygone joys!
Ein närrisch Heer von Schelmerein   A silly swarm of idle fancies
Durchschwirrt die leichte Luft.   Murmurs through the gentle air.

Ein glückhaft Wünschen macht mich froh   A happy ending so long yearned for
Nach Freuden, die ich lang verachtet: Recalls old pleasures long disdained:
O alter Duft aus Märchenzeit,   O scent of fabled yesteryear,
Berauschest wieder mich!   Befuddlng me again!

All meinen Unmut gab ich preis;	My bitter mood has turned to peace;
Aus meinem sonnumrahmten Fenster	My sundrenched window opens wide
Beschau ich frei die liebe Welt	On daytime thoughts of world I love,
Und träum hinaus in selge Weiten . . .	To daydreams of a world beyond . . .
O alter Duft—aus Märchenzeit!	O scent of fabled yesteryear!

Used by permission of Belmont Music Publishers.
English translation by Robert Erich Wolf,
Nonesuch Record H-71251.

RAVEL AND VIENNA: *LA VALSE*

Although distinctions between French and German taste in early twentieth-century art are commonly forwarded—and with some reason—it is worth recalling that a ghoulish touch fueled the sensibility of the Symbolists, from Poe and Bertrand through Baudelaire and Huysmans, as well as the nightmare visions of the Expressionists. Certain of Bertrand's verses from *Gaspard de la nuit* might have appealed to Schoenberg as much as to Ravel, and, indeed, the poet of *Pierrot lunaire*, Albert Giraud, is French.

But what holds for literature is not necessarily reflected with a direct correspondence in the world of music, and Schoenberg and Ravel would seem to paint from a palette drawn from a totally different portion of the spectrum. If occasionally we are encouraged to speak of a hint of Impressionist tracery in a work like Schoenberg's *Herzgewächse*, it may be possible to smudge the German-French distinction even further by suggesting Ravel's sympathy for Teutonic—and even in rare instances—Expressionist values.

The open antagonism against German music expressed by most Frenchmen (Cocteau, Debussy) during the period of World War I and its aftermath is not an attitude that was shared by Ravel. In refusing to join a National League for the Defense of French Music, formed in 1916 with the announced purpose of banning the performance of all music not in the public domain by German and Austrian composers, Ravel wrote, "It is of little importance to me that M. Schoenberg, for example, is of Austrian nationality. This does not prevent him from being a very fine musician, whose very interesting discoveries have had a beneficial influence on certain allied composers, and even our own."[10] Ravel's willingness not only to acknowledge but to pay tribute to Austrian traditions is apparent as early as his *Valses nobles et sentimentales* (1911), which he characterized as written in imitation of Schubert.

In 1920, Ravel went to Vienna on a concert tour sponsored by the French embassy, and was represented by two concerts of his music on October 22 and 25 as well as a third on October 23 sponsored by Schoenberg's *Verein für musikalische Privataufführungen in Wien*. The esteem in which Ravel was held—compare this with Berg's nationalistic remarks, p. 100, made at the beginning of World War I—is especially poignant in the latter program, which included only works of Ravel interlaced with compositions by Schoenberg, Berg, and Webern as follows.[11]

Ravel, *Gaspard de la nuit* (Eduard Steuermann)
Schönberg, *Fünf Lieder* aus op. 15 (Helge Lindberg, E. Steuermann)
Schönberg, *Zwei neue Klavierstücke* (Steuermann)
Webern, *Vier Stücke für Geige und Klavier*, op. 7, no. 1 (Rudolf Kolisch, E. Steuermann)

Berg, *Vier Stücke für Klarinette und Klavier*, op. 5 (Karl Gaudriot, E. Steuermann)
Ravel, *Valse nobles et sentimentales pour deux pianos à quatre mains* (Maurice Ravel
    and Alfredo Casella)
Schönberg, "Jane Grey," eine Ballade aus op. 12 (Olga Bauer-Pilecka, Ernst Bachrich)
Ravel, *Streichquartett in F-dur* (Feist-Quartett)

In later concerts, *Gaspard de la nuit* was repeatedly programmed by Steuermann, who also added the aesthetically different but technically demanding *Le tombeau de Couperin*. Ravel, in kind, sponsored the performance of Berg's pieces for clarinet and piano, op. 5, on his return to Paris. Something of this affinity carried over into his immediately ensuing *Sonata* for violin and cello (1920–22), whose contrapuntal bent, tonal ambiguities, and spare instrumentation suggest an awareness of Schoenberg's and the young Berg's achievement. In 1928, Ravel made the following revealing comment:

> The influence of Schoenberg may be overwhelming on his followers, but the significance of his art is to be identified with influences of a more subtle kind–not the system, but the aesthetic, of his art. I am quite conscious of the fact that my *Chansons madécasses* are in no way Schoenbergian, but I do not know whether I ever should have been able to write them had Schoenberg never written.[12]

But it is in the orchestral tour-de-force *La valse*, a work written in 1919–20 and originally entitled *Wien*, that Ravel was as much a commentator about the political and moral climate of Vienna as Schoenberg in his "Waltz," which closes the set of five piano pieces, op. 23 (1923). In a language that technically owes little to Schoenberg, Ravel portrays the mounting tension and ultimate collapse of Vienna's dance signature in a whirlwind of motion that carries an enormous psychological impact. Though "atonality," the apparent keystone to any definition of Viennese Expressionism, is missing, the original model (the waltz) and the attendant coloristic and phraseological distortion carry overtly Expressionist overtones, which Perle has openly compared to Berg's treatment of the idea of the march in the last of his *Three Pieces for Orchestra*, op. 6 (see p. 60). Ravel's identification of a "fantastic and fatal whirling" in *La valse* is especially audible in the closing measures of the composition where the mounting tension establishes a kind of disoriented hysteria which, for all its tonal base, projects the collapse of a collective national psyche as well as the final dissolution of pre-World War I decadent sensibilities. Schoenberg's waltz, op. 23, written shortly thereafter, is an attempt to reassemble the pieces of a fractured structure through one of his first uses of the twelve-note series. As the listener struggles to find the beat and sense the lilt of a forgotten tune, he realizes that the reordering has been only partially successful—the conductor has lost his place and the metronome is in need of a repairman.

REPERTOIRE

Munch, *The Scream* (1895), print, painting
Freud, *The Interpretation of Dreams* (1900), psychoanalytic tract
Strindberg, *Dream Play* (1902), play
Kokoschka, *Mörder, Hoffnung der Frauen* (1907), play
Kandinsky, *Der gelbe Klang* (1909), play
Schoenberg, *Erwartung* (1909), monodrama, S, orch
Schoenberg, *Pierrot lunaire* (1912), Sprechstimme, fl/pic, vn/va, cl/b cl, vc, pf
Schoenberg, *Die glückliche Hand* (1910–13), opera

Hindemith, *Mörder, Hoffnung der Frauen* (1919), opera
Ravel, *La valse* (1919–20), orch

READING

Wassily Kandinsky, *Concerning the Spiritual in Art* (New York, 1947). Originally published as *Über das Geistige in der Kunst* (Munich, 1912).

Philip Friedheim, "Rhythmic Structure in Schoenberg's Atonal Compositions," *Journal of the American Musicological Society*, xix.1 (1966), 59–72.

Herbert Buchanan, "A Key to Schoenberg's 'Erwartung'," *Journal of the American Musicological Society*, xx (1967), 434.

Elaine Padmore, "German Expressionist Opera," *Proceedings of the Royal Musical Association*, xcv (1968–9), 41.

Charles Rosen, *Schoenberg* (New York, 1975).

Schoenberg as Artist, special issue of the *Journal of the Arnold Schoenberg Institute*, ii.3 (1978).

Eberhard Freitag, "Expressionism and Schoenberg's Self-Portraits"
Georg Eisler, "Observations on Schoenberg as Painter"
Halsey Stevens, "A Conversation with Schoenberg about Painting"
Wassily Kandinsky, "The Paintings of Arnold Schoenberg"
Lawrence Schoenberg and Ellen Kravitz, "Catalog of Schoenberg's Paintings, Drawings and Sketches"
Arnold Schoenberg, "Painting Influence"

Donald Harris, "Ravel Visits the *Verein*: Alban Berg's Report," *Journal of the Arnold Schoenberg Institute*, iii.1 (1979), 75–82.

Alan Lessem, *Music and Text in the Works of Arnold Schoenberg* (Ann Arbor, 1979), 59–120, 121–163.

Carl Schorske, *Fin-de-siècle Vienna* (1980), 3–4.

Jalena Hahl-Koch, ed., *Arnold Schoenberg/Wassily Kandinsky: Letters, Pictures and Documents* (1980), Eng. trans. John C. Crawford (London, 1984).

Philip Friedheim, "Wagner and the Aesthetics of the Scream," *19th-Century music*, vii (Summer 1983), 63–79.

Pierre Boulez, "Speaking, Playing, Singing: *Pierrot lunaire* and *Le Marteau sans maître*" in *Orientations* (Cambridge, Mass., 1986), 330–43. Originally as "Dire, jouer, chanter," *Cahiers Renaud-Barrault*, xli (1963), 300–21.

CHAPTER 11

PRIMITIVISM: THE ROAD TO *THE RITE*

As Stravinsky put it, "That the first performance of *The Rite of Spring* was attended by a scandal must be known to everybody."[1] Whatever the circumstances, it was not the first musical premiere to inspire a riot, nor was the reaction sufficient to guarantee lasting notoriety, personal success, or the ultimate declaration of the work as a masterpiece.

In attempting to "explain" a masterwork, inevitably its details are analyzed and a context sought: the former in search of a constructive principle, the latter in the hope of indicating that the work in question was in many ways, including the technical, clearly prepared or even intimated in the work of other artists. The context in the present instance is especially complex and involves not only a consideration of the composer's works written prior to *The Rite*, but of the sponsoring forces and the locus of presentation: namely, the musical scene in Paris of 1909 to 1912, with special reference to Diaghilev's opera and ballet productions; and Russian nationalism as a backdrop to the emergence of a genuine avant-garde in Moscow and St. Petersburg in the early years of the twentieth century. Finally, another haunting "ism," Primitivism, deserves to be squarely faced in order to understand its relationship to current values both in France and Russia.

THE RUSSIAN AVANT-GARDE

The modern Russian movement in art is usually said to have begun with a group of artists who collected around Savva Mamontov at his estate on Abramtsevo near Moscow in the 1870s. This colony of painters, composers, singers, actors, architects, art historians, and archaeologists, who dubbed themselves "The Wanderers," represented a challenge to the official Petersburg Academy of Art, which had held sway since the time of Catherine the Great in the mid-eighteenth century. Their rallying point was a desire to create a new Russian culture. Attempting to define an art that was useful to the people, they rejected popular Western aesthetic notions of "art for art's sake" and sought to formulate an art based on their Russian national heritage.

The archaeological and historical component amongst their membership allowed a systematic search for native Russian materials, and ultimately placed a focus on Scythian civilization, medieval icons, and national peasant art and costume. This soon found expression in theatrical productions and the formation of a professional "Private Opera" in Moscow. The stage settings and costume designs of Victor Vasnetzov, which reflected the investigations and taste of Mamontov's group, were already clearly visible in the 1885 production of Rimsky-Korsakov's *The Snow Maiden* (Figure 11.1).

RIMSKY-KORSAKOV (1844–1907). Rimsky-Korsakov's tutelage under Balakirev had led naturally to a youthful realization of an *Overture on Three Russian Themes* of 1866 in obvious imitation of Balakirev's two *Overtures on Russian Themes* of 1858 and 1863. Indeed, Glinka, the father of Russian nationalist music, had early shown the way both in his opera *A Life for the Tsar* (1834–35), which made ample use of folk melodies, and especially in his popular *Kamarinskaya* (1847), an orchestral fantasy on themes of weddings and dances.[2] But Rimsky-Korsakov's two compilations of Russian folksongs (*40 Folksongs*, 1875, publ. 1882; *100 Folksongs*, 1875–76, publ. 1877) provide further evidence of the increasing consideration which the composer was to give to folk materials and themes.[3]

The first manifestation of such an interest in his own composition following the appearance of these anthologies was seen in his opera *May Night* (1878–79), based on a short story by Gogol about peasant life in the Ukraine. Of his use of folk materials in the opera he remarked, "I managed to connect, with a subject I adored, that ceremonial side of folk-life which gives expression to the survivals from ancient paganism."[4]

Figure 11.1. V. M. Vasnetzov, "The Tsar's Palace," design for Act II of Rimsky-Korsakov's *Snow Maiden* for a performance at Mamontov's private opera in Moscow, 1885. Pencil and Watercolor.

Shortly after composing *May Night*, Rimsky-Korsakov happened to reread Ostrovsky's *Snow Maiden*, a play for which Tchaikovsky had written incidental music in 1873. Although previously neutral to the work, he now reacted positively.

> My mild interest in the ancient Russian customs and heathen pantheism flamed up. There seemed no better subject than this . . . no better religion and philosophy of life than the worship of the Sun God, Yarilo.[5]

In the composition of *The Snow Maiden* during 1880–81, the employment of folk melodies gained steady ground, and both quotation as well as the construction of new melodies based on typical folk motifs abound. In his autobiographical *My Musical Life*, first published posthumously in 1909, the composer described at great length his interest in ancient musical modes as well as his specific recourse to a corpus of folk melodies, and recalled at equal length the music critics who

> having noticed both in *The Snow Maiden* and *May Night*, two or three melodies borrowed from collections of folksongs (to notice many they were powerless, as they were ill-acquainted with folk creation), proclaimed me incapable of creating my own melodies . . . despite the fact that my operas contain by far more melodies that belong to me and have never been drawn from song collections. Many melodies that I had successfully composed in folk spirit . . . they considered borrowed.[6]

Finally, in the preface to his opera *Christmas Eve* (1895), the composer spoke once again of how he had superimposed on a tale of Gogol various pagan ritual figures and, reviewing the seasonal associations of his earlier operas *May Night*, *The Snow Maiden*, and *Mlada*, claimed that he had now completed the whole solar cycle.

While audiences today know little of Rimsky-Korsakov's operas, they would be correct in assuming a totally Romantic, thoroughly Western approach without any prefiguration of the elemental primitivism associated with his two pupils, Stravinsky and Prokofiev. But both in the use of modal folk materials and his interest in pagan cultures and seasonal rites he not only provides the necessary musical link with the discoveries of the Mamontov group and a rational connection with the folk motifs of Vasnetsov's decor for *The Snow Maiden*, but also an understanding of the ease with which Stravinsky reacted to the topics of his first three ballets: *Firebird*, *Petrushka*, and *The Rite of Spring*. Technically speaking, his orchestrational prowess, his fascination for whole-tone and octatonic (alternating tone and semitone) scalar formations, and a diatonic-chromatic harmonic dichotomy were all to find immediate uses in the early works of Stravinsky (see p. 201). But before Diaghilev ever introduced Stravinsky to Paris and an international audience, he had first created an appetite for Russian music through the Russian Five. Rimsky-Korsakov, Borodin, and Mussorgsky paved the way and set the taste.

THE "WORLD OF ART"

Mamontov's neonationalist energies were soon imitated by others, and the establishment of an artist's colony in 1895 on an estate called Talashkino by Princess Maria Tenisheva (1867–1928) was openly modelled after and intended to surpass Abramtsevo. Benois, Bakst, Bilibin and Roerich were among her lists that became the basis for the "World of Art" movement formed by Diaghilev in the late 1890s. With the joint patronage of both Mamontov and Tenisheva, it soon became the rallying point for the Russian artistic avant-garde.

Based in St. Petersburg, the leadership of Alexander Benois (1870–1960) was clear from its inception. His interests in art, literature, and music were decidedly urban, and through his French, German, and Italian ancestry he brought an understanding of international culture which, branded to the burgeoning desire for a modern national tradition, was to prove crucial to the movement. Paralleling in many respects the *Art nouveau–Jugendstil* alliance, Benois' group knew and spoke publicly of Klimt and his contemporaries and, through their exhibitions organized largely through trips abroad by Serge Diaghilev, introduced the French Impressionists to Russia for the first time.

A "World of Art" magazine, under Diaghilev's direction, first appeared in 1898. Its elevated, even Messianic tone, which was at least in general terms devoted to the philosophy of "art for art's sake" and hence nominally at odds with "The Wanderers," forwarded the notion of art as a mystical experience, a tone readily relatable to Kandinsky's later *Blaue Reiter* group. It endorsed, toward this end, not only the French Impressionists but also the Viennese Secessionists, as well as the French interest in primitive and folk art that mirrored the taste of Mamontov's Ambramtsevo colony now based in Moscow. As in the later *Blaue Reiter* almanac the pages of this journal typically displayed a mixture of the cultivated and the primitive: reproductions of Puvis de Chavannes and Gustave Moreau appeared alongside photographs of peasant dress, furniture and embroidery. The idea was promoted that from the ancient ruins could spring a new art, one which honored the Russian heritage simply for its inherent beauty and not because of its subject matter.[7]

With the cessation of publication of "The World of Art" magazine in 1903, and not content with the success of his initial exhibitions in St. Petersburg, Diaghilev decided to promote a Russian section at the annual Salon d'Automne in Paris of 1906. Here Diaghilev set out to introduce Russian art to the West, and included in his massive exhibition not only icon paintings but examples of Russian art from the eighteenth and nineteenth centuries, concluding with the work of a group of the youngest Moscovites, Larionov and Goncharova, who by 1909 would launch a Russian "Primitivist" style.

Bolstered by the enormous success that followed, Diaghilev determined to introduce the music of the Russian Five in the 1907 season, and in 1908 achieved total Parisian capitulation with the Imperial Theater's production of Mussorgsky's *Boris Godunov*, with Chaliapin in the title role and Benois and Golovin as designers of the décor and costumes. Expansion of such a plan was inevitable, and in 1909 Bakst swept Paris off its feet with his fantasy décor for *Orientales* and *Sheherezade*, as did Roerich with his sets for Borodin's *Prince Igor*.

In the next five years the multiple tastes of "The World of Art" were reflected in Diaghilev's annual visits to Paris: the neoclassical attitudinizing of Benois; the Hellenistic revival of Bakst's *L'après-midi d'un faune*; the color and form of the folk-art revival in the work of Larionov and Goncharova; and the more overtly pagan-primitive evocations of Stravinsky and Roerich. An art historian has summarized the impact of these years in a manner readily understandable to the musician:

Thus in Diaghilev's ballet one can rediscover a complete microcosm of the artistic life in Russia during the reign of the 'World of Art'. In the great contribution which they made to both the Russian and Western scene, they saw their ambitions justified, and the creation of a new international culture springing from Russia as a reality.[8]

DIAGHILEV AND THE YOUNG STRAVINSKY

As early as 1902, the musical members of the "World of Art" had sponsored "Evenings of Contemporary Music," which mingled the music of the West (Mahler, Strauss, Debussy, Ravel) with contemporary Russian masters (Skriabin, Rimsky-Korsakov, Rachmaninov, Medtner). Not only did the young Prokofiev give his first public concert at one of these gatherings, but it was here in 1909 that Diaghilev was introduced to the music of a pupil of Rimsky-Korsakov, the young Igor Stravinsky. The work Diaghilev heard was the brief orchestral piece, *Fireworks*, but he was so struck by it that, following a rejected proposal to Liadov, he immediately commissioned Stravinsky to write the score for a new ballet, *The Firebird*.

It is understandable that in the young composer's first creations he would sense his relation not only to Diaghilev and the recent Parisian presentations but to the traditions of the Russian artistic and literary community of the preceding two decades. Stravinsky's musical development under the tutelage of Rimsky-Korsakov had already led him to the composition of a Symphony in E♭ (1905–07), whose scherzo discloses a strong affinity for Tchaikovsky. Also, in 1908, prior to Stravinsky's meeting with Diaghilev, he had begun a Chinese fairy-tale opera, *The Nightingale* (after Hans Christian Andersen), of which his teacher saw the preliminary sketches of the opening Act. The completion of his mentor's oriental *The Golden Cockerel* (Pushkin after Washington Irving) in 1907 indicates that a tradition was near at hand for his first operatic venture. But neither Stravinsky's near plagiarism of Debussy's "Nuages" in the orchestral introduction to *The Nightingale* nor the pentatonicism of the "Emperor's March," for all of its polytonal orientation, more than hints at the specifically Russian mode he was soon to espouse, and which with Diaghilev's encouragement was to bring the composer to international attention.

THE FIREBIRD, PETRUSHKA, AND FOLK SOURCES

Folkloristic nationalism was a central trait of the Romantic movement, and the importance of the folk song tradition to art music rose, especially in the late nineteenth century, with the appearance of numerous folksong collections in Russia, Germany, France, Spain, and England. Initially, Rimsky-Korsakov but later Stravinsky, Mahler, and Hindemith had recourse to publications of their native materials, and long before Bartók and Kodaly began their epoch-making researches into Hungarian melodies and dances, Liszt had made a half-hearted attempt to systematize Hungarian melodies in a treatise of 1859.

The distinction has frequently been made that Exoticism, the reaching out to a foreign culture for a source of inspiration, tends to appear in more advanced cultures with a clearly defined artistic tradition. Emerging national identities tend to be secured through an artistic expression that fosters the exploration of their own folk heritage and emphasizes a latent tradition from a distant past.

France in the early twentieth century is a good example of the former, Hungary of the latter.

That the compartments are not watertight is exemplified by the nineteenth-century nationalist movement in Russia, which convened both attitudes. Glinka's example with respect to Oriental and Spanish exotica in the formation of an emergent Russian music has already been discussed, but his interest in exploiting the traditions of his native homeland is equally demonstrable in his incorporation of Russian folk tunes, a model that proved fundamental to succeeding generations of Russian composers.

While native melodies inspired Stravinsky to many of his discoveries, it is intriguing to note the interest of his teacher, Rimsky-Korsakov, in such materials without a similar catalytic effect. Rimsky more clearly captured the Oriental (*The Golden Cockerel, Sheherazade*) and the Spanish (*Capriccio espagnol*) note in the popular imagination than the Russian, and this in spite of numerous works based on or incorporating Russian folk melodies. Ultimately it appears that it was less the use of Russian folk melodies or Roumanian dances than the way they were adapted and transformed by Stravinsky and Bartók that signaled their potential for Western European composers. And invariably it was such surface details as melodic grace notes, unusual scalar formations (both pentatonic and octatonic), assymetrical phraseology, or the sonority of the gamelan, sitar, and cimbalom that proved to be most readily translatable into a personal idiom.

Stravinsky's first approach to the challenge of incorporating ingredients of his own culture came as a result of his meeting with Diaghilev and the commissioning of *The Firebird*. In many ways it continued nineteenth-century traditions in its mixture of themes from Russian folklore, Tchaikovsky's *Swan Lake* and other sources. The idea of the ballet had been discussed by Diaghilev and his group earlier in 1909 before he met Stravinsky, and with the decision to move forward with the project, Fokine, who choreographed the work, developed a scenario.

That Stravinsky's method conformed to that of the late nineteenth century is verified by a 1929 Aeolian Duo-Art pianola roll played by Stravinsky, which carried a running thematic commentary on the left-hand side and a detailed description of the action on the right. This virtually measure-by-measure correspondence between music and action belongs to the venerable traditions of Tchaikovsky and Petipa. On the musical side, Stravinsky confessed that he had not yet completely broken with all the devices covered by the term "Music Drama" in his employment of a system of leitmotifs. Furthermore, in making a distinction between the forces of good and evil through the adoption of diatonic and chromatic (Ex. 11.3) ideas respectively, Stravinsky borrowed directly from the example of Rimsky's *The Golden Cockerel* (1907), which in turn had endorsed a trait traceable to Glinka's *Ruslan and Lyudmila* (1842). While the composer was usually silent on the question of folk-music sources, the diatonic tunes in Example 11.1 and 11.2, two of the best known melodies from *The Firebird*, were acknowledged as quotations of Nos. 79 and 21 respectively of Rimsky-Korsakov's *100 Russian Folk Songs* (1876).

The idea for *Petrushka* came to Stravinsky following the completion of *The Firebird* and was originally intended as a *Konzertstück* for piano and orchestra. At about this time, Diaghilev, who thought Stravinsky to be at work on *The

Example 11.1. Stravinsky, *The Firebird*, m. 1.

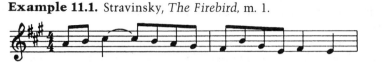

Example 11.2. Stravinsky, *The Firebird*.

Example 11.3. Stravinsky, *The Firebird*.

Molto moderato

Rite of Spring, arrived in Lausanne, and on being introduced to the music of the gestating *Petrushka*, persuaded him to turn it into a ballet. Stravinsky ultimately hit on the idea of *Petrushka*, "immortal and unhappy hero of every fair in all countries," as he later said, but in fact the pre-Lenten Carnival, familiar to post-Petrine Russia and already celebrated in the Prologue to Rimsky-Korsakov's *The Snow Maiden*, provided a ready-made tradition. Again at Diaghilev's suggestion, details of the libretto were worked out in conjunction with Alexander Benois, a devotee of Russian puppet theater who also provided set designs for the first production (Figure 11.2). The synopsis that follows appeared in the 1911 score.

Petrushka

Scene 1. *(The Admiralty Square, St. Petersburg, during the 1830s. It is a sunny winter's day, and the scene shows a corner of the Shrovetide Fair. In the background, a glimpse of roundabouts, swings and a helter-skelter. On the left, a booth with a balcony for the 'Died' (the compère of the fair). Beneath it, a table with a large samovar. In the centre, the Showman's little theatre. On the right, sweetmeat stalls and a peepshow.)*

Crowds of people are strolling about the scene—common people, gentlefolk, a group of drunkards arm-in-arm, children clustering round the peepshow, women round the stalls. A street musician appears with a hurdy-gurdy. He is accompanied by a dancer. Just as she starts to dance, a man with a musical box and another dancer turn up on the opposite side of the stage. After performing simultaneously for a short while, the rivals give up the struggle and retire. Suddenly the Showman comes out through the curtains

Figure 11.2. Benois' design for the first tableau of *Petrushka* (1911).

of the little theatre. The curtains are drawn back to reveal three puppets on their stands—Petrushka, the Ballerina and the Blackamoor. He charms them into life with his flute, and they begin to dance—at first jigging on their hooks in the little theatre, but then, to the general astonishment, stepping down from the theatre and dancing among the public in the open.

Scene II. *(Petrushka's Cell. The cardboard walls are painted black, with stars and a crescent moon upon them. Devils painted on a gold ground decorate the panels of the folding doors that lead into the Ballerina's Cell. On one of the walls is a portrait of the Showman scowling.)*

While the Showman's magic has imbued all three puppets with human feelings and emotions, it is Petrushka who feels and suffers most. Bitterly conscious of his ugliness and grotesque appearance, he feels himself to be an outsider, and he resents the way he is completely dependent on his cruel master. He tries to console himself by falling in love with the Ballerina. She visits him in his cell, and for a moment he believes he has succeeded in winning her. But she is frightened by his uncouth antics and flees. In his despair, he curses the Showman and hurls himself at his portrait, but succeeds only in tearing a hole through the cardboard wall of his cell.

Scene III. *(The Blackamoor's Cell. The wall-paper is patterned with green palm-trees and fantastic fruits on a red ground. On the right, a door leading into the Ballerina's cell.)*

The Blackamoor, clad in a magnificent costume, is lying on a divan, playing with a coconut. Though he is brutal and stupid, the Ballerina finds him most attractive and successfully uses her wiles to captivate him. Their love-scene is interrupted by the sudden arrival of Petrushka, furiously jealous. He is thrown out by the Blackamoor.

Scene IV. *(The Fair, as in Scene I.)*

It is evening, and the festivities have reached their height. A group of wet-nurses dance together. A peasant playing a pipe crosses the stage leading a performing bear. A bibulous merchant, accompanied by two gypsies, scatters handfuls of banknotes among the crowd. A group of coachmen strike up a dance and are joined by the nurses. Finally a number of masqueraders—including devil, goat and pig—rush on to the scene while Bengal flares are let off in the wings.

At this moment there is a commotion in the Showman's theatre. The rivalry between the puppets has taken a fatal turn. Petrushka rushes out from behind the curtain, pursued by the Blackamoor whom the Ballerina tries to restrain. The Blackamoor strikes down Petrushka with his scimitar. It begins to snow; and Petrushka dies, surrounded by the astonished crowd. (In the commotion the Blackamoor and the Ballerina have disappeared.) The Showman is fetched, and he reassures the by-standers that Petrushka is nothing more than a puppet with a wooden head and a body stuffed with sawdust. The crowd disperses as the night grows darker, and the Showman is left behind. But as he starts to drag the puppet off the stage, he is startled to see Petrushka's ghost appear on the roof of the little theatre, jeering and mocking at everyone whom the Showman has fooled.[9]

The presence of five principal tunes from Russian folksong collections underscores the role of native materials to Stravinsky's ballets at this time, regardless of his later soft-pedaling of their importance in his early works or their potential value to the composer in general. Perhaps Rimsky-Korsakov's brush with the critics regarding questions of originality in his incorporation of folk melodies partially explains Stravinsky's later denial regarding such elements in *The Rite of Spring*. In *Petrushka*, no admissions were necessary or denials possible because many of the tunes of the street dances, the coachmen, or the nursemaids, unlike the less familiar anthology melodies of *The Firebird*

Example 11.4. *Easter Carol* (from Rimsky-Korsakov Collection of 100 Songs, 1876). Appears at Nos. 2 and 3 in the First Pictures, and a 2 measures after 123 at the Fourth Picture.

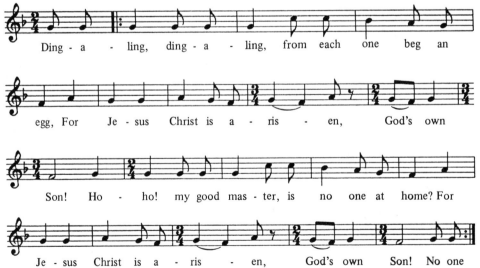

Example 11.5. *Song for St. John's Eve* (from the collection of Istomin and Liaponov, 1893). Appears from 2 measures after 34 through the measure before 41.

I am run - ning, run - ning in ___ the sun - shine ___

through the har-vest ___ field ___ run - ning I ___ reach a shrine. ___

Example 11.6. *Dance Song* (from the Rimsky-Korsakov Collection of Forty Songs, 1882). Appears 4 measures after 90. Standardized homophonic settings by both Rimsky-Korsakov and Tchaikovsky; used by Balakirev in his orchestral *Overture on Three Russian Themes* of 1858.

Ear - li - er to - night, at a ___ par - ty bright, ___

At a ___ par - ty ___ bright, ___ gos - sip - ing ga - lore.

Example 11.7. "Akh vy sieni, moi sieni" (from the Swerkoff collection). Appears beginning at 96.

Oh, you door - way, my dear door - way, Oh, my door - way new - ly

made, Door-way car - ven from new ma - ple Of a light, pret-ty shade.

Example 11.8. "O! Snow Now Thaws" (from the Prokunin-Tchaikovsky Collection). Appears at No. 109.

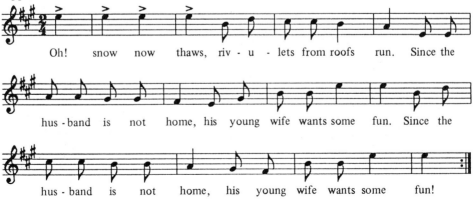

Oh! snow now thaws, riv - u - lets from roofs run. Since the

hus - band is not home, his young wife wants some fun. Since the

hus - band is not home, his young wife wants some fun!

and *The Rite*, were known to every Russian child. The use of additional popular tunes provided an easy recognizability and an intentionally brilliant exterior.

Petrushka[10]

Other quotations also occur as hurdy-gurdy tunes in scene 1: first (Ex. 11.9), a sentimental *romans* entitled "Toward Evening, in Rainy Autumn" by Nikolai Titov (1789–1843), was supplied at the composer's request by Andrey Rimsky-Korsakov (who questioned the use of such "trash"); second (Ex. 11.10), a music-hall tune, "Elle avait un' jambe en bois," Stravinsky had heard daily on a hurdy-gurdy beneath his hotel room in Beaulieu. Stravinsky was to find out that the latter tune by Emile Spencer was still under copyright, and a royalty was forthwith paid every time *Petrushka* was performed. Finally, two additional borrowings were made from Joseph Lanner's *Steyrische Tänze* (op. 165 [Ex. 11.11]) and *Die Schönbrunner* (op. 200) for the Waltz in scene 3 (Ex. 11.12).

The note of humor that Stravinsky intended can be guessed even from a casual perusal of the texts for Examples 11.4 and 11.5. The request for Easter eggs and the announcement that Christ has risen are hardly appropriate to a pre-Lenten Carnival celebration, unless, as has recently been clarified, the celebrators, singing a type of Easter carol atypical of St. Petersburg, were inebriated out-of-towners.[11] Use of the "Song for St. John's Eve" is similarly suspicious as the Feast Day for St. John is December 27. Most of the tunes

Example 11.9. Stravinsky, *Petrushka*, no. 15.

Copyright by Edition Russe de Musique. Copyright assigned to Boosey & Hawkes, Inc. Revised edition copyright 1947, 1948 by Boosey & Hawkes, Inc. Renewed 1975. Reprinted by permission of Boosey & Hawkes, Inc.

Example 11.10. Stravinsky, *Petrushka*, no. 13.

Copyright by Edition Russe de Musique. Copyright assigned to Boosey & Hawkes, Inc. Revised edition copyright 1947, 1948 by Boosey & Hawkes, Inc. Renewed 1975. Reprinted by permission of Boosey & Hawkes, Inc.

Example 11.11. Stravinsky, *Petrushka*, no. 71.

Copyright by Edition Russe de Musique. Copyright assigned to Boosey & Hawkes, Inc. Revised edition copyright 1947, 1948 by Boosey & Hawkes, Inc. Renewed 1975. Reprinted by permission of Boosey & Hawkes, Inc.

Example 11.12. Stravinsky, *Petrushka*, no. 72.

Copyright by Edition Russe de Musique. Copyright assigned to Boosey & Hawkes, Inc. Revised edition copyright 1947, 1948 by Boosey & Hawkes, Inc. Renewed 1975. Reprinted by permission of Boosey & Hawkes, Inc.

Example 11.13. Stravinsky, *Petrushka*, no. 92

possess the capacity for contrapuntal manipulation, as illustrated by Example 11.13, which juxtaposes Ex. 11.6 with a canonic presentation of the refrain figure of the opening section. Although unidentified as such, the melody of the concertant piano part suggests a potential folk origin planed in parallel 6th-chord motion (Ex. 11.14).

The arpeggiated form of the so-called *Petrushka* chord (a juxtaposition of C major and F♯ major) also emphasizes in fanfare fashion the opening fourths of

Example 11.14. Stravinsky, *Petrushka*, no. 33.

many of the *Petrushka* melodies even as it recalls an identical harmony and arpeggiation in Ravel's *Jeux d'eau* (1901).

Although the music for *Petrushka* did not evolve in Petipa-like fashion (i.e., the composer responding with small chunks of music in response to directions from a ballet master), the deployment of thematic material continues to emphasize nondevelopmental sectionalization and clear-cut repetition schemes.

Example 11.15. Stravinsky, *Petrushka*, no. 49.

Example 11.16. Ravel, *Jeux d'eau*, m. 72.

First Tableau

The Shrove-Tide Fair: ABACABA (A = Ex. 11.13; B = Ex. 11.4; C = Exs. 11.9–10)
        ends with drum roll attracting crowd to little theater.
The Magic Trick: narrative section
                30: chromaticism not only contrasts with diatonic folk-tunes but suggests magic
                        vs. natural as in *Firebird*

31: flute cadenza; perhaps inspired by Glazunov's *Raymondo*

32: 30 material; little theater curtain opens disclosing three puppets: Petrushka, a Moor, a Ballerina. Scene ends with Magician animating them with a touch of his flute.

Russian Dance: ABABA (A = Ex. 11.14; B = 11.15)

The puppets dance. Drums signal closing of scene.

Second Tableau

Petrushka's Room: a loose ABA

first conceived as *Konzertstück;* a dialogue.

48: "Petrushka's Cry," chromatic

49: "Petrushka chord" = Ex. 11.15

52: Ballerina enters; departure signaled by clarinet cadenza

60: "Petrushka's Despair." Scene closes with Ex. 11.15 + trumpet signal

Third Tableau

The Moor's Room

62: Drums announce opening of tableau

64: Syncopated rhythmic backgrounds, changing meters prefigure *Rite of Spring*

65: The Moor dances; diatonic tune against 64 followed by various changes of tempo

Dance of the Ballerina

69: cornet + percussion, arpeggios; prefigures *Histoire du soldat*

Waltz: ABA + free narrative (The Ballerina and The Moor)

71: Ex. 11.11

72: Ex. 11.12

75 = 71; 78 = 49 (Petrushka chord at quarrel with the Moor)

Fourth Tableau

The Shrove-Tide Fair

82: drums as at 47 and 62; contrary motion 3rds suggests opening of first tableau; parallel triads in oboes and violas reflects 33

Dance of the Nursemaids: localized simple forms

90: continues parallel 3rd motion + Ex. 11.6

92: figure from 1st tableau, m. 1, as counterpoint to Ex. 11.6 = Ex. 11.13

96: Ex. 11.7

98+2: Ex. 11.6 as counterpoint to Ex. 11.7

100: chromatic; peasant plays a pipe and bear walks on hind legs; cf. 30

100: folk-like; similar to Ex. 11.8

Dance of Coachmen and Stable Boys

109: Ex. 11.8

112: Ex. 11.6

The Mummers

123: Ex. 11.4

125 and 129–2: Petrushka chord + chromatics

129 = 49 + "Petrushka's lament"

130+4: Magician arrives; 30 and 32 return = Magician's chromatics

131 to end; alternating triads similar to opening

Final cadence: melody = C♯–D♯–C (rest) F♯

In 1965, at age 83, Stravinsky returned to both *The Firebird* and *Petrushka,* fashioning a "Canon on a Russian Popular Tune" for full orchestra from Ex. 11.2

and taking obvious pleasure in counterpointing Ex. 11.6 against the melody of Ex. 11.14 in a sketch.[12]

THE RITE OF SPRING

BACKGROUNDS.   The subtitle of *Le sacre du printemps*, "scenes of pagan Russia," announces not only the national origins of the composer but his country's earlier and contemporary interest in Primitivism. As noted in the beginnings of the Russian avant-garde in the preceding decades, the national tendencies of nineteenth-century Russian art were enriched by a thoroughgoing investigation of early icon painting, Scythian civilization, and numerous areas of folk-art, culminating in an openly Primitivist style by the painters Larionov and Goncharova in 1909. Presented by Diaghilev in Paris as early as 1906, these artists were soon joined in the Diaghilev circle by others with a similar inclination. Among these, none was more important for Stravinsky than Nicolas Roerich, who had worked for Mamontov's "Private Opera" during the 1880s and helped to establish the backcloth not as a decorative background but as an integral part of theater production. His passionate interest in archeology, which led to his participation in field digs from the 1890s on; his design of a Maltese cross for the tomb of Rimsky-Korsakov in 1908; and his designs for Borodin's *Prince Igor* of 1909 were all stations along the path toward the personal discovery of the latent power of primitivism. It is thus of fundamental consequence that the conception of *The Rite of Spring* was from the beginning a joint collaboration between Roerich and Stravinsky. The scenario was fashioned by the two of them, the costumes and sets realized by Roerich, and the final score dedicated to him.

Roerich's knowledge of various types of Russian preliterate theater can be assumed in the wave of interest that had focused on native Russian art. Mostly dormant for many years, they were now resurrected by Stravinsky and his collaborators in a succession of works written between 1910 and 1919. Forms devoted to pagan rituals; village weddings; minstrel animal impersonations; pre-Lenten Carnival celebrations; and stories of peasants, devils and foreign royalty played by illiterate soldiers spell the main types.[13] Stravinsky's response to each of these is clear in the scores of *The Rite of Spring, Les noces, Renard, Petrushka,* and *Histoire du soldat,* respectively.

The general temptation to connect *The Rite of Spring* with earlier Parisian achievements of such artists as Gaugin, Matisse, and Picasso is not false but unnecessarily far of the mark. True, the Fauvist's discovery of the appeal of African and Oceanic sculpture had undoubtedly served as a starting point for such a remarkable work as Brancusi's *The Kiss* of 1908 (Figure 11.3), whose reductive formalism, forecasting the importance of the nuclear oval for his later work, seems to many more primeval than primitive; and Picasso's renowned *Les demoiselles d'Avignon* of 1906–07 (Figure 11.4) had already used the planar qualities of the African mask as a springboard toward Cubism and a new definition of beauty. It is true, too, that the Franco-Russian connection was strong in artistic matters at this time. But while Picasso and Matisse had one of their most notable patrons in Sergei Shchukin, who had a room devoted to each of them in his Moscow residence, the Primitivist theme, as we have seen, had

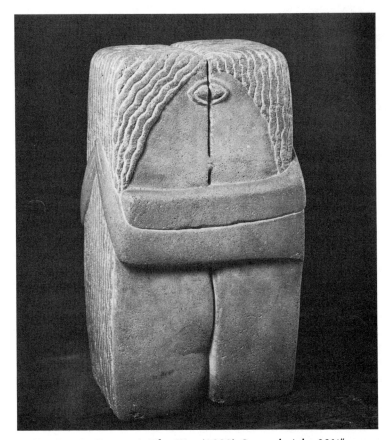

Figure 11.3. Constantin Brancusi, *The Kiss* (1908). Stone, height 22¾".
Courtesy of The Philadelphia Museum of Art. Louise and Walter Arensberg Collection. © ADAGP,
Paris/VAGA, New York, 1985.

already been completely absorbed by Russia's artistic leaders by the time of
Stravinsky's new ballet. Though Matisse's powerful and fundamental *Music* and
Dance (1909–10; Figure 11.5), which invite a natural connection with Stravinsky's "The Dance of the Adolescents," had interestingly enough been installed
in Shchukin's home as early as 1911, Kuzma Petrov-Vodkin's *The Playing Boys*
of the same year shows the absorption of similar themes and color techniques
by a native Russian. The universality of the appeal of primitive cultures as well
as the degree of artistic interchange of the time is further demonstrated by the
inclusion of seven nineteenth-century Russian peasant woodcuts in the *Blaue
Reiter* exhibition of 1911. The impression is enlarged by the procession of
countless primitive artifacts from Alaska, Brazil, Egypt, Malaysia, Mexico, New
Caledonia, the Easter Islands, and the Cameroons, together with Russian
folkprints in the *Blaue Reiter* almanac published in 1912. Their message is
compounded and sealed with the reproduction of Matisse's *The Dance* and
articles entitled "The 'Savages' of Germany" by Franz Marc and "The 'Savages' of
Russia" by D. Burliuk in the same volume (see p. 161).

   Two versions of the scenario for *The Rite of Spring* by the composer (1910,
1912) and two versions by Roerich (1912, 1913) survive. The one included here

Figure 11.4. Picasso, *Les Demoiselles d'Avignon* (1907). Oil on canvas, 8′ × 7′8″.

Collection, The Museum of Modern Art, New York. Acquired through the Lillie P. Bliss Bequest. © SPADEM, Paris/VAGA, New York, 1985.

Figure 11.5. Henri Matisse, *The Dance* (1909–10).

The Hermitage, Leningrad. © SPADEM, Paris/VAGA, New York, 1985.

is the first version of the composer, preceded by the titles of the sections from the score, which were devised by Roerich. That Stravinsky's conferences with Roerich in 1911 took place at the estate of Princess Tanisheva in Talshkino removes any doubt as to the importance of her fin-de-siècle activities for the two artists.[14]

> *Vesna Svyasschennaya (The Rite of Spring)* is a musical-choreographic work. It represents pagan Russia and is unified by a single idea: the mystery and great surge of the creative power of Spring. The piece has no plot, but the choreographic succession is as follows:
>
> First Part: The Kiss of The Earth
>
> The spring celebration. It takes place in the hills. The pipers pipe and young men tell fortunes. The old woman enters. She knows the mystery of nature and how to predict the future. Young girls with painted faces come in from the river in single file. They dance the spring dance. Games start. The Spring Khorovod. The people divide into two groups, opposing each other. The holy procession of the wise old man. The oldest and wisest interrupts the spring games, which come to a stop. The people pause trembling before the great action. The old men bless the spring earth. *The Kiss of the Earth.* The people dance passionately on the earth, sanctifying it and becoming one with it.
>
> Second Part: The Great Sacrifice
>
> At night the virgins hold mysterious games, walking in circles. One of the virgins is consecrated as the victim and is twice pointed to by fate, being caught twice in the perpetual circle. The virgins honor her, the chosen one, with a marital dance. They invoke the ancestors and entrust the chosen one to the old wise man. She sacrifices herself in the presence of the old men in the great holy dance, the great sacrifice.

THE MUSIC. The world premiere of *The Rite* was staged by Serge Diaghilev on May 29, 1913, at the Théâtre des Champs-Elysées, Paris, choreographed by Nijinsky and conducted by Pierre Monteux. The spirit of the event was captured in a caricature of the same year by Cocteau (Figure 11.6), and the details surrounding the premiere have been vividly recalled by the composer and personally read for a phonograph recording made in 1962.[15]

The Rite of Spring has been one of the most discussed and analyzed works of the twentieth century. But while the artists at Abramtsevo and Talshkino undoubtedly formed a powerful background, the absence of any musical forces more potent than Rimsky-Korsakov's *Sadko* and *Kitezh* encourages the consideration of other influences upon Stravinsky's dramatic solution in *The Rite*. Taruskin has detailed the potential importance of a movement begun by Melgunov to transcribe Russian folk tunes in a new and non-prejudicial manner. Attention was given not only to the principal melody but to the "heterophonic aspects of its performance practice."[16] The problems inherent in trying to record this practice were solved with the aid of a phonograph, and the first collections reflecting this field work were published by Evgeniia Linyova between 1904 and 1909.

That Stravinsky knew of and requested copies of Linyova's collections is proven by correspondence. Although the leap from Linyova to *The Rite* is

Figure 11.6. "The Rite of Spring," a caricature by Jean Cocteau (1913). Stravinsky energetically attacks the keyboard as the elders, youths, and sacrificial virgin are etched in "cubist" poses in the background. Regarding Cocteau and Stravinsky, see pp. 000, 000, 000–000.

immense, it is well to keep in mind that such dissonating heterophonic techniques proved important not only for this work but for those written shortly thereafter such as *Les noces* and *Renard.* Beyond the so-called Russian style, Schönberger and Andriessen have also fascinatingly detailed the force of the heterophonic unison from the *Octet* (1922–23) to *Agon* (1953–57).[17] While Stravinsky had espoused Rimsky's folklorist-diatonic and fantastic-chromatic genres in *Firebird* and *Petrushka*, in *The Rite* he sought a new solution which attempted a fusion of the two in the context which sought to submerge the folktune content and transform it on the basis of heterophonic and intersecting diatonic-octatonic formations.

Numerous features have traditionally been viewed as natural continuations of the style of *Petrushka:* (a) the reliance on Russian folktunes (Exs. 11.19–11.23; unacknowledged by Stravinsky except for the bassoon melody of Ex. 11.19);[18] (b) the view of its most familiar harmonies as bitonal conglomerations (the C major/F♯ major conjunction in *Petrushka*, Ex. 11.15, has been held as analogous to the F♭/E♭[7] juxtaposition in the "Dance of the Adolescents," Ex. 11.17, and the D[7]/E♭[7] in the "Danse sacrale," Ex. 11.18); and (c) an extrovert orchestration. The bitonal explanation of Exs. 11.17–18, encouraged by the registrally discrete projection of the components, has recently been supplemented, however, by the

Example 11.17. Stravinsky, *The Rite of Spring:* "Dance of the Youths and Maidens," opening.

view of a pervasive diatonic-octatonic linkage fundamental to Stravinsky's vocabulary from the early ballets to works of the 1950s.[19]

Equally central to the personality of the score, and the feature most frequently discussed, is its rhythmic manner. Stravinsky's music in general tends to subscribe to two kinds of rhythmic-metric constructions: (a) changing meters homorhythmically articulated by registrally and timbrally fixed components (e.g., *The Rite of Spring*, "Sacrificial Dance," Ex. 11.18); and (b) stable metrics, or consistently varying ones, serving as an ostinato against which other lines are deployed with their own noncoincidental metric life (e.g., the first of the *Three Pieces for String Quartet*, Ex. 11.25). Although the first of these types frequently gives the impression of a free primitive assault, in seminars as early as 1939 Messiaen undertook fundamental investigations that disclosed what he has labeled *personnages rythmiques*. Many years later, one of his pupils, Pierre Boulez, elaborated on Messiaen's observations, demonstrating that the three cells that articulate the opening of the "Danse sacrale" are laid out in an audible scheme as follows (the numbers indicate the number of sixteenth-notes in the pattern at each appearance; see Ex. 11.18):[20]

[A-3, A-2, A'-3], B-7, [A-2, A'-3], B-7, [A'-3], C-8, [A-2, A'-2], B-7, C-5, [A'-5, A-2, A'-2]
[A-3, A'-2, A'-3], B-4, [A'-2],   B-4, [A'-3, A-2, A'-3],   B-4, C-5, C-7

It will be noted that the A and C cells are constantly changing in duration, while the B cell remains the same for stretches of time (initially a pattern of seven sixteenths followed by one of four sixteenths). Boulez does not divide the A idea into its component parts. The recognition of A' as a related but distinct harmony, however, allows the observation of its use as a link to the opening sonority of B in every instance. The barring of each of the three A components in its own measure at the beginning provides a visual analysis of a pattern that will be systematically contracted by one measure at each of its following two appearances. Such patterning, a recurrent formalization of this rondo-like movement, is characteristic of other works of Stravinsky (see the last of the *Three Pieces for String Quartet*, 1914) and one that is fundamental to Messiaen's mature style as well (see his "Reprise par Interversions," *Livre d'orgue*, 1951, Ex. 24.3).

The bitonal clashes and the cellular rhythmic structures that prosper alongside a folk melos are the central ingredients of Stravinsky's Russian style.

Example 11.18. Stravinsky, *The Rite of Spring*: "Sacrificial Dance", no. 142–145.

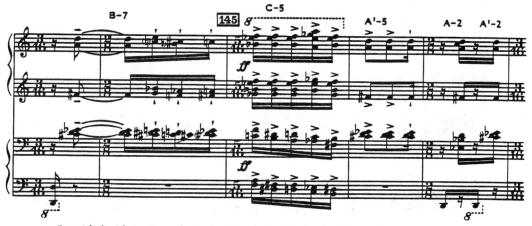

The association of such factors with a waning Exoticism or flourishing
Primitivism is only coincidental to a more fundamental import on the musical
manners of countless composers who subsequently came under the spell of *The
Rite*. As Debussy remarked shortly after the premiere:

It is not necessary to tell you of the joy I have had to see my name associated with a very beautiful thing that will be more beautiful still with the passage of time. For me, who descend the other slope of the hill but keep an intense passion for music, it is a special satisfaction to tell you how much you have enlarged the boundaries of the permissible in the empire of sound.[21]

That time has not staled its force and has only tended to support Debussy's early assessment may be judged from the following words of Boulez:

As to the composition itself, it does not *depend* on the argument of a ballet . . . In *The Rite of Spring* he stumbled upon the solution almost unaware, and rendered null and void the distinctions . . . between pure and 'programme' music, between music that is formal and that which is expressive. This ritual of 'Pagan Russia' attains a dimension quite beyond its point of departure; it has become the ritual—and the myth—of modern music."[22]

Example 11.19. Stravinsky, *The Rite of Spring.* Passages adapted from folk song. Juszkiewicz, *Litauische Volks-Weisen* (1900), No. 157:

The Rite of Spring, opening bassoon melody and No. 12:

Example 11.20. Stravinsky, *The Rite of Spring.* Passages adapted from folk song. Juszkiewicz, No. 142:

The Rite of Spring, 1 bar after 47:

Example 11.21. Stravinsky, *The Rite of Spring.* Passages adapted from folk song.

Juszkiewicz, No. 34 (also in Glazunov's *Stenka Razin,* 1885):

The Rite of Spring, 4 bars after 12; 14 through 36:

Example 11.22. Stravinsky, *The Rite of Spring.* Passages adapted from folk song.

Juszkiewicz, No. 787:

The Rite of Spring, 19 through 21:

Example 11.23. Stravinsky, *The Rite of Spring.* Passages adapted from folk song.

Juszkiewicz, No. 249:

Example 11.23 (Continued)
Juszkiewicz, No. 271:

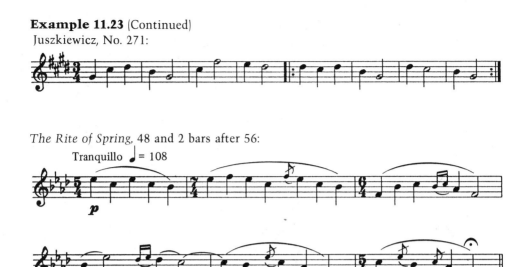

The Rite of Spring, 48 and 2 bars after 56:

Tranquillo ♩ = 108

The Rite of Spring[23]

First Part: Adoration of the Earth

Introduction: Ex. 11.19
> Rehearsal No. 1: harmonic 4th initial appearance; used chromatically at Nos. 3, 6; becomes harmonic tritone at No. 8; melodic 4th prominently used at No. 9.
> No. 12: Return of Ex.11.19 followed by first suggestion of ostinato based on Ex.11.21 (at E♭ level prefiguring bitonal complex at No. 13).

The Augurs of Spring (Les Augures Printaniers); Dances of the Young Girls (Danses des Adolescentes)
> No. 13: Basic bitonal complex: E♭ + F♭ major; bitonal complexes a semitone apart are fundamental to the *Rite*. Ostinato of Ex.11.21 continues.
> No. 19: Rising-falling scalar pattern (F–B♭) belongs to E♭ chord, underscores essential diatonic nature of materials. Ex.11.22.
> No. 25: A genuine tune, folk-like, unidentified; returns at No. 27 = *Young Girls*: continues through No. 35.

Ritual of Abduction (Jeu du Rapt)
> No. 37: alternating C^7–$E♭^7$ with material based on Ex.11.20.
> No. 41: chromatic tone clusters and linear chromatics, 39-2 and 41-2, 7ths.
> No. 44: heraldic 4ths relate to Ex.11.20 and prepare the way for the transformation of Ex.11.20 (which reappears at No. 46) into the material at No. 47 = D below.

Spring Rounds (Rondes Printanières): ABCBCDA
> A No. 48: Two melodies juxtaposed to become Ex.11.23.
> B No. 49: +3 = motif derived from Ex.11.20, mm. 3–6.
> C No. 50: Melody, unidentified, is inversion of Ex.11.22; B(No. 52); C(No. 53).
> D No. 54: Ex.11.20 in No. 47 transformation
> A No. 56: No. 48 (Ex.11.23).

Ritual of the Rival Tribes (Jeux des Cités Rivales)
> No. 57: 7ths + diatonic melody prepares for No. 60–61=Ex.11.22 in new guise, which dominates the scene to its end.

Procession of the Sage (Cortège du Sage)
> No. 67: Harmonies emphasize tritone: melody from Ex.11.20.

Dance of the Earth (Danse de la Terre)
> No. 72: Elements of whole-tone (No. 73 + 5); E–B–B♭ cluster; ostinato begins with tritone. Tritone, semitonal relationships persist, preparing for the opening of Part Two.

Second Part: The Sacrifice

Introduction
> No. 79: D–A against oscillating E♭–C♭.
> No. 80: Chord stream in similar motion prefigures Messiaen's keyboard parallelisms based on the limited modes of transposition. This continues to No. 84.

Mystic Circles of the Young Girls (Cercles Mystérieux des Adolescentes)
> No. 91: Melody of No. 81–84 continues.
> No. 93: + 4, Melody is related to openings of Exs.11.21–22.
> No. 99: No. 91 Melody.
> No. 103: End of section, concludes on two superimposed 4th chords: F♯–B♯–E♯/D♯–G♯–Cx.

Glorification of the Chosen One (Glorification de l'Élue)
> No. 104: E♭^{7} (M–m 3rd) over A pedal, 4th-chord spellings; static harmony propelled through changing meters; procedure similar to "Sacrificial Dance."
> No. 107: Duplicates No. 103, and again at No. 108.
> No. 109 & No. 109 + 1: two discrete measures, which are extended-contracted in ensuing sections over ostinati.

Evocation of the Ancestors (Evocation des Ancêtres)
> No. 121: Alternating tympani and chordal punctuations.

Ritual Action of the Ancestors (Action Rituelle des Ancêtres) (ABA)
> No. 129: Ostinato pattern set up.
> No. 132: Melody is step-wise descending through a 4th; related to Exs.11.21,22,23.
> No. 139: Return of No. 129, including chromatic melodic figuration.

Sacrificial Dance (The Chosen One): A kind of Rondo: A (142); B (149); A (167); C (172); A (180); C (181); A (186).
> No. 142: D^7 + E♭^{7} (basic *Rite* relationship).
> No. 149: Diatonic 13th chord on G to which chromatic melody No. 151 is added.
> No. 154: Movement to D-Bass over which various sonorities are projected, finally settling at No. 159 to E♭ (min/dim)
> No. 167: No. 142, only D^7 + C♯^{7}.
> No. 172–180: centered around D, alternating duplet + triplet patterns.
> No. 180: No. 142 (D^7 + single E♭).
> No. 181: Analogous to 172.
> No. 186: No. 142; Center is A; conflict with G♯–B♭.
> No. 201 + 4: Final Cadence chord is: D–A + E–G♯.

FROM *LE SACRE* TO *LES NOCES*

Except for the completion of his opera and its stepchild, *Chant du rossignol*, Stravinsky purposely avoided writing for the full orchestra during the six or seven years following the premiere of *The Rite*. For the most part, his attention is drawn to the writing of chamber works, including those for string quartet, voice with piano or instruments, and various ad hoc instrumental ensembles. While the reduction in size of the performing group seems to indicate a reaction against the style of his ballets, many of the harmonic, rhythmic, and formal qualities of *The Rite* are preserved and distilled.

Furthermore, Stravinsky's obsession during this period with the theme of animals and children, a favorite of the Russian primitivists, is typically made through Russian folk texts and constitutes a link with the past. While the melodies of the *Souvenirs* date from as early as 1906, the completion of the piano accompaniment in 1913 (orch. 1929–30) launched a series of similarly inspired pieces with unusual instrumental combinations such as the *Pribaoutki* (1914) for voice, flute, oboe, clarinet, bassoon, violin, viola, cello, and double bass.

Stravinsky has given us information that suggests a fundamental reason for the appeal of the *pribaoutki* type of text.

> The word *pribaoutki* denotes a form of popular Russian verse, to which the nearest English parallel is the limerick. According to the popular tradition they derive from a type of game in which someone says a word, which someone else then adds to, and which third and fourth persons develop, and so on, with utmost speed . . . One important characteristic of Russian popular verse is that the accents of the spoken verse are ignored when the verse is sung. The recognition of the musical possibilities inherent in this fact was one of the most rejoicing discoveries of my life.[24]

It was an attitude that Stravinsky had struck earlier in his *Japanese Lyrics* of 1912–13, without the ethnic linguistic excuse, and one that he would strike again in other works and in other languages, most notably in *Oedipus Rex* (Latin) and *Perséphone* (French). The accentuation of the first of the Japanese songs consistently runs counter to the proper Russian accent, marked ´ in the voice part (Ex. 11.24). Indeed, the English underlay is more nearly proper than the Russian—the reason that compelled Stravinsky to state that he would rather not hear his Russian songs at all than hear them sung in translation.

A letter from Miaskovsky to Prokofiev, written in June 1913, is pointed in observing that the correct declamation of the first song could be achieved by moving the music one eighth note to the left. The manuscript sketches from October 1912 show that this was indeed Stravinsky's initial solution.[25] The rationale for the composer's final accentual choices in the opening of "Akahito" appears to be provided through their association with the pitches E♭ and B♭ attended by grace notes in the accompaniment. Forecast in the opening measure, it persists as an ostinato following the entrance of the voice.

The testimony of these pieces to the continuing appeal of things Japanese is reinforced by the appearance in 1914 of an anthology of Japanese lyrics in German translation, *Japanische Frühling*, by Hans Bethge, whose *Chinesische Flöte* had served Mahler as the textual source for *Das Lied von der Erde*. The *Three Japanese Lyrics* (1912–13) were written simultaneously with the creation of *The Rite of Spring*, and their economical style seems almost to be a self-conscious antidote to the explosive language which he was developing in the ballet. Stravinsky later claimed in his autobiography that, having read a small

Example 11.24. Stravinsky, *Three Japanese Lyrics:* "Akahito," mm. 1–4.

anthology of Japanese poems in Russian translation during the summer of 1912, he was impressed with their similarity to Japanese paintings and engravings, and that "the graphic solution of problems of perspective and space shown by their art incited me to find something analogous in music."[26] While the reduction in forces is appropriate to a haiku setting, musical gestures traceable to an authentic Japanese music are, unlike Holst's *Japanese Suite* of 1916, absent beyond the grace-note style and limited pitch content of the melodies, characteristics that appear concurrently as part of Stravinsky's Russian manner.

The sketches for "Akahito," completed October 19, 1912, also include the composer's initial choices for an instrumental ensemble composed of two violins, two violas, cello, piano, piccolo, and flute. Stravinsky was in Berlin on December 4 where he attended a performance of *Petrushka* with Arnold Schoenberg, who later confessed that he had enjoyed it. On December 8,

Stravinsky heard a performance of *Pierrot lunaire* in the very hall in which it had received its premiere on October 16 of that year. The second and third of the *Japanese Lyrics* were written December 18 and January 22, 1913, respectively. Though Stravinsky's final instrumentation (2 fl, 2 cl, pf, 2 vn, va, vc) drops a viola and adds two clarinets, purportedly to conform exactly to the *Pierrot* ensemble which he admired (see pp. 113, 185), it is also possible that the original ensemble choice, made three days following the premiere of Schoenberg's melodrama, may have reflected Stravinsky's knowledge of it from press notices. In any event, the instrumental usage of the *Japanese Lyrics* shares little of the rotational variety and general coloristic sense of *Pierrot*. Indeed, the first piece is a companion to many of Stravinsky's *pribaoutki* written about the same time, while the introduction to the second piece recalls *The Nightingale*. The melodic sevenths of the last piece have encouraged some to stress its relationship to Schoenberg; the counterpart for them as well as for the ostinati of the opening song is readily to be found in *The Rite*, however, and overall the mark of the Russian prevails.

Stravinsky's two sets of *Easy Pieces* (1914–15; 1916–17) for piano duet and his *The Five Fingers* (1920–21) project a simplicity of means that may recall the invocation of Clementi in Saint-Saëns' *Carnival of the Animals* (1886) and Debussy's "Doctor Gradus ad Parnassum" (*Children's Corner Suite*, 1906–08), but their relation to the current Russian predilection for the naïf and children's art in particular as part of their preoccupation with various modes of primitivist expression is more fundamental. The directness of folksong also attracted Bartók to the writing of sets of easy pieces for children almost from his first years as a composer; and the important and stylistically more diversified *Mikrokosmos* similarly emphasized the young child in its earliest volumes. Paradoxically, these "easy pieces," whether by Stravinsky, Bartók, or Satie, frequently prove to be the breeding ground for manners that were to be used later in a more thoroughgoing fashion. Pandiatonicism,[27] polytonality, and metrical games are characteristically projected with an inimitable force precisely because the ideas have been reduced to the barest essentials. The march, waltz, and polka of the *Three Easy Pieces* (1914–15), dedicated to Casella, Satie, and Diaghilev, are marked by a directness of phraseology wedded to the discordant edge of pandiatonicism already visible in Satie's *Enfantines* (1913) and *Sports et Divertissements* (1914). More than elementary pieces with a didactic potential, they may be seen both as a mirror of Satie's "new simplicity" (p. 267) and as a preparation for the clarified Neoclassic style that was to be launched by Stravinsky in *Pulcinella* of 1919 and the *Octet* of 1922–23 (p. 316).

In more abstract terrain, the same claim may be made for the first of the *Three Pieces for String Quartet* (1914) (Ex.11.25), where the cello's ostinato (3 + 2 + 2 quarters), which defines the metric progress of the work; the first violin part, whose range is limited to a perfect fourth (g'–c"), yet whose melodic repetition encompasses an idea 23 (11 + 6 + 6) quarter notes in length; the viola's irregularly placed descending tetrachord (f♯'–c♯'), which provides both bitonal and rhythmic spice (alternating between single and double statements); and the distinctions in register and articulation for each—together make for a classic distillation of many of the properties of *The Rite*. This is especially true of the final piece of the set, where clearly alternating sections conform to Messiaen's notion of *personnages rythmiques* in the "Danse sacrale" (pp.

Example 11.25. Stravinsky, *Three Pieces for String Quartet*, Mvt. 1, mm. 1–11.

216–17). The first of Stravinsky's *Three Pieces for String Quartet* may also be seen as reasonably analogous to the premises of the Cubists in its simultaneous presentation of polytonal and temporarily displaced complementarities. The portrait of Stravinsky in the same year (1914) by Albert Gleizes, undisputed theorist of the Cubists whose tract *Du Cubisme* had appeared in 1912, encourages the connection (Figure 11.7).

Figure 11.7. Portrait of Stravinsky by Albert Gleizes (1914).
Photo courtesy of Giraudon/Art Resource. © ADAGP, Paris/VAGA, New York, 1985.

Of the immediately following works, the story of *Renard* (1915–16) was well known in numerous cultures outside of Russia, being one of the oldest beast tales from Medieval times. More importantly, the spare instrumental style is in harmony with the works mentioned earlier, and not only paves the way for *Histoire du soldat* (1918), but in its incorporation of the cimbalom projects for the first time a timbral novelty that was to reappear in *Ragtime for Eleven Instruments* (1918).

The *Berceuses du chat* ("Cat's Cradle Songs") were written during the same years as *Renard*, of which it is a mirror in microcosm. To Russian popular animal texts intoned by a contralto, Stravinsky joined the timbre of three clarinets in three ranges (E♭, A/B♭, bass clarinet). The style is as terse as the resources are economical, and the limited pitch content of the vocal part in the first song, "On the Stove," is matched by the steady gurgling ostinato of the accompaniment, which miraculously captures the mood of the epigrammatic text:

> You sleep on the stove, cat, nice and warm.
> The clock ticks: it ticks, but not for you.

The songs are dedicated to the artist Goncharova, with whom Stravinsky was to collaborate in *Les noces*, and her husband Larionov, who was assisting him at the time in the creation of *Renard* (Fig. 11.8). The internalization of the Russian folk manner of the early ballets has now led to a stylistic distillation free from melodic quotation and reflects the turn of mind of the composer, who was already at work on *Les noces*.

LES NOCES

Both text and music of Stravinsky's *Les noces* (*The Wedding*) conspired to make it a fitting climax to his so-called Russian period. The reliance on Kireyevsky's collection of Russian popular poems for this "Village Wedding" insured a native

Figure 11.8. Michael Larionov, *Renard* ("The Fox", 1921). Design for scenery made for the ballet produced by the Ballet Russe de Monte Carlo, 1922. Watercolor, 19 3/4" × 25 1/2".

quality in the subject matter. Stravinsky described the libretto, which he fashioned himself, as

> a suite of typical wedding episodes told through quotations of typical talk . . . As a collection of clichés and quotations of typical wedding sayings it might be compared to one of those scenes in *Ulysses* in which the reader seems to be overhearing scraps of conversation without the connecting thread of discourse.[28]

Not only the texts but the accompanying materials give the impression of being based on folk material, and while musical quotation is apparently limited, the vocal melos is based on the composer's already developed *pribaoutki* folk style and Russian Orthodox chant, both of which emphasize diatonicism, limited motivic content, and a free approach to accentuation. The following example from the opening illustrates the importance of a pervading three-note motif, which persists to the choral finale and chime-like coda that closes the work.

Example 11.26. Stravinsky, *Les noces* (1917).

Example 11.26 (Continued)

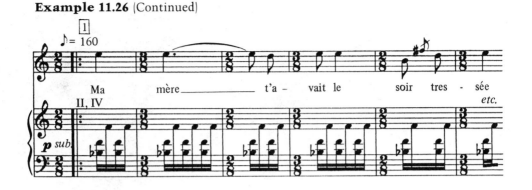

The vocal melody contains three central pitches (B,D,E) plus a grace-note F♯ compatible with E or B Dorian. The ambiguity of this potential diatonic collection is clarified at No. 1 with the introduction of B♭ and F in pianos II and IV suggesting an octatonic base (E,D,C♯,B,B♭,A♭,G,F) now allied with changes in tempo, register, and dynamics. The E–D–B cell, central not only to the section but to the work as a whole, is the link between the two formations. Such diatonic-octatonic linkage has been demonstrated by van den Toorn to be central to Stravinsky's personality from his earliest ballets through his Neoclassic period to the early serial works, and may owe its genesis to an admiration for similar formations in the works of Rimsky-Korsakov, *Sadko* in particular.[29]

As with the *Japanese Lyrics* and the *Pribaoutki*, performances of *Les noces* (a title which has persisted from the beginning) in languages other than Russian guarantee a falsification of the original accentuation. Though Stravinsky himself conducted numerous performances of the work in both French and English, his dissatisfaction with them was balanced only by the prospect of a modest increase in audience comprehension for a work whose cultural context is totally unfamiliar to non-Russians.

The instrumentation for *Les noces* proved difficult for the composer. The short score of the work had been completed as early as 1917, but his final solution for the orchestra was not achieved until 1921. Preceding this were two versions: one for large orchestra (1917) of strings and winds plus harpsichord, piano, cimbalom, and percussion; and a second version of the first and second tableaux (1919) for two cimbaloms, harmonium, pianola, and percussion (abandoned because of difficulties in the synchronization of the mechanical piano). The final version brought a further reduction: four pianos and percussion.

Diaghilev was ecstatic with *Les noces*, which on first hearing moved him to tears and the observation that it was destined to be "the most beautiful and the most purely Russian creation" of the Russian ballet. In the final production, Nijinska's choreography created a striking ethnic attitude through the insistent use of mass blockings, arched arms, and crossed legs. Goncharova created the decor and costumes based on authentic peasant designs, but in the final version the former was simplified to the point of austerity and the latter were stripped of their color at the request of the composer.

Figure 11.9. Massine, Goncharova, Larionov, Stravinsky, and Bakst (August 1915).
Photo courtesy of Robert Craft.

For all of its origins in a native folk literature and song, the effect of *Les noces* was not only new but, to Western Eufopean and American ears, exotic-primitive more than Russian. It was in fact the final distillation of impulses evident from Stravinsky's first ballets. The internalization of the various ingredients had led to the summation of the composer's first period. Its sound soon passed into the international repertoire transposed as a manifestation of Futurist tendencies (as in Antheil's *Ballet mécanique*), as a natural ally to the telling of Medieval and Classic tales (Orff, *Carmina Burana* and *Catulli Carmina*), or as an agent for sacred ritual (Messiaen, *Trois petites liturgies*, 2nd mvt.). In the composer's own career, what was seemingly a farewell to the Russian period was to return in the composer's last major work: the resounding chimes that form the coda to the wedding ritual in *Les noces* reappear with symbolic intent in the coda to Stravinsky's own final rite, the *Requiem Canticles* of 1966.

REPERTOIRE

Souvenir de mon enfance (1906; 1913), v, pf
The Firebird (1909–10), orch
The Rite of Spring (1911–13), orch
Three Japanese Lyrics (1912–13), S, 2 fl, 2 cl, pf, 2 vn, 2 va, vc
Three Pieces for String Quartet (1914)
Pribaoutki (1914), v, fl, ob/eng hn, cl, bn, vn, ba, vc, db
Les noces (1914–17; 1921–23), 4 pf, perc
Renard (1915–16), 2T, 2B, perc, str qnt, wnds, str.

Berceuses du chat (1915–16), contralto, 3 cl (E♭, B♭, bass cl)
Histoire du soldat (1918), cl, bn, corn, tbn, vn, db, perc

READING

Charles Hamm, *Petrushka,* Critical Score with Introduction and Essays (New York, 1967).

Frederick W. Sternfeld, "Some Russian Folk Songs in Stravinsky's *Petrouchka,"* in Hamm, *op. cit.,* 103–215.

Arthur Berger, "Problems of Pitch Organization in Stravinsky," in *Perspectives on Schoenberg and Stravinsky,* ed. B. Boretz and E. Cone (Princeton, 1968), 123–125.

Pierre Boulez, *Notes of an Apprenticeship* (1968).

Robert Craft, "Genesis of a Masterpiece," in *The Rite of Spring: Sketches* (London, 1969).

Allen Forte, *The Harmonic Organization of "The Rite of Spring"* (New Haven, 1978).

Vera Stravinsky and Robert Craft, *Stravinsky in Pictures and Documents* (New York, 1978): "The Firebird," 58; "Petrushka," 66; "Le Sacre du Printemps," 75; "Three Japanese Lyrics," 107; "Three Pieces for String Quartet," 126; "Les Noces," 145.

Lawrence Morton, "Footnotes to Stravinsky Studies: 'Le Sacre du Printemps'," *Tempo,* cxxviii (1979), 9–16.

Eric Walter White, *Stravinsky,* 2nd ed. (Berkeley, 1979).

François Lesure, ed., *Igor Stravinsky, "Le sacre du printemps": dossier de presse* (Geneva, 1980).

Richard Taruskin, "Russian Folk Melodies in *The Rite of Spring,"* *Journal of the American Musicological Society,* xxxiii.3 (1980), 501–543.

Boris V. Asaf'yev, *A Book about Stravinsky* (1977; Eng. trans. Richard French, Ann Arbor, MI, 1982). See review *Musical Analysis* (July, 1984), 207–8.

Simon Karlinsky, "Stravinsky and Russian Pre-Literate Theater," *19th Century Music,* vi.3 (1983), 232–240. (Concerning *The Rite of Spring, Renard, Petrushka* and *Les noces.*)

Peter van den Toorn, *The Music of Igor Stravinsky* (New Haven, 1983).

Richard Taruskin, "How the Acorn Took Root: A Tale of Russia," *19th Century Music,* vi.3 (1983), 189–212. (Concerning the use of folk themes in Glinka and Balakirev.)

Richard Taruskin, "*The Rite* Revisited: The Idea and Sources of the Scenario," *Music and Civilization: Essays in Honor of Paul Henry Lang,* ed. Maria Rika Maniates and Edomond Strainchamps (New York, 1984), 183–202.

Pierre Boulez, "Stravinsky: *The Rite of Spring"* in *Orientations* (Cambridge, Mass., 1986), 362–63. Originally a sleeve note for the recording by Boulez, CBS, MS 7293.

Jann Pasler, ed., *Confronting Stravinsky: Man, Musician, and Modernist* (Berkeley, 1986):

———. Simon Karlinsky, "Igor Stravinsky and Russian Preliterate Theater," 3.

———. Richard Taruskin, "From Subject to Style: Stravinsky and the Painters," 16.

———. Jann Pasler, "Music and Spectacle in *Petrushka* and *The Rite of Spring,"* 53.

———. David Hockney, "Set Designing for Stravinsky," 89.

———. Allen Forte, "Harmonic Syntax and Voice Leading in Stravinsky's Early Music," 130.

———. Peter C. van den Toorn, "Octatonic Pitch Structure in Stravinsky," 130.

———. Louis Cyr, "Writing *The Rite* Right," 157.

———. Jonathan D. Kramer, "Discontinuity and Proportion in the Music of Stravinsky," 174.

———. Takashi Funayama, "*Three Japanese Lyrics* and Japonisme," 273.

Claudio Spies, "Conundrums, Conjectures, Construals; or 5 vs. 3: The Influence of Russian Composers on Stravinsky" in *Stravinsky Retrospectives,* ed. E. Haimo and P. Johnson (Lincoln, 1987), 76.

Richard Taruskin, "Stravinsky's 'Rejoicing Discovery' and What It Meant: In Defense of His Notorious Text Setting" in *Stravinsky Retrospectives,* ed. E. Haimo and P. Johnson (Lincoln, 1987), 162.

PART 4

NEW ISMS AND NATIONAL IDENTITIES, 1910–1930

Between 1922 and 1930 . . . almost every year a new kind of music was created and that of the preceding year collapsed. It started with the European musicians imitating American jazz. Then followed "Machine Music" and "New Objectivity" and "Music for Every Day Use" . . . and finally "Neo-classicism."

—Arnold Schoenberg, "How One Becomes Lonely"
(1937) in *Style and Idea* (1975), 52.

Perhaps the most obvious symptom of the present crisis is its "confusion of tongues."

—Roger Sessions, "Music in Crisis,"
Modern Music, x (1932–33), 64.

The trouble with *avant-garde,* originally a term in
military tactics, is that it assumes the adventures of
individual and small-group experimenters to be justifi-
able only as they may open up a terrain through which
some larger army will then be able to pass.

—Virgil Thomson, "The Genius Type,"
The New York Review of Books,
September 26, 1968.

CHAPTER 12

FUTURISM: MANIFESTOS AND MACHINES

ITALIAN FUTURISM

The Futurist movement had its origins in an Italian turn-of-the-century sociopolitical revolt against outworn institutions whose roots were seen to reside in an uncritical acceptance of the past. This state of affairs, it was believed, had led to a state of cultural inertia in Italy, and the early figures associated with the movement shared a typical disdain for the church, socialism, and the monarchy, while in music this extended to the critics, publishers, Puccini, and melodrama. Seeking to blend the riches of the past with a dynamic present, a new, highly nationalistic view of the future was proclaimed.

The founder and leader of the movement was the Italian poet Filippo Tommaso Marinetti (1876–1944) who spelled out his new credo in *The Founding and Manifesto of Futurism* (1909):

> We will sing of great crowds excited by work, by pleasure, and by riot; we will sing of the multicoloured polyphonic tides of revolution in the modern capitals; we will sing of the vibrant nightly fervour of arsenals and shipyards blazing with violent electric moons; greedy railway stations that devour smoke-plume serpents; factories hung from clouds by the crooked lines of their smoke; bridges that stride the rivers like giant gymnasts, flashing in the sun with the litter of knives; adventurous steamers that sniff the horizon; deep-chested locomotives whose wheels paw the tracks like the hooves of enormous steel horses bridled by tubing; and the sleek flight of planes whose propellers chatter in the wind like banners and seem to cheer like an enthusiastic crowd.[1]

Marinetti's *Manifesto of Futurist Poetry* was also published in 1909, and similar manifestos soon appeared for painting (1912), sculpture (1912), and music (1910–12). In an open letter entitled "Down with the Tango and Parsifal" (1914) Marinetti decried the "effeminizing poisons of the tango," a clear reference to the rage for tango teas of the time, and the "industrialization of Baudelaire, *Fleurs du mal* weaving around the taverns of Jean Lorraine for impotent voyeurs *à la* Huysmans and inverts like Oscar Wilde." He added that "If the tango is bad, *Parsifal* is worse, because it inoculates the dancers swaying in languorous boredom with an incurable musical neurasthenia."[2] In general the masterpiece was decried, and while Debussy and Musorgsky were acknowledged as important, their influence was declared moribund.

Beyond the prolix and bellicose nature of their statements, the principal binding ingredients between the various arts were a reverence for the dynamism of urban life, a glorification of speed, and the polyphony of noises inspired by the machine age. The music of consequence that emerged from the Futurist movement directly was virtually nonexistent. Pratella (1880–1955), the only trained composer of the group and author of the principal manifestos on music, wrote a *Musica Futurista* for orchestra that was essentially too conservative to reflect properly the rhetoric of the movement. In addition to his "Manifesto of the Futurist Musicians" of 1910, Pratella wrote two additional manifestos, the "Technical Manifesto of Futurist Music" and "The Destruction of Quadrature," all three being published together in 1912. The latter of these three tracts was directly analogous to Marinetti's "Destruction of Syntax," which was obviously Symbolist inspired, and the "Technical Manifesto" explicitly recommended rhythmic irregularities, atonality, and microtones. Pratella's own composition, however, failed to demonstrate the efficacy of his theories and was judged to be too repetitive, shapeless, and reliant on whole tones.

It was Luigi Russolo, a painter by training, who brought the Futurist movement in music to a head. He opened his Futurist manifesto entitled *The Art of Noises* (1913) with the declaration,

> Ancient life was all silence. In the nineteenth century, with the invention of the machine, Noise was born. Today, Noise triumphs and reigns supreme over the sensibilities of men.

His injunction to the contemporary musician came in a passage whose lyricism vied with Marinetti.

> We must break out of this narrow circle of pure musical sounds, and conquer the infinite variety of noise-sounds . . . Let us wander through a great modern city with our ears more alert than our eyes, and enjoy distinguishing between the sounds of water, air, or gas in metal pipes, the purring of motors (which breathe and pulsate with indisputable animalism), the throbbing of valves, the pounding of pistons, the screeching of gears, the clatter of streetcars on their rails, the cracking of whips, the flapping of awnings and flags. We shall enjoy fabricating mental orchestrations of the banging of store shutters, the slamming of doors, the hustle and bustle of crowds, the din of railroad stations, foundaries, spinning mills, printing presses, electric power stations, and underground railways.

He concluded his manifesto with an alarming but refreshing admission.

> I am not a musician, I have therefore no acoustical predilections, nor any works to defend. I am a Futurist painter using a much loved art to project my determination to renew everything. And so, bolder than a professional musician could be, unconcerned by my apparent incompetence, and convinced that all rights and all possibilities open up to daring, I have been able to initiate the great renewal of music by means of the Art of Noises.[3]

Russolo's noise machines, which he labeled Intonarumori (Figure 12.1), were designed to demonstrate his theories, but their success cannot be judged

Figure 12.1. Russolo and his assistant Piatti with Noise Intoners ("Intonarumori").

because they were destroyed in World War II, and a single gramophone record that survives is inconclusive. His Noise Intoners were to be arranged into six main categories forming the basis of a Futurist orchestra:

1	2	3	4	5	6
Rumbles	Whistles	Whispers	Screeches	Noises	Voices of
Roars	Hisses	Murmurs	Creaks	obtained by	animals
Explosions	Snorts	Mumbles	Rustles	percussion	and men:
Crashes		Grumbles	Buzzes	on	Shouts
Splashes		Gurgles	Crackles	metal	Screams
Booms			Scrapes	wood	Groans
				skin	Shrieks
				stone	Howls
				terracotta,	Laughs
				etc.	Wheezes
					Sobs

A single Exploder was demonstrated in Modena in 1913, but the first concert was given in April 1914 in Milan. In a private demonstration in Marinetti's house prior to the first public performance, an illustrious audience assembled, including Marinetti, Pratella, Boccioni, Carrà, Cangiullo, Stravinsky, Diaghilev, Massine, and a Slav pianist. In his autobiography, Cangiullo—Neapolitan, Futurist poet, and painter—remembered the evening, which began with a piece by Pratella, followed by Russolo at work with eight or nine of his Noise Intoners, thus:

> A Crackler crackled and sent up a thousand sparks like a gloomy torrent. Stravinsky leapt from the divan like an exploding bedspring, with a whistle of overjoyed excitement. At the same time a Rustler rustled like silk skirts, or like new leaves in April. The frenetic composer hurled himself on the piano in an attempt to find that prodigious onomatopoetic sound, but in vain did his avid fingers explore all the semi-tones. Meanwhile, the male dancer (Massine) swung his professional legs, Diaghilev went Ah Ah like a startled quail, and that for him was the highest sign of approval. By moving his legs the dancer was trying to say that the strange symphony was danceable, while Marinetti, happier than ever, ordered tea, cakes and liqueurs. Boccioni whispered to Carrà that the guests were won over. The only person who remained unmoved was Russolo himself. He tweaked his goatee beard and said there was a lot to modify; he hated praise. As a polite murmur of disagreement started, Piatti declared that experiments would have to begin again from scratch. Stravinsky and the Slav pianist played a frenzied four-handed version of *The Firebird*, and Pratella slept soundly through it all.[4]

On April 21, 1914, three of Russolo's pieces for Noise Intoners—*The Awakening of a City, Luncheon on the Kursaal Terrace,* and *Meeting of Automobiles and Aeroplanes*—were performed in Milan. Only the month before, Russolo had forwarded a new notation (Fig. 12.4) which replaced traditional notation with a number system and a network of solid lines. Later the same year Pratella, in combining Russolo's Noise Intoners with his more traditional orchestra, wrote a piece entitled *Joy,* which made use of both standard and the newly devised notations. A footnote to the score amazingly

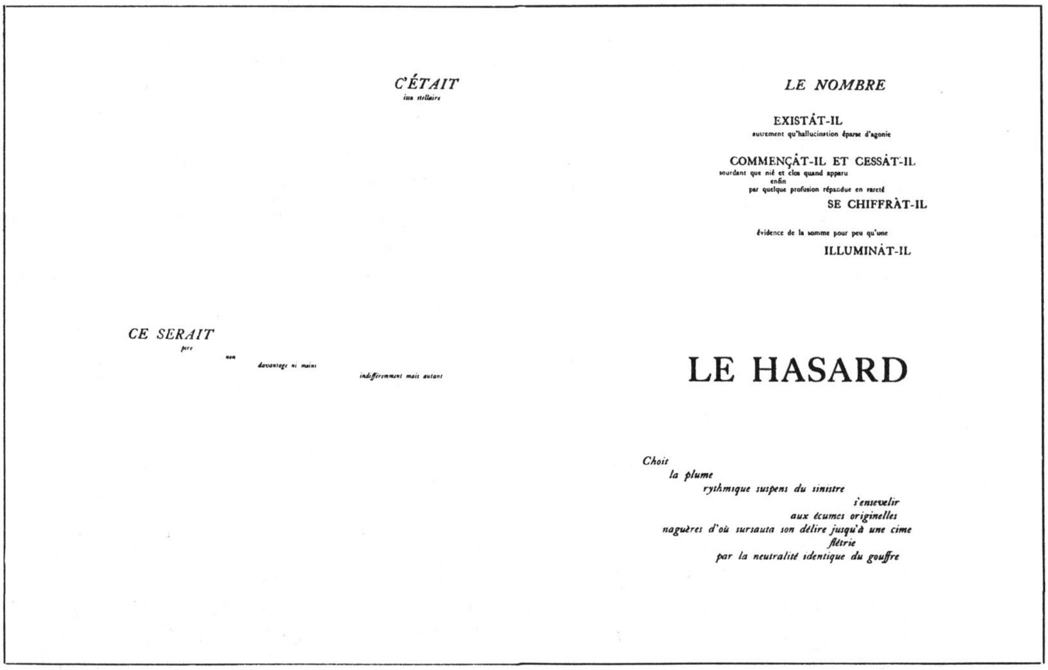
C'ÉTAIT
issu stellaire
CE SERAIT
pire
non
davantage ni moins
indifféremment mais autant
LE NOMBRE
EXISTÂT-IL
autrement qu'hallucination éparse d'agonie
COMMENÇÂT-IL ET CESSÂT-IL
sourdant que nié et clos quand apparu
enfin
par quelque profusion répandue en rareté
SE CHIFFRÂT-IL
évidence de la somme pour peu qu'une
ILLUMINÂT-IL
LE HASARD
Choit
la plume
rythmique suspens du sinistre
s'ensevelir
aux écumes originelles
naguères d'où sursauta son délire jusqu'à une cime
flétrie
par la neutralité identique du gouffre

Figure 12.2. A page from Mallarmé's *Un coup de dés* originally published in the review *Cosmopolis* (1897).

prefigures directions typically found in the scores of Cage, Stockhausen, and Reilly of a later decade:

> Immense shout from the crowd. Each single individual will attempt the most acute intonation of his own chosen tone. The intonation and the duration will be arbitrary and independent, but the entries will be rigorously observed.[5]

Just as contemporary challenges to typography may be traced from Mallarmé's *Un coup de dés* (1897; Figure 12.2) to Marinetti's various *parole in libertà* (e.g., "Turkish Captive Baloon" from *Zang Tumb Tuum*, 1914; Figure 12.3), Apollinaire's *Calligrammes* (1918), and to later configurations by numerous modern poets from Ezra Pound and e. e. cummings on, so the notational challenge of Russolo's *The Awakening of a City* (1914; Figure 12.4) signalled the beginning of a rethinking of the musical score, which persists to the present day.[6]

RUSSIAN FUTURISM

The vigorous artistic activity in Russia at precisely this time saw the appearance of a profusion of isms: Futurism, Cubo-Futurism, Suprematism, Rayonism, and later Constructivism. Lacking a significant base in the world of music, in general they need not concern us here. The appearance of the word

Figure 12.3. Marinetti, "Turkish Captive Balloon," from *Zang Tumb Tuum* (1914).

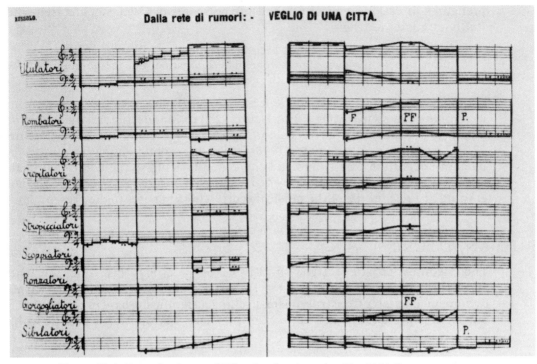

Figure 12.4. Russolo, Score of *The Awakening of a City* (1914).

Futurism, however, demands our attention. While it has been argued that Marinetti did not visit Russia until 1914, his Futurist Manifesto had appeared in translation in Russia shortly after its appearance in Paris's "Figaro" in 1909. Virtually the whole of the Primitivist movement headed by Larionov and Goncharova, interestingly, had been subsumed under the banner of Futurism from a date at least this early and probably before, and it was natural that claims of priority would be made. It was not until the period 1911–12, however, that anything even vaguely resembling Italian Futurist premises surfaced in Russian art, and even here a distinction should be made.

The appearance of the painter Kasimir Malevich (1878–1935) as successor to Larionov and Goncharova at this time was crucial for such developments. His first independent work dating from 1909 predictably depicts peasant rural themes, but by the time of *The Woodcutter* (1911) such themes had found a new and energetic rhythm, and in his pathbreaking *Scissors Grinder* of 1912 (Figure 12.5) he openly betrays the influence of the Cubists (Duchamp's *Nude Descending a Staircase*, 1912, is exactly contemporary) and, through its focus on the machine, the Italian Futurists. It has been argued that this remarkable painting manifests little of the Italian's interest in speed, that the machine itself is of a primitive type, and that the theme of the work is man's control over it and hence his destiny. Significantly, however, it also secures the easy alliance between Futurism's reductive fascination for the sounds of everyday life and urban pulse, and Primitivism's devotion to natural song and ritual rhythm.

By the end of 1913 Malevich's endorsement of Cubo-Futurism had led him to other frontiers, but Goncharova's *The Cyclist* (1912–13) and Larionov's

Figure 12.5. Kasimir Malevich, *The Scissors Grinder* (1912).
Yale University Art Gallery. Gift of Collection Société Anonyme.

Rayonist Manifesto (1913), which opens with the following words, suggest lingering Italian Futurist values:

> We declare: the genius of our days to be: trousers, jackets, shoes, tramways, buses, aeroplanes, railways, magnificent ships—what an enchantment—what a great epoch unrivalled in world history.[7]

As Larionov and Goncharova left Russia to join Diaghilev in Paris in 1915, Stravinsky could not have been unaware of the Russian developments just outlined. Their collaboration with the composer in *Renard* (1915–16) and *Les noces* (1916 and 1921), respectively, naturally enough project Primitivist values in light of their subject matter, but the presence of the two artists could hardly have failed to sensitize Stravinsky to the variegated premises of Futurism, and perhaps explain his willingness to go along with Italian Futurist experiments. Following a refusal by Stravinsky to write music for a portrayal of the Mass on stage, Diaghilev had toyed with the idea of a Futurist orchestra as an accompaniment to a projected ballet, *Liturgie* (1915), but nothing came of it. Two years later, however, on April 12, 1917, at the Rome premiere of Tommasini's *The Good-Humoured Ladies*, Diaghilev extended the Futurist theater to a presentation of Stravinsky's early *Fireworks*, with the composer conducting. For this work, Balla constructed a set of prismatic wooden shapes stretched with painted canvas. Smaller forms were translucent and capable of being illuminated from the inside. Against a black background a movement of colored lights replaced the movement of the dancers, and in the five-minute work forty-nine different sequences were projected from a keyboard activated from the prompter's box by Balla, the designer of the entire project. The relation of such Futurist experiments to the work of Skriabin and others of a slightly earlier period is apparent.

Malevich's alliance with the Russian Revolution of 1917 was inevitable, believing as he did that Cubo-Futurism was actually an artistic prophecy of and preparation for social upheaval, and Stravinsky's reaction to Revolutionary prospects was initially extremely positive as well. At the same concert that saw the Futurist production of his *Fireworks*, Stravinsky made a setting for wind instruments of *The Song of the Volga Boatmen* to replace the Russian National Anthem typically played at the beginning of the concert. His illusions about a new order in Russia even led him to contemplate ending his Swiss exile and returning to Russia. At the Rome performance, however, Stravinsky was introduced to Picasso for the first time, and their collaboration on *Pulcinella* projected. Not only his involvement in the West but news from Russia of a second Bolshevist uprising soon brought him to the realization that his hopes for the Revolution had been misplaced.

On the Italian side, Stravinsky's expressed delight over Russolo's machines at the private concert in Milan in 1914 he later claimed was feigned. Nonetheless, his own *Study for Pianola* (1917) and the piano and percussion ensemble of *Les noces* (including a mechanical piano in an early version that was abandoned because of the difficulties in synchronization) may fairly be said to reflect his interest in the experiments of the Futurists.[8] Though Stravinsky stated that his *Study* was inspired by the sounds of the mechanical pianos and orchestrinas in the streets and taverns of Madrid, elsewhere he acknowledged that his interest in player-pianos dated from 1914 following a demonstration of the pianola by the Aeolian Company in London, which offered him a commission for an original piece for the instrument. In addition to the mechanics of the instrument, Stravinsky was attracted to its capacity to rule out nuance in the fixing of tempo relationships. The importance of this to his music at large is mirrored in the transcriptions for pianola of numerous works from *Petrushka* to *Pulcinella*, *Les noces*, and *The Five Fingers* that he made for the Pleyel company in Paris—a time-consuming project "to no purpose" with which he was involved between 1921 and 1924 (Figure 12.6).

LATER REPERCUSSIONS OF FUTURISM: ANTHEIL, MILHAUD, HONEGGER, PROKOFIEV, ORNSTEIN, COWELL, VARÈSE, HINDEMITH

From the standpoint of advocates and manifestos, the Italian Futurist movement was expended by the end of the war, though its effect could be spotted throughout the next decade. Russolo's concerts in Paris in the early 1920s still engendered a certain excitement and were known to have attracted several important composers, including Ravel, Honegger, Milhaud, and Varèse. Finally, more sophisticated versions of the *Intonarumori* were advanced under the name of *Rumorarmonio* (Noise Harmonium) and Russolophone, which brought

Figure 12.6. Stravinsky at work with the Pleyela, Paris, 1923.
Photo by Vera Sudeikina.

together a collection of Noise Intoners operable from a rudimentary keyboard. The latter was promoted by Varèse in a public concert of 1929, but he was soon attracted to the thérémin and ondes martenot.

While the official "Futuristi" spawned slim musical results, their influence was more salutary than would appear at first glance. Although the emphasis placed on speed, sport, and war cast a somewhat grim political shadow over the movement (Marinetti, for example, had written an article as early as 1911–15 entitled "War, the World's Only Hygiene," and Mussolini was the patron of a Futurist architectural exhibition as late as 1928), the experimental nature of the movement fascinated numerous composers who pursued their own interpretation of the machine age in various ways.

The Futurist-inspired instrumental choices in the works of Stravinsky, for example, found an echo in the work of the American-in-Paris George Antheil, who in 1924 began a cooperative venture with painter Fernand Léger (1881–1955) and the film maker Dudley Murphy on a work already in progress, *Ballet mécanique* (1923–25). One of the earliest abstract films, its procession of gears, pots, clocks, and various types of repetitive motion was intended to be accompanied by Antheil's music performed by sixteen player pianos utilizing rolls specially cut by the Pleyel Company. Syncrhonization posed a problem, as with the second version of Stravinsky's *Les noces*, and ultimately the film and the music found independent lives. The first performance of Antheil's score included eight pianos, one player piano, four xylophones, two electric bells, two airplane propellers, tam-tam, four bass drums, and siren. Other works of a similar disposition written by Antheil about this time include his *"Airplane" Sonata* (1922) and a *Sonatina "Death of the Machines"* (1923). Antheil's *"Airplane" Sonata* undoubtedly reflects the idea of the airplane as an ideal generator of noises as pursued by Fedele Azari in his "Aerial Theater" of 1918. Russolo designed special resonators for exhaust and hood in order to amplify and modulate the timbre of the engine. Azari's *Futurist Aerial Theater* manifesto appeared in 1919 and described the "flying Intonarumori," a circus of airplanes each painted by a different Futurist painter.

A futher attempt to capture the dynamics of the machine can be seen in Honegger's *Pacific 231* (1923), a study in rhythm that portrays a train accelerating and slowing down, for which Léger also made a film. Although the same composer's *Skating Rink* (1921), with a stage design also by Léger, and *Rugby* (1928) may not have been directly inspired by the Futurists, they reinforced the movement's commitment to speed and sport.

Milhaud, one of Honegger's Parisian contemporaries, utilized patently Futurist novelties in the conjunction of speech-choruses attended by an orchestra of fifteen percussionists in the fourth, fifth, and seventh sections of *Les choëphores*, a 1915 setting based on the Oresteia trilogy of Aeschylus. While his *L'homme et son désir* of 1918 continued to place the spotlight on percussion in several episodes, the texts for his Dadaist *Machines agricoles* for voice and seven instruments of 1919 were taken from descriptions in a farm catalogue.

During this same period, Satie also made, at Cocteau's suggestion, what appears to be an obligatory reference to Futurist (*realiste*) experiments in his *Parade* in 1917. The final incorporation of sirens, typewriters, tubes (8' and 16') and roulette wheels was all that remained of Cocteau's original idea to include aeroplanes and dynamos as well. Yet as late as 1922, Satie was still heard expressing fascination for the mechanical piano:

> The *pianola* is first and foremost a different instrument from its companion the piano, with which it just has a family relationship. Igor Stravinsky, before anyone else, has really written a piece which exploits the resources unique to this instrument. The virtuosi of the keyboard should know that they could never do what an ordinary *pianola* can do; but that, on the other hand, they could never be replaced by mechanical means. Let them sleep soundly, on both ears if that pleases them. With these studies, Stravinsky brings a new and vastly rich element to Music. It is hard to anticipate the benefits which will ensue from my illustrious friend's researches. I have every confidence in him and assure him of my lasting admiration.[9]

In Russia, the Cubo-Futurists, who had portrayed the world of modern technology and the machine as early as 1911, effected a collaboration between Futurist poets Velimir Khlebnikov and Aleksei Kruchenykh with Malevich as costume and set designer in an "opera" entitled *Victory Over the Sun* of 1913. The intentionally incomprehensible nonsense of the libretto (e.g., "I eat dog/And white feets/Fried meat cake/Croaked potato/Space is limited/Print to be silent/Zheh Sheh Cheh")[10] merged with Cubist costumes forecasting

Picasso's solution for Satie's *Parade*, against a purified background of squares and diagonals that was to form the basis of Malevich's emerging Suprematism. The music was by the painter Mikhail Matiushin, who is only now being rediscovered and who, like Russolo, was not a professional composer. The score, still only partially retrieved, has been supplemented by recent manuscript discoveries that found their way into a Brooklyn Academy of Music performance on November 25, 1983.

While this multimedia show created a sensation, the immediate effect was insignificant. In a general way, however, such activities can be said to have paved the way for the emergence in the 1920s of the first generation of communist artists who designated themselves as Constructivists. Signs of their influence are clearly observable in both subject matter and musical response in works such as Mosolov's *The Steel Foundry* (1927), which uses a metal sheet to create the illusion of crashing iron and steel, and Prokofiev's "The Factory" in *Pas d'acier* (1927). The latter work was commissioned by Diaghilev in 1925 and was developed in response to a scenario by Sergei Yakulov, Soviet constructivist artist and stage designer who, unlike Prokofiev, had spent the preceding years in the Soviet Union. That it was intended to portray life in contemporary Russia is clear from Prokofiev's own description:

> The first part of the ballet would show the breakdown of the Czarist regime: meetings of workers, speeches by commissars, trains full of black-market goods, a former duchess bartering her gowns for food, a revolutionary sailor, and homeless waifs. The second part would present a picture of socialist reconstruction, the building of new plants and factories, yesterday's sailor-turned-worker, and so on.[11]

The music, which many saw as a blend of Stravinsky's Russian manner and Honegger's *Pacific 231*, as opposed to a reflection of current musical activity in Russia, was later chastised by Soviet officialdom for failing to capture the authentic spirit of Soviet culture.

One of the most engaging Russian works of exactly the same time to draw on the premises of the Futurist-Constructivists was an opera by the young Dimitri Shostakovich, *The Nose* (1927). Based on a play by Gogol about police suppression, Shostakovich fashioned the libretto himself. A lengthy interlude in the first act is written entirely for percussion instruments and is followed by a scene in which vocal noises, snores, snorts, and esophageal complexes result in a virtual human symphony. Russolo would have been pleased at this Futurist exploration, which portrays a Major Kyalov who, awakening from a deep sleep, finds that his nose has disappeared. Shostakovich insisted that he did not intend satire or parody—something he saw and disliked in Prokofiev's *The Love of Three Oranges*—only an effective treatment of an entirely serious subject. Futurist vocal and percussion explorations have here been absorbed in the service of mirroring the mechanics of bureaucracy everywhere.

A more abstract repercussion of the Futurist movement may be witnessed in the explosion of interest on the part of numerous composers to extend the resources of sound. While Russolo's *Intonarumori* according to most descriptions were reasonably primitive, the search for new sound sources of which they are indicative was paralleled by the experiments with the grand piano by two American composers: Leo Ornstein (b. 1892) and Henry Cowell (1897–1965). Leo Ornstein was born in Russia and studied as a child prodigy at the Petrograd

Conservatory. In 1907, with a professional career as accompanist and opera coach already behind him, his family fled the Russian Revolution and the fear of Jewish persecution. Suddenly transported to New York's Lower East Side, he continued his music studies and gave his first recital in 1911. The first attempts at composing music with a modern cast came with his *Danse sauvage* ("Wild Men's Dance") and *Suicide in an Airplane,* two piano works written in 1913. Both exhibit thick clusters of notes and betray in their titles Primitivist and Futurist leanings. His London recital of 1914 was openly advertised as a "Pianoforte Recital of Futurist Music"; and the critics repeatedly compared his music to Stravinsky, Skriabin, and Schoenberg, frequently concluding that Ornstein's was the most frightening and incomprehensible of the group. In "Anger" from his *Three Moods* of 1914 this tendency is continued in its alternating secondal harmonies and occasional clusters.

If such a stance by an American at this date appears surprising, it is well to recall the work of the Italo-American painter Joseph Stella (1877/79-1946). Having come to New York in 1896 to study medicine, which he soon abandoned for painting, he returned to America from a trip to Europe in 1909-12 with a commitment to translate the vitality of his adopted country into Futurist terms. His first recognition came with *Battle of Lights: Coney Island* (1913) and was sealed in his best known work, *Brooklyn Bridge* (Figure 12.7) of 1917-18. The latter drew from Cubism its natural affinity with engineering's geometric

Figure 12.7. Joseph Stella, *Brooklyn Bridge* (1917-18). Oil on canvas, 84" × 76". Yale University Art Gallery. Gift of Collection Société Anonyme.

precision, constructing an energetic network of cables that proclaimed the triumph of a mechanized society. Contemporaneous with Stella's work is *291 Machines* (1916) by another American, Morton Schamberg (1881–1918), which conjures up Picabia's *Machine tournez vite* of the same period.

The other American musician alluded to earlier—a young Californian named Henry Cowell—had employed clusters to be played by the hand and entire forearm in his *The Tides of the Manaunaun* as early as 1912, and in 1916 his investigations into new notations, clusters, dissonant counterpoint, and rhythmic complexities were reported in his *New Musical Resources*.[12] By the mid-1930s he had extended his innovatory piano techniques to include harmonics as well as the plucking and scraping of the strings, all of which are illustrated in works like *Aeolian Harp* (1923) and *The Banshee* (1925; Ex. 12.1).

Example 12.1. Cowell. "The Banshee," opening.

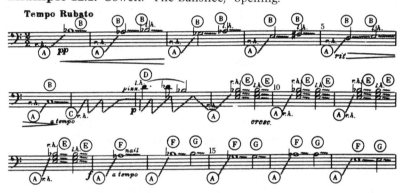

Explanation of Symbols

"The Banshee" is played on the open strings of the piano, the player standing at the crook. Another person must sit at the keyboard and hold down the damper pedal throughout the composition. The whole work should be played an octave lower than written.

R. H. stands for "right hand." L. H. stands for "left hand." Different
   ways of playing the strings are indicated by a letter over each tone,
   as follows:

(A) indicates a sweep with the flesh of the finger from the lowest string
     up to the note given.

(B) sweep lengthwise along the string of the note given with flesh of
     finger.

(C) sweep up and back from lowest A to highest B-flat given in this
     composition.

(D) pluck string with flesh of finger, where written, instead of octave
     lower.

(E) sweep along three notes together, in the same manner as (B).

(F) sweep in the manner of (B) but with the back of finger-nail instead
     of flesh.

(G) when the finger is half way along the string in the manner of (F),
     start a sweep along the same string with the flesh of the other
     finger, thus partly damping the sound.

Beginning in 1927, Cowell brought out his *New Music Edition*, which he continued to publish for twenty-five years. Prominently devoted to music of the Americas (the first issue was of Ruggles's *Of Men and Mountains*), it also included works of Schoenberg (op. 33b), Webern (op. 17, no. 2), and Varèse (*Density 21.5* and *Ionisation*). In 1927, Cowell also met Ives and soon became instrumental in the publication of his *The Fourth of July, Washington's Birthday*, and the second movement of the *Fourth Symphony*.[13]

Cowell displayed his new sonic wares in five tours of Europe between 1923 and 1933. There, numerous composers became aware of his work. Schoenberg invited him to a master class in Berlin in 1932, and this contact may account for the forearm piano clusters that figure prominently in Berg's *Lulu*. Even Bartók supposedly wrote for permission to use his clusters, though this seems a curious request in light of many of Bartók's works already composed. In 1929 Cowell, perhaps not surprisingly, created a sensation in Russia where the state publishing house printed two of his piano works. His all-encompassing interest in expanding sound resources, which led to the artistic sponsorship of people like Ives and Varèse, was paralleled by a collaboration in 1931 with Léon Thérémin (b. 1896, St. Petersburg) in the invention of an electronic machine to play complex polyrhythms which they called the "rhythmicon."

Investigations that had led Thérémin to the demonstration of his "aetherophone" as early as 1920 were echoed in the work of Friedrich Trautwein (1888–1956) and Maurice Martenot (1898–1980), whose instruments were called trautonium and ondes martenot, respectively. The differences in these electronic instruments are considerable but the net effect was similar. Though all but the ondes martenot (cultivated by Milhaud, Jolivet, Koechlin, Schmitt, Ibert, Honegger, and Messiaen) flourished only briefly, they signaled an infatuation with machine-made sound that was to lead naturally, if not inevitably, to the world of *musique concréte* and electronic music. As late as 1965, Robert A. Moog used the principle of the thérémin (body motion in relation to an antenna) in a system developed for John Cage's *Variations V*, which depends on the movement of dancers to alter the sound.

Elsewhere in Europe the emblem of Lindbergh's Atlantic flight of 1927 inspired both Weill and Hindemith to statements in praise of man and his machines, and the latter's interest during the period 1926–1931 in writing directly for the mechanical organ or for the trautonium may be seen as further evidence of Futurist fashion. Now flying under the banner of *Neue Sachlich-keit*, the machine was seen as a symbol of concision and clarity, of efficiency and objective expression.

Indeed, for his second summer festival at Baden-Baden in 1927, Hindemith proposed to feature, in addition to chamber-style cantatas, mechanical music and music for film. Having composed music in 1925 for Oskar Schlemmer's *Das Triadische Ballet*, which displayed geometric-mechanistic costumes, Hindemith now turned to the writing of music for a film, *Vormittagspuk*, transcribed directly on a pianola roll, and an animated cartoon, *Felix the Cat*, for which he utilized a synchronizing apparatus newly invented by the German engineer, Robert Blum. The seven pieces for three trautonia of 1930 and the *Konzertstück* for trautonium and strings of 1931, while confirming the stylistic attributes of two well-known contemporaneous works (*Konzertmusik* for piano, winds and two harps and another for string orchestra and brass instruments, both of 1930), also exhibit a curiosity about timbre that is frequently forgotten in the typical citation of Hindemith's sonatas for the entire range of traditional instruments.

Varèse's explorations were of a more far-reaching nature. His timbral investigations, especially into the world of percussion and noisemakers, are epitomized in three path-breaking works:

> *Hyperprism* (1923): for wind and percussion, including sleigh bells, cymbals, crash cymbals, rattles, triangle, anvil, Chinese blocks, tam-tam, Indian drum, snare drum, bass drum, tambourine, siren, a Lion's roar (a tub with a hole in the bottom through which the player pulls a rope). The work, which begins with percussion alone, contains two other passages for percussion solo as well.

> *Intégrales* (1926): 11 winds, 17 percussion played by 4 players. Four sections: 1) clarinet motif (trombone, oboe) in high register; 2) same motif in low register (hrn, tbn, perc, tutti); 3) rapid tpt: Lento, Presto, Lento, Presto; 4) Introduction by perc, ob solo; return of Presto, second Lento.

> *Ionisation* (1929–31): 13 players, 37 perc instr, including 2 sirens, 2 tam-tams, gong, bongos, maracas, sleigh bells, castanets, tambourine, anvils in two registers, chimes, celesta, piano.

The innovation of these works resides not only in the unusual instrumental ensemble, which places a premium on percussion and a highly memorable rising signature motif at the beginning of the first two (e.g., Ex. 12.2), but on a new sense of timbral condensation that shifts by turns over static harmonies (the harmony of m.5, Ex. 12.2, for example, persists for several pages) in a fashion the composer held analogous to the formation of crystals. This in turn can safely be said to have paved the way for the nonpulsed minimalism of Ligeti, Husa, and others who, eschewing thematics and pre-cut formalizations, have experimented with the transformation of curtains of sound (see p. 576). Varèse's inquiry led him to the substitution of the ondes martenot for the sirens in a 1929 performance of *Amériques* only a year after the instrument's invention; then, while composing *Ecuatorial* (1932–34) he toyed with the idea of introducing the thérémin but finally settled on two ondes martenots. Varèse's interest in electronic instruments, which culminated in *Déserts* (1934) and *Poème électronique* (1958), may be seen less as stemming from the manifestos of the Futurists, however, than sharing with them their love of mechanized urban life in which he has been compared directly to Léger and Mondrian. The search therein for new sound sources to reflect this interest defines these works as natural precursors of the electronic developments of the 1960s and 1970s.

The Futurist legacy was to remain audible long after the central movement was expended and in a variety of surroundings. Perhaps no more formidable link is to be found than in the music of Conlon Nancarrow (b. 1912), an American composer who fought in the Spanish Civil War and later moved to Mexico. Beginning in the late 1940s he had a player piano constructed especially for his purposes, and in the period from 1950 to the present he has produced a series of Studies remarkable for their diversity. The earliest, Studies 3a, b, c, were initially referred to as the "Boogie Woogie Suite" and demonstrated an affection for blues, ragtime, and later jazz styles; Study 6 is an extraordinary tango. A later group was more abstract and devoted to the consistent use of canon, while more recent explorations have developed notions akin to "metric modulation" and *musique concrète*.

Example 12.2. Varèse, *Intégrales*, mm. 1–5.

For Nancarrow the appeal of the player piano, as with Stravinsky when he transcribed so many of his works for pianola in the early 1920s, lay in its precise control over the most complex rhythmic and polyphonic textures. It is a quality that similarly appealed to Percy Grainger (1882–1962) from his early years. Following a protracted interest in making numerous rolls for the Duo Art Company, he turned to the invention of his own instruments, such as the "Kangaroo-Pouch Free-Music Machine." "Free Music," according to Grainger, was no longer to be dependent on the pitch limitations of pretuned instruments or the rhythmic limitations of performers. Some of Grainger's scores were written in a kind of graph notation so that they could be read by means of lamps and pitch-control photocells and through a series of oscillators transformed directly into sound. Though his project remained incomplete at the time of his death, it had been envisioned as early as sketches entitled *Train Music* (c. 1900) and ended well after the advent of tape decks and computers.

In France, the titles of such early examples of *musique concrète* as Pierre Shaeffer's *Etude aux chemins de fer* and *Etude aux casseroles* are sufficient to suggest that in the late 1940s, at the beginning of the electronic age, the vision of the Futurists had not been forgotten. Moreover, the "new vocalism" of the 1960s (see p. 000ff) saw composers like Berio and Crumb exploring in a fresh manner the various vocal "noises" catalogued by Russolo years before (see p. 000), while works for the more traditional orchestral ensemble, such as Eugene Kurtz's *Mécanique* (1976), Penderecki's *Symphony No. 1* (1972–73) commissioned by an English industrial firm, and Christopher Rouse's *The Infernal Machine* (1981), have openly paid homage to the clockwork energies of the Futurists.

REPERTOIRE

Pratella, *Musica Futurista* (1912)
Pratella, *L'aviatore Dro* (1911–14)
Cowell, *The Tides of Manaunaun* (1912)
Ornstein, *Danse sauvage* (1913)
Ornstein, *Suicide in an Airplane* (1913)
Ornstein, *Three Moods:* "Anger" (1914)
Russolo, *The Awakening of a City* (1914)
Milhaud, *Les choëphores* (1915)
Stravinsky, *Study for Pianola:* "Madrid" (1917)
Stravinsky, *Les noces* (1915–23)
Milhaud, *L'homme et son désir* (1918)
Milhaud, *Machines agricoles* (1919)
Honegger, *Skating rink* (1921)
Antheil, *"Airplane" Sonata* (1922), pf
Antheil, *Sonatine "Death of the Machines"* (1923)
Cowell, *Aeolian Harp* (1923), pf
Honegger, *Pacific 231* (1923)
Varèse, *Hyperprism* (1923)
Varèse, *Intégrales* (1924–25)
Antheil, *Ballet mécanique* (1925)
Cowell, *The Banshee* (1925), pf
Carpenter, *Skyscrapers* (1926)
Hindemith, *Das triadische Ballet für mechanische Orgel* (1926)
Deshevov, *Rails* (1926), pf
Chavez, *H.P. (Horsepower)* (1927)
Mosolov, *The Steel Foundry* (1927)
Prokofiev, *Pas d'acier:* "The Factory" (1927)
Shostakovich, *The Nose:* Act I, "Percussion Interlude" (1927–28)
Honegger, *Rugby* (1928)
Sabaneyev, *L'aviatrice* (1928)
Hindemith, *Lindberghflug* (1929)
Hindemith, *7 Triostücke,* 2 trautoniums (1930)
Hindemith, *Konzertstück,* trautonium, str (1931)
Varèse, *Ionisation* (1929–31)
Meytus, *The Dnieper Power Water Station* (1929–32)
Varèse, *Ecuatorial* (1932–34)

Messiaen, *Fêtes des belles eaux*, 6 ondes martenot (1937)
Schaeffer, *Etude aux chemins de fer* (1948)
Schaeffer, *Etude aux casseroles* (1948)
Nancarrow, *37 Studies for Player Piano* (1950-68)
Varèse, *Poème électronique* (1958)
Kurtz, *Mécanique* (1976)
Penderecki, *Symphony No. 1* (1972-73)
Rouse, *The Infernal Machine* (1981)

READING

Umbro Apollonio, ed. *Futurist Manifestos* (1970; Eng. trans., London, 1973):
    Filippo Marinetti, *The Founding and Manifesto of Futurism* (1909), 19.
    Francesco Pratella, *Manifesto of Futurist Musicians* (1910), 31.
    Bruno Corra, *Abstract Cinema—Chromatic Music* (1912), 66.
    Luigi Russolo, *The Art of Noises* (1913), 74.
    Carlo Carrà, *The Painting of Sounds, Noises and Smells* (1913), 111.
Henry Cowell, *New Musical Resources* (New York, 1930).
Vivian Perlis, "The Futurist Music of Leo Ornstein," *Notes*, xxxi.4 (1975), 735.
Rodney J. Payton, "The Music of Futurism: Concerts and Polemics," *Musical Quarterly*, lxii (1976), 25.
Caroline Tisdall and Angelo Bozzola, *Futurism* (London, 1977).
Richard James, *Expansion of Sound Resources in France, 1913-1940, and Its Relationship to Electronic Music* (Ph.D. dissertation, University of Michigan, 1981): Chapter 3, "The Italian Futurists"; Chapter 4, "Percussion and Noise in Music of French Provenance."
Linda Whitesitt, *The Life and Music of George Antheil, 1900-1959* (Ann Arbor, 1983).
Laurel E. Fay, "The Punch in Shostakovich's *Nose*" in *Russian and Soviet Essays for Boris Schwarz*, ed. Malcolm Brown (Ann Arbor, 1984), 229.
Terence J. O'Grady, "A Conversation with Leo Ornstein," *Perspectives of New Music*, xxiii (Fall-Winter 1984), 126-134.
Pierre Boulez, "Edgard Varèse" in *Orientations* (Cambridge, Mass., 1986), 497-98. Originally as "Arcanes Varèse" in the programme of the Domaine musical concert of 24 November 1965 on the occasion of Edgard Varèse's death.
Rex Lawson, "Stravinsky and the Pianola," *Confronting Stravinsky*, ed. J. Pasler (Berkeley, 1986), 286.
Jonathan Bernard, *The Music of Edgard Varèse* (New York, 1987).

CHAPTER 13

THE NEW SIMPLICITIES: FRANCE

FOLKSONG AND THE VOICES OF ANIMALS AND CHILDREN

The importance that Romantic German culture had placed on folk and children's art (e.g., *Des Knaben Wunderhorn*) once again surfaced in the simple, brightly colored patterns of the Vienna Art Show of 1908 (*Kunstschau Wien 1908*). Illustrations from Carl Otto Czeschka's *Die Nibelungen* as well as Oskar Kokoschka's poem *Die träumenden Knaben* ("Children Dreaming"), both of 1908, reflect not only the significance of such motifs for Wiener Werkstätte (Viennese Workshop) design of the period but also the natural alliance on this ground between Expressionism and Primitivism (see p. 161).

Although Wagner blamed the French for a predisposition toward the rational as opposed to the expressive in art, the subscription to cultural primitivism, which places a premium on the unstudied and childlike, had an equally French base from J. J. Rousseau to Henri Rousseau, Satie, and Ravel. As early as 1897, Henri Rousseau, a rare folk artist of genius, had painted a work like *The Sleeping Gypsy* (Figure 13.1) whose innocence and expressive directness was later to prompt Picasso to claim him as one of the fathers of modernism. It is a quality that is not difficult to find in many of Stravinsky's works from 1910–1920, where "primitivism" could suggest both a brusque, energetic rhythmic style and a distilled simplicity based on peasant values and conjuring up naïf as opposed to aggressive traits. Thus the attendant simplicity with respect to texture and subject matter in many of these works by Stravinsky was decidedly à la mode among numerous French artists of the time. One may conclude that there are features in Stravinsky's works that owe a debt to non-Russian sources, or at the very least that influences close at hand in France and even Germany corroborated native tendencies.

D'Indy's earlier promotion of regional French folksong at the Schola Cantorum in the 1890s probably lay in his feeling that the origins of folksong were to be found in plainchant, which he considered to be fundamental to the proper study of music. In any event, French folksong can be said to have played only a marginal role in identifying the French musical character in the late nineteenth and early twentieth centuries, even as it was in harmony with and capable of supporting the movement toward the naïf. Noteworthy examples, nonetheless, are d'Indy's own *Symphonie sur un chant montagnard français*

Figure 13.1. Henri Rousseau, *The Sleeping Gypsy* (1897). Oil on canvas 51″ × 6′ 7″.
Collection, The Museum of Modern Art, New York. Gift of Mrs. Simon Guggenheim.

(1886) or those of his pupil Canteloube, which relied heavily on the stimulus of folksong—e.g., his *Chants d'Auvergne* of 1907 and 1923–30.

Debussy's quotation of "Au claire de la lune, mon ami Pierrot" in the early *Pierrot* of 1881, of the "Marseillaise" in *Feux d'artifice*, and "Do, do, l'enfant do" together with "Nous n'irons plus au bois" in both "Jardin sous la pluie" (*Estampes*, piano) and "Rondes de printemps" (*Images*, orchestra) are rare if highly symbolic usages of French song in his music, used with the same intent as the Northumbrian tune "The Keel Row" in his "Gigues" (*Images*, orchestra). Folk tunes and popular dances also nestle comfortably alongside parodistic

Example 13.1. Debussy, *Children's Corner:* "Golliwog's Cake-walk," mm. 61–64.

Copyright 1908 Durand S.A. Editions Musicales. Used by permission of the publisher. Theodore Presser Company, sole representative U.S.A. and Canada.

references to *Faust* and *Carmen* in the ballet for piano four-hands, *Boites à joujoux* (1913), while in the *Children's Corner* (1906–08) a quotation from *Tristan* is juxtaposed against the rhythms of a cakewalk (Ex. 13.1).

Ravel, the composer of *Daphnis and Chlöe* and *Bolero*, also had a more intimate side that was in many ways closer to his fundamental nature than these popular favorites. In numerous works, an unerring sense for detail and a preference for the world of animals and children underscore Ravel's own childlike qualities. The original version of *Mother Goose* (1910) for piano four-hands carries the subtitle "Cinq pièces enfantines," but in its spare writing it is apparent that these works possess not only the assumed naïveté of a Chabrier but a precision of construction that caused Stravinsky to label the composer a "Swiss watchmaker."

The animal kingdom substituted for the voices of children in a kindred way in Ravel's slightly earlier *Histoires naturelles* (1906), where the drypoint vocal line mirrors the lithographs Toulouse-Lautrec executed in 1899 for an edition of Jules Renard's texts (Figure 13.2). While something of its burlesque element has

Figure 13.2. Toulouse-Lautrec's illustration of "La Paon" (The Peacock") for Jules Renard's *Histoire naturelles* (1899). Ravel's music for *Histoire naturelles* was composed in 1906.

been seen to reflect his admiration for Chabrier's *Six mélodies* (1890), it has also been claimed that the juxtaposition of a refined literary style with the cadence of everyday speech (reflected through changes of tempo, meter, and range) may be indebted to the speech rhythms of Musorgsky (see p. 150).[1] Final syllables are traditionally sounded in French song, though mute in normal speech, and it was in the setting of passages such as "la fiancée n'ar-rive pas" (in "The Peacock"), as a phrase of six notes approximating a conversational tone instead of the traditional nine, that a scandal was provoked at the first performance in 1907. Ravel's achievement reflects a similar preoccupation of Stravinsky not only in subject matter but with respect to matters of prosody.

Maurice Ravel, *Histoires naturelles:*

LE PAON

Il va sûrement se marier aujourd'hui.
Ce devait être pour hier.
En habit de gala, il était prêt.
Il n'attendait que sa fiancée.
Elle n'est pas venue. Elle ne peut tarder.
Glorieux, il se promène avec une allure
    de prince indien et port sur lui les
    riches présents d'usage.
L'amour avive l'éclat de ses couleurs et
    son aigrette tremble comme une lyre.
La fiancée n'arrive pas.
Il monte au haut du toit et regarde du
    côté du soleil.
Il jette son cri diabolique: Léon! Léon!
C'est ainsi qu'il appelle sa fiancée.
Il ne voit rien venir et personne ne
    répond.
Les volailles habituées ne levent même
    point la tête.
Elles sont lasses de l'admirer. Il
    redescend dans la cour, si sûr d'être
    beau qu'il est incapable de rancune.

Son mariage sera pour demain.

Et, ne sachant que faire du reste de la
    journée, il se dirige vers le perron.

Il gravit les marches, comme des marches
    de temple, d'un pas officiel.
Il relève sa robe à queue toute lourde
    des yeux qui n'ont pu se détacher
    d'elle.
Il répète encore une fois la cérémonie.

THE PEACOCK

He is surely going to be married today.
It ought to have been yesterday.
Outfitted in courtly dress, he was ready.
He waited only for his fiancée.
She didn't come. She can't tarry longer.
Glorious, he promenades with the
    carriage of an Indian prince bearing
    the rich gifts of his breed.
Love burnishes the luster of his colors,
    and his crest trembles like a lyre.
The fiancée does not arrive.
He climbs to the roof top and looks in
    the direction of the sun.
He hurls his diabolical cry: Léon! Léon!
It is thus that he calls his fiancée.
He sees nothing coming and no one
    replies.
The other fowl, accustomed to him, do
    not even lift their heads.
They are weary of admiring him. He
    descends again into the courtyard,
    so sure of being handsome that he is
    incapable of bearing malice.

His wedding will be rescheduled for
    tomorrow.

And, not knowing what to do for the
    remainder of the day, he heads for the
    flight of stairs.

He climbs the steps, as in a procession
    to a temple, with an official gait.
He raises his robe with its heavy train
    of eyes which have not been able to
    detach themselves from it.
Once more he rehearses the ceremony.

Such musical manners and subject matter were nourished in the first decade of the twentieth century at precisely the same time as attempts to spell the French personality were being made through the endorsement of various brands of exotica. Ultimately, as the usefulness of exotic imports as a determining factor in the French musical profile began to fade, they were gradually replaced not only with native folk song or approaches to the world of animals and children but with the sounds of the music hall and the cabaret, reinforced by popular styles from America and a revival of the virile French traditions of the seventeenth and eighteenth centuries. All provided an identifiable stimulus that successfully fueled burgeoning national aspirations sounded by Cocteau's anti-German call for a return to simplicity and an overtly French mode.

ERIK SATIE (1866–1925): BEFORE *PARADE*

Satie's anti-Wagnerian stance, which resulted in his earliest compositions such as *Ogives* (1886), the *Sarabandes* (1887), and *Gymnopédies* (1888), has been variously interpreted as avant-garde nihilism and as the base for the Neoclassic movement, which began around 1920. The harmonies and modal melodies of these works as well as those of *Le fils des étoiles* (1891) and the *Messe des pauvres* for organ and voices (1893–95), which court parallel ninths and quartal formations, have also been accorded the role of precursors of the language of Debussy and Ravel. The former's orchestration of the *Gymnopédies*, the latter's setting of portions of *Le fils des étoiles*, and their mutual friendship and admiration for Satie lent an initial credence to the idea.

Beyond such mainstream relationships, however, there was another side cultivated by Satie during the period of the 1890s. The nineteenth-century *café-chantant* and *café-concert* provided a vigorous tradition for the emergence of the music hall in France as early as 1867. But it was with the opening of the "Chat Noir" in 1881 that the story of the modern cabaret began. The cabaret was much more than a place for drinking, dancing, and entertainment. It was a meeting place for the artistic and literary elite, and increasingly an air of experimentation and even avant-garde pretension emerged. The fifty-year period, 1880–1930, that was the heyday of the cabaret, saw composers of greater or lesser stature visiting them, from Debussy and Satie at the turn of the century to Milhaud, Poulenc, and Jean Wiéner in the 1920s.

Satie spent over a decade of his life playing the piano and composing songs at the "Chat Noir" and the "Auberge du Clou" at precisely the time that Toulouse-Lautrec (1864–1901; *Dance at the Moulin Rouge*, 1890; *Jane Avril Dancing*, 1889–90) and Seurat (1859–1891; *Le Chahut*, 1889–90, Figure 13.3) were recording their impressions of these locales. His "La diva de l'empire" and "Je te veux" of about 1900 are charming representatives of the type of song stemming from this experience. The latter of these songs is a strophic "valse chantée" whose easy grace would be remembered by Poulenc forty years later in the composition of his *Les chemins de l'amour* (see p. 275).

Satie, *Je te veux*

J'ai compris ta détresse,	I've understood your distress,
Cher amoureux,	Dear loved one,
Et je cède à tes voeux,	And I acceed to your wish:
Fais de moi ta maîtresse.	Make me your mistress.
Loin de nous la sagesse,	Wisdom being farther from us
Plus de tristesse,	Than sadness,
J'aspire à l'instant précieux	I aspire to the precious moment

Où nous serons heureux;
Je te veux.

Je n'ai pas de regrets
Et je n'ai qu'une envie;
Près de toi, là, tout près,
Vivre toute ma vie,
Que mon coeur soit le tien
Et la lèvre la mienne,
Que ton corps soit le mien,
Et que toute ma chair soit tienne.

J'ai compris ta détresse, etc.

Oui, je vois dans tes yeux
La divine promesse
Que ton coeur amoureux
Vient chercher ma caresse.
Enlacés pour toujours,
Brûlés des mêmes flammes,
Dans des rêves d'amours
Nous échangerons nos deux âmes.

J'ai compris te détresse, etc.

Henry Pacory (Editions Salabert, Paris)

When we will be happy;
I desire you.

I've no regrets
And I have only one desire;
Near you, there, very near,
To live all my life,
That my heart should be yours
And your lips mine,
That your body should be mine,
And that all my body should be yours.

I've understood your distress, etc.

Yes, I see in your eyes
The divine promise
That your loving heart
Comes looking for my caress.
Entwined forever,
Burning in the same flames,
In dreams of love
We exchange our two souls.

I've understood your distress, etc.

Figure 13.3. Georges Seurat, *Le Chahut* (1889–90).
Rijksmuseum Kröller-Müller, Otterlo, The Netherlands.

Satie's celebrated *Trois morceaux en forme de poir* (four hands, 1890–1903) is also a seven-section anthology of pieces written in the *café-concert* idiom. The formlessness that has been charged against it is a natural consequence of its origins, and the disjunct, swiftly changing mood of music hall entertainment was to reappear in various Cocteau-inspired vehicles from the late teens and early 1920s, such as *Parade* and *Les mariés de la tour Eiffel*. The vitalizing potential of the "everyday" is also visible in the appropriation of imported popular dances by Debussy in his second book of *Preludes* (1913), where "General Lavine—eccentric" is written "Dans le style et le Mouvement d'un Cake-Walk" and "La puerta del vino" is cast in a "Mouvement de Habanera." John Philip Sousa, the American "March King," had introduced Paris to ragtimes and cakewalks as early as 1900, and by 1913 the newly arrived Argentine tango, which at that time shared the rhythm of the Cuban habanera (see p. 123), had become the rage of afternoon tea dances.

The increasing emphasis placed on simplified textures and directly appealing materials—partly in reaction to the Expressionist-Primitivist explosions of 1909–13 and partly in reaction to the Mahlerian colossus and Debussian refinements—is also evident in the piano writing of Satie's *Enfantines*, composed in 1913 some years after his return to the Schola Cantorum to study counterpoint. Such pieces are less momentous for their contrapuntal bent, however, than for the economy of means and the sly wrong notes that were a natural and contemporaneous ally of Stravinsky's sets of *Easy Pieces* (1914–17) and the slightly later *Five Fingers* (1920–21).

Enfantines is a group of three sets of three pieces, and Satie provided an elaborate text for each. The whimsy, for all the seeming innocence, is as self-conscious and clever, and occasionally as absurd, as anything the Dadaists were ever to invent. Who can fail to sympathize with the king who likes his staircase so much that he intends to have it stuffed, or with the plight of the dog who suffers from a stomach disorder because he has smoked too many cigars. The flatulent non sequiturs of the text are matched by figures that charm but fail to develop, and the aesthetic of the "new simplicity" is already secured. If Stravinsky's dedication of the waltz in his *Three Easy Pieces* (1914–15) to Satie suggests an awareness of the latter's "Valse du chocolat aux amandes" in *Enfantines*, Stravinsky's *The Five Fingers* of 1920–21 suggests an even stronger affinity with the technical limitations of Satie's set, which keeps the range to a perfect fifth in both hands.[2]

The *Chapitres tournés* also of 1913 were first performed on the same program of January 14, 1914, that saw the premiere of Ravel's Mallarmé songs and Stravinsky's *Japanese Lyrics*, together with pieces by Florent Schmitt and Maurice Delage. According to a note written by Delage on the program he sent to Stravinsky, Satie's pieces were "side-splitting." There has been considerable discussion of the meaning of Satie's commentaries that accompany his scores. A footnote to his *Heures séculaires & instantanées* (1914) states, "I forbid anyone to read the text aloud during the performance. Ignorance of my instructions will bring my righteous indignation against the audacious culprit." Some have interpreted these remarks to pertain to all of his works, though the point is arguable. What is not is Satie's periodic intention to provoke, as he indicated in the text that prefaces the opening chorale of his most important piano cycle of the time, *Sports et Divertissements* (1914): "Into it I have put all I know about boredom. I dedicate this chorale to those who do not like me. And I withdraw." The witticisms that pepper Satie's score are not only in keeping with the announced antimonumentality of the pieces they accompany but suggest not so much a joke as the intention of the artist to deflate the whole business before the listener draws the wrong conclusions from a hearing without score. In many ways, therefore, this music is not meant for public performance, a fact that helps to explain the phenomenal success of Aldo Ciccolini's recordings that allow the private listener to read the textual synopses from the record jacket in advance.

Sports et Divertissements contains the following prefatory note at the beginning of the collection:

> This publication is composed of two artistic elements: drawing and music. The drawing part consists of lines—animated lines; the musical part is represented by dots—black dots. These two parts put together—in one volume—make a whole: an album. I recommend that you turn its pages with a tolerant thumb and with a smile, for this is a work of fantasy. Let no one regard it otherwise.[3]

The means by which Satie attacked the old order include, besides the juxtaposition of numerous four-square episodes whose metric regularity is occasionally spiced with polytonality, the use of satire through quotation. Former ribbings of Mozart's Turkish music in "Tyrolienne turc" (*Croquis & Agaceries*) or a humorous citation from Chopin's renowned funeral march purposely mislabeled as a celebrated mazurka by Schubert in "d'Edriophthalma" (*Embryons desséchés*) now give way to spoofs of things associated with Debussy: (a) the quotation in "The Flirt" of the folktune "Au clair de la lune" used by Debussy in *Pierrot* (p. 183); (b) the quotation in "Les Courses" (The Races) of a snippet from the "Marseilles," as in Debussy's *Feux d'artifice* (p. 102), played delicately and pianissimo against the text "The Losers (noses pointed, ears back)"; and finally, (c) titles such as "Le feu d'artifice" (Figure 13.4) instead of "Feux d'artifice," the spelling of the final prelude to Debussy's Book II. It is a fizzled single firecracker as opposed to the dazzling shower of Debussy's lengthy and highly developed masterwork.

Some years later in his *Le coq et l'arlequin* (1918), Cocteau spoke of Satie's titles such as "Croquis & agaceries d'un gros bonhomme en bois" ("Sketches and temptations of a big wooden man"):

> One often wonders why Satie saddles his finest works with grotesque titles which mislead the least hostile sections of the public. Apart from the fact that these titles protect his works from persons obsessed by the sublime, and provide an excuse for the laughter of those who do not realize their value, they can be explained by the Debussy-ist abuse of 'previous' titles. No doubt they are meant as a good-humoured piece of ill-humour, and maliciously directed against "Lunes descendant sur le temple qui fut", "Terrasses des audiences du Clair de lune" and "Cathédrales englouties".[4]

Satie had actually alluded musically to the last of these works in the final cadence of the concluding work to *Chapitre tournés*, a work dedicated to Debussy's wife, and may account for Delage's description of the piece.

But Cocteau's remarks were made following the premiere of Satie's *Parade*, and what might have formerly been seen as "side-splitting" now became a serious business. Enemy lines were soon to be drawn, though before entering the battlefield Satie composed three of his most charming songs, the *Trois mélodies* of 1916. The texts could have been taken from Edward Lear's *Nonsense*

Figure 13.4. Page from the limited facsimile edition of Satie's *Sports et Divertissements* (1914). Translation: "*Fireworks.* (Rapidly) How dark it is! Oh, a Bengal light! A rocket! A blue, blue rocket! Everyone admires the show. An old man goes crazy. The last round of fireworks ('Le Bouquet')! April 6, 1914."

(Originally published by Publications Lucien Vogel, Paris, n.d. [c. 1925]. Dover Publications reprint 1982, with English translations by Stanley Appelbaum.)

Book or Lewis Carroll, and indeed the final poem by René Chalupt is acknowledged to be "after *Alice in Wonderland*." It is also dedicated to Igor Stravinsky. No explanations are necessary, only a text to follow, in savoring these delicious gems whose initial piece opens with an exhuberant Americanism in the piano, and whose second, following a childish confusion between "un oisetier" (a bird-tree; a nonexistent word) and a "noisetier" (a hazelnut tree), dissolves in a comprehending (?) "Ah!".

Erik Satie, *Trois mélodies*

LA STATUE DE BRONZE

La grenouille du jeu de tonneau
S'ennuie le soir sous la tonnelle
Elle en a assez d'être la statue
Qui va prononcer un grand mot, le Mot . . .
Elle aimerait mieux être avec les autres
Qui font des bulles de musique
Avec le savon de la lune.
Au bord du lavoir mordoré
Qu'on voit là-bas luire entre les branches.
On lui lance à coeur de journée,
Une pâture de pistoles
Qui la traverent sans lui profiter
Et s'en vont sonner dans les cabinets
De son piédestal numéroté.
Et le soir les insectes couchent dans sa
   bouche.

Léon-Paul Fargue

THE BRONZE STATUE

The frog of the game of "tonneau"
Becomes bored at evening under the arbor;
It is weary of being a statue
Who is about to utter an important word, the
   Word . . .
It would rather be with the others
Who are making music bubbles
With moon-soap.
Beside the reddish-brown washhouse
Which one can see shining down there
   through the branches,
All day long they toss showers of metal coins
That pass through without profit
And fall ringing into the chambers
Of its numbered pedestal.
And in the evening the insects sleep
In its mouth.

DAPHÉNÉO

Dis-moi, Daphénéo, quel est donc cet arbre
   dont les fruits sont des oiseaux qui
   pleurent?
Cet arbre, Chrysaline, est un oisetier.
Ah! . . . Je croyais que les noisetiers
   donnaient des noisettes, Daphénéo.
Oui, Chrysaline, les noisetiers donnent des
   noisettes, mais les oisetiers donnent des
   oiseaux qui pleurent.
Ah! . . .

M. Godebska

DAPHÉNÉO

Tell me, Daphénéo, what is that tree whose
   fruits are birds who weep?
That tree, Chrysaline, is a bird-tree.
Ah! . . . I thought that hazel trees bore
   hazelnuts, Daphénéo.
Yes, Chrysaline, hazel trees do have
   hazelnuts, but bird-trees have birds who
   weep.
Ah! . . .

LE CHAPELIER (d'apres "Alice au Pays des Merveilles")

Le chapelier s'étonne de constater
Que sa montre retarde de trois jours,
Bien qu'il ait eu soin de la graisser toujours
Avec du beurre de première qualité.
Mais il a laissé tomber des miettes de pain
   dans les rouages,
Et il a beau plonger sa montre dans le thé,
Ça ne la fera pas avancer davantage.

René Chalupt. © *Editions Salabert, 1917.*

THE MAD HATTER (after "Alice in Wonderland")

The hatter is astonished to find
That his watch is three days behind,
Even though he has always taken care to
   grease it
With butter of the first quality.
But he has let some breadcrumbs fall into the
   works,
And though he tries dipping his watch in the
   tea,
It fails to make it run any faster.

COCTEAU, SATIE, AND *LES SIX: PARADE* AND AFTER

"Can a small work of art have a big impact? To this my answer is: Yes, if the circumstances are right."

—E. Lowinsky, "Secret Chromatic Art Re-examined" (1972)

Jean Cocteau—writer, artist-designer, film maker, aesthetician—came to the world of music through the Ballets Russes's first Paris season in 1909. His scenario for Diaghilev's *Le dieu bleu* (1910–12) to music by Reynald Hahn was, however, the last gasp of a moribund orientalism, and following the enormous success of Stravinsky's *The Rite of Spring* Cocteau decided to take Diaghilev's dictum "Astonish me" as a personal credo.

One of his first plans (1915) was for an adaptation of *A Midsummer's Night Dream*, with music by Ravel, Satie, Schmitt, Stravinsky, and Varèse, props by Albert Gleizes, Cubist painter and theorist, and a circus scene involving members of the Cirque Medrano. While nothing came of the project, many of its ideas were carried over into his next work. Satie was the only one of the composers who came forth with a score, *Cinq grimaces*, and sensing his irreverent style Cocteau determined that he was the man for his next venture.

PARADE.   While Debussy and Ravel had orchestrated and presented several works of Satie in concerts as early as 1911, the notable popularity Satie achieved following the end of World War I was due entirely to Cocteau and *Parade* (1916–17). Cocteau spoke enthusiastically of Satie, and brought his music to the attention of artists such as Jean Wiéner, pianist and promoter of concerts; the patroness Misia Sert; and Diaghilev, who ultimately commissioned the collaboration of Cocteau (scenario), Massine (choreography), Picasso (costumes, sets), and Satie (music) in the spectacle of *Parade*.

Combining ingredients of Marinetti's variety theater (speed, instinct, surprise, practicality, and all other aspects of modern urban life); of Stravinsky's *Petrushka* (carnival; the show within a show); of the *esprit nouveau* of Apollinaire (who wrote a program note for the first performance heralding this multimedia venture and invoking the word "surrealism" for the first time); Picasso's "surrealist" curtain and "cubist" costumes; and a hint of Futurist noise-making, *Parade* was the perfect vehicle for antagonizing an audience and demonstrating its eternal incomprehension. Hardly of a piece, there was enough to offend everybody. Cocteau's contribution was minor, though he later claimed responsibility for the whole thing. The inchoate jumble of his proposed scenario, which he passed along to Satie, can be sensed from the following excerpts for "The Little American Girl" scene:

The Titanic—"Nearer My God to Thee"—elevators—the sirens of Boulogne—submarine cables—steamship apparatus—*The New York Herald*—dynamos—airplanes—short circuits—palatial cinemas—Walt Whitman—the silence of stampedes—cowboys with leather and goatskin chaps—the telegraph operator from Los Angeles who marries the detective at the end—the Sioux—the cordillera of the Andes—Negroes picking maize—beautiful Madame Astor—the declarations of President Wilson—torpedo boats—mines—the tango—projectors—arc lamps—gramophones—typewriters—the Eiffel Tower—the Brooklyn Bridge—huge automobiles of enamel and nickel—Pullman cars which cross the virgin forest—bars—saloons—ice-cream parlors—roadside taverns—Nick Carter—the Hudson and its docks—the Carolinas—my room on the seventeenth floor—panhandlers—posters—advertising—Charlie Chaplin—Christopher Columbus—the list of the victims of the Lusitania—women wearing evening gowns in the morning. . . .[5]

Parade was composed of seven sections in all, entitled Choral, Prelude of the Red Curtain (designed by Picasso, Figure 13.5), The Chinese Magician, The Little American Girl, Acrobats, Finale, and Reprise of the Red Curtain Prelude. The idea of the scenario is simple: The Chinese magician, the American ingénue, and the acrobats parade outside their tents giving free excerpts from their full performance in an effort to lure the audience into buying tickets (see Seurat's *La Parade*, Fig. 13.6). The crowd, however, mistakes their samples for the main show and disappears, ignoring the entreaty of the performers to return.

The tender irony of the opening chorale in *Sports et Divertissements* is resurrected by Satie for the solemn opening of *Parade*, which leads to the Prelude marked by a tiny fugato. Ultimately this dissolves into sliding parallel chords and Stravinskian ostinati, which characterize the Chinese Magician's music. In this movement there is only a hint of the obligatory pentatonicism, but the principal material of the woodwinds and the accompanying lower strings disclose a metric relationship similar to the first movement of Stravinsky's *Three Pieces for String Quartet* (p. 225), and the opening and closing frame of "The Little American Girl" betrays an affinity with Stravinsky's *The Nightingale*. Nothing could more clearly confirm the similarities of expression between

Figure 13.5. Picasso's "Red Curtain" for *Parade*. While Picasso's costumes for *Parade* reflected the artist's Cubist side, the opening curtain portrayed the world of the circus in fantasy-realist terms. The art of the everyday, espoused by Cocteau, Satie, and "Les Six," relied heavily on the cabaret, circus, music hall, and cinema for themes, techniques, and materials.

Figure 13.6. Georges Seurat, *La Parade* (1887–88). Canvas, 39½″ × 59¼″.

Satie and Stravinsky during the period 1913–18 already noted in a comparison of their piano works.

Though the style of *Parade* is often claimed to reflect this piano style of the teens, another work, *Le piège de Méduse*, written in 1913 though not produced until 1921, was in some ways even more prophetic. A totally Dadaist production with a stuffed monkey straight out of the pages of *Enfantines*, it is scored for clarinet, trumpet, trombone, violin, cello, double-bass, and percussion, not unlike the later ensemble for *Histoire du soldat*, and includes a Quadrille, Valse, Mazurka, and Polka. There are details that are invariably forwarded in discussing *Parade* to suggest its novelty, such as the ragtime rhythms of "The Little American Girl," which quotes Irving Berlin's "That Mysterious Rag" (Ex. 13.2), or the large intervals of the xylophone bitonally projected against the strings in the "Acrobats." But the principal novelty of the score resided in the large number of timbral oddities suggested by Cocteau, all intended to shock: typewriter, pistol shot, and sirens in "The Little American Girl"; whistles and *bouteille-ophone* in "The Acrobats"; and lottery wheel in the "Chinese Magician." There can be little doubt that Diaghilev's reports of the Futurist concert of 1914 in Milan had struck home.

In the final analysis it was undoubtedly the extramusical contributions of Diaghilev, Cocteau, Massine, Picasso, and Apollinaire that accounted for the attention originally accorded the piece. For Satie's score was a charming, though reasonably tame, example of his earlier style—compatible with the purposes at hand, but on the surface incapable of being judged a revolutionary step forward.

Example 13.2. Erik Satie, *Parade:* "Petite fille americaine," Rehearsal No. 23.

As part of a larger conception, however, its influence, though brief, was sufficient to trigger a movement. The use of a ragtime for "The Little American Girl" may leave one with the problem of how best to account for the allowance of the American strain in an aesthetic that purported to be French above all; yet it was totally in harmony with the European craze for American popular music begun at the turn of the century and that would soon reach a fever peak with the appearance of American jazz ensembles in Europe around 1920.

Stravinsky has spoken pointedly about the importance of jazz, as he conceived it, in the composition of *Histoire du soldat:*

> My choice of instruments was influenced by a very important event in my life at that time, the discovery of American jazz. (It has been pointed out that Satie's *Le Piège de Méduse* [1913] employs a combination of instruments very like that of *Histoire,* but I was completely unaware of *Le Piège de Méduse.*) The *Histoire* ensemble resembles the jazz band in that each instrumental category—strings, woodwinds, brass, percussion—is represented by both treble and bass components. The instruments themselves are jazz legitimates, too, except the bassoon, which is my substitution for the saxophone . . . The percussion part must also be considered as a manifestation of my enthusiasm for jazz . . . Jazz meant, in any case, a wholly new sound in my music, and *Histoire* marks my final break with the Russian orchestral school in which I had been fostered.[6]

Though we know that Stravinsky had seen printed scores supplied by Ansermet prior to the arrival of the American band in Europe, the specter of ragtime that surfaced in his *Histoire* (1918), *Ragtime for Eleven Instruments* (1918; Figure 13.7), and *Piano Rag Music* (1919) may owe more than a little to Satie's earlier example. The same claim may be made for Satie's "Tango" in *Sports et Divertissements* (1914) with respect to Stravinsky's tangos in *Histoire* and *The Five Fingers* (1920–21). In retrospect it is easy to see how the repetitive patterns, syncopations, and small but characteristic instrumental groupings of jazz were so readily reconcilable with the ostinati, shifting accentuation, and chamber ensembles of Stravinsky's current production. But Stravinsky may have also sensed the shift that had taken place with Diaghilev, and deemed Cocteau's descriptions of *Parade,* which appeared in *Le coq et l'arlequin* (1918), predictive as well as to his taste. There Cocteau made clear that the aim of French music was to free itself not only from the vapors of Debussy and Mallarmé but from German influences and what he called the "Russian trap." The energy, directness and, not least, the modishness of American popular music made it a momentary ally. But by 1920 Cocteau would announce in the broadsheet *Le coq* that American sources had been sufficiently tapped and proclaim "Adieu New York! Bonjour Paris!," a sentiment quickly taken up in a piece by Auric. Satie's example was deemed to consist primarily of a "return to simplicity," a "grace without pedals," a "metronomic unity," and the pursuit of "his little classic path". The last of these was mirrored in the Neoclassic line drawing which Picasso made of Satie in 1920 in a pose and chair identical to one which he executed of Stravinsky about the same time (Figure 13.8).

Figure 13.7. Picasso's front cover for the first edition (1919) of Stravinsky's piano arrangement of *Rag-time.* The two musicians are drawn in a single line.

Figure 13.8. Picasso, *Satie* (1920), drawing.
Photo courtesy of Giraudon/Art Resource. © SPADEM, Paris/VAGA, New York, 1985.

LES MARIÉS DE LA TOUR EIFFEL.   It was in this atmosphere that the formation of "Les Six" took place. Cocteau throughout the period was as important as an entrepreneur as a creative figure, though later he was to provide the ballet scenario for Milhaud's *Le boeuf sur le toit* (1920) and *Le train bleu* (1924); and texts for Honegger's *Antigone* (1922), Stravinsky's *Oedipus rex* (1926–27; Latin translation by J. Daniélou), Milhaud's *Le pauvre matelot* (1927), and Poulenc's *La voix humaine* (play, 1929; opera, 1959). He also wrote the play-ballet, *Les mariés de la Tour Eiffel* (1920–21), which introduced "Les Six" to the public.

Blaise Cendrars, announced authority on African folklore and sculpture in his postwar *Anthologie nègre*, accuser of Apollinaire as a plagiarizer in his *Calligrammes*, and early champion of Chaplin, Léger, Picasso, Chagall, Stravinsky, Honegger, and Satie, organized a concert on June 6, 1917, to celebrate the premiere of *Parade* only a few days before on May 18. Along with works of Auric and Honegger, Durey's *Carillons* received its premiere, and the concert ended with Satie playing in a four-hand arrangement of *Parade*. Half the group soon to be known as "Les Six" had made their public debut.

In *Le coq et l'arlequin* published in 1918, Cocteau announced that his principal aim was to break the spell of Debussy, openly calling Ravel "Debussyste." In the broadsheet *Le coq* (June, 1920), Satie stated "I never attack Debussy. It's only the Debussyites that annoy me. THERE IS NO SATIE SCHOOL. Satieism could never exist. I would oppose it. There must be no slavery in art. I have always tried to throw followers off the scent by both the form and content of each new work."[7] A test case came quickly with Durey, whose *Carillons* for piano, though not totally anti-Debussy on the surface, nonetheless foreshadows through repetitive patterns that go on too long the exasperating minimalisms of Satie's *Relâche* (1924) and other cellular *musique d'ameublement* (see p. 273). It was only a momentary turn, however, and Durey's career quickly took a turn totally out of view of the Satie circle.

The six composers (Poulenc, Milhaud, Honegger, Durey, Auric, Tailleferre) took their name as the result of an article published by Henri Collet in *Comoedia* (January, 1920) entitled "Les cinq russes, les six françaises et M. Satie." As pupils of Gédalge and self-styled as "Les nouveaux jeunes," they had presented concerts of their music as early as 1917. By 1918, Cocteau had become their spokesman in his *Le coq et l'arlequin* and Satie their spiritual leader. Collet's reference to the Russian Five in proclaiming a French Six was fundamental to Cocteau's chauvinistic pronouncements, which called for the elimination of foreign and especially German elements and the subscription of themes from everyday life. Toward this end the composer was encouraged to turn to the music hall, the circus, and jazz in order to emphasize directness, brevity, and a certain *sec* quality. *Trois morceaux en forme de poire*, the work that introduced Satie to Cocteau in 1915, consisting principally of arrangements of cabaret melodies, could be held up as a turn-of-the-century model. The recent example of *Parade*, with its "Little American Girl" ragtime, could be used as a current reference point.

In his play *Les mariés de la Tour Eiffel* of 1921, Cocteau enjoined "Les Six" (Durey declined) to compose the following items:

Overture	George Auric
Wedding March (entrance)	Darius Milhaud
The General's Speech	Francis Poulenc
The Trouville Bathing Beauty	Francis Poulenc
The Massacre (fugue)	Darius Milhaud
Waltz of the Radiograms	Germaine Tailleferre
Funeral March	Arthur Honegger
Quadrille	Germaine Tailleferre
Wedding March (exit)	Darius Milhaud

The action takes place on the first platform of the Eiffel Tower. Two actors, costumed as Phonographs, provide a commentary on the action and recite the lines of the various characters. Cocteau's text for Poulenc's "The Trouville Bathing Beauty" will suggest the mood, function, and context of the whole:

The Trouville Bathing Beauty

PHONO I. I am the Photographer of the Eiffel Tower and I am going to take your picture.

PHONO I AND II. Yes! Yes! Yes! Yes!

PHONO I. Arrange yourselves in a group.

The party groups itself behind the table.

PHONO II. You are wondering what has happened to the ostrich hunter and the Manager of the Eiffel Tower. The Hunter is trailing the ostrich up through every platform. The manager is trailing the Hunter, and running the Eiffel Tower. This is no sinecure. The Eiffel Tower is a world, like Notre-Dame. It is the Notre-Dame of the Left Bank.

PHONO I. It is the Queen of Paris.

PHONO II. It *was* the Queen of Paris. Now it is a telegraph girl.[8]

PHONO I. After all, a man's got to live!

PHONO II. Now, don't move. Look pleasant, please. Look straight into the camera. A little bird's going to come out.

> *A Trouville Bathing Beauty comes out of the camera. She wears a one-piece bathing suit, carries a butterfly net in which there is a heart, and has a picnic basket slung over one shoulder. Colored lights. The wedding party lifts its hands in admiration.*

PHONO I. Oh the pretty postcard!

> *Dance of the Bathing Beauty.*

But the Photographer does not share the delight of the wedding party. This is the second time today that his camera has gone back on him. He is trying to make the Trouville Bathing Beauty get back into the camera.

PHONO II. Finally the Bathing Beauty goes back into the camera. The Photographer has convinced her that it is a bathhouse.

> *End of the dance. The photographer throws a bathrobe over the girl's shoulders; she exits into the camera, skipping, throwing kisses.*

PHONOS I AND II. Bravo! Bravo! Bis! Bis! Bis![9]

In the preface to his play, Cocteau provided the manifesto for a self-consciously French art:

> The young music employs a clarity, a simplicity, a good humor, that are new. The ingenuous ear is deceived: it seems to be listening to a café orchestra, but it is as mistaken as would be an eye which could not distinguish between a loud garish material and the same material copied by Ingres.

> In *Wedding Party* we employ all the popular resources that France will have none of at home, but will approve whenever a musician, native or foreign, exploits them outside.

> Do you think, for example, that a Russian can hear the *Pétrouchka* just as we do? In addition to the charms of that musical masterpiece he finds there his childhood, his Sundays in Petrograd, the lullabies of nurses.

> Why should I deny myself this double pleasure? I assure you that the orchestra of *The Eiffel Tower Wedding Party* moves me more than any number of Russian or Spanish dances. It is not a question of honor rolls. I think I have sufficiently exalted Russian, German, and Spanish musicians (to say nothing of Negro orchestras) to permit myself this *cri du coeur.*[10]

Cocteau's reference to *Petrouchka* is telling, for in *Parade* the milling of people before sample performances designed to lure them into the main event is analogous to the opening street scene of *Petruchka* with its competing acts of organ grinder and dancer. In *Parade,* the use of white-face for the characters also simulates their puppet-like nature. Cocteau saw *The Newlyweds* as a cross between vaudeville and Greek tragedy, the two phonographs functioning in the role of the chorus. He also intended that the play be seen as a pun on the word cliché, which in French means both banality and snapshot. Instead of faithfully recording a bourgeois wedding, Cocteau seeks to explore the "negative, the underside of its poseurs." The cliché—a middle class wedding on the Eiffel Tower—becomes a cliché only when the photographer at last manages to take a snapshot.[11]

In both *Parade* and *Les mariés* the emphasis on everyday life found a natural ally in the music hall not only in the light-hearted style of the music provided by "Les Six" but in Cocteau's reliance on a series of scenes, or acts, presented without transition, much in the style of the music hall revue, and whose relation to one another was tenuous or nonexistent. Cocteau's search for a formula that was French may also be seen as a search for a panacea in a war-weary country, tired of pompous ideals and rhetoric and depersonalized by the machine age. The choice of the Eiffel Tower as the locus for his play was a natural. Built for the Paris Exhibition of 1889, it had served not only as a monument to nineteenth-century engineering skill but, as the century turned, as an expression of French cultural values and a source for the discovery of contemporary dynamics. Robert Delaunay (1885–1941) painted it more than thirty times, the most famous version being the *Red Tower* (1911–12) (Figure 13.9); Vincente Huidobro sang its praises in a poem of 1917 sprayed with syllables

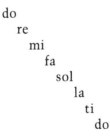

in a typographical slant and dedicated to Delaunay; and Blaise Cendrars in 1924 summarized its meaning and effect for all the world:

> No formula of art known up to now can pretend to give plastic resolution to the Eiffel Tower. Realism shrank it; the old laws of Italian perspective diminished it. The Tower rose over Paris, slender as a hatpin. When we retreated from it, it dominated Paris, stark and perpendicular. When we came close, it tilted and leaned over us. Seen from the first platform it corkscrewed around its own axis, and seen from the top it collapsed into itself, doing the splits, its neck pulled in . . .[12]

The Dadaist movement, whose negativist anti-art proclamations ultimately insured its own demise, was also in full swing. Though its tenure was brief, 1915–1922, its emphasis on the use of everyday objects, as in Duchamps *The Bride Stripped Bare by Her Bachelors, Even* (1915–1923) or less lyrically in

Figure 13.9. Robert Delaunay, *Red Eiffel Tower* (1911–12).

Solomon R. Guggenheim Museum, New York. Photo by Robert E. Mates. © ADAGP, Paris/VAGA, New York, 1985.

Kurt Schwitters' *Merzbilden* (collages made from junk or rubbish), was intended to question the moral or aesthetic bases of art and to strip it of "meaning." Appearing almost simultaneously in New York, Paris, and Zurich, the Swiss origins of the movement in the Cabaret Voltaire at the hands of such figures as the poet Tristan Tzara and the sculptor Jean Arp was naturally appealing to Cocteau and company. The degree to which they prized the absurd was picked up by the Surrealists, who took over where they left off.

Surrealism, though first used as a word by Apollinaire in a program note to *Parade*, was initially codified by the poet André Breton in his *Manifeste du surréalisme* of 1924. Drawn to the "automatic writing" techniques of the Dadaists, they were intrigued with the world of dreams and fantasies and decried the concepts of coherence, reason, and logic in art. As a substitute they forwarded the possibility of a new reality—marvelous and heightened in what they called "surrealism." As a movement its most important manifestation was in literature and painting, but to the extent that the surrealist poets (Apollinaire, Éluard) were favored by musicians, their influence was felt, and in Breton's definition of Surrealism, given here, we have a base clearly prefigured by Satie's *Descriptions automatiques* (1913) and shared by Gertrude Stein and the "automatic improvisations" of Virgil Thomson (see p. 451).

> Surrealism, n. Pure psychic automatism, by which it is intended to express whether verbally or in writing, or in any other way, the real process of thought. It is the dictation of thought, free from any control by the reason and of any aesthetic or moral preoccupation. (*Manifeste du surréalisme*, 1924.)

It is also a base from which John Cage's world of chance and "happenings" of a later date was to flourish. For Cocteau, the Dadaist-Surrealist turnover, which was taking place at this very time, offered the opportunity for a collage of five different musicians, without thought of stylistic homogeneity, in nine numbers lacking any narrative quality. *Les mariés'* celebration of the Eiffel Tower as a symbol may have promoted French culture and contemporary technological values, but the absurdity of its text, its costuming of two actors as phonographs, and the outrageous banter of the principals risk meaning in a joyous Dadaist escape into "real life."

The consequence of such a turn of mind found its ultimate expression in *Relâche*, produced by the Ballet Suédois in 1924 shortly before Satie's death. Part of a larger multimedia surrealist entertainment, Satie's contribution included an "Entr'acte cinématographique," music written to accompany a film interlude directed by René Clair in which the composer can be seen firing cannons and crawling among the gargoyles of Notre Dame. The music, when heard by itself, is marked by infuriating repetitions that sound like nothing so much as a needle stuck in the groove of a phonograph record. Lacking any technical connection with the art of the Minimalists of a later decade but disclosing an affinity with the multimediasts to come, the score finds meaning only in conjunction with a viewing of the film where the relationship of such banalities to the world of Mack Sennet (1880–1960) becomes apparent. In his vintage silent movies (1914–24), starring Buster Keaton, Charlie Chaplin, and the Keystone Kops, jerky, swiftly-paced, pseudodanger ridden, highly repetitive motion served the director in fashioning "biting parodies or incisive satires that mocked the foibles of an increasingly mechanized society."[13]

FRANCIS POULENC: FROM *LE BESTIAIRE* TO *HÔTEL*

Of all the members of "Les Six," which disbanded as a group after 1921, Poulenc (1899–1963) remained most loyal to the premises of Cocteau's manifesto. A composer who in his maturity developed a noble style for a series of religious works, he seldom left the model for simplicity or the sounds of the cabaret very far behind.

His first opus, a *Rapsodie nègre* of 1917 dedicated to Satie, was a work in five movements whose ensemble of flute, clarinet, string quartet, and piano appears to be *Pierrot* inspired. The third movement, an *intermede vocal* entitled "Honoloulou," utilized a three-stanza nonsense text of pseudo-African doggerel attributed to Makako Kangourou. The spoof was against Negro art then at the height of its fashion in Paris, and Poulenc was successful in provoking the hoped-for scandal at the premiere of the work on December 11, 1917, presented as part of a Nouveaux Jeunes concert.

His *Le bestiaire ou cortège d'Orphée* of 1918 taps the similarly titled collection of Guillaume Apollinaire (1880–1918) and uses the forces of *Rapsodie nègre* with the bassoon replacing the piano. Apollinaire was one of the fathers of Surrealism as well as one of Poulenc's favorite poets, and the texts for twenty-six additional songs as well as the libretto for his first opera *Les mamelles de Tirésias* (1947) are by him. The texts for *Le bestiaire* are a cross between those of *Histoires naturelles* and Satie's *Trois mélodies*, and numerous artists including Raoul Dufy have illustrated the collection. Poulenc's musical illustration not only captures the Dadaist-Surrealist quality of the texts but already fixes ingredients that were to remain in the language of the mature composer. The ad hoc instrumental ensemble (v, fl, cl, bn, str qt) is as fashionable as the brevity of the texts, which have something of the quality of a folk proverb concerning "The Dromedary," "The Tibetan Goat," "The Grasshopper," "The Dolphin," "The Crayfish," and "The Carp." In theme and whimsical directness of expression, the work complements the contemporaneous productions of Stravinsky and Satie. It also fed the instrumental style of the *Sonata for Two Clarinets* (1918) and another for clarinet and bassoon (1922), which secured Poulenc's link with Stravinsky in defining the Neoclassic bent of the 1920s.

Cocteau's *Le coq et l'arlequin* appeared in the spring of 1918, and in 1919 Poulenc collaborated with him in the setting of three of his chansons. Entitled *Cocardes*, they were originally scored for violin, cornet, trombone, bass drum, and triangle, which was the typical designation of the *bal musette* café orchestra. In the May 1920 issue of *Le coq*, Poulenc found his literary voice and warned that "We will never give you 'works'," which Milhaud explained to mean late-Romantic orchestral riches. Cocteau soon joined in by denouncing the idea of the masterpiece, which he said could lead nowhere. As masterpieces tend to spawn only cheap imitations (see Cage's work of this title, p. 651), he judged that the only antedote was to contradict the work of art. Its anti-art tone is Dadaist, but to the extent that the negativism is put to positive account it is in harmony with the thought of the Surrealists.

In 1921, Poulenc wrote incidental music for a play by Cocteau and Raymound Radiguet, *Gendarme incompris* (later destroyed by the composer), and contributed to the "Les Six" spectacle, *Les mariés de la tour Eiffel*, performed on June 18, 1921. Poulenc's music for "The General's Speech" and "The Trouville Bathing Beauty" conformed precisely to Cocteau's injunction for a response that was tuneful and marked by clarity, simplicity, and good humor. Diaghilev was present at the concert and asked Stravinsky to introduce him to Poulenc. The commission for a new ballet, *Les biches* (1924), was the result. In this work, and periodically throughout Poulenc's life, the spirit of the music hall was absorbed even if it did not prevail. *Les biches*, though saucy and bright, also makes use of eighteenth-century tunes and texts and attempts to evoke the lightly erotic atmosphere of Watteau's *fêtes galantes*. Its self-conscious mannerism, including the placement of singers in the orchestra pit, can best be judged in light of Stravinsky's *Pulcinella* written a few years earlier and the emerging aesthetic of Neoclassicism. Poulenc remarked in later years:

> I've often been reproached about my "street music" side. Its genuineness has been suspected, and yet there's nothing more genuine in me . . . From childhood onward I've associated café tunes with the Couperin Suites in a common love without distinguishing between them.[14]

Among the French, none sensed the spirit of the cabaret and the age of Toulouse-Lautrec more innately than Francis Poulenc, who showed a capacity to incorporate the pertness and effrontery of the music hall in the most surprising contexts, including opera (*Les mamelles de Tirésias*), ballet (*Les biches*), and the concerto (*Organ Concerto*). It is in the *valse chantée* "Les chemins de l'amour" (1940) and two songs from the set entitled *Banalités* (1940) that Poulenc strikes at the core of his Parisian heart. "Hôtel," one of the most languorous and seductive songs ever written and, as Bernac has said, "the laziest," is the perfect transformation of an art song into a torch song, while "Voyage à Paris" captures "a certain type of sentimentality and of Parisian badinage" that is inextricably associated with Maurice Chevalier. Here, as frequently before, Apollinaire provides Poulenc with the perfect texts for his purpose, totally direct in meaning and appropriately concise in expression.

HOTEL

Ma chambre a la forme d'une cage
Le soleil passe son bras par la fenêtre
Mais moi qui veut fumer
Pour faire des mirages
J'allume au feu du jour ma cigarette
Je ne veux pas travailler
Je veux fumer.

HOTEL

My room has the shape of a cage
the sun passes its arm through the window
but I who wish to smoke
to make mirages in the air
I light at the fire of day my cigarette
I do not wish to work
I just want to smoke.

VOYAGE A PARIS

Ah! la charmante chose
Quitter un pays morose
Pour Paris
Paris joli
Qu'un jour dut créer l'Amour.

TRIP TO PARIS

Ah! what a charming thing
to leave a dull place
for Paris
pretty Paris
that once upon a time love must have created.

Apollinaire, "Voyage à Paris" from Poèmes retrouvés. *(c) Editions Gallimard. Apollinaire, "Hôtel" from "Poèmes divers" in* Le guetteur mélancolique. *(c) Editions Gallimard.*

DARIUS MILHAUD: *LE BOEUF SUR LE TOIT AND LA CRÉATION DU MONDE*

When Milhaud (1892–1974) embarked on his sojourn to Brazil in 1916 as a secretary to the French foreign minister and poet, Paul Claudel, it was not only a flight from war-torn France but crucial to a developing awareness of the potential use of popular songs and dances in art music. Having earlier provided incidental music to Claudel's *Agamemnon* (1913–14), *Protée* (1913–19), and *Les choéphores* (1915), the two now collaborated on a ballet originally intended for Nijinsky, whom they met while the Ballets Russes was on tour in Brazil. The scenario by Claudel for *L'homme et son désir*, set deep in a Brazilian forest, deals with various primal qualities concerning the freeing of Man by a phantom Woman. Milhaud's musical response called for an orchestra of a dozen solo instruments; a wordless vocal quartet; and a variety of percussion including tambourines, sleigh-bells, whip, whistle, wind machine, castanets, and a plank struck by a hammer. Thus, a mixture of traditional, Dadaist, and Futurist sound sources underscore Milhaud's exercise in polytonality and Brazilian rhythms.

The score to *Parade* as well as news of its premiere had reached Milhaud in South America. Back in France by November 1918, Milhaud immediately fell in with the Cocteau circle and found his experience with Brazilian popular music to be a natural ally to Cocteau's injunction to tap the popular strain of the music hall and the circus as a source of creative stimulus. Only a month after "Les Six" had been given their name in the articles of Henri Collet, Cocteau presented a concert on February 21, 1920, which included Poulenc's *Cocardes*, a foxtrot *Adieu, New York* by Auric, and Satie's *Trois petites pièces montées*, followed by Milhaud's *Le boeuf sur le toit*.

In *Le boeuf sur le toit* ("The Ox on the Roof" or "The Nothing-Doing Bar"), Milhaud joined Cocteau in creating a work whose bitonality wedded to banal diatonic melody was to become Milhaud's most identifiable signature. The composer has sketched the background and the final scenario devised by Cocteau.

> Still haunted by memories of Brazil, I assembled a few popular melodies, tangos, maxixes, sambas, and even a Portuguese fado, and transcribed them with a rondo-like theme recurring between each two of them. I called this fantasia *Le boeuf sur le toit*, the title of a Brazilian popular song.

Originally intending his score as an accompaniment for a Charlie Chaplin silent film, he was dissuaded by Cocteau who had other plans.

> Cocteau produced a pantomime scenario that could be adapted to my music. He imagined a scene in a bar in America during Prohibition. The various characters were highly typical: A Boxer, a Negro Dwarf, a Lady of Fashion, a Redheaded Woman dressed as a man, a Bookmaker, a Gentleman in evening clothes. The barman, with a face like Antinous, offers everyone cocktails. After a few incidents and various dances, a Policeman enters, whereupon the scene is immediately transformed into a milk-bar. The clients play a rustic scene and dance a pastorale as they sip glasses of milk. The barman switches on a big fan which decapitates the Policeman. The Redheaded Woman executes a dance with the Policeman's head, ending up standing on her hands like the Salome in Rouen Cathedral. One by one the customers drift away, and the Barman presents an enormous bill to the resuscitated Policeman.[15]

Milhaud never came closer to Cocteau's dicta than in this work, where the sounds of the music hall, irreverently projected to off-key accompaniments, kept company with a mimed cast of characters drawn from the Cirque Medrano. The success of the production led to the opening in the same year of a cabaret that borrowed its title and, in establishing the concept of the American bar in Paris, became a prominent locus for the presentation of jazz and its promotion among the artistic avant-garde.

Following another set of reminiscenses of his South American adventure in the tangos of his *Saudades do Brasil* (1920–21), Milhaud, encouraged by Jean Wiéner and others, turned to an investigation of American jazz. In the London dance halls he listened intently to Billy Arnold and his band from New York, but it was only after a trip to the latter city that he wrote his most notable jazz statement, *La création du monde* (1923). The work was commissioned by Rolf de Maré and the Ballets Suédois, with Blaise Cendrars, author of *L'anthologie nègre*, contributing the scenario from African folklore, and Ferdinand Léger the scenic design (Figure 13.10).

For his part, Milhaud adopted the same orchestra of seventeen solo instruments that he had heard in Harlem (2 fl, 2 cl, ob, bsn, hn, 2 tpt, tbn, pf, perc, two vn, vc, db, sax). Through timbral novelties such as saxophone and muted trumpet, fluttering tonguing and glissandi, syncopated rhythms and blues, and

Figure 13.10. Fernand Léger, design for the first production by the Ballets Suédois of Milhaud's ballet *La création du monde* (1923).

Dansmuseet, Stockholm. © SPADEM, Paris/VAGA, New York, 1985.

the use of the piano and strings (possibly in imitation of banjos) to reinforce the rhythm section, he brought a new and fresh quality to the interpretation of primitivism. Although the fugal section that follows the langorous introduction is often cited as typical of the work's timbre and figure (Ex. 13.3), the blue notes (flat 7) in the oboe melody near the end and the equivocation between flat and

Example 13.3. Milhaud, *La création du monde*, fugue subject.

raised third in both horn and oboe are of equal interest as a direct mirror of the Gershwin idiom known to Milhaud from the early 1920s through the composer-pianist Jean Wiéner (Ex. 13.4).

Wiéner has recorded his activities at the Café Gaya where he played Gershwin in the company of Diaghilev, Misia Sert, Satie, René Clair, Jane Bathori, Maurice Chevalier, Milhaud, Poulenc, Picasso, Léger, and others.[16] And the extent of the appeal as well as the esteem accorded the popular idiom by Milhaud is vividly reflected in a lecture delivered by him at the Sorbonne on May 22, 1924, entitled "Les resources nouvelles de la musique (jazz-band et instruments méchaniques)."[17] Although Milhaud quickly became an expert on jazz for the Europeans and wrote several articles about it, by the time of his

Example 13.4. Milhaud, *La création du monde,* Rehearsal No. 51.

second trip to America in 1926 he was prepared to announce to the press that the fascination had worn off. Had he forgotten that Cocteau had already sounded its death knell in 1920 (see p. 267)?

While early in his career Milhaud had responded to Cocteau's injunction to compose a specifically French art based on sounds of the music hall, it is important to stress that not only the French and American popular modes but his Provençal origin left its indelible imprint on countless works. Many suggest that his finest music invariably reveals a Mediterranean lyricism indebted to his knowledge and not unoccasional utilization of folk melodies (*Suite provençale*, 1936; *Suite française*, 1944). Other works capture the spirit without quotation, such as *Concertino de printemps* (1934) and *Le voyage d'été* (1946). At the same time he also possessed a Teutonic seriousness that could mesh readily with his fundamentally Gallic nature (*Les malheurs d'Orphée*, 1925; *Christophe Colomb*, 1928). It was a quality equally to be found in the works of Honegger in which the proportions were almost exactly reversed.

A composer of great industry and resourcefulness whose prolific output came to more than 400 opus numbers, Milhaud's reputation, justly or not, was never higher than it was in the 1920s. But in many of the scores from this period he made fundamental contributions to the definition of an age.

ARTHUR HONEGGER (1892–1955)

"Les Six" ultimately turned out to be "Les Trois"—Poulenc, Milhaud, and Honegger—not in terms of a similar aesthetic position but in terms of international recognition. Honegger was the least French of the group, and from the inception of his career betrayed a decidedly Germanic earnestness. Yet his proximity to the Cocteau circle included, beyond his contribution to *Les mariés de la Tour Eiffel*, a jazz *Concertino* for piano and orchestra and a *Prélude et blues* for harp quartet, both from 1925, as well as Futurist-Realist scores like *Pacific 231*, *Skating Rink*, and *Rugby*. His dramatic psalm, *Le roi David* of 1921, was his first important success. Here, mining a directness of expression founded on an admiration of the Protestant chorales, he seemed to have clearly found his own voice independent of any group or attention-getting superficialities. His later symphonies No. 3 (1945–46) and No. 5 (1951) similarly possess the abiding gravity and spirituality characteristic of Milhaud's maturity and are equal to the best of their time and genre. Yet his *Symphony No. 4* ("Delicie Basilienses") signals the search for a respite and a turn to the folk melodies of Switzerland, a country in which he held a dual citizenship with his native France. In this work of 1946 we sense an affinity not only with his early *Pastorale d'été* (1920) and *Chant de joie* (1923) but with the Provençal lyricism of Milhaud. His extensive and important contributions to radio and film made use of the complete spectrum of his artistic personality.

RAVEL: FROM *L'ENFANT ET LES SORTILEGES* TO THE PIANO CONCERTI

It interested me to see what would be Ravel's attitude before this mechanical play [*Parade*] . . . Ravel listened with his bird-head forward on his shoulders, then, his eyes round and fixed, confessed to me that he didn't understand the mechanism of a music that did not bathe, he said, in a sonorous fluid . . . It was exactly the novelty of Satie not to bathe in any sonorous fluid . . . of writing, as he said himself, 'a music of everyday'.

—Jean Cocteau, "Ravel et nous," *La Revue musicale* (1938), 396.

By 1938, when Cocteau wrote these remarks, Satie and Ravel were both gone and Cocteau's memory was free to embellish. Yet Ravel, whose alternating "impressionist" (*Daphnis et Chlöe*) and "neoclassic" (*Le tombeau de Couperin*) bent suggests a capacity to mirror more than a single aesthetic and whose open-mindedness had allowed him an immediate appreciation and understanding of Stravinsky's *The Rite of Spring*, must have been troubled by the Cocteau-Satie alliance. Not so much because of *Parade*, however, as their charges against Ravel as a "Debussyste."

Ravel's reaction was not in every way predictable. That is to say, he did not change his style to conform with that of his critics. Yet, two works, begun or completed in the early 1920s, suggest a reaction to recent events. The first of these was *L'enfant et les sortilèges (The Child and the Sorceries)* and, though not completed until 1925, was begun as early as 1920. The author of *Dialogues et bêtes*, Sidonie-Gabrille Colette (1873–1954) was the ideal person to join the composer of *Histoires naturelles* to produce a lyric fantasy of animals and children. Ravel, for his part, wrote one of his most refined and inimitable scores, and also one of his most eclectic. Dances of various kinds (polka, minuet, round, foxtrot, waltz) abound and proclaim Ravel's indebtedness to the eighteenth-century opera-ballet. In addition we learn that Ravel composed *L'enfant* "in the spirit of an American operetta," and although the dance between the black Wedgwood teapot and the Chinese cup was originally planned as a bourrée, it ultimately became a rag. In the sounds of tin-pan alley (piano, sliding trombone, wood block, xylophone) we are provided the first glimpse of the jazz idiom that was to appear in the second movement (entitled "Blues") of his *Violin Sonata* (1923–27) and in the Gershwinesque rhythms and blue-note melodies of his two piano concerti (for left hand, 1929–30; in G, 1929–31). The juxtaposition of jazz and ragtime with the pentatonic melodies of the Orient, baroque dance, and coloratura virtuosity (the Fire's aria) underscores the elements of fantasy in Colette's libretto.

In an address entitled "Contemporary Music" delivered at Houston's Rice Institute in 1928, Ravel effectively pinpointed the appeal of American popular music for the composer of serious music and suggested its compatability with a variety of personal signatures.

> To my mind, the "blues" is one of your greatest musical assets, truly American despite earlier contributory influences from Africa and Spain. Musicians have asked me how I came to write "blues" as the second movement of my recently completed sonata for violin and piano. Here again the same process, to which I have already alluded, is in evidence, for, while I adopted this popular form of your music, I venture to say that nevertheless it is French music, Ravel's music, that I have written. Indeed, these popular forms are but the materials of construction, and the work of art appears only on mature conception where no detail has been left to chance. Moreover, minute stylization in the manipulation of these materials is altogether essential. To understand more fully what I mean by the process to which I refer, it would be sufficient to have these same "blues" treated by some of our own musicians and by musicians of European countries other than France,

when you would certainly find the resulting compositions to be widely divergent, most of them bearing the national characteristics of their respective composers, despite the unique nationality of their original material, the American "blues". Think of the striking and essential differences to be noted in the "jazz" and "rags" of Milhaud, Stravinsky, Casella, Hindemith, and so on. The individualities of these composers are stronger than the materials appropriated. They mould popular forms to meet the requirements of their own individual art. Again—nothing left to chance; again—minute stylization of the materials employed, while the styles become as numerous as the composers themselves.[18]

L'enfant et les sortilèges was born exactly of the time of Paul Klee's (1897–1940) *Twittering Machine* (1922). While Klee was a German master of the Bauhaus, his various "fairy tales" carry with them a markedly naive quality that stemmed from the importance he attached to the drawings of small children. A pen drawing tinted with water color, *Twittering Machine* (Figure 13.11) carries something of the same dual edge of Ravel's work though in its own terms: a fantasy piece whose childlike atmosphere at once mocks the mechanisms of modern society (the runaway clock in *L'enfant*) and yet barely conceals the sinister potential of the birds to lure unsuspecting prey (the menacing

Figure 13.11. Paul Klee, *Twittering Machine* (1922). Watercolor, pen and ink, 16¾″ × 12″ (without margins).

quality of various animals in Ravel's opera). The appeal of similar themes of animals and children was to appear in later years in numerous guises. Among others, the American Gunther Schuller (b. 1925), a tireless advocate of the power of jazz and its potential compatability with "art" music, and the Englishman Oliver Knussen (b. 1952, and a pupil of Schuller's at Tangelwood, 1970–73) both turned to a direct reconsideration of the medium and/or message of these two works by Klee and Ravel: Schuller in his orchestral *Studies on Themes of Paul Klee* (1959), one of whose movements is subtitled "Twittering Machine," and Knussen in an opera fantasy *Where the Wild Things Are* (1979–83) based on the children's classic by Maurice Sendak.

It is well to note that, in addition to the spice of popular elements that surfaced in several of his works at this time, Ravel also occasionally applied to his "sonorous fluid" the ascetic, though never quite atonal, counterpoint suggested by Schoenberg's example, without which, Ravel confessed, he could probably never have written the *Chansons madécasses* of 1925–26. Some have suggested the presence of such values in his *Sonata* for violin and cello of 1922 as well. But whatever the impetus for such a work, the economy of ensemble and spareness of writing married to an occasional discordant edge hint at a reaction (both pro and con) to the "new simplicity." Other forces at work, however, undoubtedly include Kodály, Bartók, and especially Milhaud. In an article entitled "Polytonalité et Atonalité," which appeared in *La revue musicale*, February 1923, Milhaud confessed that by 1915 he "had undertaken a thoroughgoing study of the problem of polytonality" and had composed *Les choëphores* on the basis of this research. In this same article he cited genuinely polytonal passages from the second movement of Ravel's *Sontata*, distinguishing between such music and the use of dissonant pedal point, exemplified in a citation from *Parade*. A similar use of conflicting key signatures was to reappear in the opening of the second movement, "Blues," of Ravel's *Sonata* for violin and piano (1923–27).

Example 13.5. Ravel, *Sonata for Violin and Cello*, No. 13.

Whatever the composite of resources that came to bear on Ravel's music of the 1920s, his interaction with the discoveries and inclinations of other composers is a quality seldom observed in discussions of his music. Yet, in the years following the death of Debussy, Ravel confirmed his independence and the expanding range of his expression. Of Satie in particular, Ravel was more than generous, and accorded him a role not unlike that of Schoenberg in his own development:

> While [Satie] himself may, perhaps, never have wrought out of his own discoveries a single complete work of art, nevertheless we have today many such works which might not have come into existence if Satie had never lived.[19]

"I came into the world very young at a time that was very old," Satie wrote beneath a self-portrait in neo-Socratic pose.[20] This ironic and touching view of a man who felt he was misplaced in time is perhaps more than a little self-congratulatory. His view of himself as a prophet, however, was only slightly misplaced. At least the music of numerous composers who profited from his example, such as Ravel, Poulenc, Thomson, Cage, and Ashley, clearly supports this claim. Even the first movement allegro of Stravinsky's *Octet* or the E variation of the second movement, as well as the Ragtime, Waltz, and Tango of *Histoire du soldat*, written shortly after *Parade*, would seem to owe more than a little to Satie's example (see p. 266). And Stravinsky's repetitions at the final cadence of *Pulcinella*, which are protracted to the point of absurdity, are nothing more than a mirror of the *cadence obligée* which Satie entered as a spoof of eighteenth-century manners at the end of the first and third of the *Embryons desséchés* (1913). Satie provided more than one composer with the courage not only to provoke and to bore but to lighten his touch, to scrutinize the simplest object and to smile. Ravel's reaction to Satie may have initially come as the result of a personal charge against his music. In the end, by the composer's own account, the effect had been a salutary one.

REPERTOIRE

Auric, *Adieu, New York* (1921), pf, "foxtrot"
Debussy, *Children's Corner* (1906–08): "Golliwogg's Cake-Walk"
    Préludes, Book II (1910–13): "General Lavine—eccentric" ("dans le style et Mouvement d'un Cake-walk")
Honegger, *Concertino* (1925), pf, orch
    Prélude et blues (1925), harp quartet
Martinu, *Black Bottom* (1927), pf
    La revue de cuisine (1927), ballet (including "Charleston," "Tango," "Foxtrot")
    Le jazz (1928), orch
    Jazz Suite (1928), orch: "Prelude," "Blues," "Boston," "Finale"
Milhaud, *L'homme et son désir* (1918), ballet
    Le boeuf sur le toit (1919), ballet
    Saudades do Brasil (1920–1), pf
    La création du monde (1923), ballet
    Caramel mou (1921), "shimmy" for jazz band
Poulenc, *Rapsodie nègre* (1917), Bar, fl, cl, str qt, pf
    Le bestiaire (1918), v, fl, cl, bn, str qrt
    Mouvements perpetuels (1918), pf
    Le mariés de la Tour Eiffel: "The General's Speech," "The Trouville Bathing Beauty" (1920–21)
    Les biches (1924), orch, chorus; ballet
    "Les chemins de l'amour" (1940), valse chantée
    Banalités: "Hôtel," "Voyage à Paris" (1940), v, pf
Ravel, *Histoires naturelles*: "Le paon" (1906), v, pf
    L'enfant et les sortilèges: Foxtrot, Ragtime (1920–25), opera

Sonata for Violin and Piano: 2nd mvt., "Blues" (1927)
 Piano Concerto in G, 1st mvt. (1929–31)
Roussel, "Jazz dans la nuit," op. 38 (pub. 1929)
Satie, *Trois morceaux en forme de poir* (1890–1903), pf
 "Je te veux" (c. 1900), v, pf
 Enfantines: "Valse du chocolat aux amandes" (1913), pf
 Sports et Divertissement: "The Flirt," "Le feu d'artifice," "Les courses," "Golf"
  (1914), pf
 Trois mélodies (1916), v, pf
 Parade (1917), ballet
 Relâche (1924), ballet
Stravinsky, *Histoire du soldat:* "Ragtime," "Tango" (1917)
 Ragtime for Eleven Instruments (1918)
 Piano Rag (1919)
 Three Pieces for Clarinet Solo: No. 3 (1919)
 Preludium (1936–37), jazz band
 Tango (1940), pf
 Ebony Concerto (1945), 2 cl, 5 sax, hn, gui, db, tam-tam, cym, drums
Wiéner, *Sonatine Syncopée* (1923): 2nd mvt., "Blues"
 Trois blues chantés (1924), v, pf, textless vocal part à la "saxophoniste negre"

READING

Jean Cocteau, *Le coq et l'arlequin: notes autour de la musique* (Paris, 1918). Trans. by
 Rollo H. Myers in *A Call to Order* (1926; repr. New York, 1974).
Blaise Cendrars, *L'anthologie nègre* (Paris, 1921), trans. by Margery Bianco as *The African
 Saga* (1927; repr. 1969).
Albert Jeannert, "Les Concerts Wiéner," *L'Esprit Nouveau,* xiv (1923).
Virgil Thomson, "The Cult of Jazz," *Vanity Fair,* xxiv (June 1925), 54, 118.
Darius Milhaud, "The Day After Tomorrow," *Modern Music,* iii (November–December
 1925), 22.
Darius Milhaud, "The Jazz Band and Negro Music," *Littell's Living Age,* 18 October 1924.
Darius Milhaud, "Die Entwicklung der Jazz-Band und die Nordamerikanische Neger-
 musik," *Anbruch,* vii (April 1925), 200.
Maurice Delage, "La musique de jazz," *Revue Pleyel* (April 1926), 18.
Maurice Ravel, "Contemporary Music," *Rice Institute Bulletin* (1928).
Guillaume Apollinaire, *Selected Writings,* trans. and intro. by R. Shattuck (New York,
 n.d., c. 1948). Includes Apollinaire's "The New Spirit and the Poets".
Pierre Boulez, "Satie: *Chien flasque," Revue musicale,* ccxiv (1952), 153–54. English ver-
 sion in *Orientations* (Cambridge, Mass., 1986), 323–34.
Darius Milhaud, *Notes Without Music* (London, 1952).
Roger Shattuck, *The Banquet Years* (New York, 1955; rev. 1968), 88–145.
William Austin, "Satie Before and After Cocteau," *Musical Quarterly,* xlvii (1962), 216.
Francis Poulenc, *My Friends and Myself* (1963; Eng. trans. London, 1978).
Rudi Blesh and Harriet Janis, *They All Played Ragtime* (New York, 1966).
Jean Cocteau, *My Contemporaries,* ed. and introd. by M. Crosland (London, 1967), includ-
 ing articles on Diaghilev & Nijinsky, Apollinaire, Satie, Gide, Modigliani, Picasso,
 Chaplin, Piaf, di Chirico and Colette.
Gunther Schuller, *Early Jazz* (New York, 1968).
Nancy Cunard, *Negro: An Anthology* (repr. New York, 1970).
Margaret Crosland, ed. and trans., *Cocteau's World: An Anthology of Writings by Jean
 Cocteau* (New York, 1971). Includes *Le coq et l'arlequin.*
Eileen Southern, *The Music of Black Americans* (New York, 1971).
L. Breunig, ed., S. Suleiman, trans., *Apollinaire on Art* (New York, 1972). Includes Apolli-
 naire's program note for Satie's *Parade.*
Janet Flanner, *Paris was Yesterday, 1925–1939,* ed. Irving Drutman (New York, 1972).
James Harding, *Erik Satie* (New York, 1975).

Arbie Orenstein, *Ravel, Man and Musician* (New York, 1975).

Pierre Bernac, *Francis Poulenc: The Man and His Songs,* trans. W. Radford (London, 1977).

Lisa Appignanesi, *The Cabaret* (New York, 1975).

Jay Bochner, *Blaise Cendrars: Discovery and Recreation* (New York, 1978).

Charles Hamm, *Yesterdays: Popular Song in America* (New York, 1979).

Edward Berlin, *Ragtime: A Musical and Cultural History* (Berkeley, 1980).

Robert Hughes, *The Shock of the New* (New York, 1980).

Nigel Wilkins, ed. and trans., *The Writings of Erik Satie* (London, 1980).

Lynn Haney, *Naked at the Feast: A Biography of Josephine Baker* (New York, 1981).

Robert Craft, ed., *Stravinsky: Selected Correspondence,* vol. 1 (New York, 1982). "Correspondence with Jean Cocteau, 1913–1962," 73–125.

Keith Daniel, *Francis Poulenc* (Ann Arbor, 1982).

Barbara Heyman, "Stravinsky and Ragtime," *Musical Quarterly,* lxviii.4 (1982), 543–62.

Alan Gilmor, "Erik Satie and the concept of the Avant-garde," *Musical Quarterly,* lxix.1 (1983), 104.

Charles Hamm, *Music in the New World* (New York, 1983).

John Edward Hasse, ed., *Ragtime: Its History, Composers, and Music* (New York, 1985).

Nancy Perloff, *Art and the Everyday: The Impact of Parisian Popular Entertainment on Satie, Milhaud, Poulenc and Auric* (Ph.D. diss., University of Michigan, 1986).

CHAPTER 14

THE NEW SIMPLICITIES: GERMANY

SCHOENBERG AND THE "ÜBERBRETTL"

If the French cabaret was conceived as a meeting place for artists, it also served as the stage for a confrontation with the public where not only artistic but social ideals could be projected. The "Chat Noir" became the prototype of the French cabaret and was widely imitated through new establishments and touring performers, who found an especially attentive audience in Germany.

The celebrated diseuse Yvette Guilbert (1865–1944) toured Germany in 1902 and found that the "Überbrettl," Berlin's foremost literary cabaret, had already been established as part of the Buntes Theater the year before by Ernst von Wolzogen. Seriousness of purpose claimed priority alongside hearty entertainment values, and toward this end the "Überbrettl" retained the services of Arnold Schoenberg as musical director beginning in 1901. To be sure, economic considerations played as large a part as artistic ones in his decision to leave Vienna and come to Berlin, but the respectability and currency of the movement are underscored not only by his brief presence but by Richard Strauss's burlesque opera *Feuersnot* of 1901 on a libretto of Wolzogen. The principal personalities associated with the "Überbrettl" included, besides Wolzogen and Schoenberg, Richard Dehmel (1863–1920), Frank Wedekind (1864–1918), and Otto Julius Bierbaum (1865–1910).

In 1900, Bierbaum had published a collection of lyrics whose title *Deutsche Chansons (Brettl-lieder)* accentuates the cross fertilization of French and German ideals. Schoenberg, for his part, made settings of at least seven of these *Brettl-lieder*, of which *Galathea* on a text by Frank Wedekind and *Gigerlette* with words by Bierbaum may be considered representative.

Brettl-lieder

GALATHEA

Ach, wie brenn' ich vor Verlangen,	Ah, I'm burning with desire,
Galathea, schönes Kind,	Galathea, lovely child,
Dir zu küssen deine Wangen,	Just to kiss your cheeks of fire,
Weil sie so entzückend sind.	For they're so alluring, wild.
Wonne die mir widerfahre,	How I yearn for those caresses,
Galathea, schönes Kind,	Galathea, lovely child,
Dir zu küssen deine Haare,	Just to kiss your flowing tresses,
Weil sie so verlockend sind.	For they're so alluring, wild.

Nimmer wehr' mir bis ich ende,	Evermore my heart demands,
Galathea, schönes Kind,	Galathea, lovely child,
Dir zu küssen deine Hände,	Just to kiss your graceful hands,
Weil sie so verlockend sind.	For they're so alluring, wild.
Ach, du ahnst nicht, wie ich glühe,	Ah, just see, I burn, I freeze,
Galathea, schönes Kind,	Galathea, lovely child,
Dir zu küssen deine Knie,	Just to kiss your pretty knees,
Weil sie so verlockend sind.	For they're so alluring, wild.
Und was tät ich nicht, du Süsse,	Ah, what wouldn't I do, my sweet,
Galathea, schönes Kind,	Galathea, lovely child,
Dir zu küssen deine Füsse,	Just to kiss your dainty feet,
Weil sie so verlockend sind.	For they're so alluring, wild.
Aber deinen Mund enthülle,	But to my kisses, darling maiden,
Mädchen, meinen Küssen nie,	Revealed your lips should never be,
Denn in seiner Reize Fülle,	For the fullness of their charms,
Küsst ihn nur die Phantasie.	Are only found in fantasy.

Frank Wedekind

GIGERLETTE

Fräulein Gigerlette	Fräulein Gigerlette
Lud mich ein zum Tee.	Invited me to tea.
Ihre Toilette	Her attire
War gestimmt auf Schnee;	Matched the snow's purity
Ganz wie Pierrette	Just like Pierrette
War sie angetan.	Was she all decked out.
Selbst ein Mönch, ich wette,	Even a monk, I'd bet,
Sähe Gigerlette	Would covet Gigerlette
Wohlgefällig an.	Never having doubt.
War ein rotes Zimmer,	'Twas a wine-red chamber,
Drin sie mich empfing,	Where she welcomed me,
Gelber Kerzenschimmer	Candlelight of amber
In dem Raume hing.	Around her I could see.
Und sie war wie immer	And she was as ever
Leben und Esprit.	Young life and esprit.
Nie vergess' ich's, nimmer:	I'll never forget it, never,
Weinrot war das Zimmer,	Wine-red was the chamber,
Blütenweiss war sie.	Blossom-white was she.
Und im Trab mit Vieren	And in trot with fourspan
Fuhren wir zu zweit,	We rode off, we two,
In das Land spazieren,	To a land called Pleasure,
Das heisst Heiterkeit.	Ah, what joy we knew!
Das wir nicht verlieren	That we'd not be losing
Zügel, Ziel und Lauf,	Goal and course and lane,
Sass bei dem Kutschieren	Sitting as a coachman
Mit den heissen Vieren	Above our fiery fourspan
Amor hinten auf.	Cupid held the rein.

Otto Julius Bierbaum

English translation by Barbara Zeisl.

Used by permission of Belmont Music Publishers.

Schoenberg's enforced scoring of numerous popular songs and operettas at this time in order to ensure economic survival made the period a most unhappy one, but the charm with which he executed these works betrays an experienced ear and a knowledgeable connoisseur of the genre. Written by a composer whose entire corpus includes few smiles, one can only be grateful for these gems.

A single example of Schoenberg's *Brettl-lieder*, "Nachtwandler," adds piccolo, snare drum, and trumpet to the piano accompaniment and reflects the ad hoc instrumentation that was typically pressed into service in the cabaret. It is not too difficult to entertain the notion that from such novel instrumental combinations and the *Sprechgesang* (highly inflected speech) and bodily movement of an artist like Yvette Guilbert may have sprung the instrumentation, *Sprechstimme*, and even the miming of the initial production of *Pierrot lunaire*. As distant as such a relationship may appear, the force of the German cabaret on the composer of serious art music in the 1920s was to be as great as in France. By that time the invasion of American jazz brought an additional and indisputable ingredient to the formation of a musical language increasingly placed at the service of social commentary. The war was over and the infusion of popular elements from jazz and the cabaret permitted not only a sense of entertainment and escape but the capacity—sometimes blatant, sometimes veiled—for the pronouncement of moral judgments. Although by the 1920s Schoenberg had moved irreconcilably away from the music hall and held little sympathy for those who were attracted to it, composers like Hindemith, Krenek, Weill, and even Schoenberg's own pupil Berg were to become lively if not exclusive practitioners of a language based on the recognition of popular elements and their potential message.

AMERICAN CURRENTS

Although Germany came to an appreciation of jazz and manifested an admiration for American vitality slightly later than France, the fascination in both instances was promoted by the appearance of Americans and their music in the years immediately following the end of World War I. In the late teens and early 1920s, a procession of performers, including Sydney Bechet, the Original Dixieland Jazz Band, and Paul Whiteman, brought their musical wares to Europe, where their shadow fell on both Germany and France as well as England. Dancers like Irene and Vernon Castle, known to New Yorkers and Parisians for their revues that introduced songs like "Alexander's Ragtime Band" (1911) and "Watch your Step" (1914), had early teamed up with the most popular of the black orchestras, the High Society Orchestra of James Reese Europe. With America's entry into World War I, both Europe and Vernon Castle crossed the Atlantic. Castle died with the British air force early in the war, but the formation of a group called The Hell Fighters under Europe's direction proved crucial to the introduction of American popular musical manners throughout France in the period 1918–19. The dynamism their music seemed to portray—that of a land unfettered by outworn traditions and eager to explore new horizons—was emulated in various ways, and the architect Erich Mendelsohn (*Amerika: Bilderbuch eines Architekten*, 1926) published photographs of the New York City harbor, Chicago's Michigan Avenue, New York's Wall Street, Macy's Department Store, the Chicago Tribune Building, and Detroit city buses that clearly mirrored the current infatuation with American urban life.[1]

Evidence of Germany's growing enthusiasm for jazz can also be seen in numerous periodicals of the 1920s. *Anbruch* devoted its entire April 1925 issue to the question of jazz, including an article by Milhaud, "Die Entwicklung der Jazz-Band" ("The Evolution of the Jazz-Band"). The Prague journal *Auftakt* followed in 1926 with a special issue devoted to the topic and included an article by Baresel entitled "Jazz als Rettung" ("Jazz to the Rescue"). Books devoted entirely to the subject appeared in 1927 by Paul Bernhard, *Jazz: Eine musikalische Zeitfrage* (*Jazz: A Musical Question of the Times*) and in 1929 by Alfred Baresel, *Das neue Jazzbuch* (*The New Jazz-Book*). But it was an American, Virgil Thomson, who in August 1924 wrote "the first published effort submitting jazz to the procedures of musical analysis" in H. L. Mencken's *The American Mercury.*[2]

It was another American, the black dancer Josephine Baker, who also helped to define the new uninhibitedness of her homeland for the Europeans. In 1925 both in Paris and Berlin she not only complemented the tastes of literary and artistic circles for "art negre," serving as a model for Picasso and Calder as well as Fitzgerald and Hemingway, but also created her Folies-Bergère sensation "La danse des sauvages" and introduced the new American charleston for the first time.

In this same season, Paul Whiteman (1890–1967) toured Europe with his band, now much enlarged and more than slightly removed from the original spirit of jazz. But he was enthusiastically received by audiences who quickly responded to "the precision of an elegant, well-oiled machine, a sort of Rolls-Royce of dance music".[3] Like New York, both Paris and Berlin fell in love with his renditions of Gershwin's *Rhapsody in Blue.* In a word, Western Europe had come down with an American fever. A sure sign that the temperature was elevated came with the announcement of a newly created "jazz department" in the music conservatory of Frankfurt. The first of its kind, either in Europe or America, it was headed by the composer Mátyás Seiber (1905–1960). Multiple seeds for a controversy on the proper function and arena of jazz had now clearly been sown.

PAUL HINDEMITH: JAZZ, "THE NEW OBJECTIVITY," "MUSIC FOR USE," AND FOLK TUNES.

The first use of the jazz idiom by Paul Hindemith (1895–1963) was in his instrumental works. The introduction of a foxtrot in his *Kammermusik No. 1* (1921), followed by the *Suite "1922"* for piano, which included movements entitled Shimmy, Boston, and Ragtime, suggests how readily the German infatuation extended to a diverse list of social dances. The rage of mechanical instruments such as the pianola on which to play this kind of music, exemplified in Hindemith's own composition prepared directly on punched paper rolls for Oskar Schlemmer's *Triadisches Ballet* (1926), is reflected in Hindemith's preface to the Ragtime movement of the *Suite:*

> Mode d'emploi—Direction for Use!!
>
> Pay no attention to what you have learned in your piano lessons.
> Do not consider for long whether you should play D♯ with the fourth or sixth finger.
> Play this piece very ferociously, but keep strictly in rhythm like a machine.
> Regard the piano here as an interesting kind of percussion instrument and treat it accordingly.

The alternating hands of the opening, the hints of a stride bass in the left hand, and the persistent ties across the bar line all suggest the piano rag style. But the contrary motion octaves on the black and white keys in groups of fives brings to mind the ease with which the mechanical pianos could perform such patterns, an observation confirmed by Poulenc's use of contrary-motion diatonic scales at the words "pianos mécaniques" in his *Cocardes* of 1919.

Example 14.1. Hindemith, *Suite "1922"*, "Ragtime," mm. 1-8.

Hindemith, an amateur artist, designed the cover for the piano *Suite "1922"* (Figure 14.1), and the critics were quick to pick up its message:

> The cover design, drawn by the composer himself, is already a mirror of the chaos and folly of the cabaret man, which is further reflected in the score: the pell-mell activity of the people, the vehicles, and of the arched street lamps, the offspring of electricity.[4]

The use of a foxtrot coupled with a quasi-Futurist use of sirens and whistles in his *Kammermusik No. 1* (1921) underscored Hindemith's growing reputation

Figure 14.1. Hindemith's own cover design for his *Suite "1922"*.

as a member of the avant-garde at its Donaueschingen Chamber Music Festial premiere in 1922. The work's instrumentation (fl, cl, bsn, tpt, 2 vn, va, vc, db, pf, accordion, perc) and the composer's directions that the "performers be situated out of sight of the audience" solidifed his position. His designation of the work as written "for 12 solo instruments" suggests the nature of the work, which no longer relied solely on the piano to conjure up the popular mode, and the positioning of the players "may have been an attempt to create the dance salon ambience in stark opposition to traditional concert performance practices"[5] or even to allude to the invisibility of gramophone musicians.

In these works, Hindemith posited powerful alternatives to the language of his current Expressionist-tinged operas: *Mörder, Hoffnung der Frauen* (1919) to Kokoschka's play of 1909; *Das Nusch-Nuschi* (1920), a play for Burmese marionettes in which the principal character is punished for his philandering by castration—set to a quotation from *Tristan and Isolde* that had accompanied King Mark's words "This—to me?"; and *Sancta Susanna* (1921), about a sex-starved nun who rips the loincloth from the crucified Christ, were all based on strong literary material obviously intended to shock. The free atonality and pervasive dissonance employed by Hindemith in his String Quartet No. 2 (1921) suggest that he might well have developed a natural alliance with Arnold Schoenberg. But already in these works his brand of Expressionism tends to emphasize its Romantic base and a regular phraseology far removed from Viennese developments earlier in the century.

An increasing need to simplify his creative stance as a direct reaction against such Expressionist tendencies was acted out in numerous ways throughout the 1920s and included, in addition to the works mentioned, the occasional use of jazz rhythms in *Hin und zurück* ("There and Back," 1927) and *Neues vom Tage* ("News of the Day," 1928–29). Both of these operas belonged to the category of *Zeitoper*, or operas utilizing libretti of current social significance married to popular musical idioms which, like Krenek's *Jonny spielt auf*, were for the time the rage of Europe. Both works also had libretti by Marcellus Schiffer, a writer of sketches and revues. The first deals with a couple in the throes of a divorce complicated by the interference of the media. Its retrograde action, implied by the title and reflecting contemporary film techniques, is mirrored in the music by the use of cancrizans in what can only be termed a mechanistic and cynical observation. *Neues vom Tage* is remembered primarily because of the appearance of an unclothed prima donna singing an aria in the bathtub, news of which quickly reached a shocked Adolf Hitler and later helped to stamp the composer as a *Kulturbolshevist*, paving the way for Hindemith's flight to America.

By the mid-1920s, a general reaction against sentiment and emotion by the Berlin Dadaists, whose generally negative attitude soon ensured their dissolution, led to a more useful and positive commitment, detached and cynical though it may have been, which acquired the name of *Neue Sachlichkeit* or "New Objectivity." Used as early as 1923 by artists and literary figures alike, it espoused directness of expression in the service of a politically motivated socialist realism. Such an attitude, reflected in Hindemith's increasing belief in a social function for music, led to the idea of *Gebrauchsmusik* ("Music for Use"), of which his school opera *Wir bauen eine Stadt* ("Let's Build a City," 1930) is only the most notable example of what Hindemith called "Sing und Spielmusik" intended for performance by amateurs. The continuing role of folk and popular materials in the works of Hindemith's maturity will reappear in the discussion of his opera *Mathis der Maler* (pp. 344–45). For the present it should be pointed out that the congeniality of jazz rhythms to Hindemith's musical language was sporadically evident in his later works, as in the syncopated fugue subject of the second movement of his brilliant *Symphonic Metamorphosis on Themes of Weber* (1943; Ex. 14.2).

While Germany's century-long dominance of Western European music may have suggested in its continuity less of a need for Neoclassic revival, or renewal through the importation of musical exotica or jazz, an interest in indigenous folk materials by Mahler and Berg has already been demonstrated. In both instances, however, the projection of such materials is fundamentally different from the music of Bartók and Stravinsky. German folk music in Mahler (p. 9) and Berg (p. 359) offered a symbolic element of contrast to a developingly complex language, not the source material out of which a new language was being formed. The same claim may be made with respect to the role of both jazz and/or folk sources in the music of Hindemith, Krenek, and early Weill. Schoenberg and Webern generally eschewed such references altogether. This would seem to

Example 14.2. Hindemith, *Symphonic Metamorphosis on a Theme of Weber*, Mvt. II, 11 mm. from Rehearsal nos. P through Q.

suggest a difference in orientation in the reliance on native materials between older art music cultures (Germany, France, Italy) and the younger aspiring ones (Russia, Hungary, America) or those with a discontinuous artistic history (England).

Hindemith's love for old tunes, while sharing something with Mahler and Berg, is determined by additional factors. His interest in what has commonly come to be known as *Gebrauchsmusik* was reflected in music for film, radio, and amateur performers. In the late 1920s he became familiar with the musical *Jugendbewegung*, a movement that was at the time unpolitical but devoted to the promotion of national folk music and German Renaissance popular song. Hindemith's introduction to these repertoires resuscitated an interest in melody with accompaniment that proved to be an important alternative to the essentially contrapuntal orientation of his Neoclassic style and led to the incorporation of German folk melodies in numerous works. The viola concerto entitled *Der Schwanendreher* (1935), which the composer loved to perform himself, is based entirely on early German melodies, the first movement being founded on "Zwischen Berg und tiefem Tal," well known from an early sixteenth-century setting by Heinrich Isaac. Hindemith's bible in such matters was Franz Böhme's *Altdeutsches Liederbuch* (1877), which the composer always kept near his work table. Other compositions that tapped Böhme's collection include the *Third Organ Sonata* (1940) and the opera, *Mathis der Maler* (1933–35).

CARL ORFF

Many of the issues discussed with respect to the career of Hindemith were also manifest, although in different proportion, in the music of Carl Orff (1895–1982), a composer whose career effectively began in 1924 with the formation of a school in Munich devoted to the study of music and movement. Emphasizing both Dalcrozian eurhythmics and encouraging the discovery of music through improvisation, both bodily and with simple percussion and melody instruments, his investigations forwarded simple folk and dance tunes as well as the easy manner of jazz as models, which in turn promoted the efficiency of pedal point and ostinato for improvisation. By the early 1930s his influence was sufficiently large that adoption of his methods by the German Ministry of Culture seemed imminent, but the rise of Hitler shortly thereafter curtailed all such plans. It was not until after the war that a series of broadcasts beginning in 1948 revived his educational objectives and led to the publication of his *Music for Children* (1950–54) and later his more comprehensive *Orff-Schulwerk*. The effect of these publications was international in scope, and together with different but similarly forceful methods advocated by Kodály had a profound effect on the music education of the young both in Europe and the United States.

Orff's activities in this field ought not to be separated from his activities as a composer. Intrigued with both Greek tragedy and Italian Baroque musical theater, he was a sufficiently serious student of Monteverdi to have made his own editions of "Arianna's Lament" and *Orfeo* by 1925. (Interestingly, Hindemith made his own edition of the latter work in 1943). To this dramatic foundation he added the simple and undeniably effective techniques of his improvisational researches in a language that pleased audiences by virtue of its driving ostinato rhythms, brief melodic ideas, and coloristic appeal. Though the force of his musical style has properly been seen to stem from Stravinsky's *Oedipus Rex* and *Les noces*, both works of the 1920s, this became evident only in 1937 with his first popular success, *Carmina burana*. Composed during the heyday of the Third Reich, in retrospect some have heard in the work's aggressive and repetitive figurations a reflection of the hypnotic chanting of Nazi mass rallies.

Der Mond (1939), *Catulli carmina* (1943), *Die Kluge* (1943), *Antigonae* (1949), and *Trionfo di Afrodite* (1953) appeared in succession, with an increasingly difficult metaphysical textual base but with the musical formula of his first efforts reasonably well intact. Yet in spotting the ingredients that would win audience approval, Orff also identified some of the most basic elements of all music, thereby endorsing many of the simplifying procedures prominent in various quarters during the 1920s. Perhaps his only sin was in protracting his discovery with such limited modification for the duration of a career.

ERNST KRENEK: *JOHNNY SPIELT AUF*

Krenek was born in Vienna in 1900, but already as a teenager found his way to Berlin and the musical world of Schreker, Busoni, and Scherchen. His career as a composer began with the composition of three symphonies (1921-23) dedicated to the premise of continuing the legacy of Mahler, whose daughter Anna he married. The increasingly dissonant character of these symphonies, bordering on atonality, was then applied to several operas. In the first of these, *Zwingburg* ("The Tyrant's Castle") of 1922, his interest in social and political commentary is apparent, and an organ grinder is used as the symbol of a people forced into repetitive mechanical routines. In *Der Sprung über den Schatten* ("The Leap Over the Shadow") of 1923, aspects of personal and political freedom are addressed through a musical vocabulary which, similar to Hindemith's and Weill's early efforts, was Expressionistic tinged with "pop" elements. A brush with Stravinskian Neoclassicism following a trip to Paris is evidenced in his *Second Concerto Grosso* and a *Concertino* for flute, violin, harpsichord, and strings, both of 1924, but a period in the opera houses at Kassel and Wiesbaden as conductor, composer, and director prepared his return to opera.

Krenek's initial brush with jazz had come with his move to Berlin in 1920, where two pianist-composers, Eduard Erdmann (1896–1958) and Artur Schnabel (1882–1951), introduced him to American popular music. Schnabel had toured the United States in December 1921, and in the following seasons regularly provided Krenek with samples of sheet music and possibly recordings. The first evidence of Krenek's reaction to such materials came in *Eine kleine Suite*, appended to his *Toccata und Chaconne* (1922), which included movements entitled "Allemande," "Sarabande," "Gavotte," "Walzer," "Fuge," and "Foxtrott." A *Tanzsuite* written in the same year also included a "Foxtrott" as the first movement, and both of the pieces that share this title predated the first performance of the "Foxtrott-Finale" of Hindemith's *Kammermusik No. 1* on July 31, 1922.

In spite of these and other attempts in his first operas to include popular elements, it was in *Jonny spielt auf* ("Jonny strikes up") premiered in 1927 that Krenek's rise to international stardom came.[6] It is justly considered the first example of a genuine *Zeitoper*, both with respect to its topicality and its handling of the popular musical elements. Here, the anxieties of the artist composer, symbolic of the inhibited Central European intellectual, are pitted against the uninhibitedness of Jonny, the American negro jazz fiddler. Indeed, the opening words of the opera intoned by the composer Max are "O schöner Berg"; shortly thereafter (1928), Schoenberg slyly stitched Krenek's name into the preface of his *Three Satires*, op. 28, and began an opera parodying *Zeitoper*,

Von Heute auf Morgen (1929), to a libretto by his wife, who used the nom de plume Max Blonde.

In contrasting Max with Jonny, Krenek appropriated the jazz idiom only for the latter, and for Max and Anita, the opera singer, he wrote in an openly Romantic idiom "occasionally touched up with dissonant spices and Italianizing Pucciniesque vocal exuberance."[7] For this reason he was always irritated at the application of the term "jazz opera" to *Jonny,* which he felt to be a misnomer.

At the end of the opera the composer catches the train on the first leg of his journey to America, land of dreams. Such a vision of America was shared by many Europeans in the post-World War I period and helps to account for the growing craze for her popular music.

> The journey cross the seas begins. So Jonny strikes up the dance. The new world across the ocean draws near with splendour and becomes successor to old Europe through the dance.

So sings the chorus at the final curtain. Krenek's return to the tonal idiom, seasoned with the condiments of jazz, involved not only jazz instrumentation but popular rhythms and styles, all of which abound in the first act of the opera. In the third scene, set in a Paris hotel, the sounds of Jonny's "jazzband" are heard intoning a Shimmy in "schnelles 'Grammophon' Tempo." Later in the same scene, the jazzband begins to play again, this time a Blues—introduced by a syncopated figure reminiscent of Gershwin's *Rhapsody in Blue* (Ex. 14.3)—before settling into the blues melody characterized by the flatting of the third (Ex. 14.4).

Example 14.3. Krenek, *Jonny spielt auf,* mm. 941–2.

This is soon followed by a Tango, as symbol of seduction, with the singer Anita and the composer Max accompanied by Jonny, Daniello, the virtuoso violinist, and the chorus (Ex. 14.5).

Anita and Daniello: Alle Sterne stürzen über uns zusammen!	All stars fall down upon us in our ecstasy!
Chorus: O rêverie, doucement infinie!	[O reverie, sweetly endless!]
Jonny: Dure toujours, ne finis jamais!	[Last forever, never cease.]
Chorus: Melodie seduisante, son mysterieux, rempli mon coeur de l'ivresse, de la tristesse de l'eternel amour!	[Enticing melody, mysterious sound, you fill my heart with rapture, with the sadness of eternal love.]
Anita: Comme tu es beau—si beau!	[How handsome you are—so handsome.]
Daniello: Viens, viens.	[Come, come.]

Example 14.4. Krenek, *Jonny spielt auf*, mm. 959–66.

Example 14.5. Krenek, *Jonny spielt auf*, mm. 1138–41.

(Anita draws Daniello into the room while covering his eyes with her hand. They disappear into Anita's room. Empty stage. Jonny comes up the stairs on tip-toe, without the saxophone, but weaving his hard hat. First he slinks over to the lamp and turns it off, so that the corridor is only lit by the faint gleam from the hall. Then he sneaks over to Daniello's door and puts his ear to it.)

Anita: Ah!	*Anita:* Ah!
Daniello: Je t'aime!	*Daniello:* [I love you!]
Anita and Daniello: Ma [mon] cheri!	*Anita and Daniello:* [My dearest!]
Jonny: Monsieur s'amuse! Das soll dir eine teure Nacht sein!	*Jonny:* Monsieur s'amuse! This is an expensive night for you, Sir!

(He breaks into Daniello's room with a masterkey and with the aid of a flashlight quickly finds the violin case. After a short pause for thought he takes out the violin, goes back into the corridor and locks the door again.)

Ja! so weit wär ich! Doch
jetzt wohin mit ihr? Morgen
wird alles durchsucht, behalt
ich sie, nimmt man sie mir ab.

Yes! So far, so good! But what do
I do next? Tomorrow, ev'rything will
be searched. If I keep it, they will
take it away.

(He looks about him for a moment and notices the banjo hanging on the hook in front of Anita's door.)

Aha! Da drinnen sucht sie kein
Mensch!

Aha! In here no one will look for it.

(Jonny takes down the banjo, removes it from its case, and puts the violin in its place. He is about to hang it back in its place when he realizes that the flat back of the violin lacks the roundness of the banjo. After a moment's thought he takes off his hat and fixes it to the back of the violin with a piece of string, thereby replacing the belly of the banjo. Then he hangs the case with its new contents on the hook again. During the following song, Jonny accompanies himself on the banjo.)

Auf Wiedersehn, good by, my dear,
sleep well in deine Sack. Du bist
ja doch in meine Hut, und über-
morgen holl' ich dich ab!

Auf Wiedersehn, good by, my dear,
sleep well in this here bag. You
sure belong to me, and in a couple
of days you will join your boy![8]

The mixture of French and German clearly underscores the common legacy of the French and German artistic cabaret as well as the current infatuation of those two countries with American popular song and dance. The addition of English at the end points not only to the language of Jonny's homeland and the modish polyglot infusions that persist to the present day, but to the source of jazz and the final destination of the composer at the end of the opera.

The description of the final scene by Olin Downes, music critic of *The New York Times*, captures something of the excitement and appeal of the work for its first audiences:

This [Jonny' and Max's re-arrival at the station] is done in time to catch the midnight train which connects with the boat for America. At 11:58, Max and Anita are reunited; Jonny skulking about to avoid arrest, the train steams in. In the Leipzig production it sped straight to the rim of the stage and threatened to catapult over the footlights. The guards call out, the hands of the great station clock move by seconds toward the hour. The train starts, but not before Jonny, from a scaffolding overhead, jumps for it. The train disappears. Jonny lands, instead, on the station clock. The clock becomes the world. Jonny is atop of it fiddling wildly, scornfully, lackadaisically. The characters of the opera are grouped below him. They are joined by a throng of men and women in every kind of dress and undress, who dance to Bacchanalian jazz about the base of the whirling globe. At Leipzig the stars in the sky tottered, then whirled, until, at last, the globe had become a record disk, which came gradually to a stop, with the inscription "Jonny spielt auf: Ernst Krenek, Opus 45" on it.[9]

The potential of jazz and other popular elements to serve as agents for social and political commentary is continued in *Leben des Orest* ("Life of Orestes") of 1929. During this period, Krenek also went through a "back-to-Schubert" phase, inspired perhaps by the event of Schubert's centennial in 1928 and his friendship with Artur Schnabel, who frequently performed all-Schubert concerts with his wife, a well-known singer. The theme of his next opera, *Karl V* (1933), continued to plumb the thematic possibilities of *Zeitoper* through the story of a Renaissance emperor, but for this assignment he made his first extensive entry into the world of dodecaphonic serialism, a domain that was to prove central to the remainder of his career. The first rehearsals of the opera in Vienna in 1934 were stopped by the Nazis, and his music, like Hindemith's, was outlawed. With Hitler's invasion of Austria in 1938, Krenek fled to America, where he took citizenship in 1945.

KURT WEILL

Weill (1900–1950), like Hindemith and Krenek, received his early training in Germany but spent the years of World War II in exile in the United States. With Weill, however, his total and unashamed commitment to Broadway after his move to America made for confusion on the part of audiences who had known his earlier career, and promoted the idea of the two faces of Weill.

Indeed, for those who know only *Knickerbocker Holiday* (1938), *Lady in the Dark* (1940), and *One Touch of Venus* (1943), or even his school folk opera, *Down in the Valley* of 1948, it would be difficult to imagine the reputation he had held as a leader in the German musical theater from 1925 to 1935. A student of Humperdinck and favored pupil of Busoni in Berlin, his early works included a single movement, double-function symphony (1921), which probably reflects a familiarity with the early works of Schoenberg.[10] A *Concerto for Violin and Wind Instruments* of 1924 belongs to the time of Stravinsky's *Concerto for Piano and Winds* (1924) and Berg's *Concerto for Violin, Piano and 13 Wind Instruments* (1923–25); but in its two "Nocturnes" it also reflects Mahler's *Seventh Symphony* and the mood of specific movements of Zemlinsky's *Lyric Symphony* of 1922. Mahler's *Wunderhorn*, inspired marches, which persistently found their way into his song cycles and symphonies, also found an echo in the "Alla marcia" of Weill's String Quartet No. 1, op. 8 (1923)[11] as well as in the "Kanonensong" from *Die Dreigroschenoper*, the finale to *Mahagonny* and "Der kleine Leutnant des lieben Gottes" in *Happy End*.[12]

Early on, Weill's destiny for the stage was apparent. From his *Protagonist* (1924–25) and *Royal Palace* (1926) to libretti by Georg Kaiser and Ivan Goll, important exponents of Expressionism and Dada, it was apparent that his talent for directness of expression and interest in social commentary were complementary traits. That these were well in place before Weill's first meeting with Berthold Brecht is significant.

Brecht's arrival in Berlin in 1924 already saw a figure like Erwin Piscator at work as the director of a new type of theater whose mission it was to portray society, demystify the artistic process, and expose the machinery of both art and society. The naturalistic theater was overthrown and replaced by puppets, masks, film, newspaper headlines, and placards.[13] The influence of Piscator on Brecht was momentous, and prepared the way for the Weill-Brecht collaboration in two notable productions, *The Three Penny Opera* (1928) and *Mahagonny* (1927; 1929). Between these works and his *Protagonist* of 1924, Weill wrote two works that indicate his own development independent of Brecht: *Royal Palace* (1926), which uses jazz numbers to accompany a film scene depicting various pleasures of the heroine, and *The Tsar Has His Photograph Taken* (1927), which utilizes a tango played on a gramophone to accompany the Tsar's seductions of a lady photographer.[14] In both instances, however, such use of popular or "jazz" elements is localized without infiltrating the entire score. Indeed, it is in this juxtaposition, as with Krenek's *Jonny*, that the popular mode takes on its role as social commentator and provides the key to the classification of the work as genuine *Zeitoper*.

Although Weill and Hindemith collaborated on a Brechtian-inspired *Der Lindberghflug* (1929) and Weill wrote a school opera for children, *Der Jasager* (1930), analogous to Hindemith's *Wir bauen eine Stadt*, Weill's belief in the social function of art had musically different consequences. His language became increasingly direct in every respect, not just tonally, and his use of the popular idiom moved irrevocably away from the feeling of a special effect and became an integral part of his language in works like *Three Penny Opera* and *Mahagonny*. Here he eschewed the use of parody of popular elements in the interest of forwarding them as genuine accouterments of modern urban life and a reflection of man's society not totally different from the use of a minuet or waltz in a bye-gone day. In the 1929 *Article on Jazz* Weill noted that

> Jazz appears, within a time when artistry is increasing, as a piece of nature, as the most healthy and powerful expression of an art which, because of its popular origins, has immediately become an international folk music of the broadest possible consequences.[15]

Cocteau's calls for an anti-emotional, nonsentimental expression drawn from the music hall, circus, and jazz led frequently in its earliest days to a light-hearted entertainment without pretension. Weill's similar interest in an appealing simplicity of musical expression led the composer to a consideration of his music in relation to several terms, including *Neue Sachlichkeit* ("New Objectivity") and *Gebrauchsmusik* ("Music for Use"), which enjoyed an enormous vogue in the 1920s.[16] Several of his works which were cojoined to texts with a proletarian cast had a more serious intent, and one which Weill liked to separate from the modishness of *Zeitoper*, for which he claimed no affinity. He believed that the term had become a mere catchword without substance. But of the genre's interest in jazz he spoke in an article of 1926: "The rhythm of our time is jazz. In it the slow but sure Americanisation of all our physical life finds its most notable manifestation." He also correctly cautioned against equating all popular dance elements with true jazz, which was rich but elusive in its profusion of "rhythmic complexity, of deft harmonic traits, of timbral and modulatory niceties."[17]

His adaptation of many of these ingredients can be heard in the opening of "Alabama Song" from *Mahagonny*, where a vamp accompaniment and a diatonic vocal part of limited pitch content lead to a lyric second half (Ex. 14.6). Here, the clarity of tonality projected in the left hand, the harmonic spice of the right hand, the regularity of rhythmic pulse and phraseology, the wider ranging vocal part, and syllabic projection are all characteristic of a style which the composer brought to prominence.

Example 14.6. Weill, *Mahagonny*, "Alabama Song," 9 mm.

Although the Brecht-Weill relationship was significant as well as complex, recent assessments have tended to emphasize Weill's independent preparation for their collaboration and their relatively brief association. This is helpful in trying to promote a more integral view of an artist who has been, until now, traditionally compartmentalized into a composer for the concert hall (symphony, concerto), German musical theater (*Three Penny Opera, Mahagonny*), and Broadway (*Lady in the Dark, One Touch of Venus*).

BERG, GERSHWIN, AND COMPANY

Weill's *Kleine Mahagonny*, Hindemith's *Hin und zurück*, and Krenek's *Jonny spielt auf* all created an international sensation in the 1927 season, and in some ways spelled both the climax of a movement and the beginning of its decline. Though all three composers pursued a common point of view in a small group of works, 1928 saw not only the appearance of Weill's *Three Penny Opera* but a stinging satire against the use of popular materials and the modishness of *Zeitoper* in Schoenberg's "comic" *Von Heute auf Morgen* (1928–29), whose very title suggests the fickleness of taste, which changes "from today to tomorrow". The inclusion of saxophones, piano, mandolin, and guitar in Schoenberg's opera are no more successful in capturing a genuine jazz idiom than the ensemble of Webern's *Quartet*, op. 22, composed in 1930. Dedicated to the architect Adolf Loos, Webern's work was very much a child of its time in its unusual combination of violin, clarinet, tenor saxophone, and piano. But while the instrumentation is redolent of a small jazz ensemble, the rhythmic and formal personality of the *Quartet* look in a totally different direction. Being one of his most "pointillistic" scores, the popular note would never come to mind except for the sonority of the saxophone.

If Schoenberg's response to jazz and *Zeitoper* was parodistic and satirical and Webern's superficial and negative, Berg's was positive and natural, if somewhat limited. While the use of a jazz band, ragtime numbers, and saxophones appear in Berg's *Lulu* and provide important voices for commentaries on morality and sex in Wedekind's decadent world, a no less conspicuous and equally telling use of popular materials appears in his concert aria *Der Wein* of 1929. A setting of three poems of Baudelaire, it is in some ways a preparation for *Lulu* with respect to the point in question. The appearance of a tango in the first and third songs helps not only to confirm the formal tendencies of the piece but draws attention to the visions of love of the solitary wine drinker. The use of the saxophone to intone the "Fate" motif from Wagner's *Ring*, followed by muted trumpet in the opening measures of the introduction to the work, prepares the usage of the piano and strings played "sempre pizzicato à la banjo" in support of the seductive rhythms of the tango (Ex. 14.7). If such gestures seem out of character for Berg, we should recall not only *Lulu*, an opera yet to come, but the transformation of the "Fate" rhythm that signalled Marie's murder into a jazzy polka played on a tavern piano as an accompaniment to wine and dancing in Act III, scene 3 of *Wozzeck* (Ex. 14.8). In both cases, instrumentation and rhythm take on the aspect of a quote much in the fashion of early Weill.

Gershwin and Berg would seem odd bedfellows, and any discussion of the American genius of Tin Pan Alley correspondingly irrelevant to the most sophisticated member of the Viennese trinity. Yet the issue of tango rhythms

Example 14.7. Berg, *Der Wein*, mm. 38–9.

Example 14.8. Berg, *Wozzeck*, Act III, s. 3, mm. 1–4.

and jazz instrumentation in the works of Berg in the late 1920s provides ready access to a consideration of George Gershwin (1898–1937), who was an American in Paris during the spring of 1928. Having met Maurice Ravel in New York the previous fall at a party for the Frenchman, whose only request was that Gershwin be invited, they had immediately taken to each other (Figure 14.2). Gershwin purportedly played the piano until 4 A.M., with Ravel staying to the end. Now in Paris, Gershwin actually approached Ravel, as well as Nadia Boulanger, about taking composition lessons. Both gently put him off, describing it as an inappropriate liaison. He also met and played for Milhaud, Poulenc, Auric, Prokofiev, and Walton.

His Paris visit also brought performances of the *Rhapsody in Blue* played by Wiéner and Doucet and a choreographed version by Anton Dolin for the Ballets Russes. The European premiere of his new *Concerto in F* followed in May with Dimitri Tiomkin at the piano and Vladimir Goldschman conducting. Between these two events, however, Gershwin traveled to Vienna and was delighted, if surprised, to hear the house orchestra strike up the *Rhapsody in Blue* as he entered the Café Sacher. Gershwin was indeed a celebrity in his own right. While in Vienna, Gershwin also heard Krenek's *Jonny spielt auf*, to which he reportedly reacted favorably.

Figure 14.2. A birthday party for Ravel, March 7, 1928, given by Eva Gauthier. Ravel at the piano; left to right Oskar Fried, conductor; Eva Gauthier, singer; Tedesco, conductor; Gershwin.

Wide World Photos, Inc.

By his own account, however, the most important event of the trip was a meeting with Alban Berg. He not only played his own music at some length for Berg, who was captivated, but Gershwin heard a performance of Berg's *Lyric Suite* played by the Kolisch Quartet in Berg's apartment. On his departure he took an autographed copy of the *Lyric Suite* with him, and back in Paris made repeated requests for it to be played, unimaginable as it may seem, at various receptions in his honor.[18] Years later, guests at Gershwin's home in Hollywood could find an autographed photo of Berg hanging alongside others of Irving Berlin, the Duke of Kent (later King George VI), Jack Dempsey, and a letter from Stravinsky; and through the window they might well have caught a glimpse of their host in a tennis match with Schoenberg.

The biographical evidence thus confirms that Gershwin was well known among composers of "serious" art music and that he was almost universally admired by them. Yet for all of Gershwin's familiarity with the foremost composers of his day, there is little to indicate that he took very much from them (in spite of brief periods of study with Goldmark, Cowell and Schillinger). Indeed, the evidence suggests precisely the opposite. Ravel's Piano Concerto in G (1929–31) is perhaps the most notable example of a composer with a developed musical personality partaking not only of the jazz idiom but of a mode of expression, including syncopations and blue notes, that is patently Gershwinesque. And beyond the tangos of Berg's *Der Wein*, which may have been inspired by Krenek's *Jonny* or Gershwin's recently completed *Preludes* (1926) for piano, Berg's use of an ascending clarinet glissando at the palindromic midpoint of the second song in the same work cannot help but suggest the opening gesture of Gershwin's *Rhapsody in Blue*.

Gershwin's primary success, of course, was in the musical theater, not in the concert hall, for all of his associations with Paul Whiteman and the notion of symphonic jazz. From *Strike Up the Band* (1927) and *Of Thee I Sing* (1931) to *Porgy and Bess* (1935), Gershwin left his imprint not only on American musical manners but set toes tapping and voices singing around the globe. Weill, who turned to Broadway during his American residency, not only admired Gershwin above all others but probably wondered at the secret of his art. It does not succumb easily to analysis, as Schoenberg properly noted, and the final testimony to his genius comes in the easy recognition of even so partial a list as: "The Man I Love," "I Got Rhythm," "Who Could Ask for Anything More?," "Fascinatin' Rhythm," "Oh, Lady, Be Good!," "Somebody Loves Me," "Summertime," "Bess, You is My Woman," "I Got Plenty o' Nuttin,'" "'S Wonderful," and "Embraceable You".

Gershwin's success from 1925 on helps explain the speed with which the jazz mania was assimilated by the "serious" American composer. Although John Alden Carpenter's *Krazy Kat* (1921) and *Skyscrapers* (1921) as well as Antheil's *Jazz Symphony* (1924) may claim independence from such an exposure, Grofé's *Metropolis* (1928), and Hughes' *Harlem Symphony* (1932) cannot. And, in spite of some early jazz piano pieces (1922), surely Copland's *"Jazz" Piano Concerto* of 1926 was in part prompted by the reception of Gershwin's *Rhapsody* of 1924. Copland was soon to become the champion of an American style, but he was ultimately not to find its basis in jazz, whose moods he felt were restricted to the blues and the snappy number. Although Copland, as an American, had a right to claim priority to the jazz idiom, it cannot be held that his use of it was more powerful than that of many of his European colleagues at the time. The truth of this assertion corroborates Ravel's assessment (p. 280) not only of the potency but the adaptability of jazz for composers of different nationalities. It was, for a moment in the late 1920s and 1930s, an American export and treated as a bit of exotica. The reappearance of various popular idioms in so-called "art music" beginning in the 1960s and continuing to the present day attests to their vitalizing potential for composers of disparate geographical and cultural backgrounds.

REPERTOIRE

Antheil, *Jazz Symphony* (1924)
Berg, *Der Wein* (1929)
     Lulu (1929–35)
Blacher, *Jazz-Koloraturen* (1929), v (textless S), A sax, bn.
Carpenter, *Adventures in a Perambulator* (1914)
     Skyscrapers (1923)
     Orchestra Pieces (1925–6)
Copland, *"Jazz" Piano Concerto* (1926)
Gershwin, *Rhapsody in Blue* (1924)
     Concerto in F (1925), pf, orch
     Lady Be Good (1925): "Fascinatin' Rhythm"
     An American in Paris (1928)
Grofe, *Metropolis* (1928)
Grosz, *Jazzband* (1925), vn, pf
Gruenberg, *Emperor Jones* (1932)
Haba, *Vier Tänze* (1927): "Shimmy," "Blues," "Boston," "Tango," pf
Hindemith, *Kammermusik No. 1* (1921): Finale ("Foxtrot")
     Suite "1922" (1922): "Boston," "Shimmy," "Ragtime"
     Hin und zurück (1927), opera
     Neues vom Tage (1929), opera
     Symphonic Metamorphosis on a Theme of Weber (1943), 2nd mvt.
Holst, *Jazz-Band Piece* (1932)
Krenek, *Tanzstudie* (1922), pf
     Kleine Suite (1924): "Moderner Tanz," cl, pf
     Jonny spielt auf (1927): "Tango" and "Blues"
Schoenberg, *Brettl-lieder:* "Galathea," "Gigerlette," "Nachtwandler" (1901)
Seiber, *Two Jazzolettes* (1929), 2 sax, tr, trbn, pf, perc
Shostakovich, *Jazz Suite No. 1* (1934)
     Jazz Suite No. 2 (1938)
Weill, *Der Protagonist* (1924)
     Royal Palace (1926)
     The Tsar Has His Photograph Taken (1927)
     Dreigroschenoper ("Three Penny Opera") (1928): "Moritat" ("Jack the Knife")
     Mahagonny (1927/1929): "Alabama Song"

READING

Kurt Weill, "Zeitoper," *Melos,* vii (March 1928), 106–8. Translated in Kowalke, *Kurt Weill in Europe,* 428–84.
Kurt Weill, "Notiz zum Jazz," *Anbruch,* xi (March 1929), 138. Translated in Kowalke, *Kurt Weill in Europe,* 497–98.
Arnold Schoenberg, "George Gershwin" (1938) in *Style and Idea,* ed. L. Stein (New York, 1975), 257.
Paul Hindemith, *A Composer's World* (Cambridge, Mass., 1952).
David Drew, "Music Theatre in the Weimar Republic," *Proceedings of The Royal Musical Association,* lxxx (1962).
Ian Kemp, *Paul Hindemith* (London, 1970).

Elaine Padmore, "Hindemith, Weill" in *Music in the Modern Age*, ed. Sternfeld (London, 1973), 100.

Charles Schwartz, *Gershwin, His Life and Music* (Indianapolis, 1973).

Ernst Krenek, *Horizons Circled* (Berkeley, 1974).

Geoffrey Skelton, *Paul Hindemith* (London, 1975).

Kim H. Kowalke, *Kurt Weill in Europe* (Ann Arbor, 1979).

Richard Crawford "Gershwin's Reputation: A Note on *Porgy and Bess*," *Musical Quarterly*, lxv (1979), 257.

Susan Cook, *Opera During the Weimar Republic: The Zeitopern of Ernst Krenek, Kurt Weill, and Paul Hindemith* (PhD dissertation, University of Michigan, 1985).

Kim H. Kowalke, ed., *A New Orpheus: Essays on Kurt Weill* (New Haven, 1986).

Alexander Ringer, "*Kleinkunst* and *Küchenlied* in the Socio-Musical World of Kurt Weill" in *A New Orpheus*, 37–50.

John Rockwell, "Kurt Weill's Operatic Reform and Its Context" in *A New Orpheus*, 51–60.

Stephen Hinton, "Weill: *Neue Sachlichkeit*, Surrealism, and *Gebrauchsmusik* in *A New Orpheus*, 61–82.

Susan Cook, "*Der Zar lässt sich photographieren*: Weill and Comic Opera" in *A New Orpheus*, 83–101.

Douglas Jarman, "Weill and Berg: *Lulu* as Epic Opera" in *A New Orpheus*, 147–156.

David Drew, *Kurt Weill: A Handbook* (1987).

CHAPTER 15

TOWARD NEOCLASSICISM

Of all the "isms" of the twentieth century, none is more troublesome, none more persistent in the period 1885–1935 than Neoclassicism. It has been traditionally associated with the movement begun around 1920, from the time of Stravinsky's *Pulcinella* and *Octet*, wherein the subject matter or the forms of the eighteenth century were overtly reinterpreted. For the world of music, the eighteenth century was the Classic century, and any Neoclassicism would by definition relate to it. In literature and the fine arts, however, the eighteenth century was already a Neoclassic period, one that had witnessed the revival of interest in ancient Greece and Rome. Only a sparse Greco-Roman legacy had come down to the world of music, however, and in spite of a brilliant (if largely theoretically inspired) attempt at a revival in the late sixteenth century in Italy, the later and more common designation "Classic" for the music of Haydn, Mozart, and their contemporaries had nothing to do with the idea of tapping a distant past for musical models. Rather, there was a general emphasis on proportion and balance as formal ideals and a mild revival of interest in classical subjects or texts.

FIN DE SIÈCLE PARIS

As with all revivals, the Neoclassic movement of the 1920s was well prepared, and from the first tended to encompass a taste for the seventeenth, eighteenth, and even earlier centuries. In Paris, where the movement received its strongest subscription, the poet Jean Moréas (1856–1910), whose manifesto of 1886 had helped to codify the premises of Symbolism, had by 1891 already renounced his allegiance to the movement and had proclaimed the establishment of an *école romane* devoted to fostering the art of Ronsard in the sixteenth century and La Fontaine in the seventeenth. "Today," he said, "I take pleasure in stating that the whole world turns to classicism and antiquity."[1] Among the visual artists about the same time, a similar turning to Boucher and Poussin as models can be noted in the paintings of Renoir and Cézanne, and in Dénis to the style of the Sienese and Florentine Quattrocento as well as to Ingres.[2]

Already in fin de siècle Paris we may spot the beginning of a parallel trend in music in the suites and similar formal designations of d'Indy, Saint-Saëns, and Debussy (see the Repertoire list beginning on p. 348). The search for the classic roots of a French music had been aided earlier than this, however, with the appearance of a twenty-three volume anthology of Couperin in 1862. The latter's *Pièces de clavecin* appeared in 1871 for the first time since 1700 in an edition by Chrysander and Brahms, though a native edition by Louis Diemer (1843–1919) was not to appear until 1905, shortly before Dukas' edition of Couperin's *Les gouts réunis* in 1908. The huge undertaking of a complete edition of Rameau, begun in 1895 under the general direction of Malherbe, Emmanuel, and St. Saëns, was completed only in 1911 with individual works edited by such composers as Reynaldo Hahn and Claude Debussy (*Les Fêtes de Polymnie*, 1908). D'Indy, in addition to his editions of Rameau (*Hippolyte et Aricie*, c. 1902; *Dardanus*, c. 1905), also achieved editions and revival performances of Monteverdi operas (*Orfeo, L'incoronazione di Poppea*, and *Il ritorno d'Ulisse in patria*, all c. 1904) during the same period. Although Debussy had already been busy writing his Neo-Baroque suites (e.g., *Suite Bergamasque, Pour le piano*) in the 1890s, he was never the same again, he said, following his attendance at the premiere of Rameau's newly edited and revived *Castor and Pollux* in 1903.

Such events clearly signaled the dawn of a new era with respect to an infatuation with music of a bygone age. Obviously the birth of the discipline of musicology in the nineteenth century, principally in Germany but to an important extent in France as well, had set the stage for the emergence of such an interest. Furthermore, the formation of various performing groups helped to vitalize the newly available materials. As early as 1889, Diemer had organized a group for the performance of Marais, Leclair, Rameau, Loeillet, Couperin, and Daquin on early stringed instruments and harpsichord, which led to the formation of the *Societé des instruments anciens* in 1895. Charles Bordes had also founded a chorus directed at the revival of the sacred music of the Renaissance as early as 1892, and two years later, together with Alexandre Guilmant and Vincent d'Indy, founded the Schola Cantorum. Using the study of plainsong as the basis for study, their curriculum soon extended to music of the eighteenth century. In 1894, Henry Expert published the first of several volumes devoted to French masters of the Renaissance, and this was followed by a publication of the music of early French organ masters, *Archives des Maîtres de l'Orgue*, begun in 1898.

LANDOWSKA, DEBUSSY, AND RAVEL

Wanda Landowska, the Polish harpsichordist, arrived in Paris in 1900 and immediately became acquainted with the musicians of the Schola Cantorum, as well as Erard and Pleyel, who at that time were making their first modern reconstructions of the harpsichord. Landowska, initially known for her Bach performances on the piano, received encouragement from Fauré, Dukas, and Albert Schweitzer, who by 1905 had written his first book on Bach (another Bach book appeared in the same year by Pirro) and who in the next year published a treatise on the art of French and German organ building. By 1910 and 1911, the first of a series of articles on the interpretation of Bach's keyboard music by Landowska appeared both in French and German periodicals, and by 1912 Pleyel had built a large harpsichord with 16′, 8′ and 4′ registers according to her specifications. Finally, in 1913 she was invited to create a harpsichord class at the Hochschule für Musik in Berlin. By 1921 when she performed for a congress of art historians at Versailles (Figure 15.1), her role in the musical revival of the age of Louis XIV was already legendary.

Among the works that promoted the riches of their French heritage, Debussy's Satie-inspired "Sarabande" of 1894 found an echo in the later "Hommage à Rameau" (dans le style d'une Sarabande) of his *Images*, first series, 1905, just as Ravel's *Menuet antique* for piano of 1895 was recaptured in the second movement of his *Sonatine* of 1903–05, a work with all the earmarks of an emerging Neoclassicism. The key, as noted earlier, was not only in the clarity of the sonatine structure of the first movement or the invocation of the minuet in the second, but in the restriction of the piano writing to the central portion of the keyboard, which suggests a totally new option to the Lisztian premises of Ravel's *Jeux d'eau* (1901) and an overt subscription to the manner of the clavecinists of the seventeenth and eighteenth centuries. The endorsement was never exclusive, however, and in the following years we find the language of *Jeux d'eau* expanded to a new level of virtuosity in *Gaspard de la nuit* (1908) even as the neoclassic posture was refined to a heightened degree in *Le tombeau de Couperin* (1914–17). Debussy's continuing affection for the French classic style was manifested in his last three sonatas for violin and piano; cello and piano; and flute, viola, and harp; as well as a fourth projected for oboe, horn, and harpsichord. Analogies of form and texture aside, one need only compare the opening measures of the *Prologue-overture* to Rameau's *Les fêtes de Polymnie*, edited by Debussy in 1908, with the opening measures of the *Prologue*, which serves as the opening movement to his own Sonata for cello and piano (1915) to be aware of his reliance on specific melodic-rhythmic figurations.

Figure 15.1. Landowska playing in the Hall of Mirrors at Versailles in 1921 during the Congres International de l'Histoire de l'Art.

Photo courtesy of Denise Restout.

Example 15.1. Debussy, *Sonata for Cello and Piano,* "Prologue" (1915).

Example 15.2. Rameau, *Les fêtes de Polymie:* Prologue-overture (*Oeuvres completes*, XIII, ed. by Debussy, 1908).

It is impossible to present a comprehensive list of works capable of providing a background for Neoclassicism as it emerged around 1920 because the term has been so loosely applied and viewed from so many disparate angles; yet, it would be pointless to suggest in retrospect a precision of terminology and example that was never apparent even to the principal proponents. In addition to fin de siècle developments in France it could be argued, for example, that Strauss's *Der Rosenkavalier* of 1909-10 points to a spiritual awareness of Mozart as well as a self-conscious volte-face away from the threatening Expressionism of *Elektra* (1906-8). Although the extravagance of the musical forces that project Strauss's clarified melodic and harmonic manners promotes the idea of reversionism more than of Neoclassicism, an awareness of the pairs of Mozartian wind serenades that frame his career (1881, 1884 and 1943, 1945) encourages us to search for a continuing thread. In addition, Prokofiev's claim that his "Classical" Symphony of 1916-17 was modeled directly after Haydn is confirmable both with respect to the instrumental resource and the musical syntax.

But while one may suspect that, as with Stravinsky, the influence of French taste is near at hand, for both Prokofiev and Stravinsky the reverence for Mozart shown by Tchaikovsky (*Serenade for Strings*, 1881) and Rimsky-Korsakov (*Mozart and Salieri*, 1897) provided a potent Russian tradition before either arrived in Paris. It is obvious that the backgrounds for the neoclassic taste that began to manifest itself around 1920 are to be found in various quarters prompted by highly variable points of view.

STRAVINSKY: "BACK TO . . . "

> In *Le coq et l'arlequin* I had already denounced the spells exerted by *Le sacre du printemps.* And in self-rejection Stravinsky was to outdo us all.—Jean Cocteau

If the later designation of Stravinsky's *Pulcinella* (1919-20) as the spearhead for the New Classicism was not totally unfounded, the choice falsifies as much as it informs. As we have seen, not only had an interest in the music of the eighteenth century been manifested much earlier in the century, but Stravinsky cannot even take claim for the idea of turning to the music of Pergolesi. Following the formation of a *Nouvelle societé des instruments anciens* by Henri Casadesus (1879-1947) in 1901, the ensemble toured Russia in 1909. Here they were heard by Benois, who, taken with the music of Monteclair, suggested to Diaghilev that he mount a ballet of his music. Casadesus' insistence that Monteclair's music be performed on original instruments led to Diaghilev's veto of the plan, though in the same year he approached Debussy about the possibility of a ballet with an eighteenth-century subject. In 1913, Benois again proposed a ballet based on the music of Bach and Scarlatti,[3] and although Ravel confided to Stravinsky in a letter of August 28 that "I should write again to Diaghilev that he cannot count on me for the Scarlatti ballet",[4] this was not the end of the matter. For a Scarlatti ballet, *The Good-Humoured Ladies*, was finally mounted to a score prepared by Tommasini in 1917, the same year that brought the first orchestral set of *Antiche arie e danze per liuto* by Respighi.

The Monteclair ballet was ultimately to achieve realization in an arrangement of pieces by Casadesus in 1924 with the title *Tentations de la bergère ou l'amour vainquer*, although not before Diaghilev's turn to Pergolesi, which was made in the same frame of mind. The lengthy preparation for *Pulcinella* in numerous quarters should temper the suggestion that Diaghilev's turn from the folkloristic to the neoclassic following the Russian Revolution in 1917 was solely a reflection of political developments or that he alone was responsible for leading Stravinsky single-handedly to a new-found aesthetic.

For aside from an occasional interest in neoclassic subject matter, the New Simplicity of Cocteau, purportedly defined by Satie in the world of music, had emphasized in addition to its music hall manners an economy of means and a parodistic humor observable not only in Satie's piano music of the early teens but in numerous piano works and chamber ensembles of Stravinsky written during the same period. Although Satie's "little classic path," as Cocteau put it, failed to recall a French historical legacy, many of its qualities were nonetheless in harmony with a nascent Neoclassicism. In conjunction with the French neoclassic inquiry at the turn of the century, as well as with the new *"esprit nouveau"* which Apollinaire defined as "inheriting from the classics a good solid sense . . . the sense of duty which denudes the sentiments and limits them",[5] it helped to secure the fundamental ingredients for the definition of Neoclassicism as it was to be practiced after 1920.

PULCINELLA. If *Parade* shared with *Petrushka* a common relation to the traditions of the *commedia dell'arte* secured prior to the appearance of *Pulcinella*, its individuality and force for the voyage ahead were not lost on Stravinsky, who said:

> *Parade* confirmed me still further in my conviction of Satie's merit in the part he had played in French music by opposing to the vagueness of a decrepit impressionism a language precise and firm, stripped of all pictorial embellishments.[6]

Recalling the exploration of seventeenth- and eighteenth-century musical manners twenty and thirty years before, it is a wonder that *Pulcinella* was seen as beginning anything like a movement. The explanation lies as much in the fact that *Pulcinella* was so far removed from the language of Stravinsky's early ballets as in the fact that it proved to be fundamental to his future career. As the composer stated many years later:

> *Pulcinella* was my discovery of the past, the epiphany through which the whole of my late work became possible. It was a backward look, of course—the first of many love affairs in that direction—but it was a look in the mirror, too.[7]

By combining voices that carried Pergolesi's original texts with the ballet, Stravinsky honored the French eighteenth-century tradition of joining dancing and singing and provided a model for a similar conjunction in Poulenc's forthcoming *Les biches* of 1924. On the other hand, Stravinsky's *Pulcinella* was no simple orchestration of Pergolesi numbers à la Tommasini. Transformation takes place on a number of levels, but in his instrumental choice, which excludes clarinets and percussion and includes strings divided into *concertino* and *ripieno* groupings, he honored the source of his materials. Stravinsky's reworking of Pergolesi tends to preserve the soprano and bass of the original, but his degree of involvement can be coloristic, rhythmic, and formal as well as harmonic. While Pergolesi's music dominates in the earlier sections of the ballet, Stravinsky's personal signature becomes increasingly apparent as the work progresses. Thus the G-B pedal point of the opening (Ex. 15.4) provides only the

Example 15.3. Pergolesi, *First Trio Sonata,* opening.

Example 15.4. Stravinsky, *Pulcinella* (after Giambattista Pergolesi), piano part of version for violin and piano, opening.

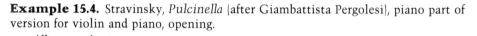

mildest harmonic coloring of the model, while the delicate rhythmic strumming of the ensuing "siciliano," conjuring up the sound of a Spanish guitar and consequently visions of a Neapolitan setting, is equally subtle. Later, however, parody and humor are more overtly interjected, most notably in the Vivo duet between double-bass and trombone, but also in the extended repetitions of the final cadence, which recalls nothing so much as Satie's spoof of eighteenth-century manners in the extended cadence ("*cadence obligée*") occupying the entire last page of the *Embryons Desséchés* (1913).

Following a perceptive notice as early as 1911 regarding the effect of contemporary musicology on composition,[8] Egon Wellesz, composer-scholar critic and one of the few who was conversant with stylistic trends in both Paris and Vienna, stated in an article of 1920 that Ravel's *Trio* and *Le tombeau de Couperin* were graced by a "wonderful clarity . . . a new classicism, a harmonious balance between form and content which can only be formed among Latin peoples, without having the stamp of academicism."[9]

The impression of some sort of universal acknowledgment of the expression's usefulness was confirmed in Diaghilev's comment of 1923, "But no, good heavens, one does not revive . . . one evolves towards neo-classicism, as Picasso evolves toward Ingres . . . my god, is it still necessary to explain such things?"[10], as well as by Stravinsky's remark to Ansermet in a letter of August 22, 1922, that Mozart was for him what Ingres was to Picasso.[11] The latter's line drawing of Stravinsky dated May 24, 1920, nine days after the premiere of *Pulcinella*, for which Picasso created the sets and costumes is vivid testimony of the composer's judgment (Figure 15.2).

By 1923 the term Neoclassicism had been so variously applied that it had come to include the possibility of an embrace of both innovation and tradition. The last charges of academicism, however, dissolved with the appearance of a series of works of sufficient originality that any such accusations could easily be set aside. The term's association with Stravinsky in that year for the very first time was one that was to prove vital.

While previously employed with numerous shades of meaning, Neoclassicism was now applied with reference to an idiom and a composer that corresponds to current usage. Its appearance in February, 1923, came in a review by Boris de Schloezer of a concert organized by Jean Wiéner, which included Stravinsky's *Symphonies of Wind Instruments* and preceded the completion of the *Octet* by only a few months.[12] As we have seen, many composers around 1920 were in search of new means of clarification following the manic-depressive assaults of Primitivism and Expressionism.

Figure 15.2. Picasso, *Igor Stravinsky*. Compare with Picasso's drawing of Satie (Figure 13.8).
Photo courtesy of Giraudon/Art Resource. © SPADEM, Paris/VAGA, New York, 1985.

OCTET. Thus, while *Pulcinella* may have been the first of Stravinsky's love affairs with the past, the decade of the 1920s was to witness the establishment of a habit. The *Octet* of 1922, using pairs of winds (fl, cl, 2 bn, 2 tpt, 2 trbn), is the first of the neoclassic pieces without reference to borrowed thematic material, but in the sequential patterns of Ex. 15.5 (m. 3–6) and the ornamental turn of Ex. 15.6 (m.2) we sense his overt stylistic posturing to which he has added his own rhythmic touch (note the metric extension in Ex. 15.5. m. 6; Ex. 15.6, m. 3). Also in the use of the title "Sinfonia" for the first movement; in the employment for the second movement of a hybrid Variation-Rondo (ABACDAE, recalling similar approaches by Haydn and Mozart who, however, typically brought back the original theme rather than the first variation, Ex. 15.7) and in a distinctively "secco" instrumental style, the eighteenth century was recalled with such a vitality and sense of originality that the viability of the approach was sealed.

Example 15.5. Stravinsky, *Octet*, Mvt. 1, Allegro.

Copyright 1924 by Edition Russe de Musique. Renewed 1952. Copyright and renewal assigned to Boosey & Hawkes, Inc. Revised version copyright 1952 Boosey & Hawkes, Inc. Renewed 1980. Reprinted by permission.

Example 15.6. Stravinsky, *Octet*, Mvt. 2, Theme.

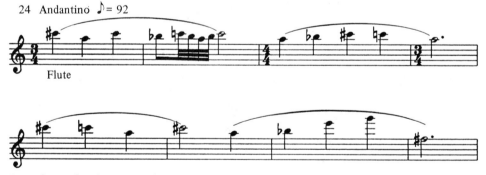

Copyright 1924 by Edition Russe de Musique. Renewed 1952. Copyright and renewal assigned to Boosey & Hawkes, Inc. Revised version copyright 1952 Boosey & Hawkes, Inc. Renewed 1980. Reprinted by permission.

If Stravinsky's *Octet* comes closer than *Pulcinella* to disclosing features that were to predominate in the ensuing decade, it is nonetheless important to remember that the refined selection of instruments in new and unusual combinations (which promoted a textural clarity typically associated with Neoclassicism) had already appeared in both fin de siècle France and Germany, in Schoenberg's *Kammersymphonie* (1906), and in numerous works written by

Example 15.7. Stravinsky, *Octet*, Mvt. 2, Variation A.

B. & H. 17281

Example 15.7 (Continued)

B. & H. 17281

Stravinsky immediately following the success of his Russian ballets: *Japanese Lyrics*, (1912–13) (S, 2 fl, 2 cl, pf, 2 vn, va, vc); *Pribaoutki*, 1914 (v, fl, ob, cl, bn, vn, va, vc, db); *Berceuse du chat*, 1915–16 (v, 3 cl); *Renard*, 1915–16; *Histoire du soldat*, 1918 (cl, bn, cornet, trbn, vn, db, perc); *Ragtime for Eleven Instruments*, 1918.

PIANO CONCERTO AND *PIANO SONATA.*   Ultimately, the suggestion that something like a "Back-to-Bach" movement had been launched came with the lean, essentially contrapuntal style of Stravinsky's *Concerto for Piano and Wind Instruments* of 1923–24, purportedly based on a study of the Bach *Three-Part Inventions*,[13] and the appearance of Schoenberg's *Three Satires* (1925), which included a highly abrasive reference to Stravinsky as "Papa Bach." Together they provided sufficient evidence to secure the notion of a Neoclassic movement in the popular imagination.

The exclusive use of wind instruments for his orchestra seemed to solidify the direction of Stravinsky's immediately preceding chamber ensembles, but in figure and design he made confirmations of a different order: the use in the first movement of the French overture form (slow introduction characterized by a dotted-note figure that also closes the movement, followed by a contrapuntal allegro); the roulades (cadenzas) of the second movement; and the contrapuntal writing of the piano part limited for the most part to the center of the keyboard—all suggest that a Baroque model is near at hand. The use of dotted rhythms in numerous later works (*Apollo, Oedipus, Orpheus, Persephone*) prompted Stravinsky to remark in his *Conversations:*

> Dotted rhythms are characteristic eighteenth-century rhythms. My uses of them in these and other works of that period, such as the introduction to my Piano Concerto, are conscious stylistic references. I attempted to build a new music on eighteenth-century classicism, using the constructive principles of that classicism ... and even evoking it stylistically by such means as dotted rhythms.[14]

In the *Piano Sonata* of 1924, Stravinsky widened his view and undertook an examination of the Beethoven sonatas, with the result that the ornamental style of the second movement is now described by the composer as "Beethoven frisé." Indeed, a comparison of the second movement with Beethoven's op. 109 (1st mvt.) and of the final movement with Beethoven's op. 54 (1st mvt.) can leave no doubt that the models are specific.

The infatuation with Bach, however, was to remain with Stravinsky to the end of his career and was to attain significance for many composers of the 1920s and 1930s. Just as Stravinsky endorsed the Bach of the *Third Brandenburg Concerto* in the opening figure of his *"Dumbarton Oaks" Concerto* of 1936, so Poulenc paid homage to the same composer's great organ *Fantasy in G. minor* (Ex. 15.8) in the texture, figure, and key of the opening of his *Concerto for Organ, Strings and Tympani* of 1938 (Ex. 15.9). And as Stravinsky tipped his hat to Haydn in his *Symphony in C* (1940), so Poulenc expressed his reverence for Mozart in the slow movement of the *Concerto for Two Pianos* (1932). Landowska's harpsichord had earlier encouraged numerous composers to rediscover the sound of her instrument, not only as an agent for the revival of old music but for the discovery of a new one, Fallas' *Concerto for Harpsichord and Five Instruments* (1923–26) and Poulenc's *Concert champêtre* (1927–28) being the most notable examples.

Example 15.8. J. S. Bach, *Organ Fantasy in G minor*, opening.

Example 15.9. Poulenc, *Concerto for Organ, Strings and tympani*, opening.

THE RAKE'S PROGRESS.   If Stravinsky never wrote for Landowska (though he knew her well from the salon of the Princess Edmond de Polignac), he did cast the harpsichord as continuo in his Neoclassic valedictory, *The Rake's Progress* (1948–51). On a chance visit to the Art Institute of Chicago in May, 1947, Stravinsky saw an exhibition of works by the eighteenth-century English artist William Hogarth (1697–1764) and was immediately struck by the dramatic potential of the cycle of eight engravings (originally paintings) entitled *A Rake's Progress* (1735). Back in California, the choice of W. H. Auden as librettist for a projected opera was made on the recommendation of Stravinsky's friend and neighbor, Aldous Huxley. That specific ideas were suggested by Stravinsky in his first letter to Auden is clear from the response of the librettist, who was already getting down to cases: "I think the Asylum finale sounds excellent, but for instance, if he is to play the fiddle then, do you want the fiddle to run through the story?"[15] Though this recollection of Stravinsky's *The Soldier's Tale* was dropped, another, the striking of a deal with the Devil, was retained. In the end, although the characters of Mother Goose and Baba the Turk were Auden's ideas, a libretto close to the final version was the result of a collaborative working period of ten days in Hollywood. Similar working relationships—with Alexander Benois (*Petrushka*) and Nicolas Roerich (*The Soldier's Tale*)—can be spotted from the beginning of Stravinsky's career.

Stravinsky and Auden restructured Hogarth's plot by introducing three wishes made by the hero. The first ("to have money") is invoked in the first scene of the opening act, followed by the introduction of Nick Shadow (the villain or devil) who announces that his uncle has died and left him all of his money. Tom engages Nick as his servant, agreeing that he will pay him after a year and a day, and sets out for London, promising to send for Anne when his affairs are in order. The original character of Sarah Young is transformed by Stravinsky and Auden into an active protagonist, frantically seeking her lover among the demimonde of London, and the orgy in a London tavern is changed into a brothel scene run by Mother Goose. Tom's marriage, not to a rich one-eyed woman, as in Hogarth, but to a bearded lady, Baba the Turk, stems from a second wish to be happy, and is undertaken as a result of Nick Shadow's suggestion that happiness can come only through freedom from Passion and Reason. A third and final wish, to wipe famine from the face of the earth, leads to Tom's loss of fortune resulting not from a trip to a gambling house (Hogarth) but from a speculative investment in the manufacture of a machine, cunningly demonstrated by Nick Shadow, that turns crockery into bread.

Auden became passionately involved with technical questions of versification, which had always interested Stravinsky from his native *pribaoutki* (a type of Russian folk verse), to *Oedipus* (Latin), *Persephone* (French), and even abstract instrument pieces (*Apollo*, where Pushkin's alexandrines served as the basis for accentual considerations). The text that Auden ultimately contrived served not only as the foundation for Stravinsky's first significant setting of the English language but proved to be one of the most artfully wrought libretti in the history of opera—a libretto whose richness can best be appreciated by a reading without music. In 1933, Stravinsky had indicated that "For *Persephone*, I wanted nothing but syllables—beautiful strong syllables—and an action. This is exactly what Gide has given me ... " Auden provided the same and more, and although there are traces of the composer's habit of superimposing musical accentuations that run counter to those of the text (a trait that infuriated Gide), the libretto as a whole is projected with a remarkable clarity.

At two and a half hours, Stravinsky's *Rake* is not only the composer's longest opera but the largest score of his entire career. Written between 1948 and 1951, it has traditionally been considered the final work of his Neoclassic period, which had begun thirty years before. Indeed, *The Rake* serves not only as a farewell to an aesthetic point of view but provides a summary of its various ingredients. During Auden's visit, librettist and composer attended a two-piano version of *Cosi fan tutte*, and Stravinsky later suggested that this was "an omen, perhaps, for *The Rake* is deeply involved in *Cosi.*"[16] Not only did the Hogarthian theme of Auden's libretto prove to be the perfect agent for Stravinsky's reinterpretation of Mozart, its rhymed verse brought the appropriate stylization for an eighteenth-century opera, suggesting in its divisions the formalization requisite to the introduction of recitative, aria, and ensemble. In a word, it is a number opera intentionally fabricated to serve a stylistic point of view.

Act I, scene 3, for Anne alone, illustrates the use of a pair of recitatives and arias to articulate an entire scene. The arias may be classified as cavatina, a simple song without da capo in the eighteenth century, and cabaletta, a vivace da capo type. Used in pairs they had found special favor in the operas of Rossini, Donizetti, Bellini, and even Verdi, whose "Ah, fors è lui" and "Sempre libera" (La *Traviata*) are well-known examples. Anne's cavatina, "Quietly, night" is a strophic aria in moderate tempo and her cabaletta, "I go to him", a quickly paced da capo. Numerous melodic clichés can be heard throughout, especially at cadences, and all of them, including the final high C, are meant to be heard as interpretive allusions to a master whom Stravinsky revered. Even the mismatch of dominant and tonic harmony at the end of the first line of the cabaletta—and tonic with supertonic at the end of the second—has the aspect, for all its wryness, of a loving if somewhat playful quotation even as it confirms a personal habit of over thirty years standing.

Example 15.10. Stravinsky, *The Rake's Progress*, Act 1, s. 3.

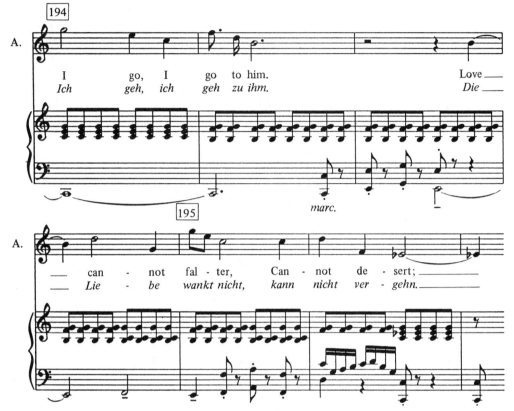

Act I, Scene 3:   The garden of Truelove's cottage. Anne has received no word from Tom, prays for his happiness and resolves to leave for London, certain that she can be of help to him. *Same as Scene One. Autumn night, full moon.* [*Anne enters from house in travelling clothes*]

Recitative:

ANNE

No word from Tom. Has Love no voice,
     can Love not keep
A Maytime vow in cities? Fades it as
     the rose
Cut for a rich display? Forgot! But no,
     to weep
Is not enough. He needs my help. Love
     hears, Love knows,
Love answers him across the silent
     miles, and goes.

Aria: Cavatina (strophic):

A: Quietly, night, O find him and caress,
    And may thou quiet find
His heart, although it be unkind,
    Nor may its beat confess,
Although I weep, it knows of loneliness.

A: Guide me, O moon chastely when I depart,
    And warmly be the same
He watches without grief or shame;
    It can not be thou art
A colder moon upon a colder heart.
[*Truelove's voice is heard calling from
    the house—"Anne, Anne"*]

Recitative:

My father! Can I desert him and his devotion for a love who has deserted me?
[*Starts walking back to the house. Then she stops suddenly.*] No, my father has strength of purpose, while Tom is weak, and needs the comfort of a helping hand.
[*She kneels*]

*(Prayer: Reprised
    Act II, s. 3):*

O God, protect dear Tom, support my
        father, and strengthen my resolve.
[*She bows her head, then rises and
        comes forward with great decision*]

ANNE

*Aria: Cabaletta
    (Da Capo; opening
    reprised Act III, s. 2):*

A: I go to him.
Love can not falter,
Can not desert;
Though it be shunned:
Or be forgotten,
Though it be hurt,
If love be love
It will not alter.

B: O should I see
My love in need
It shall not matter
What he may be.
[*She turns and starts toward the
    garden gate*]
[*Quick curtain*]

In addition to an isolated instance of canon between voice and instruments in Tom's opening Act I aria, Stravinsky has employed another structural agent that is immediately recognizable from *Oedipus Rex*: the aria reprise. Examples occur both within a single scene and between the acts: Anne's Act I, scene 3, prayer is brought back for Tom's prayer at the end of Act II; her "I go to him" from the same scene is momentarily invoked in Act III, scene 1, on Baba's insistence that she return to Tom, and even more poignantly and audibly in the next scene when Tom wins at cards with the Devil by calling on the Queen of Hearts a second time. Eschewing the use of leitmotif, which Stravinsky characterized as "a sort of check-room number" and which prompted Debussy to state that the *Ring* reminded him of a "vast musical city directory," the composer of *The Rake* has projected a powerful psychological component in terms that are closer to Mozart and Verdi than to Wagner.

The use of interlude music between the several scenes serves both a dramatic and practical function, with the color component characteristically reinforcing the formalization: The prelude to the graveyard scene, for example, employs a somber string quartet; the introduction to the idyllic first scene of Act I uses a postoral quartet of woodwinds. In the use of a chamber orchestra, and the undisguised adoption of the strophic aria (e.g., Act I, scene 2, "Love, too frequently betrayed") as well as in the introduction of the harpsichord for recitative (e.g., Act I, scene 2, "Sisters of Venus", complete with a delayed V-I cadence at the close), Stravinsky provided the audience with a composite set of readily identifiable conventions.

ACT I, SCENE 2, Excerpt.

SHADOW: (Recitative with harpsichord)

Sisters of Venus, Brothers of Mars, Fellow-worshippers in the Temple of Delight, it is my privilege to present to you a stranger to our rites who, following our custom, begs leave to sing you a song in earnest of his desire to be initiated. As you see, he is young; as you shall discover, he is rich. My master, and, if he will pardon the liberty, my friend, Mr. Tom Rakewell!

RAKEWELL: (Strophic Aria)

Love, too frequently betrayed	Love, my sorrow and my shame,
For some plausible desire	Though thou daily be forgot,
Or the world's enchanted fire,	Goddess, O forget me not.
Still thy traitor in his sleep	Lest I perish, O be nigh
Renews the vow he did not keep,	In my darkest hour that I,
Weeping, weeping,	Dying, dying,
He kneels before thy wounded shade.	May call upon thy sacred name.

Stravinsky had known the harpsichordist Wanda Landowska in Paris at least from the early 1920s, but unlike Poulenc and Falla, who wrote concertos for her during that decade, he never wrote for the instrument except in an early unpublished version of *Les noces!* In *The Rake* he seems to have retrieved its use as a vivid memory from an earlier time.

Spotting Stravinsky's "radical susceptibility to influence," a factor openly acknowledged by the composer and pointedly charged by many a critic, has proven to be a perennial pastime with virtually all the composer's scores. Beginning with the tavern talk of friends following *The Rake*'s premiere in Venice in 1951, the game of tune detection and dramatic analogy has been continuously played and has suggested references to the *Volga Boat Song* (the Mourning Chorus), *Die Meistersinger* (the beginning of Act III), *Faust* (too obvious), *Don Giovanni* (Epilogue and Graveyard Scene), Richard Strauss, and Tchaikovsky. Even the composer compounded the issue by suggesting that

"The Epilogue is a vaudeville or pasquinade, of which opera's greatest examples are in the *Seraglio* and *L'Heure espagnole*. In fact, some of *The Rake* is close to Broadway, Baba's music especially." And speaking of the opera repertory he had heard in St. Petersburg at the turn of the century, which included Bellini and Donizetti, he confessed: "I remembered the trumpet solo in *Don Pasquale*—that far back!—when I wrote *The Rake*."[17]

Outside influences aside, *The Rake* abounds with characteristics of the composer audible in works written both before and after. The opening overture, though nominally traceable to the "Toccata" that opens Monteverdi's *Orfeo* of 1607, is more clearly linkable to the fanfares of Stravinsky's own *Oedipus Rex* (1927) or the instrumental writing of the first chorus in his *Canticum Sacrum* (1955). And the canonic structure of Tom's first-act aria not only recalls the first "Eclogue" of the *Duo Concertant* (1931) but foreshadows the presence of such constructions in virtually every major work written by Stravinsky in the 1950s.[18]

For *The Rake's Progress* we have no equivalent to Eliot's annotated *Wasteland*, but Stravinsky's numerous writings throughout his life have whetted the appetite of the connoisseur for spotting allusions in his music. Recognition of such an approach is imperative to a total understanding of the composer's method as well as his message, but in the final analysis the music must stand or fall on its own. From the opening Prelude to the final Epilogue, the music alternately bristles with energy, betrays an unpredicted lyricism, or blends comedy with pathos, and at the end the composer arbitrarily winds the whole thing up with a moralization. Some critics, while acknowledging Auden's brilliant versification, have found the libretto faulty and Rakewell's progress, if not lacking in motivation, at least wanting in urgency. One hesitates to request a critique of most opera libretti by the same lofty standards (including the professed musical model, *Così fan tutte*), but one can appropriately skirt the issue of opera as drama by savoring with delectation the recurrent stylization which, if not everything, is clearly paramount. On the other hand, the "Lanterloo" chorus of Act I or the Lullaby of Act III are perfect examples of a music whose simplicity of means is as breathtaking as it is direct. Perhaps it is these moments, as much as or more than the revelation of Baba or the scene in the graveyard, that ultimately haunt the memory.

While it has been contended that *The Rake's Progress* sounded the death knell to a thirty-year flirtation, it must be noted that Stravinsky's interest in music of the past did not abate after this period. The composition of the *Vom Himmel Hoch Variations* (1955) and the *Monumentum pro Gesualdo* (1960), for example, suggest that there had always been an element of neohistoricism in Stravinsky's approach to music, and the adoption of the twelve-note series and nascent infatuation with the music of Webern about this time provided a final confirmation of an attitude that clearly transcended the narrower base of Neoclassicism. *The Rake's Progress*, however, is eloquent testimony to the suggestion that a genuine Neoclassicism had thrived and peaked. If Stravinsky's music following *The Rake* reflects a shift in interest, it should not be concluded that the basic impulse that lay behind it was to remain buried. The continued and prominent use of canon and ritornello in the early serial works of the 1950s readily confirms this judgment.

In his last years, Stravinsky surveyed the *entre deux guerres* climate with the following remarkable appraisal:

Every age is a historical unity. It may never appear as anything but either/or to its partisan contemporaries, of course, but semblance is gradual, and in time either and or come to be components of the same thing. For instance, "neoclassic" now begins to apply to all of the between-the-war composers (not that notion of the neo-classic composer as someone who rifles his predecessors and each other and then arranges the theft in a new "style"). The music of Schoenberg, Berg, and Webern in the twenties was considered extremely iconoclastic at that time but these composers now appear to have used musical form as I did, "historically". My use of it was overt, however, and theirs elaborately disguised. (Take, for example, the Rondo of Webern's *Trio*; the music is wonderfully interesting but no one hears it as a rondo.) We all explored and discovered new music in the twenties, of course, but we attached it to the very tradition we were so busily outgrowing a decade before.[19]

As a postscript it is worth noting that during the period of a thriving musical Neoclassicism, a vigorous interest was also expressed in Classical subjects as the foundation for theater works, ballets, and opera. The Greek revival hardly faltered from Strauss's *Elektra* (1906–8) to Stravinsky's *Orpheus* (1947). It was manifest in numerous works of Milhaud in the second decade (*Agamemnon*, 1913–14; *Les chöephores*, 1915; *Les euménides*, 1917–22); in a fascination for the figure of Oedipus (Yeats, 1911 and 1926; Martin, 1923 and 1924; Stravinsky, 1927; Antheil, 1929; Honegger, 1948) and Orpheus (Krenek, 1923, on a libretto of Kokoschka; Milhaud, 1924; Roger-Ducasse, 1926; Stravinsky, 1947); as well as other notable legends and stories such as Ravel's *Daphnis et Chloé* (1912), Satie's *Socrates* (1918), Honegger's *Antigone* (1921; 1924–27), Stravinsky's *Apollo* (1928), and Chavez's incidental music to Cocteau's version of Sophocles' *Antigone* (1933). The range of musical values utilized in addressing these subjects was predictably as diverse as the composers themselves, and suggested, as with the *commedia dell'arte*, the capacity of a vital literature for revival in numerous tongues. The occasional coincidence of this thematic revival with a contemporary neoclassic emphasis on refinement and proportion (as in Stravinsky's *Apollo* or Picasso's *Classic Head*, 1925) was as natural as it was undemanded.

SCHOENBERG: "ONWARD FROM . . . "

The expression *"nouveau classicisme"* had been used by the French before World War I as a derogatory reference to German instrumental music around 1900, especially Brahms.[20] The increasing hatred of the Germans and the continuing need—building on the French fin de siècle attitudes manifested in the music of Satie and Debussy—to counter nineteenth-century German hegemony with a French alternative fueled the fires which spawned the notion of a genuine Neoclassicism that was not only essentially French but frequently deemed possible only for people of Latin cultures. As we have seen (p. 314), it was a view that even the Viennese Egon Wellesz endorsed. Stravinsky's incorporation of Italian and Spanish themes was a natural concession on his part to this attitude, but the early appearance of Bach, Mozart, and even Beethoven in his list of potential models soon deflated this elitist cultural bias. It is thus all the more difficult to appreciate Schoenberg's general antipathy toward Stravinsky's aims in his music, although the anti-German tone of much of Stravinsky's

Figure 15.3. Arnold Schoenberg.
Photo by Florence Homolka. Courtesy of Arnold Schoenberg Institute.

polemical writing of the early 1920s was surely strong enough to have given offense. Schoenberg, sensing his own artistic heritage, saw no possibility in a return to anything, only a responsibility to forward the legacy and maintain the continuing superiority of German art music.

SCHOENBERG AND STRAVINSKY: *THREE SATIRES.*   If Stravinsky was anti-Wagner, he was equally anti-Brahms, if reasonably silent on the subject. That is, the post-Beethoven Germans were discounted—the ones who could provide a continuing thread; contrarily, Schoenberg endorsed them for this very reason. Thus there was a chronological as well as a cultural bias, both of which contributed to the Stravinsky-Schoenberg dichotomy at an early date.

That Stravinsky and Schoenberg had demonstrated the capacity to admire each other's music in the early teens has already been discussed (p. 223), although something of their differing historical position must have been apparent to them already from that time. In the period from 1920 to 1925, however, a number of crucial works signaled a new orientation for both, as the following chronology reveals:

May 15, 1920   Stravinsky's *Pulcinella* premiered (Paris)

July 1920   Schoenberg begins *Five Piano Pieces*, op. 23

June 10, 1921	Stravinsky's *Symphonies of Wind Instruments* premiered (London)
February 7, 1923	Schoenberg's *Five Piano Pieces* premiered (Vienna)
October 18, 1923	Stravinsky's *Octet* premiered (Paris)
May 22, 1924	Stravinsky's *Concerto* for piano and winds premiered (Paris)
July 20, 1924	Schoenberg's *Serenade* premiered (Donaueschingen)
September 13, 1924	Schoenberg's *Quintet* for woodwinds premiered (Vienna)
July 25, 1925	Stravinsky's *Sonata* for piano premiered (Donaueschingen)
September 7, 1925	Schoenberg's *Serenade* (Venice-ISCM festival)
September 8, 1925	Stravinsky's *Sonata* (Venice-ISCM festival)
September 9, 1925	Stravinsky completes *Serenade en la* for piano (Venice)
December 31, 1925	Schoenberg completes *Three Satires*, op. 28 (Vienna)

The 1925 cartoon that appeared in the Prague journal *Der Auftakt* designating Schoenberg and Stravinsky as "the founding fathers of modern music" failed to suggest the antipathy that was developing between them. While their common taste for writing serenades and sonatas, a quintet, an octet, and a concerto might seem to indicate that the composers of *Pierrot* and *Le sacre* had regrouped and were heading in the same direction, it was an opinion which neither composer would have endorsed at the time. That their positions were, in Schoenberg's mind, diametrically opposed is evident not only from the texts of *Three Satires*, wherein Stravinsky is referred to as "little Modernsky" in a wig with "authentic false hair" looking just like Papa Bach, but also from the Foreword to that publication, which sounds a warning and promotes the idea that history is in the making. Henceforth, one would be obliged to make a choice: Paris or Vienna: Stravinsky or Schoenberg; an ongoing tradition (now spelled Serialism, despite Schoenberg's railing against fashionable movements) or a retrograde Neoclassicism.

> In the first place, I wanted to hit all those who seek their personal salvation along a middle way. For the middle way is the only one that does not lead to Rome. But it is used by those who nibble at dissonances—they want to count as modern, then—but are too cautious to draw the correct conclusions . . . Next, the pseudotonalists, who think they may do anything they please, however much it shakes the foundations of tonality, so long as occasionally, at some fitting or ill-fitting moment, they offer a pinch of incense to tonality, in the form of a tonal triad . . . Secondly, I am aiming at those who pretend they are trying to 'go back to . . . ' A person like that should not try to make people believe it is *he* who controls how far back he is soon going to find himself . . . Since, moreover, we have already seen more than one "Renaissance," proclaimed with a flourish of trumpets, quickly turn out to be based on a false pregnancy (unproclaimed), let me merely put on record that such people write, of their own free will, in the same needy way that is imposed on a poor conservatoire student. Thirdly, I have pleasure in also hitting the folk-lorists who—either because they have to (from an inability to summon up themes of their own), or even though they do not have to (since an existing musical culture and tradition could, if it came to it, stand even them)—apply to the naturally primitive ideas of folk music a technique suitable only to a complicated way of thinking . . . Fourth and finally, all the " . . . ists," in whom I can see only mannerists . . .[21]

In the period 1909–1915, Schoenberg, driven by strong Expressionist currents, had composed a brief catalogue of works that sparked a creative crisis and ultimate silence. These works are by common consent Schoenberg's most radical compositions, and it is in the area of thematic delineation and surface form as much as in the question of tonality that we sense the crisis of these works. As Schoenberg himself stated:

> Intoxicated by the enthusiasm of having freed music from the shackles of tonality, I had thought to find further liberty of expression. In fact I myself and my pupils Anton von Webern and Alban Berg, and even Alois Haba believed that now music could renounce motivic features and remain coherent and comprehensible nevertheless.[22]

From this period, Schoenberg left us a handful of masterpieces in which the creative spirit burned radiantly but whose formal aspect was guided largely by intuition or a text. The ultimate rescue from his dilemma was provided by the discovery of the twelve-note series, but the rescue must be viewed as two-fold: (1) By establishing an order of pitch succession for the total chromatic, Schoenberg's newly won freedom from the "shackles of tonality" could be preserved; (2) in the same establishment of order resided the potential for the reintroduction of a pronounced motivic content that would provide an organizational gambit necessary to the composition of larger forms without text.

SUITE FOR PIANO, OP. 25   The first work to test this premise was the *Suite* for piano, op. 25 (1921–3). The net result was a melodic and harmonic style not dissimilar to Schoenberg's first "atonal" works, and Krenek's judgment that "historical perspective reveals that the advent of atonality was experienced by the public as a violent shock, while the introduction of the twelve-tone method caused hardly a ripple"[23] is confirmatory. In addition to the untransposed (Prime $= P^0$) version of the series, the transposed versions (typically identified by a superscript, 1–11, indicating the number of semitones above P^0) could be employed, as well as inversions (I), retrogrades (R), and retrograde inversions (RI) and their transpositions. The restriction to P^0 at the beginning of each movement is noteworthy, though transformations of the basic shape and layout prevent a ready confirmation of this fact. A more audible consequence of "invariance," a quality identified by Milton Babbitt and common to all twelve-note series, is exemplified by the identical positioning of certain pitch classes following inversion at any even-numbered semitonal distance. Note the pitch series for Schoenberg's op. 25, and the same position as well as adjacency of the tritone related pitches G-D♭ at $I.^6$:

P^0:	E	F	G	D♭	G♭	E♭	A♭	D	B	C	A	B♭
I^6:	B♭	A	G	D♭	A♭	B	G♭	C	E♭	D	F	E

This quality is put to highly audible account in the Musette where the tonic-dominant double-pedal implied by the dance is accorded recognition through the repeated presence of the less-stable tritone pair throughout the composition.

More problematical from the listener's standpoint is the license taken with the typical identifying rhythm and metrics of the Baroque dances whose titles are employed. The absence of a compound meter signature (either 6/8 or 9/8) or other groupings that approximate its motion for any length of time in the

Example 15.11. Schoenberg, *Piano Suite*, op. 25, "Prelude", opening.

By permission of Belmont Music Publishers.

Example 15.12. Schoenberg, *Piano Suite*, op. 25, "Gavotte," opening.

By permission of Belmont Music Publishers.

Example 15.13. Schoenberg, *Piano Suite*, op. 25, "Musette," opening.

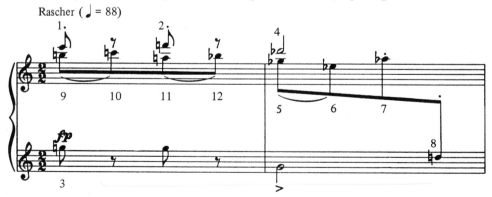

By permission of Belmont Music Publishers.

Example 15.14. Schoenberg, *Piano Suite*, op. 25, "Menuett," opening.

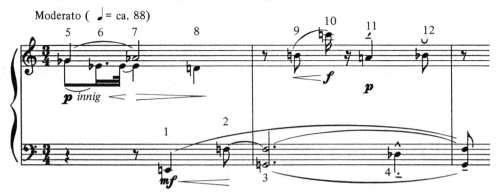

By permission of Belmont Music Publishers.

Example 15.15. Schoenberg, *Piano Suite*, op. 25, "Gigue," opening.

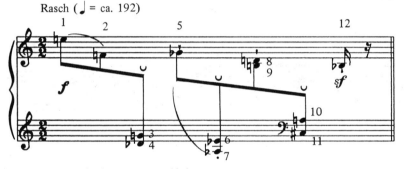

By permission of Belmont Music Publishers.

"Gigue" is paralleled by a barely detectable triple movement in the "Menuett" despite its 3/4 marking (the perception of the opening as two groups of 3/8 within the bar is a possibility). Contrarily, while an antecedent-consequent phraseology is clearly audible at the opening of the "Musette," the tonal implications of the title, discussed earlier, are addressed and modified. Such liberties with the expectations of the Baroque dance forms can be witnessed in the opening scene of Act 1 of Berg's *Wozzeck*, written slightly earlier, where Prelude, Pavane, Gigue, and Gavotte only obliquely attain to any historical authenticity.

VARIATIONS FOR ORCHESTRA, OP. 31. That the method of composing with twelve tones was a natural ally of the variation technique was demonstrated in the *Variations for Orchestra*, op. 31, Schoenberg's first major essay for orchestra since his *Five Pieces*, op. 16. Here he wed his serial technique to a form espoused as much by Brahms as by Haydn. Following a mood setting introduction and a statement of the theme in the solo cello, Schoenberg projects his melodic theme in a clearly audible form in Variation I (Ex. 15.17, bass) and Variation III (horns). Elsewhere, the Variations (II, for example) mine the motivic

Example 15.16. Schoenberg, *Variations for Orchestra*, op. 31, main theme.

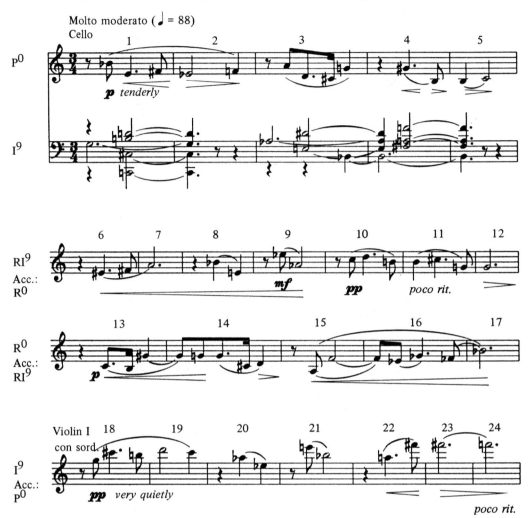

By permission of Belmont Music Publishers.

consequences of his original series in a set of developing figurations that frequently move far from the theme as melody. The BACH (Bb, A, C, B) motif,
which Schoenberg uses already in the introduction, may be seen as deducible
from the opening pitches of the first two phrases plus the concluding two
pitches of the third (a process of motivic generation readily demonstrable in the
Variations on a Recitative, op. 40, for organ).[24] Its prominent display in the high
register of the trumpets in the concluding coda functions both as crown and
homage to another master of the variation whom the composer revered.

Example 15.17. Schoenberg, *Variations for Orchestra*, op. 31, Variation I, mm. 58–59, partial score.

By permission of Belmont Music Publishers.

The matrix of the 48 versions of the series Schoenberg employs in this work is shown below (P: left to right; R: right to left; I: top to bottom; RI: bottom to top).

Bb	E	Gb	Eb	F	A	D	Db	G	Ab	B	C
E	Bb	C	A	B	Eb	Ab	G	Db	D	F	F#
D	Ab	Bb	G	A	Db	Gb	F	B	C	Eb	E
F	B	Db	Bb	C	E	A	Ab	D	Eb	Gb	G
Eb	A	B	Ab	Bb	D	G	Gb	C	Db	E	F
B	F	G	E	Gb	Bb	Eb	D	Ab	A	C	Db
F#	C	D	B	Db	F	Bb	A	Eb	E	G	Ab
G	Db	Eb	C	D	Gb	B	Bb	E	F	Ab	A
C#	G	A	F#	Ab	C	F	E	Bb	B	D	D#
C	F#	G#	F	G	B	E	Eb	A	Bb	C#	D
A	D#	F	D	E	G#	C#	C	F#	G	Bb	B
G#	D	E	C#	D#	G	C	B	F	F#	A	Bb

In practice, only a limited number of the possible orders are utilized, and the inversion beginning on G (I⁹) takes on a special importance through its hexachordally combinatorial properties with the original: The first group of six notes of P, for example, share the same pitches as the second hexachord (pitches 7–12) of I⁹, but in a different order. Schoenberg found such a structuring useful in providing accompanimental material without pitch duplication, and its readiness for such a task can be seen in the harmonization of the main theme (Ex. 15.16). The division of the melody into four statements of the row (P⁰, RI⁹, R⁰, I⁹) brings with it complementary harmonic materials derived from the same limited forms, only in reverse order. The rate at which he uses up the pitch content (e.g., a five-note melodic phrase receives a five-pitch harmonic accompaniment, a four-note and three-note phrase an identical number of accompanying pitches) ensures the desired result. In later works such as the *Violin Concerto*, op. 36, Schoenberg preferred to construct the combinatorial relationship between the original and the inversion at the interval of the perfect fifth below, I⁵.

It is revealing, however, to read the transcript of a radio talk on the *Orchestra Variations* delivered over the Frankfurt Radio in 1931. Schoenberg's tonal harmonization of the twelve-note theme, offered to would-be critics as a demonstration of his ability to compose tonally, carries with it a note of nostalgia, which is acutely underscored in his G major *Suite for String Orchestra* of 1934.

Example 15.18. Schoenberg, tonal harmonization of *Variations* melody.

By permission of Belmont Music Publishers.

Example 15.18 (Continued)

His own appraisal of this tonal harmonization invites the reader's interpretation:

> That is quite a good F major, which insistently courts G flat major, corresponding to a neapolitan sixth. Some people will prefer this treatment to the original. I don't like it, but that is a matter of taste. Why now, if I can also do it that way, do I write a different accompaniment, which is bound to have a less general appeal? Not out of malice . . .[25]

It may be concluded that Schoenberg did not view himself as a Neoclassicist during the 1920s and 1930s largely because of his sense of belonging to part of a grand tradition that he was in no sense reviving but whose continuity he was insuring. In the central movement of his *Serenade,* op. 24 (1920–23), Schoenberg's first foray into vocal writing with a twelve-note series, the choice of Petrarch for a text recalls the orchestral songs, op. 8 (1904), and the purely instrumental septet of the remaining movements adopts the plan of the eighteenth-century instrumental serenade with an opening March reprised as a Finale. Although the instrumental choice of violin, viola, cello, clarinet, and bass clarinet recalls *Pierrot lunaire,* the addition of mandolin and guitar reinforces the concept of the serenade from Mozart's *Don Giovanni* even as it reflects a sonority well known to Schoenberg from Mahler's Seventh and Eighth symphonies and *Das Lied von der Erde,* all of which employ the mandolin. The choice of texts from Bethge's *Chinesische Flöte* for the final two of a set of four choruses, op. 27 (1925), also reflects the Mahler legacy, not only in textual matters but in the simultaneous resubscription of the mandolin to join clarinet, violin, and cello in the fourth and final chorus. Similarly, in the fourth of the orchestral variations, op. 31 (1928), an excursion into *Walzertempo* discloses a similar instrumental reduction and selection, even as it momentarily recalls the rarified world of Webern's earlier op. 10, no. 3 (Ex. 3.4). Recognition of the mandolin as a timbral ingredient in the Viennese signature was later confirmed through its employment by Stravinsky in *Agon* (1953–57), one of his earliest dodecaphonic compositions, and by Boulez in *Pli selon pli* (1957–62) and *Eclat/ Multiples* (1965–   ).

At the same time it must be admitted that there is evidence in the structure and forms of Schoenberg's music during this period that a refuge had been found from the nightmare of Expressionism that had prompted an extended compositional hiatus in the late teens. This clarification, which was actively sought in various musical quarters of the 1920s, is also visible in the visual arts. Kandinsky, father of Expressionist art around 1910, retained in the 1920s his vibrant

Example 15.19. Schoenberg, *Variations for Orchestra*, op. 31, Variation IV.

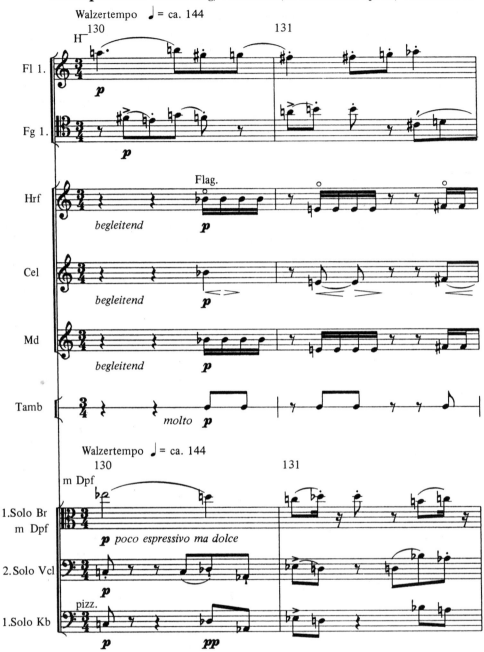

By permission of Belmont Music Publishers.

Example 15.19 (Continued)

use of color while subjecting his images to the tidying effect of geometric forms (Fig. 15.4). The invention of the pitch series and the resubscription of classical formal principles by Schoenberg, which brought order to an atonal world at exactly the same time, may be seen as directly analogous.[26]

In recent years, Boulez has judged that "Stravinsky's and Schoenberg's paths to neo-classicism differ basically only in one being diatonic and the other chromatic . . . Both composers adopt dead forms, and because they are so obsessed with them they allow them to transform their musical ideas until these too are dead."[27] In a more detailed and reasoned discussion, Charles Rosen has similarly confronted the question of "Serialism and Neoclassicism" and among other things has concluded that Serialism appeared to attempt the realization of the classical dream of a reconciliation between unity and diversity.[28] But he also spotted the consequences of Schoenberg's method in noting that

Figure 15.4. Kandinsky. *The Great Gate of Kiev* (1928). Scene XVI from a set of stage sets to accompany Mussorgsky's *Pictures at an Exhibition.* Tempera watercolor and india ink on paper, 3⅜″ × 10¾″.

Collection Theater-museum der Universität, Cologne. © VAGA, New York, 1986.

through his almost exclusive focus on the element of pitch and interval he failed to address, at least as a constructive principle, the earlier vision he had had with respect to timbre and texture. The potential misunderstanding or misuse of such a partially described method was, of course, enormous.

Schoenberg's revelation of his new course was undertaken only gradually and principally, he contended, in order to counter suggestions that he had borrowed heavily from a contemporaneous twelve-note theory introduced by Josef Matthias Hauer (1883–1959). Having known such Viennese personalities as Schoenberg as early as 1913, and Kraus, Loos, and Altenberg from 1915, Hauer had by 1919 already gradually discovered his own private vision of "a law of the twelve notes." Although their earliest musical meetings in 1917 led to Schoenberg's performances of some of Hauer's works as early as 1919 at the Verein für Musikalische Privataufführungen, a brief liaison soon turned to bitterness as Hauer began to insist on the priority of his discoveries concerning twelve-note composition, which he developed in his *Deutung des Melos* (1923), *Vom Melos zur Pauke* (1925), and *Zwölftontechnik* (1926). Making a distinction between "Melos" (atonal music) and "Rhythmus" (tonal music), he reduced his ideas not so much to a rigid system as to a method whereby the complete twelve-note chromatic was divisible into two unordered hexachordal tropes. Although the arrangement of pitches within the hexachords themselves was interchangeable, he argued from the beginning for the primacy of a "Constellation" or "Grundgestalt." Conceived as a "basic shape," it was a terminology that soon appeared in discussions of Schoenberg's dodecaphonic formations.

While attention to such technical matters invariably tended to blur rather than clarify the potential relationship between Neoclassicism and Serialism, the details of the Hauer-Schoenberg confrontation must be seen as little more than a footnote to the larger issues of an expanding tonal planetary system inevitably wedded to formal questions that consumed virtually all composers of the time. The consequences of such investigations found their way into brief tracts, occasional polemics, and endless practical demonstrations in the music itself. Although no doubt more a part of Stravinsky's age than he would ever have admitted, in later years Schoenberg seemed incapable of indicating any awareness of the common ground which they inhabited. Such a pronounced sense of isolation reflected Schoenberg's denial of any possibility for a valid Neoclassicism because, as he put it, the Neoclassicists sought "the solution by means of a historical parallel, while I have found it from within, in which I merely obeyed the subject and followed the imagination and the feeling for form."[29]

Paradoxically, many features of Neoclassicism were not only openly embraced by Germans such as Hindemith in the 1920s but periodically appropriated by Schoenberg himself: his early *Gavotte and Musette* ("in Olden Style") for strings of 1897; his later returns to the "olden style" formally (suites, op. 24, 25, 29; variations, op. 31; concerto, op. 36, 42); the "olden style" tonally (*Suite for Strings* in G major; *Theme and Variations for Wind Band*, op. 43) and quasitonally (*Variations on a Recitative*, op. 40 for organ); and transcriptions of "olden style" pieces by Handel, Bach, and Monn. It is palpably ironic that Schoenberg's *Violin Concerto* of 1936—for years considered the ultimate avant-garde concerto for its instrument and unplayable except by a few specialists—has increasingly proven to be a remarkably attractive work, whose pronounced lyricism and clear three-movement formal plan replete with audible cyclic qualities argues for its classic base.

But the national bias that had attended the first French definitions of Neoclassicism proved to be the breeding ground for his rejection. For if the French could cover over what Schoenberg saw as the mediocrity of their achievement in the nineteenth century by turning to the eighteenth century, a period of undeniable riches, then claims of the continuing superiority of German music could be blunted by what he undoubtedly saw as a historical ruse. Schoenberg's pointed assessement of Neoclassicism in the *Three Satires*, op. 28, made use of mirror canons and the old clefs not as a surprise revelation of a "back to . . ." mentality but rather as a demonstration that the new twelve-tone method was not only the logical next step following the collapse of an outworn tonality but one that was compatible with classic techniques. It proclaimed a blend of past and present in a bold new language that secured the notion of a continuing German hegemony.

Looking back on the 1920s in an article entitled "How One Becomes Lonely" (1937),[30] Schoenberg spoke frankly about his anxieties of the period but concluded with a reaffirmation of the errors of his opponents and the steadfastness of his goals.

> ... the unanimity of the rebuke was frightening ... It was the first time in my career that I lost, for a short time, my influence on youth. This took place between 1922 and 1930, and during this time almost every year a new kind of music was created and that of the preceding year collapsed. It started with the European musicians imitating American jazz. Then followed "Machine Music" and "New Objectivity" (*Neue Sachlichkeit*) and "Music for Every Day Use" (*Gebrauchmusik*) and "Play Music" or "Game Music" (*Spielmusik*) and finally "Neo-classicism". While all this happened and so many styles developed and passed away, I did not enjoy my splendid isolation very cheerfully. Although I soon realized the confusion among my opponents and although I saw with regret that many a great talent would perish through a corrupt attitude towards the arts, which aimed only for a sensational but futile success, instead of fulfilling the real task of every artist; although I knew I was right and they were wrong, I felt lonely during this period in which I was restricted to the faithfulness of ... (a) small number of pupils ...

Milton Babbitt's assessment[31] that for Stravinsky expressions like "back to Bach" and "Neoclassicism" were merely catchy slogans—tolerated for use by nonprofessionals who needed a means of establishing that they were sensitive to current trends—is only partially true. For Stravinsky's only marginal acceptance of the term in the 1920s and his later openly expressed contempt for it could not dissolve its patent usefulness in securing the notion of a Stravinsky-Schoenberg controversy and, indeed, in promoting the idea of history in the making. Neoclassicism as a concept was the rallying point around which numerous fin de siècle notions of nationality and emerging views of musical modernism were played out. It served not only to define the most prominent aesthetic positions but the personalities associated with them, and was thus as important for Schoenberg as for Stravinsky. As with most isms, once this had been accomplished, there was little need for the terminology, and individualized solutions could now be more readily introduced.

HINDEMITH: A CALL TO ORDER

EARLY CHAMBER MUSIC.   Hindemith's role in the ferment of the 1920s with respect to various trends emphasizing directness of expression (*Neue Sachlichkeit*, jazz and folksong), utilitarian values (*Gebrauchsmusik*), and social messages (*Zeitoper*) has been reviewed earlier (see pp. 292–93). But Hindemith's role in spelling the meaning of Neoclassicism for that decade was, as Stravinsky noted, equally fundamental.

> Your so-called period of formulation came only in the later 1920s, with the establishment of so-called "neoclassicism"—Schoenberg's, Hindemith's, and my own. During the fifteen years from 1930 to 1945, however, these three "neo-classic" schools were ascendant, and the fact that they can be called schools is already an indication of the onset of formulae. The Schoenberg, or, as it is now called, the dodecaphonic school, for all its great merits, was obsessed by an artificial need to abnegate any suggestion of triadic "tonality"—a very difficult thing to do. And, curiously, its music was heavily founded in the most turgid and graceless Brahms.
>
> As for my imitators, my "school" if you prefer, their trouble was that they imitated not so much my music as my person in my music. They were noted for their rhythms, their *ostinatos,* their "unexpected" accents, their diatonic "lines," their "dissonances," and for their final C-major chords with B natural or A in them. The characteristics of the Hindemith school were its interminable 9/8 movements,

its endless fourths, and its fugues with subjects at least thirty-two bars long. Other schools existed, of course—the Broadway, the Appalachian, the Neo-Neanderthal (Orff), the *arrière-garde*, etc., but these three were principal and paramount.

All three schools had come to a stalemate, however, when at the end of the war in 1945 a new period of exploration and revolution began precisely with the rediscovery of the masterpieces of 1912, and the music of Webern in general.[32]

Just as France had provided an extended preparation for the emergence of neoclassic values, so in Germany Reger (*Suite in E minor*, 1895; *Variations and Fugue on a Theme of Bach*, 1904), and Busoni (*Tre pezzi nello stilo antico*, 1882; *Kleine Suite* for cello, 1886) had early indicated their classical orientation (see Repertoire list, p. 350). The latter's inclination was manifest in the somewhat more elaborate formulations of later years such as *Arlecchino* (1917). Here, Neoclassicism is visible not only in the utilization of masks to promote a certain objectivity but also in the quotation or parody of musical ideas from *Don Giovanni*, Beethoven's Fifth Symphony, and *Fidelio*.

The novelist Thomas Mann had enlisted the expression "neue Klassizität" as early as 1911, and Feruccio Busoni's introduction of the term "junge Klassizität" in an open letter of 1920 had mirrored Mann in his espousal of Goethe's analogy between the development of plants and artistic creation. The emulation consisted of an emphasis on an all-encompassing unity derived from a single source, on the horizontal element in music as opposed to the vertical, and a rejection of tone painting and overripe harmonies. In retrospect, however, both Mann's and Busoni's terms appear to correspond roughly to the French notion of "nouveau classicisme" as a German alternative to Wagner, albeit in the French view of things an alternative that had courted academicism.

By 1921, in the press and also by reason of his *Toccata: Preludio, Fantasia, Ciaccona* of that year, Busoni became increasingly, if briefly, associated with the expression "neue Klassizität." But by 1924, the year of his death, Neoclassicism was already receiving a new and practical definition in the works of other German composers, including Krenek (*Toccata and Chaccone*, 1922), Weill (*Fantasia, Passacaglia, Hymn*, 1922), and Hindemith, as Busoni's role in the succeeding evolution of the aesthetic was reduced to a historical footnote. It is well to recall that the first three of this German quartet were contemporaneously active later in the decade in the definition of *Zeitoper*, an operatic genre only marginally indebted to Neoclassicism.

Although Hindemith's first major works, such as *Mörder, Hoffnung der Frauen* (1919) on a text of Kokoschka, or *Das Nusch-Nuschi* (1920) and *Sancta Susanna* (1921), seemed to signal the continuation of the Expressionist movement begun ten years earlier, it was not long before his experience as an instrumentalist led him to explore the possibilities of an economical but coloristically variable style suggested by *Pierrot lunaire* and *Histoire du soldat*. Hindemith's numerous highly contrapuntal pieces written under the title of *Kammermusik* in the 1920s and 1930s, together with a procession of sonatas for virtually every instrument that extended over an even longer period, earned for the composer a reputation as one of the liveliest of the Neoclassicists.

The *Kammermusik No. 1* (1921) for twelve solo instruments (including fl/picc, cl, bsn, pf, 2 vn, vla, vc, cb, accordion, trumpet, siren, and various percussion) seems at first sight to be more allied with the Futurists and Dadaists than the Neoclassicists, and the quotation of a foxtrot openly foreshadowed his jazz inspired *Suite "1922"* for piano (see p. 290). This was followed, however, by a series of chamber concertos for piano, violin, viola, and organ—works that in their textural clarity, repetitive rhythms, and balanced phraseology recalled the Brandenburg concertos. Turning aside at this point from the Expressionist-Bartókian mixture of his *Third String Quartet* (1922), Hindemith continued to explore various Baroque forms in the *Fourth String Quartet* (1923), whose movements are labeled fugue, chorale prelude, march, and passacaglia. The final group of songs from the cycle *Das Marienleben* (1922–23) are similarly organized as ground bass, theme and variations, and chorale fantasia. But the potential for a reconciliation between such Baroque ideals and Expressionist drama was finally demonstrated in *Cardillac*, where the sequence of numbers carrying both symbolic and formal implications share something of Berg's approach in *Wozzeck*.

MATHIS DER MALER.   While Hindemith's experience in the 1920s with *Zeitoper* (see pp. 292–93) may have presaged his later concern about larger social issues, and particularly the artist in society, his most notable theatrical success following *Hin und zurück* and *Neues vom Tage*—namely, *Mathis der Maler*—had clearly cast aside the modish jazz trappings of the genre. Pieces written prior to *Mathis* included the controversial *Lehrstück*, with a libretto by Bertold Brecht. Featured at the Baden-Baden festival of 1929, the story tells of an airplane pilot injured in a crash who turns to his fellow man for aid. The moral implications of its most notorious scene, which depicts clowns relieving the aches of an ailing giant by sawing off its limbs, created a scandal at the first performance. An eventual rift ensued between Hindemith, who suggested that the clown scene could be omitted, and Brecht, who insisted on its inclusion.

Following the more patently didactic and participatory children's opera, *Wir bauen eine Stadt*, Willy Strecker of the publishing house of Schott Söhne encouraged Hindemith to consider writing an opera based on the life of the German painter Matthias Grünewald. It would be an allegory about the role of the artist in society told against a backdrop of the Peasant's Revolt (1524–25), where Catholic and Protestant rivalries were temporarily set aside in an effort to crush the peasant uprising. As Strecker noted in a letter to Hindemith, there would be ample opportunity to draw parallels with present times. The hero-artist's initial support of the peasants, his ultimate rejection of politics, and the return to his art is the theme that paralleled Hindemith's personal struggle during the period following Hitler's rise to power. In 1934, Hindemith's music was branded as "cultural Bolshevism" and performances were momentarily banned. This was allegedly due to the immorality of his early Expressionist operas as well as the later *Neues vom Tage*. Further accusations included his association with Jews and the seeming parody of a Bavarian military march heard at Nazi rallies in the finale of his *Kammermusik No. 5* (1927). Indeed, at the conclusion of the work, which is a viola concerto, the march seems to sputter and dissolve rather than end on a triumphant note.

Although the opera itself was not yet complete, Hindemith arranged three important orchestral interludes into a *Mathis der Maler* symphony, which received its premiere under Furtwängler in March 1934. Its enormous public success was soon tarnished by news the following month that word had reached the Reichsmusikkamer of critical remarks purportedly made by Hindemith about Hitler. A radio ban of all his music was immediately imposed, and with it came the beginning of troubles with the Nazi Ministry of the Arts. Over the next years the roles of various personalities, including Strauss and Furtwängler, changed from month to month, and the fact that Hindemith's wife was half Jewish was only a minor factor in an otherwise complex scenario. Furtwängler had hoped in a newspaper article, published on November 25, 1934, on the front page of Berlin's *Deutsche Allgemeine Zeitung*, to win Hitler's support for a production of *Mathis*. Furtwängler diplomatically listed Hindemith's achievements, dismissed his Jewish associations as irrelevant, and allowing for past mistakes emphasized the need of the artist to have a free voice without official interference. Goering, Goebbels, and Hitler himself quickly expressed outrage at such an attempt to dictate an official policy toward the arts. In a public statement in which Goebbels spoke of "how deeply the Jewish intellectual infection has eaten into the body of our own people" and made the cautionary injunction that a true German composer "must be a real artist, not just a producer of atonal noises," he also read a telegram from the president of the Reichsmusikkammer, Richard Strauss, congratulating Goebbels on his success in "weeding out undesirable elements." Though Strauss later denied that he ever sent such a telegram, Hindemith's fate was clearly sealed.[33]

A trip to America for performances of his music in 1937 intervened before the premiere performance of the opera, *Mathis der Maler*, not in Germany but in Zurich on May 28, 1938. Hindemith soon left for Switzerland, where he lived for fifteen months prior to his departure in February 1940 for America and a wartime exile, first in Buffalo, then at Yale.

Although the opera *Mathis der Maler* may accurately be called a number opera, its neoclassical base is not so obvious as his Handel-inspired *Cardillac* of a few years earlier. While in *Mathis* ternary aria, plainchant hymn and folksong duet articulate the opening scene of the opera, recitative and arioso are also used to blend the separate units into a music with a seamless forward-moving continuity. Even more central to the opera is the consolidation of harmonic values, which dramatize a subscription to the premises of tonality. A few years later, in his *Unterweisung im Tonsatz* (1937, rev. 1940; Eng. trans., *Craft of Musical Composition*, 1942, rev. 1948), Hindemith explained his feelings not only about the importance of a tonal logic in music but also his belief that the triad "can never be avoided for more than a short time without completely confusing the listener."

Hindemith had fashioned a three-movement symphony from *Mathis* for practical reasons similar to Berg's casting of symphonic excerpts from his operas *Wozzeck* and *Lulu*. Each movement represented a panel from Grünewald's renowned Isenheim altarpiece (Fig. 15.5): "Concert of Angels," "Entombment," and "The Temptation of St. Anthony." The idea of "The Temptation" as the dramatic climax of the opera came quite late to Hindemith and provided the resolution to a number of structural difficulties he had encountered. In the opera, Mathis, taking refuge in a forest, has a vision in which each of the characters of the opera appears in a symbolic form corresponding to one of the figures in the paintings of Grünewald's "Temptation." In spite of their urgings to join in the Peasant's Revolt, Matthias determines to return to his God-given

Figure 15.5. Mathias Grunewald, Isenheim Altarpiece (c. 1510–15). Left to right: "Consort of Angels"; "The Temptations of St. Anthony"; "Entombment" (pradella, below).

Musée Unterlinden, Colmar.

calling, that of a painter. The first movement of the symphony serves as the prelude to the opera, and the second movement is an instrumental interlude that attends Mathis' watch over the death of Regina.

   Hindemith himself claimed that "Old folk songs, war songs of the Reformation period, and Gregorian chant were the nourishing foundation of the *Mathis* music." Indeed, although folk tunes are not featured prominently in either the opera or the symphony, their character is an important stylistic determinant in both. Regina's folksong "Es wollt ein Maidlein waschen gehn" in the first scene of the opera, for example, prompts a complementary though original response from Mathis. Two further quotations are prominent in the symphonic version: "Es sungen drei Engel" ("Three angels sang", Böhme No. 540), which appears in the introduction to the opening movement, and the plainchant, "Lauda Sion Salvatorem," which serves as a crown to the finale. In the opera, the tonal plan moves chromatically from C♯ to the E of the central scene and then returns. But in the orchestral version, not a symphony in the traditional sense except for the three-movement fast-slow-fast sequence, tunes of Ex. 15.20 and 15.21 are made to serve a tonal and dialectic organization different from the stage version, thus marking the piece as a natural successor to the narrative dramas of Mahler's symphonies. The D♭ tonality of "Es sungen drei Engel (Ex. 15.20) identifies the principal struggle with the central key (G) of the first movement promoted in the opening measure and in the principal theme (Ex. 15.22). The argument is pursued in the progression from C (the subdominant to G) to C♯ in the second movement ("Entombment") and in the ultimate resolution on D♭ for the finale (Ex. 15.21). Such tonal maneuvering recalls the tonal frames for several of Mahler's symphonies, such as the Second (C minor-E♭ major, symbolizing Death–Resurrection). The point is dramatized with the knowledge that "Lauda Sion" appears in E♭ in the opera, whereas it is transposed to D♭ in the symphonic version.

Example 15.20. Hindemith, *Mathis der Maler*, Mvt. 1, 9 mm. taken from Rehearsal no. 1.

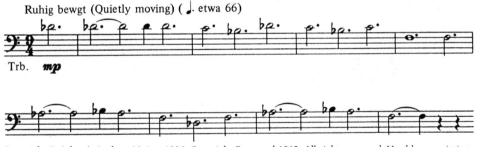

Example 15.21. 'Lauda Sion Salvatorem" (plainchant).

Hindemith's tunes (both plainchant and German folk melodies), whether they appear in concerto, sonata, or opera, invariably sound at home in a world marked by formal balance and tonal stability and where the metric accents of the march and the chorale never seem very far away (see pp. 292–94). In this latter quality we can also spot a natural affinity for the world of Mahler, which

Example 15.22. Hindemith, *Mathis der Maler*, Mvt. 1, 7 mm. taken from Rehearsal no. 2.

explains the ease with which the end of the first movement of Hindemith's *Symphonic Metamorphosis on Themes of Weber* (1943) quotes *notatim* from the close of the third movement of Mahler's *Ninth Symphony*. Refusing any connection with the aesthetic of Schoenberg and Webern, the works of Hindemith's maturity assert his devotion to his German heritage and at the same time seemingly attempt, like Berg, to promote and stabilize the legacy of Mahler, though in highly personal yet readily identifiable terms.

HINDEMITH AS THEORIST.   Hindemith's interest in a rational order for harmony and melody led to the codification of two fundamental theories: (a) that the twelve degrees of the chromatic scale have an innate hierarchical relationship based on acoustical principles, demonstrating a diminishing relationship to the first note in the following series: (b) that harmonic intervals may be similarly grouped in invertible pairs (except the octave and the tritone):

Example 15.23. Series I:

Example 15.24. Series II:

Hindemith's series speak of intervalic relationships not thematics or motifs and are consequently immediately distinguishable from the speculations of Schoenberg and Hauer (see p. 338). Attention to the weight of these relationships promoted the recomposition of such large-scale works as the song cycle *Das Marienleben* (1923, rev. 1948) and the opera *Cardillac* (1926, rev. 1952). That Hindemith considered these revisions as "improvements" he left no doubt, speaking of the original version of *Das Marienleben* as "essentially a series of songs, held together by the text and the action as it developed from that, but otherwise following no overall musical plan."[34] In the reworking of the cycle, not only is the harmony revised according to the relative tensions of his Series II, but a symbolic use of tonality clearly founded on the relationships of his Series I also appears in which Christ is represented by a tonic E, the Virgin Mary by the dominant B, the divine by A, eternity by C, etc. A similar reliance on the logic of Series I is observable in the succession of fugues and interludes for piano that make up his *Ludus Tonalis* (1942), a work frequently referred to as a modern-day *Well-Tempered Clavier*. And the tritone (G-D♭) relationship addressed in *Mathis der Maler*, discussed earlier, involves the most distant tension of the same series.

By taking into account the relationship of all tones in the complete chromatic, Hindemith sought to provide a rationale for those notes that are outside the diatonic and to confect what he called a "tonal planetary system" quite distinct from that of the polytonalists or atonalists whom he deplored.[35] This logical release from "the tyranny of the major and minor" was, he believed, a natural consequence of a movement begun by Wagner in *Tristan and Isolde*. As a pedagogical tool, Hindemith's *Craft of Musical Composition* had a limited acceptance, though in March, 1937, Nadia Boulanger, having seen proofs, made a trip from Paris to Berlin to discuss with Hindemith the possibility of making a French translation. The stipulation that she be allowed to print her objections in a preface to such an edition undoubtedly spelled the end to any possible realization of the project, for in the event nothing came of the plan. Boulanger's continuing admiration for Hindemith could nonetheless be spotted in her utilization of his *Elementary Training for Musicians* as a pedagogical tool to the end of her career.

Hindemith's belief in such precepts occupied him to his death, and although it failed to win the universal acceptance for which he had hoped, it proved to be the anchor for his late style and compatible with his basic neoclassic bent. Attempts late in life to expand his language, as in the twelve-note theme of the *Tuba Sonata* (1955), failed to erode his lifelong faith in the venerability of the major triad, a cadence sonority that became a Hindemithian signature. His devotion to tonality, a melodic style based on the four-phrase sentence derived from folk song, chorale, and march, and a metric accentuation drawn from similar models yielded a personal profile already well established by the 1930s. In his best works, such as the *Concert Music for Piano, Winds and Two Harps* (1930), *Mathis der Maler* (1933–35); *Organ Sonata No. 1* (1937), *Piano Sonata*, 4h. (1938), *Nobilissima Visione* (1938), *The Four Temperaments* for piano and strings (1940), and the *Symphonic Metamorphosis on Themes by Weber* (1943), Hindemith escaped for all time whatever charges might be leveled against him as a composer hopelessly chained to repetitive Baroque motor rhythms, a restructured tonality, or impractical theories. His fashion, somewhat faded at the time of his death, may well return as the full dimension of his best work becomes better known to a younger generation now somewhat distanced from its original impact.

REPERTOIRE: Toward Neoclassicism, France

Castillon, *Cinq pièces dans le style ancien* (1871)
Chaminade, *Pièce dans le style ancien* (1893)
Debussy, *Petite Suite* (1889): En bateau, Cortège, Menuet, Ballet
    Suite bergamasque (1890–1905): Prélude, Menuet, Clair de lune, Passepied
    Pour le piano (1894–1901): Prélude, Sarabande, Toccata
    Images, Book II (1896): "Hommage à Rameau," pf
    Sonata for cello and piano (1915)
    Sonata for flute, viola and harp (1916)
    Sonata for piano and violin (1917)
Delibes, *Six air de danse dans le style ancien* (1882)
Dukas, *Variations, Interlude et Final sur un thème de Rameau* (1899–1902)
Falla, *Concerto* (1923–6), harpsichord, 5 solo instr
Honegger, *Fugue et choral* (1917), org
    Trois contrepoints (1923), fl, eng hn, vn, vc
    Partita (1930), 2 pf
    Les noces d'Amour et de Psyché (after Bach French Suites, 1930)
    Concerto da camera (1949), fl, eng hn, str
d'Indy, *Suite en rè dans le style ancien* (1886), tr, 2 fl, str
    Douze petites pièces faciles dans le style classique de la fin du XVIIIe siècle
    (1908–15)

>*Menuet sur le nom d'Haydn* (1909), pf
>*Six chansons anciennes du Vivarais* (1926)
>*Suite* (1927), fl, str trio, harp
>*Madrigal à deux voix* (Charles d'Orleans) (1928)

Martin, *Suite* (1913)
>*Sonata da chiesa* (1938)

Martinu, *Partita* (1931)
>*Concerto for harpsichord* (1935), chamb orch

Milhaud, *Suite* (1913), pf
>*Chamber Symphonies Nos. 1–6* (1917–23)

Pierné, *Pastorale variée dans le style ancien* (1894)
>*Ballet de cour, six airs de danse dans le style ancien* (1905)

Poulenc, *Sonata* (1918, rev. 1945), 2 cl
>*Suite en ut* (1920), pf
>*Sonata* (1922), hn, tpt, trbn
>*Les biches* (1923), ballet, 17th c. texts for chorus, orch
>*Concert champêtre* (1927–28), hpd, orch
>*Aubade* (1929), pf, 18 instr
>*Sextet* (1932–39), fl, ob, cl, bsn, hn, pf
>*Concerto* (1932), 2 pf, orch
>*Suite française*, after Gervaise (1935), 2 ob, 2 tpt, 3 trmb, perc, hpd
>*Mass* (1937), unacc. chorus
>*Concerto* (1938), org, str, tymp

Ravel, *Menuet antique* (1895), pf
>*Sonatine* (1905): Modéré, Menuet, Animé
>*Le tombeau de Couperin* (1914–17): Prélude, Fugue, Forlane Rigaudon, Menuet, Toccata
>*Sonata for violin and cello* (1922)

Respighi, *Antiche arie e danze per liuto*, Set 1 (1917), orch

Saint-Saëns, *Oratorio de Noël*: "Prélude dans le style de J.S. Bach" (1854)
>*Suite for Orchestra* (1877): Prélude, Sarabande, Gavotte, Romance, Final
>*Septet* (1882): Prélude, Menuet, Intermede, Gavotte en final; tpt, str qt
>*Suite for Piano* (1892): Prélude and Fugue, Menuet, Gavotte, Gigue
>*Sarabande et Rigaudon* (1892), str orch

Stravinsky, *Pulcinella* (1919–20), ballet with song (S, T, B), orch
>*Symphonies of Wind Instruments* (1920)
>*Octet* (1922–23), fl, cl, 2 bn, 2 tpt, 2 trmb
>*Concerto for Piano and Winds* (1923–24)
>*Sonata for Piano* (1924)
>*Serenade in A* (1925–26), pf
>*Oedipus Rex* (1926–27), opera-oratorio
>*Apollo* (1927–28), ballet, str
>*Capriccio for Piano and Orchestra* (1928–29)
>*Symphony of Psalms* (1930), chorus, orch
>*Concerto in D* (1931), vn, orch
>*Duo Concertant* (1931–32), vn, pf
>*Concerto in E flat, "Dumbarton Oaks"* (1937–38)
>*Symphony in C* (1939–40)
>*The Rake's Progress* (1948–51), opera

Tommasini, *The Good-Humoured Ladies* (1916), ballet

READING: Toward Neoclassicism, France

Igor Stravinsky, *An Autobiography* (New York, 1936).

Igor Stravinsky and Robert Craft, *Memories and Commentaries* (Garden City, N.Y., 1960), 89, 117–18.

Edward T. Cone, "The Uses of Convention: Stravinsky and his Models," *Musical Quarterly*, xlvii (1962), 287.

William Austin, *Music in the Twentieth Century* (New York, 1966), 330-344.

Charles B. Paul, "Rameau, d'Indy and French Nationalism," *Musical Quarterly*, lviii (1972), 46.

Pierre Boulez, "Stravinsky: Style or Idea? In Praise of Amnesia" in *Orientations* (1986), 349-59. Appeared originally as "Style ou idée?—éloge de l'amnésie," *Musique en jeu*, iv (1971), 4-14.

Pierre Boulez, *Conversations with Célestin Deliège* (1975; Eng. trans., London, 1976).

Paul Griffiths, *The Rake's Progress* (Cambridge, 1982).

Karl Geiringer, "Brahms as a Musicologist," *Musical Quarterly*, lxix.4 (1983), 463.

Scott Messing, *Neo-Classicism: The Origins of the Term and its Use in the Schoenberg/Stravinsky Polemic in the 1920's* (PhD dissertation, University of Michigan, 1986).

Glenn Watkins, "The Canon and Stravinsky's Late Style" in *Confronting Stravinsky*, ed. J. Pasler (Berkeley, 1986), 217.

Ethan Haimo, "Problems of Hierarchy in Stravinsky's Octet" in *Stravinsky Retrospectives*, ed. E. Haimo and P. Johnson (Lincoln, 1987), 36.

Joseph Straus, "Sonata Form in Stravinsky" in *Stravinsky Retrospectives*, ed. E. Haimo and P. Johnson (Lincoln, 1987), 141.

REPERTOIRE: Toward Neoclassicism, Germany

Busoni, *Tre pezzi nello stilo antico* (1882), pf
    Kleine Suite (1886), vc, pf
    Fantasia contrapuntistica (1910), pf
    Arlecchino (1917), opera
Hindemith, *Kammermusik No. 1* (1921), 12 solo instruments
    String Quartet Nos. 2-4 (1921-23)
    Das Marienleben (1922-23), v, pf
    Kammermusiken Nos. 2-7 (1924-27), concertos for pf, vc, vn, va, va d'amore, org
    Konzertmusik (1931), pf, brass, 2 harps
    Mathis der Maler (1933), opera; sym suite
    Ludus Tonalis (1943), pf
    Sonatas (1917-55), various instr
    Concerto (1962), org, orch
Reger, *Suite "Den Manen J.S. Bachs"* (1894-95), org
    Variations and Fugue on a Theme of J.S. Bach (1904), pf
    Konzert im alten Stil (1912), orch
    Kanons und Fuguen in alten Stil (1914), 2 vns
Schoenberg, *Serenade*, op. 24 (1920-23), cl, b cl, mand, gui, vn, va, vc, B (mvt. 4)
    Suite, op. 25 (1921-23), pf
    Two Chorale-Preludes by J.S. Bach: "Komm, Gott, Schöpfer, heiliger Geist," "Schmücke dich, O liebe Seele" (1922), orch
    Suite (1925-26), E♭ cl/fl, cl, b cl/bn, pf, vn, va, vc
    Three Satires, op. 28 (1925), SATB: "Am Scheideweg"; "Vielseitigkeit"; "Der neue Klassizismus" with v, vc, pf
    Variations, op. 31 (1925-28), orch
    String Quartet No. 3, op. 30 (1927)
    Prelude and Fugue in E flat major by J.S. Bach (1928), trans. for orch
    Concerto for cello and orchestra (after a harpsichord concerto by G. M. Monn) (1932-33)
    Concerto for string quartet and orchestra (after Handel) (1933)
    Suite in G major (1934), str orch
    Violin Concerto, op. 36 (1936)
    String Quartet No. 4, op. 37 (1936)
    Piano Quartet in G minor by Brahms (1937), trans. for orch
    Chamber Symphony No. 2, op. 38 (1906/1939)
    Variations on a Recitative, op. 40 (1941), org
    Theme and Variations, op. 43 (1942), wind band
    Piano Concerto, op. 42 (1942)
    String Trio, op. 45 (1946)

READING: Schoenberg

Arnold Schoenberg, *Style and Idea*, ed. L. Stein (New York, 1975): "Hauer's Theories" (1923), 209. "Tonality and Form" (1925), 255. "Igor Stravinsky: *Der Restaurateur*" (1926), 481. "Stravinsky's *Oedipus*" (1928), 482. "New Music, Outmoded Music, Style and Idea" (1946), 113. "My Evolution" (1949), 79. Part V: *Twelve-Tone Composition* (six articles), 207–250.

Arnold Schoenberg, Preface to *Drei Satiren*, op. 28 (1925).

Arnold Schoenberg, "Variations for Orchestra, op. 30" (Frankfurt radio talk, 1931), *The Score*, July 1960, 33.

René Leibowitz, *Schönberg et son école* (Paris, 1947; Eng. trans., 1949).

Dika Newlin, *Bruckner, Mahler, Schoenberg* (New York, 1947).

H. H. Stuckenschmidt, *Arnold Schönberg* (Zurich, 1951; Eng. trans., 1959).

Josef Rufer, *Die Komposition mit zwölf Tönen* (Berlin, 1952; Eng. trans., 1954).

Anthony Payne, *Schoenberg* (London, 1968).

Willi Reich, *Schoenberg oder der konservative Revolutionär* (Vienna, 1968; Eng. trans., *Schoenberg: a critical biography*, London, 1971).

B. Boretz and E. Cone, eds., *Perspectives on Schoenberg and Stravinsky* (Princeton, 1968).

Glenn Watkins, "Schoenberg and the Organ," *Perspectives on Schoenberg and Stravinsky* (1968), 93–109.

J. Maegaard, *Studien zur Entwicklung des dodekaphonen Satzes bei Arnold Schönberg* (Copenhagen, 1972).

Pierre Boulez, "Schoenberg the Unloved?" *Die Welt*, September 7, 1974, for the Schoenberg centenary. English translation in *Orientations* (Cambridge, Mass., 1986), 325–29.

Pierre Boulez, *Par volonté et par hasard: entrétiens avec Célestin Deliège* (Paris, 1975; Eng. trans. 1976), 31.

Charles Rosen, *Arnold Schoenberg* (New York, 1975), 70–105.

Journal of the Arnold Schoenberg Institute (1976–   ).

M. Macdonald, *Schoenberg* (London, 1976).

Glenn Watkins, "Schoenberg Re-Cycled" in *Essays on Music for Charles Warren Fox* (Eastman School of Music Press, 1979), 72.

Dika Newlin, *Schoenberg Remembered: Diaries and Recollections (1938–76)*, (New York, 1980).

A. Lessem, "Schoenberg, Stravinsky, and Neo-Classicism: The Issues Reexamined," *Musical Quarterly*, lxvii.4 (1982), 527–42.

Scott Messing, *Neo-Classicism: The Origins of the Term and its Use in the Schoenberg/Stravinsky Polemic in the 1920's* (PhD dissertation, University of Michigan, 1986).

Leonard Stein, "Schoenberg and 'Kleine Modernsky'," *Confronting Stravinsky*, ed. J. Pasler (Berkeley, 1986), 310.

Glenn Watkins, "The Canon and Stravinsky's Late Style," *Confronting Stravinsky*, ed. J. Pasler (Berkeley, 1986), especially 237–46.

READING: Hindemith

Paul Hindemith, *Unterweisung im Tonsatz, i: Theoretischer Teil* (Mainz, 1937, rev. 1940; Eng. trans. by Arthur Mendel as *The Craft of Musical Composition*, New York, 1942).

Paul Hindemith, *A Composer's World* (Cambridge, Mass., 1952).

R. Stephan, "Hindemith's Marienleben," *Music Review*, xv (1954), 275.

Hans Tischler, "Hindemith's Ludus Tonalis and Bach's Well-Tempered Clavier," *Music Review*, xx (1959), 217.

William Austin, *Music in the 20th Century* (New York, 1966), 396–408.

Ian Kemp, *Hindemith* (London, 1970).

A. Briner, *Paul Hindemith* (Zurich and Mainz, 1971).

G. Skelton, *Paul Hindemith* (London, 1975).

Ian Kemp, "Hindemith" in *The New Grove Dictionary of Music* (1980), vol. 8, 573–87.

H. Wiley Hitchcock, "Trinitarian Symbolism in the 'Engelkonzert' of Hindemith's *Mathis der Maler*" in *A Festschrift for Albert Seay* (Colorado College, 1982), 217–29.

David Neumeyer, *The Music of Paul Hindemith* (New Haven, 1986).

CHAPTER 16

ZEMLINSKY'S *LYRIC SYMPHONY:* AGAINST THE TIDE

Zemlinsky (1871–1942) is remembered today more for his personal connection with Schoenberg, Berg, and Webern than for his own music. Schoenberg accorded him the central position in his musical formation, and while Zemlinsky's admiration for all of Schoenberg's music was not unconditional, his loyalty was unswerving. Beyond the string quartets, which are occasionally performed, the *Lyric Symphony* of 1922–23 is one of the few works of Zemlinsky to have survived in the concert hall. Its reliance on the poems of Rabindranath Tagore is slightly outmoded for its time, but suggests lingering traits that continued to appeal to a small group of composers. The source is Tagore's *The Gardener* of 1885. Tagore's winning of the Nobel Prize for literature in 1911 pointed to the need for translation, and an English edition closely supervised by Tagore appeared in 1913, followed by the German translation of Hans Effenberger in 1914. It is interesting to note in this connection that the American composer John Alden Carpenter wrote his *Gitanjali* song cycle on Tagore texts in 1913.

MAHLER AND BERG

Carpenter's emphasis on themes of children ("The Sleep that Flits in Baby's Eyes", "When I Bring to you Coloured Toys") was a theme dear to Tagore, but Zemlinsky's choices for his *Lyric Symphony* are of another order and more varied. The moods of the seven poems range from the opulent decadence of the second number to the expressionist nocturnes of the fourth and sixth. But there is also a recurrent hint of *Weltschmerz* and a reverence for intoxication that recalls the lines of Li-Tai-Po. Zemlinsky's admission in 1922 that "I wrote something during the summer along the lines of *Das Lied von der Erde*" encourages us to seek parallels beyond the obvious use of two voices in alternation and the choice of texts by an oriental poet. The connection can be observed on varying levels:

Movement 1. A structure in three stanzas for the opening poem occurs in both cycles (see pp. 18–19). In addition, each possesses a concluding refrain:

"Dunkel ist das Leben, ist der Tod" (Mahler) and "Ich vergesse, ich vergesse immer" (Zemlinsky) for each of the stanzas. Zemlinsky has emphasized another textual constituent of Tagore's poem, "O keen call of thy flute", which appears in the middle of all three stanzas, by bringing it back at the conclusion of the third.

Ich bin friedlos,	I am restless,
ich bin durstig von fernen Dingen.	I am athirst for far-away things.
Meine Seele schweift in Sehnsucht,	My soul goes out in a longing
den Saum der dunklen Weite zu berühren.	to touch the skirt of the dim distance.
O grosses Jenseits,	O Great Beyond,
o ungestümes Rufen deiner Flöte,	o keen call of thy flute!
Ich vergesse, ich vergesse immer,	I forget, I ever forget,
dass ich keine Schwingen zum Fliegen habe,	that I have no wings to fly,
dass ich an dieses Stück Erde	that I am bound in this spot evermore.
gefesselt bin für alle Zeit.	
Ich bin voll Verlangen und wachsam,	I am eager and wakeful,
ich bin ein Fremder im fremden Land—	I am a stranger in a strange land.
dein Odem kommt zu mir	Thy breath comes to me
und raunt mir unmögliche Hoffnungen zu.	whispering an impossible hope.
Diese Sprache klingt meinem Herze	Thy tongue is known to my heart
vertraut wie seine eig'ne.	as its very own.
O Ziel in Fernen,	O Far-to-seek,
o ungestümes Rufen deiner Flöte.	o the keen call of thy flute!
Ich vergesse, iche vergesse immer,	I forget, I ever forget,
dass ich nicht den Weg weiss,	that I know not the way,
dass ich das beschwingte Ross nicht habe.	that I have not the winged horse.
Ich bin ruh'los,	I am listless,
ich bin ein Wanderer in meinem Herzen.	I am a wanderer in my heart.
Im sonnigen Nebel der zögernden Stunden,	In the sunny haze of the languid hours,
welch gewaltiges Gesicht von dir	what vast vision of thine
wird Gestalt in der Bläue des Himmels.	takes shape in the blue of the sky!
O fernstes Ende,	O Farthest End,
o ungestümes Rufen deiner Flöte.	o the keen call of thy flute!
Ich vergesse, ich vergesse immer,	I forget, I ever forget,
dass die Türen überall verschlossen sind	that the gates are shut everywhere
in dem Hause wo ich einsam wohne,	in the house where I dwell alone!
o fernstes Ende,	(O Farthest End,
o ungestümes Rufen deiner Flöte.	o the keen call of thy flute!)

Movement 2. Mahler's jade dust strewn over delicate blossoms is mirrored by Zemlinsky's dust of rubies (a girl flings her necklace beneath the wheel's of a Prince's passing chariot).

Movement 3. The parallel in the third song is momentarily with Strauss: "Deine Lippen sind bittersüss vom Geschmack des Weins aus meinen Leide" recalls the closing lines of Salome's apostrophe to the head of John the Baptist: "Ich habe ihn geküsst deinen Mund, es war ein bitterer Geschmack auf deinen Lippen" (see p. 149). Furthermore, the music which Zemlinsky weds to these lines is thematically linkable with Strauss's musical setting to the opening lines of the same section at the text, "Ah, thou wouldst not suffer me to kiss thy mouth. Well! I will kiss it now. I will bite it with my teeth as one bites a ripe fruit." (See p. 147, motif no. 14).

There is a further reference to be found in this movement, not to Mahler or Strauss, but to Berg, whose *Lyric Suite* of 1926 took its title from Zemlinsky's work. Furthermore, there is a musical citation in Berg's fourth movement taken from the third movement of the present work, and the use of quotation marks in the score is accompanied by a foot-note citing its origins in Zemlinsky. The text at this pont in Zemlinsky's symphony is "Du bist mein Eigen, mein Eigen," but the fuller text, "I have caught you and wrapt you, my love, in the net of my music. You are my own, my own." carries a secret message and has recently been discovered to refer to a "faraway loved one," Hanna Fuchs, sister of Franz Werfel and Alma Mahler's sister-in-law, whom Berg had met in 1925 as he began to compose the *Lyric Suite*.

Example 16.1. Berg, *Lyric Suite*, Mvt. 4, mm. 46–50.

Du bist die Abendwolke,	You are the evening cloud
die am Himmel meiner Träume hinzieht.	floating in the sky of my dreams.
Ich schmücke dich und kleide dich immer	I paint you and fashion you ever
mit den Wünschen meiner Seele.	with my love longings.
Du bist mein Eigen, mein Eigen,	You are my own, my own,
Du, die in meinen endlosen Träumen wohnt.	Dweller in my endless dreams!
Deine Füsse sind rosigrot	Your feet are rosy-red
von der Glut meines sehnsüchtigen Herzens.	with the glow of my heart's desire,
Du, die meine Abendlieder erntet.	Gleaner of my sunset songs!
Deine Lippen sind bittersüss	Your lips are bitter-sweet
vom Geschmack des Weins aus meinen	with the taste of my wine of pain.
Leiden.	
Du bist mein Eigen, mein Eigen.	You are my own, my own,
Du, die in meinen einsamen Träumen wohnt.	Dweller in my lonesome dreams!
Mit dem Schatten meiner Leidenschaft	With the shadow of my passion
hab' ich deine Augen geschwärzt,	have I darkened your eyes,
gewohnter Gast in meines Blickes Tiefe	Haunter of the depth of my gaze!

Ich hab' dich gefangen und dich eingesponne,
  Geliebte,
in das Netz meiner Musik.
Du bist mein Eigen, mein Eigen.
Du, die in meinen unsterblichen Träumen
  wohnt.

I have caught you and wrapt you,
  my love,
in the net of my music.
You are my own, my own,
Dweller in my deathless dreams!

Movement 4. A freely dissonant vocal line arches over long pedals in a highly Expressionistic nocturne, a mood that is intensified in the sixth movement.

Movement 5. "Feurig und kraftvoll": The contrast between movements four and six encompasses once again a more Mahlerian vocabulary, including his march-like rhythms.

Movement 6. Zemlinsky's final two movements both mirror Mahler's conclusion (also a conflation of two poems) with their note of farewell. The eerie, disjunct vocal line of the sixth song, which in spite of underlying pedals courts atonality, is marked by orchestral punctuations carrying an enormous psychological impact. The soaring climax achieved by voice and orchestra with the final line is extraordinary and occupies the twilight zone between Mahlerian ectasy and the Bergian *Höhepunkt.*

Vollende denn das letzte Lied
und lass uns auseinander gehn;
vergiss diese Nacht, wenn die Nacht um ist.
Wen müh' ich mich mit meinen Armen zu
  umfassen?
Träume lassen sich nicht einfangen,
meine gierigen Hände drücken Leere an
  mein Herz
und es zermürbt meine Brust.

Then finish the last song
and let us leave.
Forget this night when the night is no more.
Whom do I try to clasp in my arms?

Dreams can never be made captive.
My eager hands press emptiness to
  my heart
and it bruises my breast.

Movement 7. The textual parallels with Mahler in the seventh song are obviously meant to be noted: Mahler's "Flowers grow pale in the twilight" (see p. 20) recalls Zemlinsky's gentle touch of the hands "like the flower of the night"; but especially Mahler's concluding "Still ist mein Herz und harret seiner Stunde" cannot fail to remind the listener of Zemlinsky's "Steh' still, steh' still, o wundervolles Ende."

Friede, mein Herz,
lass die Zeit, für das Scheiden süss sein,
lass es nicht einen Tod sein, sondern
  Vollendung.
Lass Liebe in Erinn'rung schmelzen
und Schmerz in Lieder.
Lass die letzte Berührung deiner Hände
  sanft sein,
wie die Blume der Nacht.
Steh' still, steh' still, o wundervolles
  Ende,
für einen Augenblick,
Und sage deine letzten Worte in Schweigen.
Ich neige mich vor dir,
ich halte meine Lampe in die Höhe,
um dir auf deinen Weg zu leuchten.

Peace, my heart,
let the time for the parting be sweet.
Let it not be a death but
  completeness.
Let love melt into memory
and pain into songs.
(Let the flight through the sky
end in the folding of the wings over the nest.)
Let the last touch of your hands be gentle
like the flower of the night.
Stand still, O Beautiful End,
for a moment,
and say your last words in silence.
I bow to you
and hold up my lamp
to light you on your way.

German translation by Hans Effenberger in Der Gärtner *(Leipzig: K. Wolff, 1914).*

Original text in Bengali. English translation adapted from Tagore in The Gardner *(London: Macmillan Press, 1913).*

Zemlinsky's choice of Rabindranath Tagore for his *Lyric Symphony* speaks no more and no less of orientalism than Mahler's *Das Lied von der Erde*, even as it alternately discourses on the intoxicating force of love and nature in a fashion that underscores the common ground of East and West and its fascination for both the nineteenth and twentieth centuries.

POSTHUMOUS REPUTATION

The musical language of the *Lyric Symphony*, which subscribed to Late Romantic values on the brink of Expressionism, may have been viewed in 1922 as moving decidedly against the current tides of Serialism, Neoclassicism or the New Simplicity. As Zemlinsky was a Viennese intimate of Schoenberg, Berg, and Webern, the issue must have been compounded. From another point of view it reminds us that not all music of the time endorsed one trend or the other, and that lingering Romantic values continued to play a vital role throughout the 1930s and 1940s in such substantial composers outside the avant-garde as Vaughan-Williams, Barber, Prokofiev, Bloch, Britten, Shostakovich, and Rachmaninov. Even Schoenberg's periodic returns to tonality in works such as the *Suite for String Orchestra* (1934) and the *Variations on a Recitative* for organ, op. 40 (1941), or his orchestral transcription of Brahms's *Piano Quartet* in G minor (1937) reveal a lingering and irrepressible Romanticism. Unfashionable as it may seem, through their example the New Romanticism of the 1970s and 1980s was undoubtedly more readily accomplished. That the reintroduction of Zemlinsky's works, the *Lyric Symphony* in particular, into the concert repertoire not only followed the Mahler revival in the 1950s and 1960s but coincided with the rising fashion in the 1970s of the music of Alban Berg, the most Romantic of the Viennese trinity, is already a matter of history. It also cautions writers of such histories to take the measure of their story from a broader range than the narrow edge of the avant-garde.

REPERTOIRE: Zemlinsky

Ehetanzlied und andere Gesänge (c. 1900), v, pf (Bierbaum, Morgenstern)
"Jane Grey" (1907), v, pf (also set by Schönberg)
Sechs Gesänge (1910–13), Mez/Bar, pf, orchestrated (Maeterlinck)
String Quartet No. 2 (1914)
Eine florentinische Tragödie (1915–16), opera (Wilde)
Der Zwerg (1920–21), opera (after Wilde's *The Birthday of the Infanta*)
Lyrische Symphonie (1923), S, Bar, orch (Tagore)
String Quartet No. 3 (1923)

READING

H.-L. de la Grange, *Mahler*, i (New York, 1973).
Alexander Ringer, "Schoenbergiana in Jerusalem," *Musical Quarterly*, lix (1973), 1.
Horst Weber, *Alexander Zemlinsky* (Vienna, 1977).
M. S. Cole, "*Afrika singt:* Austro-German Echoes of the Harlem Renaissance," *Journal of the American Musicological Society*, xxx (1977), 72.
George Perle, "The Secret Program of the *Lyric Suite*," *International Alban Berg Society Newsletter*, v (June 1977), 4.
R. Stephan, *Alexander Zemlinsky: ein unbekannter Meister der Wiener Schule* (Kiel and Vienna, 1978).

CHAPTER 17

BERG: *WOZZECK* AND THE *VIOLIN CONCERTO*

The importance of Mahler and Schoenberg in the formulation of Berg's youthful musical personality has already been detailed. It now remains to consider two works representative of his middle and late maturity, the opera *Wozzeck* (1917–22) and the *Violin Concerto* (1935), and to test their relation to contemporaneous musical developments.

WOZZECK

As early as 1914, Berg had seen the Viennese premiere of Büchner's *Woyzeck* (the original spelling), which had survived only in sketches at the dramatist's death in 1837. The advent of World War I, however, brought Berg into uniform for the next three years, and although he made some initial sketches on leave in 1917, he was not able to turn his attention seriously to the project until he was mustered out in 1918.

BÜCHNER AND THE *WUNDERHORN* TRADITION.   An opera whose story can be as readily summarized as *Wozzeck* by anyone who has seen or heard it would not appear to qualify as Expressionist. Compared with *Erwartung* it would seem to be the purist *verismo*, and indeed Marie can be correctly labeled as *Hausfrau* with the most elemental passions. No nameless Woman she. Her cradle song and reading from the Bible are scenes as touching as can be found in all opera; her stirrings in response to the seductions of the Drum Major are as full-blooded as Tosca's; and we identify with her plight on a highly personal level.

But there is another dimension to the story by George Büchner (1813–1837), which Berg transformed from its original twenty-five loosely connected episodes into a more coherently structured drama, and it is a dimension associated with the title figure, Wozzeck. While he asks us for our sympathy in a recurrent motif of lament ("Wir arme Leut"—"We poor people"; Ex. 17.1), we also sense from the first scene that he is a person who is deeply disturbed, a factor that is seized upon by the Doctor as he uses him as a guinea pig for his psychoanalytic experiments. Berg has highlighted the contrasting qualities of human reality and Expressionist unreality by layering his scenes in such a way as to create a fusion between the two. The first act, for example, would make a suitable story for a nineteenth-century opera in its scenes one, three, and five. Scenes two and

Example 17.1. Berg, *Wozzeck,* "Wir arme Leut!"

four, however, introduce visions, confusion, and hallucination. Berg's textual solution was as important to the final success of the work as the music, and the subtle balance of variable degrees of reality that informs the finely crafted libretto is matched by a similar sensitivity in the fluctuating choice of musical language.

A perusal of Georg Büchner's *Woyzeck* reveals that in tapping this work as a textual source, Berg had the ready-made ingredients for the incorporation of folksong. Scene after scene (including some not utilized by Berg) finds the various characters breaking into rhymed verse with the indication that it should be sung. In the Tavern Scene of *Wozzeck* immediately following Marie's murder, for example, Wozzeck begins:

Es ritten drei Reiter wohl an den Rhein	Three riders came riding up to the Rhine,
Bei einter Frau Wirtin da kehrten sie ein.	And went to my hostess to taste of her wine.

Example 17.2. Berg, *Wozzeck,* Act III, s. 3, mm. 145–6.

Not only does Berg's musical response (compare with Ex. 17.7) signal his awareness of the folk quality of its rhyme, but the imagery is clearly reminiscent of numerous texts that appear in the *Wunderhorn* anthology of 1804. The following examples taken from that collection argue that it was Büchner's intention that the allusion would be sensed.

Es ritten drei Reiter zum Tor hinaus
  or
Es waren drei Soldatensöhn
Sie haben Lust, in Krieg zu gehn
Frau Wirtin, hat sie die Gewalt,
Ein'n Reiter über Nacht aus zu behalten

The apprentices in Act II, scene 4 similarly intone a song that begins:

Ein Jäger aus der Pfalz	A hunter from the South
Ritt einst durch einen grünen Wald!	Was riding through a shady grove

which suggests the following *Wunderhorn* lyric:

Es ritt ein Jäger wohlgemut
Wohl in der Morgen stunde,
Wollt jagen in dem grünen Wald
Mit seinem Ross und Hunde

The ritual of children's games ("Ringel, ringel, Rosenkranz"), so poignantly introduced at the finale of the opera, is actually a transposition of a lyric in Büchner's original sung by an old woman to the play of children as Marie watches on. Its relation to the *Ringelreihe-lied* of the *Wunderhorn* collection is inescapable, just as Marie's lullaby "Eia popeia" has numerous counterparts in the same anthology (*Eia popeia et cetera, Wiegenlied,* and *Walte Gott Vater* in particular).

It has been noted by Büchner scholars that in none of his other works does the folksong predominate to such an extent: A total of thirteen different songs appear in the series of fragments that occupy only twenty-five pages in a standard German edition. And it has also been remarked that no play before *Woyzeck* employs them so profusely.

Berg's musical response to these and other similar folk song texts is telling. While for the most part he appears not to be quoting melodies that had originally been associated with the folk texts in question (a procedure occasionally endorsed by Mahler in his setting of *Wunderhorn* lyrics), he nevertheless adopts the manner of folk melody with respect to phraseology and melodic interval. That this was consciously done can be determined from an article of 1929 wherein Berg himself related how he

> coped with the necessity of including music of a 'folky' and singable character, i.e. with the necessity to establish an appreciable relationship between art-music and folk-music in this opera—a matter of course in a tonally conceived work. It was by no means easy to express their differentiation of levels in so-called atonal harmony. I believe I have succeeded by composing all sections requiring that atmosphere of *Volkstümlichkeit* in a primitive manner ... That particular manner favours a symmetrical arrangement of periods and sections, it utilizes harmonies in thirds and especially in fourths and a type of melody in which whole-tone scales and perfect fourths play an integral part, in contrast with the diminished and augmented intervals which usually dominate the atonal music of the 'Vienna School'. Also the so-called polytonality may be counted among the devices of a more primitive brand of harmony. We find a popular element in them in the Military March (with its intentionally 'wrong basses") [Ex. 17.5] and in Marie's Lullaby (with its harmonies in fourths) [Ex. 17.7].[1]

Berg's assurance of distinct levels of musical speech can readily be perceived by the listener. In Act 1, scene 2, the designation of the scene as a Rhapsody should be amplified to indicate an alternating structure between the Rhapsody proper and the accumulating strophes of a hunting song—the former associated with Wozzeck's hallucinations and identified by a three-chord progression (frequently limited to the first two; Ex. 17.3), the latter (Ex. 17.4) wedded to interval (fourth) and metrics (duple compound), which reappear in a similar context in the next scene (see Ex. 17.7).

Example 17.3. Berg, *Wozzeck*, Act I, s. 2, "Rhapsody" chords.

Example 17.4. Berg, *Wozzeck*, Act I, s. 2, mm. 212–14.

Zweite Szene: Rhapsody (Andres)   Scene Two

(Freies Feld, die Stadt in der Ferne. Spätnachmittag. Wozzeck und Andres schneiden Stöcke im Gebüsch.)

(An open field outside the town. Late afternoon. Wozzeck and Andres are cutting sticks in the bushes.)

WOZZECK (Rhapsody)

Du, der Platz ist verflucht!

WOZZECK

Hey! This place is accursed.

ANDRES ("Hunting Song," strophe 1)

Ach was! (singt vor sich hin)

Das ist die schöne Jägerei,
Schiessen steht Jedem frei!
Da möcht ich Jäger sein,
Da möcht ich hin.

ANDRES

How now! *(sings)*

The huntsman's life is gay and free,
Shooting is free for all!
There would I huntsman be,
There would I be.

WOZZECK (Rhapsody)

Der Platz ist verflucht! Siehst Du den lichten Streif da über das Gras hin, wo die Schwämme so nachwachsen? Da rollt Abends ein Kopf. Hob ihn einmal Einer auf, meint', es wär' ein Igel. Drei Tage und drei Nächte drauf, und er lag auf den Hobelspänen.

WOZZECK

This place is accursed! See how the mist is floating above the grass there, where the toadstools are springing up. There rolls at dusk a head! Once a man did lift it up, thought it was a hedgehog. Three days and three nights then, and he lay in his wooden coffin.

ANDRES ("Hunting Song," strophe 2)

Es wird finster, das macht Dir angst. Ei was! *(hört mit der Arbeit auf, stellt sich in Positur und singt)*

Läuft dort ein Has vorbei,
Fragt mich, ob ich Jäger sei?
Jäger bin ich auch schon gewesen,
Schiessen kann ich aber nit!

ANDRES

It gets darker. You are afraid. How now! *(He stops working, strikes a stance and sings)*

Runs there a hare so free,
Asks me if I huntsman be?
Huntsman have I long since been,
Try to shoot it, I can not!

WOZZECK (Rhapsody and "Hunting Song," strophe 3)

WOZZECK

Still, Andres! Das waren die Freimaurer! Ich hab's! Die Freimaurer! Still! Still!

ANDRES

Sassen dort zwei Hasen,
Frassen ab das grüne Gras.

(unterbricht den Gesang. Beide lauschen angestrengt. Dann selbst etwas beunruhigt; wie um Wozzeck und sich zu beruhigen)

Sing lieber mit!
Frassen ab das grüne Gras
Bis auf den Rasen . . .

WOZZECK (Rhapsody)

(stampft auf) Hohl! Alles hohl! Ein Schlund! Es schwankt! *(er taumelt)* Hörst Du, es wandert was mit uns da unten! *(in höchster Angst)* Fort, fort!

ANDRES

(hält Wozzeck zurück) He, bist Du toll?

Still, Andres, that must be the Freemasons! That's it! The Freemasons! Still! Still!

ANDRES

Two fat hares were sitting,
Eating off the greeny grass.

(Stops singing, himself rather uneasy. Then, in order to calm down Wozzeck and himself)

Sing it with me! . . .
Eating off the greeny grass,
Down to the roots . . .

WOZZECK

(stamping on the ground) Hollow, all quite hollow! A gulf! It quakes! *(he staggers)* Listen, there's something moving with us down there. *(in mounting fear)* Away!

ANDRES

(holding Wozzeck back) Hey! Are you mad?

In the following scene (Act 1, scene 3), a Military March with Trio and Da Capo is signaled not only by its march rhythms but by a "Quasi-Trio" directly relatable to the folk song idea in general and of the *Wunderhorn* collection in particular. Following a harangue with Margret at the sound of the approaching band, Marie breaks into a lusty phrase as the military parade passes beneath her window:

Soldaten, soldaten, sind schöne Burschen!

The soldiers, the soldiers are splendid fellows!

Redlich was the first to note the similarity between Marie's opening phrase (Ex. 17.5) and that of the third strophe of Mahler's *Revelge* (Ex. 17.6) but failed to sug-

Example 17.5. Berg, *Wozzeck*, Act I, s. 3, mm. 346–50.

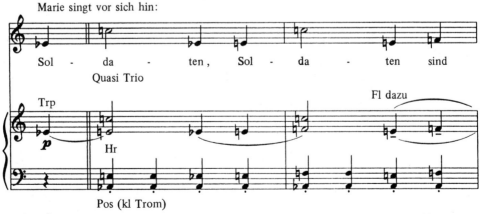

Example 17.5 (Continued)

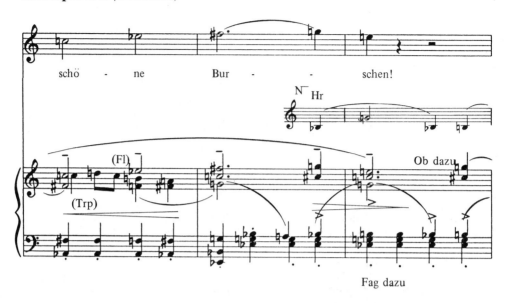

gest the appropriateness of the quotation. The text of *Revelge* (see p. 8) similarly speaks of a soldier marching along the road with his troops gradually approaching the window of his beloved. The allusion to the *Wunderhorn* text through Mahler's music is thus not only poignant but musically symbolic. The comparison is to be drawn not only between the dramatic context and melodic head-motif but in the military march music that precedes it and continues as an accompaniment. The beginning of the Da Capo of the march is cut short with the slamming of the window and Marie's turn to her child. The remainder of the scene is given over to another formalization, a two-strophe Cradle Song (Ex. 17.7), whose inten-

Example 17.6. Mahler, *Des Knaben Wunderhorn:* "Revelge," 8 mm. from third stanza.

Example 17.6 (Continued)

Example 17.7. Berg, *Wozzeck*, Act I, s. 3, mm. 372–5.

Example 17.7 (Continued)

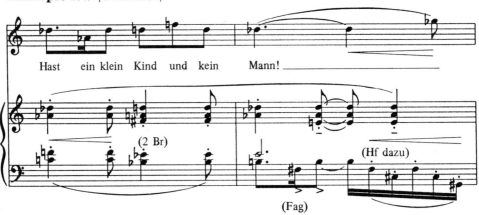

tional folk character was noted by Berg, followed by a concluding through-composed episode at the entrance of Wozzeck lacking in any such orientation. While the folk element in Büchner's drama and in Berg's response to it are important ingredients to stress in coming to terms with the opera, it would be a mistake to imply that its total message can be understood within the context of the *Wunderhorn* folk tradition. There are ingredients in Büchner's play that are rightly labeled as proto-Expressionist in character frequently tinged by attendant intellectualizations, ingredients of which Berg was equally aware and for which he also found a musical counterpart. It is the mixture of these two qualities that provides much of the fascination for the work.

Dritte Szene: Military March & Cradle Song

(Mariens Stube. Abends. Die Militärmusik nähert sich. Marie mit ihrem Kinde am Arm beim Fenster.)

MARIE (Military March)

Tschin Bum, Tschin Bum, Bum, Bum, Bum! Hörst Bub? Da kommen sie! *(Die Militärmusik, mit dem Tambourmajor an der Spitze, gelangt in die Strasse vor Mariens Fenster.)*

MARGRET

(auf der Strasse, sieht zum Fenster herein und spricht mit Marie) Was, ein Mann! Wie ein Baum!

MARIE

(spricht zum Fenster hinaus) Er steht auf seinen Füssen wie ein Löw'. *(Der Tambourmajor grüsst herein. Marie winkt freundlich hinaus.)*

Scene Three

(Marie's room. Evening. The military band approaches. Marie stands with her child in her arms at the window.)

MARIE

Chin, boom, chin, boom, boom, boom, boom. Do you hear, boy? They're coming now! *(The band, headed by the Drum Major, comes into the street before Marie's window.)*

MARGRET

(peers into the window and says to Marie) What a man! Like a tree!

MARIE

(through the window to Margret) He stands on his feet like a lion. *(The Drum Major greets Marie, who waves to him.)*

MARGRET

Ei was freundliche Augen, Frau Nachbarin! So was is man an ihr nit gewohnt!

MARIE (Quasi-Trio)

(singt vor sich hin)
Soldaten, Soldaten
sind schöne Burschen!

MARGRET

Ihre Augen glänzen ja!

MARIE

Und wenn! Was geht Sie's an? Trag' Sie ihre Augen zum luden und lass Sie sie putzen: vielleicht glänzen sie auch noch, dass man sie für zwei Knöpf' verkaufen könnt'.

MARGRET

Was Sie, Sie "Frau Jungfer"! Ich bin eine honette Person, aber Sie, das weiss jeder, Sie guckt sieben Paar lederne Hosen durch!

MARIE (Da Capo, beginning; Introduction to "Cradle Song")

(schreit sie an) Luder! *(schlägt das Fenster zu. Die Militärmusik ist plötzlich, als Folge des zugeschlagenen Fensters, unhörbar geworden. Marie ist allein mit dem Kind.)* Komm, mein Bub! Was die Leute wollen! Bist nur ein arm' Hurenkind und machst Deiner Mutter doch so viel Freud' mit Deinem unehrlichen Gesicht! *(wiegt das Kind)*

Eia popeia . . .

("Cradle Song," strophe 1)

Mädel, was fangst Du jetzt an?
Hast ein klein Kind und kein Mann!
Ei, was frag' ich darnach,
Sing' ich die ganze Nacht:
Eia popeia, mein süsser Bu',
Gibt mir kein Mensch nix dazu!

("Cradle Song," strophe 2)

Hansel, spann' Deine sechs Schimmel an,
Gib sie zu fressen auf's neu,
Kein Haber fresse sie,
Kein Wasser saufe sie,
Lauter kühle Wein muss es sein!

(Das Kind ist eingeschlafen.)

Lauter kühle Wein muss es sein!

MARGRET

Oho! What friendly glances, neighbour! We're not used to that from you.

MARIE

(singing to herself)
The soldiers, the soldiers
are splendid fellows!

MARGRET

Your eyes are sparkling!

MARIE

What if they are? What's that to do with you? Take your eyes to the Jew and have them polished; perhaps they'll be bright enough for two buttons.

MARGRET

How dare you, you "madam!" I'm an honest woman, but everyone knows that you can't keep your eyes off any man.

MARIE

(shouting at her) Hussy!! *(She slams the window, the band is no longer heard, Marie is alone with her child.)* Come, my child. We shan't hear their slanders. You are just an innocent and give to your mother so pure a joy, although no priest blessed your little face. *(She rocks the child.)*

Hush-a-bye, baby . . .

Maiden, what song shall you sing?
You have a child, but no ring.
Why such sorrow pursue?
Singing the whole night through:
Hush-a-bye, baby, my darling son,
nobody cares, ne'er a one.

Jackie, go saddle your horses now,
Give them to eat and to spare,
No oats to eat today,
No water to drink today,
Purest, coolest wine shall it be . . .

(She notices that the child is asleep.)

Purest, coolest wine shall it be!

FORMAL ISSUES. The conventional foundations on which Berg based his musical language, their relation to the world of Mahler, and their potential for development have been discussed in an earlier section (Chapter 4). The retention at this point in his career of a Wagnerian system of leitmotifs, therefore, should come as no surprise, even as the formal construction of sonatas and passacaglias must be viewed as a decidedly modish gesture totally in harmony with the compulsion for formal clarification that marked so much music of the 1920s.

As early as August, 1918, Berg indicated in a letter to Webern that he had already begun to sense the ultimate structural plan for his opera:

> It is not only the fate of this poor man, exploited and tormented by *all the world,* that touches me so closely, but also the unheard-of intensity of mood of the individual scenes. The combining of four or five scenes into *one* act through orchestral interludes tempts me also, of course. (You find something similar in the *Pelleas* of Maeterlinck-Debussy!) I have also given thought to a great variety of musical forms to correspond to the diversity in the character of the individual scenes. For example, normal operatic scenes with thematic development, then others *without* any thematic material, in the manner of *Erwartung* (understand me rightly: this is a question of forms, not of the imitation of a style!), song forms, variations, etc.[2]

Willi Reich, Berg's biographer, has supplied a much-quoted diagram that illustrates the composer's formal responses to the three acts and fifteen scenes:[3]

DRAMATIC	MUSICAL
	ACT I
Exposition	
Wozzeck and his relation to his environment.	Five Character Sketches.
Scene	Scene
1. The Captain	1. Suite
2. Andres	2. Rhapsody
3. Marie	3. Military March and Cradle Song
4. The Physician	4. Passacaglia
5. The Drum Major	5. Andante affetuoso (quasi Rondo)
	ACT II
Denouement	
Wozzeck is gradually convinced of Marie's infidelity.	Symphony in five movements.
Scene	Scene
1. Wozzeck's first suspicion	1. Sonata form
2. Wozzeck is mocked	2. Fantasie and Fugue
3. Wozzeck accuses Marie	3. Largo
4. Marie and Drum Major dance	4. Scherzo
5. The Drum Major trounces Wozzeck	5. Rondo marziale

ACT III

Catastrophe

Wozzeck murders Marie and atones through suicide.	Six Inventions
Scene	Scene
1. Marie's remorse	1. Invention on a Theme
2. Death of Marie	2. Invention on a Tone
3. Wozzeck tries to forget	3. Invention on a Rhythm
4. Wozzeck drowns in the pond (Instrumental interlude with closed curtain)	4. Invention on a 6-note chord (Invention on a Key)
5. Marie's son plays unconcerned	5. Invention on a Persistent Rhythm (Perpetuum mobile)

Berg encouraged the listener to forget all about such constructions, and it cannot be denied that for the novice as well as for the connoisseur there is little point in trying to hear the component parts of the Suite that make up Act I, scene 1: Prelude, Pavane, (Cadenza for viola), Gigue, (Cadenza for bassoon), Gavotte (with two Doubles), Air, and Reprise. Indeed, while the seriousness of the topic at hand (Captain: "It makes me afraid for the world to think of eternity.") may be held as complementary to the historical traditions of the designated Pavane, any attempt to relate it aurally to its expected metrics (2/2 with upbeat) will fall as short as expectations for the appearance of compound metrics in the Gigue (though once again the more light-hearted nature of the Gigue seems to mirror in a general way the action of the moment wherein the Captain discourses about the wind that always seems to him like a mouse, now blowing from the South-North). If the general relation of mood to chosen dance designation seems to imply a reasonable if loose analogy, the idea of using Baroque titles in the first place can only be judged against the emerging Neoclassicism of the 1920s and the immediately preceding example of pieces like Ravel's *Le tombeau de Couperin* (1914–17). It is of more than passing interest that Berg's music for Act I was already complete by 1919, well before Schoenberg's first excursion into the realm of Baroque dance designations in his *Suite for Piano*, op. 25 (1921–23).

More in keeping with a fundamental Bergian perspective is the choice of a sonata design for Act II, scene 1. Here, the inherent dialectic and latent drama of the sonata is chosen for its approximation to dramatic values that articulate the scene as follows:

Introduction (mm. 1–6) (Curtain down): alternating chords recall end of Act I. C established as pitch center.

Exposition	1st Reprise	Development	2nd Reprise (Recap.)
Main Theme	Main Theme	Main Theme and Closing Theme	Main Theme
(mm. 6/7–28) Marie alone; admires earrings given to her by Drum Major	(mm. 59/60–80) Marie alone; compares herself with rich people; admires earrings	(mm. 96–108) Marie and Wozzeck; argument over jewelry	(mm. 127/8–150) Marie alone; despairs that man, woman and child all go to the devil; (C major glissando down; Curtain down)
Transition (mm. 28–9: V–vi cadence in C) (mm. 29–42) Marie tells child to close its eyes; hint of threat	Transition (mm. 81–9) Marie orders baby to close its eyes	Transition (mm. 108–45) Wozzeck alone; concern for child: "Wir arme Leut!" climaxes on twelve-note chord	Interlude: Thematic reprise
2nd Theme (mm. 43–52) Marie's gypsy song further frightens child (music derived from Act I, scene 3)	2nd Theme (mm. 90–2) Marie threatens child with blindness	No development of 2nd Theme	Main Theme and 2nd Theme
Closing Theme (mm. 53–9) Child's fear conjures Wozzeck's music (whole tone melody in sixteenths)	Closing Theme (mm. 93–6) Wozzeck's entrance (whole tone music in eighth notes)	Recitative (mm. 116–127) Wozzeck gives Marie his earrings (C major triad held, mm. 116–124)	Closing Theme (mm. 162–170) Long silence (166–9) (Curtain up: C major glissando up)

The deployment of the sonata idea in programmatic or texted surroundings is something to which Berg fell natural heir through the tone poems of Strauss and Schoenberg as well as the symphonies of Mahler. Its continuing appeal in later works such as *Der Wein* and his final opera *Lulu* is worthy of note.

A less difficult premise underlies the six inventions of the final act, especially in scenes two and three where the underlying pedal and rhythm respectively are clearly audible even to first-time listeners. Scene two, an invention on the tone "B", seeds a mounting tension over this pedal note that leads to Wozzeck's murder of Marie. Following a "Todeschrei" that looks back to *Erwartung* ("Hilfe"; Ex. 10.2) and ahead to *Lulu*, the orchestra mounts a twice-stated crescendo on this pitch, which is interrupted by a proclamation of the rhythm of the next scene on the tympani. The application of this "Death Rhythm" (see pp. 58–59) as a foundation for the entire ensuing scene is a masterstroke, especially as its initial appearance is associated with the sounds of a tavern piano (Ex. 14.8) and the strains of a folk song creating a decidedly frivolous surface mood. That the ominous consequences of Wozzeck's deeds cannot be washed away by wine, however, is quickly made clear as the polyphony of speeds to which the pattern is subjected leads to Margret's discovery of blood on Wozzeck and his ultimate departure in search of the murder weapon he has thrown into a pond.

Zweite Szene: Invention on a Tone

Marie

Was zitterst? *(spring auf)* Was willst?

Wozzeck

Ich nicht. Marie! Und kein Andrer auch nicht! *(packt sie an und stosst ihr das Messer in den Hals)*

Marie

Hilfe! *(sinkt nieder. Wozzeck beugt sich über sie. Marie stirbt.)*

Wozzeck

Tot! *(richtet sich scheu auf und stürzt geräuschlos davon)*

Dritte Szene: Invention on a Rhythm

(Eine Schenke. Nacht. Schwaches Licht. Dirnen, unter ihnen Margret, und Burschen tanzen eine wilde Schnellpolka. Wozzeck sitzt an einem der Tische.)

Wozzeck (Polka)

Tanzt Alle: tanzt nur zu, springt, schwitzt und stinkt, es holt Euch doch noch einmal der Teufel! *(stürzt ein Glas Wein hinunter; den Klavierspieler überschreiend)*

Scene Two (Conclusion)

Marie

You shiver? *(She jumps up)* What now?

Wozzeck

No one, Marie! If not me, then no one! *(He seizes her and plunges the knife into her throat.)*

Marie

Help! *(She sinks down. Wozzeck bends over her. She dies.)*

Wozzeck

Dead! *(He rises to his feet anxiously, and then rushes silently away.)*

Scene Three (Beginning)

(A tavern. Night. Badly lit. Girls, among them Margret, and apprentices are dancing a wild and rapid polka. Wozzeck is seated at one of the tables.)

Wozzeck

Dance, all you, dance away! Leap, sweat and reek. For some day he'll fetch you, the Devil! *(Dashes down his glass; then, shouting down the pianist)*

(Song)

Es ritten drei Reiter wohl an den Rhein,	Three riders came riding up to the Rhine,
Bei einer Frau Wirtin da kehrten sie ein.	And went to my hostess to taste of her wine.
Mein Wein ist gut, mein Bier ist klar,	My wine is good, my beer is clear,
Mein Töchterlein liegt auf der . . .	My daughter dear lies on her . . .

Verdammt! *(springt auf)* Komm, Margret! *(tanzt mit Margret ein paar Sprunge. Bleibt plötzlich stehen)* Komm, setz Dich her. Margret! *(fuhrt sie an seinen Tisch und zieht sie auf seinen Schoss nieder)* Margret, Du bist so heiss *(drückt sie an sich: lässt sie los)* Wart nur, wirst auch kalt werden! Kannst nicht singen?

Be damned! *(jumps up)* Come, Margret. *(Dances a few steps with her, then suddenly stops)* Come, let's sit down, Margret. *(leads Margret to his table, and pulls her onto his lap)* Margret, you're hot as fire. *(Presses her to him; lets her go)* But wait till you're cold also! Can't you sing, girl?

Margret

Margret

(vom Klavierspieler auf der Bühne begleitet, singt)

(the little out-of-tune piano accompanying her)

(Song)

In's Schwabenland, da mag ich nit,	To Swabia I will not go,
Und lange Kleider trag ich nit,	And your long dresses I'll not wear,
Denn lange Kleider, spitze Schuh,	For trailing dresses, pointed shoes,
Die kommen keiner Dienstmagd zu.	Do not belong to servant girls.

Wozzeck

Wozzeck

(auffahrend) (Nein! keine Schuh, man kann auch blossfüssig in die Holl' geh'n! Ich möcht heut raufen, raufen . . .

(flaming up) No! Wear no shoes! For one can barefooted go to hell-fire. I want to wrestle, wrestle . . .

Unsuccessful in his attempt to retrieve the knife, Wozzeck drowns to the chilling cry "Das Wasser is blut" ("The water is blood") and the sound of chromatically rising bubbles, which are patently inspired by the closing measures of Schoenberg's *Erwartung*. The orchestral interlude that follows serves not only as a transition to the final scene but also as a symbolic statement of the entire drama as musical materials are recalled in a compelling summation. The climax on a shattering twelve-note chord (a device later to be resurrected at an analogous point in *Lulu*) is followed by a series of V-I patterns in D minor that appear

Example 17.8. Berg, *Wozzeck*, Act III, mm. 362–5.

to proclaim not so much the securing of a tonality as a resolution of the central themes of the opera.

In the final scene the now parentless child rides his hobby-horse. A singing game of ring-around-the rosey ("Ringel, Ringel Rosenkranz") by children playing nearby is interrupted by news that everyone has gone to the pond. In their rush to join the crowd one of them taunts Marie's child with the hurtful "You! Your mother is dead." ("Du! Dein Mutter ist tot.") Guileless and unfathoming he continues to ride, "Hop, hop. Hop, hop," before finally deciding to follow them. Ultimately, even as the listener may occasionally be aware of numerous fascinating structural details, every gesture is seen to feed the drama that sweeps us inexorably to the final curtain.

Berg's observation of the similarities to *Pelléas* should not go unnoticed, even as his more individualized and integrated solution should be emphasized. While the separate scenes are formally self-contained, the oscillating chords that close the end of Act I reappear at the opening of Act II and provide the final sonority at the end of Act III. Similarly, the recall of motifs associated with Marie's cradle song of Act I, scene 3, in these final moments marked by the innocence and incomprehension of children, and the return of brightness of morning that opened Act I, scene 1, suggest a master craftsman at work.

Because of such a network of formal reference points, Berg's system of leitmotifs assumes a much less heavy burden. They are, however, projected with an unusual clarity and underscore the melodic, rhythmic, and harmonic style of more abstract formulations throughout the opera. Thus, the b-f dyad that many analysts have seen to rest at the foundation of the opera can be spotted in several motifs (Exs. 17.9–11) and in important cadential figures that close the several acts, just as common harmonic formations are shared by others. The extent of this extraordinary integration has recently been explored by numerous authors (see especially Perle, Hyde, Schmalfeldt, and Jarman in the Reading List at the end of the chapter), who have extracted not so much a method from a study of the score as the profile of a composer whose technique instinctively promoted solutions with a compelling logic and a dramatic potential.

Example 17.9. Berg, *Wozzeck*, "Fanfare" leitmotif[4]

Example 17.10. Berg, *Wozzeck*, "Military March" leitmotif

Example 17.11. Berg, *Wozzeck*, "Marie's Aimless Waiting" leitmotif

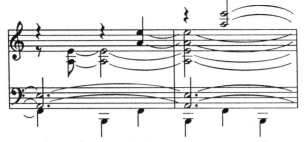

Thus to a Wagnerian system of leitmotifs Berg wedded a symbolic use of rhythm and a bifocal view of melody and harmony indebted to his idol Gustav Mahler. But the loosening of tonality and metrics; the extension of the means of vocal expression, such as *Sprechstimme* or Marie's two-octave downward leap on the word "Hilfe" at the moment of her death; and a timbral palette that includes the use of a chamber orchestra identical in makeup to Schoenberg's *Kammersymphonie*, op. 9 (and so advertised in the score), all point to the work of his mentor as a final model for his own private vision. *Wozzeck* thus reflects a composite set of influences, yet stands as one of the most individual works of the modern theater. The continuing success that followed the Berlin premiere of Berg's *Wozzeck* in 1923 is unmatched by any contemporary opera, but the blend of such disparate elements fails to explain the source of the appeal. The answer must lie in the fact that the magic is not in the formula but in a grand intuition and a dramatic instinct that is given to few composers.

THE VIOLIN CONCERTO

FORM, SERIES, AND QUOTATION   Berg's last completed work was a *Violin Concerto* (1935) laid out in two parts, each with two movements played without pause.[5]

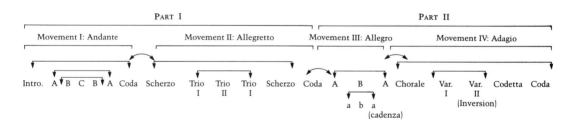

The various internal symmetries suggested by the arrows also extend to the presentation of a Carinthian folk tune in the second and fourth movement Codas, the sharing of material in movements two and three, and the presentation of the music of mm. 1–2 in the final two bars of the work. Such arch structures are omnipresent in virtually all the mature works of Berg and elsewhere typically include palindromic movement as well.

Recalling his juxtaposition of atonal materials with overtly folk inspired melodies in *Wozzeck,* Berg here alternately employs the folk tune and chorale with the resources of a twelve-note series, albeit one with strong triadic implications. The solo violin may be heard at the beginning of the concerto intoning arpeggiations based on the following pitch successions of the row (Ex. 17.12): 1-3-5-7; 2-4-6-8; 3-5-7-9; 11-10-1-12. This in turn leads to an ascending melodic announcement of the entire series played by the solo violin that is immediately complemented by a descending statement of the inversion.

Example 17.12. Berg, Prime set of the *Violin Concerto.*

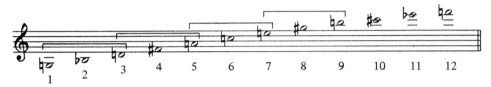

That the work, for all its purely instrumental character, is another "latent drama" like the *Lyric Suite* (see p. 354), has been widely discussed. Here, however, Berg seemingly sought to clarify his intensions through his pupil Willi Reich, and to lay the mystery to rest in advance. The dedication "to the memory of an angel" refers to Manon Gropius, daughter of Alma Mahler, and close friend of the Bergs who had died at the age of eighteen. In this light, the quotation of the funeral chorale "Es ist genug" as the theme for a set of variations is not only appropriate but openly perceivable to the listener. In its initial statement as a theme, the paired phraseological structure of the original chorale (ABC/ABC, D/D, E/E) is highlighted through alternating presentations of the melody by the solo violin answered by woodwinds that preserve the essence of Bach's harmonization.

Example 17.13. J.S. Bach, Harmonization of chorale, *Es ist genug so nimm, Herr.*

Es ist genug; so nimm, Herr

Example 17.13 (Continued)

Beyond this, however, there is an additional quotation of a Carinthian folksong that has only recently been identified and discussed with respect to its potentially hidden message. As background to a consideration of this issue it is necessary to recall that, like Mahler, the writing of abstract instrumental pieces always caused Berg some indecision, and not until a context closely linked to a human situation was fixed could he see his way clearly to its completion.

We have the evidence not only of the early *Orchestra Pieces* and the later *Lyric Suite* to back this contention but also Berg's only other concerto, the *Chamber Concerto* for violin, piano, and thirteen instruments. In the latter work, the choice of fifteen solo instruments parallels the number used by Schoenberg in his *Chamber Symphony*, op. 9. In addition, he begins the work with three musical motifs that link the names Alban Berg, Anton Webern, and Arnold Schoenberg in a fashion literal enough to have pleased his German ancestors from Bach to Schumann (Ex. 17.4).

Berg had accepted the commission for the *Violin Concerto* from Louis Krasner somewhat reluctantly (as he was busily involved with *Lulu*), and it was only after he had begun work on it that the death of Manon Gropius sparked the sense of urgency so vital to all of Berg's creative endeavors. While the symbolic intent of the chorale is clear, the symbol is universal as opposed to personal—similar in nature to the introduction of the *Dies irae* in numerous works of the nineteenth century. It also provides the note of resolution to the drama and carries with it the quality of redemption or resurrection analogous to Mahler's choice of an ode to close his *Second Symphony.*

THE SECRET PROGRAM.   The significance of the Carinthian folk tune, which occurs in the coda to Parts I and II, has only recently been made clear, however.[6] The first movement opens with a Prelude and is followed by a Scherzo with two

Example 17.14. Berg, *Chamber Concerto* for vn, pf, and thirteen wind instr., opening motto theme (five measures).

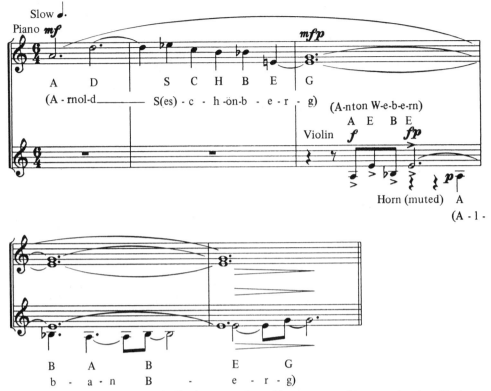

Trios, which Reich informs us is intended to portray the youthful spirit of the young girl. In the service of painting such a portrait, Berg introduces three ideas at the opening of the Scherzo described as *scherzando, wienerisch,* and *rustico.* The Viennese section emphasizes the thirds and leaps of a Strauss waltz, while the "rustic" section contains yodeling figures. In the second trio, Berg underscores the folk character of the music by the introduction of regular two- and four-bar phrases that prepare the introduction of a Carinthian folktune. Until 1976, however, this tune had never been identified, nor its text retrieved. In that year, a one-page article by Herwig Knaus appeared in *The Musical Times* that discussed the origins of the melody. While Berg had labeled the tune "Kärtner Volksweise," Redlich had suggested in 1957 that it was a "stylized yodler" and attempted to derive the melody from transpositions of the "wienerisch" material that preceded it. Knaus, after systematic sifting through early and modern song collections, located the tune in a volume entitled *Wulfenia-Blüten,* a collection by Karl Liebleitner, printed in 1892, and noted that Berg's tune (Ex. 17.16) was a literal reproduction, except for key and speed, of the song "A Vögele af'n Zweschpm-bam" (Ex. 17.15): It will be noted that the secondary melody (or *Übersingen*) classifies the tune, as Redlich suspected,[7] as a yodler, and Berg

Example 17.15. "A Vögele af'n Zweschpm-bam."

A Ve - ga-le af'n Zwesch_pm_bam hat me auf - gweckt,

tri - di - e, tri - di - e i - ri tu - li - e! sist

hiatt i ver - schla - fn in der Miaza - le ihrn Bett,

tri - di - e, ri tu - li - - e_____!

Example 17.16. Alban Berg, *Violin Concerto*, 14 mm. quoting "A Vögele af'n Zweschpm-bam."

retains the upper part in the solo violin exactly as it appears in Liebleitner's collection. The following text accompanies the melody:

A bird on the plumtree has wakened me,
Tridie, tridie, iri, tulilei!
Otherwise I would have overslept in Mizzi's bed
Tridie, etc.

If everybody wants a rich and handsome girl
Tridie, etc.
Where ought the devil take the ugly one?
Tridie, etc.

The girl is Catholic and I am a Protestant
Tridie, etc.
She surely will put away the rosary in bed,
Tridie, etc.

Knaus was somewhat nonplussed by the text, which he bypassed without interpretation, stating that "Berg chose his song, despite its somewhat risqué text, from the musical treasures of his second motherland, Carinthia."[8]

Indeed, on the surface the text appears to be something of an embarrassment in the context of the work. But it is difficult to believe, in light of what we have seen of Berg's predisposition elsewhere, that he chose the tune indiscriminately or without regard to the textual message. That he may have relied on the fact that the message would remain secret is in keeping with what we now know of the *Lyric Suite* and his claims for the *Chamber Concerto*. Once again, available biographical information suggests an answer.

In September 1903, when he was eighteen (the same age as Manon Gropius when she died), Berg attempted suicide—largely, it was thought, because he was distraught at having done poorly in his exams the preceding year and now faced with the prospect of spending an extra year in school. It has recently been revealed, however, that there was more to the source of suffering than academic failure.[9] In the immediately preceding summer, Berg fathered an illegitimate daughter, the result of a liason with a girl in Carinthia, the area in which he traditionally spent his summer vacations. Contrary to the repressed sexuality so vividly portrayed by Klimt and Kokoschka of middle- and upper-class Viennese woman who were expected to maintain their innocence until married, the Viennese young man typically exploited lower-class working women generically referred to as *süsse Mädel* ("sweet young things"). The interest of Adolf Loos, Peter Altenberg, and Egon Schiele in adolescent girls reflects an ongoing fascination with the stimulations of innocence earlier addressed by Wedekind in *Spring's Awakening* and with unequal relationships outside social convention.[10]

Thus, though Berg's behavior was in conformity with a person of his age, time, place, and station, his sense of remorse in later years at the "loss" of a daughter whom he could not claim is undoubtedly reflected in the quotation of the Carinthian folk tune. Not only his status as an eighteen-year-old struggling to finish the Gymnasium but also perhaps religious differences, alluded to in the final strophe of the text, contributed to the impossibility of the situation. A secondary interpretation may be placed alongside this theory, however: The girl's name in the song is Mizzi, which was not only the nickname for Berg's Carinthian girlfriend but also virtually identical to the one he used in addressing Manon ("Mutzi") Gropius. She, too, had been deprived of a father when Alma Mahler left the architect, Walter Gropius, shortly after Manon's birth. They had been married in August, 1915; Manon had been born in 1916. But in August 1918 we find Alma Mahler being tended by Helene Berg after the birth of a son by the playwright, Franz Werfel. The liason with Gropius was, thus, extremely brief, and Manon never really knew her father. Berg, who adored the little girl from childhood, may in such circumstances have felt an unusual degree of compensation in befriending the child, and consequently felt a heightened sense of loss at her passing.

Furthermore, the text of the second stanza of the Carinthian melody strikes at another bit of biographical evidence. Manon's mother Alma was reportedly one of the most beautiful women in Vienna, and to judge from the list of men who pursued her, her charm must have been extraordinary. That she was indeed fixated on the question of her own beauty is proven by innumerable comments, including her own. While she had children by Mahler, we never hear talk of their beauty, but with Manon Gropius it is a different matter. The following passage taken from her autobiography *And the Bridge is Love* indicates the sense of pride and personal fulfillment she took in the physical beauty of this child and the relation of this issue to her father:

> Why had this marriage with Gropius not worked out? He was *strikingly handsome,* a highly gifted artist, a man of my kind, *of my blood* . . . But what homogeneity means—this I would see in my child from Walter Gropius. *The miracle of sameness*—which I would shun otherwise—was born in her. She was the *most beautiful* human being in every sense . . .[11]

Reading the second and third verse of the Carinthian folktune, we realize that Berg could hardly have highlighted the issue more dramatically had he written the text himself.

The residual message that underlies virtually every score of Berg, whether instrumental or vocal, is exemplified in his use of folk text and tune in a pointedly referential manner. The tendency is Romantic, but for all of its indebtedness to Mahler specifically it is one of the most individualizing characteristics of Berg's musical language.

The same claim may be made with respect to Berg's symbolic use of rhythmic devices, and the connecting links to Mahler put forward earlier with respect to *Wozzeck* and *Lulu* (see pp. 58–59) can be sealed once again in the *Violin Concerto.* Thus the first part of the second movement, marked "Cadenza," is the tragic climax of the work, and is associated with the death of Manon Gropius. The palindromic motive that permeates the entire section is Mahlerian in its effect—colossal in gesture and impact. With the deletion of the final note, Berg's rhythm is identical to the fully developed motif (long, short, long, long) of Mahler's Ninth Symphony, first movement (see p. 57). With the addition of the figure in parenthesis (Ex. 17.17), its relation to the Fate motive of Mahler's Sixth Symphony as well as his own *Wozzeck* is revealed. Once the listener is so tuned, the world of Mahler is recalled in other ways. Thus the cyclic reprise of

Example 17.17. Berg, *Violin concerto,* Mvt. 2., "Hauptrhythmus."

the opening measure of the first movement in the closing measures of the last is not only in harmony with a larger Mahlerian premise but by now has taken on a new brand of cyclicism that is Berg's own. In *Wozzeck, Der Wein,* and the *Violin Concerto,* among other works of his maturity, the sense of a circular return to the beginning as the music closes suggests a form without end, just as, in a different fashion, the words "Ewig, ewig" in the fading measures of Mahler's *Das Lied von der Erde* seem to linger long after the music has finished. In the latter instance it is the lack of resolution of the vocal part and the hanging sixth above the final major triad that seem to negate any sense of finality. There should be little doubt, with the composite evidence put forward here, that the final sonority of the *Violin Concerto*—which follows a set of variations on the chorale "O Ewigkeit, du Donnerwort" and similarly reveals a prominently sounded sixth above a major triad—was meant to invoke a recognition on the part of the connoisseur and to act as a gesture of personal farewell, referential, and unending (see p. 19). The same musical ingredients at the close of *Lulu* (two dyads: A–E, B–F) promote a similar interpretation in light of the concluding text:

GRAFIN GESCHWITZ:	COUNTESS GESCHWITZ:
Lulu!—Mein Engel! Lass dich noch einmal sehen!—Ich bin dir nah!—Bleibe dir nah—in Ewigkeit!	Lulu! My angel! Let me see you once more! I am near you! Forever near you! For eternity!

POST-MORTEM: *LULU,* WEDEKIND AND BERG

If Berg's approach to folk song was to approximate its qualities and thereby effect a contrast in a manner that parallels Mahler's method, it may also be said that such practice rarely brought with it a spontaneous gaiety, but contrarily seemed to sharpen the bittersweet qualities that potentially reside in such a juxtaposition. This can be dramatically observed in his opera *Lulu* in the use of barrel-organ music and the quotation of Wedekind's *Lautenlied* in Act III (the "Variations" movement of the *Lulu Symphony*). For all the compatability of various diatonic tunes with a typical Bergian dodecaphonic series, here the overtly C-major quality of the melody is striking, and in its initial appearance Berg makes no effort to cloud its origins. Only with Wedekind's text at hand,

Example 17.18. Berg, *Lulu,* Act III, s.2, mm. 693–708, Wedekind's "Lautenlied."

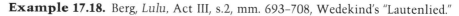

however, do we sense the quiet desparation that lies beneath the innocent sound of the melody. Here the musical quotation simultaneously alludes to an unspoken text. Entitled *Konfession,* Wedekind's Lied begins:

> 1. With joy, by every oath, I swear before Almighty God, who is my judge that I would far rather be a whore than richly possessed of fame and fortune.

2. In me, world, you have lost a woman, a woman self-possessed and free from inhibition. Was there ever anyone born for the business of love as I was born for it?[12]

A comparison of this unspoken text with the words of "Lied der Lulu" clarifies the appropriateness of the citation of Wedekind's tune. As with the allusion in *Wozzeck* to a *Wunderhorn* lyric, the significance of the musical idea is revealed only when the associative text is known.

LULU

Wenn sich die Menschen um meinetwillen umgebracht haben, so setzt das meinen Wert nicht herab. Du hast so gut gewusst, weswegen Du mich zur Frau nahmst, wie ich gewusst habe, weswegen ich Dich zum Mann nahm. Du hattest Deine besten Freunde mit mir betrogen, Du konntest nicht gut auch noch Dich selber mit mir betrügen. Wenn Du mir Deinen Lebensabend zum Opfer bringst, so hast Du meine ganze Jugend dafür gehabt. Ich habe nie in der Welt etwas anderes scheinen wollen, also wofür man mich genommen hat. Und man hat mich nie in der Welt für etwas anderes genommen, als was ich bin. Nein, nein, nein!

LULU

Even though men may kill themselves or others because of me, that doesn't make me worthless. You know why you wanted to make me your wife, just as I knew why I wanted to marry you. You let your closest friends get caught up in your deception, yet you can't really deceive yourself. And even if you have given me the best of your late years, you have had the flower of my youth in return. I've never in the world pretended to be anything I am not. And no one has ever taken me for anything but what I am. No, no, no!

To speak of Berg's opera *Lulu* in the context of the Decadent movement is an anachronism; to speak of Wedekind its author is not. Frank Wedekind (1864–1918), lame from birth and attracted to the life of the circus with its athletes and acrobats, found his way in an early wanderlust life to the first literary cabaret in Munich. There he sang to his own lute accompaniments original songs filled with cynical sentiments about a bourgeoise society (see p. 286). His first play, *Spring's Awakening* of 1891, dealt with the taboo subject of children's sexuality, and various details, including a scene with explicit self stimulation, drove it from the stage for more than a decade. The Lulu plays written between 1892 and 1895 and published in various formats with the titles of *Erdgeist* (*Earth Spirit*) and *Die Büchse der Pandora* (*Pandora's Box*) explored the even more complex topic of the involuntary "femme fatale," exerting a power over men that is beyond her control. As with *Pelléas*, Fate transcends human understanding or alteration. But the depravity of the characters and the casualness with which the themes of murder, prostitution, lesbianism, innocence, and degeneracy are treated—in a bewildering procession of events that seem to catapult the heroine and those in her orbit to inevitable extinction—was also deemed unfit for the public stage from the start.

A private performance was seen by the young composer Alban Berg in 1905, shortly after his twentieth birthday, but he would wait another twenty years before returning to a consideration of its message. In a technical sense, Berg's ultimate *construction*, both in terms of the libretto and musical vocabulary, could not have been envisioned at the time of his original exposure to the drama. In terms of the literary and musical *message* and their complementary natures, the opera *Lulu*, unfinished but essentially complete at the time of Berg's death in 1935, may be seen as belonging to the time of the play. Wedekind's focus reinforces Freud's sexual inquiry of the same decades with equal honesty. Although his treatment of the demimonde has more than a trace of the Decadent predilection of the period as well, in retrospect the vividness of his themes appear to be served up less to entertain than to probe and disquieten his audience into a new and questioning attitude. His insistence on presenting exaggerated action, personality, or forum as a norm has pegged him as a transitional figure in the movement toward Expressionist theater. The social conscience that underscores the choice and whose inquiry is meant to disturb more than to titillate can also be seen to presage many of the impulses of a brand of musical theater that would be dubbed *Zeitoper* in the 1920s.

While a discussion of Berg's creative method in composing *Lulu* may easily side-step the issues attendant to the birth of the play by emphasizing its pitch-serial structure (Schoenberg), rhythmic symbolism (Mahler), or the vastly complex issue of formal planning, Wedekind's fin-de-siècle morality play must be seen to belong to the same age that allowed Wilde to reinterpret the Biblical story of *Salome* with a psychosexual frankness that was both powerful, new, and not intended for the weak at heart. While Berg's *Lulu*, like Satie's *Parade*, begins with a circus manager outside his tent with samples of his wares inviting the audience to enter, Wedekind's metaphor is of a heightened psychological order and fraught with implication through the presentation of Lulu dressed as a serpent. In spite of such modish incorporations such as a jazz orchestra, a film sequence, and Futurist machinery (electric doorbell, coffee machine, telephone, stock exchange reports, and revolvers), today's audiences, innocent of serial and dramaturgical analysis, have properly come to sense the essentially late-Romantic foundation for Berg's final score, and to hear it, for all its technical advance, as a somewhat ripened version of first decade musical manners.

REPERTOIRE

Wozzeck (1917–22)
Chamber Concerto (1923–25), pf, vn, winds
Lyric Suite (1925–26), str qt
Der Wein (1929), S, orch
Lulu (1929–35), opera; *Lulu Suite* (1934), S, orch
Violin Concerto (1935)

READING

Alban Berg, "A Word About Wozzeck," *Modern Music*, v. 1 (November–December, 1927), 22ff.
George Perle, "The Secret Programme of the Lyric Suite," *Musical Times*, cxviii (1977), 629, 709, 809.
Pierre Boulez, *Alban Berg: Lulu* (1979); extracts in the accompanying booklet to Boulez's recording of the opera, DGG 2740 213. English translation in *Orientations* (Cambridge, Mass., 1986), 380–403.
Douglas Jarman, *The Music of Alban Berg* (Berkeley, 1979).
Karen Monson, *Alban Berg* (Boston, 1979), 142–189, 284–297, 323–334.

George Perle, *The Operas of Alban Berg.* Volume One: *Wozzeck* (Berkeley, 1980).

Glenn Watkins, "New Perspectives on Mahler and Berg," *Michigan Quarterly Review,* xx.2 (Spring 1981), 134–143.

Douglas Jarman, "Alban Berg, Wilhelm Fliess and the Secret Programme of the Violin Concerto," *The International Alban Berg Society Newsletter,* no. 12 (1982), 5–11.

Janet Schmalfeldt, *Berg's Wozzeck: Harmonic Language and Dramatic Design* (New Haven, 1983).

George Perle, *The Operas of Alban Berg.* Volume Two: *Lulu* (Berkeley, 1984).

CHAPTER 18

WEBERN'S PATH TO THE NEW MUSIC

Webern's development in the post-World War I years showed less concern for the various stylistic options of the period than most composers of the time. Though his adoption of Schoenberg's method of composing with twelve tones in retrospect seems inevitable, it effected only a minor transformation in the surface appearance of his music and in essence argued only for greater economy and integration of his musical materials. His rejection of jazz rhythms or sonorities (the saxophone of op. 22 is the only concession and is in no way redolent of an American popular instrument), of *Zeitoper* or folk tunes, is matched, however, by the same unspoken subscription of neoclassic textures and formalities (symphony, quartet, concerto, cantata) observable in the contemporaneous productions of his mentor, Arnold Schoenberg. Yet his continuing devotion to a pointillistic rhythmic and color component largely disguises this concern, while his choice of texts frequently reinforces an earlier disposition.

TRAKL-LIEDER, OP. 14, AND THE *LATIN CANONS*, OP. 16

Although the setting of Goethe, *Wunderhorn*, and Chinese texts in Webern's songs, opp. 12–19 emphasizes the composer's orientation to folk verse piety and themes from nature, other textual choices in this same group by Strindberg and Trakl suggest that he was not totally oblivious to Expressionist literary currents. In the six *Trakl-lieder*, op. 14 (1919–21) it is possible to test the extent of the attraction. In spite of a pervasive introverted quality, the brevity and the leanness of his textures coupled to an essential quietness which seems to refuse the scream as an expressive gesture—all appear to disclaim any connection with the central premises of Expressionism. Trakl's poetry, however, provides an opportunity to take note of Webern's reaction to openly Expressionist lines and to remember its effect when we meet it in other surroundings. There can be no denying that Trakl's life provides an incentive for a careful scrutiny of the values inherent in his poetry: A victim of alcohol, drugs, and war, haunted by visions of incest and suicide, he speaks in these songs of the elements of despair and death that disturbed the work of many poets and artists both before and immediately following World War I. Trakl's grim message, which speaks of both personal catastrophe and political and social disintegration, indeed helps us to understand that Schoenberg's silence during these years can be viewed as more than a period of reflection in search of a theory of composing with twelve tones.

Although Webern's songs, op. 13 (1914–18), for soprano and orchestra of thirteen instruments, had displayed the coloristic acuity that was so pronounced in his *Five Orchestra Pieces*, op. 10 (1911–13), in the *Trakl-lieder* Webern reduced his orchestra to an even sparer chamber grouping of clarinet, bass clarinet, violin, and cello. It is clear that the rotation of this instrumental quartet (first and final songs for the complete quartet; the second for bass clarinet and strings; the third for clarinet and strings; the fourth for clarinets and cello; the fifth for clarinets and violin) demands a recognition of the indebtedness of the cycle to Schoenberg's *Pierrot lunaire*. Beyond the coloristic component, Webern's response mirrors the essence of Trakl's lyrics through the disorienting language of atonality and a vocal style characterized by an exaggerated intervallic structure. Webern's atomized phraseology is the perfect complement to Trakl's refined intensity, but structurally it derives from the Expressionist predilection, more clearly observable in a libretto like *Erwartung*, to substitute the individual word for the involved syntactical construction and in so doing to place a premium on silence and the pause.

Example 18.1. Webern, *Six Trakl-Lieder*, op. 14, no. 6, mm. 12–13.

Dunkler Odem in grünen Gezweig.   Dark haze in green branches.
Blaue Blümchen umschwebern das Antlitz   Blue flowerets float round the head of
   des Einsamen,   the lonely one,
     den goldnen Schritt   the golden step
       ersterbend unter dem Oelbaum.   dying beneath the olive tree.

Aufflattert mit trunknem Flügel die Nacht.
So leise blutet Demut,
   Tau, der langsam tropft
      vom blühenden Dorn.
Strahlender Arme Erbarmen
   umfängt ein brechendes Herz.

The night flutters up on drunken wings.
So gently bleeds humbleness,
   dew, falling slowly
      from the flowering thorn.
The mercy of glowing arms
   embraces a breaking heart.

English translation by Leroy Linick.

Although Webern had earlier begun to raise this technique to the level of an artistic credo both in the service of texts with a different aesthetic orientation and in total instrumental abstractions (see p. 42), it is tempting to suggest as one of its sources the clipped verse and elliptical punctuation of Expressionist drama and poetry. The increasingly obscure tonal orientation, the preference for melodic sevenths and ninths, the rhythmic variety through manipulation of triplet figures as well as the discontinuous phraseology promoted through the prominent use of the rest, once established, all remain as part of the mature language of the composer. Thus in Webern's return to a *Wunderhorn* text in "Dormi Jesu" (*Five Canons on Latin Texts*, op. 16, 1924) the naive piety of "Der Tag ist vergangen" (Ex. 3.1) is treated to a musical response reflective less of the *Volkslied* style of the latter than of Webern's continuing preoccupation with the contrapuntal virtuosity of Heinrich Isaac and the canonic art of other Netherlanders of the High Renaissance.

Example 18.2. Webern, op. 16, no. 2, mm. 1–3.

Dormi Jesu, mater ridet,
quae tam dulcem somnum videt,
dormi Jesu blandule.
Si non dormis, mater plorat,
inter fila cantans orat:
blande veni somnule.

Sleep, my Jesus; mother smiles when
She can see you sweetly sleeping.
Sleep, my Jesus, tenderly.
When you don't sleep, mother weeps and
Plucks the strings and sings a prayer
Calling tender sleep to you.

WEBERN AND THE SERIES: *SYMPHONY,* OP. 21; *CONCERTO,* OP. 24; *CANTATA,* OP. 29

Together with Schoenberg's concept of *Klangfarbenmelodie,* this rhythmic-contrapuntal conjunction provided the basis of Webern's personal style—a style already well in place before his espousal of Schoenberg's method of composing with twelve tones. His first use of the twelve-note series, which followed imme-diately in opus 17 (1924), leads only to increasing conciseness of expression and economy of motivic content. Though Webern's *String Quartet* of 1905 had early demonstrated his proclivity for a similar motivic restriction, with the adoption of Schoenberg's method a reliance on three- and four-note motifs subjected to contrapuntal manipulation (inversion, retrograde, retrograde inversion) becomes the center of his art and one that increasingly displays a devotion to canons, palindromes and other symmetrical structures.

Example 18.3. Webern's Series.

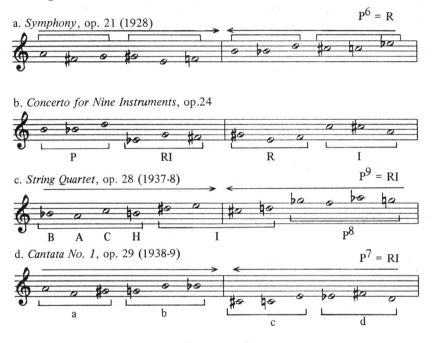

a. *Symphony*, op. 21 (1928)

b. *Concerto for Nine Instruments*, op.24

c. *String Quartet*, op. 28 (1937-8)

d. *Cantata No. 1*, op. 29 (1938-9)

The series for the *Symphony*, op. 21, is so typically structured and the contrapuntal layout so ingenious that it has become the *locus classicus* of the mature Webern style. Webern himself spoke of the second movement thus:

> [The series] has the peculiarity that the second half is the retrograde of the first half. This is a very intimate unity. So here only 24 forms are possible, as two are always identical with each other. At the beginning the retrograde appears in the accompaniment of the theme, the first variation is, in the melody, a transposition of the series starting on C. The accompaniment is a double canon.—Greater unity cannot be achieved. Even the Netherlanders never managed this.—In the fourth variation there are constant mirror forms. This variation itself is the central point of the whole movement, and after this everything goes backwards. So the whole movement itself is a double canon by retrograde motion . . . What you see here— retrograde, canon, etc.,—it's always the same—mustn't be thought of as "stunts"— that would be absurd!—As many connections as possible were to be created, and you must admit that there are many connections here![1]

Webern's manipulation of the series rarely reveals twelve-note themes as in Schoenberg's *Variations for Orchestra*, op. 31, principally because of the registral, temporal, timbral, and dynamic variety of the original presentation. The exposition of the musical material in such a fashion frequently renders larger formal events, such as development, reprise, or variation, difficult to distinguish. Much of the fascination of Webern analysis has turned on the observation of the interaction of micro- and macro-formal elements; of color, motif, and rhythm in the service of canon, variation, rondo, scherzo, and sonata forms. The potentially disastrous formal consequences of the art of the *Trakl-lieder* is ultimately counterbalanced by Webern's devotion to Goethe's artistic but scientifically enlightened view of an ordered universe, where the smallest organisms constantly reappear—"always the same, always different". Herein must lie the ultimate appeal of the series for Webern's mature works.

This judgment may be illustrated by his *Concerto for Nine Instruments*, op. 24 (1934). A work of his maturity, the basic set (Ex. 18.3b) is constructed from symmetrical three-note groups which, true to Webern's earlier predilection, are characteristically isolated through color and the rest.

Example 18.4. Webern, *Concerto for Nine Instruments*, op. 24, Mvt. 1, mm. 1–5.

Example 18.4 (Continued)

b.

In the *Cantata No. 1*, op. 29 (1938–39), the motivic content (Ex. 18.3d) is familiar. The "c" group is the same as the principal motif of his *String Quartet* of 1905, the "d" group identical to the generating motif of Schoenberg's passacaglia (No. 8) in *Pierrot lunaire* (Ex. 10.6). The middle two triads are intervallically identical to the second and first three-note motifs of op. 24, yet part of a larger hexachordal relationship: The interval content of the first six notes is the same as the retrograde inversion of the second six. Although three-note and six-note groupings are identified in the instrumental introduction of the first movement through color and the rest, other divisions are also endorsed. Thus four different versions of the series that constitute the choral opening of the first movement are divided into phrases of five, four, and three notes respectively, a division identical to the theme of Schoenberg's orchestral *Variations*, op. 31 (Ex. 15.16).

Example 18.5. Webern, *Cantata No. 1*, op. 29, Mvt. 1, mm. 14–19.

Example 18.5 (Continued)

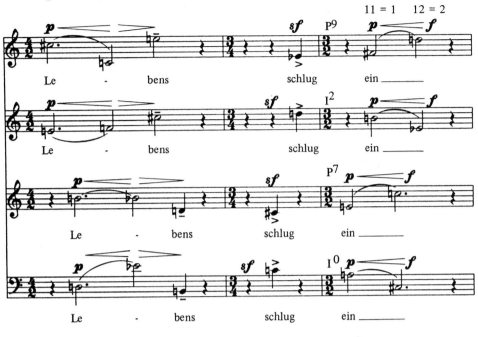

In the following text of the first movement, the appearance of rests, indicated by hash marks, reflects a continuing preoccupation of the composer and leads not so much to a syntactical confusion of the text as to a delicate aeration with the potential for textual emphasis and relief.

Webern, Cantata No. 1

I.

[Chorus]
Zündender Lichtblitz / des Lebens /
schlug / ein / aus der Wolke des Wortes. /
Donner / der Herzschlag / folgt nach, /
bis / er / in Frieden / verebbt.

II.

[Soprano solo]
Kleiner Flügel Ahornsamen
schwebst im Winde!
Musst doch in der Erde Dunkel sinken.
Aber du wirst auferstehn dem Tage,

all den Düften und der Frühlingszeit;
wirst aus Wurzeln in das Helle steigen,

bald im Himmel auch verwurzelt sein.

Wieder wirst aus dir du kleine Flügel senden,

I.

Lightning, the kindler of Being.
struck, flashed from the word in the storm
Thunder, the heart beat, follows, [cloud.
at last dissolving in peace.

II.

Little winged seed of maple,
borne by the breezes!
Thou must fall to earth and lie in darkness.
But then thou shalt rise again to the
   daylight,
to the fragrance and the air of Spring;
from thy earth-roots shalt thou rise to
   brightness,
soon in heaven too shalt have thy roots.

And again shalt put thy wings out, little
   maple,

die in sich schon tragen deine ganze
schweigend Leben sagende Gestalt.

which already carry thy entire silent form,
the bearer of new life.

III.

III.

[*Chorus*]
Tönen die seligen Saiten Apolls,
wer nennt sie Chariten?
Spielt er sein Lied durch den wachsenden
wer denket Apollon?   [Abend

Hearing the blessed strings of the Sun-god,
who senses the Graces?
Echoes his song in the darkening evening,
who thinks of Apollo?

Sind doch im Klange die früheren Namen alle
   verklungen;
sind doch im Worte die schwächeren Worte
   lange gestorben;
und auch blasseren Bilder zum Siegel des
   Spektrums geschmolzen.

Have not the earlier names all been
   gathered, lost in that music?
Have not the weaker words long ago
   perished, slain by the word's might?
Also the fainter image is melted as seal of
   the spectrum.

[*Soprano solo*]
Charis, die Gabe des Höchsten:
die Anmut der Gnade erglänzet!
[*Chorus*]
Schenkt sich im Dunkel
[*Solo*]
dem werdenden Herzen
[*Chorus*]
als Tau
[*Solo*]
der Vollendung.

Charis, the gift of the highest:
the grace of her favour is sparkling!

She comes in darkness,

the ripening heart's gift,

as dew

of perfection.

The close of the work discloses the magic that Webern could distill from such constructions. The final "dew of perfection" is cradled in a richly harmonic "als Tau" sung by the chorus and the mobile tracery of the soprano on "der Vollendung," while the briefest of instrumental codas concluded on the pizzicato of the harp recalls the composer of the early orchestral works.

POST-MORTEMS

Webern's meteoric ascension and ultimate canonization beginning in the early 1950s came at the close of World War II when the musical world was in need of revitalization and a fresh start. Webern's music, previously almost totally unknown, served the need for an underexposed model admirably. Stravinsky's assessment of 1960 expressed not only the breadth of Webern's influence by that time but also forecast uncannily his ultimate eclipse by later, more fashionable trends. His centennial year in 1983 went almost unmarked, if performances, symposia and other testimonials to his art are any indication—a fate hardly imaginable for Berg in 1985.

Stravinsky's judgment that Webern was "too original—i.e., too purely himself" suggests the limits of his appeal as well as his inimitability, and justifies his conclusion:

Of course the entire world had to imitate him; of course it would fail; of course it will blame Webern. No matter, though. The desparate contrivance of most of the music now being charged to his name can neither diminish his strength nor stale his perfection.[2]

REPERTOIRE

Six Songs (Trakl), op. 14 (1919–21), S, cl/Eb cl, b cl, vn, vc
Five Canons on Latin Texts, op. 16 (1923–24), S, cl, b cl
Two Songs (Goethe), op. 19 (1926), SATB, cl, b cl, cel, gui, vn
Symphony, op. 21 (1928)
Quartet, op. 22 (1930), cl, t sax, pf, vn
Concerto, op. 24 (1931–34), fl, ob, cl, hn, tpt, trbn, pf, vn, va
Cantata No. 1 (Jone), op. 29 (1938–39), S, SATB, orch
Variations, op. 30 (1940), orch
Cantata No. 2 (Jone), op. 31 (1941–43), S, B, SATB, orch

READING

Anton Webern, Preface to *Choralis Constantinus II* of Heinrich Isaac in *DTÖ*, xxxii, Jg. xvi/1 (1909), Eng. trans. in H. Moldenhauer, *Anton von Webern* (New York, 1978), 84–5.
Colin Mason, "Webern's Later Chamber Music," *Music and Letters*, xxxviii (1957), 232.
Walter Kolneder, *Anton Webern* (1961; Eng. trans., Berkeley, 1968).
Hans Moldenhauer and Demar Irvine, eds., *Anton von Webern: Perspectives* (Seattle, 1966).
D. Saturen, "Symmetrical Relationships in Webern's First Cantata," *Perspectives of New Music*, vi.1 (1967), 142.
Martin Boykan, "The Webern Concerto Revisited," *Proceedings of the American Society of University Composers*, iii (1968), 74.
Scott Goldthwaite, "Historical Awareness in Anton Webern's *Symphony*, op. 21," *Essays in Musicology: in Honor of Dragan Plamenac* (Pittsburgh, 1969), 65.
Hans Moldenhauer, *Anton von Webern* (New York, 1978).
Glenn Watkins, "The Canon and Stravinsky's Late Style" in *Confronting Stravinsky*, ed. J. Pasler (Berkeley, 1986), 222, 245.

PART 5

EMERGING NATIONAL ASPIRATIONS: 1910–1945

Actually, it seems to me that, in order to create an indigenous music of universal significance, three conditions are imperative. First, the composer must be part of a nation that has a profile of its own—that is the most important; second, the composer must have in his background some sense of musical culture and, if possible, a basis in folk or popular art; and third, a super-structure of organized musical activities must exist—to some extent, at least—at the service of the native composer.

—Aaron Copland, *Music and Imagination*
(Harvard University Press, 1952), 79.

CHAPTER 19

HUNGARY:
BÉLA BARTÓK

In retrospect, the extent to which national biases helped to spell the personalities and movements of the opening decades of the twentieth century may be deemed extraordinary. Yet the orientation can be seen not only as derivative from a thoroughly nineteenth-century turn of mind but also increasingly by non-German nations as an attempt to counteract German hegemony established during the Romantic Age. In addition, emerging national aspirations among countries such as Hungary, the Soviet Union, and the United States of America, as well as the renaissance of musical impulses in countries with a discontinuous artistic history, as with Spain and England, served to compound the variable national imprints of the prevailing French-Russian-German axis at the turn of the century.

BACKGROUNDS AND INFLUENCES

Although a few compositions from the first two decades of the century suggest that Béla Bartók (1881–1945) was involved with issues beyond his national borders (e.g., the symbolist vagaries of *Duke Bluebeard's Castle* of 1911 or the Oriental-Primitivist decadence of *The Miraculous Mandarin* of 1919), a perusal of the titles of Bartók's compositions confirms the popular impression that his music was from the beginning highly dependent on native folk songs and dances. His interest in this music was not superficial and continued throughout his lifetime; works that incorporate folk materials or are dependent on its directness of expression (such as the various didactic and children's pieces) account for a large percentage of his total output.

There are several reasons for this: first, his independent researches into Hungarian, Bulgarian, Roumanian, Slavic and Arabic folk music begun as early 1904 and continued to the end of his career (see Fig. 19.1.); second, his lifelong faithfulness to the folk melos as a compositional resource in an attempt to establish a Hungarian national music, a quest in which he was joined by his compatriot Zoltán Kodály (1882–1967). While Stravinsky's indebtedness to Russian tunes and texts is clear, our final impression of the composer tends to accentuate his variable stylistic alliances, including a rejuvenating Neoclassicism and a filtered Serialism. If something of the Russian always prevailed, his outlook was extremely cosmopolitan, his taste catholic. Bartók, in spite of an

Figure 19.1. Bartók transcribing folk music (c. 1930).

awareness of contemporary movements and trends which was manifest in his own music in subtle ways, ultimately achieved a synthesis in his music which seemed always to affirm the folk element.

In his early years the influence of Liszt (*Rhapsody* for piano and orchestra, 1904) and Strauss (*First Orchestral Suite*, 1905) can be observed. More profound and lasting, after being introduced to it by Kodály in 1907, was the example of Claude Debussy, whose scalar and improvisatory style haunted Bartók to the end. Debussy's piano prelude *Feux d'artifice* provides an excellent touchstone: the opening bitonal wash (Ex. 5.12), the following tritone punctuations in the right hand (Ex. 19.2), the crushed minor seconds in rapid alternation (Ex. 5.13), the nonfunctional parallel harmonic structures (Ex. 5.11), and the quotation of national materials (Ex. 5.15) could only have appealed to Bartók's developing personality and is directly reflected in a work like "The Night's Music" from the *Out of Doors* suite for piano of 1926 (Ex. 19.1). The numerous movements dominated by nocturnal sounds which appear throughout Bartók's career (e.g., Piano Concerto No. 2, mvt. 2; *Music for Strings, Percussion and Celesta*, mvt. 3) are vivid testimony to his lifelong fascination for Debussy's approach to sonority. The stamp which he gave to it, however, was sufficiently personal that it was capable of being appropriated fifty years later by a composer such as George Crumb as a direct gesture of homage to Bartók. An especially clear example can be heard in the eerie landscape drawn from the Piano Concerto No. 2 (1930–31,

Example 19.1. Bartók, *Out of Doors:* "The Night's Music" (1926), 3 mm.

mvt. 2; see p. 408) which Crumb used as the foundation for his *Star Child* of 1983.

According to his autobiography (1918), Bartók had felt as early as 1902 that he had a role to play in the shaping of a Hungarian style largely in response to his growing nationalistic feelings and anti-Hapsburg sentiment. While he had already made his first arrangements of Hungarian folk songs in that year, by the time of the *Ten Easy Pieces* for piano of 1908 he was combining settings of pentatonic folk melodies ("Evening in a Village") with original compositions that extract the essence of folk dances ("Bear Dance"). However much he seemed to have relied from time to time on the music of Debussy or Stravinsky, or to have acknowledged the importance of Beethoven and Bach in the formation of a personal style, it was only when he had found a counterpart in peasant music that he seemed to feel that his choice had been legitimized. If Schoenberg

Example 19.2. Debussy, *Préludes*, Book II: "Feux d'artifice" (1913), mm. 9–12.

looked to the German tradition for justification of his innovations; Debussy to Rameau for his sense of vocal recitative; and Ravel to Couperin and the clavecinists as one of the sources for a keyboard style, so Bartók looked to the folk music of his native Hungary as well as to contemporary Western trends. This mixture of the vernacular and the cultivated in his music was repeatedly discussed by Bartók throughout his career.

MELODY AND HARMONY

Bartók's melodies and harmonies can typically be seen to spring from the same scalar source, and a comprehensive investigation of Bartók's tonal and harmonic system by Lendvai has identified the prevalence of three interval-repeating scales without final note implication. Classified according to their semitonal content, model 1:5 (c, c#, f#, g, c), model 1:3 (c, c#, e, f, g#, a, c), and model 1:2 (c, c#, d#, e, f#, g, a, b flat, c) are basic to a variety of folk musics. In turn, Lendvai has demonstrated that the interval relationship of these and other scales utilized by Bartók disclose an abiding relationship to the Golden Section (see p. 96) or the Fibonacci series (2-3-5-8-13-etc.).[1]

Although the prevalence of harmonic and melodic fourths and tritones (model 1:5) in his music has been traced to Hungarian and Slovak song repertoires, respectively, they are intervals that are found contemporaneously in abundance in the music of Debussy, Ravel, Schoenberg, Berg, and Skriabin as well as in Stravinsky's early music based on Russian melodies. The more char-

Example 19.3. Bartók, *Miraculous Mandarin* (1918), 4 mm. from Rehearsal no. 66.

acteristic sound of melodies using a mixture of minor seconds and minor thirds (model 1:3), however, is one that has rightly been credited to Arabic influences, while the pattern of alternating major and minor seconds (model 1:2) is equivalent to the octatonic scale employed by Stravinsky and the second mode of limited transposition of Messiaen.

Just as Stravinsky's melodies were characterized by ornamental figures, such as the mordent and particularly the grace note (see the *Japanese Lyrics*, Ex. 11.24), so Bartók's knowledge of Croatian melodies is reflected in a variety of melodic embellishments and inflections among which the glissando (especially for trombone, strings, and tympani) became a signpost of his style in numerous abstract works of his maturity (Ex. 19.4).

In the realm of harmony, his vertical relationships frequently reinforce the interval content of his folk melodies. The prominence of the interval of the melodic and harmonic fourth in some of his earlier works can thus be traced to

Example 19.4. Bartók, *String Quartet No. 4*, mm. 77–82.

Example 19.4 (Continued)

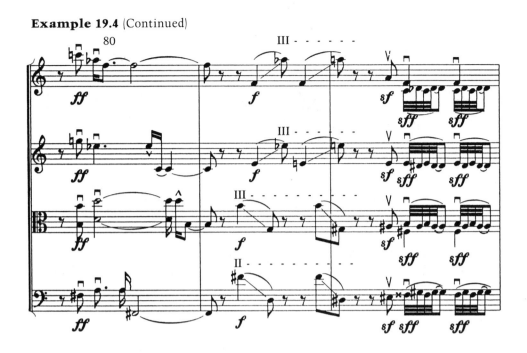

both native materials and a knowledge of Debussy, some of whose music Kodály had brought back from Paris as early as 1907. Yet regardless of the numerous potential sources for his harmonic clusters, it is remarkable that Bartók acknowledged Henry Cowell when he wrote the composer asking for permission to incorporate his dense harmonic congestions into his own music. Nothing could better illustrate the composite set of justifications that typically abides as a backdrop to an idea before Bartók makes it his own: Debussy, *Feux d'artifice*; Scarlatti's *acciacature*; Cowell's clusters; Mozart, *Sonata*, K. 310, l.h. opening (Ex. 19.5).

As early as 1908, Bartók had written one of the earliest examples of bitonality operating under the force of multiple key signatures in the first of the *Fourteen Bagatelles* (Ex. 19.6). Antedating the examples of Stravinsky (p. 225) and Milhaud in the teens or the samples by Ravel (p. 282) in the 1920s, the following

Example 19.5. Bartók, *Piano Sonata* (1926), Mvt. 3, mm. 83–93.

Example 19.5 (Continued)

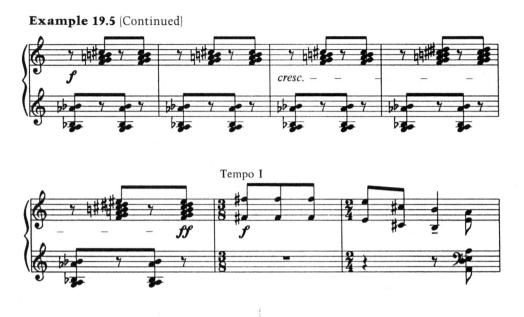

juxtaposition of an Aeolian strain on C♯ with a Phrygian melody on C proclaims a quasi-Ivesian sensibility and an ear willing to test the range of possibilities. But in spite of such progressive evidence, Bartók's harmonic-melodic language typically adapted to an overriding sense of tonality, and except for a few works in the early 1920s, notably the Violin Sonatas, Bartók never seriously flirted with an abortive atonality.

Example 19.6. Bartók, *Fourteen Bagatelles*, op. 6, no. 1, mm. 1–9.

RHYTHM

Finally, the rhythm of numerous Eastern European folk songs had a profound impact on the development of Bartók's musical language: (a) the parlando-rubato style, an assymetrical, declamatory style based on textual accentuation, which in the Hungarian language almost always occurs on the first syllable; (b) the *tempo giusto* based on more regularized dance patterns. The imitation of both the parlando-rubato and giusto styles can easily be heard in "Evening in a Village" of the *Ten Easy Piano Pieces,* and in the *Allegro barbaro* a complex of motivic repetition, extension, and interpolation reflect the distillation of numerous folk music practices. Perhaps most audible of all are the additive rhythms that Bartók assimilated from Bulgarian folk songs. Examples include the 3+2+2+3/8 meter utilized in the Scherzo of the *Fifth Quartet* and the 3+3+2/8 in the last of the six dances in Bulgarian rhythms from *Mikrokosmos,* Book VI (1939).

Example 19.7. Bartók, *Mikrokosmos,* Book VI, "Dances in Bulgarian Rhythms," no. 6, mm. 1–4.

Copyright 1940 by Hawkes & Son (London) Ltd. Renewed 1967. Reprinted by permission of Boosey & Hawkes, Inc.

Bartók's reliance on peasant music ranges from arrangements of folk tunes to concert pieces involving quotation of such material to pieces that distill and transform intervallic and metric elements of various ethnic source materials. Its importance to Bartók's art cannot be overestimated any more than the spark of originality that fueled it. The need for composers of less imposing musical cultures such as Bartók and Stravinsky to rely on the one thing they could claim as a tradition proved to be as fortunate as it was understandable. Such an emphasis on mining the consequences of a rich local tradition (heretofore untapped and hence especially potent) obviated the necessity for either composer to indulge to any great extent in the brands of exotica favored by Western European composers. In turn, their solutions held the potential for being viewed and adopted by others as an additional coloristic resource.

FORM AND FIGURE: AT THE CROSSROADS WITH STRAVINSKY AND SCHOENBERG

In the final two decades of Bartók's life it is from works like the last three quartets (1928, 1934, 1939), the *Music for Strings, Percussion and Celesta* (1936), the *Sonata for Two Pianos and Percussion* (1937), the second and third piano concerti (1931, 1945), and the *Concerto for Orchestra* (1945) that we draw our central impression. While his interest in folk materials is manifest in virtually all of these pieces, a pervasive interest in larger architectural designs and abstract formalization becomes increasingly apparent. In testing the style of composers who came of age or who moved to a new stage of development in the 1920s against the aesthetic dualism of Stravinsky and Schoenberg that was formulated at this time, there is a tendency to place Bartók in the Stravinsky camp and to suggest a natural antipathy on his part toward Vienna. Indeed, while proclaiming Stravinsky and Schoenberg as the two principal geniuses of the day in a statement of 1924, Bartók openly acknowledged a closer proximity to Stravinsky and proclaimed *Le sacre du printemps* as the most imposing work written in the previous thirty years. Bartók's position is readily understood: His reliance on folk melody and rhythm suggests a similarity of approach to the works of Stravinsky; and Schoenberg's general dislike of the "folklorists" and the "primitivists" would seem to place him at a considerable aesthetic distance from Bartók.

PIANO CONCERTO NO. 1.   Nonetheless, Bartók's fascination with Schoenberg at this time is repeatedly confirmed and encourages us to determine the source of his interest and the extent of his familiarity with Schoenberg's music. In a letter of November 1920, Bartók stated that "of Schoenberg I know only his *Klavier-stücke . . .* His music is a little foreign to me, but he has demonstrated some new possibilities in music which had only been hinted at before him."[2] While Bartók had been familiar with Schoenberg's op. 11 piano pieces since 1912, it was not until April 1921 that Bartók performed, in a program that included Stravinsky's *Piano Rag Music* (1919), the first two pieces of Schoenberg's op. 11 in concert in Budapest. His attraction to certain figurations in the first of these pieces is still observable in passages from the *Piano Concerto No. 1* of 1926 (Exs. 19.8-9).

   In this very concerto, however, as well as in the *Nine Little Piano Pieces* also of 1926, there are also suggestions that Bartók was not unaware of the Neoclassic movement and even of the potential of direct modeling. Bartók had in fact been interested in Italian and French harpsichord music of the 1700s

Example 19.8a. Schoenberg, *Three Piano Pieces*, op. 11, no. 1, m. 12.

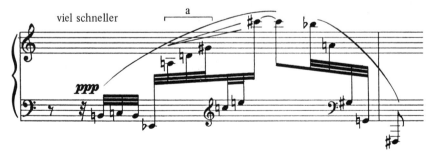

By permission of Belmont Music Publishers.

Example 19.8b. Bartók, *Piano Concerto No. 1*, Mvt. 1, 3 mm. from Rehearsal no. 23.

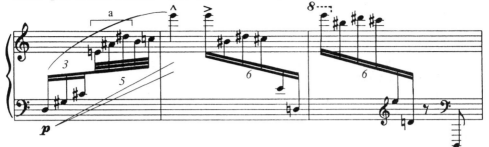

Example 19.9a. Schoenberg, *Three Piano Pieces*, op. 11, no. 1, m. 40.

Example 19.9b. Bartók, *Piano Concerto No. 1*, Mvt. 2, 2 mm. from Rehearsal no. 2.

much earlier than this, as his essay *The Performance of Works Written for the Clavecin* (1912) and the introduction to his editions of the *Well-Tempered Clavier* (1907) and the music of Scarlatti, Couperin, and Rameau (1921) attest. In a letter to a friend, however, Bartók provided the final clue:

> In my youth, Bach and Mozart were not my ideals of the beautiful, but rather Beethoven. During the past few years I have been occupied with pre-Bach music

and I think that traces of these studies are revealed in the *Piano Concerto* (No. 1) and the *Nine Little Piano Pieces*.[3]

In support of Bartók's claim we need not look far in order to spot both texture and figure of the earlier masters at work. If passages by Bach in identical (Ex. 19.10) and dominant-related (Ex. 19.11) keys appear as probable models for the fourth of the *Nine Little Piano Pieces*, even more dramatic are the examples drawn from Bartók's own editions of the Scarlatti sonatas, which appear to have served in his *First Piano Concerto* (Exs. 19.12–14).

Example 19.10a. Bach, *Two-Part Inventions*, E♭ major, opening.

Example 19.10b. Bartók, *Nine Little Piano Pieces*, No. 4, opening.

Example 19.11a. Bach, *Well-Tempered Clavier*, Book I: Fugue in F♯ minor, opening.

Example 19.11b. Bartók, *Nine Little Piano Pieces*, development.

Example 19.12a. Scarlatti, *Sonata No. 6*, p. 6, line 1.

Example 19.12b. Bartók, *Piano Concerto No. 1*, Mvt. 1, 4 mm. from Rehearsal no. 8.

Example 19.13a. Scarlatti, *Sonata No. 5*, p. 19, mm. 10–11.

Example 19.13b. Bartók, *Piano Concerto No. 1,* Mvt. 3, 4 mm. from Rehearsal no. 1.

Example 19.14a. Scarlatti, *Sonata No. 5,* p. 20, mm. 1–2.

Example 19. 14b. Bartók, *Piano Concerto No. 1,* Mvt. 3, 4 mm. from Rehearsal no. 12.

With Stravinsky, Bartók shared a fundamental grounding in a native folk melos, which both tapped throughout their life. The effects of this grounding can be seen in melody, rhythm, and harmony. The accentuations and melodic-harmonic colorings that derived from various folk scales encouraged, if it did not demand, that both maintain an essentially tonal approach to music. This property in turn allowed the easy incorporation of figural quotations from an earlier tonally based music. Nonetheless, in the decade of the 1920s when the Stravinsky-Schoenberg polarity was initially being defined, encouraging composers to strike an allegiance either with Serialism or Neoclassicism, Bartók flirted briefly with the former as well as with the latter. It should be stressed, however, that the main contribution of the Neoclassic dalliance (which may not be as superficial as previously thought) was for Bartók, as for most composers of the 1920s, a much needed purgation following the manic-depressive assaults of Primitivism and Expressionism in the early teens. In Bartók's case, the clarification that the study of classical counterpoint brought was reinforced by a clarification of form influenced by a study of Beethoven and Liszt; an awareness of the continuing German tradition in the works of Schoenberg and Berg; and an attraction to the constructive proportions of the Fibonacci series (1-2-3-5-8-13-etc.) and the Golden Section (see p. 96) that lay at the heart of Cubist theory as propounded by Gleizes (see p. 225).

The search for a compositionally clarifying model, however, is observable in virtually all composers of the time, as the music of Bach and his precursors achieved virtually cult status. Schoenberg's endorsement of the idea of the suite in several works and orchestrations of three organ works of Bach, including two chorale preludes (1922) and the great Prelude and Fugue in E^b major from *Klavierübung*, Part III (1928), suggest that virtually no one was immune from the fever. Against this observation, however, should be placed the pronounced disdain for neoclassic tendencies on the part of Schoenberg and his pupils; the appetite for composers of the German Baroque merely confirmed the Viennese contention of the continuing superiority of their tradition and even of a projected dominance of German music "for the next hundred years" through the discovery of the method of composing with twelve tones. Whether or not we invoke the term Neoclassicism or make use of the slogans "Back to Bach" (Stravinsky) or "Onward from Mozart and Beethoven" (Schoenberg), Bartók shared with most important twentieth-century masters an historical awareness and an increasing literacy of earlier music that was a mark of the age.

Bartók's seeming flirtation with certain aspects of both a burgeoning Neoclassicism and a flourishing atonality on the brink of Serialism is a fascinating thing to observe. For all of Bartók's claim of an interest in Bach that would seem to have replaced a youthful veneration for Beethoven, in a preponderance of his works written from the late 1920s on his early admiration for the master from Bonn is still very much in evidence. It is an interest in Beethoven that is reasonably analogous to Stravinsky's professed study of the keyboard sonatas in preparation for his own sonata of 1924.

LAST STRING QUARTETS; PIANO CONCERTOS NO. 2 and 3.   The last three string quartets of Bartók (1928, 1934, 1939), however, all possess a grandeur of architecture unprecedented in the works of the composer to that time. The attention accorded large-scale formal issues involving arch forms, symmetricalities, and cyclic features proclaims Beethoven and Liszt as ancestors and, by extension, Schoenberg as spiritual cousin. To the composer's infatuation with counterpoint has been added a consuming attention to the architectonics of form. If the *Third String Quartet* of 1927 exemplifies Bartók's endorsement of Baroque polyphony as a natural ally in the projection of folk materials, the use therein of canon, inversion, and augmentation together with his contemporaneous concern for proportional formalistic schemes emphasizing the Golden Section and proto-serial pitch manipulation discloses a decided Viennese affinity. Bartók's insistence that developing variation was an attribute of Eastern folk practice does not disguise the relationship of such a technique with the concentrated language of Berg's *Lyric Suite* (1927), whose motivic quality and cyclic aspects were known to have appealed to Bartók.

Both the *Fourth* (1928) and *Fifth* (1934) *String Quartets* pursue a five-movement organizational plan that may be described as palindromic—A B C B' A'—but with the fourth and fifth movements typically providing more than variation as they search out a compelling, forward-moving drama. In *String Quartet No. 4*, the second and fourth movements are a pair of scherzos interrupted by a third movement given over to one of Bartók's signature evocations of the sounds of night; in *String Quartet No. 5*, the second and fourth movements are slow movements separated by a "Scherzo alla bulgarese." The central movements themselves are rounded three-part forms so that the palindromic plan is complete.

Something of this same structural outline is also preserved in a three-movement work such as the *Piano Concerto No. 2* (1930–31) as follows:

> 1st mvt.: Allegro (Exposition-Development-Recapitulation) for winds and percussion.
> 2nd mvt.: Adagio ("Night Music") for muted strings and percussion.
>   Scherzo (ABA') for strings, winds, and percussion.
>   Adagio ("Night Music") for muted strings and percussion.
> 3rd mvt.: Rondo, termed a free variation of the first movement by Bartók, for full orchestra.

It would be possible to multiply the number of examples that demonstrate these principles, but the end results seldom give any hint of a formula at work. In later pieces like the *Music for Strings, Percussion and Celesta* (1936), one of his most ingenious and attractive works, integration takes place through the use of a generating chromatic subject at the opening of all the movements. And evidence of palindromic movement appears in the retrograde form of the nocturnal third movement as well as in the statement of the first-movement imitative material whose entrances alternate at levels a fifth higher and lower—moving from A at the beginning to E♭ at the climax (A-E-D-B-G-F♯-C-C♯-F-A♭-B♭-E♭) and returning to A (Ex. 19.15).

Bartók's claim that "For an artist it is not only right to have roots in the art of some former times, it is a necessity"[4] confirms a sensibility observable not only in his music of the 1920s but also in his final maturity. For in works such as the *Sonata* for solo violin (1944) and the *Third Piano Concerto* (1945) of his last years, the Bach of the unaccompanied *Chaconne* and the Beethoven of the

Example 19.15. Bartók, *Music for Strings, Percussion and Celesta*, Mvt. 1, mm. 1–3.

Example 19.16a. Beethoven, *String Quartet*, op. 132, Mvt. 3, beginning.

Example 19.16b. Bartók, *Piano Concerto No. 3*, Mvt. 2, beginning.

Example 19.16b (Continued)

Pf.

op. 132 quartet (the "Heiligen Dankgesang" movement) glow radiantly as a backdrop (Ex. 19.16). The use of such materials welded to a highly individual personality rooted in the traditions of his native Hungary marks Bartók as one of the grand synthesizers of the first half of the twentieth century.

To attempt an assessment of Bartók in relation to the towering figures of Stravinsky and Schoenberg is to do him no injustice and is clarifying with respect to the position of all three. A lecture delivered at Harvard in 1943 provides vivid testimony to the value that Bartók placed on the works of Stravinsky and Schoenberg and illustrates a capacity to relate his own development to each. That Bartók's language is as individual and recognizable as that of the other two is due in large measure to factors which are traceable to the folk legacy of his native Hungary; that he ultimately wrote music which transcended its provincial origins is due in no small part to the attention he gave to resolving questions of a more universal order. To the extent that his interpretation of the legacy of the Western European composer brought him face to face with the stylistic tenets of the Neoclassicists and the structural premises of the Serialists, his message is less insular than had he relied more exclusively on the musical values of his native Hungary. In the confrontation and resolution of these two traditions Bartók gave birth to a vigorous and personal art.

REPERTOIRE

Sonata No. 1 (1921), vn, pf
Sonata No. 2 (1923), vn, pf
Piano Sonata (1926)
Out of Doors (1926), pf
Nine Little Piano Pieces (1926)
Piano Concerto No. 1 (1926)
String Quartet No. 3 (1927)
String Quartet No. 4 (1928)
Piano Concerto No. 2 (1930–31)
String Quartet No. 5 (1934)
Music for Strings, Percussion and Celesta (1936)
Sonata for Two Pianos and Percussion (1937)
Mikrokosmos, Book VI (1939)
String Quartet No. 6 (1939)
Concerto for Orchestra (1943, rev. 1945)
Piano Concerto No. 3 (1945)

READING

Milton Babbitt, "The String Quartets of Bartók," *Musical Quarterly*, xxxv (1949), 377.

Colin Mason, "Béla Bartók and Folksong," *Music Review*, xi (1950), 292.

Colin Mason, "An Essay in Analysis: Tonality, Symmetry and Latent Serialism in Bartók's Fourth Quartet," *Music Review*, xviii (1957), 189.

Allen Forte, "Bartók's Serial Composition," *Musical Quarterly*, xlvi (1960), 233.

F. Bónis, "Quotations in Bartók's Music," *Studia musicologica Academiae scientiarum hungaricae*, v (1963), 355.

Halsey Stevens, *The Life and Music of Béla Bartók* (New York, 1964).

László Somfai, "'Per finire': some Aspects of the Finale in Bartók's Cyclic Form," *Studia musicologica Academiae scientiarum hungaricae*, xi (1969), 391.

Jonathan Kramer, "The Fibonacci Series in Twentieth-Century Music," *Journal of Music Theory*, 17 (1972), 110–48.

Benjamin Suchoff, ed., *Béla Bartók Essays* (London, 1976).

George Perle, "The String Quartets of Béla Bartók," *A Musical Offering: Essays in Honor of Martin Bernstein* (New York, 1977).

Vera Lampert and László Somfai, "Béla Bartók" in *The New Grove Dictionary of Music and Musicians* (1980).

Elliot Antokoletz, *The Music of Béla Bartók: a Study of Tonality and Progression in Twentieth-Century Music* (Berkeley, 1984).

Pierre Boulez, "Bartók: *Music for strings, percussion and celesta*" in *Orientations* (Cambridge, Mass., 1986), 346–48. Originally a sleeve note for the recording by Boulez, Columbia 7206.

CHAPTER 20

RUSSIANS ABROAD
AND AT HOME

PROKOFIEV

Stravinsky's early career capitalized on his Russian origins in the establishment of a personal style. Prokofiev (1891–1953), ten years his junior, from the beginning showed his awareness of these successes, and without relying on native folk materials to any great extent emulated something of the senior composer's audacious manner. Although Skriabin, Reger, Strauss, and Debussy were among his first conscious influences, Prokofiev had already shown "modern" tendencies in his *Suggestion diabolique* (1908). In his affection for the symbolist poet Balmont (1910–16: op. 9, 23, 27) he also reflected a contemporary sympathy of Stravinsky and a taste for Skriabinesque harmonies, but in his *Toccata* and the first of the *Sarcasms*—piano works from 1912—he demonstrated his capacity for the barbaric as well as for the ironic—characteristics in tune with the productions of both Bartók and Stravinsky at the time.

His introduction to Diaghilev's company in 1914 was one of signal importance for his career, and while the resulting ballet, *Ala and Lolly,* was not to be performed until 1921, the *Scythian Suite* drawn from it was completed in 1915. Diaghilev's commission for a ballet on a "prehistoric" Russian subject found Prokofiev with a considerably greater literary heritage than a musical one. Working in tandem with Gorodetsky, who researched Russian mythology minutely, they devised a scenario that owes more than a little to Rimsky-Korsakov's *Snow Maiden.* Ultimately, not only the paganism of the scenario but the musical manners of the score indicate that it was written heavily under the shadow of Stravinsky's *Le sacre du printemps,* which also fell strongly on the two works immediately following, *Chout* ("The Tale of the Buffoon") of 1915 and the cantata *They are Seven* on texts of Balmont of 1917–18. Although it is tempting to suggest that Prokofiev had already struck a "primitivist" note as early as his piano *Toccata* of 1912, prior to the premiere of *Le sacre,* by Prokofiev's admission that work as written directly under the influence of Schumann's *Toccata,* which he was studying at the time as a student in the St. Petersburg Conservatory. Regardless of the genesis of the trait, or the label applied to it, Prokofiev early discovered a driving rhythmic manner with an obligatory discordant edge whose spirit was to persist for the rest of the composer's life. A particularly notable later example with a strong spiritual affinity is the finale to the *Piano Sonata No. 7* of 1942.

412

If after the 1920s Prokofiev was to decry Stravinsky's "pseudo-Bachism," he had nonetheless had an early brush with Neoclassicism himself in the *Ten Pieces* for piano of 1906–13 (which includes a Gavotte, Rigaudon, Prelude, and Allemande); in his Haydnesque *"Classical" Symphony* (1916–17); and in the *Four Pieces* for piano of 1918 (Dance, Minuet, Gavotte, Waltz). Later in his career, Prokofiev was to identify four main characteristics of his style: the search for innovation (which included primitivist and grotesque attitudes), the neoclassic, the lyric, and the element of toccata. We are encouraged to judge from this that although Neoclassic labels may be absent in many works of his maturity, its clarifying influence is a constant, as his devotion to large forms and a veneration of the sonata idea confirms.

Prokofiev's ability to square such formalisms with contemporary trends can be seen in the *mécanique* qualities of his *Symphony No. 2* (1924–25) which immediately preceded *Pas d'acier* (1925–26). In the latter work the age of "iron and steel," as previewed by the Futurists (many of whom Prokofiev had met on a trip to Italy in 1915), was mirrored in a ballet concerning Soviet industrialization directly commissioned by Diaghilev to be set to a scenario by the constructivist painter Yakulov. Musically speaking, the rhythmic energy of a residual primitivism was obviously at hand to serve a new theme. Two further ballets, *L'enfant prodigue* (1928–29) and *On the Dnieper* (1930–31), though similar in musical idiom, were not equally successful. That the Ukranian peasant setting of the latter work failed to move Prokofiev suggests a fundamental distinction between the motivating forces behind Prokofiev and Stravinsky.

The period 1918–22, which saw the composer in the United States, and the period 1922–36, which he spent in Paris, was followed by a return to Russia in 1936, where he remained until his death. His original exile had been prompted by the unsettling climate of the Russian Revolution, and gradually he had accommodated to the West as his professional successes grew there. Ultimately, the need to be amongst his friends in his native land brought his return, but it was not without its consequences. On the positive side it must be stressed that many of Prokofiev's most impressive scores come from these last years. *Lieutenant Kijé* (1934), which was the first of his Soviet commissions, had prompted two trips to Moscow in 1933. With a permanent change in residence, the following major scores appeared: *Violin Concerto No. 2* (1935); *Romeo and Juliet* (1935–36); *Alexander Nevsky* (1939); *Symphony No. 5* (1944); *Piano Sonata No. 7* (1939–42); *Sonata for Flute and Piano* (1943); *War and Peace* (1941–43; rev. 1946–52).

But there was a darker side stemming from his return to Russia. The first rumblings of a new order had appeared in 1929 with the pronouncement of "The Ideological Platform of the Russian Association of Proletarian Musicians".[1] A period of artistic isolation from the music of Western Europe followed in 1932, and the establishment of the Union of Soviet Composers brought with it guidelines for the composer, who was advised to address his music to the people and, in fashioning music with a general appeal, to rediscover the traditions of Russia's past and particularly its native folk materials. Further intimations of a new era of censorship came with *Pravda's* rebuke of Shostakovich's *Lady Macbeth of Mtsensk* in January, 1936, just prior to Prokofiev's arrival in the spring. Whether due to this indictment or to the Soviet's rejection of *Romeo and Juliet* the year before as unsuitable for dancing, Prokofiev turned to the writing of pieces with a studied simplicity—*Music for Children* for piano,

Three Children's Songs, and *Peter and the Wolf*—recalling Stravinsky's interest of twenty years before. In observation of the national celebrations of 1937 he composed the *Cantata for the Twentieth Anniversary of the October Revolution* in an obvious attempt to respond to the call for Soviet realism. Scored for two choruses, orchestra, military band, and percussion band and calling for gunshots, machine-gun fire, and sirens, it should have been enough to please the most enthusiastic patriot. Yet the composer's motives were questioned in the setting of texts by Marx and Lenin, a note of satire was noted, and the premiere of what eventually turned out to be an extremely forceful work was delayed until 1966.

While Prokofiev's collaboration with Eisenstein on the music for the film *Alexander Nevsky* (1938), a thirteenth-century hero of the Russian people, proved more successful, his cantata *Hail to Stalin* (1939) and his opera *Semyon Kotko* (1940), based on Katayev's civil war story *I am the Son of the Working People,* once more proved abortive. Still, the period of the war was one of the composer's most productive, and his *Fifth Symphony* of 1944 was considered by many to be his finest. Then in 1947 for the 30th anniversary of the Revolution, Prokofiev composed the festive poem *30 Years* and another cantata *Flourish, mightly homeland,* both of which were cooly received in official quarters. In 1948 the state intervened to correct what it termed a lax state of musical affairs, and in an official party decree pronounced the works of Prokofiev and most other prominent composers as "marked with formalist perversions . . . alien to the Soviet people." *War and Peace* was particularly denigrated and numerous earlier works of Prokofiev were banned.

By "formalist perversions," they indicated, was meant a separation of form from content, which in practice meant "modernism" of any sort, but particularly angular, unsingable melodies, primitivist rhythms, Futurist noises, and especially dodecaphony. In a letter to the General Assembly of Soviet Composers regarding the Resolution of the Central Committee of February 10, 1948, Prokofiev admitted to "formalism," advocated a return to memorable melody, a turning away from atonality toward a simple harmonic language, and a reinstatement of polyphony capable of incorporating Russian folk melodies.[2]

Many of these qualities had already appeared even in his abstract works from the time of his return to the Soviet Union in the 1930s, of which the opening unaccompanied violin melody (Ex. 20.1a) and ringing cantabile of the second theme (Ex. 20.1b) in the *Violin Concerto No. 2* provide ample testimony. However, the orchestral entrance in B minor following the opening, and the tendency of even the most lyric moments (as Ex. 20.1b) to slide almost imperceptibly into distant tonal terrain, are the marks not only of a tonalist but of a composer with an enriched harmonic sense sufficient to defy any critical

Example 20.1a. Prokofiev, *Violin Concerto No. 2,* Mvt. 1, mm. 1–4.

Example 20.1b. Prokofiev, *Violin Concerto No. 2*, Mvt. 1, second subject.

condemnation as simply conservative. The same may be said about many of his mature works, including the powerful *Symphony No. 5*.

The final judgment that Prokofiev's last works were less provocative than his early ones is no more an indictment than a similar charge frequently leveled against Bartók. But the difference in the consequences of their attention to national aspirations is dramatic. Bartók's language developed gradually and steadily from a fundamental investigation into the music of his native land, building on yet transcending the foundational voice. Prokofiev's career was more cosmopolitan, including a long period of exile, and his development was largely allied to the production of symphony (7), sonata (piano, 10; violin, 2; cello, 1), concerto (piano, 5; violin, 2; cello, 2), and ballet. The final attempts to secure a national expression under pressure can only be deemed unfortunate. Yet, as with Shostakovich, the capacity to maintain his integrity in the separate production of an impressive corpus of "unofficial" works proved to be a mark of the true artist, and not all of his work that openly utilized Russian themes was propaganda in the narrowest sense (unless a work like Copland's *Lincoln Portrait* can be considered propaganda).

In *Alexander Nevsky*, for example, national aspirations and a high order of creative talent fuse naturally. Sergei Eisenstein, who had revealed a new potential for film in his moving story of mutiny on the *Battleship Potemkin* (1924), approached the tale of Alexander Nevsky in 1938 on the wave of a renewed Russian interest in its own history. Nevsky, immortal hero, twice protected his people from advances, first by the Swedes and then by the Germans in 1242. It is the latter defense, with its climactic battle on the ice, that inspired Eisenstein; and Prokofiev, who had been commissioned to write the music for the film, determined to expand his original contribution to a full-length cantata for chorus, orchestra, and mezzo-soprano. The cantata was completed in Moscow in February 1939, but first performances took place in various foreign capitals in the early 1940s, and together with his opera *War and Peace* of 1941–43 constituted less an indictment against war than a testimony to the indomitable spirit of the Russian people in times of war.

While Prokofiev's career can be seen to mirror both social and musical developments of the time, it would be difficult to cast him as innovative figure of the avant-garde. Indeed, the popularity of his music covering the range of his career suggests as much, and there are few composers of his generation whose music can sustain whole concerts with such universal appeal (e.g., *Piano Concerto No. 3; "Classical" Symphony; Romeo and Juliet; Symphony No. 5*). The potential for envy, not to say snobbery, among more provocative or influential composers is obvious. The least that most would concede was his importance in establishing the profile of a genuinely Russian music in the first half of the twentieth century.

Prokofiev's death on March 5, 1953, only hours before the passing of Josef Stalin, went almost unnoticed in the press. While millions of Soviet citizens paid their last respects to Stalin, only ten individuals, including Kabalevsky, Shostakovich, and Khachaturian, were present at a memorial service on March 7, where David Oistrakh played the first and third movements of Prokofiev's Violin Sonata. Although Khrennikov, the party taste maker, was understandably not in attendance, we now know that many others, who knew and loved Prokofiev's music and who under different circumstances would have come, stayed away through fear of reprisals.

DMITRI SHOSTAKOVICH

Unlike Stravinsky and Prokofiev, the entire career of Shostakovich (1906–1975) is associated with his native homeland in the period following the Revolution in 1917. Still, he is much closer to Prokofiev in expression even as he alternately reflects characteristics of Tchaikovsky and Stravinsky in technique.

His career was launched with his *Symphony No. 1*, written as a graduation piece from the Leningrad Conservatory in 1925. But for all the sardonic twist of the scherzo reminiscent of Prokofiev or the polytonal trumpet calls, the work, remarkable for a composer of nineteen, has a predictable classic stamp. Shostakovich soon made gestures, however, that placed him among the avant-garde with works such as his opera, *The Nose* (1927–28), where extraordinary vocal sounds and protracted percussion interludes signal that the composer has taken a more adventurous turn (p. 245). Shostakovich's treatment of bureaucracy everywhere in his opera was paralleled by the juxtaposition of social ideologies in the contemporaneous ballet *The Age of Gold* (1927–30), a satire set at an industrial fair somewhere in Western Europe. The arrival of a Soviet football team as honored guests soon allows them to become the object of a variety of intrigues at the hands of the capitalists. The well-known "Polka," frequently extracted from the ballet, is a mocking burlesque about a League of Nations disarmament conference.

The lack of approval by Soviet authorities for this and other works of the period, such as the industrial ballet *The Bolt* concerning Soviet productivity, was based on the question of proper nuancing of social ideologies and not on the progressive nature of the music. Indeed, the openness of the Soviet Union to the latest productions of the West was remarkable during this very period: Krenek's *Jonny spielt auf* was performed thirty-five times in Leningrad during a six-week period in 1929; and works like Stravinsky's *Renard* and *Pulcinella* as well as Berg's *Wozzeck* had appeared earlier than that. While the political climate and the attendant censorship of the Iron Curtain may have been prefigured in this period, it had not yet begun to prevent an open interchange between East and West on artistic grounds.

While Shostakovich later in life referred to his *Second* and *Third Symphonies* (1927, 1929) as "youthful experiments", their subtitles, "To October" and "The First of May," respectively, indicate that he is a son of the Soviet Union—a point of view that is still visible in his *Symphony No. 11* (1957), subtitled "The Year 1905" and written for the 40th anniversary of the Revolution, as well as the *Symphony No. 12* (1961), subtitled "The Year 1917" and dedicated to the memory of Lenin.

Indeed, the fifteen symphonies Shotakovich wrote between 1925 and 1971 are in many ways a mirror of the composer's career. They were also seen in retrospect as a mirror of the Russian intelligentsia who were powerless to speak. The *Fourth Symphony* (1935–36) was modeled after Mahler, but shortly after rehearsals had begun it was apparent that official condemnation was in the offing. The story that the premiere of the work in 1961 was delayed due to the composer's self-criticism was later denied in Shostakovich's *Testimony* (published in 1979) and the fear of reprisals openly acknowledged. The criticism surrounding *The Lady Macbeth of the Mtsensk District* (1930–32), now known to have stemmed principally from a sexually explicit passage of 123 measures with a provocative instrumental component,[3] brought forth the *Symphony No. 5* (1937), a work that ushered in a second creative period extending to 1966. The description of this symphony as "an artist's creative answer to justified criticism"[4] was a confection of party officials, though ·Shostakovich did not protest its use. Far from being a capitulation to the tenets of socialist realism, however, it is an abstract symphonic work lacking either elaborate program or reference to folk materials. As such it also forces us to recall the craft and power of such works as Shostakovich's *24 Preludes* (1932–33) and *24 Preludes and Fugues* (1950–51). Even had the *Fifth Symphony* lacked a provocative social context, it would have rightly become, as it did, one of his most highly proclaimed and frequently performed works.

SYMPHONY NO. 5. Written in a traditional four-movement design, the *Fifth Symphony* opens with a first movement whose sonata form is defined by two themes in the first group,

Example 20.2. Shostakovich, *Symphony No. 5*, Mvt. 1, mm. 1–2.

Used by permission of European American Music Distributors Corporation, sole U.S. agent for Ernst Eulenburg, Ltd.

Example 20.3. Shostakovich, *Symphony No. 5*, Mvt. 1, mm. 5–9.

Used by permission of European American Music Distributors Corporation, sole U.S. agent for Ernst Eulenburg, Ltd.

followed by the extraordinarily powerful melody of the second-theme melody.

Example 20.4. Shostakovich, *Symphony No. 5*, Mvt. 1, mm. 51–59.

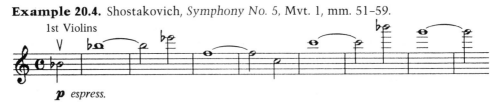

Both the contrapuntal bent evidenced in the canonic treatment of Ex. 20.2 and the broadly arching quality of the melody in Ex. 20.4 proved to be personal signatures of the maturing composer.

Following a raucous scherzo (song and trio), which recalls the young composer, and a third movement Largo, comes the finale, which is a march. Owing as much to the composer's Russian heritage (Tchaikovsky in particular) as to Mahler, the imprint of the conclusion was to resurface in exaggerated fashion in the "invasion theme" of his *Seventh Symphony* (1941). The march-like first theme (Ex. 20.5) is followed by dervish-like contrasting material (Ex. 20.6.) A horn call ushers in a quieter central section, followed by a return of the opening material and a coda based on a solemn presentation of Ex. 20.5.

Example 20.5. Shostakovich, *Symphony No. 5*, Mvt. 4, mm. 3–4 after No. 97.

Example 20.6. Shostakovich, *Symphony No. 5*, Mvt. 4, mm. 2–4 after No. 98.

The seventh and eighth symphonies were written during the war years, the seventh achieving a level of popularity that transformed it into a symbol of victory for the Allies in many quarters. The *Eighth String Quartet* (1960), written "in memory of the victims of fascism and war," utilizes motifs from earlier works as well as the quotation of a Russian revolutionary song, "Languishing in Prison." An autobiographical component is clearly evident in the employment of musical equivalents of the composer's name D-S-C-H (D-E♭-C-B).

The somewhat liberalized atmosphere in Russia that followed the death of Stalin (1954) is mirrored in the work of Solzhenitsyn (*A Day in the Life of Ivan Denisovich*, 1962) and the outspoken poetry of Yevtushenko. It was the latter source that Shostakovich tapped for his *Symphony No. 13* (1962) for baritone solo, male chorus, and orchestra. The texts, though purportedly about the Nazi massacre of the Jews, were widely understood and dramatically approved as a criticism of the Stalin era before conservative forces forced the rewording of certain of Yevtushenko's lines from *Babi Yar* that were deemed offensive.

SYMPHONY NO. 14.   While the *Symphony No. 14*, which followed in 1969, may be viewed as a song symphony in the tradition of *Das Lied von der Erde*, the looseness of structure and the literary texts recall Mahler's independent orchestral songs from *Des Knaben Wunderhorn*. The opening theme of "On Watch" (No. 5) ("In the trench he will die before the coming of night") recalls Mahler's "Serenade of the Sentry" and "Reveille," just as "In Prison" (No. 7) evokes the plight of "The Drummer-Boy". Similarly Apollinaire's "Lorelei" (No. 3: "Three knights . . . are going along a road . . . at the bend of the Rhine"), which is prepared by Garcia Lorca's tavern song of death (No. 2), inevitably suggests Wozzeck's tavern song, "Es ritten drei Reiter wohl an den Rhein" (see p. 358). Shostakovich's admiration for Berg can be confirmed in this work in numerous subtle musical details such as the use of an accelerating chromatic crescendo which ends abruptly at the close of "The Suicide" recalling Wozzeck's drowning scene. Furthermore, the palindromic dyads intoned on the vibraphone at the opening and close of "Lulu's Lied" find a direct mirror in both figure and sonority at the close of "Lorelei". With a knowledge of Lulu's text ("Even though men may kill themselves or others because of me"), the appropriateness of the reference in "Lorelei" ("To the golden-haired witch men flocked, Nigh maddened with love.") is clarified.

The only Russian who appears in the company of the Western poets, Lorca, Apollinaire, and Rilke, is the little known Küchelbecker (1797–1846). A participant in the Decembrist uprising of 1825 in an attempt to overthrow the Czars, he was imprisoned for ten years and spent the final years of his life in Siberia. From there he sent verses to his friends, including the poet Anton Delvig, a contemporary and friend of Pushkin. In "O Delvig, Delvig!" (No. 9) lies the key to Shostakovich's message: "What is the reward for lofty deeds and poetry? For talent, what is there and where is the comfort among villains and fools?" "The Death of the Poet" (No. 10) follows, and with the intonation of the "Dies irae" in the upper strings clearly suggests a reprise of this material that figured so prominently in the opening movement, "De Profundis."

The note of pessimism and the spectre of death, which are omnipresent in these songs, reaches its most poignant level in the concluding song, where at the end it is easy to believe that the "bonelike rattle of percussion" is a reminder "of the skeleton beneath the flesh, awaiting its inevitable day."[5] Written for an orchestra of strings and percussion with soprano and bass soloists, it is dedicated to Benjamin Britten, whose friendship the composer cherished. The discordant terrain of the work, which is as bleak as it is sardonic, lies far removed from the world of Russian folk-song quotation observable in

Symphony No. 11. Yet the autobiographical mixes poignantly, if obliquely, with commentary on the aspirations of a socialist regime that had criticized yet supported the composer's entire career.

That Shotakovich shared Prokofiev's devotion to the large received musical forms is dramatized in a prolific production that included fifteen symphonies, fifteen string quartets, and six concerti. That he, like Prokofiev, managed to withstand the threats and taunts of governmental control over artistic matters suggests that he felt little need to argue matters verbally, only musically. His *Testimony,* posthumously edited and published by Solomon Volkov against varying charges of authenticity, enigmatically discloses the various forces at work on a productive Soviet artist. Together with Stravinsky and Prokofiev, Shostakovich sealed the idea of a variable and powerful twentieth-century Russian musical expression. The extent of their achievement can be judged by comparing their language with that of Sergei Rachmaninov, the last of the great Russian Romantics, who lived until 1943. Of the four, Shostakovich was the only one whose entire career was spent at work in his native homeland.

READING (Prokofiev)

Toccata, op. 11 (1912), pf
Scythian Suite, op. 20 (1915), orch
Chout, op. 21 (1915), ballet
Symphony No. 1 ("Classical"), op. 25 (1916–17)
Piano Concerto No. 3, op. 26 (1917–21)
Le pas d'acier ("The Steel Step"), op. 41 (1925–26)
Violin Concerto No. 2, op. 63 (1935)
Romeo and Juliet, op. 64 (1935–36)
Peter and the Wolf, op. 67 (1936)
Cantata for the 20th Anniversary of the October Revolution, op. 74 (1937).
Alexander Nevsky, op. 78 (1939), cantata; Mez, chorus, orch
Piano Sonata No. 7, op. 83 (1939–42)
War and Peace, op. 91 (1941–43), opera
Sonata for Flute and Piano, op. 94 (1943)
Symphony No. 5, op. 100 (1944)

READING (Prokofiev)

William Austin, "Prokofiev's Fifth Symphony," *Music Review,* xvii (1956), 205.
Andrew Porter, "Prokofiev's Late Operas," *The Musical Times,* cviii (1967), 312.
Victor Seroff, *Sergei Prokofiev: A Soviet Tragedy* (New York, 1968).
Rita McAllister, "Natural and Supernatural in 'The Fiery Angel'," *The Musical Times,* cxi (1970), 785.
Nicolas Slonimsky, ed., *Music Since 1900,* 4th ed. (New York, 1971). "The Ideological Platform of the Russian Association of Proletarian Musicians" (1929), 1353–57. S. Prokofiev, "Letter to the General Assembly of Soviet Composers" (1948), 1373–74.
Malcolm H. Brown, "Prokofiev's *War and Peace:* á Chronicle," *The Musical Quarterly,* lxiii (1977), 297–326.
Malcolm H. Brown, "Stravinsky and Prokofiev: Sizing up the Competition" in *Confronting Stravinsky: Man, Musician and Modernist,* ed. J. Pasler, (Berkeley, 1986), 39.

REPERTOIRE (Shostakovich)

Symphony No. 1 (1925)
Symphony No. 2: "To October" (1927)
The Nose (1927–28), opera
The Age of Gold (1927–30), ballet

Lady Macbeth of the Mtsensk District (1930–32), opera
Jazz Suite (1934, 1938)
Symphony No. 5 (1937)
Symphony No. 7, "Leningrad" (1941)
Symphony No. 11, "The Year 1905" (1957)
Symphony No. 12, "The Year 1912" (1961)
Symphony No. 13, "Babi Yar" (1961)
Symphony No. 14 (1969), S, Bar, orch
Symphony No. 15 (1971)
Sonata (1975), va, pf

READING (Shostakovich)

Virgil Thomson, "Socialism at the Metropolitan," *Modern Music,* xiii (1935).

Norman Kay, *Shostakovich* (London, 1971).

Solomon Volkov, ed., *Testimony: the Memoirs of Shostakovich* (New York, 1979).

Boris Schwarz, "Shostakovich," *The New Grove Dictionary of Music and Musicians* (1980), XVII, 264–275.

Boris Schwarz, *Music and Musical Life in Soviet Russia, 1917–1981* (New York, 1983).

Royal S. Brown, "The Three Faces of Lady Macbeth" in *Russian and Soviet Music: Essays for Boris Schwarz,* ed. M. Brown (Ann Arbor, 1984), 246.

Laurel E. Fay, "The Punch in Shostakovich's *Nose*" in *Russian and Soviet Music: Essays for Boris Schwarz* (1984), 229.

CHAPTER 21

THE TWENTIETH-CENTURY SPANISH AND ENGLISH RENAISSANCE; RENEWALS IN ITALY

SPAIN

The French and Russian view of Spain as an exotic locale has been noted from the 1840s through the 1890s. But Spain's folk music, together with its distinguished legacy of sacred church music in the Renaissance, had also been the object of research by a native musician, Felipe Pedrell (1841–1922), from the 1880s on. His numerous editions of early Spanish composers and his complete edition of the Spanish master Victoria (1548–1611) were momentous and achieved for him a reputation as founder of modern Spanish musicology. Together with his critical writings on Spanish popular song and a study of counterpoint, they served as the basis of instruction for his most famous pupils—Albeniz, Granados, Falla, and Gerhard—who collectively heralded a new Renaissance in Spanish music. After such a protracted national silence in the world of music, it is understandable that the young composers would have been moved to the creation not only of a new music but one that was identifiably Spanish. While Albeniz's *Iberia* and Granados' *Goyescas* achieved a considerable popularity, it was Falla's career more than the others that helped to focus world-wide attention on the Iberian peninsula.

MANUEL DE FALLA.   As with Albeniz and Granados, Falla (1876–1946) found in Paris a second home where he was on intimate terms with Debussy and Ravel, and from them he absorbed the idea of "truth without authenticity," which had guided much of their music on Spanish themes. He soon decided that it was his aim to achieve a music that was universal as well as national.

The earliest notable sign of his Spanish manner appeared in his *Pièces espagnoles* for piano (1902–08), written before he had heard Albeniz's *Iberia* (1906–08). *La vida breve* (1904–05) was the first work to bring his name before the French capital, and the *Siete canciones populares españolas* (1914–15) led to his first significant success, *El amor brujo* (1915), a ballet with songs inspired by Spanish folk art and the *cante jondo,* the primitive song of Andalusia. Although Falla had become a serious student of this native vocal style, it became increasingly clear that it was his primary aim to attempt an "imaginary folk art" wherein the rhythm and sonority of his native Spain would be projected via the French and Russian orchestral traditions. His renowned "Ritual Fire Dance" from *El amor brujo* is a perfect example of such a success without resorting to quotation.

Originally written as a "farsa mimica" (*El Corregidor,* 1916–17), the fashioning of *The Three-Cornered Hat* into a ballet came at the suggestion of Diaghilev, who produced it in his 1919 season with choreography by Massine and decor and costumes by Picasso. With much of the music stemming from popular sources (seguidilla, fandango) and the orchestra frequently projecting the sonority and the manner of a guitar ("The Miller's Dance"), it proved to be one of Falla's most light-hearted and appealing works.

El retablo de maese Pedro (1919–20), which followed, is taken from *Don Quixote* and belongs to the theater of reduced resources espoused by Stravinsky in *Renard* (1915–16) and *Histoire du soldat* (1918). The three singers are characterized by different styles: Maese Pedro, popular; Don Quixote, lyrical and neo-Renaissance; Trujaman, sacred song, popular cries, and old romances. Similarly in his concerto of 1923–26 for harpsichord (an instrument used first in *El retablo*) and five solo instruments (fl, ob, cl, vn, vc), which he wrote for Landowska, the three movements highlight the popular, religious, and courtly styles of old Spain through references to a Renaissance madrigal, "De los álamos vengo, madre," to a *Tantum ergo* in the Visigothic mode, and to Scarlatti. In addition to an obvious nod to contemporaneous Neoclassic ideals with respect to models and instrumental choice, the gravity and twangy dissonances of the second movement confirm the differences between this work and Poulenc's *Concert champêtre*—the latter bucolic and lit with the pastels of Watteau, the former an incisive pen and ink drawing by Goya.

Atlántida, an extended oratorio for chorus and orchestra, occupied Falla on and off for the last two decades of his life (1925–46) and was left incomplete at his death. Like *El retablo* and the harpsichord concerto, it was premised on a synthesis of the vernacular and sacred, early and contemporary styles. Such a range of models and sources of inspiration (which included thirteenth-century Spanish songs in the fashioning of incidental music for *Auto de los reyes magos,* 1923) made Falla very much a composer of his time, even as he succeeded in finding a personal voice that emphasized a national bias.

It is a curiosity that the search for a genuine Spanish musical expression by native composers should have followed in the wake of repeated attempts by foreigners to tap the colors and especially the rhythms of the Hispanic peninsula. From Glinka's *Jota aragonesa* (1845) and Liszt's *Rhapsodie espagnole* ('Folies d'Espagne et jota aragonesa,' c. 1863) to other works of the second half of the nineteenth century by Balakirev, Rimsky-Korsakov, and Glazunov, (see p. 117), attempts to capture a genuine Spanish manner had been numerous and well-received. The continuing infatuation with a limited number of Spanish moods and models reached its high point with a group of works by Debussy and Ravel (p. 123) at a time that also saw native Spanish composers at work trying to define a version of their musical language worthy of export. Ultimately, the achievements of the Russians and the French proved to be more vivid in the popular imagination than products nourished on native Spanish soil, and probably no work by any composer defined the essence of the Spanish spirit more indelibly for the man in the street than Bizet's *Carmen*. Thus the Spanish composer's legitimate search for a national expression came after other countries had appropriated its surface characteristics in the popular pursuit of exotic manners. Oddly, Debussy's "La soirée dans Grenade" (1903) or Ravel's *Rapsodie espagnole* (1907) and *Bolero* (1928) ultimately came to symbolize an authentic Spanish expression as much or more than Falla's renowned "Ritual Fire Dance" or Granados's "The Maid and the Nightingale" from the *Goyescas* of 1911.

Falla's search for a genuinely Spanish music parallels similar developments in other countries. Yet while some have claimed that his art did not admit of ready continuation and that it signalled an exhaustion of the possibilities of Spanish nationalism, this is surely too narrow a view. An interesting if not final chapter to the Spanish story comes with Roberto Gerhard (1896-1970), also a pupil of Pedrell (until 1922) as well as Schoenberg (1923-28), whose early *Cançons populars catalanes* (1928) was conducted by Webern in Vienna at the International Society for Contemporary Music (ISCM) festival of 1932. If the *Cancionero de Pedrell* and the ballet *Don Quixote,* both of 1941, effectively brought an end to his involvement with Spanish themes, there can be no doubt that the foundation of his style in a native folk art had an important and ameliorating effect on his final endorsement of a brand of Schoenbergian serialism in his mature years. Equally significant, though from a more distant geographical angle, the protracted interest of the American George Crumb in Lorcan texts and Spanish rhythms and colors confirms that Iberian motifs and sonorities still have the potential to fire the imagination of the late twentieth-century composer.

ENGLAND

VAUGHAN WILLIAMS.   In England, where no major composer had surfaced between Purcell and Elgar, it was natural that Ralph Vaughan Williams (1872-1958) and Gustav Holst (1874-1934) should rely on the character of English folk song and the traditions of Elizabethan music to assist in the promotion of an English style. The English Folk Song Society, devoted to the collection and publication of native melodies, was founded in 1898 and proved to be a natural ally to a generation of composers who sought to develop a national music distinguishable from Continental practice. Similarly, the formation of a Purcell Society in 1876 led to the first volume of a projected complete edition in 1878. *The Old English Edition*, devoted to the music of Arne, Blow, Byrd, Campion, and others, appeared between 1889 and 1902, and after the turn of the century a series of volumes devoted to *The English Madrigal School* (Weelkes, Wilbye, Morley) appeared beginning in 1913. Finally, the monumental *Tudor Church Music,* including the sacred works of Byrd, Gibbons, Tallis, and Taverner, began issuing from the press in 1922. Arkwright, Fellowes, and others who served as editors of these collections thus served a similar function to Pedrell in Spain in spotlighting both native folk and early polyphonic music, and in the process served to heighten the national conscience with respect to its musical traditions.

Vaughan Williams had begun as early as 1903 to gather and edit English folk melodies (in all he collected over 800 songs) and to edit music for the Purcell Society. His work on *The English Hymnal* (1906) also led to his acquaintance with the English hymn tune repertoire, to his adaptation of thirty-five to forty from folk songs, and to the composition of new ones, of which his *Sine nomine* ("For all the saints") is justly the most celebrated. The influence of folk song in original works is first witnessed in his *Norfolk Rhapsodies* (1905–06) and in the quotation of two tunes in *A Sea Symphony* (1903–09) to texts of Walt Whitman, but his personal voice first emerged in his *Fantasia on a Theme by Thomas Tallis* for double string orchestra (1910). He had been initially introduced to Tallis's Phrygian melody while working on *The English Hymnal* (Ex. 21.1), and discovered in working out its potential for divided string groups a harmonic, rhythmic, and spatial language that was to remain fundamental to the end of his career. Here, chordal blocking and the alternating triple and quintuple metrics blend with modal melodies and harmonic cross-relations traceable to the practice of Tudor musicians.

Vaughan Williams argued the question of nationalism and the use of folk melodies in numerous articles,[1] and in so doing took on the attending question of originality. For him the only obligation of the composer was to find the *mot*

Example 21.1. Tallis, Third Mode Melody.

Third Mode Melody
With deep feeling

Thomas Tallis, 1567

Example 21.1 (Continued)

juste, which meant the right music for the right occasion. Acknowledging that the influence of the folk-song collector Cecil Sharp (1859–1924) had helped to sharpen his views on the topic, he also spoke candidly of his protracted exposure to hymn tunes:

> In 1904 I undertook to edit the music of a hymn-book. This meant two years with no "original" work except a few hymn-tunes. I wondered then if I were "wasting my time." The years were passing and I was adding nothing to the sum of musical invention. But I know now that two years of close association with some of the best (as well as some of the worst) tunes in the world was a better musical education than any amount of sonatas and fugues.[2]

Eventually, Vaughan Williams' development saw the absorption of qualities first encountered in native repertoires ultimately transcend any evidence of dependency, though works based on folk songs were composed to the last decade of his life. The easy pastoral style of his earliest works, which blends polymodalities traceable to indigenous repertoires with a sensitive awareness of the orchestral manners of the French impressionists, is clearly audible in his *Third Symphony* ("Pastoral") of 1921. The work's unrelenting sameness of mood, favored by some but prompting the English composer Peter Warlock to state that "it is all too much like a cow looking over a gate," was followed, however, by the ballet score *Job: A Masque for Dancing* (1927–30) after William Blake. Invoking a more varied syntax, an occasional Dionysian manner, and a rethinking of orchestral sonority (including a prominent use of the saxophone as an impersonation of the Devil and the sounds of the full organ to underscore massive orchestral blockings), Vaughan Williams prepared the way for his most archly dissonant symphony, the Fourth in F minor of 1931–35.

Two principal motives heard at the outset of the work bind the traditional four-movement structure compared by some critics to Beethoven's Fifth, and provide a cohesiveness that is easy to follow:

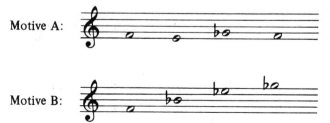

The use of a tuba to project the fugato theme of the Scherzo's trio in the third movement underscores the composer's interest in unusual sonorities evident as late as his *Romance* for harmonica, strings, and piano of 1951; his *Tuba Concerto* of 1954; and even his opus ultimum, the Ninth Symphony of 1950, where three saxophones are cojoined with flügelhorn.

The legacy of his nine symphonies is imposing among his contemporaries, and together with many choral works and ballets, of which *Job* must be considered a masterwork, guarantee him a permanent and special position among composers of his generation.

WALTON.   Besides Vaughan Williams, no English composer active during the period of the 1920s through the 1940s achieved greater renown than William Walton (1902–83), who was popularly viewed as the epitome of the British composer. His earliest success, following his departure as a student from Oxford, was the entertainment *Façade* (1921–22, rev. 1942) for reciter and instrumental ensemble (fl/pic, cl/b cl, sax, tpt, perc, vc). Using experimental verses of Edith Sitwell, the convergence of numerous ingredients is clearly visible in the use of recitation to a hybrid ensemble related to *Pierrot lunaire* (flute and clarinet doublings, cello) and *Histoire du soldat* (trumpet, percussion). In his incorporation of the saxophone, Walton set the stage for the use of popular dances of the time, including the foxtrot (No. 20) and tango (No. 6), which had only recently been adopted by Hindemith (*Kammermusik No. 1*, 1920–21) and Stravinsky (*Histoire du soldat*, 1918) respectively. The Spanish note is caught in several numbers (4, 5, 6, 9) through rhythms (especially the habanera rhythm of the "Tango-Pasodoble") and coloristic effects (muted trumpet, castanets, and string pizzicato simulating a guitar), while others are bathed in a lazy-hazy mock "impressionism" ("En famille" and "Lullaby for Jumbo"). In addition, the witty urbanity of Sitwell's seminonsense verses helped to cast Walton as a member of the young avant-garde in the years immediately preceding the first Stein-Thomson collaborations. But in spite of Walton's intimate friendship with Sitwell's brothers, Osbert and Sacheverell, who tried to persuade him of a natural intellectualism, Walton resisted and gradually relinquished the early profile secured by *Façade*.

For Walton's ultimate reputation as a composer was neither as a practitioner of modernist tendencies nor English national aspirations but as a craftsman who owed as much to continental composers (Hindemith, Ravel, Stravinsky) as to any identifiable English strain. Yet, many of the themes of his works such as the coronation marches *Crown Imperial* (1937), *Orb and Sceptre* (1953), and the *Coronation Te Deum* (1952–53) marked him as the "official" state composer of the period, and in his work for Laurence Olivier's Shakespeare films (*Henry V*, 1943–44; *Hamlet*, 1947; *Richard III*, 1955) the impression was confirmed.

In his two impressive solo concertos, one for viola of 1928–29 (premiered by Hindemith) and another for violin of 1938–39 (commissioned by Jascha Heifetz), Walton composed two staples of the repertoire for their respective instruments. But the latter's open Romanticism and beguiling lyricism cojoined to a dazzling virtuosity spoke of a bygone age to many who now found his *Belshazzar's Feast* (1930–31), for Baritone, chorus, and orchestra, effective but traditional. While in the latter instance, public acceptance and critical response in certain quarters may have been at odds, few failed to recognize the power with which Walton addressed the venerable English choral tradition in a highly dramatic and extraordinarily brilliant score.

His later *Troilus and Cressida* (1950–54), after Chaucer, confirmed a native bias with respect to textual matters, but two works of the 1960s—orchestral pieces on themes by Hindemith and Britten—point not only to personal affinities but to a concern for craftmanship that was apparent from the time of his *Symphony No. 1* (1932–35). Ultimately, Walton would probably not have been displeased with the final judgment that in *Belshazzar's Feast* and the *Violin Concerto* he had composed the two finest examples of English oratorio and solo concerto since Elgar.

BRITTEN.   Benjamin Britten (1913–1976) was England's most internationally acclaimed composer among those who emerged just prior to the beginning of World War II. His debt to English predecessors like Vaughan Williams and Holst may be taken for granted, yet the beginning of his career was marked by a search for stylistic independence from native sources. After seeing a performance of *Wozzeck* in 1934 he expressed a desire to go to Vienna to study with Berg, but family objections prevailed. By 1939, already a collaborator with as well as a friend of W. H. Auden, he followed the English poet to New York, and during this period composed verses from Rimbaud's *Les Illuminations* (1939) as a gesture of growing freedom as well as developing sensitivity to problems of versification. Later settings of Michelangelo, Hölderlin, and Pushkin in their original languages are equally marks of an attitude sensitive to the resolution of linguistic questions.

The discovery of Purcell and Crabbe (1754–1832) inspired Britten to a reconsideration of English declamation and English themes, respectively, and his return to England brought the first evidence of this new orientation in *A Ceremony of Carols* (1942), *Rejoice in the Lamb* (1943), and the immensely evocative and characteristic *Serenade* (1943) for tenor, horn, and strings. Confecting an anthology of English poems ranging from fifteenth-century anonymous sources to Ben Johnson, Blake, Keats, and Tennyson, Britten fashioned a unity in the *Serenade* largely through a pervasive reference to nocturnal motifs, which he framed with a pair of horn solos. The exuberant writing for both horn and voice in Tennyson's "Nocturne" is counterbalanced by the haunting ground of the "Lyke-Wake Dirge," a text Stravinsky was to appropriate in his *Cantata* of 1952. While the work reflects the extent to which nineteenth-century musical values persisted in many quarters through the period of World War II, it also discloses the discovery of a highly personal voice attuned to the nuances of the English language, a refined harmonic sense aware of the potential of the modes as well as the power of tritonal juxtapositions, an ear sensitive to the shadings of pitch (as the quarter-tone bending of the horn at the close of Blake's "Elegy" or the untempered pitches of the natural horn in the Prelude and Postlude), and an instinctive sense of dramatic shaping, which was soon to find release in the world of opera.

BLAKE, *Elegy*

O rose, thou art sick;
The invisible worm
That flies in the night,
In the howling storm,

Has found out thy bed of crimson joy;
And his dark, secret love
Does thy life destroy.

TENNYSON, *Nocturne*

The splendour falls on castle walls
And snowy summits old in story:
The long night shakes across the lakes,
And the wild cataract leaps in glory:

Blow, bugle, blow, set the wild echoes flying,
Bugle, blow; answer, echoes, answer, dying.

O hark, O hear, how thin and clear,
And thinner, clearer, farther going!
O sweet and far from cliff and scar
The horns of Elfland faintly blowing!

Blow, let us hear the purple glens replying:
Bugle, blow; answer, echoes, answer, dying.

O love, they die in yon rich sky,
They faint on hill or field or river:
Our echoes roll from soul to soul
And grow for ever and for ever.

Blow, bugle, blow, set the wild echoes flying;
And answer, echoes, answer, dying.

Dirge (Anon., 15th cent.)

This ae nighte, this ae nighte,
Every nighte and alle,
Fire and fleet and candle-lighte,
And Christe receive thy saule.

When thou from hence away art past,
Every nighte and alle,
To Whinnymuir thou com'st at last;
And Christe receive thy saule.

If ever thou gav'st hoe'n and shoen
Every nighte and alle,
Sit thee down and put them on;
And Christe receive thy saule.

The opera *Peter Grimes* followed a reading of the Suffolk poet George Crabbe, a poet who with pervasive psychological insight dwelt on themes of misery and guilt among ordinary folk. A work that brought international attention and whose power still holds the operatic stage, it proved to be the beginning of the rejuvenation of English opera for the first time since Purcell. To his predilection for Phrygian and Lydian modalities and the harmonic and textual advances of the *Serenade*, Britten added the operatic conventions of aria and set orchestral piece. In the latter category, the four "Sea Interludes and Passacaglia" have achieved a notable popularity and dramatize Britten's indebtedness to Debussy's *Pelléas*, Berg's *Wozzeck*, and especially to Musorgsky's *Boris Godunov* in the second interlude, "Sunday Morning," where church bells resound with echoes of the Coronation Scene.

Example 21.2. Britten, *Peter Grimes:* "Sunday Morning."

Copyright 1945 by Boosey & Hawkes, Ltd. Renewed 1972. Reprinted by permission of Boosey & Hawkes, Inc.

Britten's interest in his English heritage continued to manifest itself throughout his career not only in his choice of texts (Shakespeare's *Midsummer Night's Dream*, 1960; *Canticle II:* "Abraham and Isaac," a Chester miracle play, 1952; Eliot, *Canticle IV and V*, 1971, 1975) but in the setting of innumerable English folk songs, including the orchestral *Suite on English Folk Tunes* (1966–75) and numerous arrangements of the music of Henry Purcell, including his well known *The Young Person's Guide to the Orchestra* ("Variations and Fugue on a Theme of Purcell") of 1946.

In addition to these native forces, however, Britten's admiration for Mahler, Berg, and Stravinsky is to be noted throughout his career, though a derivative quality is not openly perceivable after the early works. In a more general sense, however, he reinforced Stravinsky's interest in textual problems and Neoclassic clarity, Berg's formal and harmonic sense, and Mahler's march rhythms and brooding philosophical inquiry. True, as late as *A Midsummer Night's Dream* (1960; p. 552) and *A War Requiem* (1961; see p. 495), Britten's devotion to English textual sources continued to reinforce a native point of view. But even though in the *War Requiem* Britten married the English choral traditions (including boys' voices) to the pervasive themes of innocence and wickedness found in his operas, his message is now unmistakably universal. And just as the engineering of twelve-note complexes in his Shakespeare opera suggests that the composer's purview is not restricted to geographical or cultural boundaries, so the adaptations from Japanese nō drama in *Curlew River* (1964) confirmed his ecumenical vision.[3] The mixture of the various ingredients, however, always remained Britten's own and resulted in an art notable for its communicative power.

A War Requiem of 1962, which made an enormous impression in its first seasons, was somewhat neglected if not dismissed in the following years. It may yet prove to be Britten's masterpiece, and will be considered among the messages of hope (Chapter 23) written by composers of various nationalities who, while preserving their native dialect, sought to address issues that transcend provincial aspirations.

It should not be judged from this brief overview of a thriving English musical conscience tuned to national traditions that England's contribution to the contemporary musical scene was limited to such a point of view. From the turn of the century through the decade of the 1940s, a procession of composers whose inclination ranged from Edwardian Romanticism to the folk-song movement, Neoclassicism, Serialism, and various avant-garde manners can be seen in an extensive list: Elgar, Delius, Bantock, Davies, Vaughan Williams, Havergal Brian, Holst, Bax, Ireland, Bridge, Cyril Scott, Percy Grainger, Bliss, Walton, Constant Lambert, Lord Berners, Peter Warlock, Lennox Berkeley, Howells, Rubbra, Finzi, Elizabeth Luytens, Tippett, and Britten.

In the post-World War II period in particular, an extraordinarily vital musical culture continued to produce personalities whose position in the international avant-garde vied with the best and most provocative anywhere. The names of Peter Maxwell Davies, Harrison Birtwistle, Alexander Goehr, Robin Holloway, Richard Rodney Bennett, John Tavener, and Oliver Knussen are sufficient to suggest the diversity of expression among their lists. Consideration of these composers will surface in subsequent chapters topically and without special concern for national origins.

ITALY

Italy's musical importance in the nineteenth century rested primariy in the realm of opera as the names of Bellini, Donizetti, and Verdi will attest. If her cultivation of instrumental music after 1850 was negligible, the rise of a group of composers born around 1880 known as the "generazione dell'ottanta" gave promise of a change in the situation.

Several aesthetic strains can be readily identified in Italian musical culture at the turn of the century involving these men. While Puccini (1858–1924) was clearly the senior and most successful composer among them, the cult of *verismo* was also promoted at the hands of Montemezzi (1875–1952) and Zandonai (1883–1944). But in addition, an interest in Italy's rich musical traditions prior to the nineteenth century was also apparent in the work of composers like Casella (1883–1947), Ghedini (1892–1965), Pizzetti (1880–1968), and Malipiero (1882–1973), who collectively shared a neoclassical inclination that paralleled developments in other Western European countries (see Chapter 15). A concern for assisting the revival of such important early Italian masters as Monteverdi and Vivaldi led to complete editions of their works by Malipiero, and the resulting enthusiasm for this heritage could be spotted in numerous composers of the next generation such as Dallapiccola. Furthermore, even so popular a composer as Respighi (1879–1936) responded directly to such native repertoires in his adoption of plainsong (the Roman orchestral works; a violin concerto on Gregorian themes) as well as the music of the seventeenth and eighteenth centuries (*Gli Uccelli, Ancient Airs and Dances*) which led him to the discovery of a glittering impressionist style that courted both the heroic and a more restrained neoclassic vein. Thus Italy opened the twentieth century with memories of a rich legacy and evidence of talent sufficient to capitalize on it.

In retrospect it is observable that Casella and Busoni proved to be the strongest pedagogical influences—the former having taught Dallapiccola, Petrassi, and Malipiero; the latter Malipiero and Ghedini. But Busoni's lengthy stay abroad early in his career was counter-balanced only by a brief tenure (c. 1913) at the Liceo musicale in Bologna where he soon felt his hopes for promoting a musical revolution were misplaced. Among their pupils born shortly after the turn of the century, Petrassi (b. 1904) and especially Dallpiccola (1904–75; see pp. 488–93) were the first to show their potential for involvement in the issues of the avant-garde. We should not forget, too, that in Russolo (see pp. 236–40), a non-musician, we have already seen the possibility for the creation of a radical movement on Italian soil. It seemed almost logical that Milan, the birthplace of Futurism, should have proved to be the site for the first electronic developments in 1955 (see p. 595).

Casella's Società Italiana di Musica Moderna (1917–19) provided a momentary impetus to composers of various stripes (Malipiero, Castelnuovo-Tedesco, Pizzetti, Respighi, Zandonai) in the promotion of progressive musical values, but soon led to the denouncement by the last three of these of what they saw as harmful progressive trends. Casella and Malipiero regrouped with the support of the poet D'Annunzio in the formation of the Corporazione delle Nuovi Musiche (1923–28) which pledged to introduce to Italy "the latest expressions and the most recent researches of contemporary musical art." Performances of works like *Pierrot lunaire*, conducted by Schoenberg, and Stravinsky's *Les noces* promoted throughout the country a vigorous musical life that soon merged with the International Society for Contemporary Music that had been formed in 1922.

The World War II years, a period of anti-semitic censorship akin to that found in Germany, found pressure being brought to bear against most new works less because of their radical idiom than because of their lack of Italian qualities. Furthermore, the number of institutions established during the 1920s and 1930s for the promotion of new music and early music alike is remarkable; the Venice Festival of Contemporary Music (1930) and the Maggio Musicale Fiorentino (1933) persist to this day.

Among the generation of composers who came to the fore for the first time in the 1930s, Dallapiccola (see p. 488-93) and Petrassi were the most important. But the generation that was born about this time and that surfaced in the decade following the end of World War II was both larger and richer in variety. Building upon the diverse legacy of the first half of the century, this generation would contribute to the musical scene in a manner disproportionate to the size of their country (see p. 595).

REPERTOIRE

Falla, *La vida breve* (1904-05), lyric drama
    El amor brujo (1914-15), ballet
    El sombrero de tres picos (1919), ballet
    El retablo de maese Pedro (1919-22), puppet opera
    Concerto (1923-26), hpd, fl, ob, cl, vn, vc
    Atlántida (1926-46, inc.), oratorio
Vaughan Williams, *A Sea Symphony* (1903-09)
    Norfolk Rhapsodies (1905-06)
    Fantasia on a Theme by Thomas Tallis (1910)
    Job: A Masque for Dancing (1927-30), ballet
    Symphony No. 4, f minor (1931-35)
Holst, *A Somerset Rhapsody* (1906-07)
    Four Old English Carols (1907)
    Two Psalms (1912)
    The Planets (1914-16)
Britten, *A Ceremony of Carols* (1942)
    Rejoice in the Lamb (1943)
    Serenade (1943), T, hn, str
    Peter Grimes (1945), opera
    Variations and Fugue on a Theme by Purcell (1946)
    A Midsummer Night's Dream (1960), opera
    War Requiem (1961), S, T, Bar, boys' chorus, chorus
    Songs and Proverbs of William Blake (1965), Bar, pf
    Suite on English Folk Tunes (1966-75)

READING

Ralph Vaughan Williams, "Who Wants the English Composer?" (1912), repr. in H. J. Foss, *Ralph Vaughan Williams* (London, 1950).

Ralph Vaughan Williams, "Should Music be National?" from *National Music* (1934), repr. in *Composers on Music*, ed. S. Morgenstern (New York, 1956).

Benjamin Britten, "On Behalf of Gustav Mahler," *Tempo*, ii (1942).

Erwin Stein, "Britten Seen Against His English Background" in *Orpheus in New Guises* (London, 1953).

Manuel de Falla, "Cante Jondo" in S. Morgenstern, ed., *Composers on Music* (New York, 1956), 402-09.

Benjamin Britten, "On Realizing the Continuo in Purcell's Songs," *Henry Purcell: 1659-1695*, ed. I. Holst (London, 1959).

Gilbert Chase, *The Music of Spain* (New York, 1959).

Eric Walter White, *Benjamin Britten: His Life and Operas* (London, 1970).

Peter Evans, *The Music of Benjamin Britten* (London, 1979).

Enrique Franco, "Manuel de Falla" in *New Grove Dictionary of Music and Musicians* (1980), VI, 371-74.

Michael Trend, *The Music Makers: Heirs and Rebels of the English Musical Renaissance, Edward Elgar to Benjamin Britten* (London, 1985).

CHAPTER 22

AN "AMERICAN" MUSIC FOR AMERICA

If English folksong and the traditions of Tudor church music assisted in the development of an English style at the turn of the century, in America, a country that was musically just beginning to come of age, the challenge to develop a national music through recourse to the music of the Indians and the Negros was sounded by Dvořák.

One of the first American spokesmen for the cause was Arthur Farwell, who in establishing the Wa-Wan Press (1901) called on American composers to follow a program using American folk material (ragtime, black, Indian and cowboy songs) as a basis. Paradoxically, although MacDowell, as a product of French and German training, rejected Dvořák's advice and Farwell's invitation, he wrote one of the most durable pieces of the type in his *Indian Suite* (1891–95) for orchestra. Other composers turned to minstrel show-tunes and spirituals, and Henry Gilbert (1868–1928) lavished Creole melodies from Louisiana in his *The Dance in Place Congo* (1908). Many who were given neither to Indianist nor folklorist ventures occasionally succumbed to the temptation to write such works as a demonstration of their independence from German influence.

Simultaneously, however, the French influence persisted in the music of Charles Martin Loeffler (1861–1935) and Charles Griffes (1884–1920). While Loeffler's French strain leaned toward the Symbolist poets (Verlaine, Maeterlinck), Griffes' taste was more for Oriental motifs and a species of musical exoticism. His *Sho-jo* (a Japanese pantomime for fl, ob, cl, hrp, Chinese drum, tam-tam, str of 1917) and *The Pleasure Dome of Kubla-Khan* (pf, 1912; orch, 1917) typify the endorsement of European tastes by those who were unconcerned about discovering an independent American style.

CHARLES IVES

BACKGROUNDS; SONGS, 1897–1917.   The most notable example of an American composer at the turn of the century who was instinctively drawn to America's repertory of melodies and particularly to its hymnody was Charles Ives, 1874–1954 (Figure 22.1). For all of his iconoclastic disposition and seemingly modern tendencies, in his use of such materials and the value he placed on them he represented the end of the Romantic era. In his philosophy—namely, the transcendentalism of Emerson and Thoreau—he is similarly of the nineteenth

Figure 22.1. Charles Ives.
Photo by Eugene Smith.

century. It is instructive to begin a consideration of Ives' music with the sound of the early songs he wrote on texts formerly set by Schumann and Brahms, *Ich grolle nicht* (1899) and *Feldeinsamkeit* (1897), in order to appreciate that his ear for Wolf and Debussy was as keen as that for competing brass bands. In the latter of these songs the occasional pentatonicisms yield to the larger impression that the young composer has set for himself a lyric task familiar to Gounod in casting a new melody ("Ave Maria") over the framework of J. S. Bach's C major Prelude (*Well-Tempered Clavier*, Book I) whose insistent arpeggiation Ives maintains in the piano accompaniment.

Feldeinsamkeit (1897)

Ich ruhe still im hohen, grünen Gras
Und sende lange meinen Blick nach
  oben,
Von Grillen rings umschwirrt ohn'
  Unterlass,
Von Himmelsbläue wundersam umwoben.

Loneliness of the Open Country

I lie quietly in the tall, green grass,
And gaze longingly into the depths
  above,
Surrounded by the incessant buzzing
  of the crickets
And the wondrous blue of Heaven.

Die schönen weissen Wolken zieh'n dahin	The beautiful white clouds drift along
Durch's tiefe Blau wie schöne stille Träume.	Through the deep azure like beautiful, silent dreams.
Mir ist als ob ich längst gestorben bin	I feel as though I had died long ago,
Und ziehe selig mit durch ew'ge Räume.	And drift with them blissfully through eternal realms.
Ich ruhe still im hohen, grünen Gras	I lie quietly in the tall, green grass,
Und sende lange meinen Blick nach oben.	And gaze longingly into the depths above.

Herman Almers

Ives' dependency on the tunes of his native land, however, can be seen as early as his *Variations on "America"* (1891) for organ. It was a taste he was never to lose and a feature that was so persistent that the listener who is nonconversant with them is seriously deprived of the fundamental impact of his message.

Ives's modernism, which seems to have developed largely without reference to current European developments, includes a prominent experimentation with the use of multiple sound sources emphasizing a sense of musical space. This in turn can lead to rhythmic simultaneities involving multiple tempi and multiple metric conjunctions. His interest, encouraged from an early age by his father, in stretching his ears to accommodate all manner of sonorities led also to the direct use of polytonality, atonality, the use of quarter-tones and tone clusters, and even a toying with proto-serial and proto-aleatoric passages. In much of his music the confusion is counterbalanced by a mystical transcendentalism stated on occasion in a language very close to Mahler's (Ives's Fourth Symphony, third movement) and at other times evoking the world of Debussy (*Three Places in New England:* "The Housatonic at Stockbridge").

Ives is a composer of his time in other ways. His concern for the issue of war led him not only to crusade for the Liberty Bond sales in World War I but to numerous poignant musical statements. The use of the tune "In the Sweet Bye and Bye" in his *Second Orchestral Set* (1915) stemmed from an experience following the sinking of the *Lusitania,* when he heard people in a New York subway station break voluntarily into song. His *Tom Sails Away* (1917) is as heart-rending as (and in some ways unwittingly prepares the ground for) Barber's *Knoxville: Summer 1915* (1945) as it projects George M. Cohan's "Over There" in the penultimate line with a caution that miraculously escapes sentimentality.

Tom Sails Away (1917)

Scenes from my childhood are with me.
I'm in the lot behind our house up on the hill,
A spring day's sun is setting,
Mother with Tom in her arms is coming
Towards the garden; the lettuce rows are showing green.

Thinner grows the smoke o'er the town,
Stronger comes the breeze from the ridge,
'Tis after six, the whistles have blown.
The milk train's gone down the valley.
Daddy is coming up the hill from the mill,
We run down the lane to meet him.

But today! Today Tom sailed away for,
For over there, over there, over there!
Scenes from my childhood are floating before my eyes.

Charles Ives
From: Nineteen Songs. © *1935 Merion Music, Inc.*
Used by permission of the publisher.

The openly maudlin text of John McCrae's *In Flanders Fields* is similarly delivered from a cloying treatment through an ingenious combination of the "Marseillaise," "America" ("God Save the Queen"), and "Columbia, the Gem of the Ocean." The symbolism is not difficult to read, though less obvious is a possible reference to Debussy, who had also placed "God Save the Queen" in octaves in the bass of his "Hommage à S. Pickwick Esq. P.P.M.P.C." and the identical interior snippet from the "Marseilles" in the soprano of his "Feux d'artifice," both *Preludes* from Book II published only a few years before in 1913.

In Flanders Fields (1917)

In Flanders fields the poppies blow
Between the crosses, row on row,
That mark our place, and in the sky
The larks still bravely singing fly,
Scarce heard amidst the guns below.
We are the dead. Short days ago
We lived, felt dawn, saw sunset glow,
Loved and were loved, and now we lie
In Flanders fields.

Take up our quarrel with the foe!
To you from falling hands we throw
The torch. Be yours to hold it high.
If ye break faith with us who die
We shall not sleep though the poppies grow
In Flanders fields.

John McCrae

Example 22.1. Ives, *In Flanders Fields*, mm. 28–37.

Copyright 1955 by Peer International Corporation. Copyright renewed. Used by permission.

Example 22.1 (Continued)

The revivals, camp meetings, and holiday celebrations that Ives repeatedly portrayed in his compositions incorporate a healthy arsenal of popular songs, dance tunes, and gospel hymns. In every instance they reflect musical messages received as a child in his native Connecticut. Works that draw heavily on this childhood experience include "Children's Day" from *Symphony No. 3* (1904), "The Fourth of July" (1911-13), "Declaration Day" (1912), "The Children's Holiday at Putnam's Camp" from the *First Orchestral Set* (1912), and the *Sonata for Violin and Piano No. 4* (1916), subtitled "Children's Day at the Camp Meeting."

His use of ragtime (*Ragtime Pieces*, 1902-04) antedates its appearance in the music of European composers by a decade and a half, even if it was not through his example that the latter were finally introduced to it. Ultimately, Ives must be seen both as special case and symptomatic figure of his day. The age of German hegemony in music was dying at the very moment the United States was struggling to find its own artistic voice. Ives was educated at Yale, and he composed with reference to the music he knew from his community and church. No quantity of Indianist music could ever have protested the prospect of a burgeoning American music as forcefully as Ives, and later only Copland and Harris applied a somewhat distant formula with equal success.

Although Schoenberg repeatedly expressed his negative feelings regarding the use of folk materials in the polemical foreword to *Three Satires*, op. 28 (1925) and in the articles *Folk-Music and Art-Music* (c. 1926) and *Why no Great American Music?* (1934), after his death the following remarks were found among his papers:

> There is a great Man living in this Country—a composer. He has solved the problem how to preserve one's self and to learn. He responds to negligence by contempt. He is not forced to accept praise or blame. His name is Ives.[1]

SYMPHONY NO. 4.   *The Unanswered Question* of 1906 is a work for three performing bodies: an off-stage group of strings that plays a continuous stream of triads in a dream-like atmosphere that suggests an existence beyond time; a separate solo trumpet part, rhythmically uncoordinated with the strings, that periodically restates the same atonal musical idea; and four flutes who, in an increasingly agitated fashion, angrily respond in dense polyrhythmic clusters by way of an answer to the "silence of the druids" (strings) and the "perennial question of existence" (trumpet). Both the use of a literary idea to generate a form and the spatial juxtaposition of opposing forces reflect in microcosm many of the principal features of Ives's Fourth Symphony.

Composed between 1909 and 1916, the Fourth Symphony had to wait until 1965 for a complete performance, though its first two movements had been performed in 1927. Ives specialists judge it to be a synthesis of his career, which as a composer ended in the early 1920s. The work is in four movements: Prelude: Maestoso; Allegretto, Fugue; Andante moderato; Largo maestoso. Of this symphony Ives wrote, "The aesthetic program of the work is that of the searching questions of 'What?' and 'Why?', which the spirit of man asks of life. This is particularly the sense of the Prelude. The three succeeding movements are the diverse answers in which existence replies."[2]

Already in the Prelude there is a division of the musical resources into a main orchestra (including piano and optional voices) and a distant chamber ensemble of harp and solo strings, which softly intones an interior phrase from *Nearer My God to Thee* against the protestations of the orchestral basses.[3] Aside from this tune and another, *In the Sweet Bye and Bye*, the central statement is a setting of the hymn *Watchman, Tell Us of the Night* sung by the chorus:

Watchman, tell us of the night,
What the signs of promise are:
Traveler, o'er yon mountains height,
See that Glory-beaming star!

Watchman, aught of joy or hope?
Traveler, yes; it brings the day,
Promised day of Israel.
Dost thou see its beauteous ray?

Example 22.2. Ives, *Symphony No. 4*, Mvts. 1 and 4: "Nearer My God to Thee."

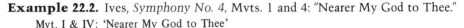

Mvt. I & IV: 'Nearer My God to Thee'
(opening)

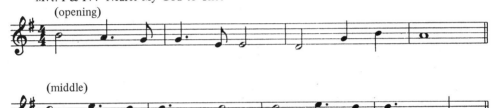

(middle)

Example 22.3. Ives, *Symphony No. 4*, Mvts. 1 and 2: "In the Sweet By and By," opening.

Mvts. I & II: 'In the Sweet By and By' (opening)

The second movement is the first of three replies to the questions posed by the Prelude. The composer wrote:

> "The second movement is not a scherzo in an accepted sense of the word, but rather a comedy—in which an exciting, easy and worldly progress through life is contrasted with the trials of the Pilgrims in their journey through the swamps and rough country. The occasional slow episodes—Pilgrims' hymns—are constantly crowded out and overwhelmed by the former. The dream, or fantasy, ends with an interruption of reality—the Fourth of July in Concord—brass bands, drum corps, etc."

The movement is marked by complexities of rhythm and tonality and a profusion of quotations: *Marching Through Georgia, In the Sweet Bye and Bye, Turkey in the Straw, Camptown Races, Throw Out the Lifeline, Beulah Land, Yankee Doodle, Jesus, Lover of My Soul,* and *Columbia the Gem of the Ocean.* Many of these tunes appear recurrently in other works of Ives.

Example 22.4. "Beulah Land," opening.

Mvt. II: 'Beulah Land' (opening)

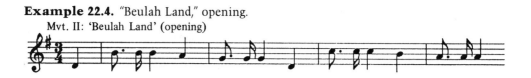

Example 22.5. "Jesus Lover of My Soul," opening.

'Jesus Lover of My Soul' (opening)

Ives spoke of the third movement as "an expression of the reaction of life into formalism and ritualism." A double fugue on the hymns *From Greenland's Icy Mountains* and *All Hail the Power*, its origins are in the first movement of his First String Quartet (1896). Ives' command of counterpoint seems easy and occasionally reminiscent of Mahler's slow movements. Near the end, an interior phrase from Brahms' *Alto Rhapsody* is clearly heard ("From Thy Psalter, Father of Love, a strain is clearly audible"), but the final gesture is reserved for the quotation of a passage from Handel's *Joy to the World.*

Example 22.6. Mvt. 3: "From Greenland's Icy Mountains," opening.

Mvt. III: 'From Greenland's Icy Mountains' (opening)

Example 22.7. "All Hail the Power of Jesus' Name," closing.

'All Hail the Power of Jesus' Name' (closing)

Example 22.8. Brahms, *Alto Rhapsody:* "Ist auf deinem Psalter," mm. 116–117.

Ist   auf   dei - nem   Psal - ter

"The last movement," Ives concludes, "is an apotheosis of the preceding content, in terms that have something to do with the reality of existence and its religious experience." Three independent forces are discernible: the percussion, the main orchestra, and the distant ensemble; the principal material is that of *Nearer My God to Thee* recalled from the first movement.

Replacing *Wunderhorn* lyric and melody with tunes and texts from his native America, Ives' idea of the symphony discloses more than a casual affinity with Mahler, both technically and spiritually. The text to the opening of Ives' *Fourth Symphony*, "Watchman, tell us of the night," which was inspired by the appearance of Haley's Comet in 1910, may be compared directly with Nietzsche's *Mitternachtlied* in Mahler's Third Symphony. And in numerous details such as the quotation of diatonic tunes in chromatic surroundings, the juxtaposition of the vernacular and the cultivated, the preoccupation with fate motifs, the concluding slow movements, cyclic manipulation, and competing brass bands, the affinity is secured. The recognition of these features, which suggest parallels in the music of Berg, in no way smudges his American profile or compromises an extraordinary individuality.

PIANO SONATA NO. 2. Ives' *Second Piano Sonata* ("Concord, Mass., 1840–1860") was written between 1910 and 1915 and captures for many the quintessential expression of his New England transcendentalism even more forcefully than the contemporaneous Fourth Symphony. Flourishing between 1830 and 1860, the New England transcendental literary-philosophical movement was most eloquently epitomized by Ralph Waldo Emerson and Henry David Thoreau, and, although lacking in any rigorous system, nonetheless held to the importance of human intuition and the rejection of traditional authority. Emerson's essay on "Self-Reliance" (1841) can be seen as a mirror of the kind of creative individualism that so appealed to Ives, who came increasingly to believe in the spontaneous adaptability of familiar material to the creative process. He also agreed with Emerson on the distinctions between "substance," or spiritual quality, and "manner," the means by which the former was translated in the creative act. He was also bold enough to suggest that Debussy might have been a better composer had his spiritual premise been stronger and his "form," "perfume," and "manner" less obviously in control.

Some have viewed such a philosophy as a kind of rationale for Ives' own brand of music making, as an excuse not only to place a premium on quotation of the commonplace but to serve it up in imaginative ways that do not always suggest the presence of a highly developed technique. An extraordinarily difficult work whose textures range from dense harmonic clusters to simple hymn-like passages, the *Concord Sonata* is a sprawling but powerful work whose four movements are entitled "Emerson," "Hawthorne," "The Alcotts," and "Thoreau." Something of the relationship Ives frequently observed between materials of widely differing origins can be seen in this sonata in his use of the similar opening motifs from Beethoven's Fifth Symphony and the hymn tune "Jesus, Lover of My Soul" (Ex. 22.5). There is no better way to sense the meaning of their appearance and juxtaposition than to read Ives' own words in his *Essays Before a Sonata*, of which the following is an excerpt from "The Alcotts".[4]

> Concord village itself reminds one of that common virtue lying at the height and root of all the Concord divinities. As one walks down the broad-arched street—passing the white house of Emerson, ascetic guard of a former prophetic beauty—he comes presently beneath the old elms overspreading the Alcott House . . . Within the house, on every side, lie remembrances of what imagination can do for the better amusement of fortunate children who had to do for themselves—much-needed lessons in these days of automatic, ready-made, easy entertainments which deaden rather than stimulate the creative faculty. And there sits the little old spinet piano Sophia Thoreau gave to the Alcott children, on which Beth played the old Scotch airs, and played at the *Fifth Symphony.*

> . . . All around you, under the Concord sky, there still floats the influence of that human-faith melody—transcendent and sentimental enough for the enthusiast or the cynic, respectively—reflecting an innate hope, a common interest in common things and common men—a tune the Concord bards are ever playing while they pound away at the immensities with a Beethoven-like sublimity, and with, may we say, a vehemence and perseverance, for that part of greatness is not so difficult to emulate.

AMERICAN COMPOSERS, ISSUES, AND ORGANIZATIONS IN THE 1920s

VARÈSE'S INTERNATIONAL COMPOSERS' GUILD AND COWELL'S *NEW MUSIC EDITION.* One of Ives' closest musical friends and his biographer, Henry Cowell (1897–1965), was born in California, and from the first disclosed an expanded outlook beyond the provincial, if dominant, influence of composers working on the Eastern seaboard. Though later this was to encompass a look westward across the Pacific to the cultures of the Orient, his initial investigations, as detailed in Chapter 12, primarily underscored an interest in amplifying the universe of sound sources and rhythmic relationships. A similar disposition, though with quite different results, on the part of Edgard Varèse (1883–1965; see Chapters 12 and 28), did not prevent these two composers from sensing a creative mission that was specifically American, a fact clearly reflected in the title of Varèse's *Amériques* (1918–21). Their mission was not, however, the promotion of a singular "American" style based on indigenous materials, but to establish a freedom of expression from conservative European models.

In 1921, Varèse and the harpist Carlos Salzedo founded the International Composers' Guild (ICG) with the idea of promoting performances of contemporary music. That its purview was not exclusively American is apparent from the name of their organization, but the insistence on programming only those works that had been previously unperformed soon led to a splinter group, which was to be known as the League of Composers. During the brief period of its activity, which lasted until 1927, the ICG sponsored many important first performances, including those of Varèse's *Hyperprism, Octandre,* and *Intégrales,* and the American premieres of Berg's *Kammerkonzert,* Schoenberg's *Pierrot lunaire,* Stravinsky's *Les noces,* and Webern's op. 5, conducted by such notables as Klemperer, Reiner, and Stokowski.

Beginning in 1927, the year of the ICG's demise, Cowell inaugurated his *New Music Edition,* a rare American forum for the publication of contemporary music.[5] Remaining active for a quarter of a century, it saw through the press such works as Varèse's *Density 21.5* and *Ionisation,* several works by Ives, including the second movement of the *Fourth Symphony,* and Schoenberg's op. 33b and Webern's op. 17, no. 2.

CARL RUGGLES.   Also prominently associated with the ICG was the American individualist, Carl Ruggles (1876–1971). Acknowledging Ives as a kind of spiritual godfather, he together with Cowell, Varèse, Wallingford Riegger (1885–1961), and John Becker (1886–1961) were sometimes referred to as the "American Five." But all of them shared not so much an interest in American themes as an awareness that a new opportunity lay ahead for them in forging a new music relatively free from outmoded ideals. Ruggles' *Angels* for muted brass of 1922 already betrays a sympathy with the aims of Cowell and Varèse with respect to the exploration of sonority and was performed at the 1925 festival of the new European-based International Society for Contemporary Musicians (ISCM), inaugurated in 1922. Though intensely chromatic and given to favoring minor seconds, tritones, and octave displacements, Ruggles' music only rarely uses twelve-note successions and is in no way serial in method. *Suntreader* (1926–31), for an orchestra with quintuple winds, is by common consent the most important work of Ruggles' maturity. Its biting dissonances and angular melodies are more than a little reminiscent of the orchestral style of Schoenberg's op. 16, no. 5, but the drama of the opening and recurring tympani strokes recalls nothing so much as Brahms's First Symphony. Although his *Men and Mountains* appeared in the first issue of Cowells' quarterly publication *New Music,* Ruggles' independence from the aesthetic of his friends such as Cowell, Ives, and Varèse, as well as Berg, whose music he admired, is noteworthy throughout his production and combines both delicacy and strength of expression.

RIEGGER AND BECKER.   The same may be said in the main of Riegger, whose *Study in Sonority* of 1926–27 for ten violins (or multiples thereof) is based on two dissonant harmonies, and whose *Dichotomy* for chamber orchestra of 1931–32 uses two rows of ten and eleven notes, respectively. Such a personal approach to the total chromatic led in his later years to the adoption of the twelve-note method as a source for motivic organization and culminated in his *Third Symphony* (premiered 1948), a work that brought him a belated recognition.

John Becker's *Sinfonia Brevis* (1929), whose spirited subtitles (I. A Scherzo in the Spirit of Mockery; II. Memories of War—Sorrow—Struggle—A Protest!) sound worse than their bite, and his *The Abongo* (1933), a work for percussion ensemble subtitled "A Primitive Dance," though less interesting and individual, conform to the progressive intentions and announced iconoclasm of the group with which he was associated. All of their careers, however, had to await their deaths for a comprehensive appraisal to begin and, in some instances, for performances to occur.

COPLAND: 1920 THROUGH WORLD WAR II

AN AMERICAN IN PARIS AND NEW YORK.   Although Copland (b. 1900) had seen a copy of the *"Concord" Sonata* on Goldmark's piano when he was his student (1917–19), Ives' music was not to be a primary formative influence. Copland has remarked that in 1919 he had heard Leo Ornstein (see p. 245) play his Futurist "Danse sauvage," but also that the opportunity to hear contemporary music of any kind in New York was rare and that he knew the names of only a handful of American composers, among whom John Alden Carpenter and Charles Griffes figured prominently.[6]

In 1920, Copland set off for France to study at a new school for American musicians in Fontainebleau. On his first evening in Paris, June 19, 1921, he noticed an advertisement for the premiere performance of *Les mariés de la tour Eiffel* by the Ballet Suédois at the Théâtre des Champs Elysées (see pp. 268–73), which he attended. Later Copland recalled the audience's reaction, which included whistles and hoots, and concluded that "It was the perfect way to spend one of my first nights in Paris—to get right into the action, where controversial music and dance were happening."[7]

At the school in Fontainebleau, founded by the American conductor Walter Damrosch, Copland studied composition with Paul Vidal, and only through the enthusiastic reports of a fellow student ultimately began attending harmony classes taught by Nadia Boulanger. Because of her, Copland decided to stay on the next year. Under her tutelage he (and several generations of American composers following him) was exposed to Fauré and Stravinsky and simultaneously to the French fascination for American jazz. Things happened quickly after that. His *The Cat and the Mouse* was accepted for publication by the venerable publishing house of Durand; and a visit to the cinema to see the Expressionist horror sensation *Nosferatu* led to the subject of his first ballet, *Grohg.* An extract, "Cortège macabre," was later premiered by the Eastman Philharmonia as one of six pieces from a field of forty-eight applicants at the first of Howard Hanson's American Composers' Concerts (May 2, 1925).

Before this latter event, however, Copland had returned home (June 1924) with an express commission to write an *Organ Symphony* for Nadia Boulanger to be presented January 11, 1925, with the New York Symphony orchestra under the baton of Damrosch himself. The latter's announcement from the stage following the performance could not have been better calculated to bring an unknown composer to the attention of the public: "Ladies and gentlemen, I am sure you will agree that if a gifted young man can write a symphony like this at twenty-three—within five years he will be ready to commit murder."[8] Virgil Thomson felt it to be a work of a new American generation; Lawrence Gilman, critic of the *Herald Tribune,* was enthusiastic; the work was repeated shortly thereafter on Boulanger's recommendation by the Boston Symphony Orchestra (BSO) under Koussevitsky; and the venerable Paul Rosenfeld, along with Minna Lederman, editor of the newly founded *The League of Composers' Review* (later known as *Modern Music*), undertook to find the appropriate patronage so that Copland could continue to compose.

Such details are worth mentioning for a variety of reasons, not least of which is the fact that but for such a turn of events Copland's ensuing career might have been quite different. He was one of the few composers of his and the following generation who ultimately made a living from writing music without obligatory recourse to teaching or writing—although in fact he did some of both from time to time. Furthermore, the introduction of Copland's work by Koussevitsky and the BSO signaled the beginning of a rare kind of leadership, which saw the first performance of sixty-six American pieces during Koussevitsky's reign there (1924-1949).

While Copland had initially gone to Europe to learn the art of composition, he had also discovered an "American" voice being used there by such composers as Debussy, Ravel, Stravinsky, and Milhaud (see Chapter 13). In America, among "serious" composers only John Alden Carpenter and Louis Gruenberg had employed ragtime and jazz rhythms, but George Gershwin's *Rhapsody in Blue* had been premiered in New York in February 1924, prior to Copland's return home in June.

The first work Copland wrote following the *Organ Symphony* was a commission from the League of Composers, and Claire Reis, managing director of the League, approached Koussevitzky with the idea of a premiere with the Boston Symphony Orchestra. The piece was written in the summer of 1925 at the MacDowell Colony, where Copland met Roy Harris for the first time. *Music for the Theatre*, as it came to be called, contained the syncopations and the "blue" notes that Copland hoped would label him as an American composer. This was followed by his *"Jazz" Piano Concerto* of 1926, a work that could hardly have been written totally innocent of Gershwin's *Rhapsody* (1924) or his *Piano Concerto* of 1925, although Copland has been hesitant to claim them as models. By 1927, Milhaud would pronounce the European infatuation with American jazz passé, even as Copland in the same year announced its importance for the American composer in an article, "Jazz Structure and Influence",[9] written for *Modern Music*. While Ravel, Berg, and a few others would champion the use of jazz for a few more years, Copland, too, tired of a too heavy reliance on what he claimed were its limitations to two principal moods—the blues and the snappy number. Conversely, he later properly noted that its influence was to persist throughout his career in numerous polyrhythmic explorations.

PIANO VARIATIONS.   The American strain that appeared in these early works and that was complemented by the Copland-Sessions Concerts of 1928–31 devoted to the promotion of American music[10], disappeared momentarily in works such as the *Piano Variations* (1930) and the *Short Symphony* (1933)—compositions that suggested a personal assimilation not only of Stravinsky's Neoclassicism but of features he had heard in the music of Schoenberg (piano harmonics), Webern (large intervals), and Bartók (additive rhythms) and others on numerous trips to Berlin, Vienna, and elsewhere. In the following example, which compares the opening of the theme of the *Variations* (a) with the opening of Variation 2 (b), it is possible to note many of these characteristics in addition to the use of register changes and doublings at the semitone (b) as a variational technique while still restricting the pitch content to the opening four pitches of the theme.

Example 22.9. Copland, *Piano Variations:* a) Theme; b) Variation 2 (opening).

Example 22.9 (Continued)

*) ◇ press down silently

Copland has spoken openly about the relation of his *Variations* to Schoenberg:

> The *Variations* incorporates a four-note motive on which the entire piece is based. Almost every note and chord in the piece relates back to these four notes. The *Variations* cannot be said to have been written according to all the rules of Schoenberg's method—for example, I repeat tones in their original form—but I have no doubt that the construction of the piece shows his influence. We were all at that time influenced by both Stravinsky and Schoenberg to some degree. I never rejected Schoenberg's ideas, even though I was closer to the French way of doing things. I believe that any method which proves itself so forceful an influence on the music of our times must be of considerable interest. In fact, I lectured about serialism at the New School as early as 1928. For me as a composer, the twelve-tone method was a way of thinking about music from a different perspective, somewhat like looking at a picture from a different angle so that you see things you might not have noticed otherwise. It was an aid in freshening the way I wrote at a time when I felt the need of change, and so I view it as an enrichment. It forced me into a different, more fragmented kind of melodic writing that in turn resulted in chords I had rarely used before. Thus my harmonic writing was affected in the *Piano Variations*, and in the works that followed . . . These pieces are more dissonant than my earlier works, yet I did not give up tonality. If a composer is secure in his judgment, his sense of what is musically valid does not change when he adopts a

"new" method . . . As for the traditional theme and variations form, this also I adapted to my own use. The twenty brief variations divide into two sections of ten without episodes or breaks between them, resulting in a sound that flows freely without discernible divisions.[11]

With the dissolution of the Copland-Sessions Concerts in December 1931, Copland planned the First Festival of Contemporary Music at Yaddo in April–May 1932, programming, in addition to many pieces from the loosely organized Young Composers' Group, Sessions' new *Piano Sonata*, his own *Variations*, and seven songs by Charles Ives. As Copland later stated, ". . . this was the first time a group of professional musicians were paying serious attention to Ives. It was a turning point in the recognition of his music."[12]

A SIMPLER LANGUAGE.   If the *Piano Variations* spelled the beginning of an interest in serial writing, as Copland later claimed, it was an interest that was laid aside in the period of the Depression years of the 1930s and the war years of the first half of the 1940s. Copland's retreat from a progressive, international language and return to a simpler style was due not to his encounters with the music of Satie, as it was to a certain degree in the music of his friend and fellow Boulanger-pupil Virgil Thomson (Fig. 22.2), nor to his discovery of Ives, but to a

Figure 22.2. Left to right: Samuel Barber, Virgil Thomson, Aaron Copland, Gian Carlo Menotti, and William Schuman in Thomson's apartment.
Photo by John Stewart

subscription to folk elements—both American and Latin-American—in the service of an increasing sensitivity to social issues of the time.

The hemispheric isolationism that prevailed during the Depression of the 1930s no doubt promoted the adoption of Americanist themes, an attitude that the coming of World War II did nothing to dispel. A champion of Chavez, Copland visited Mexico in 1932, and the ensuing *El salón Mexico* (1933–36) and *Billy the Kid* (1938) were the first evidence of this new style, which was to flourish until 1950 and under whose imprint the Copland name was to become established internationally. Copland's friendship with numerous leftist actors and musicians, including those of the Composers Collective, also prompted an attitude that it was the composer's responsibility to meet the people at least half way.[13] His first use of North American folk materials appeared in his *Second Hurricane*, a "play opera" of 1936, but the incorporation of them in later works, while highly memorable, never assumed major status. In his approach to music for the people, or music for use, Copland made friends and worked with personalities in the world of ballet, theater, radio, and the movies. With Agnes de Mille, who spawned the idea for *Rodeo*, he found himself in collaboration with not only a dancer but a choreographer whose directions could be as specific as Petipa's were to Tchaikovsky.[14] Other works that endorsed this aspect of his personality were *Lincoln Portrait* (with speaker, 1942), *Symphony No. 3* (1944–46), and *Red Pony* (music for a film, 1948). While a work like *Lincoln Portrait* combined "Yankee Doodle" with "Camptown Races" in a somewhat Ivesian manner, *Appalachian Spring* (1944) projected the Shaker tune "Simple Gifts" as a set of variations in such a forceful manner that it has entered the public conscience, having been adopted by folk singers and television commercials alike. On a more abstract level the bold and sturdy fourths and fifths of his "Fanfare for the Common Man" (1942, later incorporated into his *Symphony No. 3*), have also been accepted, though perhaps unidentified, as American copyrighted material for use at festivals and athletic contests.

Example 22.10. Copland, *Appalachian Spring:* "Simple Gifts."

Simple Gifts:

Example 22.11. Copland, *Fanfare for the Common Man.*

Although Copland's intermittent turn to serialism after 1950 was seen in some quarters as a capitulation, Copland had always had a lighter and a more severe style, as exemplified by *Appalachian Spring* and the *Piano Variations*, respectively. The consequences of this dualism will be pursued in Chapter 25.

ROY HARRIS

Harris's study in Los Angeles with Arthur Farwell virtually guaranteed a self-consciousness about the responsibilities of the American composer to write an "American" music. But as with Copland, Piston, Thomson, and many others, Harris (1898–1979) perfected his craft abroad under the watchful eye of Nadia Boulanger in Paris. Even there his development was to an extent due to his own investigations of music as diverse as Bach, Lassus, the French clavecinists, and early English composers. This continued after his return to the United States, where he pursued his study of early music at the Library of Congress.

In 1933, Serge Koussevitzky, the director of the Boston Symphony Orchestra, called for a "great symphony from the west" and Harris responded with his *First Symphony*. He was later to write his *Third* and *Fifth Symphonies* for Koussevitzky as well. Farwell was happy to label the young American composer as a rebel of the human soul, "though more especially the Western American soul." His melodic style, in particular, has been deemed to be deeply evocative of the American character, and Copland, Hanson, and others were quick to suggest its base in Celtic folk song and Protestant hymnody.

SYMPHONY NO. 3.   While titles such as *When Johnny Comes Marching Home* (1935), *Folksong Symphony* (No. 4, 1940), *Abraham Lincoln Walks at Midnight* (1953), and *Folk Fantasy for Festivals* (1956) suggest a continuing devotion to his American roots, it was in his untitled Third Symphony more than any other work that Harris made his deepest impression. Whatever claims may be made for his music are most forcefully encountered in this work. A symphony in five sections, the piece begins with a lyrical cantilena typical of Harris in its persistent modality as well as its long arches which could only have pleased Boulanger who always prodded her students to search for the "grande ligne" (Ex. 22.12). The

Example 22.12. Harris, *Symphony No. 3.*

work ends with a vigorous and dramatic fugue (Ex. 22.13), where material from the third and fourth sections are combined. The finale, which the composer described as "Dramatic, tragic," is marked by the arching melodic style of the opening, followed by a concluding coda characterized by repetitive strokes on the tympani.

Example 22.13. Harris, *Symphony No. 3*

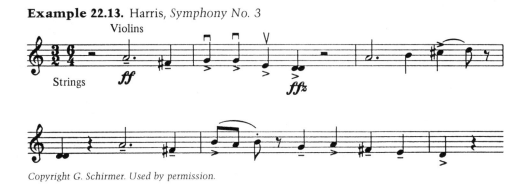

For all of Harris's association with such folk figures as Burl Ives, the Lomaxes, Woody Guthrie, and Carl Sandburg, and in spite of critic Paul Rosenfeld's claim of an indebtedness to the open spaces of the Western prairies for his expansive lyric style, Harris's symphonies persistently search out a heroic note. It is a quality he shared with the more Romantic Howard Hanson, who gave Harris his first public performance in 1926 as part of the newly established American Composers' Concerts and Festivals of American Music at the Eastman School of Music.

Harris's search to expand his vocabulary included a systematic study of the modes and metrics. But while his awareness of developing technologies led him to write a work in 1942 for flute and string quartet entitled *Four Minutes and Twenty Seconds* (the maximum time alloted to a side on a 78 rpm disc) and a concerto for amplified piano (1968), his essential language was established in his first works. If the promise of the Third Symphony faded somewhat in the last years of his life, it was not due to any lack of energy on the part of a composer who left a large corpus of music, including fourteen symphonies.

VIRGIL THOMSON

PARIS-BOSTON-PARIS. While Virgil Thomson (b. 1896), like Copland and Harris, went to Paris to study with Nadia Boulanger, his career reflects a different aspect of the Parisian experience. His first trip abroad in 1921–22 found him studying organ as well as counterpoint, a fact attested to by his organ *Passacaglia* and *Pastorale on a Christmas Plainsong,* both of 1922. During this time he was introduced to Cocteau, Les Six, and Satie. Back in Boston in 1923 he conducted the American premiere of Satie's *Socrate* at Harvard and finished his undergraduate degree, which he had begun in 1919.

In 1925 he returned to Paris, where he was to remain until 1940. The first work to be completed, the *Sonata da chiesa* of 1926, would seem to reflect the

Neoclassic fashion of the time in its outer movements, a Chorale and Fugue, but the inclusion of a Tango for the middle movement indicates that examples by both Satie (*Sports et Divertissements*) and Stravinsky (*Histoire du soldat*) were near at hand to provide an added pinch of spice. With this sonata, his work with Boulanger ended, and there immediately followed a set of *Variations and Fugues on Sunday School Tunes* (1926), whose willful "mis-harmonizations" are more than a little reminiscent of Ives's *Variations on "America"*. The American strain continued with his *Symphony on a Hymn Tune* (1928), a work that revealed a young composer tapping his experience as a young organist at the Calvary Baptist Church in Kansas City perhaps more than at King's Chapel, Boston.

GERTRUDE STEIN AND *FOUR SAINTS IN THREE ACTS.* Thomson's first meeting with Gertrude Stein, the American expatriate writer who had been living in Paris since 1903, took place in 1926, and it was the American "Bad Boy of Music," George Antheil, who made the introduction. Stein must have sensed from the first that in Thomson's feigned naïveté and witty urbanity there resided the perfect ingredients for a collaboration. While Thomson was at work setting two Stein texts, including *Capitals, Capitals* (1927) for four male voices and piano, they began to make plans for an opera.

Stein's initial contribution to *Four Saints in Three Acts* was a rambling text without scenes or scenario, which Thomson, through pruning and rearrangement with a friend, brought into a workable shape. Eschewing narrative or any sense of plot, Stein's libretto employed repetition, rhythm, and a deflated rhetoric in the service of a new syntax whose meaning was its sound. If the French traditions from Mallarmé to Apollinaire served as a useful starting point, the irrationality and absurdity so prized by the Dadaists served as a final catalyst. Stein's description of her creation explains all and nothing:

> A saint as a real saint never does anything, a martyr does something but a really good saint does nothing, and so I wanted to have Four Saints who did nothing and I wrote the Fourt Saints in Three Acts and they did nothing and that was everything.[15]

Thomson was clearer about his hopes of solving for all time the essential questions about English musical declamation:

> My theory was that if a text is set correctly for the sound of it, the meaning will take care of itself. And the Stein texts, for prosidizing in this way, were manna. With meanings already abstracted, or absent, or so multiplied that choice among them was impossible, there was no temptation toward tonal illustration, say of birdie babbling by the brook . . . you could make a setting for sound and syntax only, then add, if needed, an accompaniment equally functional.[16]

Thomson's response to Stein's text began with daily improvisation at the piano. Writing nothing down, he knew that the music was set when it repeatedly began to improvise itself in the same way—an attitude more than marginally in harmony with the Dadaist notion that "the slighest erasure is a violation of spontaneity."[17] Such spontaneity resulted in an objectification of the creative act, a process akin to automatic writing that frequently led to a kind of stalling technique as in the following from the Prologue: "Four Saints two at a time have to have to have to have to." Thomson reinforced Stein's method and language through an agglomeration of simple, highly identifiable components whose matter-of-factness is matched by the irrationality of the various juxtapositions. As Cage whimsically noted in his discussion of *Four Saints*, Thomson used 111 tonic/dominants, 178 scale passages, 632 sequences, 38 references to nursery tunes, and one quotation of "My Country, 'tis of Thee".[18] The opening measures of the Prologue suggest the potential result: A four-square chorus part receives a mismatched harmonization due to the latter's triple metric organization in a style not unrelated to Thomson's organ variations on Sunday school tunes both with respect to method and ingredients.

The ensuing four (sic) acts, with many more saints than the title suggests, require little preparation to follow, only a suspension of disbelief. The series of Sunday school tableaux set in the Spanish Baroque are rich in imagery but not in narrative, and the memory of the work properly hinges on such famous lines as "Pigeons on the grass alas" and Thomson's heady mixture of tango from the dance hall, accordion from the cabaret, reed organ from the country church, and recitation tone derived from liturgical chant.

Example 22.14. Thomson, *Four Saints in Three Acts*, "Prologue," mm. 1–8.

Copyright 1934 Beekman Music, Inc. Used by permission of the publisher.

Example 22.14 (Continued)

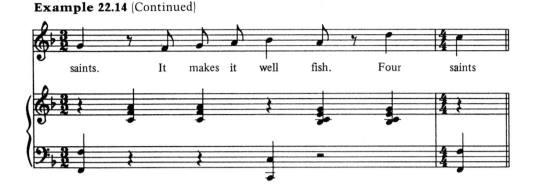

LATER WORKS AND WRITINGS. With *Four Saints in Three Acts* Thomson redefined the European "new simplicity" for Americans in a fashion that was outrageously avant-garde. It was an attitude which he was to pursue in another collaboration with Stein, *Mother of Us All* (1947), and transform and distill to a more compelling and expressive language in such works as the *Five Songs from William Blake* (1951), where his capacity for imagery and poignant sentiment in "The Divine Image" and "Tiger! Tiger!" proved to be extraordinarily powerful and direct.

Virgil Thomson, *Five Songs from William Blake*

THE DIVINE IMAGE

To Mercy, Pity, Peace, and Love
All pray in their distress;
And to these virtues of delight
Return their thankfulness.

For Mercy, Pity, Peace, and Love
Is God, our Father dear,
And Mercy, Pity, Peace, and Love
Is man, His child and care.

For Mercy has a human heart,
Pity a human face,
And Love, the human form divine,
And Peace, the human dress.

Then ev'ry man, of ev'ry clime
That prays in his distress,
Prays to the human form divine,
Love, Mercy, Pity, Peace.

And all must love the human form,
In heathen, Turk or Jew;
Where Mercy, Love, and Pity dwell
There God is dwelling too.

TIGER! TIGER!

Tiger! Tiger! burning bright
In the forests of the night,
What immortal hand or eye
Could frame thy fearful symmetry?

In what distant deeps or skies
Burnt the fire of thine eyes?
On what wings dare he aspire?
What the hand dare seize the fire?

And what shoulder, and what art,
Could twist the sinews of thy heart?
And when the heart began to beat,
What dread hand? and what dread
      feat?

What the hammer? what the chain?
In what furnace was thy brain?
What the anvil? what dread grasp
Dare its deadly terror clasp?

When the stars threw down their spears,	Tiger! Tiger! burning bright
And water'd heav'n with their tears,	In the forests of the night,
Did he smile his work to see?	What immortal hand or eye,
Did he who made the Lamb make thee?	Dare frame thy fearful symmetry?

In later years, the American note was also repeatedly sounded and frequently with a captivating lyricism and charm (*The Plow that Broke the Plains*, 1936; *Filling Station*, 1937; *Louisiana Story*, 1948). On other occasions, a language marked by harmonic planing tinged with modal coloring suggests an ear for the art of Vaughan Williams and Britten as in his "Seine at Night" (1947) from *Three Pictures for Orchestra*, a work which he called a postcard from the Seine to the folks back in Kansas City, where he was raised as a boy.

As music critic of the *New York Herald Tribune* from 1940 to 1954, Thomson was a vital voice with respect to issues both at home and abroad. An article of 1941 proved to be one of the most eloquent apologies for French music from Satie to Milhaud that had appeared to that time. His dismissal therein of Schoenberg's music as "the purest Romantic chromaticism"; of Hindemith and Stravinsky as Neoclassicists with ears, like Brahms, "glued firmly to the past"; and even of *The Rite of Spring* and *Petrushka* as "Wagnerian theater symphony and the nineteenth-century cult of nationalistic folklore applied to ballet," led not surprisingly to the conclusion that because of its renunciation of the impressive and the heroic, "The Satie music aesthetic is the only twentieth-century musical aesthetic in the Western World."[19] Only a few years later, however, when the end of World War II signaled the end of America as a musical backwater, he was one of the first to encourage the abandonment of the notion of a self-conscious American music and the recognition of the multiple aesthetic forces at work from both native (Sessions, Cowell, Varèse, Ruggles) and expatriot (Schoenberg, Stravinsky, Krenek, Hindemith) composers alike.[20] It went hand in hand with his simultaneous recognition of the power and appeal of Schoenbergian atonality among the younger generation of composers who were just then emerging.[21] In spite of, or rather like, the abiding harmonic conservatism of his music, his critical vision with respect to the contemporary scene was both up-to-date and provocative. It proved ultimately to be one of the major measures of the man.

WALTER PISTON AND ROSS LEE FINNEY

Following his undergraduate studies at Harvard (1920–24), Walter Piston (1894–1976) followed the footsteps of Copland, Harris, and Thomson and went to Paris to study with Nadia Boulanger and also with Dukas. For Piston, however, the Parisian experience was one in which the exposure to developing Neoclassic traits in the 1920s proved to be the most lasting. The "grand line" that Boulanger emphasized to all of her pupils found its outlet in arching melodies that vie with those of Harris and Schuman, and the rhythmic syncopations that reflect the almost obligatory American jazz element are also occasionally audible. Piston's eight symphonies are testaments to his craft, which also frequently found expression in chamber works such as the *Suite* for oboe and piano (1931) and the *Partita* for organ, violin, and viola (1944), where a strong contrapuntal bent and a pronounced reliance on Baroque instrumental structures prevail.

For all of the conservatism in America during the 1930s and 1940s of which his music is reflective, his exploration with twelve-note sets, though invariably with a tonal base, can be seen not only in his works after 1960, when dodecaphonic procedures achieved vogue status, but already as early as his *Chromatic Study on the Name of Bach* for organ of 1940. Piston's impact as a pedagogue was strongly felt (his pupils included Carter, Bernstein, Berger, and Fine) in a career spent entirely at Harvard, where he wrote the fundamental textbooks, *Harmony* (1941), *Counterpoint* (1947), and *Orchestration* (1955).

Something of the same mix of ingredients can be seen in the career of Ross Lee Finney (b. 1906). An early exposure to the guitar and the repertoire of American folk melodies had a pronounced influence on his music, audible even as late as his retelling of Chaucer in *The Nun's Priest's Tale* of 1966 for solo voices, SATB, narrator, folk singer, electric guitar, and small orchestra. But like so many in the 1920s and 1930s, he also found his way to Paris and Boulanger (1927–28), though this was followed by study with Roger Sessions at Harvard (1928–29) and Alban Berg in Vienna (1931–32).

It was during the war years, however, that something of this international exposure was turned to a more nationalistic account in works that patently endorsed native folk materials, such as the Third String Quartet (1941) or music by native figures such as William Billings in his *Hymn, Fuguing Tune and Holiday* (1943). From 1950, a continually enriching musical vocabulary led to an investigation of serial techniques, a delayed reaction, no doubt, to his studies with Berg. With a mature career strongly identified with the University of Michigan, he was, like Piston, a teacher with a strong impact and counted among his students composers of such variable persuasions as Albright, Bassett, Crumb, and Reynolds. The collective list of Piston's and Finney's protégés confirms that their teachers' personal mix of neoclassic, serial, and native source material was happily balanced by the absence of a doctrinaire approach to pedagogy. While neither group ever formed a school, their geographically scattered presences proved to be as important for the American musical scene as the more readily identifiable orbits surrounding Princeton and Columbia.

SAMUEL BARBER

The traditionalism of Barber (1910–1981) has been typically described as Romantic by inclination. It is a view encouraged by his early popular successes, *Adagio for Strings* (1936) and *Essay for Orchestra No. 1* (1937), both promoted by Arturo Toscanini, as well as by his later operas, *Vanessa* (1958) and *Anthony and Cleopatra* (1966), the latter commissioned for the opening of Lincoln Center in New York. Other works, however, revealed a neoclassic bent, such as the *Capricorn Concerto* (1945), a concerto grosso for flute, oboe, trumpet and strings; a willingness to work with twelve tone material, observable in his impressive and virtuosic *Piano Sonata* of 1949 (Ex. 25.2) premiered by Vladimir Horowitz; or an interest in incorporating American folk materials, as in *Four Excursions* (1944) for piano.

While the American aspect of Barber's personality has never been particularly stressed, few composers of any persuasion have written a work more thoroughly imbued with a sense of their native land than *Knoxville: Summer 1915* (1947) for soprano and orchestra. James Agee's text is a prose poem of enormous impact, pointedly local in tone but universal in message. Barber responded to the words of the unwitting philosopher-child with a magical lyric style that at once catapulted the work to the status of an American classic. The instrumental accompaniment that both supports the voice and provides a running commentary to the text is a chamber orchestra of the dimension of the composer's *Capricorn Concerto*, and the musical idiom is as simple and direct as the folk-inspired melodies of his *Four Excursions*.

Eleanor Steber, who commissioned the work and sang the world premiere with Koussevitzky and the Boston Symphony, has pointed to its ineffable American quality with the observation: "The very sounds of the words in *Knoxville* evoke for us a sense of childhood, of being loved and protected and part of a tradition."[22]

Knoxville "Summer of 1915"

[We are talking now of summer evenings in Knoxville, Tennessee in the time that I lived there so successfully disguised to myself as a child.]

. . . It has become that time of evening when people sit on their porches, rocking gently and talking gently and watching the street and the standing up into their sphere of possession of the trees, of birds' hung havens, hangars. People go by; things go by. A horse, drawing a buggy, breaking his hollow iron music on the asphalt: a loud auto: people in pairs, not in a hurry, scuffling, switching their weight of aestival body, talking casually, the taste hovering over them of vanilla, strawberry, pasteboard, and starched milk, the image upon them of lovers and horsemen, squared with clowns in hueless amber. A streetcar raising its iron moan; stopping; belling and starting, stertorous; rousing and raising again its iron increasing moan and swimming its gold windows and straw seats on past and past and past, the bleak spark crackling and cursing above it like a small malignant spirit set to dog its tracks; the iron whine rises on rising speed; still risen, faints; halts; the faint stinging bell; rises again, still fainter; fainting, lifting, faints foregone: forgotten. Now is the night one blue dew.

Now is the night one blue dew, my father has drained, he has coiled the hose.
Low on the length of lawns, a frailing of fire who breathes . . .
Parents on porches: rock and rock: From damp strings morning glories hang their ancient faces.
The dry and exalted noise of the locusts from all the air at once enchants my eardrums.

On the rough wet grass of the back yard my father and mother have spread quilts. We all lie there, my mother, my father, my uncle, my aunt, and I too am lying there . . . They are not talking much, and the talk is quiet, of nothing in particular, of nothing at all in particular, of nothing at all. The stars are wide and alive, they seem each like a smile of great sweetness, and they seem very near. All my people are larger bodies than mine . . . with voices gentle and meaningless like the voices of sleeping birds. One is an artist, he is living at home. One is a musician, she is living at home. One is my mother who is good to me. One is my father who is good to me. By some chance, here they are, all on this earth; and who shall ever tell the sorrow of being on this earth, lying, on quilts, on the grass, in a summer's evening, among the sounds of the night. May God bless my people, my uncle, my aunt, my mother, my good father, oh, remember them kindly in their time of trouble; and in the hour of their taking away.

After a little, I am taken in and put to bed. Sleep, soft smiling, draws me unto her: and those receive me, who gently treat me, as one familiar and well-beloved in that home: but will not, oh, will not, not now, not ever; but will not ever tell me who I am.

Reprinted by permission of Grosset & Dunlap from A Death in the Family *by James Agee, copyright © 1957 by The James Agee Trust, copyright renewed 1985 by Mia Agee.*

WILLIAM SCHUMAN

William Schuman (b. 1910) has been one of the vital musical presences in American music for forty years as composer, educator, and administrator. The most dominant influence in his compositional style was that of his teacher Roy Harris, to whom it is possible to attribute the long-breathed cantilena and the rich triadically-based polyharmonies. Like Piston and Harris, he was not immune to neo-Baroque structures such as passacaglia and fugue and extended canonic writing (as the opening of the Ninth Symphony). It was this solid craftmanship in works like *Symphony No. 3* (1941) and the *Symphony for Strings* (No. 5, 1943) that gained for Schuman his first recognition.

In spite of his reputation as a symphonist, which also reflects a preoccupation of Harris who wrote fourteen, identification with his American heritage is observable from the early *American Festival Overture* (1939) through such works as *George Washington Bridge* (1950); *New England Triptych:* "Be Glad Then, America," "When Jesus Wept," and "Chester" (1956), an arrangement of Ives' *Variations on "America"* (1963); *To Thee Old Cause* (1968) and *Casey at the Bat* (1976; arr. from his opera *The Might Casey*, 1953); and the bicentennial commission, *Symphony No. 10: "American Muse"* (1975). That he was also capable of writing works with a more universal significance is attested to by the program of his *Symphony No. 9* ("The Ardeatine Caves").

His extended tenure as director of the Julliard School of Music and then Lincoln Center for the Performing Arts also touched American musical life in general as much as it did that of New York City in particular.

OTHER AMERICANS

To the names of composers already mentioned who were born around the turn of the century and who contributed to the definition of American music, several could rightly demand equal attention, including Leo Sowerby (1895–1968), student of Boulanger and first recipient of the American Prix de Rome (1921–24); and Howard Hanson (1896–1981), first director of the Eastman School of Music, where his American Music Festivals became an important forum from the 1930s for the showcasing of young American talent, including first performances of works by Copland and Harris. Also, from a different quarter, Douglas Moore (1893–1969) studied with Parker at Yale and later with d'Indy and Boulanger in Paris (1919–21). His preference for pioneer and rural subjects ultimately confirmed, however, his commitment to the discovery of an American lyric theater (*The Devil and Daniel Webster*, 1939; *The Ballad of Baby Doe*, 1956), a quality later mirrored in the music of Carlisle Floyd and Jack Beeson.

Yet a healthy share of the burden of music-making in America to the end of World War II rested upon another group of composers born between 1910 and

1950 who came to maturity during that period and who helped to secure the notion of an American school. The composers of distinction from this time—a number of whom continued to compose into the 1930s—would include Milton Babbitt, Arthur Berger, Leonard Bernstein, Marc Blitzstein, Henry Brant, John Cage, Elliott Carter, Ruth Crawford Seeger, Paul Creston, Ingolf Dahl, Norman Dello Joio, David Diamond, Irving Fine, Lukas Foss, Lou Harrison, Ulysses Kay, Leon Kirchner, Pauline Oliveros, Vincent Persichetti, Elie Siegmeister, William Grant Still, Deems Taylor, Randall Thompson, and Ben Weber.

Names like Babbitt and Cage became prominent among the lists of the international avant-garde and helped to dispel the notion of the American composer as one concerned only with the struggle to secure a national musical language. Others continued to be drawn to American themes as evidenced in their titles and their texts. But still more prominent were a group of composers whose training either in Europe or at home was reflected in a music which was carefully crafted, attractively colored, and frequently contrapuntal: Diamond (b. 1913) who, following studies at Eastman, worked with Boulanger and lived from 1951–65 in Italy; Siegmeister (b. 1909) who studied at Columbia and then with Boulanger; Berger (b. 1912) who studied with Piston at Harvard and then Milhaud at Mills; Dello Joio (b. 1913) a pupil of Wagenaar at Julliard and Hindemith at Yale.

The somewhat discrete mixture of native values and European-styled training gradually gave way during this period to a blend of the two, which soon became the mark of a new American training now made available in its own universities. Whatever charges of academicism were later to be made, it is important to note the prominence of some of the most prestigious European personalities in establishing these faculties—from Schoenberg, Hindemith, Milhaud, and their pupils to the countless students of Boulanger. By the end of World War II, the European factor had somewhat diminished, but it continued with renewed vigor beginning in the 1950s with the inauguration of the Fulbright scholar program. Once again an invigorating agency had surfaced to promote the cross-fertilization of American and European musical values. By this time, however, the currents had begun to move in both directions: Babbitt had already preceded the European composers in his first attempts at total serialism, and John Cage introduced a new dimension which, for a moment at least, left the avant-garde in almost total disarray. The American story could no longer be defined principally through the use of native materials but increasingly by virtue of the residency of its protagonists (see Chapters 25 and 27). It almost seemed to vindicate George Antheil's earlier prediction that "An 'American school' of music will come about only when, finally, we stop planning methodically to catch ourselves one."[23]

REPERTOIRE (Ives)

"Feldeinsamkeit" (1897), v, pf
Variations on America (1891), org
Ragtime Pieces (1902–04), small orch
"The Unanswered Question" (1906), tpt, 4 fl, str
"The Housatonic at Stockbridge" (*Three Places in New England,* 1908–14), orch
Sonata No. 2 ("Concord, Mass., 1840–1860") (1910–15), pf
Symphony No. 4 (1909–16)
"Flanders Field" (1917), v, pf

"Tom Sails Away" (1917), v, pf
"Ann Street" (1921), v, pf

READING (Ives)

Charles Ives, *Essays Before a Sonata (1920) and Other Writings*, ed. H. Boatwright (New York, 1970).

Charles Ives, "Some Quarter-Tone Impressions" (1925) in *Essays Before a Sonata and Other Writings*, ed. H. Boatwright (New York, 1970), 109–11.

Aaron Copland, "The Ives Case," *Our New Music* (New York, 1941), 149.

Elliott Carter, "Ives Today: his Vision and Challenge," *Modern Music*, xxi.4 (1944), 199.

Henry and S. Cowell, *Charles Ives and his Music* (New York, 1955).

Sondra Rae Clark, "The Element of Choice in Ives's *Concord Sonata*," *Musical Quarterly*, lx (1974), 167.

Vivian Perlis, *Charles Ives Remembered* (New Haven, 1974).

Frank Rossiter, *Charles Ives and his America* (New York, 1975).

H. Wiley Hitchcock, *Ives* (London, 1977).

H. Wiley Hitchcock and Vivian Perlis, *An Ives Celebration* (Urbana, Ill., 1977).

Robert P. Morgan, "Ives and Mahler: Mutual Responses at the End of an Era," *19th Century Music*, ii.1 (1978), 72–81.

Christopher Ballantine, "Charles Ives and the Meaning of Quotation in Music," *Musical Quarterly*, lxv (1979), 167.

J. Peter Burkholder, "'Quotation' and Emulation: Charles Ives's Uses of His Models," *Musical Quarterly*, lxxi.1 (1985), 1.

REPERTOIRE (American Composers, 1920s)*

Ruggles, *Angels* (1922), 6 tpt
Ruggles, *Men and Mountains* (1924), small orch
Ruggles, *Suntreader* (1926–31), orch
Riegger, *Study in Sonority*, 10 vn (1926–27)
Riegger, *Dichotomy* (1931–32), chamb orch
Riegger, *Symphony No. 3* (1946–47), orch
Becker, *Sinfonia Brevis* (1929), orch
Becker, *The Abongo* (1933), perc ens

READING (American Composers, 1920s)

Charles Seeger, "Carl Ruggles," *Musical Quarterly*, xviii (1932), 578.

Henry Cowell, "John Becker," *American Composers on American Music* (Stanford, Calif., 1933, R1926), 82.

Lou Harrison, "About Carl Ruggles" (1946), repr. in *The Score*, xii (1955), 5.

Elliott Carter, "Wallingford Riegger," *Bulletin of American Composers Alliance*, ii.1 (1952), 3.

Henry Cowell, "Current Chronicle: New York," in *Musical Quarterly*, xxxix (1953), 426.

Henry Cowell, "A Note on Wallingford Riegger," *Julliard Review*, ii (1955).

John Kirkpatrick, "The Evolution of Carl Ruggles: A Chronicle Largely in his Own Words," *Perspectives of New Music*, vi.2 (1968), 146.

Steven E. Gilbert, "Carl Ruggles (1876–1971): an Appreciation" and Charles Seeger, "In memoriam: Carl Ruggles (1876–1971), *Perspectives of New Music*, xi.1 (1972), 224 and x.2 (1972), 171.

Don C. Gillespie, "John Becker, Musical Crusader of St. Paul," *Musical Quarterly*, lxii (1976), 195.

Barbara Zuck, *A History of Musical Americanism* (Ann Arbor, 1980).

Rita Mead, *Henry Cowell's New Music 1925–36: The Society, the Music Editions, and the Recordings* (Ann Arbor, 1981).

*For Cowell and Varèse see Chapter 12, p. 251.

REPERTOIRE (Copland)

Symphony No. 1 (1924), org, orch
Music for the Theater (1925), orch
Piano Concerto ("Jazz") (1926)
Piano Variations (1930)
Short Symphony (1932–33)
El salón Mexico (1933–36), orch
Billy the Kid (1938), ballet
Fanfare for the Common Man (1942), brass, perc
Lincoln Portrait (1942), narr, orch
Rodeo (1942), ballet
Appalachian Spring (1944), ballet
Symphony No. 3 (1944–46)
Red Pony (1948), film score

READING (Copland)

Edmund Wilson, Jr., "The Aesthetic Upheaval in France: The Influence of Jazz in Paris
    and Americanization of French Literature and Art," *Vanity Fair* (February 1922), 49.
Virgil Thomson, "The Cult of Jazz," *Vanity Fair*, xxiv.4 (1925), 54.
Virgil Thomson, "Aaron Copland," *Modern Music*, ix (1932), 67.
Arthur Berger, "The Piano Variations of Aaron Copland," *Musical Mercury*, i (1934), 85.
Arthur Berger, "Copland's Piano Sonata," *Partisan Review*, x (1943), 187.
Elliott Carter, "Theater and Films," *Modern Music*, xxi (1943), 50.
Arthur Berger, *Aaron Copland* (New York, 1953).
J. F. Smith, *Aaron Copland: His Work and Contribution to American Music* (New York,
    1955).
Aaron Copland, *Copland on Music* (New York, 1960).
Caroline Oja, "The Copland-Sessions Concerts and their Reception in the Contemporary
    Press," *Musical Quarterly*, lxv (1979), 212.
Aaron Copland and Vivian Perlis, *Copland, 1900 through 1942* (New York, 1984).
See also *Reading* list for Chapters 13, 14, and 25.

REPERTOIRE (Jazz-Influenced Works by Americans, c. 1915–1930)

Gilbert, *The Dance in Place Congo* (c 1908, rev. 1916), performed 1918 at Metropolitan
    Opera company and at 1927 ISCM Festival
Carpenter, *Piano Concertino* (1915), use of ragtime
Carpenter, *Tango americaine* (1920), pf
Carpenter, *Krazy Kat* (1921), jazz pantomime
Copland, *Trois esquisses* (1921), mvt. 3, "Jazzy"
Antheil, *Symphony No. 1* (1922), ragtimes
Gershwin, *Blue Monday Blues* (1922), 1 act jazz opera
Antheil, *Jazz Sonata* (1923), pf
Copland, *Two Pieces* (1928), str qt, mvt. 2 "rondino"
Gilbert, *Dance for Jazzband* (1924)
Gruenberg, *Daniel Jazz* (1925), v, orch (1925 ISCM in Venice)
Carpenter, *Skyscrapers* (1924), ballet
Gershwin, *Rhapsody in Blue* (1924)
E. B. Hill, *Jazz Studies* (1924), 2 pf
Antheil, *A Jazz Symphony* (1925)
Copland, *Music for the Theater* (1925)
Gruenberg, *Jazz Masks* (1925), pf, takeoffs on Mendelssohn, Chopin, Rubinstein,
    Offenbach
Gruenberg, *Jazzberries* (1925), pf, fox-trot, blues, waltz, syncopep
Gershwin, *Concerto in F* (1925), pf, orch
Sowerby, *Monotony* and *Syncopation* (1925) for Paul Whiteman's orch
Carpenter, *Jazz Orchestra Pieces* (1926), mvt. "A Little Bit of Jazz" for Paul Whiteman

Gershwin, *An American in Paris* (1928), orch
R. Thompson, *Jazz Poem* (1928), pf, orch
Antheil, *Transatlantic* (1930), opera, dance rhythms
H. Forrest, *Camilee* (1930), opera, updating of *La Traviata* with foxtrots and charlestons
W. G. Still, *Afro-American Symphony* (1930), 2nd mvt. uses blue notes
Gruenberg, *Emperor Jones* (1933), opera

REPERTOIRE (Harris)

When Johnny Comes Marching Home (1935), band
Piano Quintet (1936)
Symphony No. 3 (1937)
Symphony No. 4: "Folksong Symphony" (1940), chorus, orch
Folk Fantasy for Festivals (1956), solo vv, folk singers, choruses, pf
Abraham Lincoln Walks at Midnight (1953), A, pf trio
Epilogue to Profiles in Courage: J.F.K. (1964), orch
Symphony No. 10: "Abraham Lincoln" (1965), chorus, brass, perc, 2 amp pf

READING (Harris)

Arthur Farwell, "Roy Harris," *Musical Quarterly*, xviii (1932), 18.
Paul Rosenfeld, *Discoveries of a Music Critic* (New York, 1936), 324ff.
Arthur Mendel, "The Quintet of Roy Harris," *Modern Music*, xvii.1 (1939), 25.
Nicolas Slonimsky, "Roy Harris," *Musical Quarterly*, xxxiii (1947), 17.

REPERTOIRE (Thomson)

Sonata da chiesa (1926), cl, hn, tpt, trbn, vn
Variations and Fugues on Sunday School Tunes (1926), org
Capitals, Capitals (1927), male voices, pf
Four Saints in Three Acts (1927–28, orch. 1933), opera
Symphony on a Hymn Tune (1928)
The Plow that Broke the Plains (1936), orch
Filling Station (1937), ballet
Mother of Us All (1947), opera
Louisiana Story (1948), film score
Three Pictures for Orchestra (1947–52)
Five Songs of William Blake (1951), Bar, orch

READING (Thomson)

Virgil Thomson, *The State of Music* (New York, 1939).
Virgil Thomson, *The Musical Scene* (New York, 1945).
Virgil Thomson, *The Art of Judging Music* (New York, 1948).
Virgil Thomson, *Music, Right and Left* (New York, 1951).
Kathleen Hoover and John Cage, *Virgil Thomson: His Life and Music* (New York, 1959).
Virgil Thomson, *Virgil Thomson* (New York, 1966).
Virgil Thomson, *Music Reviewed 1940-1954* (New York, 1967).
Virgil Thomson, *American Music Since 1910* (New York, 1971).
Virgil Thomson, *A Virgil Thomson Reader* (New York, 1981).

REPERTOIRE (Piston, Finney, Barber, Schuman)

Piston *Suite* (1931), ob, pf
The Incredible Flutist (1938), ballet suite
Chromatic Study on the Name of Bach (1940), org
Partita (1944), org, vn, va
Symphony No. 3 (1947)
Symphony No. 7 (1960)

Finney *String Quartet No. 3* (1941)
    Hymn, Fuguing Tune and Holiday (1943)
    Piano Quintet (1948)
    Variations on a Theme of Alban Berg (1952), pf
    The Nun's Priest's Tale (1966), solo vv, narrator, folk singer, SATB, elec gui, small orch
Barber *Adagio for Strings* (1936)
    Essay for Orchestra No. 1 (1937)
    Four Excursions (1944), pf
    Capricorn Concerto (1944), fl, ob, tpt, str
    Piano Sonata (1949)
    Knoxville: Summer of 1915 (1947), S, orch
    Vanessa (1957), opera
    Antony and Cleopatra (1965–66), opera
Schuman *American Festival Overture* (1939)
    Symphony No. 5 (Symphony for Strings) (1943)
    William Billings Overture (1943)
    George Washington Bridge (1950), wind band
    The Mighty Casey (1953), opera
    New England Triptych (1956): "Be Glad Then, America," "When Jesus Wept," and "Chester Overture"
    Variations on "America", arr. of Ives's organ work (1963)
    To Thee Old Cause (1968)
    Symphony No. 10 ("American Muse") (1975)

READING (Piston, Finney, Barber, Schuman)

Ross Lee Finney, "Piston's Violin Sonata," *Modern Music*, xvii (1939–40), 210.

Leonard Bernstein, "Young American—William Schuman," *Modern Music*, xix.2 (1942), 97.

Nathan Broder, "The Music of William Schuman," *Musical Quarterly*, xxxi (1945), 17.

Elliott Carter, "Walter Piston," *Music Quarterly*, xxxii (1946), 354.

Nathan Broder, *Samuel Barber* (New York, 1954).

Paul Cooper, "The Music of Ross Lee Finney," *Musical Quarterly*, liii (1967), 1.

Peter Westergaard, "Conversation with Walter Piston," *Perspectives of New Music*, vii.1 (1968), 3.

William Schuman, "Introduction" to *The Orchestral Composer's Point of View*, ed. Robert Hines (Norman, Okla., 1970).

Christopher Rouse, *William Schuman Documentary* (New York, 1980).

PART VI

BEYOND NATIONALISM: 1920–1950

"Whether or not the Church was the wisest patron—though I think it was; we commit fewer musical sins in church—it was rich in musical forms. How much poorer we are without the sacred musical services, without the Masses, the Passions, the round-the-calendar cantatas of the Protestants, the motets and sacred concerts, and vespers and so many others. These are not merely defunct forms but parts of the musical spirit in disuse."

—Igor Stravinsky, *Conversations* (1959), 141.

CHAPTER 23

RITUALS, LITURGIES, AND VOICES OF WAR

If the Futurists' glorification of speed and the machine can be seen as a natural reflection of man's technological prowess but also of his periodic compulsion to make war; the Dadaist message of Cocteau-Satie and some of the early works of Milhaud and Poulenc primarily as an expression of the absurdity of life; the straining at national identities as a natural but frequently self-conscious action of countries anxious for artistic self-esteem; and the craze for jazz as a confection of the escapists balancing the Neoclassicist's and Serialist's obsession with order following a world holocaust, it must not be concluded that the capacity of music to aspire to man's nobler instincts remained dormant during the period between the end of World War I and the renewal of global combat in the 1940s.

By turns the composer sought to express man's alarm and outrage at the carnal ravage of international conflict and to turn to the Scriptures as well as to the contemporary poets as a source of spiritual sustenance. In this observation we are once again reminded that the history of any art is not just a story of technical advance and/or change but of the themes of expression and the account to which stylistic developments are put. At various junctures throughout the twentieth century, man's search for spiritual values has surfaced in opera, symphony, and Mass; mystery play, ballet, and cantata. Yet the period before the beginning of World War I to the conclusion of hostilities was not notable for a musical corpus with a pronounced spiritual base, and while the anxiety of a society on the eve of a global conflict has frequently been seen at the root of the Expressionist movement, the number of musical statements that speak directly of the war of 1914–18 are few. Although in the twentieth century, a time marked by two colossal struggles to "end all wars," the musician has reacted in curious patterns of silence and protest, the period of World War II was far more responsive, with clear and frequently powerfully defined messages.

That numerous composers, active at the time of the earlier conflict, felt its paralyzing effect, however, is suggested in Ravel's postcard of April 1916, concerning a mission when he was in uniform:

> It consisted of going to X . . . in order to bring back a requisitioned vehicle, abandoned would be more correct. Nothing troublesome happened to me. I did not need my helmet, my gas mask remained in my pocket. I saw a hallucinating thing: a nightmarish city, horribly deserted and mute. It isn't the fracas above, or the small balloons of white smoke which align the very pure sky; it's not this formidable and

invisible struggle which is anguishing, but rather to feel alone in the center of this city which rests in a sinister sleep, under the brilliant light of a beautiful summer day. Undoubtedly, I will see things which will be more frightful and repugnant; I don't believe I will ever experience a more profound and stranger emotion, than this sort of mute terror.[1]

Ravel's *Le tombeau de Couperin*, which was written during the period 1914-17, is a lament in the manner of Couperin's *tombeaux* for Lully and Corelli, but there is a more personal message behind the Neoclassic pose. Each movement is dedicated to a friend of the composer who was slain in the war, and on the title page Ravel drew a symbolic funerary urn. Ravel's response to his own personal experience of the horrors of war is thus oblique and served up in a language of restraint and control.

Though Debussy's *En blanc et noir* (1915) may carry a symbolic message in the quotation of "Ein feste Burg," his most direct expression of the inhumanity of war came in a minor song, *Noël des enfants* of 1915. On a text by the composer, it exists in two versions: one for voice and piano, another for children's choir. A time of personal crisis and illness, the period of this work also witnessed the exploration of Neoclassical principles by Debussy in a set of sonatas for various instruments.

It is intriguing that Berg, too, in his contemporaneously composed *Wozzeck* (1915-22) dealt not only with the plight of the soldier but with formalistic matters that parallel those of Debussy and Ravel. In a letter of November 8, 1914, Berg had written:

Today I saw a long column of wounded soldiers—horrible. And soon afterwards a company of soldiers shouting and singing, on their way to the front. These are memories that won't be wiped out in a hurry. I sometimes feel here as if I were living outside this world.[2]

It may not be too fanciful to suggest that the need to bring a degree of order in such a period of chaos can partially explain the formalisms of all three composers at this time.

Although the utilitarian and popular motifs that fed the New Simplicity at the turn of the second and third decades were in general harmony with the tidying effects of both Neoclassicism and Serialism, and while a search for order seemed paramount, it appeared to be impossible for music to be more precise about the general disillusionment following World War I. A sense of clarification, of nostalgia for a bygone age, or a toying with meaning and reality, perhaps, but very few sermons.

The first articulate signs came naturally enough in the world of literature where, among writers in the English language, T. S. Eliot's *The Waste Land* (1922) combined something of the raw edge and force of Ezra Pound, to whom it was dedicated, with a style rich in classic allusion and the expression of modern man's lust and fears. The underlying story of the search for the Grail mirrored a concern for personal salvation that soon became an obsession on the part of many artists in the 1920s. Stations along the way for Eliot included his confirmation in the Church of England in 1927, followed by his *Ash Wednesday* of 1930 and *Murder in the Cathedral* of 1935. Analogously, Cocteau's struggle for personal esteem and against an addiction to opium led first to the health clinics and then to his open *Letter to Jacques Maritain*, written in 1925, wherein he sought a momentary salvation in the neo-Thomism of the philosopher. Cocteau had initially met Maritain and his wife, Catholic converts from Judaism and Protestantism, in 1924 through the composer Auric, but later on numerous occasions at the Maritain's legendary Sunday open houses, which cultivated the artistic avant-garde. There the topics of discussion, as well as the guests whose regulars numbered Claudel, Chagall, Rouault, and Max Jacob, were often the same as those to be found at the *Boeuf sur le toit*. Cocteau rationalized his conversion as totally in harmony with his previous orientation when he stated that "conformism is the new anticonformism of the twentieth century." In so doing he preached the compatibility of religion and freedom in art—an attitude that was to prove attractive to numerous intellectuals and artists and to offer a humanizing touch to the technical rigours of several aesthetic points of view.

STRAVINSKY

We know from a letter of May 1, 1926, that copies of Cocteau's *Lettre à Maritain* and Maritain's *Réponse à Jean Cocteau*, both inscribed by their respective authors, were sent to Stravinsky shortly after their appearance in print.[3] Stravinsky first met Maritain in June of the same year, but in a letter from Maritain of July 1935,[4] following publication of Stravinsky's *Autobiography* in April, there is evidence that their philosophies were not totally in harmony with each other. Stravinsky's dictum that "Music is powerless to express anything at all," properly understood as a belief in the absolute autonomy of music, was questioned and pitted against Maritain's view concerning "creative emotion and intuition"—a subject totally beside the point.

Apart from Cocteau, one of the most significant agents in Stravinsky's awareness of Maritain's neo-Thomist views of the correlation of aesthetics and ethics was Arthur Lourié. Music commisar in St. Petersburg from 1918 following the Revolution and a cultivated composer who had experimented with atonal and quarter-tone music in the teens, he had come to Paris by 1924 via Berlin. Introduced to Stravinsky by Vera Sudeikina (Stravinsky's mistress and later his second wife), he soon became Stravinsky's confidant, musical adjutant, and mouthpiece in numerous writings. In addition to the potential influence on Stravinsky's philosophy, Lourié's knowledge of Russian Orthodox music was also at the ready, and his keen interest in questions of modality and the repertoire of Byzantine chant, as well as his continuing search for a Slavonic sonority (as in the *Sonata liturgica* of 1928 or the *Concerto spirituale* of 1929 for piano, voices, and orchestra minus woodwinds and upper strings) undoubtedly did not go unnoticed. Although Lourié's music achieved only minor recognition, the full import of his relation to Stravinsky remains to be detailed. Of his influential role—though somewhat delayed reaction—in casting Schoenberg and Stravinsky as Thesis and Antithesis, initially forwarded in an article "Neo-Gothic and Neo-Classic" in *Modern Music* (1928), there can be no doubt.

According to Stravinsky, however, his literal reconversion to Orthodoxy was due to a religious experience in the Basilica in Padua in 1926 on the occasion of the 700th anniversary of St. Anthony. The first musical reflection of this conversion was an a cappella setting of the *Pater noster* in Slavonic. After the Russian Revolution, Stravinsky's turning away from Russian themes and toward a Western-oriented Neoclassicism undoubtedly left a sense of void, which the use of his childhood language for prayers now addressed. Its association with a spiritual turn, which was by definition supranational, was also natural and led quickly to his preference for Latin as the language best suited to the expression of universal truths.

Stravinsky's choice of Cocteau at this time as the librettist for *Oedipus Rex* was based on an admiration for Cocteau's updated French version of *Antigone* (1922), a text Honegger was already busy composing (1924–27). But it occurred to Stravinsky that for such a formidable task, both with respect to the subject matter and the fact that it was to be his first composition using a non-Russian text, Latin offered him "a medium not dead but turned to stone and so monumentalized as to have become immune from all risk of vulgarization."[5] Cocteau's original was in French, but was subjected to a considerable shearing and was translated into Latin by the Abbé Daniélou.

SYMPHONY OF PSALMS. Stravinsky's first attempt at setting a sacred Latin text was thus prepared by the experience of *Oedipus* and associations with Cocteau, Maritain, and Lourié. It is a work of stark spirituality and uncommon power; a manifestation of the composer's desire always to keep his expression severely under control; in part a suppression of the ego "dedicated to the glory of God"; and on the technical side an expression of his current Neoclassic tendencies married to a new search for sonority and a highly personal and unorthodox formal plan. The orchestra, which in part may have been indebted to Lourié's example (*Concerto spirituale*) in the omission of violins and violas, relies heavily on Stravinsky's experience with winds (*Symphonies*, 1920; *Piano Concerto*, 1924). The use of pianos is a coloristic marking that had surfaced as early as *Petrushka* and would reappear in his *Symphony in Three Movements* and virtually all of the sacred pieces of his last years (*Threni; Sermon, Narrative and Prayer; Introitus; Requiem Canticles*). Stravinsky's prior experience in writing for chorus, limited principally to secular works such as *Les noces* and *Oedipus Rex*, was put to good account in the choral writing of his psalm symphony. Both the narrow range choral recitation and the energizing instrumental ostinato that characterize the opening of *Oedipus* are mirrored in the setting of Psalm 39 in the first movement.

Example 23.1. Stravinsky, *Oedipus Rex*, Rehearsal no. 2 (partial score).

Example 23.1 (Continued)

Example 23.2. Stravinsky, *Symphony of Psalms*, Rehearsal no. 4.

The first Brussels performance listed the three movements as *Prelude, Double Fugue,* and *Allegro symphonique.* Although later dropped, they provide a helpful indication to the construction of the symphony. The second movement begins with an instrumental fugue whose head motif continues to play with the minor thirds of the first movement ostinato (transpose all notes to the same octave in the first three measures of Ex. 23.3 and compare with the B-D, A#-C# ostinato of Ex. 23.2). With the entrance of the chorus, a new fugal structure is introduced together with the initial instrumental one.

Example 23.3. Stravinsky, *Symphony of Psalms,* Mvt. 2, mm. 1–7.

Example 23.4. Stravinsky, *Symphony of Psalms,* Mvt. 2, Rehearsal No. 5.

The final movement is the longest and is marked by a transition from the serenity of the opening "Alleluia" to a climax at "Laudate eum in sono tubae" and a return to the opening. Praise is the watchword and the Dionysian element is allowed to surface only briefly. The end of the work relates not only to the composer's preference for stasis as a closing gesture (*Three Pieces for String Quartet, Symphonies of Winds, Les noces, Symphony in C, Requiem Canticles*) but to his predisposition toward a chant-like writing (the composer himself spoke of it as "Igorian chant"), which was to appear in numerous Latin texted works of his later years (*Canticum Sacrum, Threni, Requiem Canticles*).

Example 23.5. Stravinsky, *Symphony of Psalms*, Mvt. 3, 2 mm. before Rehearsal No. 1.

Copyright 1931 by Edition Russe de Musique. Renewed 1958. Copyright and renewal assigned to Boosey & Hawkes, Inc. Revised edition copyright 1948 by Boosey & Hawkes, Inc. Renewed 1975. Reprinted by permission of Boosey & Hawkes, Inc.

MASS AND LATER WORKS   The *Mass* of 1944–48 is in many of its particulars a distillation of the tendencies observable in the Psalm symphony. The use of a double wind quintet (2 ob, eng hn, 2 bn, 2 tpt, 3 trbn) may be related less to the *Octet* than to the supression of upper strings in his work of 1930. The choral writing also strikes many familiar poses, but in its cantorial solos (Ex. 23.6a) and particularly in the duets of the Gloria (Ex. 23.6b), which typically cadence on open fifths, a new starkness is achieved that is redolent of a Medieval liturgy.

Although Machaut has been proposed as a model, Stravinsky denied that he knew that composer's *Mass* at the time. The limitations and even dangers of invoking Stravinsky's heightened historical awareness to explain his musical manners are emphasized.

Example 23.6a. Stravinsky, *Mass,* "Gloria," voices only, nos. 11–12.

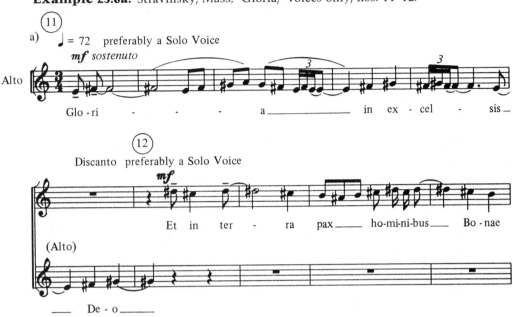

Example 23.6b. Stravinsky, *Mass,* "Gloria," voices only, nos. 17–19.

Example 23.6b (Continued)

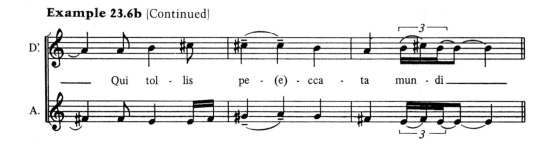

The importance of the element of ritual in the works of Stravinsky has frequently been noted. While the initial observation carries a special ring because of an automatic association with his legendary *Le sacre du printemps,* the assertion is valid far beyond the province of pagan rites. The celebration of birth and the rituals of marriage and death are openly addressed in *Les noces* (1915–23), *Greetings Prelude* (1955), and *Requiem Canticles* (1966). Yet while his *Mass* (1948) was intended to be used liturgically, many of his statements of praise and lamentation are to be found in the nonliturgical setting of Latin texts such as a *Symphony of Psalms* (1930), *Canticum Sacrum* (1955), and *Threni* (1957; see discussion on pp. 542–47) or English ones such as *A Sermon, a Narrative and a Prayer* (1960–61) and *Anthem* (1962), an a cappella setting of T. S. Eliot's biblical paraphrase, "A dove descending."

The memorial piece for a friend spans his entire career and begins with his *Chant funèbre* (1908) in memory of his teacher Rimsky-Korsakov and continues with the *Symphonies of Wind Instruments* (1920) dedicated to the memory of Claude Debussy and described by Stravinsky as "an austere ritual." Later works such as *In Memoriam Dylan Thomas* (1954), *Elegy for J.F.K.* (1963), *Introitus* for T.S. Eliot (1965), and the *Variations* for Aldous Huxley (1963–64) are freighted with the additional poignancy of the loss of friends by a man living into old age. The tribute was ultimately to be returned to him in numerous memorial works written by Krenek, Davies, Carter, Copland, Sessions and others (see p. 682).

Stravinsky, *Symphony of Psalms*

PSALMUS XXXVIII (VULGATE)
Verses 13 and 14

Exaudi orationem meam, Domine,
et deprecationem meam:
auribus percipe lacrymas meas.

Ne sileas, quoniam advena ego apud te,
et peregrinus, sicut omnes patres mei.

Remitte mihi,
ut refrigerer priusque abeam,
et amplius non ero.

PSALMUS XXXIX (VULGATE)
Verses 2, 3 and 4

Expectans expectavi Dominum,
et intendit mihi.

PSALM XXXIX (KING JAMES VERSION)
Verses 12 and 13

Hear my prayer, O Lord,
and give ear unto my cry;
hold not Thy peace at my tears.

For I am a stranger with Thee,
and a sojourner, as all my fathers were.

O spare me,
that I may recover strength,
before I go hence, and be no more.

PSALM XL (KING JAMES VERSION)
Verses 1, 2 and 3

I waited patiently for the Lord;
and he inclined to me,

Et exaudivit preces meas:
et eduxit me de lacu miseriae,
et de luto faecis.

Et statuit supra petram pedes meos;
et direxit gressus meos.

Et immisit in os meum canticum novum,
carmen Deo nostro.

Videbunt multi et timebunt,
et sperabunt in Domino.

and heard my cry.
And he brought me up also out of a horrible pit,
out of the miry clay,

and set my feet upon a rock,
and established my goings.

And He hath put a new song in my mouth,
even praise unto our God;

Many shall see it, and fear,
and shall trust in the Lord.

PSALMUS CL (VULGATE)

Alleluia.

Laudate Dominum in sanctis ejus:
laudate eum in firmamento virtutis ejus.

Laudate eum in virtutibus ejus:
laudate eum secundum multitudinem
    magnitudinis ejus.

Laudate eum in sono tubae:
laudate eum in psalterio et cithara.

Laudate eum in tympano et choro:
laudate eum in chordis et organo.

Laudate eum in cymbalis bene sonantibus:
laudate eum in cymbalis jubilationis:
omnis spiritus laudet Dominum.

Alleluia.

PSALM CL (KING JAMES VERSION)

Praise ye the Lord.

Praise God in His Sanctuary.
praise Him in the firmament of His power.

Praise Him for His mighty acts:
praise Him according to His excellent
    greatness.

Praise Him with the sound of the trumpet:
praise Him with the psaltery and the harp.

Praise Him with the timbrel and dance:
praise Him with stringed instruments and
    organs.

Praise Him upon the loud cymbals:
praise Him upon the high sounding cymbals.
Let everything that hath breath praise the
    Lord.

Praise ye the Lord.

Mass

KYRIE

Kyrie eleison.
Christe eleison.
Kyrie eleison.

Lord have mercy upon us.
Christ have mercy upon us.
Lord have mercy upon us.

GLORIA

Gloria in excelsis Deo.
Et in terra pax hominibus
bonae voluntatis. Laudamus te,
benedicimus te,
adoramus te,
glorificamus te;
gratias agimus tibi
propter magnam gloriam tuam;
Domine Deus,
Rex coelestis,
Deus pater omnipotens.
Domine Fili unigenite,
Jesu Christe;
Domine Deus,

Glory to God on high.
And on earth peace to men
of good will. We praise Thee,
we bless Thee,
we adore Thee,
we glorify Thee;
thanks we give unto Thee
for Thy great glory;
Lord God,
King of heaven,
God the Father Almighty.
O Lord, only-begotten Son,
Jesus Christ;
O Lord God,

Agnus Dei,
Filius Patris;
Qui tollis
   peccata mundi,
miserere nobis.
Qui tollis
   peccata mundi,
suscipe deprecationem nostram.
Qui sedes
   ad dexteram Patris,
miserere nobis;
quoniam tu solus Sanctus,
tu solus Dominus
tu solus altissimus, Jesu Christe,
cum Sancto Spiritu
in gloria Dei Patris.
Amen.

Credo in unum Deum,
Patrem omnipotentem,
factorem coeli et terrae,
visibilium omnium
et invisibilium;
Et in unum Dominum,
Jesum Christum,
Filium Dei unigenitum,
et ex Patre natum
ante omnia saecula,
Deum de Deo,
lumen de lumine,
Deum verum de Deo vero,
genitum, non factum,
consubstantialem Patri,
per quem omnia facta sunt;
Qui propter nos homines
et propter nostram salutem
descendit de coelis,
et incarnatus est
de Spiritu Sancto

ex Maria Virgine,
et homo factus est;
crucifixus etiam pro nobis,
sub Pontio Pilato passus
et sepultus est;
et resurrexit tertia die
secundum Scripturas;
et ascendit in coelum;
sedet ad dexteram Patris,
et iterum venturus est cum gloria
judicare vivos et mortuos,
cujus regni non erit finis;
et in Spiritum Sanctum
Dominum et vivificatem,
qui ex Patre Filioque
   procedit,
Qui cum Patre et Filio
simul adoratur et conglorificatur,

Lamb of God,
Son of the Father;
Thou that takest away
   the sins of the world,
have mercy upon us.
Thou that takest away
   the sins of the world,
receive our prayer.
Thou that sittest
   at the right hand of the Father,
have mercy upon us.
For Thou alone art holy,
Thou alone art Lord,
Thou alone art most high, Jesus Christ,
with the Holy Ghost
in the glory of God the Father.
Amen.

I believe in one God,
the Father Almighty,
Maker of heaven and earth,
of all things visible
and invisible;
and in one Lord,
Jesus Christ,
only-begotten Son of God,
and begotten of the Father
before all worlds,
God of God,
Light of Light,
true God of true God,
begotten, not made,
of one substance with the Father,
by whom all things were made;
Who for us men
and for our salvation
came down from heaven,
and was made incarnate
by the Holy Ghost

of the Virgin Mary
and was made man;
He was crucified also for us,
He suffered under Pontius Pilate
and was buried:
and He rose again on the third day
according to the scriptures;
and ascended into heaven;
He sitteth on the right hand of the Father,
and He shall come again with glory
to judge the quick and the dead,
whose kingdom shall have no end;
and I believe in the Holy Ghost,
the Lord and Giver of life,
Who proceeds from the Father
   and the Son,
Who with the Father and Son
together is worshipped and glorified,

Qui locotus est per Prophetas;	Who spoke through the Prophets;
et unam sanctam catholicam	and in one holy Catholic
et apostolicam ecclesiam;	and Apostolic Church;
confiteor unum baptisma	I acknowledge one baptism
in remissionem peccatorum,	for the remission of sins,
et expecto resurrectionem mortuorum,	and I look for the resurrection of the dead,
et vitam venturi saeculi.	and life in the world to come.
Amen.	Amen.

SANCTUS

Sanctus, sanctus, sanctus,	Holy, holy, holy,
Dominus Deus Sabaoth.	Lord God of Hosts.
Pleni sunt coeli et terra	Heaven and earth are full
gloria tua;	of Thy glory;
Hosanna in excelsis.	Hosanna in the highest.
Benedictus qui venit	Blessed is He that cometh
in nomine Domini.	in the name of the Lord.
Hosanna in excelsis.	Hosanna in the highest.

AGNUS DEI

Agnus Dei, qui tollis	Lamb of God. Who takest away
peccata mundi,	the sins of the world,
miserere nobis.	have mercy on us.
Agnus Dei, qui tollis	Lamb of God, Who takest away
peccata mundi,	the sins of the world,
dona nobis pacem.	give us peace.

POULENC

The image of Stravinsky introducing Diaghilev to Poulenc (1899–1963) following the premiere of *Les mariés de la tour Eiffel* in 1921 and the latter's subsequent composition of *Les biches* (1924) and the *Concert champêtre* (1927), both from the world of Watteau, were sufficient to dub Poulenc's recipe as developed from a Stravinskian base, lightly sauced by Satie. While the recognition of the formative ingredients is fair, it fails to take into account Poulenc's increasingly original manner founded on his natural gifts as a melodist and a spiritual orientation that characterized numerous works from the mid-1930s to the end of his life.

MASS AND OTHER LATIN WORKS.   Poulenc's return to the church and consequent search for an appropriate mode of expression followed the death of a friend and a pilgrimage to Notre Dame de Rocamadour in 1936. The peripatetic decade of the 1920s was behind him, the memory of World War I not too distant, and the war clouds of a new conflict already gathering. The composer's first statement following a reconversion to the Roman Catholic faith of his childhood was the *Litanies à la vierge noire* (1936), patron saint of Rocamadour, for women's voices and organ. The organ, which also served him in his concerto of 1937, is the liturgical instrument par excellence and accounts for Poulenc's consideration of this latter Janus-faced composition as being "on the outskirts" of his religious music. In both works, dramatic dissonances proclaimed by the organ (Ex. 15.9) alternate with melodies that frequently betray their origin in plainchant.

In his *Mass* in G of 1937, Poulenc endorsed many of these same features together with an abiding allegiance to chromatically and modally colored tonality. In the Kyrie and Agnus Dei, in particular, lengthy pedal-points sustain floating melismas that recall the organum style of twelfth-century St. Martial at Limoges (Ex. 23.7) but also provide a foundation for the richly harmonic (eight to ten voices *divisi*) style of other dramatically contrasting sections (Ex. 23.8).

Example 23.7. Poulenc, *Mass*, "Kyrie."

The *Mass* quickly became a classic of the choral repertoire and secured a new dimension for Poulenc's art. A devotion to similar musical values continued to be in evidence in the a cappella writing of numerous motets that followed (*Quatre motets pour un temps de pénitence*, 1938–39; *Quatre motets pour le temps de Noël*, 1951–52) as well as in the larger choral works with orchestra (*Stabat mater*, 1950; *Gloria*, 1959), and his religious opera *Dialogues des carmélites* (1953–56). In his opus ultimum, the *Sept répons de ténèbres* (1961), Poulenc achieved a final distillation in an elliptical style that marks an awareness of the world of Webern without abdicating his private vision.

FIGURE HUMAINE AND "*C*". Poulenc may have achieved his most powerfully spiritual statement, however, in a work that is neither liturgical nor sacred. It is the a cappella cantata, *Figure humaine*, written in 1943 on a text of Paul Éluard. Poulenc met Éluard for the first time in 1917 and sensed an immediate affinity for his poetry. In time his texts were to provide the source for no less than thirty-four songs for voice and piano and several choral works. Poulenc said of

Example 23.8. Poulenc, *Mass*, "Agnus Dei," Rehearsal No. 49.

Copyright Editions Salabert. Used by permission of G. Schirmer.

him: "He is the only Surrealist who could tolerate music, and all his poetry is musical vibration." Although we may not search in his poetry for exact meanings, which can ultimately only be intuited, the message as well as the sentiment seem somehow always clear and the cumulative drama frequently breathtaking.

Poulenc has spoken of the origins of his cantata for double mixed chorus a cappella in the receipt of typescripts of Éluard's poetry by mail during the years of the German occupation of France. Poulenc determined, following another votive pilgrimage to Rocamadour in the summer of 1943, to prepare and print in secret a work based on these poems that was to be performed on the day of liberation. *Figure humaine* was completed quickly, published sub rosa by his friend and publisher Paul Rouart, and immediately after the liberation sent to London, where, before the end of the war, the first performance was given by the BBC chorus.

During this same year Jean Lurçat (1892–1966), one of the modern masters of tapestry, created a related and remarkable work (Figure 23.1). Incorporating the ninth and tenth stanzas of Éluard's *Liberté* in its margins, the final word itself is set in a blazing emblem of victory. Poulenc closes his cantata with this very poem, and, using all of its 21 stanzas, capitalizes on the mounting tension created by the recurrence of the same concluding line for each ("J'écris ton nom")

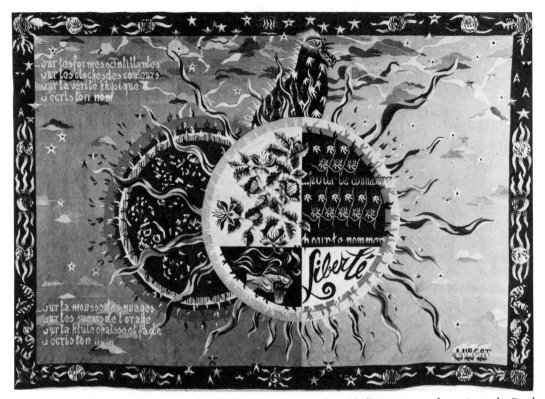

Figure 23.1. *Liberté*, a tapestry by Jean Lurçat (1943), "Inspiré par le poème de Paul Éluard." Poulenc set the text as the final number of his cantata *Figure humaine* (1943).
Musée national d'art moderne, Centre Georges Pompidou, Paris. © ADAGP, Paris/VAGA, New York, 1985.

and the ultimate resolution of the poem in the capture of the word "Liberté", whose final syllable resounds to a major triad.

The dedication of *Figure humaine* to Picasso speaks not only of Poulenc's friendship with the painter but of the mesmerizing impact of *Guernica* (1937) as an indictment of war. Its musical language reflects the reverence secured in the *Mass* written six years before but now turned to an even more personalized, secular but no less spiritual account. Because of its enormous difficulty it is rarely performed (though well represented on recording), and it may well stand as the final testament of the multiple values—literary and musical—of the artist. On the subject of war, its message was never surpassed by the composer except, perhaps, in his setting of a single lyric, "C," also of 1943, on a poem of Louis Aragon, whose clearer imagery is infused by a pervading tenderness and a heart-breaking quality at the final couplet.

C

J'ai traversé les ponts de Cé	I have crossed the bridges of C
C'est là que tout a commencé	It is there that it all began
Une chanson des temps passés	A song of times past
Parle d'un chevalier blessé	Speaks of a injured knight

D'une rose sur la chaussée
Et d'un corsage délacé
Du château d'un duc insensé
Et des cygnes dans les fossés

Of a rose in the roadway
And an unlaced bodice
Of the castle of a mad duke
And of swans in the moats

De la prairie où vient danser
Une éternelle fiancée
Et j'ai bu comme un lait glacé
Le long lai des gloires faussées

Of the meadow where comes dancing
One eternally betrothed
And I drank like iced milk
The long poem of false glories

La Loire emporte mes pensées
Avec les voitures versées
Et les armes désamorcées
Et les larmes mal effacées

The Loire transports my thoughts
With the overturned cars
And the unprimed weapons
And the ill dried tears

Ô ma France ô ma délaissée
J'ai traversé les ponts de Cé.

O my France o my forsaken one
I have crossed the bridges of C.

Louis Aragon, used by permission of Editions Seghers, Paris.

Figure Humaine

No. 1, BIENTÔT

De tous les printemps du monde
Celui-ci est le plus laid
Entre toutes mes façons d'être
La confiante est la meilleure

Of all the world's springs
This one is the ugliest
Of all my states of mind
Confidence is the best

L'herbe soulève la neige
Comme la pierre d'un tombeau
Moi je dors dans la tempête
Et je m'éveille les yeux clairs

The grass pushes up the snow
Like a gravestone
As for me I sleep through the storm
And wake up with my eyes bright

Le lent le petit temps s'acheve
Où toute rue devait passer
Par mes plus intimes retraites
Pour que je rencontre quelqu'un

The slow the petty time is finishing
Where every road was bound to pass
In my inmost retreats
So that I can meet somebody

Je n'entends pas parier les monstres
Je les connais ils ont tout dit
Je ne vois que les beaux visages
Les bons visages sûrs d'eux mêmes

I can't hear the monsters talking
I know them they have said everything
I only see the beautiful faces
The good faces sure of themselves

Sûrs de ruiner bientôt leurs maîtres.

Sure that they are soon going to ruin their masters.

Paul Éluard, extracted from Sur les pentes inférieures, *© Editions Gallimard. Used by permission.*

No. 8, LIBERTÉ

Sur me cahiers d'écolier
Sur mon pupitre et les arbres
Sur sable sur la neige
J'écris ton nom

On the pages of my exercise-books
On my school desk and on the trees
On sand and on snow
I write your name

Sur toutes les pages lues
Sur toutes les pages blanches
Pierre sang papier ou cendre
J'écris ton nom

On all the pages I have read
On all the white pages
Stone blood paper or ash
I write your name

Sur les images corées
Sur les armes des guerriers

On the gilded images
On the weapons of warriors

Sur la couronne des rois	On the crowns of kings
J'écris ton nom	I write your name
Sur la jungle et le désert	On the jungle and the desert
Sur les nids sur les genêts	On the nests and on the wild gorse
Sur l'écho de mon enfance	On the echoes of my childhood
J'écris ton nom	I write your name
Sur les merveilles des nuits	On the marvels of the night
Sur le pain blanc des journées	On the white bread of the day
Sur les saisons fiancées	On the seasons in their betrothals
J'écris ton nom	I write your name
Sur tous mes chiffons d'azur	On all my rages of azure
Sur l'étang soleil moisi	On the pond of mildewed sunlight
Sur le lac lune vivante	On the lake of living moonlight
J'écris ton nom	I write your name
Sur les champs sur l'horizon	On the fields on the horizon
Sur les ailes des oiseaux	On the wings of birds
Et sur le moulin des ombres	And on the windmill of shadows
J'écris ton nom	I write your name
Sur chaque bouffée d'aurore	On every puff of dawn
Sur le mer sur les bateaux	On the sea on boats
Sur la montagne démente	On the crazy mountain
J'écris ton nom	I write your name
Sur le mousse des nuages	On the foaming clouds
Sur les sueurs de l'orage	On the sweating storms
Sur le pluie épaisse et fade	On the thick insipid rain
J'écris ton nom	I write your name
Sur les formes scintillantes	On the scintillating shapes
Sur les cloches des couleurs	On the bells of colour
Sur la vérité physique	On scientific truth
J'écris ton nom	I write your name
Sur les sentiers éveillés	On newly-awakened pathways
Sur les routes déployées	On roads unfolding before us
Sur les places qui débordent	On squares filled to overflowing
J'écris ton nom	I write your name
Sur la lampe qui s'allume	On the lamp that is lit
Sur la lampe qui s'éteint	On the lamp that is put out
Sur mes maisons réunies	On my reunited houses
J'écris ton nom	I write your name
Sur le fruit coupé en deux	On a fruit cut in two
Du miroir et de ma chambre	From the mirror and from my room
Sur mon lit coquille vide	On my bed's empty shell
J'écris ton nom	I write your name
Sur mon chien gourmand et tendre	On my greedy affectionate dog
Sur ses oreilles dressées	On his pricked-up ears
Sur sa patte maladroite	On his clumsy paws
J'écris ton nom	I write your name
Sur le tremplin de ma porte	On the diving-board of my door
Sur les objets familiers	On the everyday objects
Sur le flot du feu béni	On the sea of sacred fire
J'écris ton nom	I write your name
Sur tout chair accordée	On all reconciled bodies
Sur le front de mes amis	On the foreheads of my friends

Sur chaque main qui se tend J'écris ton nom	On every outstretched hand I write your name
Sur la vitre des surprises Sur les lèvres attentives Bien au-dessus du silence J'écris ton nom	On the window of surprises On lips eager with attention Far beyond mere silence I write your name
Sur mes refuges détruits Sur mes phares écroulés Sur les murs de mon ennui J'écris ton nom	On my exploded hiding-places On my ruined lighthouses On the walls of my boredom I write your name
Sur l'absence sans désir Sur la solitude nue Sur les marches de la mort J'écris ton nom	On absence without desire On naked solitude On the staircase of death I write your name
Sur la santé revenue Sur le risque disparu Sur l'espoir sans souvenir J'écris ton nom	On health restored On dangers that are gone On hope without remembrance I write your name
Et par le pouvoir d'un mot Je recommence ma vie Je suis né pour te connaître Pour te nommer	And through the power of a word I can begin to live once more I was born to know you And to call you
Liberté.	Liberty.

Paul Éluard, © *Les Editions de Minuit. Used by permission.*   *English translation courtesy of Erato records, STU 70924.*

OLIVIER MESSIAEN

Poulenc's defense of Stravinsky's Neoclassicism against the "Messiaenistes" in the period immediately following the end of World War II cannot disguise the fact that all three had previously inhabited a common terrain not only in their choice of religious themes but also in certain of their harmonic manners. But unlike Stravinsky or Poulenc, Messiaen's story contains no conversion, and he has stated that:

> I have had the good fortune to be a Catholic; I was born a believer . . . A number of my works are dedicated to shedding light on the theological truths of the Catholic faith. That is the most important aspect of my music . . . perhaps the only one I shall not be ashamed of in the hour of death.[6]

EARLY ORGAN WORKS.   Messiaen (b. 1908) began his career as a composer in the late 1920s, and already in *Le banquet céleste* (1928) a mixture of received attitudes as well as a prefiguration of those to come is observable. In its parallel harmonic chains he demonstrated a knowledge of Debussy, but in its rhythmic manner, which did not so much evade a feeling of the bar line as suspend a sense of time in a work of twenty-five measures that takes six minutes to perform, he launched a new and fundamental perspective. It proved, in fact, to be the seed not only for such endless melodies as the final "Louange" of his *Quatuor pour la fin du temps* (1941), the "Combat de la mort et de la vie" from *Les corps glorieux* (1939), or for the final chord of "Prière du Christ montant vers son Père" (*L'Ascension*, 1933), which lasts some fifty-seven seconds. It was the beginning of a new attitude toward music as nonbeginning and unending, eternal and beyond time, and sharing more than a little with the hypnotic stasis of many of Stravinsky's slow tempo codas noted earlier. The force of the idea was to remain remarkably strong in many of Messiaen's later compositions and prove adaptable, as an element of ritual, in the works of many other composers as well, Stockhausen's *Inori* (1973–74) and Boulez's *Rituel* (1974–75) being notable examples.

The gradual development of a personal language in the 1930s and 1940s was almost exclusively allied with instrumental works supplied with religious titles and texts, and more rarely with works for chorus. Among the latter, *O sacrum convivium* (1937) captures the quiet spirituality of his slow organ movements while employing a rich harmonic vocabulary that betrays a kinship with Poulenc. Elsewhere, as in the second movement of *Trois petites liturgies* (1944), the ritual energies—both rhythmic and timbral—of *Les noces* prevail in the company of the ondes martenot as a voice of mystic exaltation. In the organ works, scriptural quotations typically adorn his scores, which disclose an unmatched technical virtuosity ranging from the French styled toccatas of Vierne and Dupré ("Transports de joie", *L'Ascension*, 1933; "Dieu parmi nous", *La Nativité*, 1934) to monophonic passages ("Alleluias sereins d'un âme que désire le ciel," *L'Ascension*, Ex. 30.2) and pieces ("Force et agilité des corps glorieux," *Les corps glorieux*, 1939) that give the allusion of an elaborately colored chant.

THE TECHNIQUE OF MY MUSICAL LANGUAGE: Les corps glorieux; Quatuor pour la fin du temps; Messe de la Pentecôte:"Communion". Messiaen's interest in the irrational values of Chopin and in Debussy's rhythms no longer dependent on tonality or pulse contributed to a supple metricality that underscored his mystical bent. Contrarily, his fascination for the "vers mesurés à la antique" of Claude Le Jeune (1530–1600), especially in his *Cinq rechants* (1949), and the rigorous rhythmic structures of Greek and Hindu music complemented his investigation into the question of rhythmic and pitch modes. The latter, visible in his works from the mid-1930s on, was given a detailed explication in his *Technique de mon langage musical* (1944). The number of the first three modes is coincidentally equivalent to the number of transpositions that are possible without redundancy; Mode 1 is thus the whole-tone scale (T, T). Mode 2, alternating minor and major seconds (S, T), Mode 3 (S, T, S), and Mode 4 (S, S, m3, S) are the most frequently used by Messiaen, while Modes 5 through 7 are rarely employed. The modes govern both the melodic and harmonic aspect of a composition, and thus share features with both traditional tonality and emerging serial tenets.

"L'Ange aux parfums" from *Les corps glorieux* (1939) illustrates the simultaneous use of Modes 1, 2, and 3 (A, B, C) in their exclusive deployment in the Pedals, Positive, and Great manuals respectively, together with associative rhythms (X, Y, Z). The relationship of the materials is constantly changing, however: repetitions of material on the middle staff are separated by an eighth-note rest while those of the right-hand are repeated without pause, and after three statements each in this fashion the patterns themselves begin to contract—all of this against the unchanging and persistent ostinato of the pedal, whose rhythm (Z) is "non-retrogradable", i.e. it reads the same forwards as backwards.

Example 23.9. Modes of Limited Transposition; Retrograde and Nonretrogradable rhythms.

1st Mode:

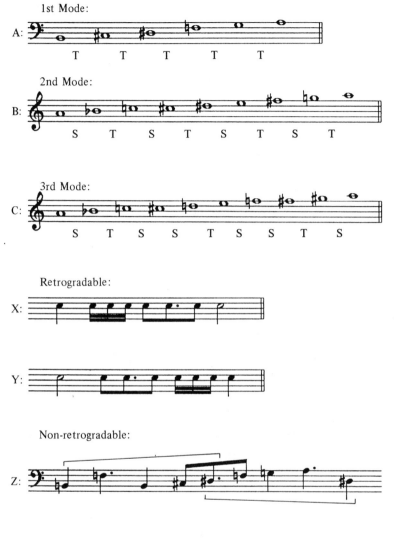

2nd Mode:

3rd Mode:

Retrogradable:

Non-retrogradable:

Example 23.10. Messiaen, *Les corps glorieux:* "L'Ange aux parfums."

Example 23.10 (Continued)

In 1940, as a prisoner of war of the Germans, Messiaen wrote the extraordinary *Quatuor pour la fin du temps*. Beyond the spiritual vision of the work, which seems to reject the thought of analysis, is a structural premise that, were it not for its compelling aural qualities, could logically be called academic. The quartet of violin, clarinet, cello, and piano begins the first movement, "Liturgie de cristal," with the soprano instruments portraying a blackbird and a nightingale celebrating the arrival of dawn. The cello, however, lays down a changing grid of five pitches projected over a rhythmic pattern of fifteen values while the piano plays a twenty-nine-note ostinato wedded to a rhythmic pedal of seventeen values. The relation of such formal planning to the Medieval isorhythmic motet naturally comes to mind. But an interest in such procedures in the twentieth century had already been demonstrated in the first of Stravinsky's *Three Pieces for String Quartet* (Ex. 11.25) as well as in one of Schoenberg's first serial ventures, the setting of a Petrarch sonnet in the *Serenade*, op. 24, where a twelve-pitch series is juxtaposed onto a phraseology determined by the eleven syllables of each line of the poem.

While *Mode de valeurs* (1949), as we shall see, momentarily promoted the rigorous integration of all parameters, Messiaen was never essentially committed to the Schoenbergian notion of the pitch series, but rather to the concept of the pitch mode, which implies neither order nor use of the complete chromatic.

That Mode 1 is the whole-tone scale associated with Debussy and Mode 2 is the octatonic scale so fundamental to Stravinsky dramatizes that Messiaen's orientation is one of pitch placement, which has lead in Messiaen's music to a consideration of resonance or, as he would phrase it, "added resonance." This may be described as the relationship between a note or chord played softly above a louder principal sound ("upper resonance") or below it ("inferior resonance"). Successfully employed, the resonance is absorbed into the fundamental and effects a transformation of timbre rather than becoming a part of the harmony. Visible in Messiaen's music already from the early *Préludes* (1929), Messiaen speaks directly to the issue in his *Technique de mon langage musical* (1944):

> In the resonance of a low C, a very acute ear can hear an F♯ (the eleventh harmonic). Therefore, we are justified in treating this F♯ as an added note in the basic triad.[7]

A particularly dramatic example of Messiaen's attention to such resonance factors, even in a final cadence chord, can be seen in the following example from the *Messe de la Pentecôte* (1950), where the distance between the low pedal C (at 16' and 32'—i.e., sounding one and two octaves below the written pitch)—and the highest F♯ (registered for a 1' piccolo solo—i.e., sounding three octaves above the written pitch), traverses over nine octaves. The resulting sonority is a mysterious blend that, properly recorded or heard on a fine instrument, must be heard to be believed. Attention to such factors was not lost on Messiaen's pupil,

Example 23.11. Messiaen, *Messe de la Pentecôte:* Communion ("Les oiseaux et les sources").

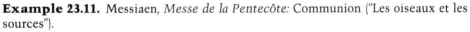

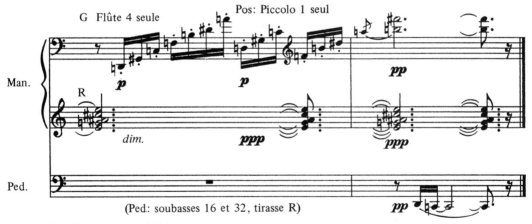

Used by permission of Alphonse Leduc.

Pierre Boulez, who in his work from the 1960s on has disclosed his fascination for the phenomenon. The opening measures of *Eclat* are a good example, and his more recent *Répons* (1980–) makes conscious use of the contrast between resonating and non-resonating sounds.

Such technical matters were for Messiaen, however, invariably related to a philosophical inquiry that repeatedly pointed to his French Symbolist roots, his

Catholic faith, and a fascination for exotic (non-Western) systems. The synesthetic mysteries of the Symbolists, for example, have continued to flourish in the homilies of Messiaen, whose cosmic mysticism is always awash in a blaze of colors. While Aldous Huxley and Henri Michaux have experimented with mescalin to induce synesthetic phenomena, Messiaen's response is a natural aural-optic reality. In his *Couleurs de la cité céleste* (1963) the emphasis placed on color associations in a blinding vision of the Apocalypse can only be understood (not personally experienced by the listener) in light of the specific color equations that Messiaen has made with the various Modes of Limited Transposition. The following illustrations, which are Messiaen's own, are extraordinary in their precision and subtlety.[8]

MODE 2

    First transposition: blue and violet
    Second transposition: gold and brown
    Third transposition: green

MODE 3

    First transposition: orange-colored halos of milky white with rose reflections, spotted with a little red, like an opal, with some green pigmentation and specks of gold.
    Second transposition: grey, gold, and mauve
    Third transposition: blue and green
    Fourth transposition: orange streaked with red and a little blue

The combination of Modes 2 and 3, which occurs frequently, reveals for Messiaen a purplish-blue flecked with red, gold, and silver. Manifestations of Messiaen's involvement with such a musical kaleidoscope can be seen in the text of his *Trois petites liturgies*, where "rainbows of love" are reflected in "red and violet song in praise of the Father" in the first movement, and where in the third a set of "correspondances" recalls Baudelaire:

Envelop me in Thy tenderness.
Yellow-violet, vision,
White veil, subtlety,
Orange-blue, strength and joy,
Celestial arrow, ability,
Give me the flower and the foliage of Thy Love.

It is worthy of note that Messiaen's record jackets, which the composer oversees much in the same manner as Debussy with his publisher Durand, typically emphasize violet, his favorite color, with touches of the complementary colors blue and orange.

In recent years, the austerities of *Mode de valeurs* (1949) and *Livre d'orgue* (1951; see discussion on pp. 506–9) have been replaced by the retrospective style of *La transfiguration* (1969), and the mystical qualities apparent in his style of the 1930s and 1940s have returned frequently wedded to newly devised formal complexities (e.g., the "langage communicable" of his *Méditations sur le mystère de la Sainte Trinité*, 1969). The five-hour opera on the life of St. Francis of Assisi (1983), prematurely and incorrectly announced as his final work, testifies to the composer's dual emphasis on irrational mysticism and rationally controlled structures reflective of a natural marriage between Christian-Nature symbolism and an intricate, highly personal formalism.

SCHOENBERG

No composer's career expresses more clearly than Arnold Schoenberg's the fact that the history of any art is not just a story of technical advance and/or change but of the themes of expression and the account to which stylistic developments are put. It is surely no accident, too, that the period that saw the interaction of ethics and aesthetics in a group of Parisian-based composers also proved to be pivotal for the interaction of personal faith and creation in the works of numerous composers in other countries.

Arnold Schoenberg (1874–1951) had been raised in the orthodox Jewish faith in Vienna, though in 1898 at age fourteen he had converted to Lutheranism. In the period following World War I, Schoenberg, according to his own testimony, began a fourteen-year preparation (1919–33) for his return to Judaism. The first outward manifestation of the struggle appears in the uncompleted score of *Jacob's Ladder*, whose libretto was written in 1915 and for which music was composed between 1917 and 1922. The examination of life and its obligations is undertaken from every possible angle, a theme treated in more allegorical terms in his play without music, *The Biblical Way* (1926–27), which attempts, in Schoenberg's words, "a very up-to-date treatment of the story of how the Jews became a people."[9]

Schoenberg's most important musical testament to such an inquiry is his opera *Moses and Aaron*, composed between 1930 and 1932, for which two acts are provided with music and a third remains solely as a text. Schoenberg's increasing awareness of the growing wave of anti-Semitism in Germany as well as in Vienna led to his eventual flight from Germany and his reconversion to Judaism in a private ceremony in Paris on July 24, 1933.

Less than two weeks later, in a letter to Webern, Schoenberg announced future plans to work for the Jewish national cause, most immediately through a long tour of America, then perhaps a world tour "to persuade people to help the Jews in Germany."[10] The problems attendant to settling into a new life in America, first in Boston (October, 1933) and then in Los Angeles (autumn, 1934), and to recurring bouts with ill health left him little time or energy to fulfill his dreams, but musical evidence, such as his setting of the *Kol Nidre* (1938) intended for synagogue use, throughout the American years points to his passionate and continuing attention to these announced concerns.

A Survivor from Warsaw of 1947, like so many of Schoenberg's works, finds the composer engaged in ethical and moral judgments. In *Die glückliche Hand* (1910–13), *Von Heute auf Morgen* (1928), and *Moses and Aaron* (1930–32) Schoenberg had delivered himself via Expressionist drama, *Zeitoper*, and Biblical play of messages central to his personal and artistic nature. In *A Survivor from Warsaw*, for narrator, male chorus, and orchestra, ingredients from all these works surface naturally and forcefully. As in his *Kol Nidre*, where Expressionist anxieties and attendant colorings and dissonances stand next to moments of prayerful tonality, the music traverses a range in keeping with the unfolding narrative, and includes passages of direct text painting, which are rare in Schoenberg. The libretto, based on stories from the Warsaw Ghetto, is in Schoenberg's inimitable English, with passages in German to portray the voice of the Nazi sergeant and in Hebrew for the choral chant, "Shema Yisroel," which closes the work. Having fled Europe himself in 1933, Schoenberg's message is both painful and personal.

Five years earlier, Schoenberg had written his *Ode to Napoleon Bonaparte* (1942) for speaker, piano, and string quartet, and in some ways it may be viewed as a preparatory and parallel composition. The text by Byron is openly anti-Napoleonic; the opening motif from Beethoven's *Fifth Symphony* (used as a popular victory theme in World War II) to accompany the words "earthquake voice of victory," and the conclusion of an Eb chord (the key of Beethoven's "Eroica") all suggest a precisely pointed message.

In a group of final works for chorus—*Dreimal tausend Jahre*, op. 50a (1949), *De profundis*, op. 50b (1950), and the *Modern Psalm*, op. 50c (1950)—Schoenberg essayed a valedictory that summed up his ultimate concern: life as a pattern of change and religion as a quest. It has been suggested that the justification for his break with tonality, which eluded him in theory, he eventually found in religion,[11] but it is also possible to see as a corollary the idea that his invention of the series not only provided a law but allowed the exercise of freedom through intuition. The distance on this point from the contemporary neo-Thomism of Maritain, though dialectically alien, is not great.

Schoenberg's understandable paranoia with respect to both racial and artistic persecution left him with no doubt as to the nobility of his mission. But a periodic nostalgia for tonality, the one thing whose demise he had been responsible for bringing about, lured him into writing a series of works during his American years that caused many of his disciples to question his steadfastness. Beginning with the *Suite* for string orchestra of 1934, the *Kol Nidre*, op. 39 (1938), the *Chamber Symphony No. 2*, op. 38 (1939; begun in 1906), and continuing through the *Variations on a Recitative* for organ, op. 40 (1941), the *Theme and Variations* for winds, op. 43a (1943), and to an extent such serial works as the *Ode to Napoleon*, op. 41, and the *Piano Concerto*, op. 42 (1942), Schoenberg satisfied a periodic inner need to return to tonality, which he touchingly addressed in one of his final essays, "On revient toujours" ("One always returns") of 1948. In writing these works, he argued, he had let nobody down, least of all himself, and had only exercised a fundamental creative and expressive need: ". . . a longing to return to the older style was always vigorous in me; and from time to time I had to yield to that urge."[12] Apparently there were matters of musical faith as well.

DALLAPICCOLA: *CANTI DI PRIGIONIA* AND *SICUT UMBRA*

Born into an Italian family at Pisino d'Istrai, then under the jurisdiction of the Austrian empire, Luigi Dallapiccola (1904-1975) was interned at Graz with his parents as a teenager (March 1917–November 1918) for suspected Italian sympathies. Such an early introduction to the force of politics on the human condition would prove to be a major theme in his later work as a composer. Though an early infatuation with Debussy and early Italian music, especially Monteverdi and Gesualdo, provided an early grounding for the young composer, later confrontations with the world of Schoenberg (especially *Pierrot lunaire*), Berg (the dramatic works), and Webern (both instrumental and vocal styles) proved to be seminal.

The quotation of music originally associated with medieval texts (his own *Tre laudi*, 1936–37) alongside that composed to tell the story of modern man's search for a glimpse of eternity first occurred in his setting of Saint-Exupéry's *Volo di notte* (1937–39) as an opera. Such stylistic juxtaposition found a powerful new expression in his first work of protest, the *Canti di prigionia* (1938–41), the first part of a trilogy that was later to include the *Canti di liberazione* (1951–55) and *Requiescant* (1957–58). Written following the announcement of anti-Semitic policies by Mussolini (Dallapiccola's wife was a Jew), the work is dedicated to the theme of tyranny and its consequences, and is scored for chorus (mixed in the outer movements, female in the middle one), two pianos, two harps, six tympani, xylophone, vibraphone, ten bells, cymbals, three tamtams, triangle, and side-, snare-, and bass-drums.

The texts Dallapiccola chose were those of three illustrious prisoners who "had fought for liberty and for the triumph of justice":[13] Mary Stuart (Queen of Scots), the sixth-century philosopher Boethius, and Girolamo Savanarola, the Florentine preacher-monk in the most troubled days of the Medicis.

Canti Di Prigionia

I. Preghiera di Maria Stuarda.
> O Domine Deus! Sperevi in Te.
>
> O care mi Jesu! Nunc libera me.
> In dura catena, in misera poena,
>   desidero Te.
> Languendo, gemendo et genu flectende,
> Adoro, imploro, ut liberes me.
> (Maria Stuart)

II. Invocazione di Boezio.
> Felix qui potuit boni fontem visere
>   lucidum,
> Felix qui potuit gravis terrae solvere
>   vincula.
> (Boetius: De Consolatione Philosophiae,
>   III, 12)

III. Gongedo di Girolamo Savonarola.
> Premat mundus, insurgens hostes, nihil
>   timeo,
> Quoniam in Te Domine speravi,
> Quonium Tu es spes mea,
> Quonium Tu altissimum posuisti
>   refugium tuum.
> (Savonarola: Meditation in
>   Psalmum XXXI)

Songs of Prison

I. Prayer of Mary Stuart.
> O my Lord and God! I have hoped unto
>   Thee.
> O my beloved Jesus! Now set me free.
> In hard chains, in pain and misery, I long
>   for Thee.
> Languishing, lamenting, bending my knee,
> I adore Thee and implore Thee, that Thou
>   settest me free.

II. Invocation of Boetius.
> Happy he who able to see the luminous
>   source of Good,
> Happy he who can free himself from the
>   heavy bonds of the earth.

III. Leave of Girolamo Savonarola.
> May the world oppress me, may the
>   enemies arise, I fear nothing,
> For into Thee, my Lord, I have put my
>   hope,
> For Thou arest my hope,
> For Thou arest my highest and last refuge.

In each movement to the material provided by two twelve-note series is wedded a fragment of the "Dies irae," whose visions of the Last Judgement seemed appropriate to Dallapiccola during the dark days of the war. The series serves as the basis for the more agitated sections and even as the harmonizing material for the plainchant in the final section, but the austerity of the first movement suggests nothing so much as the quiet fervor of the finale of Stravinsky's *Symphony of Psalms*. The composer's "hope of convincing people that even a composer very much in sympathy with the twelve-tone technique is not a person detached from life but one who, like every man, lives his own life with many sorrows and some joy"[14] can be said to have been achieved.

While the first complete performance of *Canti di prigionia* took place in Rome, December 1941, it was its presentation at the ISCM concerts of 1946 following the end of World War II that brought Dallapiccola to the notice of the musical world. Though its theme reappeared in numerous works, his vocabulary sought an ever greater refinement that moved increasingly close to the world of Webern. That a pronounced lyricism also prevailed is evident in works like the *Goethe Lieder* of 1953 for mezzo-soprano and three clarinets.

His last major work, the opera *Ulisse* completed in 1968, recalls the fact that he had prepared a modern performing edition of Monteverdi's *Il ritorno di Ulisse in patria* in 1941-42, while one of his final creations, *Sicut umbra* for mezzo-soprano and twelve instruments reminds us of his early "night flight" with Saint-Exupéry (*Volo di notte*). Here he invokes the delicate tracery of the stars through a direct projection of maps of the night sky into musical figures and a haunting contemplation of death. Using three groups of instruments recalling the *Pierrot lunaire* ensemble (piccolo, flute in C, alto flute; clarinets in Eb, Bb, and bass clarinet; violin, viola, cello) softened by a fourth reflective of *Herzgewächse* (vibraphone, celesta, harp), Dallapiccola provides an introduction for flutes followed by a setting of three poems by Juan Ramón Jiménez for clarinet and strings; flutes, clarinet, and strings; and the total ensemble. The reservation of the celestial instruments for the final poem, "Ideal Epitaph for a Sailor," is a masterstroke in its crystalline etching of the constellations. It was also a mark of Dallapiccola's art to have significantly addressed the unanswerable questions of humanity and existence with a rare combination of intellect and poetry.

Sicut Umbra (1970)

EL OLIVIDO

! Olvido, hermoso olvido,
libertador final
de nuestro nombre puro,
en la imajinación del tiempo feo!

—Hombres, hombres, hombres . . . , ay!—

! Oh, venideros días,
en que el alma, olvidada con su nombre,
habrá estado, en si, en todo,
y no estará, con otro, en nada!

EL RECUERDO

Como médanos de oro,
que vienen y que van, son los recuerdos.

El viento se los lleva,
y donde están, están,
y están donde estuvieron,
y donde habrán de estár . . .—Médanos de
    oro—.

Lo llenan todo, mar
total de oro inefable,
con todo el viento en él . . .—Son los
    recuerdos—.

FORGETFULNESS

Forgetfulness, beautiful forgetfulness,
final liberator
of our immaculate name,
in the imagination of an ugly time!

—Mankind, mankind, mankind . . . Ah!—

Oh, future days,
in which the soul, with its name forgotten,
will have been, in itself, in all,
and will not be, with another, in nothing!

MEMORIES

Like golden sand-dunes,
that come and go, such are remembrances.

The wind carries them away,
and where they are, they are,
and they are where they were,
and where they ought to be . . .—Golden
    sand-dunes—.

They permeate all,
absolute sea of ineffable gold,
with the wind ever present . . .—Such are
    remembrances—.

EPITAFIO IDEAL DE UN MARINERO

(mm. 139–200)
1, 2

Hay que buscar, para saber
3 tu tumba, por el firmamiento. **4, 5, 6**
—Llueve tu muerte de una estrella. **7**
La losa no te pesa, que es un universo
de ensueño—.   **8, 9**
En la ignorancia, estás
en todo (cielo, mar y tierra) muerto.

Spanish texts by Juan Ramón Jiménez.

IDEAL EPITAPH FOR A SAILOR

We must look, if we want to find
your grave, overhead in the sky.
—Your death rains from a star.
The tombstone is light upon you,
for it is a dream universe—.
Unknowing, you dwell
in all—sky, sea earth—dead.

*English trans. by J. L. Gili used by permission of Aquilar,
Madrid, and D. Francisco Hernàndez-Pinzón Jimenez.*

Example 23.12. Dallapiccola, *Sicut Umbra.*

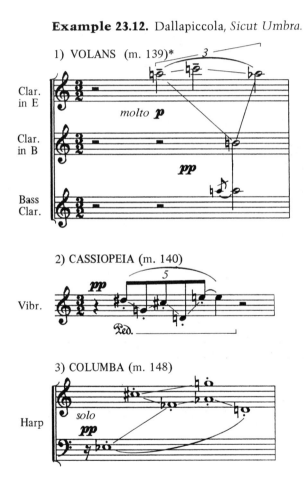

*The number and measure of each figure refers to its first appearance.

Example 23.12 (Continued)

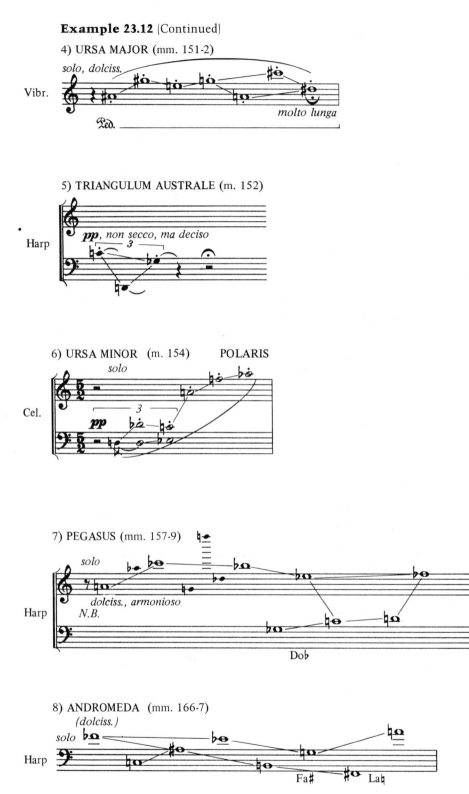

4) URSA MAJOR (mm. 151-2)

5) TRIANGULUM AUSTRALE (m. 152)

6) URSA MINOR (m. 154)   POLARIS

7) PEGASUS (mm. 157-9)

8) ANDROMEDA (mm. 166-7)

Example 23.12 (Continued)

9) LIBRA (mm. 168-9)

VAUGHAN WILLIAMS AND HARTMANN: WHITMAN AS WAR POET

The appeal of verses by the American poet Walt Whitman (1819–92) is apparent among a group of English composers from the end of the nineteenth century and the beginning of the twentieth. Not only Stanford and Hamilton Harty, but especially Delius, Holst, and Vaughan Williams were attracted to the rhythm and sonority of his free-verse style. Both Holst and Vaughan Williams set Whitman's *Toward the Unknown Region* in 1905–06, and it was this work that launched Williams's public career. He turned again to a setting of Whitman for his first symphony, *A Sea Symphony* (1903–09) and for *A Dirge for Two Veterans*, which followed in 1911.

In spite of Vaughan Williams's important work on *The English Hymnal* (1906) and his own contributions as a hymn writer, he was never a practicising Christian and, as his second wife put it, "he later drifted into a cheerful agnosticism."[15] This in no way, however, kept him from assuming the role of the visionary whose inquiry into the aspirations of the common man carried its own note of spirituality and anguish. Such was the background for works like his *Sancta civitas* (1923–25), an oratorio on texts from Revelations, or *Job* (1927–30), a ballet intended for Diaghilev, based on Blake's *Illustrations to the Book of Job* and one of the most powerful scores of any composer of the period. While his unaccompanied *Mass in G minor* (1920–21) is properly seen in light of the revival of early English polyphony, and William Byrd in particular at Westminster Cathedral, his *Dona nobis pacem* of 1936 openly addresses the spectre of war.

Here he returned to the poetry of Whitman, and resurrecting his *Dirge for Two Veterans*, written on the eve of World War I but never performed or published, he interfaced additional texts from Whitman's *Drum Taps* (1865) with words from the Scriptures in a fashion that cannot help but be seen as a prefiguration of Britten's *War Requiem* (1962). The opening movement is an intonation of the Agnus Dei, "O Lamb of God, who takest away the sins of the world," followed immediately by a Whitman chorus, "Beat! beat! drums" and a movement for baritone soloist and chorus, which concludes with the words:

For my enemy is dead, a man divine as myself is dead,
I look where he lies white-faced and still in the coffin—I draw near,
Bend down and touch lightly with my lips the white face in the coffin.

Such is the stuff that was later to make up the haunting images of the English war poets, Sassoon and Owen. The revived dirge on a Whitman text is the fourth movement, and the work closes with words by John Bright, Liberal and Quaker politician, uttered in a speech before Parliament in 1854 during the Crimean War:

> The Angel of Death has been abroad throughout the land; you may almost hear the beating of his wings.

and an adaptation of Scriptures from numerous sources including Jeremiah, Daniel, Psalms, Isaiah, and Luke.

The force of Whitman's lines replete with war imagery also appealed at exactly the same time to an American, Howard Hanson (1896–1981), whose *Drum Taps* for chorus and orchestra dates from 1935, as well as to a German, Karl Amadeus Hartmann (1905–1963), whose *First Symphony* subtitled "Versuch eines Requiems" ("An Attempted Requiem") dates from 1935–36. Hartmann's symphony began its life with an independent performance of the first movement under the title "Miserere" at the ISCM concert in Prague in August 1935, which also saw the premiere of Berg's *Lulu Symphony*. It is in five movements, of which only the third is purely orchestral, the remaining four relying on texts from Whitman to focus on the mounting concern for what many at the time saw as another inevitable conflict. The collective message is unmistakable. The second movement text is familiar as the lament on the death of Lincoln, "When lilacs last in the dooryard bloom'd," later set by Hindemith in 1945, Sessions in 1970, and Crumb in 1980 (*Apparition: Elegiac Songs and Vocalises*), while the fourth movement text is known from Delius's *Sea Drift*. The sentiment of the opening movement is as powerful as it is pointed, and Hartmann's tarnished fanfares capture the newsreel quality of rallies held by the Third Reich in the period during which it was written. The contrasting vocal recitative of the movement creates a vision for the listener that persists to the end of the work.

Elend

Ich sitze und schaue auf alle Plagen
   der Welt und auf alle Bedrängnis
   und Schmach,
ich sehe die Müsal der Schlacht, Pestilenz,
   Tyrannei, sehe Märtyrer und Gefangene,
ich beobacht die Geringschätzung und
   Erniedrigung, die die Armen von dem
   Hochmütigen zu erleiden haben;
auf all Gemeinheit und Qual ohne Ende
   schaue ich sitzend hin,
Sehe und höre.

Misery

I sit and I look out upon all the
   sorrows of the world and upon all
   oppression and shame . . .
I see the workings of battle,
   pestilence, tyrany, I see martyrs
   and prisoners.
I observe the slights and
   degradations cast by arrogant
   persons upon laborers . . .
All these—all the meanness and
   agony without end I, sitting, look
   out upon,
See, hear and am silent.

Hartmann, who composed eight symphonies, is considered by many as one of the most important exponents of symphonic form in this century in spite of a lack of widespread recognition. But though many of his later works disclose an inclination toward Neoclassicism in their repeated attention to variation, fugue, and mirror forms, the humanitarian sense of urgency that informs his first symphony appears repeatedly. An opera tuned to the theme of a popular revolt against repression and force was in its planning stages at the time of his death, and the incomplete but performable *Gesangsszene* for baritone and orchestra on a text from Giraudoux's *Sodom and Gomorrha* (1963) announces the final destruction of civilization at its close with the words, "It is the end of the world. The saddest of all . . . "

That Whitman's words continued to stir and to sound the note of pity in man's eternal stumbling toward war was powerfully captured in Ned Rorem's *War Scenes* (1969) for baritone and piano. The impulse behind the cycle was clearly marked in the dedication: "To those who died in Vietnam, both sides, during the composition: 20–30 June 1969."

BRITTEN: *THE WAR REQUIEM*

Victory in Europe came on May 7, 1945, and in the Pacific on August 15. The death of Webern as the result of an accidental shooting by an American soldier on September 15 and of Bartók in impecunious surroundings on September 26 signaled not only the loss of two major musicians but the end of an era as well. Krenek's *Elegy* for strings of 1946 in memory of Anton Webern is one of his most moving utterances and was obviously written under the direct impact of personal loss, though Lutosławski's *Funeral Music* (1954–58) for Bartók, symbolic in both title and dedication of a new stylistic turn for the composer, was not written until the following decade.

Similarly delayed reactions to the tragedies of war began to surface in the 1960s. Britten's *War Requiem* did not appear until 1962, following an understandably protracted period of gestation. The work was written to celebrate the consecration of St. Michael's Cathedral in Coventry, the original church having been destroyed in one of the most devastating air raids of the Battle of Britain. For many of the early performances of the work, the choice of an Englishman (Peter Pears), a German (Dietrich Fischer-Dieskau), and a Russian (Galina Vishnevskaya) in the three prominent solo roles was potently symbolic.

The conception of the work as a setting of the Latin Mass for the Dead troped by poems of Wilfred Owen (1893–1918) is one of the most moving to have come out of the conflict. The poems were carefully chosen to reinforce the vivid and concrete imagery of the Requiem and the burial service. The quotation at the beginning of the score is from the preface to a collection the poet was preparing shortly before his death:

> My subject is War, and the pity of War.
> The Poetry is in the pity.
> All a poet can do is warn.

Although Rupert Brooke may have been the most popular poet of World War I in the English language, his idealist view of a sacrificing youth ran counter to the message of Owen. Killed in France at the age of 25, Owen spoke of the horrors of war, stripped of any glamor, and suggested questions about man's capacity for slaughter that remain disturbing to this day.

To the quality of pity Owen has added a note of reconciliation, which marks the verses as peculiarly suited to the task of achieving a synthesis with the Mass, worked out by Britten according to the following plan:

I. *Requiem aeternam*

> Requiem aeternam (Chorus); Te decet hymnus (Boys); Requiem aeternum
> "What passing-bells for these who die as cattle?" (Tenor Solo)
> Kyrie eleison (Chorus)

II. *Dies irae*

> Dies irae, dies illa (Chorus)
> "Bugles sang, sadd'ning the evening air" (Baritone Solo)
> Liber scriptus proferetur (Soprano Solo and semi-chorus)
> "Out there, we've walked quite friendly up to Death" (Tenor & Baritone Solos)
> Recordare Jesu pie (Chorus)
> "Be slowly lifted up, thou long black arm" (Baritone Solo)
> Dies irae (Chorus)
> Lacrimosa dies illa (Soprano Solo and Chorus)
> "Move him, Move him into the sun" (Tenor Solo)
> Pie Jesu Domine (Chorus)

III. *Offertorium*

> Domine Jesu Christe (Boys)
> Sed signifer sanctus Michael (Chorus)
> "So Abram rose, and clave the wood, and went" (Tenor and Baritone Solos)
> Hostias et preces tibit Domine (Boys)
> Quam olim Abrahae promisisti (Chorus)

IV. *Sanctus*

> Sanctus, Sanctus Dominus Deus Sabaoth (Soprano Solo and Chorus)
> "After the blast of lightning from the East" (Baritone Solo)

V. *Agnus Dei*

> "One ever hangs where shelled roads part" (Tenor Solo)
> Agnus Dei, qui tollis peccata mundi (Chorus)

VI. *Libera me*

> Libera me; Dies illa, dies irae; Libera me (Soprano Solo and Chorus)
> "It seemed that out of battle I escaped" (Tenor Solo)
> "'None,' said the other, 'save the undone years'" (Baritone Solo)
> "Let us sleep now . . . " (Tenor and Baritone Solos)
> In paradisum deductant te Angeli (Boys, Soprano Solo & Chorus)
> Requiem aeternam dona eis, Domine (Boys)
> Requiescant in pace. Amen. (Chorus)

Though Britten's plan is more comprehensive and unified, a similar interfacing of secular war poems with texts from the Scriptures and the Mass has been noted in Vaughan Williams's *Dona nobis pacem* of 1936, which may well have served as a model. There the secular poet was Whitman and the war of which he spoke was the American Civil War, but the imagery of "Beat! beat! drums!—blow! bugles! blow!" and "For my enemy is dead, a man divine as myself is dead" parallel in a dramatic way sentiments expressed by Owen in "Bugles sang" and the closing "Strange Meeting," which finishes with the words:

I am the enemy you killed, my friend.
I knew you in this dark; for so you frowned
Yesterday through me as you jabbed and killed.

I parried; but my hands were loath and cold.
let us sleep now . . . .*

Britten deploys his musical forces on three distinct spatial planes: the tenor and baritone soloists, who intone Owen's poems, in the foreground with their own chamber orchestra; the chorus, occasionally reinforced by the soprano soloist, with the full orchestra in the middle ground; and the boys' voices with organ placed in the background, presiding over the whole with a liturgical calmness. He also reminds us of his prior concern for the themes of the work through allusion to his own *Sinfonia da Requiem* (1940) in the Antiphon and to his *Canticle II: Abraham and Isaac* (1952) in the Offertorium at the text "Thou didst promise unto Abraham and his seed." A passing reference to Verdi's *Requiem* in the Introit also recalls a similar homage by Stravinsky in the "Libera me" of his *Requiem Canticles.*

From the quietly brooding tritones of the Introit to the thundering statement of the "Dies irae," which invokes the flying bugles of Britten's early *Serenade* wedded to Mahler's harrowing march rhythms, to the haunting reveries of "Let us sleep now," which draws on the recurring textual theme of the healing power of sleep throughout Britten's career, the work is a remarkable blend of liturgical and personal drama. While intercut (e.g., the "Lacrimosa" is four times interrupted by Owen's poem) and combination (e.g., "Let us sleep now" is sung as counterpoint to the beginning of "In paradisum") may rule over development in the whole, something of Britten's interest in a symbolic tonal dialectic, perceivable in numerous earlier works, is audible in the persistent tritones. They serve not only schematic function in single movements; such as the ostinato of the Agnus Dei,

(F#-E-D#-C#-B-C-D-E-F-G :‖ A-B-C-Bb-Ab-F#, da capo),

but are heard as a framing arch that reaches from the final cadence of the opening Introit through the "Pie Jesu Domine" at the close of the "Dies irae" to the final "Requiescant in Pace." In each instance the persistent C-F# is ultimately provided an F major resolution. This gesture of closure also provides the final memory for the piece:

> Into Paradise may the Angels lead thee; at thy coming may the Martyrs receive thee, and bring thee into the holy city Jerusalem. May the Choir of Angels receive thee, and with Lazarus, once poor, mayest thou have eternal rest. Rest eternal grant unto them, O Lord: and let eternal light shine upon them. May they rest in peace. Amen.

WAR WITHOUT WORDS: SYMBOLS AND SCENARIOS

In the period 1920-50 the composer made numerous statements about war and peace and not always with a text to make the message explicit. Thus Villa-Lobos's symphonic sequence (Nos. 3, 4, 5) of 1919-20 carries the subtitles "A guerra," "A vittoria," and "A paz," respectively. And Ives, before penning "Flanders Field" and "Tom Sails Away" in 1917 used the hymn tune "Sweet Bye and

---

*Wilfred Owen, Collected Poems. Copyright 1963 by Chatto & Windus. Reprinted by permission of New Directions Publishing Corporation.

Bye" in his *Second Orchestral Set* (1915) to recall a personal experience where people spontaneously broke into song in the New York subways following the sinking of the Lusitania. Other symbolic quotations include Shostakovich's use of a German beer drinking song in his *Symphony No. 7* (1941), which dealt with the defense of Leningrad. It was a note of irony that was remembered and picked up by Bartók in his *Concerto for Orchestra* (1943).

The power of an implicit scenario to transform what we hear is nowhere more vividly demonstrated than in Stravinsky's revelation in 1962 (*Dialogues and a Diary*) that the *Symphony in Three Movements* (1942–45) "was written under the impression of world events," that the "finale contains the genesis of a war plot," that the first movement was "likewise inspired by a war film, this time of scorched earth tactics in China," and that the final "rather too commercial, D-flat sixth chord . . . in some ways tokens my extra exuberance in the Allied triumph."[16] Two other symphonies written at the close of hostilities are Milhaud's *Symphony No. 3* (1946), whose subtitle "Te Deum" connotes a hymn of Thanksgiving, and Honegger's *Symphony No. 3* (1945–46), whose designation "Liturgique" is further amplified in the several movements, which are labeled "Dies irae," "De profundis clamavi," and "Dona nobis pacem." Though such titles in Honegger's symphony may recall or prefigure Dallapiccola, Messiaen, and Vaughan Williams, respectively, the listener cannot fail to note how the language of *Pacific 231*, which had served as a model for the *musique des machines* in the 1920s, has now been transferred to the first movement as an expression of the machines of war. The impact is cinematographic, reminiscent of the soundtrack of numerous newsreels and movies that appeared during World War II. The march, which is adopted with a similar intention in the final movements of that work, shares with Hindemith and Shostakovich a legacy in the symphonies of Mahler, now infused with an updated message.

In the decades that followed, Penderecki's *Threnody to the Victims of Hiroshima* (1960), completed the year before the *War Requiem*, reflected less the maturation of a language available to the composer before the war, as with Britten, than the exploration of a new sonic world with traditional instruments (see pp. 000–00). The popularity the piece achieved was undoubtedly due to the imagery which audiences drew from its title, though the composer denied explicit reference to airplane drones, whistling bombs in freefall, or catastrophic explosions.

In Messiaen's *Et exspecto resurrectionem mortuorum* ("And I await the Resurrection of the Dead") of 1964, a work commissioned by the French government for the dead of two world wars, the composer continued to spell his visions of the Apocalypse replete with color imagery, Indian rhythms, and bird calls found in other works both before and after. Scored for a large ensemble of winds and percussion which, the composer stated, indicates the need for performance in vast spaces (cathedrals, open air, even mountain heights), Messiaen eschewed the setting of texts, but in a fashion typical of his abstract instrumental works of the 1930s and 1940s used scriptural quotation as prefatory material instead. Thus the first movement, which carries the text of the *De profundis* ("Out of the depths have I cried unto thee, O Lord"), is mirrored by a theme in the lower brass harmonized by "six horns in colored clusters—a cry from the Abyss!"[17] It is a sonic image that would be recalled by Boulez in his *Rituel: In Memory of Bruno Maderna* of 1974–75.

The recurring spectres of Guernica, Leningrad, Auschwitz, and Hiroshima (see the Repertoire List on p. 503) would seem to indicate not only that music is capable of becoming an agent for social protest but that the horrors of World War II have imposing implications for our time and will not readily dissolve. In all, the means of musical projection have been as varied as the message has been insistent. Works written in the 1960s that plumbed the civilized world's memory of its darkest hour included those by other such well-known figures as William Schuman, Luigi Nono, and R. Murray Schafer, by which time new world events had transpired, capable of provoking composers to speak of more immediately impending issues. Ned Rorem's *War Scenes* once again demonstrated the power of Whitman's texts to sound a warning—this time about a war newly begun and angrily protested.

Terry Riley's *A Rainbow in Curved Air* (1970) resounds in its score with the processes of the minimalists and in its textual preface with the sentiments of the Flower Children.

> And then all wars ended / Arms of every kind were outlawed and the masses gladly contributed them to giant foundries in which they were melted down and the metal poured back into the earth / The Pentagon was turned on its side and painted purple, yellow & green / All boundaries were dissolved / The slaughter of animals was forbidden / The whole of lower Manhattan became a meadow in which unfortunates from the Bowery were allowed to live out their fantasies in the sunshine and were cured / People swam in the sparkling rivers under blue skies streaked only with incense pouring from the new factories / The energy from dismantled nuclear weapons provided free heat and light / World health was restored / An abundance of organic vegetables, fruits and grains was growing wild along the discarded highways / National flags were sewn together into brightly colored circus tents under which politicians were allowed to perform harmless theatrical games / The concept of work was forgotten.[18]

And demonstrating the intercultural anxiety for the issue at hand, Richard Wernick (b. 1934) wrote his *Kaddish-Requiem* (1971), subtitled "A Secular Service for the Victims of Indochina," for an extended *Pierrot* ensemble of mezzo-soprano, cantor, pic, fl, alto fl, cl, bass cl, vn, vc, sitar, pf and percussion.

More recently, the young American Steven Rouse (b. 1957) voiced a renewed concern of his generation for the problem of nuclear disarmament in a work entitled *Dense Pack* (1983–84) for a cappella chorus and tam-tam. Based on a dismemberment of "The Star-Spangled Banner" reassembled in clusters, it protests man's folly not by invoking the memory of prior conflicts but by posing a symbolic question about man's current behavior. It is heartening to note that a complete list of those who have been moved to make such statements since World War II would tellingly reveal the names of Russian, Canadian, Polish, Czech, French, Italian, British, and American composers alike.

To this survey of some typical examples of music as a reflection of man's nobler instincts or as commentary on his baser ones, it is well to add that works politically motivated by the belief in the necessity of class revolution (e.g., Henze, Nono) have appeared with increasing frequency in the post World War II period. Certainly this is not the first time in history, nor even in the twentieth century, when music has mirrored the social-political scene (Hindemith's *Mathis der Maler* or Schoenberg's *A Survivor from Warsaw*, for example). But Stockhausen, while decrying the lack of governmental support of the arts worldwide, has also recently warned against "all propaganda that music should be politically committed, or that it is only 'entertainment'," suggesting that both are primary contributors to the lowering of the prestige that arts can enjoy in any society.[19] Nonetheless, it is obvious that music not only has the power to do both but that it has devoted an important portion of its energies to such missions in our century.

REPERTOIRE (Stravinsky)

Pater noster (1926); *Credo* (1932); *Ave Maria* (1934), chorus (originally in Slavonic)
Symphony of Psalms (1930), chorus, orch
Mass (1944–48), TrATB, 2 ob, eng hn, two bn, two tpt, 3 trbn
Canticum Sacrum (1955), T, Bar, chorus, orch
Threni: id est Lamentationes Jeremiae prophetae (1957–58), soli, chorus, orch
A Sermon, a Narrative and a Prayer (1960–61), A, T, speaker, chorus, orch
The Flood (1962), soloists, chorus, orch
Anthem: "The Dove descending breaks the air" (Eliot) (1962)
Introitus: "Requiem aeternam", ded. to Eliot (1965), T, B, harp, pf, 2 tmp, 2 tam-tam, va, db
Requiem Canticles (1965–66), A, B, chorus, orch

READING (Stravinsky)

Arthur Lourié, "Neo-Gothic and Neo-Classic," *Modern Music,* v.3 (1928), 3.
Jean Maritain, *Creative Intuition in Art and Poetry* (Princeton, 1953).
Igor Stravinsky, *Chroniques de ma vie* (Paris, 1935–36; Eng. trans. *An Autobiography,* 1936).
Frederick Brown, *An Impersonation of Angels: A Biography of Jean Cocteau* (New York, 1968).
Vera Stravinsky and Robert Craft, *Stravinsky in Pictures and Documents* (New York, 1978).
Eric Walter White, *Stravinsky: The Composer and his Works* (2nd ed., Berkeley, 1979).
Robert M. Copland, "The Christian Message of Igor Stravinsky," *Musical Quarterly,* lxvii.4 (1982), 563–79.
Gilbert Amy, "Aspects of the Religious Music of Stravinsky" in *Confronting Stravinsky: Man, Musician and Modernist,* ed. J. Pasler (Berkeley, 1986), 195.

REPERTOIRE (Poulenc)

Litanies à la vierge noire (1936), women's vv, org
Mass (1937), SATB
Quatre motets pour un temps de pénitence (1938–39), SATB
Figure humaine (1943), cantata, 12 vv
Stabat mater (1950), S, SATBarB, orch
Gloria (1959), S, chorus, orch
Sept répons de ténèbres (1961), child S, male vv, boys' vv, orch

READING (Poulenc)

Henri Hell, *Francis Poulenc* (New York, 1959).
D. Cox, "Poulenc and Surrealism," *The Listener* (July 11, 1963), 69.
Francis Poulenc, *Moi et mes amis* (Paris, 1963; Eng. trans. *My Friends and Myself,* 1978).
Pierre Bernac, *Francis Poulenc* (Paris, 1977; Eng. trans., 1977).

REPERTOIRE (Messiaen)

La banquet céleste (1928), org
L'ascension (orch, 1933; org, 1934)

La nativité du Seigneur (1935), org
Les corps glorieux (1939), org
Quatuor pour la fin du temps (1940), cl, pf, vn, vc
Visions de l'amen (1943), 2 pf
Vingt regards sur l'enfant Jésus (1944), pf
Trois petites liturgies (1944), 18 S, pf, ondes martenot, cel, vib, 3 perc, str
Turangalîla-symphonie (1946–48), pf, ondes martenot, orch
Mode de valeurs et d'intensités (1949), pf
Messe de la Pentecôte (1950), org
Livre d'orgue (1951), org
Oiseaux exotiques (1956), pf, 11 winds, xyl, glock, 2 perc
Chronochromie (1960), orch
Couleurs de la cité céleste (1963),pf, 13 winds, xyl, xylorimba, mar, 4 perc
Et exspecto resurrectionem mortuorum (1964), 18 ww, 16 brass, 3 perc
Méditations sur le mystère de la sainte Trinité (1969), 100 vv chorus, pf, vc, fl, cl, vib, mar,
    xylorimba, orch
Saint François d'Assise (1983), opera
Livre du Saint Sacrement (1986), org

READING (Messiaen)

Olivier Messiaen, "Le rhythm chez Strawinsky," Le revue musicale, no. 191 (1939), 331.
Olivier Messiaen, Technique de mon langage musical (Paris, 1944; Eng. trans. 1957).
Claude Samuel, Entretiens avec Olivier Messiaen (Paris, 1967; Eng. trans. 1976).
Roger Smalley, "Debussy and Messiaen," Musical Times, cix (1968), 128.
Stuart Waumsley, The Organ Music of Olivier Messiaen (Paris, 1969). . .
Trevor Hold, "Messiaen's Birds," Music and Letters, lii (1971), 113.
Robert Sherlaw Johnson, Messiaen (London, 1975).
Roger Nichols, Messiaen (London, 1975).
Paul Griffiths, "Catalogue de couleurs: Notes on Messiaen's Tone Colours on his 70th
    Birthday," Musical Times, cxix (1978), 1035.
Paul Griffiths, Olivier Messiaen and the Music of Time (London, 1985).

REPERTOIRE (Schoenberg)

Jakobsleiter (1917–22), oratorio, solo vv, choruses, orch
Moses and Aron (1930–32), opera, Act 3 not composed
Kol Nidre, op. 39 (1938), speaker, chorus, orch
Ode to Napoleon, op. 41 (1942), reciter, pf, str qt/str orch
A Survivor from Warsaw, op. 46 (1947), narrator, male vv, orch
Dreimal tausend Jahre, op. 50a (1949), SATB
De profundis, op. 50b (1950), SSATBB
Modern Psalm, op. 50c (1950), speaker, chorus, orch

READING (Schoenberg)

Karl H. Wörner, Schoenberg's Moses and Aron (Heidelberg, 1959; Eng. trans., rev. 1963).
Peter Gradenwitz, "Schoenberg's Religious Works," Music Review, xxi (1960), 19.
Alexander Ringer, "Schoenbergiana in Jerusalem," Musical Quarterly, lix (1973), 1.
Oliver W. Neighbour, "Arnold Schoenberg: 4. Personality and Beliefs," The New Grove
    Dictionary of Music and Musicians (1980), XVI, 706–08.

REPERTOIRE (Dallapiccola)

Sei cori di Michelangelo Buonarrote il giovane (1933–36)
Canti di prigionia (1938–41)
Volo di notte (1937–39), opera
Il prigioniero (1944–48), opera
Liriche greche (1944–45), voice and instruments

Goethe Lieder (1953), mezzo, 3 clar
Ulisse (1968), opera
Sicut umbra (1970), mezzo, 12 instr

READING (Dallapiccola)

Luigi Dallapiccola, "The Genesis of the *Canti di prigionia* and *Il prigioniero*," *Musical Quarterly*, xxxix (1953), 355.
Roman Vlad, *Luigi Dallapiccola*, trans. by Cynthia Jolly (Milan, 1957).
Hans Nathan, "The Twelve-Tone Compositions of Luigi Dallapiccola," *Musical Quarterly*, xliv (1958), 289.
James Dapogny, *Style and Method in Three Compositions of Luigi Dallapiccola* (Ph.D. diss., U. of Illinois, 1971).

REPERTOIRE: (Whitman as War Poet)

Vaughan Williams, *A Dirge for Two Veterans* (1911)
Vaughan Williams, *Dona nobis pacem* (1936), S, Bar, SATB, orch
Hanson, *Drum Taps* (1935), Bar, chorus, orch
Hartmann, *Symphony No. 1* (1935–36), A, orch
Hindemith, *A Requiem for Those We Love* ("When Lilacs Last in the Dooryard Bloom'd") (1945), Mez, Bar, chorus, orch
Hartman, *Gesangsszene:* "Sodom and Gomorrha" (1963), Bar, orch
Rorem, *War Scenes* (1969), Bar, pf
Sessions, "When Lilacs Last in the Dooryard Bloom'd" (1970), S, A, Bar, vv, orch
Crumb, *Apparition: Elegiac Songs and Vocalises* ("When Lilacs Last in the Dooryard Bloom'd") (1980), S, pf

REPERTOIRE (Britten)

Sinfonia da requiem (1940), orch
A Ceremony of Carols (1942), boys' vv, harp
St. Nicolas (1948), T, S, A, 4 Tr, SATB, str, pf 4 hands, perc, org
Missa brevis (1959), boys' vv, org
Noye's Fludde (1957), children's opera (Chester miracle play)
War Requiem (1961), S, T, Bar, boys' vv, mixed vv, orch, cham orch, org
Cantata misericordium (1963), T, Bar, small chorus, str qt, str orch, pf, harp, timp
Children's Crusade (*Kinderkreuzzug*, Brecht, trans. H. Keller) (1968), children's vv, perc, 2 pf, org

REPERTOIRE (Other Rituals and Liturgies)

Barber, *Prayers of Kierkegaard* (1954), S, A ad lib, T ad lib, chorus, orch
Berio, *Nones* (1954), orch
Bernstein, *Symphony No. 1* ("Jeremiah") (1943)
Bernstein, *Symphony No. 3* ("Kadish") (1961–63)
Boulez, *Rituel: In memoriam Bruno Maderna* (1974), wind, perc
Feldman, *Rothko Chapel* (1972), chorus, 2 vv, cel, perc, va
Lutosławski, *Funeral Music* (1958)
Penderecki, *Stabat mater* (1962)
Penderecki, *Passion according to St. Luke* (1965)
Penderecki, *Utrenia* (1970)
Penderecki, *Polish Requiem* (1980–84)
Stockhausen, *Sternklang* (1971)
Stockhausen, *Inori* (1974)

REPERTOIRE (Other Voices of War)

Barber, *Symphony No. 2* (1944): 2nd mvt. rev. as *Night Flight* (1964)
Barber, *A Stopwatch and an Ordinance Map* (1940), male vv, brass, timp
Bliss, *The Beatitudes* (1962), for Coventry
Crumb, *Black Angels* ("in tempore belli") (1970), elec str qt
Debussy, *Noël des enfants* (1915), v, pf
Debussy, *En blanc et noir* (1915), 2 pf
Holst, *Dirge for Two Veterans* (1914)
Honegger, *Symphony No. 3* ("Liturgique") (1945–46)
Husa, *Music for Prague* (1968)
Ives, *Second Orchestral Set* (1909–1915)
Ives, *Tom Sails Away* (1917), v, pf
Ives, *In Flanders Field* (1917), v, pf
Milhaud, *Symphony No. 3* ("Te Deum") (1946)
Nono, *La Victoire de Guernica* (1954)
Nono, *Variazioni canoniche sulla serie dell' op. 41 di Schoenberg* (1950)
Nono, *Canti di vita e d'amore: sul ponte di Hiroshima* (1962)
Nono, *Ricorda cosa ti hanno fatto in Auschwitz* (1966)
Nono, *Siamo in gioventù del Vietnam* (1973)
Penderecki, *Threnody to the Victims of Hiroshima* (1960)
Penderecki, *Dies irae:* "Auschwitz Oratorio" (1967)
Ravel, *Le tombeau de Couperin* (1914–17), pf
Riley, *A Rainbow in Curved Air* (1970)
Schmitt, *Chant de guerre* (1914)
Schuman, *Symphony No. 9:* "The Ardeatine Caves" (1967)
Shafer, *Canzoni for Prisoners* (1962)
Schafer, *Threnody* (for Japanese children) (1966)
Shostakovich, *Symphony No. 7* ("The Leningrad") (1941)
Shostakovich, *Symphony No. 8* (1943)
Shostakovich, *String Quartet No. 8* (1960) ("To the Victims of Fascism and War")
Stravinsky, *Symphony in Three Movements* (1942–45)
Villa-Lobos, *Symphony No. 3:* "A guerra" (1919)
Villa-Lobos, *Symphony No. 4:* "A vittoria" (1919)
Villa-Lobos, *Symphony No. 5:* "A paz" (1920)
Weill, *Johnny Johnson* (1936) (an antiwar musical with Paul Green)

PART VII

POSTWAR SERIALISM AND THE RISE OF AN INTERNATIONAL AVANT-GARDE

"When I read your letter, you can't imagine how delighted I was to see that we are both on our way to making more discoveries, and in step with each other."

—Pierre Boulez, Letter to John Cage, 1951.
Reprinted in *Orientations* (1986), 135.

CHAPTER 24

EUROPE: IN SEARCH OF A COMMON PRACTICE

At the end of World War II the musical world was eager to pursue somewhat selectively the explorations of the first half of the century. The voices of war, steadily sounded throughout the conflict (Shostakovich, Stravinsky, Poulenc), continued to be heard (Penderecki, Britten). But other more purely formalistic issues impatiently awaited a reexamination. If tonal Neoclassicism, following a final flourish in the late 1940s, was finally laid to rest with Stravinsky's *The Rake's Progress* (1948–1951), the Serialism of Schoenberg and his followers, which had been pronounced a dead end by many a critic in the 1930s and 1940s, was not taken up with an individualizing touch by composers of various nationalities and stylistic inclinations. The message their new works carried was that any aesthetic is capable of being reinterpreted and vitalized in highly personal terms. The early recognition that serial organization need not imply a style was a revelation to many, and the consequent fervor of the subscription cannot help but suggest that in part it was a reflection of an almost compulsive search for order following a period of world-wide chaos. The hope in many quarters that it might prove to offer an international common practice seemed for a moment almost legitimate.

The seminal postwar figures in the exploration of the efficacy of various brands of pitch and rhythmic organization were Olivier Messiaen in Paris and Milton Babbitt in America. Through their pupils, a new generation vigorously pursued the possibilities of applying serial procedures to parameters other than pitch, even as an older generation of established composers (Stravinsky, Copland, Sessions, Shostakovich, Britten), perhaps sensing the fashionableness as well as the potential creative revitalization of such a method, also began to investigate, with various degrees of rigour, the possibilities of the twelve-note pitch series.

MESSIAEN: *MODE DE VALEURS ET D'INTENSITÉ; LIVRE D'ORGUE*

The explorations of Olivier Messiaen (b. 1908) into pitch and rhythm in the 1930s, which were detailed in his *Technique de mon langage musical* (1944) and extended to include formalisms with respect to dynamics and register in *Cantéyodjayâ* (1948), forecast an interest in an broadened organizational spectrum. It was only in his *Mode de valeurs et d'intensité* of 1949, however,

Example 24.1. Messiaen, *Mode de valeurs et d'intensité*, three division modes.

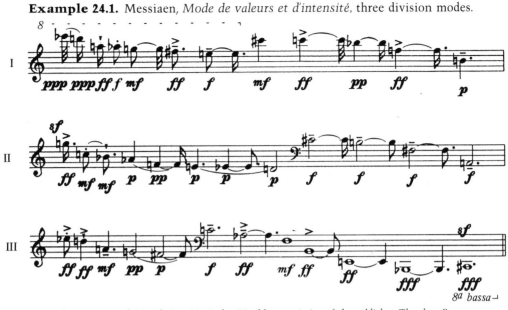

that he introduced nonordered twelve-member sets of numerous parameters (pitch, rhythm, dynamics, density, intensity, attack, register) for the first time. A work for solo piano written on three staves, each division is characterized by a different set of determinants. That the sets are not deployed serially (i.e., in a fixed order), however, is apparent from the opening measures of the piece. While influential for a group of younger composers including Boulez and Stockhausen, who were initially transfixed by it, the piece proved to be something of a dead end for the composer, and led not to the use of a Schoenbergian pitch series but

Example 24.2. Messiaen, *Mode de valeurs et d'intensité*, opening measures.

Example 24.2 (Continued)

rather to an extension of previously established pitch modes and rhythmic manners involving statement, expansion, and contraction of patterns intricately associated with color and dynamic.

Though Messiaen made an early recording of it, in many ways *Mode de valeurs* was a performance fiction. Such subtle gradations of dynamic and attack (the nearest equivalent to color transformation) were nearly impossible to achieve on the piano, and it is therefore not surprising that in his next works Messiaen turned to the organ, whose capacity, unlike the piano, to fix the color and dynamic component as accurately as the pitch he knew intimately from his years as a performer on the instrument. In the *Messe de la Pentecôte* (1950) he seemed momentarily to continue directly from the consequences of his last organ cycle, *Les corps glorieux* (1939), but in *Livre d'orgue* of 1951 he pared his newly considered language to the bone and reinforced the surface impression that he was flirting with the possibility of a rapprochement with the world of Webern.

The "Reprise par Interversion" that opens the cycle is characterized by a twelve-pitch all-interval series, a detail that may be claimed to reflect a knowledge of Berg's *Lyric Suite*, which Messiaen had taught in his classes in the 1940s (compare also with Ex. 4.9, mm. 5–9). The piece as whole, however, reflects less any growing allegiance to Schoenbergian or Bergian serialism in general than a continuation of his earlier studies of Stravinsky's *Le sacre du printemps* in particular. This led to the identification of what he called "personnages rhythmiques," rhythmic cells that remain the same, expand, or contract (Ex. 24.3), and the promotion of the concept of chromatic durations. Three Hindu rhythms, each with a distinctive color component, appear: "pratàpecekhara" (bourdon 16', oboe, cymbale), augmenting by a thirty-second note at each repetition; "gajajhampa" (prestant 4', nazard 2⅔', tierce 1⅗', piccolo 1' + pedal bombarde 16'), decreasing by the same value; "sârasa" (bourdon 16', bourdon 8', flute 4'), remaining the same. Each of these is involved in the evolution of the larger form of the movement, the first section being repeated by taking notes (pitch, duration, color) in alteration from the extremes to the center, then again from the center outward, and finally the whole being presented in retrograde. While the consequences of such an attitude continued to

Example 24.3. Messiaen, *Livre d'orgue:* "Reprises par Interversion," opening.

R: bourdon **16**, hautbois, cymbale | Pos: prestant **4**, nazard **2 ⅔**, tierce **1⅗**, piccolo **1** | G: bourdon **16**, bourdon **8**, flûte **4** | Péd: bombarde **16** seule|

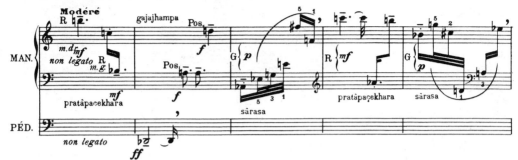

be explored throughout the decade and found one of its most resourceful expressions in *Chronochromie* of 1960 for orchestra, the prominence accorded monophonic writing in much of *Livre d'orgue* argues for Messiaen's recognition that the collective rhythms of a polyphonic structure could quickly obscure the organizational properties of a piece that was serial in every parameter.

BOULEZ

Nonetheless, Messiaen's example soon led to similarly systematic and serial explorations in the works of his pupils. Boulez (Figure 24.1) had studied privately with Messiaen in 1944–45, and beginning in 1946 he had demonstrated a serialist bent and an appreciation of the single movement structure of

Figure 24.1. Pierre Boulez and Olivier Messiaen in rehearsal at the Théatre de la Ville for the 10th anniversary concert of the Ensemble Intercontemporain, January 23, 1987. Photo Jean Pierre Leloir.

Schoenberg's op. 9 in his *Sonatine* for flute and piano. Following hard on the heels of an article with a strong sense of history and a need to turn its course,[1] Boulez proceeded to tackle a larger Beethoven-like four-movement form in the guise of his *Second Piano Sonata* (1947–48). Here, nonrepetitive, nonhierarchical rhythms (purportedly by way of analogy with pitch serialism) achieve a welter of polyphonies and relationships that, in spite of a demonstrable cellular structure with respect to both pitch and rhythm, no ear could reasonably be expected to hear. It is little wonder, then, that the potentially clarifying method demonstrated by Messiaen's *Mode de valeurs* was received as prophetic.

Boulez's first work to register an awareness of Messiaen's score was the *Livre pour quatuor* (1948–49), though the freedom to choose which movements were to be performed prefigured developments of a different kind. Shortly thereafter, in 1950, Boulez wrote an article for the journal *Contrepoint* in which, on the occasion of the 200th anniversary of Bach's death, he suggested that Leibowitz's claim of a historical parallel between Bach and Schoenberg was misplaced, and that a more accurate one could be drawn between Bach and Webern. Performances of Webern's *Second Cantata* at the ISCM in 1950 helped to seal the connection in the discussions of the avant-garde, and finally Boulez's polemical article "Schoenberg is DEAD!" in the English journal *The Score* aimed not only at the demolition of the Schoenberg cult led by Leibowitz but in effect announced the formation of a Webern cult with Boulez as the leader.

It is easy to forget that a certain Webern also labored; to be sure, one never hears this discussed anymore . . .

Perhaps we can see that the series is a logically historical consequence, or—depending on what one wishes—a historically logical one. Perhaps, like that certain Webern, one could pursue the sound-EVIDENCE by trying to derive the structure from the material . . .

Perhaps one could generalize the serial principle to the four sound constituents: pitch, duration, intensity and attack, timbre. Perhaps . . . perhaps . . . one could demand from a composer some imagination, a certain dose of asceticism, even a little intelligence, and finally a sensibility that will not be toppled by the smallest breeze . . .

It has become indispensable to demolish a misunderstanding that is full of ambiguity and contradiction: it is time to neutralize the setback. That correction will be accomplished not by any gratuitous bragging, much less any sanctimonious fatuity, but by rigor free of weakness and compromise. Therefore I do not hesitate to write, not out of any desire to provoke a stupid scandal, but equally without bashful hypocrisy and pointless melancholy: SCHOENBERG IS DEAD![2]

No doubt canonization of Webern was made easier because the music was almost totally unknown, heightening the sense of discovery. The first familiarity of his scores was frequently achieved, however, by composers in search of a justification for a mission only dimly perceived but undertaken with a Messianic fervor. A search for the extension of serial procedures to patterns of duration and register in the music of Webern (especially the *Symphony*, op. 21, and the *Variations*, op. 30) confirms that at an early date Webern's music was not only rediscovered but reread to provide the basis for a new aesthetic. By 1953, Robert Craft had begun his project to record the entire *oeuvre*, and Stravinsky's attendance at rehearsals was symptomatic of the interest in Webern's music that had permeated to virtually every quarter.

STRUCTURES 1a. Boulez's continuing investigation into the organizing potential of expanding and contracting rhythmic cells was forwarded in *Polyphonie X* for eighteen solo instruments, but following a scandalous premiere at the Donaueschingen Festival in October 1951, the work was withdrawn. Boulez was hailed a genius in some quarters, hissed and booed in others. The next step in the search for total control of materials, an *Etude* for one-track tape (1952) realized at the French radio studio under the direction of Pierre Schaeffer, also proved momentarily abortive, but with *Structures*, Book I, of the same year Boulez finally succeeded in fixing a grammar. Divided into three pieces (1a, 1b, 1c) each concentrates on specific elements: (a) pitch and duration; (b) attack; (c) dynamics. As a performance convenience the piece is arranged for two pianos, though still demanding a high degree of concentration from the executants.

The opening of *Structures 1a*, shown in the following example, reveals Boulez's adaptation of one of Messiaen's pitch modes from *Mode de valeurs*:

Piano I (original order): Eb-D-A-Ab-G-F#-E-C#-C-Bb-F-B
Piano II (inversion): Eb-E-A-Bb-B-C-D-F-F#-Ab-C#-G

while limiting his rhythmic values to the same range,

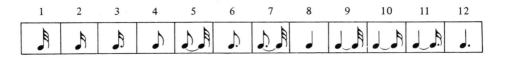

though in the following order:

Primo: 12, 11, 9, 10, 3, 6, 7, 1, 2, 8, 4, 5
Secondo: 5, 8, 6, 4, 3, 9, 2, 1, 7, 11, 10, 12

Reliance on the charts Boulez constructed for the purposes of composing *Structures 1a* discloses a direct equation between pitch and duration, the order of the Primo being that of RI (bottom to top) on G and the Secondo that of R (right to left) on the pitch B. All numbers in the matrix refer to pitches as they appear in P^0 and are translatable to numbers in the duration chart.[3]

Piano I: pitch >

	1/E♭	2/D	3/A	4/A♭	5/G	6/F♯	7/E	8/C♯	9/C	10/B♭	11/F	12/B
Piano II: pitch ∨	7/E	1	10	3	4/A♭	5	11	2	8	12	6	9
	3/A	4	1	2	8/C♯	9	10	5	6	7	12	11
	10/B♭	3	7	1	2/D	8	12	4	5	11	9	6
	12/B	10/B♭	11/F	7/E	1/E♭	2/D	9/C	3/A	4/A♭	6/F♯	8/C♯	5/G
	9/C	12	6	11	7/E	1	8	10	3	5	2	4
	2/D	8	4	5	6/F♯	11	1	9	12	3	7	10
	11/F	7	12	10	3/A	4	6	1	2	9	5	8
	6/F♯	11	9	12	10/B♭	3	5	7	1	8	4	2
	4/G♯	5	2	8	9/C	12	3	6	11	1	10	7
	8/C♯	9	5	6	11/F	7	2	12	10	4	1	3
	5/G	6	8	9	12/B	10	4	11	7	2	3	1

< Piano II: rhythm

∧
Piano I: rhythm

Pitch–rhythm matrix for Boulez's *Structures 1a.*

LE MARTEAU SANS MAITRE.   Having promoted an all-encompassing order in *Structures*, Book I, Boulez realized that he had written something that was, as he put it, not only "total" but "totalitarian." This led to a loosening of the technique in *Le marteau sans maître* (1952–54) where the serial orders are, by the composer's own admission, virtually undecipherable by the analyst. In 1977, following leads initially introduced by Boulez, Lev Koblyakov[4] finally succeeded in determining the work's serial basis: twelve pitches are divided into five segments (f'-e♭" / b-d'-b♭'-c♯" / a-c' / g♯' / g'-e"-f♯") that were subjected to "multiplication". Designating the five segments as A through E, A × B is obtained by constructing the minor 7th of the first segment above each of the pitches of the second segment: b-a'; d'-c"; b♭'-a♭"; c♯"-b"). The elimination of the redundant pitch b results in a group of seven different pitches. The seven-note series described here (actually AB which is equivalent to BA) can be seen in the opening measure of the alto flute at the beginning of the third movement (Ex. 24.5). Similar manipulations, involving a specific plan of transposition, generate the pitch content for succeeding measures of the introduction through

Example 24.4. Boulez, *Structures 1a*, mm. 1–7.

multiplications of B (BB: 9 pitches: BC: 6 pitches: BD: 4 pitches; BE: 8 pitches). By the time of Koblyakov's disclosures, however, such information seemed largely irrelevant—largely because a first generation of listeners had already come to terms with the work without regard to its serial properties, although Boulez's compositional method continued to develop along such lines.[5] While the idea of pitch group and register was to retain its vitality for Boulez, the notion of the series as an ordered sequence of pitches was to be largely abandoned (see Exs. 24.7 and 30.1).

Example 24.5. Boulez, *Le marteau sans maître*, "l'artisanat furieux," Mvt. 3, mm. 1–15.

In *Le marteau sans maître* three texts by René Char serve as the basis for a composition in nine movements for mezzo-soprano and an ensemble which includes flute, xylophone, vibraphone, percussion, guitar and viola.

I. "L'ARTISANAT FURIEUX"

la roulotte rouge au bord du clou
et cadavre dans le panier
et chevaux de labours dans le fer à cheval
je rêve la tête sur la point de mon couteau
  le Pérou

II. "BEL ÉDIFICE ET LES PRESSENTIMENTS"

j'écoute marcher dans mes jambes
la mer morte vagues par-dessus tête

I. FURIOUS ARTISANS

The red caravan at the edge of the prison
And a corpse in the basket
And workhorses in the horseshoe
I dream, head on the point of my knife,
  Peru

II. BEAUTIFUL BUILDING AND PREMONITIONS

I hear walking in my legs
The dead sea waves over my head

enfant la jetée-promenade sauvage	Child—the wild promenade-pier
homme l'illusion imitée	Man—the imitated illusion
des yeux purs dans les bois	Pure eyes in the woods
cherchent et pleurant le tête habitable	Seek, weeping, a head to live in

III. "BOURREAUX DE SOLITUDE"

III. HANGMEN OF SOLITUDE

le pas s'est eloigné, le marcheur s'est tu	The step has receded, the walker is silent
sur le cadran de l'limitation	On the dial of imitation
le balancier lance sa charge de granit réflexe	The pendulum thrusts its load of reflex granite

Used by permission of Librarie José Corti.

The texts are set only in Movements 3, 5, 6, and 9, the last being a second version of Movement 5. The idea of the parenthesis, the trope and the gloss—terms used by Boulez in his *Third Piano Sonata*—operates here as a formal principle that promotes three levels of unification in an asymmetrical plan.

1. avant "l'artisanant furieux"
    2. commentaire 1 de "bourreaux de solitude"
3. "l'artisanant furieux"
    4. commentaire II de "bourreaux de solitude"
        5. "bel édifice et les pressentiments"
          (version première)
    6. "bourreaux de solitude"
7. après "l'artisanat furieux"
    8. commentaire III de "bourreaux de solitude"
        9. "bell édifice et les pressentiments"
          (double)

Boulez advised the listener to familiarize himself with the texts prior to a hearing, a reasonable injunction in view of both the difficulty of the surrealist poetry and the melismatic vocal style, which does not always promote textual intelligibility. "L'artisanat furieux" is entrusted to a quartet of instruments in its prelude (1), a trio in its postlude (7), and to a duo for voice and flute in the setting of the text itself (3), where a kinship to "Nacht" in *Pierrot lunaire* seems inescapable (Ex. 24.5). In the course of the cycle the means of textual projection range from standard vocalization, *Sprechstimme* (Schoenberg, *Pierrot lunaire*), singing with a closed mouth (Berg, *Altenberglieder*, vocal entrance of the first song), and virtuosic coloratura (Berg, *Lulu*; see especially the "Prologue" for a catalogue of vocalizations).

"Bourreaux de solitude" is the heart of the composition and the most complex, ranging from the light ritualistic drumming of the first commentary (2) to the lengthy pauses that separate the outbursts of the second (4) to the use of the full ensemble in Movement 6, which sets the text. Regarding the instrumental sonority, Boulez acknowledged that the composition of *Le marteau sans maître* was "influenced by non-European models ... the xylophone representing the African balafron, the vibraphone the Balinese gender and the guitar recalling the Japanese koto,"[6] although he denied that either style or instrumental usage had any connection with the musical civilizations in question. That Boulez's most extended observations regarding the work came in an article, subtitled *"Pierrot lunaire* and *Le marteau sans maître,"* that does not skirt the opportunity to compare and contrast the two cycles, speaks not only of Boulez's awareness of the emblems of musical modernity but of his relation to them.

PLI SELON PLI. Boulez's next major cycle was entitled *Pli selon pli* on three texts of Mallarmé: "Le vierge, le vivace et le bel aujourd'hui", "Une dentelle s'abolit," and "A la nue accablante tu," which are designated Improvisation I, II, and III. Acting as a frame are the opening *Don* and closing *Tombeau* for an enlarged orchestral resource, which contrasts with the more chamber-like ensembles accompanying the improvisations. The vocal style is even more lavish than *Le marteau*, but the opening of "Le vierge, le vivace et le bel aujourd'hui" demonstrates the use of fixed association between pitch and register, which can be traced to *Mode de valeurs.*

Example 24.6. Boulez, *Pli selon pli:* "Le vierge, le vivace et le bel aujourd'hui," mm. 1–8.

Mallarmé became a guiding star for Boulez throughout this period, and it is not surprising that the composer's commentary about *Pli selon pli* (1957–62) emphasizes literary values and larger issues of design. The syntactical revolution begun by Baudelaire and brought to its apex by Mallarmé had once again been revived in the name of legitimizing a new sense of musical order. In later works, Boulez continued to tap Mallarmé not as a textual source but as a structural model, combining strictness in construction and a modified serialism with an open-ended sense of form. His view of many of his compositions as "works in progress"—e.g., *Eclat-Multiples, Livre pour cordes, Third Piano Sonata, Répons*—is also reflective not only of a familiarity with the work of John Cage but of a twentieth-century literary bias. The syntactical challenge, while having its roots in the Symbolist literary movement, extends naturally from Mallarmé's *Un coup de dés* (1897) through the Futurist writings of Marinetti, the calligrams of Apollinaire, and the mainstream of modern literature, which encompasses Joyce and Eliot. Thus other formal components than serial pitch ones were to prove fundamental in the years ahead. And while Boulez's early relation to Stockhausen and Cage has changed through the years, traces of his association with both were to remain apparent.

STOCKHAUSEN: FROM SERIES TO FORMULA

Beginning his studies at the Cologne Hochschule für Musik in 1947, Karlheinz Stockhausen (b. 1928) studied composition with Frank Martin and simultaneously musicology, philology, and philosophy at Cologne University. The composer and theorist Herbert Eimert, who was a decisive influence on Stockhausen at this time, suggested that he attend the summer school at Darmstadt in 1951, and it was there that he was introduced to Messiaen's *Etudes rhythmiques* and the first movement of Goeyvaerts *Sonata for Two Pianos*, a work predicated on a knowledge of the most recent work of Messiaen. The only Webern he had heard to that time were the *Five Movements* for string quartet of 1909.

KREUZSPIEL.   Stockhausen's first individualized statements as a composer followed and only to an extent flowed from these brief encounters and limited repertoire. The most important of these was the highly attractive, totally nonacademic sounding *Kreuzspiel* (1951) for oboe, bass clarinet, piano, and percussion (tumbas and tom-toms). Here "the timbres are directly linked to the registers of pitch construction, and both are serial,"[7] articulating the structure of what Stockhausen called his "point" sound-world of isolated events. The leanness of texture propelled by the persistent drumming (six drums pitched in alternating fourths and tritones) sets up a magical field that is at once seductive and, on the surface, light years away from Boulez's *Structures 1a*, begun in the same year. Yet the serialism, which is of a non-Schoenbergian brand, rigorously explores various parameters in a consistent plan: In the first section, for example, two hexachords (Eb, D, E, G, A, Ab; Db, C, Bb, F, B, Gb), laid out at the beginning in the piano in the high and low registers respectively, begin to infiltrate each other and cross over until at the end of the section they have exchanged registral positions. Similarly the pitch order is derived from permutations in the row involving the gradual shifting of internal members to the outside. These several evidences of mediation between the extremes reflect not only the title of the work (*Kreuzspiel* = "Cross-play") and an impending preoccupation with Stockhausen, but contemporaneous concerns of Messiaen manifest in his "Reprises par Interversion" from *Livre d'orgue* (Ex. 24.3), which also dates from 1951.

In January 1952, Stockhausen left for Paris to study with Messiaen. Here he also met Boulez, already at work on *Structures 1a*, and began a study of *musique concrète*, an interest originally prompted by tapes that Meyer-Eppler had played for Stockhausen before he left for Paris. Investigation of this terrain was now made possible through an arrangement Boulez made with Pierre Schaeffer for a few studio hours every week at the French radio. Though his single *Etude* for one-track tape of 1952 was of itself no more important than Boulez's similar venture written at the same time, it sowed the first seeds of his acoustical investigations into timbre, which he was to pursue on his return to Cologne. During his fourteen-month period of study in Paris, a shift in emphasis from his so-called "point" style to a more homogeneous collection of points that he called "groups" occurred in works like *Kontra-Punkte* and the first of his *Klavierstücke*, both of 1952–53.

The extraordinary demands made on the performer in his *Klavierstücke I-IV* mirrored the world of Messiaen's *Mode de valeurs* and Boulez's *Structures I*, and Stockhausen, undoubtedly sensing that an impasse had been reached, sought to leave more to the performer by introducing the choice of a relative set of values in a new collection, *Klavierstücke V-X* (1954–55). Numerous works written in the late 1950s spell out Stockhausen's developing ideas with respect to serialism, electronic music, spatial music, and the composer-performer relationship.

FROM *ZEITMASZE* TO *TIERKREIS*. Three works of 1956 provide a reasonable measure of the diversity of his interest at that time: *Zeitmasze*, *Klavierstücke XI*, and *Gesang der Jünglinge*. *Zeitmasze* ("tempi") for woodwind quintet, uses a scale of tempi related to the longest and shortest note values that can be comfortably executed by a performer. Verbal tempi such as "so rasch wie möglich" (as fast as possible; see Ex. 24.7, rehearsal no. 164) reflect less the impossibilities of Schumann's G minor *Piano Sonata*, where it is followed by "noch schneller" (faster still), than a practical way of fixing performance coordinates. Mixing points and groups in "collective form," Stockhausen threw an exuberant challenge to the performer not so much with respect to the isolated playability of any given part than with respect to the problems of ensemble.

Klavierstücke XI, written in the same year, posited a new approach to the ordering of musical events. The score consists of nineteen "groups" on a single sheet that can be played in any order, with appropriate instructions for connection depending on the performer's choice. The implications of this work were duly noted by Boulez and others (see p. 557), and for a moment a breakdown in the new serial fraternity seemed imminent.

Gesang der Jünglinge, an electronic work also of 1956, followed the preliminary investigations of *Studie I* (1953) and *Studie II* (1954). The possibility of another kind of serial alliance was evident in the serial deployment of a boy's voice reciting the "Benedicite" in conjunction with electronically produced sounds projected through five spatially separated loudspeakers. Other works written about this time that involved the spatial element as an important component were *Gruppen* (1955–57) for three orchestras and *Carré* (1959–60) for four orchestras and four choruses.

To each new area under consideration Stockhausen typically brought the organizing potential of the serial idea. Thus, alongside the spatial question of

Example 24.7. Stockhausen, *Zeitmasze*, nos. 161–164.

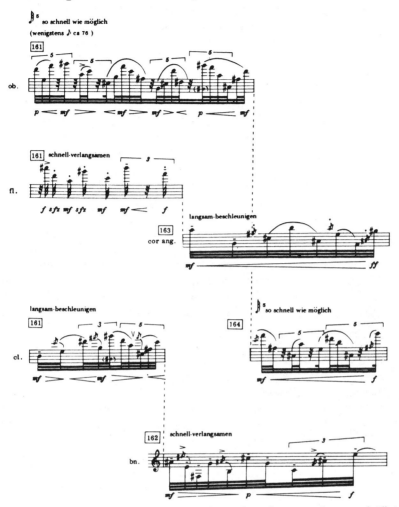

Gruppen he sought out an answer to the tempo relationships of the three orchestras developed along serial lines where durational succession not only paralleled melodic succession but a logarithmic scale of twelve tempi replaced Messiaen's chromatic duration scale and further associations were sought between register and color.[8]

Through the period of the 1960s and 1970s Stockhausen left virtually no frontier uninvestigated, and his relation to various other fields of inquiry will be taken up in their appropriate context. Increasingly, the idea of the melodic formula, generally using the complete chromatic, came to the fore and has persisted to the present day. Although the rigour of application that marked his works of the early 1950s has been periodically modified, the basis for all of his later work has been in the serial premise expressed in a melodic formula (*formel*). The melodic foundation, typically subjected to phraseological partitioning, can already be observed in so early a work as *Formel* (1951) which was written immediately after *Kreuzspiel* but suppressed until the 1970s when the composer realized its relation to newly composed works like *Mantra* (1970), *Inori* (1972), and *Tierkreis* (1975; Ex. 30.3). From such formulae came the idea of deriving large-scale structures, including different but related works. From the *Tierkreis* melodies that provide the foundation for *Musik im Bauch* (1975) and *Sirius* (1975–77) to the formulations that underlie the seven-day opera cycle in-progress, *Licht* (1979–   ), Stockhausen has addressed the organizing potential of melody in a manner and scope which unavoidably recalls Wagner.

The degree to which the names of Boulez and Stockhausen have been linked over the years is a natural consequence of their beginnings as pupils of Messiaen and their first ventures into total serialism around 1951–52 prompted by the association. Following their initial efforts, both Boulez and Stockhausen increasingly moved away from orthodox Schoenbergian dodecaphony as well as the rigours of their own total serial discoveries. But the issues uncovered in these initial works proved to be central far beyond the work that lay immediately ahead. If the nuancing and categorization of vocal sound as sound (as opposed to any role it might have as a transmitter of semantic meaning) in both Boulez's *Le marteau sans maître* and Stockhausen's *Gesang der Jünglinge* can properly be attributed to each composer's experience with total serialism, the same may be said about much of the music they were to write for the remainder of their careers.

Ultimately, their compositional stances proved to be more complementary than identical. Stockhausen's investigation of electronic music persisted from the 1950s through the 1980s, while Boulez, following an abortive early electronic *Etude* kept his distance until the 1970s. The relation of both to John Cage (see pp. 561–65) and those who challenged the premises of the serialists has been characterized by brief flirtations and ultimate departures in search of individual solutions. Much of what follows in succeeding chapters will take at least a momentary bearing from one of these three figures.

20TH-CENTURY ANALYSIS: THE COMPOSER, THE THEORIST, THE LISTENER

Musical analysis as commonly understood today had its beginnings in the eighteenth century in a philosophical base that spawned the notion of aesthetics as an attitude concerned with the contemplation of the beautiful. The language developed in this pursuit quickly began to embrace not so much a poetic description as a logical, number-based quantification of the proportions of musical structure that purportedly reinforced the ideal of an objective observation.[9]

The dramatic increase in the twentieth-century composer's interest in writing about music continues a trend since Beethoven that reflects a change in music's role, as Berio has properly noted, from an objective activity (fulfilling a specific social function) to a subjective one (as a vehicle of expression and for personal ideas).[10] In addition, the early twentieth century witnessed numerous attempts by theorists and musicologists at viewing both older repertoires and newer ones. The notion that theoretical analysis could serve a goal beyond instruction in composition was based on a heightened historical awareness in the nineteenth century as witnessed in studies by Baini of Palestrina (1828), by Winterfeld of Giovanni Gabrieli (1834), Spitta of J. S. Bach (1873–80) and by Kretzschmar of repertoires from Monteverdi to Mahler (1887–1905). Something of this same reverence for the past and the role that musical analysis could play in its recapture was still to be seen in the significantly new approaches to perception by Prout and Leichtentritt based upon emerging principles of Gestalt psychology. Questions of perception, which led to the development of "reduction" techniques, whereby larger musical gestures could be overviewed, were undertaken by Arnold Schering (1911–12) and Heinrich Schenker, first in his *Harmonielehre* of 1906, and later in numerous studies culminating in *Der freie Satz* (posthumously published in 1935). Equally important for an analytical method based on an historical awareness was the work of Guido Adler, whose emphasis on style criticism was seen as central to the task of the musicologist. The capacity to view the musical object accurately and dispassionately with respect to its component parts, and irrespective of the attached composer's name, was his fundamental concern.

Later pupils of Adler, such as Ernst Kurth, placed a correlative emphasis on three levels of perception: physical (by the ear); sensory (by the nervous system); and psychological (mirroring contemporary trends of the Gestalt theorists and Freud). Evidence of the importance of such points of view can readily be made by readers of this volume in a review of the works of Schoenberg, both with respect to his own theoretical treatises (*Harmonielehre*, 1911; *Models for Beginners in Composition*, 1942; *Structural Functions of Harmony*, 1954) and to the aesthetic basis of his compositions from the time of *Erwartung* (1909) and *Die glückliche Hand* (1910–1913). Berg's analyses of several Schoenberg scores (*Pelleas und Melisande; Kammersymphonie; Gurrelieder*) and Webern's later *The Path to the New Music* all reflect a common Viennese preoccupation. Berio has spoken of Schoenberg's theoretical involvement in the *Harmonielehre* in an especially provocative light:

> The fact that Schoenberg tended to overvalue the harmonic dimension as such, to functionalize and formalize it in scholastic fashion as an independent musical dimension—thus echoing Schenker despite himself—just at the moment when he was himself creating music in which all musical dimensions (with the partial exception of rhythm) were short-circuiting, might lead one to think that the *Harmonielehre* acted as a sort of psychological life-line for him."[11]

The nostalgia that Schoenberg would experience for harmony for the rest of his career is betrayed on its every page. It is, incidentally, a sentiment shared by many composers of the 1970s and 80s, including Boulez and Stockhausen as well as Rochberg and Del Tredici, who individually have sought ways to effect its restoration.[12]

Such a brief review serves only to emphasize the heady activity with respect to musical analysis that has dominated the twentieth century from its first years. With such a variety of accumulating techniques at the disposal of the composer, it is little wonder that the first attempts at total serialization by post-World War II composers should have been accompanied by a barrage of technical polemics. The relevance of numerous discussions and the identity of the intended audience for such observations was not always made clear. For while the identification of a composer's grammar (theories intended as compositional instruction) and a concern for questions of perception purportedly aimed at the development of a listening grammar were frequently addressed, a complex, often highly mathematical and redundant verbalization frequently sounded like nothing so much as an attempt on the part of the composer to convince himself of the validity of his approach. Perhaps, unavoidably, such investigations frequently succeeded principally in fixing only a theoretical grammar: ways to view a score only marginally related to the original compositional process or the potential for hearing by the human ear. Ultimately, the lingering suspicion surfaced that a great deal of such number analysis flourished not only because of its potential empirical validation for an elusive repertoire, but because it was as pedagogically addressable as Fux's species counterpoint.

The decade of the 1950s was especially taken with such polemical activity, and the journal *Die Reihe* is a mirror of the variety of investigations which were undertaken to justify a burgeoning Serialism. Boulez, who was as devoted to the crusade as anyone during that period, later spoke of the early 1950s as theoretical years virtually without analogy except, perhaps, for the late 14th century, and even as "years during which theoretical endeavour was such that research and composition became incompatible." It is not surprising, then, that when querried in 1975 as to whether or not *Structures* ought still to be performed, he responded, "Certainly. A work such as my *Structures* for two pianos . . . can still be played as a document . . ."[13] The identification of the serial procedures which were operative in *Le marteau sans maître* by Koblyakov in 1977 seemed by that date of antiquarian interest even to the knowledgeable listener.

Other composers who have been fundamentally concerned with a personal theoretical basis of composition (with occasional attempts to insist on its relevance for listeners) have included such varied and formidable exponents as Hindemith, Messiaen, and Babbitt. The consequences of their systems for others have ranged from marginal to nonexistant. At the same time, no one would deny them either their private vision, its importance to the act of creation, or the fact that there are audible consequences stemming from their structural premises. The considerable attention devoted to such a range of complex problems of structure and perception tended, nevertheless, to defeat many a reader and encourage the admission of failure in coming to terms with the music. Such a rush to judgement may have been as natural as it was unreasonable. But a lesson may have been learned: namely that a theory can justify a music no more than a venerable model. It has been a lesson hard won by numerous musicians from the 1920s to the present.

After 1955 Boulez, having vigorously promoted a serial approach to composition, helped lead the way out of a maze which was in large measure of his own making. Modifications to orthodox Serialism could also be seen from this time in the works of Stockhausen. With the serial *Nones* (1955) just behind him Luciano Berio proclaimed in 1959 that "serial procedure guarantees nothing", and finally sought to put the issue to rest with a total rejection (*Christian Science Monitor*, 1965): "Any attempt to codify musical reality into a kind of imitation grammar (I refer mainly to the efforts associated with the twelve-tone system) is a brand of fetishism which shares with Fascism and racism the tendency to reduce live processes to immobile, labelled objects, the tendency to deal with formalities rather than substance." The debate was not yet ended, but the notion that all music that was not serial was "useless" (to recall Boulez's judgement) had been stilled. Freedom from Serialism, however, did not mean the end of theoretical speculation on the part of analysts or composers, who continued to verbalize a varied set of philosophical values in a lively and continuing discourse.

The final question of the perceptibility of serial constructions in music, if not silenced, now no longer seemed the burning issue it had been in the decade of the 1950s. Meyer expressed concern based on early training in tonal music; the small degree of redundancy in serial music; the variety of serial procedures used from one piece to the next; and the lack of emphasis on the simpler intervallic relationships such as octaves and fifths.[14] Levi-Strauss found the serial problem to reside in the lack of a hierarchical relationship between tones which necessarily leads to listener expectation;[15] Ruwet forwarded these arguments and others based upon structural linguistics.[16] Most of the discourse revolved not around the composer's aesthetic preferences but the potential for the listener to hear such structures, a question which the American Milton Babbitt had already taken head on (see p. 530).

REPERTOIRE (Messiaen and Boulez)

Messiaen, *Cantéyodjayâ* (1948), pf
Messiaen, *Mode de valeurs et d'intensité* (1949), pf
Messiaen, *Chronochromie* (1960), orch
Messiaen, *Méditations sur le mystère de la Sainte Trinité* (1969), org
Boulez, *Sonatina* (1946), fl, pf
Boulez, *Second Piano Sonata* (1947–48)
Boulez, *Structures*, Book I (1951–52), 2 pf
Boulez, *Le marteau sans maître* (1952–54), A, a fl, gui, vib, xylorimba, perc, va
Boulez, *Piano Sonata No. 3* (1955–57)
Boulez, *Pli selon pli* (1957–62): "Don," "Improvisations sur Mallarmé I-III," "Tombeau," S, orch
Boulez, *Eclat/Multiples* (1965–70, in progress), 15 instr
Boulez, *Rituel* (1974–75), wind, perc

READING (Messiaen and Boulez)

Pierre Boulez, "Sound, Word, Synthesis" in *Orientations* (Cambridge, Mass., 1986), 177–82. First part of two initially published as "Son, verbe, synthèse" in German in *Melos*, xxv.10 (1958), 310–13. Complete text first published in French in *Points de repère* (1985).

Gyorgy Ligeti, "Pierre Boulez: Entscheidung und Automatik in der Structure Ia," *Die Reihe* (1958), no. 4, 33; Eng. trans. in *Die Reihe* (1960), no. 4, 36.

Pierre Boulez, "Olivier Messiaen" in *Orientations* (Cambridge, Mass., 1986), 404–20. Original as "Une classe et ses chimèmres," a tribute to Messiaen on his fiftieth birthday in the programme for the Domaine musical concert of April 1959.

Karlheinz Stockhausen, "Musik und Sprache," *Die Reihe* (1960), no. 6, 36; Eng. trans. in *Die Reihe* (1964), no. 6, 40.

Pierre Boulez, "Constructing an Improvisation: *Deuxième Improvisation sur Mallarmé*" in *Orientations* (Cambridge, Mass., 1986), 155–73. Original German text from October 1961; revised 1981.

Pierre Boulez, "Poetry—Centre and Absence—Music" in *Orientations* (1986), 183–98. Originally given as a lecture, "Poésie—centre et absence—musique" at Donaueschingen in 1962; published in German in *Melos*, xxx.2 (1963), 33–40.

Pierre Boulez, "Speaking, Playing, Singing: *Pierrot lunaire* and *Le marteau sans maître*" in *Orientations* (1986), 330–43. Originally as "Dire, jouer, chanter," *Cahiers Renaud-Barrault*, No. 41 (1963), 300–21.

Pierre Boulez, *Penser la musique aujourd'hui* (Paris, 1963); Eng. trans as *Boulez on Music Today* (London, 1971).

Pierre Boulez, *Relevés d'apprenti* (Paris, 1966); Eng. trans as *Notes of an Apprenticeship* (New York, 1968).

G. W. Hopkins, "Debussy and Boulez," *Musical Times*, cix (1968), 710.

Pierre Boulez, "On Musical Analysis" in *Orientations* (Cambridge, Mass., 1986), 116. Based on an interview of 1970 and revised by the author in 1980.

Pierre Boulez, *Par volonté et par hasard; entretiens avec Célestin Deliège* (Paris, 1975); Eng. trans. as *Conversations with Célestin Deliège* (London, 1976).

Robert Sherlaw Johnson, *Messiaen* (London, 1975).

Roger Nichols, *Messiaen* (London, 1975).

Anne Trenkamp, "The Concept of 'Aléa' in Boulez's 'Constellation-Miroir'," *Music and Letters*, lvii (1976), 1.

Joan Peyser, *Boulez: Composer, Conductor, Enigma* (New York, 1976).

Paul Griffiths, *Boulez* (London, 1978).

REPERTOIRE (Stockhausen)

Kreuzspiel (1951), ob, b cl, pf, 3 perc
Klavierstücke I–IV (1952–53)
Klavierstücke V–X (1954–55)
Klavierstücke XI (1956)
Zeitmasze (1955–56), fl, ob, eng hn, cl, bn
Gruppen (1955–57), 3 orchs
Gesang der Jünglinge (1955–56), 5 1-track tapes
Carré (1959–60), 4 choruses, 4 orchs
Kontakte (1959–60), 4-track tape, (pf, perc)
Momente (1961–64; 1972), S, 4 choruses, ens

READING (Stockhausen)

Karlheinz Stockhausen, "Electronic and Instrumental Music," *Die Reihe* (1961), no. 5, 59.

Karlheinz Stockhausen, "The Concept of Unity of Electronic Music," *Perspectives of New Music*, i.1 (1962), 39.

Karl H. Wörner, *Karlheinz Stockhausen* (Rodenkirchen, 1963; Eng. trans., enlarged, 1973).

Karlheinz Stockhausen, "Music and Speech," *Die Reihe* (1964), no. 6, 40.

Roger Smalley, "Stockhausen's Gruppen," *Musical Times*, cviii (1967), 794.

Jonathan Cott, ed., *Stockhausen: Conversations with the Composer* (New York, 1973).

Jonathan Harvey, *The Music of Stockhausen: an Introduction* (London, 1975).

Robert P. Morgan, "Stockhausen's Writings on Music," *Musical Quarterly*, lxi (1975), 1.

Robin Maconie, *The Works of Karlheinz Stockhausen* (London, 1976).

Jerome Kohl, "The Evolution of Macro and Micro-Time Relations in Stockhausen's Recent Music," *Perspectives of New Music*, vol. 22 (1983–84), 147–85.

READING (20th-Century Analysis: The Composer, The Theorist, The Listener)

Heinrich Schenker, *Harmonielehre* (Berlin, 1906; Eng. trans., 1954).

Guido Adler, *Der Still in der Musik* (Leipzig, 1911; expanded into *Methode der Musikgeschichte*, 1919).

Hugo Leichtentritt, *Musikalische Formenlehre* (Leipzig, 1911; rev. 1927; Eng. trans. 1951).

Arnold Schoenberg, *Harmonielehre* (Vienna, 1911; rev. 1921; Eng. trans. Roy E. Carter, *Theory of Harmony*, 1978).

A. O. Lorenz, *Gedanken und Studien zur musikalischen Formgebung in R. Wagner's 'Ring des Nibelungen'* (diss., U. of Frankfurt am Main, 1922).

Heinrich Schenker, *Fünf Urlinie-Tafeln* (Vienna, 1932; Eng. trans. *Five Graphic Analyses*, 1969).

J. Yasser, *A Theory of Evolving Tonality* (New York, 1932).

Heinrich Schenker, *Der freie Satz* (Vienna, 1935; Eng. trans. 1960).

Donald F. Tovey, *Essays in Musical Analysis* (London, 1935–39).

Paul Hindemith, *Unterweisung im Tonsatz* (Mainz, 1937; rev. 1940; Eng. trans. Arthur Mendel as *Craft of Musical Composition*, 1942).

J. Schillinger, *The Schillinger System of Musical Composition* (New York, 1946).

Olivier Messiaen, *Technique de mon langage musical* (Paris, 1944; Eng. trans. 1956).

Arnold Schoenberg, *Style and Idea* (New York, 1950; enlarged, ed. L. Stein, 1975).

Josef Rufer, *Die Komposition mit zwölf Tönen* (Berlin, 1952; Eng., trans. Humphrey Searle, *Composition with Twelve Notes*, 1969).

Felix Salzer, *Structural Hearing: Tonal Coherence in Music*, 2 vols. (New York, 1952).

Arnold Schoenberg, *Structural Functions of Harmony* (London, 1954; rev. 1969).

Milton Babbitt, "Some Aspects of Twelve-Tone Composition," *The Score and I.M.A. Magazine*, xii (1955), 53.

George Rochberg, *The Hexachord and its Relation to the Twelve-Tone Row* (Bryn Mawr, Penn., 1955).

Leonard B. Meyer, *Emotion and Meaning in Music* (Chicago, 1956).

Jan LaRue, "A System of Symbols for Formal Analysis," *Journal of the American Musicological Society*, x (1957), 25.

György Ligeti, "Pierre Boulez: Entscheidung und Automatik in der *Structure la*," *Die Reihe*, iv (1958), 33; Eng. trans. in *Die Reihe*, iv (1960), 36.

Rudolph Reti, *Tonality, Atonality, Pantonality: A Study of Some Trends in Twentieth-Century Music* (London, 1958).

Karlheinz Stockhausen, "Musik und Sprache," *Die Reihe*, vi (1960), 36; Eng. trans. in *Die Reihe*, vi (1964), 40.

L. A. Hiller and L. M. Isaacson, *Experimental Music: Composition With an Electronic Computer* (New York, 1959).

W. Meyer-Eppler, *Grundlagen und Anwendungen der Informationstheorie* (Berlin, 1959).

Allen Forte, "Schenker's Conception of Musical Structure," *Journal of Music Theory*, v (1959), 1–30.

George Rochberg, "The Harmonic Tendency of the Hexachord," *Journal of Music Theory*, iii (1959), 208.

N. Ruwet, "Contradictions du langage sériel," *Revue belge de musicologie*, xiii (1959), 83.

Milton Babbitt, "Twelve-Tone Invariants as Compositional Determinants," *Musical Quarterly*, xlvi (1960), 246.

Edward T. Cone, "Analysis Today," *Musical Quarterly*, xlvi (1960), 172.

G. W. Cooper and L. B. Meyer, *The Rhythmic Structure of Music* (Chicago, 1960).

Carl Dahlhaus, "Zur Kritik musiktheoretischer Allgemeinprinzipien," *Musikalische Zeitfragen*, ix (1960), 68.

Howard Smither, *Theories of Rhythm in the Nineteenth and Twentieth Centuries, With a Contribution to the Theory of Rhythm for the Study of Twentieth-century Music* (diss., Cornell Univ., 1960).

Ernst Ansermet, *Les fondements de la musique dans la conscience humaine* (Neuchâtel, 1961).

Milton Babbitt, "Set Structure as a Compositional Determinant," *Journal of Music Theory*, v (1961), 72.

Allen Forte, *The Compositional Matrix* (New York, 1961).

Leonard B. Meyer, "On Rehearing Music," *Journal of the American Musicological Society*, xiv (1961), 257.

N. Ruwet, "Fonction de la parole dans la musique vocale," *Revue belge de musicologie* (1961), 8.

E. Karkoschka, "Musik un Semantik," *Melos*, xxxii (1962), 252.

W. Kolneder, "Visuelle und auditive Analyse," *Veröffentlichungen des Instituts für Neue Musik und Musikerziehung Darmstadt*, iii (1962), 57.

Jan LaRue, "On Style Analysis," *Journal of Music Theory*, vi (1962), 91.

W. Meyer-Eppler, "Informationstheoretische Probleme der musikalischen Kommunikationen," *Die Reihe*, viii (1962), 7; Eng. trans., *Die Reihe*, viii (1968), 7.

P. Westergaard, "Some Problems in Rhythmic Theory and Analysis," *Perspectives of New Music,* i.1 (1962), 180.

Pierre Boulez, *Musikdenken heute* (Darmstadt, 1963); Fr. orig. as *Penser la musique aujourd'hui* (1964); Eng. trans. as *Boulez on Music Today* (1971).

Karlheinz Stockhausen, *Texte,* ed. D. Schnebel: *Texte zu elektronischen und instrumental Musik,* i (Cologne, 1963); *Texte/zu eigenen Werken/zur Kunst anderer/ Aktuelles,* ii (Cologne, 1964). No Eng. trans.

I. Xenakis, *Musiques formelles: nouveaux principes formels de composition musicale* (Paris 1963; Eng. trans., *Formalized Music: Thought and Mathematics in Composition,* 1971).

Allen Forte, "A Theory of Set-complexes for Music," *Journal of Music Theory,* viii (1964), 136–83.

Lucian Berio, "The Composer and His Work" in *Christian Science Monitor,* 15 July 1965.

Claudio Spies, "Notes on Stravinsky's Variations" (1965) and "Some Notes on Stravinsky's Requiem Settings" (1967) in *Perspectives on Schoenberg and Stravinsky* (1968).

Henri Pousseur, "The Question of Order in New Music," *Perspectives of New Music,* v.1 (1966), 93.

Jan LaRue, "Two Problems in Musical Analysis: The Computer Lends a Hand," in *Computers in Humanistic Research: Readings and Perspectives,* ed. E. A. Bowles (Englewood Cliffs, 1967).

Leonard B. Meyer, *Music, the Arts and Ideas: Patterns and Predictions in Twentieth-Century Culture* (Chicago, 1967).

Gary E. Wittlich, *An Examination of some Set-Theoretic Applications in the Analysis of Non-Serial Music* (diss., Univ. of Iowa, 1969).

Pierre Boulez, "On Musical Analysis" in *Orientations* (Cambridge, Mass., 1986), 116. Based on an interview of 1970 and revised by the author in 1980.

Jan LaRue, *Guidelines for Style Analysis* (New York, 1970).

E. Lendvai, *Béla Bartók: An Analysis of his Music* (London, 1971).

I. Xenakis, *Musique, architecture* (Paris, 1971).

Milton Babbitt, "Set Structure as a Compositional Determinant" in *Perspectives on Contemporary Music Theory,* eds. Benjamin Boretz and Edward T. Cone (New York, 1972).

N. Ruwet, *Langage, musique, poésie* (Paris, 1972; includes earlier articles).

Allen Forte, *Structure of Atonal Music* (New Haven, 1973).

Leonard B. Meyer, *Explaining Music: Essays and Explorations* (Berkeley, 1973).

Carl Dahlhaus, "Schoenberg and Schenker," *Proceedings of the Royal Music Association,* c (1973–74), 209.

Alexander Goehr, "The Theoretical Writings of Arnold Schoenberg," *Proceedings of the Royal Music Association,* c (1973–74), 85.

Brian Fennelly, "Twelve-Tone Techniques" in *Dictionary of Contemporary Music,* ed. John Vinton (New York, 1974).

Ernst Krenek, "Serialism" in *Dictionary of Contemporary Music,* ed. John Vinton (New York, 1974).

Howard E. Smither, "Rhythm" in *Dictionary of Contemporary Music,* ed. John Vinton (New York, 1974).

Wallace Berry, *Structural Functions in Music* (Englewood Cliffs, 1975).

Robert Morgan, "Dissonant Prolongations: Theoretical and Compositional Precedents," *Journal of Music Theory,* xx (1976).

C. Schachter, "Rhythm and Linear Analysis: A Preliminary Study," *Music Forum,* iv (1976), 281–334.

M. Yeston, *The Stratification of Musical Rhythm* (London, 1976).

Lev Koblyakov, "P. Boulez, 'Le Marteau sans Maître,' Analysis of Pitch Structure," *Zeitschrift für Musiktheorie,* vii.1 (1977), 24–39.

E. Narmour, *Beyond Schenkerism: The Need for Alternatives in Musical Analysis* (Chicago, 1977).

Jim Samson, *Music in Transition: A Study of Tonal Expansion and Atonality, 1900–1920* (New York, 1977).

M. Yeston, ed., *Readings in Schenker Analysis and other Approaches* (New Haven, 1977).

Charles Wuorinen, *Simple Composition* (New York, 1979).

Ian D. Bent, "Analysis" in *New Groves Dictionary of Music and Musicians* (1980).

Allen Forte and Steven E. Gilbert, *Introduction to Schenkerian Analysis* (New York, 1982).

Oswald Jonas, *Introduction to the Theory of Heinrich Schenker*, trans. and ed. John Rothgeb (New York, 1982).

James M. Baker, "Schenkerian Analysis and Post-Tonal Music" in *Aspects of Schenkerian Theory*, ed. David Beach (New Haven, 1983).

Janet Schmalfeldt, "Pitch-Class Set Theory: Historical Perspective" in *Berg's Wozzeck* (New Haven, 1983).

Fred Lerdahl, "Cognitive Constraints on Compositional Systems" in J. Sloboda, ed., *Generative Processes in Music* (New York, 1987).

CHAPTER 25

THE UNITED STATES OF AMERICA

A list of American-born composers with established reputations before World War II who in the first postwar years adopted serial principles, however momentarily, is as diverse as it is fascinating and would include names like Sessions and Copland, who were known in the 1920s for their espousal of the cause of American music. Many composers of the next generation, however, made their initial reputation through a subscription to serial procedures, an endorsement that for a time from the mid-1950s on seemed almost a requirement for artistic survival. As Druckman has stated: "not being a serialist on the East Coast of the United States in the sixties was like not being a Catholic in Rome in the thirteenth century. It was the respectable thing to do, at least once."[1]

BABBITT: FROM *THREE COMPOSITIONS FOR PIANO* TO *RELATA I*

Although the intimidating remarks of Boulez, who stated that he considered all music that was not serial to be useless, had their effect, the quasimathematical approach of Milton Babbitt (b. 1916), whose speculations led to totally controlled pieces such as *Three Compositions for Piano* as early as 1947, more directly influenced a decade of American composers loosely aligned as the Princeton Group. Babbitt's interest in serial structure, in symmetrical types of sets, and particularly in combinatoriality demonstrated a loyalty to the precepts of Schoenberg that was not shared by Boulez. Furthermore, Babbitt's first attempts at total serialism marginally antedate those of his European colleagues, and in any event were independently arrived at. The parallel with the simultaneous but separate investigations of Schoenberg and Hauer in the early 1920s with respect to dodecaphonic organization is brought to mind.

The structure of Babbitt's *Three Compositions for Piano* (1947–48) entails numerous features of which the following are prominent:

1. The use of an all-combinatorial set: P with a transposition of itself (P-0/P-6, mm. 1-2); P with I (P-0/I-1 = R-0/RI-1, mm. 2–4); I with R (I-1/R-6, mm. 7–8); and naturally P with R (equivalent to I-7/RI-7, mm. 5–6).

2. The use of durational sets: P = 5,1,4,2; R = 2,4,1,5; I = 1,5,2,4; RI = 4,2,5,1. The integer identifies the number of sixteenth-notes that occur before a

longer note or a rest intervenes to signal pattern closure. The association of P, R, I and RI duration series with the corresponding pitch series is observable in the example.

3. Dynamic levels associated with serial forms: *mp* with P; *mf* with R; *f* with I; *p* with RI.

4. Registral choices determined by serial procedures.[2]

Example 25.1. Babbitt, *Three Compositions for Piano*, No. 1, mm. 1–8.

A phraseological reliance on groups of six pitches, a charge occasionally leveled against Schoenberg's *Violin Concerto* (1936) and a factor that persistently attends Ex. 25.1, is ready compensation for the listener who may experience difficulties following the multiple relationships of Babbitt's language. While the extension of serial procedures to parameters other than pitch was launched in this work, Babbitt extended his inquiry to the use of the "chromatic" duration scale of Messiaen (although apparently developed independently of him) in his *Composition for Twelve Instruments* (1948, rev. 1954).[3] Continuing dissatisfaction with the incompatibilities of serial procedures used for pitch and rhythm led Babbitt in 1957 to the idea of "time point sets" wherein the various note-values are identified by their position at the point of attack within the bar. Here the obvious need for a clear and audible metric organization is acute if such an organization is to have any meaning for the listener. One of the first works to invoke this principle was *All Set* for jazz ensemble of 1957, and from that time on Babbitt has continued its use.

During the period of consolidation in the mid-1950s, Babbitt's article "Some Aspects of Twelve-Tone Compositions"[4] made an enormous impact. There his clarification of the principles of combinatoriality, derived from a study of Schoenberg's music (see pp. 333–34) and applied in as early a work as *Three Compositions for Piano*, and derivation, having to do with the symmetrical qualities of series like Webern's op. 24 (see p. 386) and their potential for giving rise to other derived sets, sounded a warning to his European colleagues that they had failed to note properly the implications of the classics of the serial repertoire. The resounding challenge of Boulez's "Schoenberg is Dead" was met head on.

Three years later in a much discussed article entitled "Who Cares if You Listen?"[5], Babbitt protested the implications of the various ordered parameters not only as compositional ideal but as performer-listener challenge. He put forward four points with respect to the new "serious," "advanced" contemporary music that was his domain: (1) the music is more efficient, reducing "redundancy" of language and demanding more of performer and listener; (2) the total serial organization of pitch, register, dynamic, duration, and timbre creates a structure of intense interrelationships; the failure to perform or perceive a value or a dynamic correctly, for example, will lead to the false identification of other elements; (3) the structure of a work tends to be piece-specific, with less opportunity for the performer or listener to draw on prior experience; (4) the development of an analytical theory in tandem with this music places new responsibilities on performer and listener to understand the basis of construction.

In discussing the growing distance between the composer and his public, Babbitt compared developments in music to the revolution in theoretical physics in the nineteenth century. Advancing the notion of the composer as a researcher-scholar whose mission it is to advance the frontiers of knowledge, he advocated the consolidation of the retreat of the composer to the ivory tower— i.e., the university. In this he struck a direct parallel with Schoenberg's Society for Private Musical Performances founded in Vienna in 1918 which, bypassing the masses, addressed itself to a clientele of connoiseurs.[6]

Although few would claim that either listener or performer has experienced a notable success in following aurally many of the complex relationships in the works of Boulez, Babbitt, or Messiaen, serial exploration has a natural history with respect to both pitch and rhythm that extends back to the isorhythmic motet of the fourteenth century, where the audibility of such constructions was equally problematical. Furthermore, Babbitt's early elucidations of the twelve-tone matrix (a grid that provides all forty-eight versions—transpositions, inversions, retrogrades—of the series; see p. 333 for an example) and his clarification of the concepts of combinatoriality and derivation has entered the common parlance of all who would claim to be conversant with the consequences of Serialism.

The recurring emphasis on such architectural elements, as well as the complexity of their relationship, sent Babbitt as naturally to the electronic studio in search of a means of control as it had Messiaen, Boulez, and Stockhausen somewhat earlier in Paris. His involvement with the RCA synthesizer at the Columbia-Princeton Electronic Music Center in New York in the mid-1950s (Figure 25.1) ultimately found its first expression in his *Composition for Synthesizer* of 1961. Serial organization and electronic manipulation were to be the prime movers behind his mature works, of which *Philomel* (1964) for soprano and tape may be said to have found the largest

Figure 25.1. Milton Babbitt and the RCA Synthesizer used in the creation of all his electronic works.

Photo courtesy of Milton Babbitt.

audience. Yet the performance problems inherent in works for larger ensembles, such as *Relata I* for orchestra of 1965, forced him to note with chagrin following a performance with the New York Philarmonic that

> only about 80 per cent of the notes of the composition were played at all, and only about 60 per cent of these were played accurately rhythmically, and only about 40 per cent of these were played with any regard for dynamic values . . . composers of such works who have access to electronic media will, with fewer and fainter pangs of renunciation, enter their electronic studios with their compositions in their heads, and leave those studios with their performances on the tapes in their hands.[7]

In the following years, however, with the aid of a new breed of virtuoso performer, Babbitt continued to explore the humanizing capacity of live performance cojoined with tape begun in *Vision and Prayer* (1961) and *Philomel* (1964) in works such as *Phonemena* (soprano and piano, 1970; soprano and tape, 1974) and *Reflections for Piano and Tape* (1974), as well as the nonelectronic *Arie da capo* for flute, clarinet/bass clarinet, piano, and violin.

SESSIONS AND COPLAND AS SERIALISTS

It must not be thought that Babbitt was an isolated figure in America through the decades of the 1950s and 1960s. His numerous distinguished pupils, who were frequently students of Roger Sessions as well, include Peter Westergaard (b. 1931), Eric Salzman (b. 1933), Donald Martino (b. 1931), and Benjamin Boretz (b. 1934). In addition, associations with the Columbia-Princeton Center provided exposure to a receptive "New York Group," such as Charles Wuorinen (b. 1938) and Harvey Sollberger (b. 1939), whose interest in serial approaches to composition was advanced through his presence. All felt the force of his ideas as well as his pedagogy, while turning their experiences with total serial organization to individual account.

But there were other American personalities, such as Wallingford Riegger, Ross Lee Finney, and Roger Sessions, whose language had already been well formed before the war, who now adopted serial procedures as an enriching option without sense of obligation. The introduction of Roger Sessions (1896–1985) in a list of American serialists may seem to do as much violence to the progression of his career as it does in the case of his friend and contemporary Aaron Copland, a coprotagonist for the cause of "American Music" in the 1920s. Yet his association with many of the serialists, including his pupils Andrew Imbrie (b. 1921), Seymour Shifrin (b. 1926), and Leon Kirchner (b. 1919), is a matter of history. Babbitt's teacher and colleague at Princeton and long esteemed as one of America's venerable musical figures, Sessions in his earlier years had disclosed a degree of dependence on Stravinsky in surface manner and to Schoenberg in expressive gesture.

In a revealing historical overview of the state of musical affairs in 1933, Sessions showed an appreciation of the German composer's attempt to respond to the musical needs of the people in certain works by Hindemith and Weill; spoke of the "ambiguous nature" and "extraordinary lack of coherence between the music heard and . . . its theoretical structure" in much of the music of Schoenberg and his pupils; and, calling for the abandonment of the term

"Neoclassicism," openly allied himself with the aesthetic of Stravinsky.[8] While he had known the early serial works of Schoenberg from their first appearance in print, he had continued to develop the total chromatic in a highly personal way in works such as the *Violin Concerto* (1935) and *String Quartet No. 1* (1936). It was not until the solo *Violin Sonata* of 1953, however, that the increasingly prevalent interest in Schoenbergian serialism led to its natural incorporation in his own music. The *String Quartet* of 1958 further illustrated the extent to which the pitch series could be allied in a functional way to distinctively chosen rhythmic units.

With these works behind him it was no surprise to hear the composer state in his essay "Problems and Issues Facing the Composer Today" of 1960 that "The serial organization of tones must be, and for the most part is, today regarded as a settled fact."[9] His discussion of the serial organization of elements other than pitch and the future of electronic music was optimistic but cautionary, holding to the pragmatic notion that "it is only results that matter." In works of the following years, the *Third Piano Sonata* (1965), *Symphony No. 8* (1968), and *When Lilacs Last in the Dooryard Bloom'd* (1970) for soloists, chorus, and orchestra, technique and expression blend impressively as one.

While Copland's claim to a severe as well as a more popular idiom, both of which he tapped from time to time, provided a palpable rationale for his ultimate serial ventures, Sessions' progression toward the same, though personalized, technical goal was perhaps more predictable because of a more homogeneous development. In 1950, Copland (b. 1900) for the first time introduced the principles of the twelve-tone technique in his *Piano Quartet*. The use of a twelve-note ostinato for the adagio of Samuel Barber's *Piano Sonata* (1949) the preceding year is indicative of the fashionableness of experimenting with twelve-note ideas in the early post-war years.

Example 25.2. Barber, *Piano Sonata*, Adagio, mm. 1–3.

Copyright G. Schirmer. Used by permission.

Copland's *Piano Fantasy* (1957) effectively blended serial procedures with the rugged language of the *Piano Variations* (1930). His break in the 1930s with the style of the earlier variations (see pp. 445–47) had been prompted by a desire to incorporate American folk elements in an effort to achieve a more direct line of communication with his public during a period of economic and social depression. The subscription to serial procedures was recognized by the composer as a kind of return. The composer has commented:

Example 25.3. Copland, *Piano Fantasy.*

I can see now that the *Piano Variations* of 1930, because of the concentration there on a few notes, was the real beginning of my interest in serial writing. In my youth, I didn't feel at all sympathetic to Schoenberg, Berg and Webern. I considered them as still writing German music, the influence of which I, as an American composer, was trying to escape. The expressive quality, the esthetic, seemed to be essentially an old, Wagnerian one. (This was, of course, before the emotionally cool later works of Webern.) I found the new method interesting, but it didn't occur to me to try and separate the method from the esthetic.

At the end of the Second World War, younger men, like Pierre Boulez, effectively demonstrated that the twelve-tone method could be retained without the German esthetic, and, by 1950, I was involved. I was interested in the simple outlines of the theory and in adapting them to my own purposes. As a result, I began to hear chords I wouldn't have heard otherwise: Here was a new way of moving tones about that had a freshening effect on one's technique and approach. This, to me, was and remains the principal attraction of serial writing.[10]

Two works for orchestra, *Connotations* (1962) and *Inscape* (1967), secured Copland's commitment to the exploration of serial procedures and proved to be works of a powerful expression. The initial comments of Leonard Bernstein following the premiere of *Connotations* ("Copland tried to catch up with twelve-tone music just as it too was becoming old-fashioned to the young") were soon modified by his reaction to *Inscape* following its premiere in Ann Arbor ("Aaron, it's amazing how, even when you compose in a completely 'foreign' idiom, the music *still* comes out sounding like you!") While it is of interest to recall that Copland, like Bartók, had been taken with Berg's *Lyric Suite* at the ISCM festival of 1927, it would be stretching the point to claim a genuine affinity for the music of the Second Viennese School in general. The point seemed to be that, whether the principal material of a given work was pandiatonic or dodecaphonic, Copland's tendency to partition his pitch materials into locally operative cells was the fundamental feature that rhythm, phraseology, and color helped to seal as a personal signature.

When questioned about the plainness of style apparent in the *Duo for Flute and Piano* (1971) and whether or not it might be viewed as anachronistic in light of *Connotations* and *Inscape*, Copland responded:

> Perhaps, although I've done this sort of thing before—in the 1950s, for instance, when the diatonic *Old American Songs* came soon after the serially oriented *Piano Quartet*. Whether a piece is to be in my so-called "simple" or "severe" style depends essentially upon the musical materials I begin with. In my *Night Thoughts* for piano, written in 1972, you will actually find a combination of both kinds of material.[11]

Obviously Copland views the series as an option with potential stylistic consequences but without obligatory suppression of a personal manner. In later years, looking back on his *Short Symphony* of 1931–33, he spoke of the first movement in the following terms: "All melodic figures result from a nine-note sequence—a kind of row—from the opening two bars."[12] Contrarily, as he pointed out with respect to *Connotations*, "the dodecaphonic method supplies the building blocks, but it does not create the edifice. The composer must do that." Here his source material is initially announced in block chordal fashion leading, in the composer's words, to "a free treatment of the Baroque form of the Chaconne."

Example 25.4. Copland, *Connotations*, opening.

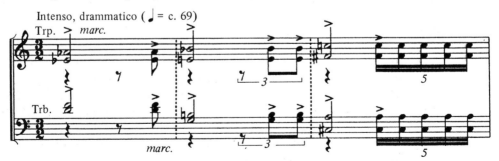

BROADENING SERIAL HORIZONS: PERLE, WUORINEN, AND OTHERS

Of Babbitt's age but independent of Princeton associations, George Perle (b. 1915), through a comprehensive study of the Viennese trinity as early as the 1930s, arrived at a theory of twelve-note usage that, although endorsing set order, rejected pitch equivalency through the establishment of hierarchies analogous to mode and key. His investigations also led him to the idea of "metrical modulation," frequently associated with Carter (see p. 537) but independently arrived at by Perle. His compositions, while typically anchored in some brand of serialism (*Three Movements* for orchestra, 1960; *String Quartet No. 7*, 1973), have also endorsed free or intuitive choices and sought always for an immediacy of understanding that he felt was missing in the work of many serialists. His *Serenade No. 3*, an enormously attractive and energetic score of 1983, and his *Concertino* for piano, winds, and percussion of 1979 both provide ample evidence of his success in such a quest: Winds, percussion, and a virile concertante piano part alternately and fleetingly redolent of Berg (*Chamber Concerto; Der Wein*), Schoenberg (*Piano Concerto*), and Stravinsky (e.g., the use of the piano in *Requiem Canticles*) engage in an invigorating dialogue that is fresh, totally contemporary in speech, but direct in its effect without any semblance of avant-garde protest. Perle's investigations in recent years into the works of Berg, particularly the *Lyric Suite, Wozzeck*, and *Lulu* (see p. 381f), as well as his influential *Serial Composition and Atonality* (1962; 4th ed., 1978) have proven fundamental to an understanding of both subject and author.

During the decade of the 1960s, as noted (see p. 520ff), the difficulties inherent in the perception of serial music by the listener was discussed on various levels, and many composers began to readdress themselves to the problem of communication with an audience. While Babbitt and his circle claimed a responsibility on the part of the listener (see p. 530) and promised dividends, the willingness as well as the size of audiences for most serial music had dwindled to the point that it was considered by many as music for the cognoscenti. Yet the repertoire of pieces indebted to dodecaphonic principles was sufficiently large by 1961 to call forth Ann Phillips Basart's *Serial Music: A Classified Bibliography of Writings on Twelve-Tone and Electronic Music*, reflecting a voluminous technical literature on the subject in numerous periodicals including the German-language *Die Reihe* (1955–62, trans. into English, 1958–68); the English-based *Tempo* (1939–), and *The Score* (1949–1961); and the American serials *The Musical Quarterly* (1915–), *Journal of Music Theory* (1957–), and *Perspectives of New Music* (1962–).

By the late 1960s, many of the generation who had been committed to serial composition, especially in matters of pitch, began to veer away from an exclusive loyalty to such precepts, to modify and personalize its stamp, and ultimately to consider it as only one among numerous options. Statements by Rochberg (see pp. 647–48) and Wuorinen, both formerly arch-serialists, concerning their *String Quartet No. 3* (1972)[13] and *Grand Bamboula* (1970), respectively, were indicative of a loosening attitude without sense of forfeiture. Wuorinen stated candidly:

> In a way, the *Grand Bamboula* demonstrates as clearly as any work my present attitude toward the organizing powers of the twelve-tone system. It has become for

me a musical system of such encompassing size that it seems to merge into a yet larger organism that embraces western tonal music too. In the *Bamboula,* the set can never be heard in the foreground; rather it is shape-defining, harmony-generative of foreground detail. But many of the concerns that are presumed basic to twelve-tone music (aggregate formation, clear presentation of sets or segments of them in the foreground, etc.) have no place here, and seem to me contextual matters, perhaps essential to a given work, but not to the Schoenbergian universe as a whole. And to repeat: what strikes me most is the sense that different though their classic expositions be, the tonal and twelve-tone systems are non-dichotomous and complementary—overlapping, moreover, and converging in the kind of musical continuity that may be said to underlie all western music. Credo in unam musicam.[14]

The truth of this assertion is confirmable even to first-time listeners of this work, who, were they innocent of its author and his serial orientation, might be forgiven for judging its natural affinity to certain post-Bartókian manners of the Polish School that developed in the 1960s (see p. 619).

CARTER: A SPECIAL CASE

The music of Elliott Carter (b. 1908) in his maturity is best discussed in relation to such developing points of view, and suggests something of the loosening hold of strict serialism, its usefulness both as a structural model and an object of commentary. For while Carter by admission was never an inveterate serialist, it has been in the juxtaposition of the carefully drawn and the freely structured, interstitched or simultaneously projected, that he has fashioned a new expression made up of equal parts of order and seeming chaos based on techniques known to literature and the cinema.

Carter, who like Sessions knew the first twelve-note works of Schoenberg from the time of their initial publication in the 1920s, followed a path through the late 1940s that principally reflected his exposure to Neoclassic principles as a pupil of Nadia Boulanger. His recognition as a composer began about the time of his *Cello Sonata* (1948) wherein many of the organizational approaches to meter and pitch that were to be the mark of the mature composer emerged for the first time. Leaving Neoclassicism aside, he did not become a serialist in any accepted meaning of the term; yet his interest in intricate pitch and rhythmic constructions in the service of large-scale form complemented the activity of the so-called serialists.

In addition to an inclination toward the nonserial use of the total chromatic, two concepts—metrical modulation and layered textural forms—have become inextricably associated with Carter. The former refers to the fastidious manner in which Carter smoothly controls changes in tempo from one section of a composition to another through the maintenance of a steady pulse. That the unit that binds the movement into and out of these changes of tempo is seldom the same is illustrated in Example 25.5 from his *Second String Quartet* (1959).

Carter's concept of metrical modulation, which followed from a considera-tion of Indian *talas*, Arabic and Balinese systems, Cowell's *New Musical Resources*, as well as the music of the fifteenth century, Skriabin, and Ives, has proven to be one of his most identifiable traits. By extension, his interest in

Example 25.5. Carter, *Second String Quartet* (1955), a) Mvt. 2, violin 1, mm. 181–86. b) Mvt. 2, violin 1, mm. 231–233.

manipulating timbral and temporal groupings as an aspect of form is also reflected in the *Second String Quartet,* where a four-movement structure (Allegro fantastico; Presto scherzando; Andante espressivo; Allegro, each led by a different instrument) is framed by an introduction and conclusion. The movements themselves are interrupted by a set of cadenzas by the viola, cello, and first violin, while the second violin "acts as a moderating influence, using its pizzicato and arco notes to mark regular time, its half, or double—always at the same speed."[15] In its characterization of the individual members of the quartet as well as in the use of cadenzas, Carter's *Second Quartet* (1959) looks back to the *Quartet No. 2* of Charles Ives (1907–13) and ahead to the second quartet of Jacob Druckman (1966). Carter's interest in the juxtaposition of opposing bodies, however, was to prove fundamental for many works that followed, including the *Double Concerto for Harpsichord and Piano with Two Chamber Orchestras* (1961) and his *String Quartet No. 3* (1971). In the latter work the composer divides the quartet into two duos, one of which plays four movements (Furioso; Leggerissimo; Andante espressivo; and Giocoso) in a quasi rubato, "expressively intense, impulsive style," while the other plays six movements (Maestoso; Grazioso; Pizzicato giusto, meccanico; Scorrevole; Largo tranquillo; Appassionato) in a metrically strict fashion. The movements are fragmented and "played in other orders than the four listed for Duo I and the six for Duo II so there is a constant interlacing of moods and materials."[16]

In 1971, the year of his *String Quartet No. 3*, Carter talked retrospectively about his concern for the importance of time, which he held to be the most crucial element of all. Claiming that music had tried every conceivable harmonic and timbral combination, he argued that in spite of the important and fundamental contributions to rhythm by Stravinsky, Bartók, Varèse, and Ives in the twentieth century, which had been primarily concerned with rhythm on the micro level, very little attention had been paid to the organization of musical time in larger structures. While the omission of Messiaen in such a discussion may seem remarkable, Carter openly addressed the contribution from Darmstadt. Condemning the idea of "moment-form" as an irresponsible solution to the anxiety of dispensing with older notions of antecedent-consequent movement, he also charged that much music of today was of a kind in which

> "first you do this for a while, then you do that". I wanted to mix up the "this" and the "that" and make them interact in other ways than by linear succession . . . Musical discourse, it became obvious to me, required as thorough re-thinking as harmony had been subjected to at the beginning of the century.[17]

Carter's *Symphony of Three Orchestras* (1976) is not only one of the more recent manifestations of this point of view but, prompted by a poem of Hart Crane, reflects an increasing interest in both literary sources and vocal settings, of which *A Mirror on Which to Dwell* (1975) on texts of Elizabeth Bishop and *Syringa* (1978), with ancient Greek texts juxtaposed to contemporary verses of John Ashbery, may be held as representative. The composer's unswerving interest in addressing and expanding the fundamental questions of formal organization has led some to compare him with Berg, although for others the density and complexity of ideas, which border on the chaotic in such a work as *Night Fantasies* (1983) for solo piano, tends to obscure a potentially equivalent drama.

Though Carter's mixture is his own, and the originality of his language incontestable, knowledge of his affection for such disparate artists as Ives, Ruggles, Varèse, Stravinsky, and certain serialists helps to account for the diversity of his expression, which he has fashioned into a bold and uncompromising personal blend without hint of pastiche.

REPERTOIRE (Babbitt)

Three Compositions for Piano (1947–48)
Composition for Twelve Instruments (1948, rev. 1954)
Du (1951), S, pf
All Set (1957), a sax, t sax, tpt, trbn, db, drums, vib, pf
Composition for Synthesizer (1961)
Vision and Prayer (1961), S, tape
Philomel (1964), S, tape
Relata I (1965), orch
Phonemena (1970; 1974), S, pf/tape
Arie da capo (1973–74), fl, cl/b cl, pf, vn, vc
Reflections (1974), pf, tape

READING (Babbitt)

Milton Babbitt, "Some Aspects of Twelve-Tone Composition," *The Score*, xii (1955), 53.

Milton Babbitt, "Who Cares if You Listen?", *Contemporary Composers on Contemporary Music*, E. Schwartz and B. Childs, eds. (New York, 1967).

Milton Babbitt, "Twelve-Tone Rhythmic Structure and the Electronic Medium," *Perspectives of New Music*, i.1 (1962), 49–79.

George Perle, *Serial Composition and Atonality* (Los Angeles and London, 1962, rev. 1978), 99–101, 135–6, 139–41.

Milton Babbitt, "On Relata I," *The Orchestral Composer's Point of View: Essays on Twentieth-Century Music by Those Who Wrote It*, ed. Robert Stephan Hines (Norman, Okla., 1970); reprinted in *Perspectives of New Music*, ix.1 (1970), 1.

REPERTOIRE (Sessions and Copland)

Sessions, *Violin Sonata* (1953)
    Montezuma (1941–63), opera
    Third Piano Sonata (1965)
    Symphony No. 8 (1968)
    When Lilacs Last in the Dooryard Bloom'd (1970)
Copland, *Piano Quartet* (1950)
    Piano Fantasy (1957)
    Nonet (1960), 3 vn, 3 va, 3 vc
    Connotations (1962), orch
    Inscape (1967), orch
    Threnody I: Igor Stravinsky in memoriam (1970), fl, str trio
    Duo (1971), fl, pf
    Night Thoughts (Homage to Ives) (1972), pf

READING (Sessions and Copland)

Roger Sessions, "Music in Crisis: Some Notes on Recent Musical History," *Modern Music*, x (1932–33), 63–78.

Roger Sessions, "Problems and Issues Facing the Composer Today," *Musical Quarterly*, xlvi (1960), 159–171.

Edward T. Cone, "Conversations with Roger Sessions," *Perspectives of New Music*, iv.2 (1966).

Roger Sessions, *Questions about Music* (Cambridge, Mass., 1970).

Arthur Berger, "Aaron Copland's Piano Fantasy," *Julliard Review*, v. 1 (1957), 13.

Eric Salzman and P. Des Marais, "Aaron Copland's Nonet: Two Views," *Perspectives of New Music*, i.1 (1962), 172.

Peter Evans, "Copland on the Serial Road: an Analysis of Connotations," *Perspectives of New Music*, ii.2 (1964), 141.

Aaron Copland, "The Contemporary Scene," *Saturday Review*, xlix.26 (1966), 49.

Edward T. Cone, "Conversation with Aaron Copland," *Perspectives of New Music*, vi.2 (1968), 57.

Aaron Copland, "Is the University Too much With Us?," *New York Times* (July 26, 1970), D13, 22.

Aaron Copland and Vivian Perlis, *Copland, 1900 through 1942* (New York, 1984).

REPERTOIRE (Perle, Wuorinen, Carter)

Perle, *Three Movements* (1965), orch
Perle, *String Quartet No. 7* (1973)
Wuorinen, *Grand Bamboula* (1970)
Carter, *String Quartet No. 2* (1959)
Carter, *Double Concerto for Harpsichord and Piano* (1961)
Carter, *String Quartet No. 3* (1971)
Carter, *Syringa* (1974), Mez/B, 11 insts

Carter, *Symphony of Three Orchestras* (1976)
Carter, *Night Fantasies* (1983), pf

READING (Carter)

Allen Edwards, *Flawed Words and Stubborn Sounds: A Conversation with Elliott Carter* (New York, 1971).
David Schiff, *The Music of Elliott Carter* (New York, 1983).

CHAPTER 26

SERIALISM AND THE EUROPEAN OLD GUARD

It would be fictitious to suggest that in the post-war period Serialism prospered exclusively in Paris, Darmstadt, and Princeton. Indeed, its capacity to accommodate differing aesthetic points of view proved in many ways remarkable. The variable appeal of various serial or, more specifically, twelve-note compositional approaches to the younger and middle generation of composers such as Fortner, Libermann, Blacher, Henze, Dallapiccola, Seiber, Searle, Hamilton, Goehr, Baird, Lutosławski, and Denisov in Germany, France, Italy, England, Poland, and Russia was a natural consequence of the vigorous creative inquiry already discussed. But the most dramatic indication of the virility and all-encompassing nature of the Serialist movement in the 1950s and 1960s is to be found in the adoption and personalization of dodecaphonic procedures by a number of European composers in their middle and late maturity whose language had previously been identifiably tonal. The idea of an orthodox Serialism had by this time, however, been totally set aside. Indeed, the serial component itself, implying an ordered set, seemed to give way to a more general integration of the total chromatic, leading to a preference for expressions such as "12-note composition." This was natural in light of the tendency of the term Serialism to imply a rigid casting of an ideal series in a repetitive sequence of readily decipherable transformations rather than the presence of a twelve-note set at various background and foreground levels. For all that, some composers' path to dodecaphonic composition, including Stravinsky's, was prepared by a rigorously serial, nondodecaphonic, approach.

STRAVINSKY: *IN MEMORIAM DYLAN THOMAS, CANTICUM SACRUM, MOVEMENTS,* AND THE LAST WORKS

Evidence of a serialist predisposition has been claimed, though not always with a compelling logic, in the music of Stravinsky from the time of *The Five Fingers* (1920–21) through the *Sonata for Two Pianos* (1943–44) and *Orpheus* (1947). Whatever hindsight may be invoked, there can be little argument that Stravinsky's adoption of the "Method of Composing with Twelve Tones" for the first time in the tenor aria "Surge aquilo" (*Canticum Sacrum*, 1955) had been preceded by a number of works that had foreshadowed its appearance.

The use of canon and cancrizans in the "Ricercars" of his *Cantata* (1952) heralds a renewed attention to contrapuntal manipulation, and the bracketed indications and verbal identifications of these structures in the score carried something of the force of a newly announced credo, an impending turn. In the immediately ensuing *Septet* (1953), composed coincidentally with his exposure to Schoenberg's *Septet*, op. 29, his use of sixteen-note ("Passacaglia") and eight-note ("Gigue") series prepares the way for the even more economical and rigorously applied five-note series of *In Memoriam Dylan Thomas* (1954) for tenor, string quartet and trombone quartet. Here interval content and shape of the basic motif (E-E♭-C-C♯-D) are identical with the opening figure of Bartók's

Example 26.1. Stravinsky, *In memoriam Dylan Thomas*: "Dirge-Canons (Prelude)," for Tenor Voice, String Quartet, Four Trombones; opening.

Music for Strings, Percussion and Celesta, but the use to which it is put is of an entirely different order. Once again marking his printed score with brackets and identifications (left inadvertently, the composer later protested, from the manuscript version), the work's pitch content is shown to be totally derived from this single cell. Carrying a personal message as a consequence of the poet's death and aborted plans for collaboration on an opera, the setting of Dylan Thomas's poem ("Do not go gentle into that good night") is for tenor and string quartet and reflects in its ritornello structure the refrain properties of the poem ("Rage, rage against the dying of the light") and in its insistence on the number five something of the decasyllabic content of each line. In the framing "Dirge Canons," however, Stravinsky weds cellular, contrapuntal manipulation to a discrete alternation of the instrumental color component (string quartet and trombone quartet). Something of the force of this immiscible approach to color had been observable throughout the composer's career, but its potential usefulness as a formal constituent in the serial works to come now became evident. As a new orientation is announced, timbre and tone betray remnants of a dying Neoclassicism in a formalization tht emphasizes the ritornello and Baroque structure. Serialism thus not only showed its capacity to accommodate the older forms (Schoenberg had already demonstrated this in the 1920s) but also to serve the personal language of such an individual composer as Stravinsky.

The achievement of a twelve-note serial usage finally came with *Canticum Sacrum* (1955), a five-movement work for tenor and baritone soloists with chorus and orchestra. The extension of serial procedures to a twelve-pitch order, in spite of the orderly preparation in the immediately preceding works, was taken in some quarters as evidence of the final conquest of Schoenberg's aesthetic, and in others as a devastating and unfortunate capitulation. Many a pedagogue, including Nadia Boulanger, who had for decades held up the works of Stravinsky against the examples of Viennese dodecaphony, were now forced to a reconsideration. Hearing prior to the premiere that *Canticum Sacrum* was to include an organ part for the first time in Stravinsky's career, Boulanger ecstatically prophesied that "Perhaps the 20th century will finally give the instrument another Bach."[1] Hope turned momentarily to chagrin when the organ part revealed unison twelve-note rows in several of the movements.

In the first movement, however, the organ's function in providing stately contrapuntal interludes to the fast tempo sections (characterized by diatonic choral melodies supported by the organ and pungent repeated notes in the brass) does attain to a reasonable analogy with a Bach Toccata, or even more plausibly to the late sixteenth-century Venetian composer Claudio Merulo. For as the opening lines prior to the first movement proper tell us, the dedication of the work is to the city of Venice and its patron Saint Mark. Though the accompanying trombones of the "Dedicatio" may recall the recent *In Memoriam Dylan Thomas,* the opening harmony of the ensuing first movement is a bitonal juxtaposition (Bb-D/B-D-F#), or diatonic-octatonic linkage, familiar from the Russian period. But the organ interludes that twice interrupt the first movement are pure white-note diatonic music, with each of the five voices moving in a restricted compass—five, four, three, and two notes, respectively, in the manuals and six in the pedals—recalling the period of the late teens and early 1920s (see p. 226). The five alternating sections that make up the first movement also serve as a frame to the piece as a whole, with the entire movement performed in exact retrograde, to a different text, in the concluding fifth movement.

It is only in *Canticum Sacrum*'s central three movements, however, that use is made of a group of related twelve-note pitch series. Evidence of the gradual manner and radical ease with which Stravinsky absorbed the series without straining for stylistic homogeneity can nowhere be better viewed and heard than in his ballet *Agon*. Begun in 1953, it was completed after the experience of *Canticum Sacrum*, and the clear tonality of the opening and closing fanfare material contrasts vividly with the "Pas de deux" which, though texturally and intervallically indebted to Webern and timbrally through the use of the mandolin to the Viennese in general (see p. 335), is rhythmically identifiable as pure Stravinsky. Berio has spoken affectionately of the work and its importance:

> *Agon* is a triumph not only of invention and, in its own way, of awareness and of courage, but also of the transformation of materials. Onto a subcutaneous tissue (as Schoenberg would have called it) that is, a harmonic structure that glides from G major to a Webernian series (and back again) through various stages of chromatic corruption, there unfolds in remorseless, exemplary and naive fashion, the hyper-intelligent parable of a "short history of music" that performs a lucid, but tragic autopsy on itself under the pretext of a game.[2]

The suggestion that in his serial works Stravinsky always sounded like Stravinsky should not be taken to indicate that there were no consequences of his adoption of the method. While *Threni* (1957) for chorus and orchestra, his first completely twelve-tone serial work, embraced a smooth, contrapuntal style almost Renaissance in character, echoes of Webern in the slightly later *Movements* for piano and orchestra (1959) were due as much to disjunct intervals, sparse linear textures, and instrumental choice as to the use of the series. The signals that continued to reach the listener suggesting that the old Stravinsky was not dead included a continuing emphasis on melodies with oscillations between two notes (Ex. 26.2, mm. 48, 51, 53–4), punctuations that

Example 26.2. Stravinsky, *Canticum Sacrum:* "Surge aquilo," mm. 46–57.

Example 26.2 (Continued)

endorsed prominent harmonic fifths (*Movements* for piano and orchestra, final measure of Ex. 26.3) and formalizations emphasizing canon,[3] ritornello patterns, and symmetrical structures. All these features helped to secure the impression that with Stravinsky, tonal impication, Russian melodic manner, and audible sectionalization were compatible with the series. Stravinsky's claim that his *Movements* was the "most advanced music from the point of view of construction of anything I have composed" refers principally to the complexity of the serial relationships and the rhythm. Concerning the rhythmic manner of the piece, his remark, "Though parallels are not equivalents, look at Josquin for a parallel: that marvelous second *Agnus Dei* in the *Missa l'homme armé*, or at Baude Cordier's *pour le deffault de dieu Bacchus* . . . . ,"[4] suggests that his

Example 26.3. Stravinsky, *Movements for Piano and Orchestra*, Mvt. 1, opening.

Copyright 1960 by Hawkes & Son (London) Ltd. Reprinted by permission of Boosey & Hawkes, Inc.

Example 26.3 (Continued)

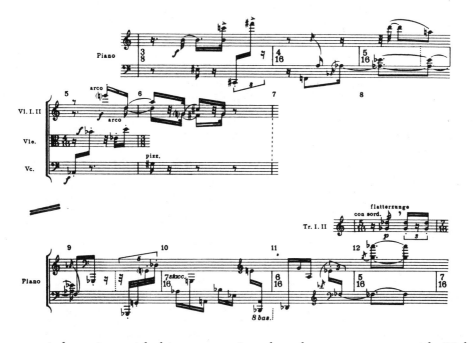

infatuation with history continued to be as strong as with Webern. The movement toward an increased antitonality that he claimed for the work was not a tendency he was to pursue. *Movements* was a brief though magical flirtation with the rigours of serialism before turning its properties to a more personal and retrospective account in the last group of works that followed (*Sermon, Narrative and Prayer, Variations, Introitus, Requiem Canticles*).

It is noteworthy that his last major opus was a work that was essentially his own requiem—one that was stylistically a *summa* of his entire career, melding the insistent repetitions of *Le sacre* to the "Prelude"; the choral intonations of the *Symphony of Psalms* to the "Exaudi"; the energizing keyboard writing of the *Piano Concerto* and the *Symphony in Three Movements* as well as the cymbalom flourishes of *Renard* to the "Dies irae"; the fanfares of *Oedipus* and *The Rake* to the "Tuba mirum"; the isolated long-short punctuations from the *Symphonies of Winds* (an "austere ritual" dedicated to the memory of Debussy) to the "Interlude"; and the tolling bells of *Les noces* to the final "Postlude." No work could more properly demonstrate that Stravinsky's turn to serialism was essentially not a rapprochement, let alone a capitulation, to the sound world of Arnold Schoenberg, but rather an extension of a personal language through his typical confrontation of a stylistically alien, but potentially enriching, model.

Canticum Sacrum

DEDICATIO

Urbi Venetiae, in laude Sancti sui Presidis, Beati Marci Apostoli.

DEDICATION

To the City of Venice, in praise of its Patron Saint, the Blessed Mark, Apostle.

I

Euntes in mundum universum, praedicate evangelium omni creaturae.

Go ye into all the world, and preach the gospel to every creature.

II

Surge, aquilo; et veni, auster;
perfla hortum meum, et fluant aromata illius.
Veniat dilectus meus in hortum suum,
et comedat fructum pomorum suorum.
Veni in hortum meum, soror mea, sponsa;
messui myrrham meam cum aromatibus meis;
comedi favum meum cum melle meo;
bibi vinum meum cum lacte meo.
Comedite, amici, et bibite;
et inebriamini, carissimi.

Awake, O north wind; and come, thou south;
blow upon my garden, that the spices thereof
may flow out.
Let my beloved come into his garden,
and eat his pleasant fruits.
I am come into my garden, my sister, my
spouse;
I have gathered my myrrh with my spice;
I have eaten my honeycomb with my honey;
I have drunk my wine with my milk:
eat, O friends; drink,
yea, drink abundantly, O beloved.

III

Caritas

Diliges Dominum Deum tuum ex toto corde tuo, et ex tota anima tua, et ex tota fortitundina tua.

Thou shalt love the Lord thy God with all thine heart, and with all thy soul, and with all thy might.

Diligamus nos invicem, quia charitas ex Deo est; et omnis qui diligit ex Deo natus est, et cognoscit Deum.

Beloved, let us love one another: for love is of God; and everyone that loveth is born of God, and knoweth God.

Spes

Qui confidunt in Domino, sicut mons Sion;
non commovebitur in aeternum, qui habitat in Jerusalem.
Sustinuit anima mea in verbo ejus; speravit anima mea in Domino, a custodia matutina usque ad noctem.

They that trust in the Lord, shall be as mount Zion, which cannot be removed but abideth for ever.
My soul doth wait, and in his word do I hope.
My soul waiteth for the Lord more than they that watch for the morning.

Fides

Credidi, propter quod locutus sum; ego autem humiliatus sum nimis.

I believed, therefore have I spoken: I was greatly afflicted.

IV

Jesus autem ait illi: Si potes credere, omnia possibilia sunt credenti. Et continuo exclamans pater pueri, cum lacrimis aiebat: Credo, Domine; adjuva incredulitatem meam.

Jesus said unto him, If thou canst believe, all things are possible to him that believeth. And straightway the father of the child cried out, and said with tears, Lord I believe; help thou my unbelief.

V

Ille autem profecti praedicaverunt ubique, Domino cooperante et sermonem confirmante, sequentibus signis.
Amen.

And they went forth, and preached everywhere, the Lord working with them, and confirming the word with signs following.
Amen.

Requiem Canticles

Prelude

Exaudi orationem meam,	Hear my prayer,
ad te omnis caro veniet.	unto Thee shall all flesh come.

Dies irae, dies illa,	Day of wrath and doom impending,
Solvet saeclum in favilla,	Heaven and earth in ashes ending!
Teste David cum Sibyllla.	David's words with Sibyl's blending!

Quantus tremor est futurus	Oh, what fear man's bosom rendeth
Judex est venturus,	when from heaven the judge descendeth,
Cuncta stricte discussurus!	on whose sentence all dependeth!

Tuba mirum spargens sonum	Wondrous sound the trumpet flingeth
Per sepulchra regionum	through earth's sepulchres it ringeth,
Coget omnes ante thronum.	all before the throne it bringeth.

Interlude

Rex tremendae majestatis	King of majesty tremendous,
Qui salvandos salvas gratis,	Who dost free salvation send,
Salva me, fons pietatis.	Fount of pity, then befriend us!

Lacrimosa dies illa,	Ah! that day of tears and mourning!
Qua resurget ex favilla	From the dust of earth returning,
Judicandus homo reus:	man for judgement must prepare him:
Huic ergo parce Deus.	Spare, O God, in mercy spare him!

Pie Jesu Domine,	Lord, all-pitying, Jesu blest,
dona eis requiem. Amen.	grant them rest. Amen.

Libera me, Domine, de morte aeterna,	Deliver me, O Lord, from death eternal,
in die illa tremenda:	in that fearful day:
Quando coeli movendi sunt et terra:	When the heavens and the earth shall be
Dum veneris judicare saeculum per ignem.	shaken:
Tremens factus sum ego, et timeo,	When Thou shalt come to judge the world by
dum sicsussio venerit, atque venture ira.	fire.
Quando coeli movendi sunt et terra.	I am in fear and trembling
Dies illa, dies irae, calamitatis et miseriae,	till the sifting be upon us, and the wrath to
dies magna et amara valde.	come.
Libera me.	When the heavens and the earth shall be
	shaken.
	O that day, that day of wrath, of calamity and
	misery,
	a great day and exceeding bitter.
	Deliver me, O Lord.

Postlude

SHOSTAKOVICH, SOVIET RUSSIA, AND SERIALISM

The time of jubilation in Russia following the fall of Berlin on May 1, 1945, was short. For not only were many of the severities of daily wartime existence extended, but in artistic matters questions relating to national ideologies and aspirations, momentarily set aside during the war years, were revived in a series of cultural purges during the years 1946 to 1948. The man in charge was Andrei Zhdanov, already known from the middle 1930s as one of the primary voices in the definition of Socialist Realism for the arts; his return as the man at the top in 1946 was ominous. The series of "creative debates," which typically ended in the slandering of the intellegentsia, ultimately culminated in the First All-Union Congress of Composers held in Moscow from April 19–25, 1948, with open attacks against Miaskovsky, Prokofiev, Shostakovich, and Khachaturian—all internationally well-known figures at the time. A Resolution from the Central Committee published on February 10, 1948 charged them with Formalism, Modernism, and Westernism, all of which were anathema to Soviet ideals. Something of this state of affairs has been discussed earlier (see pp. 414, 417), but the importance of this declaration was to resound over the following decades during which time Tikhon Khrennikov (b. 1913) presided as chairman of the Composers' Union.

Khrennikov's stern antimodernist policy not only dictated the composition of Soviet Realist works but proscribed the use of avant-garde techniques from the West. Serialism, thus, was a natural target for censure, and its absence in the scores of Soviet composers through the final Stalin years and those of his successor, Nikita Khruschev, was predictable. The reactions of the most famous composers during this period were, on the whole, restrained and mildly apologetic, though it would be fair to say that the quality of the music of the most important members of the Old Guard, Prokofiev and Shostakovich, did not suffer notably—the sizable dash of anti-Soviet criticism in the West notwithstanding. The sense of repression that prohibited a freedom of inquiry, however, is decidedly manifest in the period through the decade of the 1960s, in spite of a certain liberalization in the period following Stalin's death, 1953–64. For in a speech of March 8, 1963, the Soviet premiere, Nikita Khruschev, restated a longstanding premise of Soviet Realism that melody must be the watchword of all music if it was to appeal to the masses, and he observed that

> . . . You can meet young people who try to prove that melody in music has lost the right to exist and that its place is now being taken by 'new' music—'dodecaphony,' the music of noises. It is hard for a normal person to understand what the word 'dodecaphony' means, but apparently it means the same as the word 'cacophony.' Well, we flatly reject this cacophonous music. Our people can't use this garbage as a tool of their ideology.[5]

Echoes of Khruschev's shoe-slamming antics at the United Nations in New York flash across the mind.

The appearance of Rodion Shchedrin (b. 1932), then in his early thirties, at a Plenary Meeting of the Board of Soviet Composers in Moscow from March 23–30, 1963, indicated a modest shift in interest toward the development of the younger generation. The history of state policy over the next twenty years is tortuous, mercurial, and ideologically never very far from the conservative, repressionist tastes of the late 1940s. But little by little, the possibility of extending techniques to include dodecaphony emerged, and a whole range of expression, including that of an unofficial group of post-Webernists, intermittently surfaced. It is very difficult to judge the musical personalities of composers like Volkonsky, Pyart, Tishchenko, Karayev, Shnitke, and Denisov from the small evidence that has filtered through to the West, but the ease with which such an "official" composer as Shchderin has incorporated elements of jazz as well as twelve-tone and aleatoric principles into his second and third piano concertos of 1966 and 1973 cannot go unnoticed.

It was much in the same ambivalent spirit that Shostakovich in 1968 cautioned against the destructive tendencies of avant-gardism while allowing a sensitive expansion of the means of expression. On the one hand he condemned such progressive tendencies as

> a deliberate attempt . . . to achieve a new quality in music merely through the repudiation of historically evolved norms and rules. This is a gross theoretical error . . . We Soviet artists resolutely reject 'avantgardism.'[6]

and on the other allowed that

> . . . As for the use of strictly technical devices from such musical 'systems' as, say, the twelve-tone or the aleatory . . . everything is good in moderation . . . The use of elements from these complex systems is entirely justified if it is dictated by the idea of the composition . . . Please understand that the formula 'the end justifies the means' to some extent seems right to me in music. Any means? Any, as long as they convey the goal.[7]

Shostakovich went on to declare Mahler, Prokofiev, Miaskovsky, Stravinsky, Bartók, and Berg as among the classics of the twentieth century, suggesting at least a momentary rehabilitation of the reputation of Stravinsky and the composer of *Wozzeck*, whose opera had been known to Leningrad audiences as early as 1927. Something of the rising appeal of the music of Berg in particular is evidenced in Mikhail Tarakanov's *The Musical Theatre of Alban Berg* (Moscow, 1976), whose preface by Shchedrin opens with the judgment that Berg was one of the most striking and original musical personalities of the twentieth century.

Evidence of this freer attitude appeared in Shostakovich's *Violin Sonata* of 1968, where the first theme of the first movement is twelve-note, as is the opening of *String Quartet No. 12* of the same year. While the use of a twelve-note idea in neither case led to a thorough-going investigation of serial procedures, the systematic exploration of the total chromatic did enrich Shostakovich's vocabulary in several of his last works and concomitantly emphasized his contrapuntal bent without sacrificing a basic tonal orientation. It is a claim that can similarly be made for his younger compatriot Edison Denisov (b. 1929), whose use of twelve-note serialism combined with an interest in Russian folk material resulted in a formidable interpretation of the Stravinsky legacy in a work like *Plachi* ("Laments") of 1966. With the appearance and interpretation of dodecaphonic ideas in music from such alien and previously antagonistic cultures—and at a time that still saw Khrennikov at the head of the musical ministry—the long debate over the viability, not to mention the adaptability, of Schoenberg's method seemed to have come to an end.

BRITTEN, ENGLAND, AND SERIALISM

Shostakovich's friend Benjamin Britten also explored the possibilities of twelve note composition without exploiting the full ramifications of a serialist approach. In the *Songs and Proverbs of William Blake* (1965), Britten fashioned a twelve-note idea in several Proverbs that separates the Songs and functions somewhat in the manner of a ritornello. As with Shostakovich, however, such practices did not disturb Britten's essential language but only provided a momentary organizational solution.

Somewhat more characteristically, Britten worked first with twelve-note tertian harmonic fields in an extended and audible fashion in the "Sleep Music" that closes Act II of *A Midsummer Night's Dream* (1960). In the dialogue that precedes the final chorus, a single chord sustains for extended periods of time, changing only with the commentary of a new character. In the final chorus, however, the harmonic rhythms of the same sequence accelerate and assume a structural significance (note the chord changes in the following libretto).

Example 26.4. Britten, *A Midsummer Night's Dream*, twelve-note chord progression.

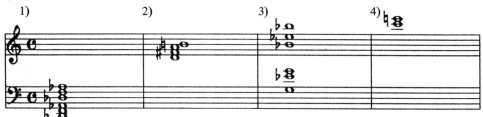

Benjamin Britten, *A Midsummer Night's Dream*, Act II: Postlude

LYSANDER:

    1: When I come, where he calls, then he is gone,
    And I am fall'n in dark uneven way,
    And here will rest me. Come, thou gentle day.
    (Lies down)
    For if but once thou show me thy grey light
    I'll find Demetrius, and revenge this spite.
    (He sleeps)
    (Enter Puck and Demetrius)

PUCK:

    2: Ho, ho, coward, why com'st thou not?

DEMETRIUS:

    Abide me if thou dar'st. Where art thou now?

PUCK:

    Come hither, I am here.

DEMETRIUS:

    Nay, then, thou mock'st me; thou shalt buy this dear,
    If ever I thy face by daylight see.
    Now go thy way; faintness constrineth me
    To measure out my length on this cold bed.

By day's approach look to be visited.
(Lies down and sleeps)
(Enter Helena)

HELENA:

3: O weary night, O long and tedious night,
Abate thy hours, shine comforts from the East,
And sleep that sometimes shuts up sorrow's eye
Steal me awhile from mine own company.
(Sleeps)

PUCK:

Yet but three? Come one more,
Two of both kinds make up four.
(Enter Hermia)
Here she comes, curst and sad,
Cupid is a knavish lad
Thus to make poor females mad.

HERMIA:

4: Never so weary, never so in woe,
Bedabbled with the dew, and torn with briers,
I can no further crawl, no further go,
My legs can keep no pace with my desires.
Here will I rest me till the break of day.
Heaven shield Lysander, if they mean a fray.
(She sleeps)
(Enter Fairies, very stealthily)

MOTH, MUSTARDSEED, COBWEB, PEASEBLOSSOM, FAIRIES:

1: On the ground, 2: sleep sound;
3: He'll apply to your eye,
4: Gentle lover, 1: remedy.
2: When thou wak'st, 3: thou tak'st
4: True delight in the sight
1: Of thy 2: former 3: lady's 4: eye:
1: And the 2: country 3: proverb 4: known,
3: In your waking 2: shall be 1: shown:
1: Jack shall have Jill,
2: Nought shall go ill,
3: The man shall have his 4: mare again,
1: And all shall be well 2: all shall be well
3: all shall be well, shall be 4: well
(Puck squeezes juice on Lysander's eyes)
1, 2, 3, 4 (Exeunt Puck and Fairies)
1

Though the systematic use of the total chromatic is verifiable visually, aurally the listener is reminded of the English predisposition toward tertian sonorities from the faburden and gymel techniques of the Middle Ages to the composed triads of Dunstable and Leonel Power, which Walter Frye already labeled the "contenance Angloise" in the fifteenth century. Indeed, Britten's melodic and harmonic sequence is more than a little reminiscent of the Orcadian "Hymn to St. Magnus", a work that was to attract the younger Englishman, Peter Maxwell Davies, in a setting of 1972.

Davies (b. 1934) showed an early interest in dodecaphonic structures, and one of his first performing groups was called the Pierrot Players, renowned for performances of Schoenberg's work and others written for the resources of its ensemble. Ultimately, his serial inclination was to take him in another direction, but it was in part reflective of a vigorous presence in England of musicians and composers trained in Vienna, such as Egon Wellesz (1885–1974) and Roberto Gerhard (1896–1970), both pupils of Schoenberg; Humphrey Searle (b. 1915), a pupil of Webern; and the remarkable Elizabeth Lutyens (b. 1906), whose first essays in serialism were achieved in virtual isolation in the late 1930s.

Of Davies' age, and associated with him for a time in Manchester along with Harrison Birtwistle (b. 1934), was Alexander Goehr (b. 1932), son of the conductor Walter Goehr, a pupil of Schoenberg. The young Goehr was early led to an appreciation of both Schoenberg and Messiaen, with whom he studied briefly, and finally Boulez. This led to an amalgam of various "bloc sonore" procedures and doubling techniques over a cantus firmus, combinatorial serialism, and an interest in early (Janequin, Le Jeune, Monteverdi) and exotic (Japanese Noh drama) music.

OTHER COUNTRIES

The diversity of interest and intent in so-called twelve-tone writing had already by the 1960s confirmed the notion of its adaptability to radically different surface textures and tonal orientations. Any notion that dodecaphonic music had by definition to sound like that of the post-Webernites had been effectively dispelled in numerous quarters including the avant-garde itself.

To recite the names of the legion of composers who have used some brand of a strict or modified serial technique would be virtually to make a list of the most active composers before 1970 and would include in addition to those living in France, Germany, Austria, the United States, England, and Russia, mentioned earlier, composers active in Italy, Hungary, Poland, and Argentina. To explore examples of each strictly from the standpoint of serialism would take us into a consideration of individual careers more than add to the overview already presented. Yet such a roster would include some of the most notable musical luminaries of the age, a number of whom will be considered later in relation to questions other than serialism: Dallapiccola, Berio, Nono, Maderna, Bussotti (Italy); Lutosławski, Baird (Poland); Ligeti (Hungary); Husa (Czecho-slavakia); and Ginastera (Argentina).

Among the older guard, dodecaphonic procedures were typically allowed to function as a revivifying ingredient for a language essentially already defined; among the avant-garde the continuing search for new expressive means frequently developed quickly away from Viennese, Parisian or American models to a freer exploration of surface sounds, moving textural masses and a new investigation into the properties of time, space, and silence. Thus Ligeti's identification with Darmstadt and as analyst-apologist for Boulez's *Structures* in the late 1950s quickly turned to a consideration of nonserial questions in a group of works of the early 1960s (see p. 576). Similarly, the exploratory gestures in dodecaphonic manipulation of Lutosławski's *Funeral Music* (1956) proved liberating in the same way as his probe of aleatoric procedures in *Venetian Games* (1961), without securing an undivided allegiance in either instance. And Ginastera's infatuation with twelve-note ideas from his earliest works (*Panambi,* *1934–36*) through the *Piano Sonata* (1952) and his final operatic successes (*Don Rodrigo, Bomarzo, Beatrix Cenci*) could not disguise an essentially Bergian freedom of approach to the use of such materials in the service of a fundamentally Dionysian language. In virtually all these instances, some premise more fundamental than Serialism was invariably at work as an identifying constituent.

REPERTOIRE (Stravinsky)

Cantata (1952), S, T, fem chorus, 2 fl, ob, eng hn/ob2, vc
Septet (1953), cl, hn, bn, pf, vn, va, vc
Three Shakespeare Songs (1953), Mezz, fl, cl, va
In Memoriam Dylan Thomas (1954), T, str qt, 4 trmb
Canticum Sacrum (1955), T, Bar, chorus, orch
Agon (1953–57), harp, mandoline, pf, tim, 3 tom-toms, xyl, castanets, str qnt; ballet
Threni (1957–58), soli, mixed chorus, orch
Movements (1958–59), pf, orch
Double Canon (1959), str qt
A Sermon, a Narrative and a Prayer (1960–61), A, T, speaker, chorus, orch
The Flood (1961–62), dance drama, narrator, soloists, chorus, orch
Abraham and Isaac (1962–63), Bar, cham orch
Elegy for J.F.K. (1964), Bar, 3 cl (2 B♭, 1 alto)
Variations (1963–64), orch
Introitus (1965), tenors, basses, harp, pf, 2 timp, 2 tam-tams, solo va and dbs
Requiem Canticles (1966), A, B, chorus, orch

READING

Milton Babbitt, "Remarks on the Recent Stravinsky," *Perspectives on Schoenberg and Stravinsky* (Princeton, 1968), 165–85.
Claudio Spies, "Some Notes on Stravinsky's Requiem Settings," *Perspectives on Schoenberg and Stravinsky* (1968), 223–49.
Peter van den Toorn, *The Music of Igor Stravinsky* (New Haven, 1983).
Milton Babbitt, "Order, Symmetry, and Centricity in Late Stravinsky" in *Confronting Stravinsky,* ed. J. Pasler (Berkeley, 1986), 247.
Glenn Watkins, "The Canon and Stravinsky's Late Style," *Confronting Stravinsky,* ed. J. Pasler (Berkeley, 1986), 217.
Charles Wuorinen and Jeffrey Kresky, "On the Significance of Stravinsky's Last Works" in *Confronting Stravinsky,* ed. J. Pasler (Berkeley, 1986), 262.
William Austin, "Stravinsky's 'Fortunate Continuities' and 'Legitimate Accidents,' 1882–1982" in *Stravinsky Retrospectives,* ed. E. Haimo and P. Johnson (Lincoln, 1987), 1.
Milton Babbitt, "Stravinsky's Verticals and Schoenberg's Diagonals: A Twist of Fate" in *Stravinsky Retrospectives,* ed. E. Haimo and P. Johnson (Lincoln, 1987), 15.
Paul Johnson, "Cross-Collectional Techniques of Structure in Stravinsky's Centric Music" in *Stravinsky Retrospectives,* ed. E. Haimo and P. Johnson (Lincoln, 1987), 55.

REPERTOIRE (Shostakovich and Soviet Russia)

Shchedrin, *Piano Concerto No. 2* (1966)
Shchedrin, *Piano Concerto No. 3* (1973)
Denisov, *Plachi* ("Laments") (1966)
Shnitke, *Quasi una sonata* (1968), vn, pf
Volkonsky, *Musica stricta* (1956), pf
Volkonsky, *Mirror Suite* (1960), v (Lorca), fl, gui, perc, ch org, vn
Shostakovich, *Violin Sonata* (1968), vn, pf
Shostakovich, *String Quartet No. 12* (1968)

READING (Shostakovich and Soviet Russia)

"Resolution of the Central Committee: 'On the Opera *Velikaya Druzhba* by Muradeli" of
February 10, 1948; Eng. trans. N. Slonimsky in *Music since 1900*, 4th ed. (New York,
1971), 684–88.
Alexander Werth, *Musical Uproar in Moscow* (London, 1949).
Victor Seroff, *Dmitri Shostakovich* (New York, 1943, rev. 1970).
R. S. Brown, "An Interview with Shostakovich," *High Fidelity*, xxiii (1973), 86.
Solomon Volkov, ed., *Testimony: the Memoirs of Shostakovich* (New York, 1979).
Boris Schwarz, *Music and Musical Life in Soviet Russia, 1917–1981* (Bloomington, 1983).

REPERTOIRE (Britten, England, and Other Countries)

Britten, *Songs and Proverbs of William Blake* (1965), Bar, pf
Britten, *A Midsummer Night's Dream* (1960), opera
Davies, *Hymn to St. Magnus* (1972), S, fl, basset cl, pf/hpd/cel, perc, va, vc
Ginastera, *Panambi* (1934–35), ballet
Ginastera, *Piano Sonata* (1952)
Ginastera, *Don Rodrigo* (1963–64), opera
Ginastera, *Bomarzo* (1966–67), opera
Goehr, *Piano Trio* (1966)
Lutosławski, *Funeral Music* (1958)

CHAPTER 27

THE INTERNATIONAL AVANT-GARDE: CHOICE AND CHANCE

The gradual adoption of variable dodecaphonic procedures witnessed in the preceding chapter suggests that the hope of a small group of composers for its ultimate triumph as a common practice was not totally unfounded. Yet the prospect ultimately proved to be illusory and common agreement among its practitioners momentary. In retrospect it is a remarkable thing to realize that in the early 1950s, just at the moment of a supposed coming together in a new and binding musical fraternity, the seeds of its demise were already surfacing. It was only a matter of time until the aspirations of an all-encompassing Serialism as a universal language were to be threatened and then toppled.

That such reactive phenomena can be observed periodically throughout the history of any art is attested to by contrasting Baudelaire's observation that he pitied poets who were guided only by instinct with his own later remarkable confession:

> I have tried more than once, like all my friends, to enclose myself in a system in order to preach there at my ease. But a system is a sort of damnation which thrusts us into a perpetual rejection . . . I have come back to seek shelter in impeccable naïveté . . . It is there that my philosophical conscience has found rest.[1]

As an avid admirer of Baudelaire whom he repeatedly quoted, Boulez had the poet's support for diametrically opposing views. By 1960, invoking still other literary models, he began to argue for an expanded view of form:

> It must be our concern in future to follow the examples of Joyce and Mallarmé and to jettison the concept of a work as a simple journey starting with a departure and ending with an arrival . . . The modern conception of the maze in a work of art is certainly one of the most considerable advances in Western thought, and one upon which it is impossible to go back.[2]

But in 1962, in spite of his attraction to some of the alternatives to Serialism, Boulez felt compelled to register his dismay at the current state of affairs:

> At the first opportunity there was a break-out from the stifling prison of *number*, and then EVERYTHING was allowed including the most idiotic and vulgar exhibitionism. Did anyone expect thus to escape the only reality? And what did this

permissiveness and these long holidays from thought signify, if not a continued flight from responsibility?[3]

EASTERN BACKGROUNDS: SONORITIES AND STRUCTURES

The backgrounds for the rise of both colorist and formal-constructive alternatives can be seen in the explorations of the first part of the century in the works of Debussy and Delage, Ravel and Roussel, and a host of other composers who were in search of new Eastern hues to blend with a more traditional Western musical values. Among the next generation of French composers, none found a more fundamental application of this resource than Olivier Messiaen, whose titles such as *Turangalila-symphonie* (Hindu poems of love), *Harawi* (Peruvian folklore), and *Sept Haikai* (following a trip to Japan in 1962) bear ample testimony. The infatuation, needless to say, was not only with textual matters but with a consuming interest in questions of color and rhythm, of which the latter led to a detailed study of Greek and Hindu patterns and forms.

But it was not in Europe alone that the value of such an exploration was sensed, for in America interest in Pacific cultures quickened under the impulse of a group of California-based composers: Henry Cowell (*Madras, Ongaku,* Koto concertos), Colin McPhee (*Tabuh-tabuhan, Balinese Ceremonial Music*), Lou Harrison (*Double Music, Moogunkwha*), and to an extent Harry Partch, whose percussion inventions in special tunings seemed an extension of the gamelan. As early as the mid-1920s, Cowell had turned to the serious study of non-European musics, working with ethnomusicologists in Berlin under a Guggenheim grant. His interest with new sounds shifted to an exploration of ethnic music both from the standpoint of sound and organization. This led to the idea of "elastic form," one of his most revolutionary ideas, in which the notion of indeterminacy is put forward, suggesting that the performer, as in his *"Mosaic" String Quartet* (1934), could assume a role with the composer in determining the order in which composed segments would be presented. It remained for John Cage, however, to translate these impulses not so much into compositions as into a point of view capable of stimulating composers of widely divergent aesthetic orientations.

JOHN CAGE

In his "Music Lovers' Field Companion" of 1954, John Cage (b. 1912), noting Stockhausen's interest in "global structures" and Boulez' fondness for "parentheses and *italics*", declared "I prefer my own choice of the mushroom. Furthermore it is avant-garde."[4] Its veiled note of accuracy and whimsy cannot help but recall Satie, about whom he has also written,[5] but the references to Boulez (*Third Piano Sonata*) and Stockhausen were not idle. For by 1954 Cage, formerly a student of Cowell and Schoenberg, was busy solidifying a posture dependent-independent of both, even as he dangled his views in the face of the European avant-garde. It is remarkable that the decades of the 1930s and 1940s, which had seen the rise of "Americanism" in music and the repeatedly expressed need to define an American music distinct from its European counterparts based on the use of indigenous materials, should be followed in the 1950s by an American challenge to European hegemony with respect to international avant-gardism.

Purportedly engaged in fashioning a path for the future that all composers could travel, the Europeans saw their sense of camaraderie begin to dissolve almost from the beginning, and Cage did not fail to note that the time was ripe to show his hand.

Born in California, Cage went to New York in 1933 where he studied with Adoph Weiss, and non-Western, folk, and contemporary music with Henry Cowell. Returning to California in the fall of 1934 he began studies with Schoenberg. His first compositions, which reflect the exposure to his earliest teachers, disclose an interest in the systematic use of the total chromatic (*Six Short Inventions*, 1933) and twelve-note serial manipulations (*Metamorphosis*, 1938) as well as percussion ensembles (*First Construction [in Metal]*, 1939). In the performance of many of his early percussion pieces he was joined by the composer Lou Harrison, whose interest in non-Western source materials and just intonation was reinforcing.

Continuing his interest in unusual percussion ensembles, he moved first to Chicago in 1941 and then the next year to New York, which was to become his permanent home. Here his music was first brought to public attention under the auspices of the League of Composers in a concert given at the Museum of Modern Art in February 1943. Joining with the dancer Merce Cunningham, his music through the 1940s continued the exploration of a wide range of percussion instruments, including the prepared piano. Building on the pioneering work of Henry Cowell with the piano (Ex. 12.1), Cage's search for new sounds led to the insertion of various objects between the strings, turning this familiar keyboard instrument into an exotic vari-timbred percussion instrument. The first piece for his new invention was entitled *Bacchanale* of 1938, a work whose published score includes a chart indicating how each pitch is to be modified (small bolt, weather stripping, screw with nuts). Furthermore, its limited pitch content and highly repetitious figurations clearly look back to the music of Satie as well as ahead to the Minimalist music of the 1960s, even as it betrays a knowledge of the music of Bali, black Africa, and India.

A series of pieces for prepared piano followed in rapid succession, including *A Book of Music* (2 prepared pf, 1944), *Three Dances* (2 prepared pf, 1945), *Sonatas and Interludes* (prepared pf, 1946–48), and the *Concerto* for prepared piano and chamber orchestra of 1951. It was a performance of the *Sonatas and Interludes* at Carnegie Hall by Maro Ajemian in January 1949 that not only created a stir but brought the degree of recognition and patronage that allowed developments of the years immediately following.

Cage's interest in exploring and extending the realms of sound reflects an attitude already clarified at some length in an article *The Future of Music: Credo*, written as early as 1937, in which he stated his belief in the use of various kinds of noise he felt would ultimately culminate in the electronic production of all imaginable sounds. In this he mirrored not only the Futurist legacy but the contemporary passion of both Cowell and Varèse, and by 1942 he had produced his *Imaginary Landscape no. 3*, which employed audio-frequency oscillators, variable-speed turntables, electric buzzer, and amplified marimba in a work purportedly for six percussionists.

The indeterminate pitch of many of the "noises" of Cage's early compositions naturally led to an emphasis on rhythmic structure. Thus in the opening of *First Construction (in Metal)*, 1939, the pattern 4+3+2+3+4 is repeated sixteen times, while lengthier and more complex designs were incorporated in the *String Quartet* of 1950 and *Music for Marcel Duchamp* (prepared pf, 1947). Such exploration of additive rhythmic patterns recalls not only the Bulgarian rhythms of Bartók but the Greek and Hindu patterns being manipulated by Messiaen at about the same time.

Beginning in 1951, however, Cage's infatuation with Oriental philosophy led him to a new liberating structural argument, which in the eyes of many seemed to threaten chaos. Cage, who had begun to work with the concept of the Magic Square, found in the Oriental *I Ching* ("Book of Changes") a work that illustrates the generation of random numbers by throwing coins or yarrow stalks. Intrigued by the similarity of this philosophy with his own, he set about to write *Music of Changes* (1951). Each detail of his score was determined by the toss of three coins six times, which directed him to a specific number in *I Ching*; this in turn sent him to a numbered position on one of twenty-six charts he had devised. Thus a single pitch was determined. The procedure was then repeated in the determination of duration, timbre, and other parameters. The process, while purportedly based on chance, required for the forty-three-minute piece an incalculable number of tosses, a rigorous mathematical method, and a precisely notated score whose directions to the performer were ultraspecific. As Peyser has stated, "The *Music of Changes* was to be Cage's *Structures*," and Boulez himself, who frequently corresponded with Cage at the time, openly observed in an article, "Eventuellement," that "The direction of John Cage's experiments is too near that of my own for me not to take note of it."[6] A piano recital given by David Tudor on New Year's Day, 1952 (see Figure 27.1), which programmed both Boulez's *Second Sonata* and Cage's *Music of Changes*, vividly registered their compatability at the time (see epigram, p. 504).

Though the genesis of the score of *Music of Changes* was determined by aleatoric operations, its performance was not. In his *Imaginary Landscape No. 4*

THE LIVING THEATRE PRESENTS A PIANO RECITAL BY
DAVID TUDOR, JANUARY FIRST, 1952, 8:00 P.M., IN THE
CHERRY LANE THEATRE, 38 COMMERCE STREET.

PROGRAM:

2ème SONATE   PIERRE BOULEZ
    Extrêmement rapide
    Lent
    Modéré, presque vif
    Vif

FOR PREPARED PIANO   CHRISTIAN WOLFF
    4 pieces

INTERSECTION 2   MORTON FELDMAN

MUSIC OF CHANGES   JOHN CAGE
    4 parts

THIS IS THE FIRST PERFORMANCE OF THE INTERSECTION AND THE CHANGES, AND THE FIRST NEW YORK PERFORMANCE OF THE PIECES BY CHRISTIAN WOLFF.

Figure 27.1. Program designed by John Cage for Living Theater recital, New York, January 1, 1952.

Photo courtesy of John Cage.

(1951) for twelve radios and twenty-four players and a conductor, the composer further freed the choice of materials while maintaining firm control over its form by directing the receivers according to a precisely determined schedule of duration and dynamics. Finally, in the *Concert* for prepared piano and chamber orchestra of 1957–58, Cage wrote a work without master score but with each part written in detail. The piano part is a book of eighty-four different kinds of related and unrelated materials that may be played in whole or in part and in any sequence. The orchestral accompaniment may involve any number of players, and the work may be of any length, the determination of which is made by the conductor. The composer's statement that he considered the work to be "in progress" was soon to be mirrored in numerous works of Boulez, who, if in need of a French model, could rightly point to Mallarmé.

CAGE VIS À VIS BOULEZ AND STOCKHAUSEN

Although Boulez had been impressed with the gamelan sounds and the rhythmic organization of Cage's *First Construction (In Metal)* at a concert in Paris in 1949, with his first trip to New York in the autumn of 1952 Boulez became convinced that he and Cage were on totally different paths. Their correspondence stopped, and Cage's further influence on the European avant-garde at large was to be delayed until 1958 when he returned to give lectures at Darmstadt. In 1954, however, during a European concert tour with the pianist David Tudor, Stockhausen was introduced to and was impressed with the piano music of both Cage and Morton Feldman. Stockhausen's own *Piano Pieces V–X* (1954–55) have been held to reflect this confrontation.

Boulez soon charged Cage with the adoption of "a philosophy tinged with Orientalism that masks a basic weakness in compositional techniques,"[7] and the two composer's assessment of *Changes* dramatized the widening gulf between them.

> **Cage:** "Structure, which is the division of the whole into parts; method, which is the note-to-note procedure; form, which is the expressive content, the morphology of the continuity; and materials, the sounds and silences of the composition, are all determined . . . the fact that these things that constitute it, though only sounds, have come together to control a human being, the performer, gives the work the alarming aspect of a Frankenstein monster."[8]

> **Boulez:** "Schematization, quite simply takes the place of invention; imagination—an auxiliary—limits itself to giving birth to a complex mechanism which takes care of engendering microscopic and macroscopic structures until, in the absence of any further possible combinations, the piece comes to an end."[9]

The seeming culmination of such an attitude came in Stockhausen's *"Piano Piece XI* of 1956, a work in nineteen groups on a single sheet of paper from which the performer, beginning with the group "he sees first," continues in any order until one group has been played three times. A connecting link is guaranteed at the end of each group by the indication of tempo, dynamic and touch for the next group.

In spite of several articles by Cage which appeared in Stockhausen's journal *Die Reihe* and a photograph taken of the two composers together in 1958 (Figure 27.2), it is well to note Stockhausen's claims of independence from his American

Figure 27.2. "Flying Together": John Cage with Karlheinz Stockhausen, about 1958.
Photo courtesy of John Cage.

friend. Having studied statistics with Werner Meyer-Eppler at Bonn University in 1953, Stockhausen had already explored ideas of redundancy in randomly created texts and the aleatoric manipulation of electronic controls according to various curves in the composition of *Gesang der Jünglinge* (1955–56), resulting in "an aleatoric layer of individual pulses which, in general, speeded up statistically."[10] Stockhausen warned, however, that it would be "quite wrong . . . to trace the European tendencies to 'open forms' back to American influences" and insisted that the sources for his approach were to be found in contemporary European investigations in mathematics and the natural sciences.[11] Admitting that Meyer-Eppler had informed his students of similar interests in aleatoric procedures in America, Stockhausen has disclaimed knowledge of specific examples at the time except in the world of painting. It is intriguing to consider the roughly simultaneous explorations—similar in concept but independently executed—that have occurred periodically amongst members of the avant-garde in the 20th century (Schoenberg and Hauer, Messiaen and Babbitt, Stockhausen and Cage), and to contemplate the possibility of *Zeitgeist* phenomena that would promote the likelihood of such an eventuality.

Although Boulez's *Third Piano Sonata* (1956–57), a purported example of "mobile" form with eight possible manners of ordering the five movements, would also attest to more than a fleeting kinship, the composer distanced himself from Cage and Stockhausen in several pronouncements. Of Stockhausen's *Klavierstücke XI*, Boulez charged that it represented "a new sort of automatism, one which for all its apparent opening the gates to freedom, has only really let in an element of risk that seems to be absolutely inimical to the integrity of the work."[12]

Boulez's aesthetic touchstone for his *Third Sonata* was Mallarmé's *Un coup de dés* ("A Throw of the Dice," Fig. 12.2); its variable fonts and typographical layouts on the page provoked a rethinking not only of the conventional musical score but also the order in which its constituent elements were to be reassembled in performance. With only two of the five movements completed to date, he nonetheless established "Constellation/Constellation-Miroir" as the obligatory third movement, the position of the others remaining free. The structure of the movement is also fixed in its alternation of lighter and heavier textures, labeled as *points* and *blocs* and printed in green and red ink, respectively. While there are performance options with respect to the order of certain segments, the choice is limited and a formal coherency for the work is sealed.[13] It was in his fundamental article entitled "Aléa" (Latin: "dice") that Boulez acknowledged the despairing persistence of chance in the act of composition and the need for the composer to absorb and control it.

Later works by Boulez, such as *Domaines* (1968) and *Rituel* (1974–75), continued to leave a certain discretion of order or entrance to the performer or conductor, and in *Domaines*, for solo clarinet or clarinet and orchestra, not only the order but the forces to be used are left open. In the version with orchestra, the clarinetist moves among six instrumental groups located separately on the stage, so that the mobile quality of the work is not only conceptual but visible in live performance. The conception was clearly in harmony with a tenet of Cage, who argued elsewhere:

> (This) separation in space will facilitate the independent action of each performer, who, not constrained by the performance of a part which has been extracted from a score, has turned his mind in the direction of no matter what eventuality. There is the possibility when people are crowded together that they will act like sheep rather than nobly. That is why separation in space is spoken of as facilitating independent action on the part of each performer.[14]

Boulez's *Poèsies pour Pouvoir* (Michaux) for five-track tape and orchestra of 1958, which explored orchestral spatial relationships in the wake of Stockhausen's *Gruppen* for three orchestras (1955–57), was withdrawn, but following *Domaines* the spatial component continued to be featured prominently. . . . *explosant-fixe* . . . (1971), for example, has its eight performers occupying distinct locations on the stage. In this work, communication between the groups

> is established in two ways: either the sound is lifted from its direct source and made to move about the hall, without being transformed; or else it is transformed by another instrument.[15]

In the portion of *Multiples* completed and performed as of 1974 as well as in his *Rituel* (see pp. 672–73) of the same year, Boulez seemed to be allowing other breezes to flow through his music: the primacy of interval in nondodecaphonic melodies; a touch of Stravinsky's energizing rhythms; the extended breath of Messiaen's ornithological melismas, and the full-throated coloring of his brasses. In all, a mixture of tightly controlled structures softened by a degree of performer freedom and spatial designation typically under the control of the composer-conductor suggests the posture that led Boulez to his research institute (Institute for Research and Coordination of Acoustics/Music: IRCAM) with its notable "Espace de Projection" (Fig. 32.2).

In *Kontakte* (1959–60), for four-track tape or alternatively with the addition of a piano and percussion part, Stockhausen moved from the concept of the interdependent "group" to that of the autonomous "moment." Each unit is to be experienced individually, none is more important than any other, and the listener's attention may vary without detriment to the whole, in harmony with the idea that each "moment" is dispensable. Thus a "moment"-form may be said to be without beginning or end and reflects a

> concentration on the Now–on every Now–as if it were a vertical slice dominating over any horizontal conception of time and reaching into timelessness, which I call eternity . . .[16]

In the rejection of the principle that music must be constructed of ideas in an antecedent-consequent fashion, Stockhausen had many fellow-travelers who were concerned with the question of the linkage of musical events. But some charged that this failure to take into account "the problem of time-continuity and of producing feelings of tension and release and therefore of musical motion in the listener"[17] had its natural roots in the problematical notion of total serialism. Begun with *Kontakte* (1956), the final embodiment of this concept of form was achieved in *Momente* (1961) for soprano solo, four choral groups, and thirteen instrumentalists. The notion, however, that the several versions of the work that have been performed result from the potential for random addition or omission is incorrect, as Stockhausen has taken pains to explain:

> *No* "moments" may be omitted except the "moment" I (m) *backwards. No* additional "moments" have been inserted freely. The *Formscheme* was composed *first* in 1961 and included all the moments which have been composed later. It is true that *Momente* has been performed twice in shorter versions because it was not yet ready.[18]

Recognizing perhaps that his moment of influence had come, if only in his rejection—total or partial—by other composers, Cage was content throughout the 1960s and 1970s to preach his anarchy, which increasingly courted anti-art in a fashion reminiscent of the Dadaists of the early 1920s. Yet the anti-ego, anti-masterpiece mentality that nurtures such a view is not only in harmony with Satie but with Eastern philosophy, which had supported Cage's art from its inception. Noting that the purpose of the Indian rhythmic system of *tals* was "to sober and quiet the mind, thus rendering it susceptible to divine influence," Cage determined

> that this *was* the proper purpose of music. In time, I also came to see that all art before the Renaissance, both Oriental and Western, had shared this same basis, that Oriental art had continued to do so right along, and that the Renaissance idea of self-expressive art was therefore heretical.[19]

Cage's attempt to restore the balance, to negate the past traditions of Western music, had found its most radical statement in *4' 33"* (1952). In the first performance David Tudor, appearing on stage, placed a score on the piano. He made no gesture during the allotted time of the title, and at the conclusion closed the lid of the piano and departed. In this spirit, Cage emphasized the role of silence as a frame for sound and suggested a freedom from typical Western modes that few would deny has been salutary. Referring to works like *4' 33"* and others that place a premium on its inherent premise, Cage has stated:

> . . . in this new music nothing takes place but sounds: those that are notated and those that are not. Those that are not notated appear in the written music as silences, opening the doors of the music to the sounds that happen to be in the

environment. This openness exists in the fields of sculpture and architecture. The glass houses of Mies van der Rohe reflect their environment, presenting to the eye images of clouds, trees, or grass, according to the situation. And while looking at the constructions in wire of the sculptor Richard Lippold, it is inevitable that one will see other things, and people too, if they happen to be there at the same time, through the network of wires. There is no such things as an empty space or an empty time. There is always something to see, something to hear. In fact, try as we may to make a silence, we cannot.[20]

While few have taken the elements of silence and chance to Cage's extremes and many have felt the quality of negation inherent in his philosophy of music both perilous and punitive to the creative urge, the use of aleatory passages within more traditional schemes was, as we shall see, to mark Cage's presence on the twentieth-century musical scene not only as catalytic but fundamental to a newly won sensibility.

BROWN, FELDMAN, AND WOLFF

Three composers early joined Cage in New York in helping to establish his aesthetic while developing individual personalities of their own.

Earle Brown (b. 1926) was an early devotee of the Schillinger system whose mathematical basis and graphic components meshed naturally with an early interest in the question of notational alternatives. His *Folio* series of 1952–53 for unspecified instruments contained the first pieces written in graphic notation, which Cage had already taken up by the time of his *Concert* for piano and

Figure 27.3. Earle Brown, score of "December 1952."

orchestra of 1956–57. In the first of the set, entitled "November 1952 (Synergy)," the standard staff was eliminated in favor of a full sheet of 50 lines with conventional note-heads; instruments, clefs, attacks, and the like were to be decided by the performer. In "December 1952" from the same set, Brown achieved his first wholly graphic score with the suppression of all familiar notational devices and the placement of black rectangles of various sizes in a pleasing but irregular pattern on the page. The result (Figure 27.3) says as much about the composer's admiration for the art of Jackson Pollock and Piet Mondrian (Figure 27.4) as it does about how any performance drawn from it might sound.

Figure 27.4. Piet Mondrian, *Pier and Ocean* (1915).

His *Twenty-Five Pages* (1953), in a patent reflection of Calder's mobiles, was the first of his "open-form" compositions, where the order and combination of the specifically written score is left to the performer, while in *Available Forms I* (1961), the first of his orchestral open forms, the conductor determines the inclusion, omission, repetition, and order of materials to be performed. The score is made up of six loose pages, all of which are in view of the eighteen performers, and the conductor indicates which sections are to be played by moving an arrow on a large board which contains the number 1 to 6. Brown's announced aim was not only to cleanse the score of the punishing complexities of the total-serialists, but to encourage the performer thereby to a newly won spontaneity. Both the graphic element and the concept of the open form have continued to characterize Brown's music, which in the 1960s had a considerable vogue.

In the 1930s, Alexander Calder (1898–1976) developed the mobile sculpture—precisely balanced constructions of metal wire, hinged together and weighted so as to move with the slightest current of air (Figure 27.5). Following contact with the Surrealists, who alerted him to the poetic riches of natural as opposed to controlled movement, he abandoned the idea of motor-driven sculptures and settled on random responses to the environment for his mobiles. The analogy with the aesthetic and emerging notations of Brown, Feldman, and others is not only clear but claimed by the composers themselves. While the analogy can hold for the performer as well (confronted with the choices of the score before him), it of necessity diminishes or disappears altogether for the average listener without benefit of notation or knowledge of the performing premise.

Morton Feldman (b. 1926) had studied with Riegger and Wolpe before he met Cage in 1950. From that time on he was intimately associated with Cage, Brown, Wolff, and Tudor, as well as the abstract expressionist painters in New York. His developments in graphic notation are related to but separate from those of Brown, and he has tried various solutions, which include: (a) a reasonably precise notation with free durational values; (b) the use of specific pitches without rhythmic association; (c) the construction of a single part to be played independently by a group of players, thus setting up a field of reverberation from a limited sound source (e.g., *Piece for 4 Pianos*, 1957). The last of these complements Cage's earliest contributions (e.g., *Bacchanale*) to the formation of what was to be dubbed the Minimalist movement (see p. 572). His use of notation that places emphasis on the preselection and ordering of registers (high, middle, low), timbres, densities, and pulse without specification of rhythm or pitch succession can be seen in his *The King of Denmark* (1964) for percussion soloist. Here the notation is as clear and pure as its sound, and the legend at the beginning of the score (Ex. 27.2), which became a hallmark of much music of the 1960s, is the performer's key to making his own version of a piece that, in detail and design, is still very much under the control of the composer.

Example 27.1. Brown, *Available Forms I.*

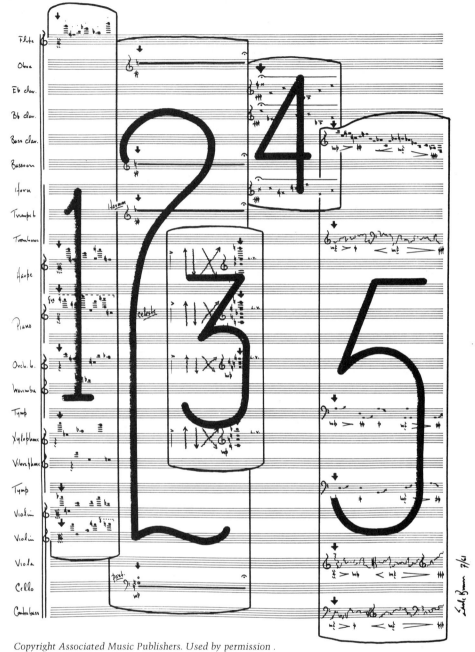

THE KING OF DENMARK (Solo percussionist)

1. Graphed high, middle, and low, with each box equal to MM 66–92. The top line or slightly above the top line, very high. The bottom line or slightly beneath, very low.

2. Numbers represent the amount of sounds to be played in each box.

Figure 27.5. Alexander Calder, *Lobster Trap and Fish Tail* (1939). Hanging mobile: painted steel wire and sheet aluminum, about 8′ 6″ × 9′ 6″.

Collection of The Museum of Modern Art, New York. Commissioned by the Advisory Committee for the stairwell of the Museum. Copyright © ADAGP, Paris/VAGA, New York, 1985.

3. All instruments to be played without sticks or mallets. The performer may use fingers, hand, or any part of his arm.

4. Dynamics are extremely low, and as equal as possible.

5. The thick horizontal line designates clusters. (Instruments should be varied when possible.)

6. Roman numerals represent simultaneous sounds.

7. Large numbers (encompassing high, middle, and low) indicate single sounds to be played in all registers and in any time sequence.

8. Broken lines indicate sustained sounds.

9. Vibraphone is played without motor.

Symbols Used: B—Bell-like sounds; S—Skin instruments; C—Cymbal; G—Gong; R—Roll; T.R.—Tympani roll; △—Triangle; G.R.—Gong Roll.

In the main, Feldman's music since 1970 has relied on conventional notations while preserving the same quietude and absence of dramatic gesture that was the mark of his earlier music. *Rothko Chapel* (1971) for soprano, viola, and

Example 27.2. Feldman, *The King of Denmark*, 2nd system from end.

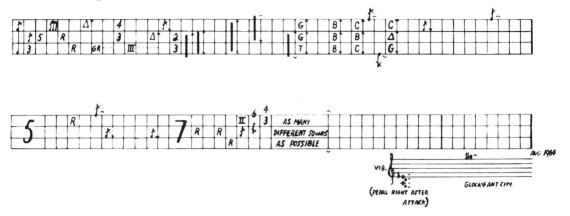

percussion, and a high point of his maturity, is the perfect counterpart to the sanctuary for which it was commissioned—a Houston chapel of stark simplicity articulated by fourteen canvases by Mark Rothko. A hushed and delicate stasis marks the four sections distinguished by subtle changes in color and motion, and a pitch world that is unordered and intuitive.

Christian Wolff (b. 1934), though born in France, came to the United States in 1941 and already by the early 1950s was associated with the group of composers discussed in this section. His earliest scores are completely notated economies involving a minimum number of pitches (three pitches only for both *Duo for Violins*, 1950, and *Serenade*, 1951), which is minimalist with respect to pitch but arbitrary though explicit with respect to orders of repetition or duration. Later in works such as *Duo for Pianists II* (1958) and *In Between Pieces* (1963) for three players, Wolff liberated his performers to listen attentively to each other. Rejecting the idea of the conductor, he provided his musicians with the basic raw materials sufficient to construct a music through a set of cues played within a specific time span.

CONCEPTUALISTS AND CONSERVATIVES

In the early 1960s, Cage's influence was further manifested in the so-called Fluxus movement, whose practitioners seemed like nothing so much as revivifiers of the Dadaist absurdities of the 1920s. One who joined their ranks was La Monte Young (b. 1935), but unlike most of them he had been introduced to Cage's music while a pupil of Stockhausen at the Darmstadt courses in 1959. His scores, alternately titled simply "Composition" or with extravagant word assemblages of paragraph length worthy of Satie, were typically verbal instructions with an inescapable charm. *Composition 1960 no. 5* instructs that a butterfly should be set free in a performance area with the doors open, the composition ending when the butterfly flies out. *Composition 1960 no. 7*, which states only that a notated perfect fifth be held for a long time, focuses on the composer's infatuation with the purest materials contemplated over an extended time span.

The whole category of "conceptual" music, of which Young's butterfly music is representative, held brief sway in numerous quarters. Paralleling a movement in the visual arts wherein an image is conceived and described but not executed, Nelson Howe's *Fur Music* (a piece of notched carpet is stroked and a music imagined) is an extreme example of a trend that was momentarily explored by Stockhausen in *Aus den sieben Tagen* (1968) and *Für kommende Zeiten* (1968–70), whose scores are made up solely of verbal directions. For the subsection entitled "Es" from the former set, the composer provided the following description:

> *Es* reaches an extreme of intuitive playing in the instruction to play only when he has achieved the state of *non thinking,* and to stop whenever one begins to think. By this means a state of playing should be achieved in which one acts and reacts purely intuitively. As soon as a player thinks of something (e.g., *that* he is playing; *what* he is playing; *what* someone else is playing or has played; *how* he should react; *that* a car is driving past outside, etc.), he should stop, and only start again when he is *just* listening, and at one with what is heard.[21]

His *Sternklang* of 1971, while anchored in a multiple-chord base, is a meditational exercise of necessity performed out of doors on a clear night wherein rhythm, tone-color, and interval are drawn from a reading of the star constellations and "is intended as a preparation for beings from other stars and for the day of their arrival."[22] Its relation to Cage's *Atlas eclipticalis* (1961) and Dallapiccola's *Sicut umbra* (1970), both of which contain passages whose pitches were derived from placing star maps across the staves, is apparent. At each turn of his career, Stockhausen has insisted on the legitimacy as well as the compatability of such intuitive gestures linked to a highly developed structural plan; ultimately intended for realization they fail to qualify as classical Concept Art. Others more totally committed to an aesthetic whose vision attains to Tom Johnson's *Celestial Music for Imaginary Trumpets* (1974)—a single five-note chord written between the 99th and 103rd leger line above the treble clef—must nonetheless be haunted by the seemingly unsurpassable reduction of Cage's *4' 33"*, which only he could follow with *0' 00"*.

Beyond the New York group identified with Cage and the Conceptualists, interest in harnessing some of their more viable premises also began to surface among more traditional European musicians. Many composers sought both to further challenge the stance of the serialists and to promote a sense of inquiry regarding the essence of sound and its manipulation, function, and performance. The aesthetic distance between them was often chasmic. Following his first use of twelve-note series in *Funeral Music* (1956), the introduction of aleatoric or chance ingredients by Lutosławski in his *Venetian Games* (1961) is symptomatic of the generalized use to which many of the attitudes of Cage and company were put beginning in the 1960s. Prompted by a hearing of Cage's *Concert for piano and orchestra* of 1958, Lutosławski's endorsement was neither anti-serial nor pro-Zen with respect to theoretical or philosophical base, but rather practical and conceived as an isolated detail technique. In assessing the importance of aleatoric procedures to the composer's creative arsenal, he spoke of "the possibility it admits of expanding a work's rhythmic interest without an increase of performance difficulties, and the scope it gives to individual instruments within the orchestra to play freely. In my work, however, the composer remains the directing force."[23]

Ultimately both the sense of game, or performer participation, and sonic freedom that had been won through Cage's fresh inquiry led to an ever-widening field of possibilities. The listener without benefit of score could scarcely be aware of whatever sense of exhiliration might have been felt in the live performance by the players of music by Cage, Feldman, or Wolff. But with Ligeti, as well as with Lutosławski, the surface features that led to immediately perceptible textures; with Xenakis, whose architectural training and mathematical base led to the construction of a "stochastic" music that placed a premium on revolving sonorous masses; and with the pulsed Minimalists, who laid out an audible process that was perceptible as well as hypnotizing, some of the consequences and future potential of an important pioneering movement became apparent to all.

MINIMALISM: A NEWER SIMPLICITY

In the inordinately sustained or repetitive use of simple materials characterized by a fondness for intervals with the simplest ratios, La Monte Young (b. 1935) revealed a kinship with Harry Partch's and Lou Harrison's preference for just intonation and a decidedly Eastern philosophical bias. But it was not only scores like Young's *Composition 1960 No. 7* (consisting solely of a notated perfect 5th "to be held for a long time") and other unending pieces conceived for the Theater of Eternal Music, founded in 1964, that helped to prepare the way for the advent of Minimalism. The hypnotic repetitions subtly propelled by changing accents in Cowell's percussion piece, *Ostinato Pianissimo*, of 1934; the mesmerizing pulse figurations of many of Cage's earliest works for prepared piano; and the static quietude of Morton Feldman's numerous nonevent scores had also helped to establish a new way of thinking about and listening to music. Quickly, however, a group of younger American composers of a similar orientation extended such beginnings to include improvisation and the idea of "process" to the arena of reduced means.

RILEY, REICH, AND GLASS

Riley. Terry Riley (b. 1935) belongs with Steve Reich (b. 1936) and Philip Glass (b. 1937) to this founding group of composers generally referred to as Minimalists because of their general reduction of materials and emphasis on repetitive schemes and stasis. First associated with Young and the Fluxus group in New York, Riley went to Europe in 1962 where he worked in the French radio-television studios investigating the potential of pattern, pulse, and phrase. The patterns were short, the pulse was steady, and the phase relationships were based on the idea of gradual nonsynchronization. The tape loop, a recurring ostinato, and the various modifiers available in the studio were ready-made for his investigations into La Monte Young's dream world, the first result of which was his *Mescalin Mix* (1962–63). Riley soon moved to live performance in his *Keyboard Studies* (1963), built from a four-note phrase repeated at a swift tempo, and then to his well-known ensemble piece, *In C* (1964). This work is developed from the repetition of fifty-three figures of which the opening five are:

Example 27.3. Riley, *In C*, opening.

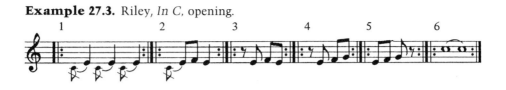

Any number of players may participate; listening to the Pulse ("even octave eighth notes drummed steadily on the top two Cs of the keyboard throughout the duration of a performance")[24] and to each other, they determine in improvisatory fashion the number of repetitions of a given figure, the placement of accents within the figures, and how often and how long to rest between repetitions. The gradual extensions and contractions of brief patterns, establish a hypnotic ever-changing atmosphere whose perceptual ambiguity has been held analogous to the visual shifts of op art.

In early works such as *In C* which contributed to the first definitions of Minimalism, a collection of endorsements as well as rejections were apparent: the music carried an openly tonal bias, though clearly many of its premises could have been worked out in non-tonal terrain; the music may have endorsed an anti-masterpiece mentality but its dimensions were typically monumental; while seeming to reject the idea of composing in the procrustean forms, its devotion to the idea of process from germinal sources suggested a link with classic repertoires whose formal foundation resided in the potential for working out musical ideas of a highly organic nature; the indeterminate (e.g., the number of repetitions for each pattern of *In C*) is coupled with a total control over the nature and quantity of the materials (limited time values, tonal orientation, 53 figures). Appearing a decade after the appearance of Boulez's *Structures 1a*, Stockhausen's *Kreuzspiel* and Cage's *Music of Changes*, the Minimalist movement endorsed neither total control or chance as an exclusive credo. In its freedom and in its rigidity it partook of the experience of both. While this may have resulted primarily as a result of an infatuation with exotic music systems, it would be impossible to claim innocence of the Western avant-garde for its chief protagonists.

After *In C* Riley returned to the studio to develop his "time-lag accumulator," a series of tape recorders with delayed playback, which enables the live solo performer to project successively played sequences simultaneously. His *A Rainbow in Curved Air* (1970; see p. 499) utilizes this equipment in an improvisation based on modal scales and rhythmic patterns that may be likened to the *talas* of Indian music, of which Riley has become a serious student.

Reich.   Steve Reich, a student of African drumming, has also put his interest in exotic music to personal account in a series of pieces that has emphasized ensembles of the same instruments, either live or together with electronically modified versions, as in *Piano Phase* (1967) for two pianos; *Violin Phase* (1967) for violin and three-track tape or four violins; *Four Organs* (1970) for four electronic organs and maracas; or *Drumming* (1971) for eight small tuned drums, three maracas, three glockenspiels, voices, and piccolo. A trend toward greater timbral diversity is apparent in his *Music for 18 Musicians* (1975), which undoubtedly reflects the growth of his own ensemble, Steve Reich and Musicians, the formation of which secured his desire that his music should be performed only by groups of which he is a member. Concerning *Four Organs*, which may be taken as a representative work, Reich describes the gradual process that is the piece:

> *Four Organs* . . . begins with a short pulsing chord which gradually gets longer and longer in duration. As the chord stretches out, slowly resolving and unresolving, a sort of slow motion music is created. The maracas lay down a steady time grid of even eighth notes throughout, enabling the performers to play together while mentally counting up to as much as 200 beats and more on a given cycle of sustained tones. *Four Organs* is the only piece of music I am aware of that is composed exclusively of the gradual augmentation (lengthening) of individual tones within a single chord. From beginning to end there are no changes of pitch or timbre, all changes are rhythmic and simply consist of gradually increasing durations.[25]

Schoenberg's single chord for the third of his *Five Pieces for Orchestra*, op. 16, may be seen as only a dim ancestor because of the introduction of shifting color and modulation, but in its use of canon (Ex. 2.9) it is a spiritual cousin to Reich and Riley, both of whom are fascinated with such properties. This is especially audible in Reich's *Come Out* (1966), which utilizes a brief spoken phrase ("come out to show them") recorded on two channels which, beginning together in unison, gradually separate into two, four, and eight voices.

In "Music as a Gradual Process," Reich summed up his point of view and his approach in a series of aphorisms, two of which read:

> I am interested in perceptible processes. I want to be able to hear the process happening throughout the sounding music.

> Though I may have the pleasure of discovering musical processes and composing the musical material to run through them, once the process is set up and loaded it runs by itself.[26]

As the Minimalists' mesmerizing repetitions began to spell a new sense of time, to some they seemed psychedelically in tune with the opium reveries of Baudelaire. Producing the effect of a hypnotically reiterated mantra (see Stockhausen's piece by that name) or subtly changing raga (Messiaen), the wave motion compositions of the Impressionist-Symbolists typically bathed in a halo of pedal had been transformed into Phase music seen in some quarters during the troubled years of the Vietnam War in the early 1970s as the ideal background for a mind trip with Timothy Leary. Debussy's *Les sons et les parfums tournent dans l'air du soir* had given way to Riley's *A Rainbow in Curved Air*. Though controlled experiments with mescalin and other stimulants were openly discussed by Michaux, Huxley, Kagel, and numerous others, the necessity for such agents in the service of an expanded perception was widely rejected by most composers, the practice deemed not only injurious but passé. Nonetheless, it is only fair to report that the rise of Minimalism coincided with the age of the Flower Children, Haight-Ashbury in San Francisco, and the increased use of marijuana and other drugs. The initial search for a heightened aural perception by both performer and audience found a momentary, if potentially dangerous, ally.

Glass. The extension of minimalist procedures into the world of music theater has been notably accomplished by Philip Glass, whose training included

Example 27.4. Reich, *Four Organs*, mm. 1–4, m. 42.

work not only with Nadia Boulanger but also Ravi Shankar. The gradual contraction and extension of simple, diatonic formulae in a work like his *Music in Similar Motion* (1969) strikes a close affinity with the procedures of Riley's *In C*, but the highly repetitive surfaces of a series of theater pieces from *Einstein on the Beach* (1975) and *Satyagraha* (1980) to *The Photographer* (1982) and *Akhnaten* (1984) has found a new context and a new audience. Like Reich, Glass insists on control of all performances of his music, and the persona aspect of his presentations coupled with a music of loud dynamic, strong pulse, and diatonic tunefulness has openly invaded the world of the rock enthusiast.

The use of minimalist procedures in the confection of full-fledged operas, however, shares an even more intimate connection with the minimalist qualities of numerous earlier "happenings" and brands of music-theater, particularly pieces by Robert Ashley (from *Wolfman*, 1964, to *Perfect Lives (Private Parts*, completed in 1981) and others of the ONCE group formed in Ann Arbor in the early 1960s (see p. 599). Their reliance on various electronic and video components emphasized the compatability of Minimalism and mixed media.

NONPULSED MINIMALISM.   The surface quality of much minimalist music shares a common corridor with other music that is precisely notated, lacking in a regular and insistent pulse, and typically viewed from a different vantage point. Among non-American composers, the Hungarian György Ligeti shares a similar approach in many of his works such as *Atmosphères* (1961) for large orchestra (used as a sound track for the film *2001*), *Continuum* (1968) for harpsichord—a piece whose persistent figurations carry a not-so-distant affinity with the opening of Debussy's *Feux d'artifice*)—and *Volumina* (1961–62) for organ (see p. 622). Typically in these works the sense of ebb and flow of sound masses emerges from densely polyphonic constructions. Dubbed "micropolyphony" by the composer, the number and crowding of the various parts completely obscures the individual voices. From the middle 1960s, Ligeti sought to clarify the components somewhat, while still holding to the same general constructive outlook. In his orchestral *Melodien* (1971), for example, melodic fragments in a revolving textural mass persistently disappear at the moment of recognition, while other melodic ideas—extracted and illuminated from a murky background—are afforded only a fleeting presentation. The *Double Concerto* (1972) for flute, oboe, and orchestra is in two movements, and may serve as a *locus classicus* of the two moods of Ligeti's nonpulsed Minimalism: The first movement, an extended moment of stasis awash in a blend of microtones from the principal instruments, which offers a new alternative to the idea of diatonic versus chromatic; and a second movement which, in the composer's words, "Starts with gentle undulations and gradually rises to an insane prestissimo requiring tremendous virtuosity."[27] Numerous texturally related works appeared in the decade of the 1960s and 1970s by composers such as Karel Husa (*The Apotheosis of This Earth,* 1970) or even Mauricio Kagel, whose *Transición I* (1958–60) differed from most electronic pieces of the period in its employment of slow changes in timbre in a nonchanging pitch field.

The reduction of materials and the sense of fluctuating stasis of all such music may be traced, however, to numerous previous sources beyond Cage and company: to Schoenberg's op. 16, no. 3, where a single chord is filtered through various colors; to the subtle metamorphosis of Skriabin's mystic chord in

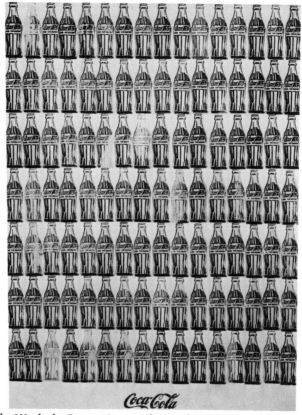

Figure 27.6. Andy Warhol, *Green Coca-Cola Bottles* (1962). Oil. 82½" × 57". Warhol's repetitive use of familiar figures (Marilyn Monroe, Campbell Soup Cans, Coca-Cola bottles), sometimes presented without change, sometimes with slight modification, has been held to be analogous to the practices of the Minimalist composers.

Collection of Whitney Museum of American Art. Gift of the Friends of the Whitney Museum of American Art. Acq. #68.25. © VAGA, New York, 1986.

Prometheus; to Varèse's *Intégrales,* whose static opening the composer likened unto a crystal; to Stravinsky's numerous static codas (from *Les noces* and the *Symphony of Psalms* to the *Symphony in C* and the *Requiem Canticles*); and to countless works by Messiaen such as the final movement in the *Quartet for the End of Time,* where spellbinding repetitions in the piano not only support a violin solo of great lyric beauty but also induce a suspension of time.

Although the ancestry of phase (minimal) music as well as other brands of musical stasis is traceable in part to such specific Western precursors, its foundation in Eastern traditions is also apparent, as its most noted practitioners will insist. Thus it is obvious that this new sense of time without end, of a music that seems to continue after the music has stopped, is not the creation of the Minimalists. The repetitive pentatonic field audible in the final movement of George Crumb's *Makrokosmos III: "Music for a Summer Evening"* (1974) exemplifies the efficacy of the idea in a language spiritually indebted to the time legacy of Debussy-Schoenberg-Varèse-Messiaen-Reich-Ligeti while sounding like none of them. And Gorecki's *Symphony No. 3* (1976) for soprano and orchestra, though linked by musical ideas that are spiritually akin to Prokofiev, develops its limited materials at such a leisurely pace that it seems to create a fusion of the Mahlerian adagio and the Minimalist's unlabored turnover of events. At the present moment it appears that Minimalism as a limited American movement may have crested and faded; the larger field of which it is representative, however, may have only just been tapped.

REPERTOIRE (International Avant-garde)

Cage, *Six Short Inventions* (1933)
> *First Construction in Metal* (1939), perc
> *Bacchanale* (1938), prepared pf
> *Imaginary Landscape No. 1* (1939), 2 variable-speed turntables, frequency recording, muted pf, cymbal
> *A Book of Music* (1944)
> *Three Dances* (1945), 2 prepared pf
> *Sonatas and Interludes* (1946–48), prepared pf
> *Concerto* (1951), prepared pf, orch
> *Imaginary Landscape No. 4* (1951), 12 radios, 24 players
> *Music of Changes* (1951), pf
> *Imaginary Landscape* (1952), any 42 recordings
> *4' 33"* (1952), tacet for any inst/insts
> *Concert for Piano and Orchestra* (1957–58)
Brown, *Folio* series (1952–53), unspecified instr: "November 1952," "December 1952"
> *Twenty-five pages* (1953)
> *Available Forms I* (1961)
Feldman, *Piece for 4 Pianos* (1957)
> *The King of Denmark* (1964), perc
> *The Rothko Chapel* (1971), chorus 2vv, cel, perc, va
Wolff, *Duo for Violins* (1950)
> *Serenade* (1951)
> *Duo for Pianists II* (1958)
> *In Between Pieces* (1963)
Young, *Composition 1960 no. 5*
> *Composition 1960 no. 7*
Howe, *Fur Music*
Stockhausen, *Aus den sieben Tagen* (1968)
> *Für kommende Zeiten* (1968–70)
> *Sternklang* (1971)
Lutosławski, *Venetian Games* (1961), orch

READING (International Avant-garde)

Pierre Boulez, "Aléa," *Nouvelle Revue francaise*, no. 59, November 1, 1957; Eng. trans. in *Perspectives of New Music*, iii.1 (1964), 42–53, and in *Notes of an Apprenticeship* (New York, 1968), 35–51.
Antonie Goléa, *Recontres avec Pierre Boulez* (Paris, 1958), 229.
John Cage, *Silence* (Middletown, Conn., 1961): "To Describe the Process of Composition Used in *Music of Changes* and *Imaginary Landscape no. 4*," 57–59; "The Future of Music: Credo," 3–6; "Experimental Music," 7–12; "History of Experimental Music in the United States," 68–75.
Pierre Boulez, "Sonate, que me veux-tu?" trans. D. Noakes and P. Jacobs in *Perspectives of New Music*, i.2 (1963), 32–94, and in *Orientations* (Cambridge, Mass., 1986), 143–54.
Karlheinz Stockhausen, "Momentform" in *Text*, i (1963), 189–210.
John Cage, *A Year from Monday* (Middletown, Conn., 1967).
Leonard B. Meyer, "The End of the Renaissance" in *Music, the Arts and Ideas* (Chicago, 1967).

Pierre Boulez, "Eventuellement" in *Notes of an Apprenticeship* (New York, 1968), 175.

John Cage, *Notations* (New York, 1969).

Eric Salzman, "Milton Babbitt and John Cage, Parallels and Paradoxes," *Stereo Review*, xxii.4 (1969), 60.

R. C. Clark, "Total Control and Chance in Musics: A Philosophical Analysis," *Journal of Aesthetics and Art Criticism*, xxviii (1970), 335; xxix (1970), 53.

Richard Kostelanetz, ed., *John Cage* (New York, 1970).

Pierre Boulez, *Penser la musique aujourd'hui* (Paris, 1963). Eng. trans. by S. Bradshaw and R. R. Bennett as *Boulez on Music Today* (Cambridge, Mass., 1971), 26.

Chou Wen-Chung, "Asian Concepts and Twentieth-Century Western Composers," *Musical Quarterly*, lvii (1971), 211.

Michael Nyman, "Cage and Satie," *The Musical Times*, cxiv (1973), 1227.

Karl H. Wörner, *Stockhausen: His Life and work* (Rodenkirchen, 1963; Eng. trans., enlarged, 1973), 110.

Pierre Boulez, *Par volonté et par hasard: entretiens avec Célestin Deliège* (Paris, 1975); English translation as *Conversations with Célestin Deliège* (London, 1976), especially Chapter XII: "The Concept of Mobility: *The Third Piano Sonata—Éclat—Domaines*," 81–88.

Roger Maconie, *The Works of Karlheinz Stockhausen* (London, 1976).

Anne Trenkamp, "The Concept of 'Aléa' in Boulez's 'Constellation-Miroir'," *Music and Letters*, li.1 (January 1976), 1–10.

Paul Griffiths, *Modern Music: The Avant-Garde Since 1945* (London, 1981): Chapter 4, "New York, 1951–53: Cage and the Road to Silence"; Chapter 7, "Chance and Choice"; Chapter 10, "Indeterminacy: Changing the System."

REPERTOIRE (Minimalism)

Adams, *Grand Pianola Music* (1982)
Ashley, *Perfect Lives (Private Parts)* (1981)
Glass, *Einstein on the Beach* (1975)
Glass, *Satyagraha* (1981)
Glass, *The Photographer* (1982)
Glass, *Akhnaten* (1984)
Kagel, *Transición I* (1958–60)
Ligeti, *Atmosphères* (1961), orch
Ligeti, *Volumina* (1961–62), org
Ligeti, *Continuum* (1968), hpd
Ligeti, *Melodien* (1971), orch
Ligeti, *Double Concerto* (1972), fl, ob, orch
Reich, *Come Out* (1966)
Reich, *Violin Phase* (1967), vn and 3-track tape or 4 vn
Reich, *Four Organs* (1970), 4 elec org and maracas
Reich, *Drumming* (1971), 8 small tuned drums, 3 maracas, 3 glockenspiels, vv, pic
Reich, *Clapping Music* (1972)
Reich, *Six Pianos* (1973)
Reich, *Music for Eighteen Musicians* (1976)
Reich, *Octet* (1979), 2 pf, str qrt, 2 cl, bass cl, fl, pic
Reich, *Tehillim* (1981)
Reich, *The Desert Music* (1983)
Reich, *Sextet* (1984)
Riley, *Mescalin Mix* (1962–63)
Riley, *Keyboard Studies* (1963)
Riley, *In C* (1964), melody insts
Riley, *A Rainbow in Curved Air* (1970), partly improvised, multiple recording techniques
Riley, *Poppy Nogood's Phantom Band* (1970), as above
Young, *Composition 1960 No. 7* (1960), a held perfect 5th

READING (Minimalism)

La Monte Young and Marian Zazeela, *Selected Writings* (Munich, 1970).

Erhard Karkoschka, *Notation in New Music* (New York, 1972).

H. Wiley Hitchcock, *Music in the United States*, 2nd ed. (Engelwood Cliffs, 1974).

Michael Nyman, *Experimental Music: Cage and Beyond* (London, 1974).

Steve Reich, *Writings about Music* (Halifax, 1974).

Eric Salzman, *Twentieth-Century Music: An Introduction* (Englewood Cliffs, 1974), 186–189.

David Cope, *New Music Notation* (Dubuque, 1976).

Paul Griffiths, *Modern Music: The Avant-Garde Since 1945* (London, 1981), 176–181.

K. Robert Schwarz, "Steve Reich: Music As a Gradual Process," *Perspectives of New Music*, xix (1980–81), 373–92; xx (1981–82), 225–86.

John Rockwell, "Philip Glass: The Orient, the Visual Arts and the Evolution of Minimalism" and "Robert Ashley: Post-Cageian Experimentation and New Kinds of Collaboration" in *All American Music: Composition in the Late Twentieth Century* (New York, 1983), 96–108, 109–122.

Wem Mertens, *American Minimal Music* (New York, 1983).

H. Wiley Hitchcock, "Henry Cowell's *Ostinato Pianissimo*," *Musical Quarterly*, lxx.1 (1984), 23–44.

Keith Potter, "The Recent Phases of Steve Reich," *Contact*, xxix (Spring 1985), 28–34.

Keith Potter, "Steve Reich: Thoughts for His 50th-Birthday Year," *Musical Times* (January 1986), 13–17.

PART VIII

THE QUEST FOR NEW SOUNDS

Today with the technical means that exist and are easily adaptable, the differentiation of the various masses and different planes as well as these beams of sound, could be made discernible to the listener by means of certain acoustical arrangements. Moreover, such an acoustical arrangement would permit the delimitation of what I call "zones of intensities." These zones would be differentiated by various timbres or colors and different loudnesses . . . The role of color or timbre would be completely changed from being incidental, anecdotal, sensual, or picturesque; it would become an agent of delineation, like the different colors on a map separating different areas, and an integral part of form. . . .

Moreover, the new musical apparatus I envisage, able to emit sounds of any number of frequencies, will extend the limits of the lowest and highest registers, hence new organizations of the vertical resultants; chords, their arrangements, their spacings—that is, their oxygenation . . . The never-before-thought-of use of the inferior resultants and of the differential and additional sounds may also be expected. An entirely new magic of sound!

—Edgard Varèse, "New Instruments and New Music" (1936) from *The Liberation of Sound* (ed. and annotated by Chou Wen-chung), *Perspectives of New Music*, v. 1 (Fall–Winter 1966), 11–19.

CHAPTER 28

ELECTRONICS AND EXPLORATIONS OF DURATION, TIMBRE, AND SPACE

BACKGROUNDS

In 1904, Schoenberg wrote an article entitled "The Future of the Organ" in which he envisioned a highly portable instrument capable of being played like a typewriter by two to four players, with a range of dynamics from the softest pianissimo to the loudest fortissimo, a range of seven to eight octaves, and a spectrum of sixty to seventy different colors.[1] Two years later, the invention of the vacuum tube by Lee De Forest and of the gargantuan Dynamophone, weighing 200 tons, by Thaddeus Cahill prompted Busoni to speak further of the potential of music-making machines, and the period of the 1920s, as we have seen, brought forth the inventions of Thérémin, Trautwein, and Martenot.

Throughout this period, and continuing through the early 1930s, various artists associated with the Bauhaus, founded in 1919 in Germany by the architect Walter Gropius, continually exploited the interplay of architecture, photography, film, painting, light, and sound transformation. Lothar Schreyer, Oskar Schlemmer, Gertrude Grunow, Ludwig Hirschfeld-Mack, Laszlo Moholy-Nagy, and Paul Hindemith are only some of the more important names associated with this group, whose investigations were paralleled by Laurens Hammond, Varèse, Hoérée, Honegger, and Toch in other countries. Inquiry ranged from the possibilities of variable turntables, reverse turntables, groove scratching, film sound-track composition, megaphones, and speech modification.[2] The advances in electronically produced sounds during the 1920s remained largely undeveloped throughout the 1930s and 1940s, however, although arguably envisioned by numerous composers. In the period following the end of World War II the new technology found a counterpart to The Bomb as image in the Electronic Studio as apparatus, provoking numerous sonic explosions that made many wonder if technology as the plaything of the composer had not achieved the upper hand.

The emergence of the tape recorder and a ready network of radio studios in Europe combined to set the stage for three independent centers: Paris (Club d'Essai,

1948, reorganized as Groupe de Récherche de Musique Concrète, 1951, and again as Groupe de Récherches Musicales, 1958, with Schaeffer, Henry, Varèse, and Xenakis as the principal figures); Cologne (Studio für Elektronische Musik, 1951, with Eimert and Stockhausen); and New York (Luening and Ussachevsky, privately from 1952; Varèse, privately from 1953; Columbia-Princeton Electronic Music Center, 1959, with Babbitt, Luening, Ussachevsky, Sessions, Varèse, Davidovsky, and Wuorinen). The distinctions in the early years between what the French called *musique concrète* (manipulation of sounds found in nature), the German *elektronische musik* (based on electronically generated sounds), and the American fascination for the modification of produced or imitated instrumental sounds soon dissolved as studios in Toronto, Tokyo, Milan, Brussels, and Warsaw appeared devoted to the exploration of the whole range of sonic generation and manipulation.

The advantage of the tape recorder was the ease with which it permitted transformations known from earlier experiments with phono-discs. Regardless of the origins of the sound material, the tape recording quickly demonstrated its capacity to allow the following: (1) alteration of speed; (2) direction reversal, changing not only note order but attack characteristics; (3) splicing, editing, and isolation of components; (4) addition of reverberation, filtering, mixing; (5) volume control; and (6) the confection of loops that constituted a kind of ostinato technique to be used in conjunction with other materials.

FRANCE AND THE NETHERLANDS: SCHAEFFER, VARÈSE'S *POÈME ÉLECTRONIQUE*, XENAKIS

As early as 1948, Schaeffer's *Etude aux chemins de fer*, a three-minute work based on the manipulation (juxtaposition and reassemblage without sonic modification) of the sound of railway trains, and his *Etude aux casseroles*, utilizing the sound of saucepans, were broadcast over French radio in a program billed as a "concert of noises." The direct manipulation of sound without recourse to the abstractions of a musical score led him to label his music *concrète*. Although Schaefer denied with a curious vehemence the legacy of a loosely defined Futurist Succession via Russolo's Intonarumori, Antheil's *Ballet mécanique*, and Honegger's *Pacific 231*, his titles, perhaps unwittingly, acknowledged it.[3] Schaeffer's accomplishments attracted many composers, among them Messiaen and his pupils Pierre Henry, Karlheinz Stockhausen, and Pierre Boulez, all of whom at one point or another made pilgrimages to Schaeffer's studio. Henry's *Symphonie pour un homme seul* of 1949–50 was a work derived solely from human noise (virtually the whole catalogue of Futurist vocalisations; see p. 237) wedded to instrumental and percussion sounds. The climax to this phase in France came with his *Veil of Orpheus*, drawn from an earlier opera written in collaboration with Schaeffer and exhibiting a resplendent array of virtually all the techniques known at the time: spoken chorus, voice and instruments subjected to speed changes, glissandi, reverberation, and the like. While Henry was to remain close to Schaeffer's domain, Messiaen after a single work for tape entitled *Timbres-durées* (1952) and Boulez following two *Etudes* (1951–52), all of which have remained unpublished, moved in other directions. Boulez's essential suspicion of electronically produced music or electronically modified live performance was to remain until the 1970s.

The hope of the American Edgard Varèse for a new break-through in the realms of timbre and space had been suggested both by his compositions and his essays during the period of the 1920s through the 1940s. By his own admission, the touchstone for his development had been Busoni's *Sketch for a New Aesthetic of Music* (1906), and in works like *Amériques* (1918–21), *Hyperprism* (1922–23), and *Ionisation* (1929–31) his use of unusal percussion ensembles and such Futurist-sounding items as sirens stemmed principally from his urge to explore and extend the realm of sound more than from any desire to subscribe to a particular aesthetic. His visions for an electronic future, shared by Cage in the 1930s, were, however, not to be quickly realized. Disappointment in 1933 over the lack of support from the Bell Telephone Co. and the Guggenheim Foundation for a proposed center for electric-instrument research led to personal depression and virtual creative silence during the period 1936–47. Although his interest in electronic instruments was manifested as early as *Ecuatorial* (1932–34) in the projected use of a Thérémin and eventual inclusion of two ondes martenots, it was not until 1953 with the gift of an Ampex tape recorder that he could begin to tackle many of the questions that had been haunting him for years.

Although at work on *Déserts* (1950–54) for fourteen winds, piano, and five percussion instruments, he set about composing three optional electronic interludes based on factory noises and percussion instruments. He was invited by Schaeffer to come to the Paris radio-television studios in 1954 to complete the piece, which was given the first live stereo broadcast in France later that year. He was back in New York in 1955, but with the commission of the *Poème électronique* for the Brussels Exposition of 1958 he returned to Europe in 1957 to work at the Philips laboratories in Eindhoven, the Netherlands. In this composition distinctions between French (*musique concrète*) and German (*electronische Musik*) attitudes with respect to source materials were dissolved.

Utilizing not only piano, percussion (including drums and temple bells or gongs) and organ, solo and choral voices, and a collection of machine noises (among which the sound of a jet airplane is readily identifiable), he constructed the *concrète* portion of his composition through subtle modifications of attack, reverberation, and timbral filtration. The gong motive at the beginning of the composition is modified by six different attack characteristics, the last of these being filtered so as to lower the pitch approximately an octave. The use of changes in tape speed (e.g., the solo female voice near the end where the range is extended beyond human capacity) and tape editing (cutoffs, splicing) play an equally important role in the work. To the *concrète* elements Varèse has added electronic sounds that range from simple sine-wave sounds (containing no overtones) to white-noise (including all possible frequencies).

The form of the piece can be discussed as any other with respect to the recurrence of motivic or, especially, timbral ideas. David Cope has constructed a particularly clear diagram of its principal ideas that serves the same function for the listener as the *Hörpartitur* constructed for Stockhausen's *Studie II* (Ex. 28.5) or Ligeti's *Artikulation* (Ex. 28.6), and has concluded that several types of rondo forms may be heard.[4] He distinguishes the following basic materials: gongs (large bells); long, held tones (pedals); sawtooth-type noise elements; rising motive (2nds); drums; rising glissandi; voice(s). In addition to various rondo patterns fashioned out of this material, he has also properly noted the possibility of hearing the work as a simple three-part form, each of which begins similarly with gongs followed by long pedal notes.

In spite of its sonic variety, the piece is a remarkably integrated collage. Varèse took pains, however, to distinguish between his approach to electronic composition and that of another fellow American in a statement that is both clarifying and accurate:

I respect and admire Milton Babbitt, but he certainly represents a completely different view of electronic music from mine. It seems to me that he wants to exercise maximum control over certain materials, as if he were *above* them. But I want to be *in* the material, part of the acoustical vibration, so to speak. Babbitt composes his material first and then gives it to the synthesizer, while I want to generate something directly by electronic means. In other words, I think of musical space as open rather than bounded, which is why I speak about projection in the sense that I want simply to project a sound, a musical thought, to initiate it, and then to let it take its own course. I do not want an *a priori* control of all its aspects.[5]

Intended for projection over some 350 speakers placed in architectural conjunction with an edifice designed by Corbusier, one can only imagine from the available stereo recording and the diagram of the sound paths (Figure 28.1) the effect of *Poème électronique* in its original surroundings, now destroyed. David Ernst has described it thus:

The taped sounds were distributed by telephone relays among various combinations of loudspeakers. These "sound paths" were determined by a fifteen channel

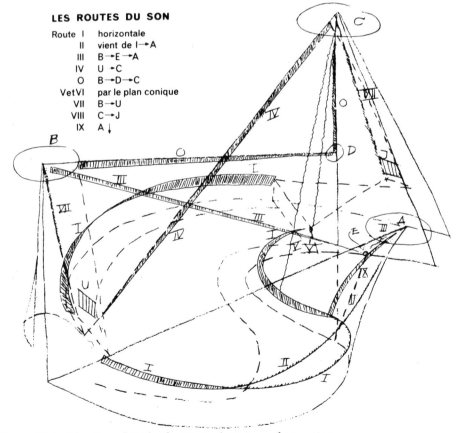

Figure 28.1. The Sound Paths for Varèse's *Poème électronique*.
Fondation Le Corbusier, Paris.

control tape, each track of which contained twelve separate signals. Therefore, 180 (15 × 12) control signals were available to regulate the sound routes, lighting effects and a variety of light sources which consisted of film projectors and projection lanterns, spotlights, ultra violet lamps, bulbs, and fluorescent lamps of various colors.[6]

To say "designed by Corbusier" is something of an overstatement. While the project was under his direction, his chosen collaborators were Varèse and another architect-composer, Iannis Xenakis. He insisted, over the preference of the Philips company for a native composer, that it was to be Varèse, take it or leave it. And to Xenakis, a young architectural assistant, he entrusted the basic design of the pavilion—a design that, in an exceptional authorization, he agreed to cosign as a testimony of respect. However, Corbusier was actively engaged in overseeing many details of the project, including the choice of images that were to be projected during the performance of Varèse's music: animals, idols, *masques et visages*, paintings, manuscripts, and diverse scenes. Synchronization was out of the question (recall the collaboration between Léger and Antheil in *Ballet mécanique*), but Corbusier had stipulated originally only that, toward the middle of the piece, a sudden and total silence should take place accompanied by the "brutality of a white light." Even this seemingly simple suggestion was not honored, however; Varèse, speaking of his *Poème électronique* in-progress, told him: "My dear Corbu, I cannot realize this silence; it [the middle] is precisely the moment of the greatest noise in the entire piece."

Although Stockhausen's *Gesang der Jünglinge* for five-track tape had received its public premiere in Cologne on May 30, 1956, the inaugural performance of Varèse's *Poème électronique* on May 2, 1958 in Brussels was undoubtedly perceived as a breakthrough by all those present. Witnesses included Stockhausen, Kagel, Berio, Maderna, Pousseur, Brown, Schaeffer, and John Cage. In a photograph made at the occasion, Cage irreverently (or symbolically exploring spatial relationships?) rests horizontally at their feet (Figure 28.2). Discovery was obviously in the air.

Among those present Badings (b. 1907), a native of the Netherlands and already an established composer since the late 1930s, had turned to electronics in the early 1950s. For the Brussels Exposition he composed a work entitled *Genese* for five audio-frequency oscillators. A work of almost ten-minutes duration, it is more substantial than, and lacks the preludial functions of, Xenakis's *Concert P-H*, a two-track tape of two and a half minutes also written especially for the Philips pavilion.

A richly illustrated volume devoted to the Corbusier-Varèse collaboration (Figure 28.3) published in 1958[7] emphasizes, however, the extent to which the Greek architect-composer Iannis Xenakis (b. 1922) was involved in the project beyond his short composition. Following an active role in the Greek Resistance during World War II, he found his way to Paris in 1947 where he met Honegger, Milhaud, and Messiaen. An introduction to the architect Le Corbusier led to collaborative efforts, including the construction of surfaces derived from the hyperbolic paraboloid for the Philips pavilion at the Brussels Exposition (Figure 28.4). His interest in various branches of mathematics led to their use as models in his own musical constructions. Thus in *Metastasis* (1953–54), the principle of the straight line continuously displaced—visible in many of his architectural schemes and later in the surface of the Philips pavilion—was adapted to the

Figure 28.2. Brussels World's Fair (1958). Front row, left to right: Mauricio Kagel, Earle Brown, Luciano Berio, Karlheinz Stockhausen; back row, left to right: Henk Badings, André Boucourechliev, Bruno Maderna, Henri Pousseur, Mlle. Seriahine, Luc Ferrari, and Pierre Schaeffer. Supine: John Cage.

Photo by Faider, Brussels.

two-dimensional staff representing a series of converging and separating glissandi. There followed two works of pure *musique concrète: Concret P-H*, the two-track tape written especially for the Philips pavilion and using smoldering charcoal as a sound source; and *Bohor I*, a four-track tape of 1962 composed in Schaeffer's electronic studio in Paris and derived from the limited resource of various Oriental bracelets and a Laotian mouth organ. The appeal of natural masses, as in smoldering charcoal, rain, or swarms of insects, is also manifest in numerous nonelectronic pieces by Xenakis and, together with the appeal of probability theory, helps to explain his preference for masses that he calls "clouds" and "galaxies"; it also points to his antipathy for contemporary music viewed from the standpoint of isolated points, a view he discussed in the essay "Le crise de la musique sérielle" of 1955.[8]

The mathematical basis for much of Xenakis' music has unduly emphasized the cerebral aspect of his music; contrarily, a term such as "stochastic"—frequently applied to his music and implying the controlled use of a very large number of elements that gives the false impression of aleatory or chance procedures—has incorrectly tended to signify the opposite point of view. His

Figure 28.3. Corbusier and Varèse (1958).
Fondation Le Corbusier, Paris

concern for the spatial element was pursued in pieces like *Hibiki-hana-ma* (twelve-track tape conceived for the same space as Stockhausen's *Spiral*, Osaka Expo 1970, see Figure 28.5), and in the mid-1970s he became increasingly interested in the role of the computer both for compositional calculation and for sound generation. Yet his interest in Byzantine traditions and the music of ancient Greece (e.g., *Oresteia*, 1966; *Medea*, 1967) and other musics from the distant past underscores an abiding humanistic orientation fundamental to all his work that belies an exclusive intellectual bias.

GERMANY: STOCKHAUSEN FROM *STUDIE I* TO *MANTRA*

Stockhausen, too, immediately realized the potential of tape not only for articulating the nuances of attack and rhythmic intricacies of the total serialists but also, through sound generation, for its capacity to control the realms of timbre and space through the construction, cataloguing, and placement of a corpus of sonorities. An early single-track *Etude* was achieved in Paris in 1952, but it was not until his return to Cologne in 1953 that Stockhausen confected his first important electronic creations. Research at Bonn University's Institute of Phonetics, a series of Darmstadt lectures, and a Cologne Radio broadcast led to the

Figure 28.4. The Philips Pavilion at the Brussels World's Fair deisgned by Le Corbusier (1958).

Fondation Le Corbusier, Paris.

installation of an electronic music studio at the Cologne Radio under its first director Herbert Eimert.

The composer has recently clarified the record by stating that

> When I was hired in May 1953 by WDR Cologne to work in the Electronic Music Studio, the studio was officially opened in a press conference and a public announcement. Eimert had not set up a studio. There was no studio before May 1953. Eimert and Beyer had made a few experiments before this time in an ordinary sound studio, mixing a few tapes with sound which had been provided by Meyer Eppler from Bonn ('Bode-Melochord') . . . Eimert has never 'worked together with me' in the studio. As a matter of fact, Eimert sat only a few times in a studio together with the technician Heinz Schüte and later Leopold von Knobelsdorff (both still at the WDR) who both *made* Eimert 'compositions'. Eimert has never worked in the studio *himself*, and he was not at all what I would call a composer. He helped me because he was in charge as the administrator of the studio.[9]

In Cologne, Stockhausen quickly produced his first electronic invention, *Studie I* (1953), constructed entirely from sine-wave sounds (containing no overtones). *Studie II* (1954) followed, but, contrary to prevalent descriptions of the piece, Stockhausen has recently protested that it contains "*no* white noises, and

I have used *no* filters whatsoever. The process of synthesizing sound spectra with sine waves is precisely described in the score. I have used an echo chamber. Who gave this strange idea that I used white noise?"[10]

Stockhausen's score for his *Elektronische Studie II* of 1954 (Figure 28.5) was the first of its kind to be published. The synthesized spectra with sine waves is portrayed here by a three-tiered system: (a) the upper level indicates the pitch level with frequencies indicated in Hertzes on a scale from 100 to 17,200 cps; (b) the middle level indicates duration in centimeters, where 76.2 cm of tape = 1 second; (c) the lower level provides an intensity scale between 0 and −40 decibels (dB). Heavier shading indicates overlapping note mixtures, and all changes, including such overlays, are marked by a vertical stroke on the time line.

The "aural score" or "Hörpartitur" devised by Renier Wehinger in 1970 for György Ligeti's *Artikulation* (Figure 28.6), a work also realized at the West German Radio in Cologne in 1956, similarly indicates the number of seconds of elapsed time at the bottom, while the symbols above the score (a circle divided into four quadrants) indicates which of four tape tracks is operating in the score below. The score is printed in colors which, along with the individual shapes, spell the sound source (e.g., sine wave, noise, filters, etc.). Such scores are unnecessary for the listener but may be useful for study purposes. Some of the more fanciful ones, like the Ligeti, have achieved the status of an art print. For other solutions to a rethinking of the score, which in part stemmed from such electronic pictures, see the examples by Lutosławski and Penderecki (Exs. 29.2 and 29.3), as well as the nontraditional but efficient solutions by Brown and Feldman (Exs. 27.1 and 27.2).

There were several electronic generators, in addition to those that produced "sine waves", which were soon developed at Cologne and elsewhere. These were capable of producing variable "colors" that quickly became part of

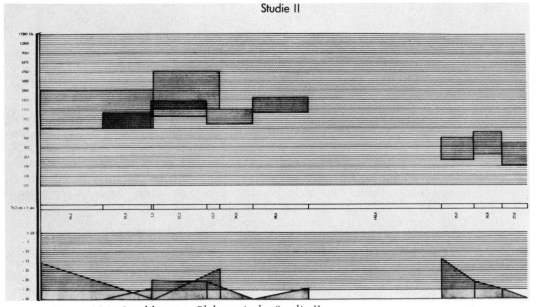

Figure 28.5. Stockhausen, *Elektronische Studie II.*

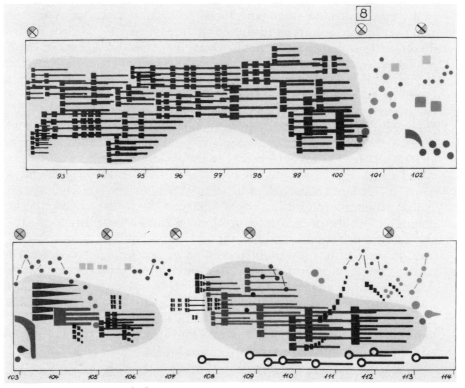

Figure 28.6. Ligeti, *Artikulation.*

Copyright B. Schott's Söhne, Mainz, 1970. Used by permission of European-American Music Distributors Corporation, sole U.S. agents for Universal Edition Ltd.

the indispensable apparatus of the composer's studio: (a) the "sawtooth-wave" generator, producing a sound with all overtones and a characteristic nasal quality; (b) the "white-noise" generator, producing a curtain of all possible frequencies and hence of indefinite pitch frequently likened unto the sound of a waterfall; and (c) "inharmonic" generators" with irregular overtone patterns producing a bell-like tone. Devices to modify these basic sound spectra were also brought into play: (a) "modulators", which act upon two different signals to produce a new one; the "ring modulator" suppresses the originals of two sounds while producing the sum as well as the differences of these frequencies; (b) "filters", which promote color change through the emphasis and reduction of certain overtones; (c) "reverberators," which introduce echoes. The device of the tape "loop" does not belong to these categories; rather than generating or transforming sound, its function is to produce a recurring "ostinato" through a fan-belt looking piece of tape containing a musical idea or sequence.

The distinctions between French and German aims with respect to source material quickly began to dissolve, and in Stockhausen's *Gesang der Jünglinge* (1956) a boy's voice reading from the Book of Daniel was mixed with electronically produced sounds. (Correcting another widely repeated misunderstanding Stockhausen has stated: "The boy's voice in *Gesang der Jünglinge* has never been transformed. *All* the recorded sounds of the boy's voice are composed together with the electronic music *untransformed* as they were recorded.") Originally written for five-track tape, the score calls for five groups of loudspeakers to be set up surrounding the audience. One of the first works thus "to use the direction of sounds and their movement in space as aspects of the form," its impact was soon to appear in compositions such as Varèse's *Poème électronique* (1958). While the use of space as an architectural component of sound can be traced at least as far back as the Gabrielis in Venice's San Marco at the end of the sixteenth century (if not a much earlier responsorial psalmody), neither their view of the spatial component, nor Berlioz's as exhibited in his *Grand messe des morts* (1837), nor Schoenberg's somewhat enlarged view in his *Jakobsleiter* of 1915–17 prefigure except in the most elementary way the marriage of architecture and music fundamental to works like Varèse's *Poème*, Xenakis's *Concret P-H*, Stockhausen's *Spiral*, which called for the construction of a special hall at the Osaka World Fair of 1970 (Figure 28.8) or Boulez's *Répons* (1981–   ) conceived for his "Espace de projection" in Paris (Figure 32.2).

Stockhausen's career following these early electronic works was, as we have already seen, in no way exclusively tied to or even related to such modes or media—serial, aleatoric, conceptual and theater approaches alternately or simultaneously commanding his attention. While since the middle 1970s he has turned to other more conventional performance sources and means of notation, from the 1960s to his current opera cycle *Licht* (Figure 28.7) a series of works have explored the various relationships of electronics to the world of sound. The principal works include:

> *Kontakte* (1959–60), for four-track tape; a second version adds piano and percussion; the music was also used for a theater piece entitled *Originale* (1961).

> *Mikrophonie I* (1964), for tam-tam, two microphones, two filters, and potentiometers, where the two players activate the single tam-tam, and through various approaches and actual physical contact of the microphones with the surface of the instrument alter the sound.

> *Mixtur* (1964), for five orchestral groups, sine-wave generators, four ring modulators (which suppress the original two sounds while producing the sum as well as the differences of these frequencies). Stockhausen has clarified the interaction between the components thus: "It is completely wrong that in *Mixtur* orchestral sounds are mixed with sounds generated electronically. Orchestral sounds are *ring-modulated*, which means that the sine waves which modulate the orchestral sounds are *never heard* (should not be heard). The term *Mixture* comes from the professional terminology of organ playing: in German the organ stops produced "*Mixturen*" (parallel frequencies). I therefore use this term also in orchestral composition."[11]

> *Telemusik* (1966), for four-track tape, composed in the Japanese Radio studio, involving the electronic manipulation of materials drawn from folk and traditional sources. Rather than a collage, however, Stockhausen subjects the materials to what he called "intermodulation", a process achieved through ring modulators such that the various properties of melody, rhythm, amplitude, etc. from one source transforms the analogous property of another.

> *Hymnen* (1967), for four-track tape; a second version with instruments; an attempt at a synthesis of *Musique concrète* and *elektronische Musik* lasting two hours using a large number of national anthems in an attempt, not unlike *Telemusik*, to write a "music of the whole world".

Figure 28.7. Stockhausen in the control room of Studio II at the West German Radio (WGR) Cologne in August 1985 while producing "sound scenes" for *Monday from Light*. This is the same studio in which Stockhausen produced, from 1953 to 1956, *Elektronische Studien I und II* (Electronic Studies I and II) and *Gesang der Jünglinge* (Song of the Youths).

Photo by Clive Barda.

Kurzwellen (1968), for four instruments, four shortwave receivers, microphones, filters, potentionmeters, wherein the 4 players operate according to a set of instructions, imitating sounds which they have picked up on their shortwave receivers; all of this acted upon by a microphonist much in the manner of *Mikrophonie I* who thus determines the final transformation of the player's music. In 1969 the idea was extended, under the title *Kurzwellen mit Beethoven (Stockhoven-Beethausen, Opus 1970)*, involving individually prepared tapes for each of the players made up of fragments from the works of Beethoven.

Spiral (1969), a work for soloist(s) and shortwave receiver, drew upon the experience of *Kurzwellen*, and received its most notable successes in hundreds of performances given in a specially constructed auditorium for the Osaka World Exposition 1970 (Figure 28.8). In the auditorium the public sat somewhat below (ideally *at*) the level of the sphere's equator on a circular, sound transparent platform. Soloists in the performance of *Spiral* played or sang either on a podium at one side (P), or one of six balconies, place in a circle about 3.5 meters above the audience

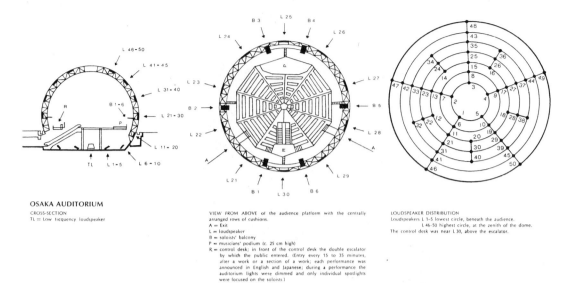

OSAKA AUDITORIUM
CROSS-SECTION
TL = Low frequency loudspeaker

VIEW FROM ABOVE of the audience platform with the centrally
arranged rows of cushions.
A = Exit
L = loudspeaker
B = soloists' balcony
P = musicians' podium (c. 25 cm high)
R = control desk; in front of the control desk the double escalator
by which the public entered. (Entry every 15 to 35 minutes,
after a work or a section of a work; each performance was
announced in English and Japanese; during a performance the
auditorium lights were dimmed and only individual spotlights
were focused on the soloists.)

LOUDSPEAKER DISTRIBUTION
Loudspeakers L 1-5 lowest circle, beneath the audience.
L 46-50 highest circle, at the zenith of the dome.
The control desk was near L 30, above the escalator.

Figure 28.8. Osaka Auditorium, Expo 70. Cross-section, view from above, and loud-speaker distribution for the spherical auditorium of the German Pavilion. Developed by architect F. Bornemann on the basis of proposals by Stockhausen. The electroacoustic installation, including the control desk, was designed by Stockhausen and constructed by the firm of Siemens.

Diagram used by permission of the composer.

platform (B 1-6). All instrumental or vocal sounds and all shortwave sounds were fed into a control desk (R) by means of microphones and contact microphones, and from there they were projected into the auditorium over fifty loudspeakers arranged in seven circles one above another in ten vertical rows. For performances of *Spiral* voices, instruments and shortwave receiver were normally switched to two or three master faders and were connected to a so-called rotation mill (1-10 outputs consecutively connectable by a handle turned manually in a circular fashion at a maximum speed of about 4 revolutions per second). The spatial projection with potentiometers and rotation mill was freely improvised by Stockhausen or his assistants.

Mantra (1970), for two pianists, completely notated but composed from a single melodic formula (like many of his non-electronic works of the 1970s) repeated and modified by a ring modulator.

CAGE AND MILAN: BERIO, POUSSEUR

Just as Cage had been an early articulator of total serialism and chance, he had preceded the European avant-garde to a consideration of sound and its sources. Following his essay *The Future of Music: Credo* (1937), echoing Varèse's vision of an impending world of electronics, Cage composed his first work reflective of his interest in and awareness of such developments in *Imaginary Landscape No. 1* (1939), which utilized two variable turntables, frequency recordings, muted piano, and cymbal. A similar panel of equipment was used in his *Imaginary Landscape No. 3* (1942), but it was not until *Imaginary Landscape No. 5* (1952) that he prepared his first piece for magnetic tape. Though the tape recording machine had been invented by 1935, it was not commercially available until after the war, and Cage's first tape piece put old habits to work in the service of the new technology: Forty-two phonograph records were transferred to tape, which was then sliced into segments of varying lengths, the reassemblage being accomplished according to chance operations. The method bears a striking resemblance to that of the Dadaist Tristan Tzara in his chance poems of 1919 wherein words clipped from a newspaper article were tossed into a paper bag and copied anew in the order in which they were removed (a procedure still operative in György Ligeti's *Artikulation* for four-track tape of 1958). Cage's *Williams Mix*, also of 1952, was even more complex, composed from 600 tapes similarly dissected and rejoined according to the principles of *I Ching*.

Cage, who did not connect with the Princeton-Columbia group forming in the early 1950s, set out for Europe. There he joined Berio and Maderna who, following their exposure to Schaeffer's electronic studio in Paris, had opened the Studio di Fonologia Musicale in Milan in 1955. In 1958, three works were realized there: Berio's *Omaggio à Joyce*, Pousseur's *Scambi*, and Cage's *Fontana Mix*. The score for Cage's work was nothing more than a set of transparent sheets with lines and dots, reminiscent of Brown's graphic notation of a few years before. They were in effect a kit for the realization of a tape piece of which Cage provided only a sample solution in the Milan studio. As such they represented a new approach. While the cutting and splicing of *Williams Mix* was carefully controlled by chance operations, as Cage later put it "This was characteristic of an old period, before indeterminacy in performance, you see; for all I was doing then was renouncing my intention. Although my choices were controlled by chance operations, I was still making an object. For that reason, this piece, I later said, in an article called 'Indeterminacy,' was equivalent to producing a Frankenstein. I denounced my own work." Asked if he would still allow it to be played, his response was similar to Boulez (p. 522) with respect to *Structures:* "Of course. I made it perfectly clear what I think it is; so if people use it, they know what they are up against."[12]

While in Milan, Cage also created two solo theater works for television, *Sounds of Venice* and *Water Walk* (1959). The idea of the "happening," or unstructured events for several performers, had been explored by Cage as early as 1952, but in two works of 1960, *Theatre Piece* and *Cartridge Music* (see p. 595), he created the first examples of live electronic music involving several players to create sounds through the insertion of objects into phonograph cartridges or by the action of these objects supplied with contact microphones on pieces of furniture. The stage had been set, obviously, for Stockhausen's *Mikrophonie I* of 1964 and innumerable electronic performer-theater pieces to come, including Pousseur's *Répons* (1960, rev. 1965).

Berio (b. 1925), having been exposed to both Neoclassicism and Serialism through his teachers Ghedini (Milan, 1948–50) and Dallapiccola (Tanglewood, 1951), respectively, was also stimulated by his acquaintance with the early work of Luening and Ussachevsky in 1952 on a visit to America. Single-track tape pieces from 1953–55 led to his *Perspectives*, a two-track tape of 1957, by which time he had made the acquaintance of Pousseur, Stockhausen, and Maderna (Basle, 1954) and with the latter had established the Milan Studio (June, 1955). Berio's *Thema*, subtitled *Omaggio à Joyce*, from the same season as *Fontana Mix*, investigated a different premise from Cage's altogether. As early as 1952 Pierre Henry (b. 1927) had written a piece entitled *Vocalise* constructed solely from manipulations of the syllable "ah," an idea picked up by the composer Takemitsu in his *Vocalism Ai* of 1956, which used only the two syllables of the Japanese word for "love". Now Berio extracted a text from Joyce's *Ulysses* and proceeded to dismember and filter its constituent parts into an absorbing sonic adventure. Although even with text at hand, comprehension is elusive, nothing could have more clearly captured one of the central premises of Joyce's novel nor forecast more accurately one of the future directions of Berio's music, which was soon to investigate in a more thorough-going fashion the idea of words both as meaning and as phonetic sounds. In part it was from such inquiries that the "new vocalism" (p. 605) was born, incorporating both electronic (*Visage*, 1961) and traditional means (*Circles*, 1960; *Recital for Cathy I*, 1972).

BACKGROUNDS FOR AN ITALIAN AVANT-GARDE.   The preceding appraisal of Berio demands a momentary review of the multiple musical values endorsed by native Italian composers in the 20th century. From the *verismo* of Puccini (1858–1924), Montemezzi (1875–1952) and Zandonai (1883–1944); to the neo-classical inclinations of composers like Casella (1883–1947), Ghedini (1892–1965), Pizzetti (1880–1968) and Malipiero (1882–1973); to such a popular figure as Respighi (1879–1936), Italy opened the 20th century with memories of a rich legacy (Donizetti, Bellini, Verdi) and evidence of talent sufficient to capitalize upon it.

We have noted before that it seemed almost logical that Milan, the birthplace of Futurism, should have proved to be the site for the first electronic developments. But in addition to Berio (a pupil of Ghedini who was strongly influenced by Dallapiccola), there were other Italian figures whose careers developed in a somewhat different direction yet whose voices were soon recognized on the international scene. The senior of these musicians were: Bruno Maderna (1920–73; a pupil of Malipiero), as influential as a conductor and promoter of contemporary music (Boulez, Stockhausen, Nono) as he was as a composer; and Luigi Nono (b. 1924), pupil of Malipiero and Maderna, son-in-law of Schoenberg, and early serial advocate whose music frequently addressed the issues of left-wing politics. Both Maderna and Nono had been at the 1951 Darmstadt sessions along with Stockhausen, and this association was to prove crucial.

A slightly younger group would include Clementi (b. 1925; pupil of Petrassi), whose associations with Maderna and Stockhausen at Darmstadt finally led to a principal alignment with Cage's aleatory techniques; Donatoni (b. 1927; pupil of Pizzetti), whose career has ranged from a confrontation with Boulez and Stockhausen to Cageian indeterminacy and has currently settled into a more traditional mode enriched by his previous experiences; Bussotti (b. 1931), whose similar reactions to Cage and Boulez led to a highly theatrical and intensely virtuosic style which courted both the quietly seductive and the aggressively violent; and Castiglioni (b. 1932; pupil of Ghedini), whose early interest in Boulez soon encompassed a surprising affection for late Romanticism in the development of a personal style which studiously avoided the fashions of the international avant-garde at any given moment.

The lineage of these several composers with the principal figures and aesthetic options of the post-World War II period is easily discernible, and in spite of a generally non-aggressive campaign to promote their works outside of their native land, their contribution forms a critical chapter for the period in question. Although the heralded establishment of an electronic studio in Milan in 1955 was to prove less indicative of the specific future direction of most Italian composers than of a generally inquisitive turn of mind, it clearly forecast the multiple energies of the period just ahead. The performances of the Nuovo Consonanza at Rome from 1961 and those of the Settimana Internazionale di Nuovo Musica, irregularly convened at Palermo from 1960–68, proved to be not only important platforms for new music but more tuned to the avant-garde than the Venice Biennale. All in all Italy has not only fostered a musical climate disproportionately rich to its size but continues to be a lively participant in the contemporary musical scene today.

AMERICA: LUENING, USSACHEVSKY, BABBITT

By 1952, Otto Luening (b. 1900) and Vladimir Ussachevsky (b. 1911), already acknowledged composers of a more traditional music, began their experiments with tape. In October of that year, a concert of their music, the first of its kind in the United States, was presented at New York's Museum of Modern Art. Works performed included Ussachevsky's *Sonic Contours* and Luening's *Fantasy in Space*, both singled out by the critics as especially effective. In these works, Luening's restriction to manipulations of flute sonorities and Ussachevsky's investigations into the properties of piano sound were typical of the time in their reliance on traditional instruments as source material. Quickly, however, both composers moved to a consideration of expanded resources, mirroring Stockhausen's developments of the period. Their *A Poem in Cycles and Bells*, which utilizes material from *Fantasy in Space* and *Sonic Contours*, is a work for tape and live orchestra, while Ussachevsky's *A Piece for Tape Recorder* (1956) combines electronically generated sounds with instruments. The initial geographic distinctions with respect to primary source material had by this time obviously faded, a fact only corroborated by Pierre Henry's turn to the juxtaposition of *musique concrète* and electronically produced sounds in 1958.

In 1955, the construction of the Olson-Belar Sound Synthesizer at the RCA laboratories in Princeton led to the coordination of efforts in 1959 in what was called the Columbia-Princeton Electronic Music Center, largely due to the guiding spirit of Babbitt and Sessions of Princeton and Luening and Ussachevsky of Columbia University. Babbitt's initial efforts were less concerned with the investigation of timbral novelties than in the exploration of the control such a machine could effect over structural matters. The main advantage of the RCA synthesizer was its capacity to produce a succession of sounds from a coded input tape that could specify virtually any timbre or duration. Difficult to use and considerably bulkier than the later modular, voltage-controlled synthesizer, it nonetheless marked the beginnings of the systematic investigation into the variety of electronic alternatives that had by that time surfaced elsewhere in the world.

The first concert of music to demonstrate the potential of the new center was held at Columbia University in May 1961 and included Davidovsky's electronically generated *Electronic Study No. 1* and Luening's *Gargoyles* for live violinst and tape as well as Babbitt's *Composition for Synthesizer*. The latter work emphasized Babbitt's interest in instrumental timbres and well-tempered pitches in what seemed like a direct transference of preelectronic compositional aims.

The development of the keyboarded Moog synthesizer, as well as another similar principle developed by Buchla, not only provided greater ease for the composer but, through their proliferation, greater accessibility, which soon touched the world at large through numerous rock ensembles and novelties such as Walter Carlos's *Switched-On Bach* (1968). The electronic age was in full swing, and the serious composer began to compose directly for the record companies. Morton Subotnick's *Silver Apples of the Moon* (1966–67) for electronic music synthesizer was one of the earliest of these commissions, which was soon followed by *The Wild Bull* (1968)—both works without an obligatory concert hall destination, although readily capable of appropriation by modern dance companies.

While Subotnick was composing on his Buchla synthesizer and activities at the Columbia-Princeton Center continued, numerous American universities installed electronic studios in the 1960s, to the point where it clearly became a matter of prestige to claim a certain degree of sophistication in the available equipment. Kenneth Gaburo (b. 1926), having begun his first electronic explorations in the 1950s, pursued his work at the University of Illinois (and later in San Diego) where he wrote a group of five tape compositions during 1964–65, of which *For Harry* (Partch) and *Lemon Drops* may be held as representative. Mixing *concrète* and electronically generated sounds, he produced in *Lemon Drops* a work whose charm seems to prefigure a combination of Stockhausen's music boxes in *Tierkreis* (not yet composed) and Partch's cloud chamber bowls with the easy wit of a small jazz ensemble.

The Machine in the form of computer had earlier made its debut in the mid-1950s at the University of Illinois under the direction of Lejaren Hiller and Leonard Isaacson. The computer quickly displayed its power to play a role both in the making of compositional choices to be played by standard ensembles (Hiller-Isaacson, *Illiac Suite* for string quartet, 1957, was the first substantial digitally programmed piece) as well as in the generation of sounds to be stored and retrieved according to a compositional program (Hiller-Cage *HPSCHD* for "one to seven live harpsichords and one to fifty-one computer generated tapes" of 1969).

That Babbitt and others of his circle had been interested primarily in using the synthesizer as a reliable articulator of highly complex music essentially instrumental in character is confirmed by alternative versions for voice and piano or voice and tape of Babbitt's *Phonemena* of 1974 and Benjamin Boretz's *Group Variations* (1964–73), a work originally scored for chamber orchestra and later transferred to the computer. Such a point of view was in harmony with the serial structures of these composers in their preelectronic music and contrasts vividly with the approach to electronic composition by Varèse, which had nothing to with transferring materials conceived from without but with the transformation and projection of materials discovered from within (see p. 000). Others who shared both Varèse's and Stockhausen's interest in exploring realms of sound and texture unimaginable with traditional performing forces were Charles Dodge (*Earth's Magnetic Field*, 1970) and James K. Randall (*Quartersines*, 1969). By the time Charles Wuorinen's *Time's Encomium* (1969) had won a Pulitzer Prize in 1970, the natural compatibility of well-tempered dodecaphonic serialism with synthesized, electronically processed sounds had been forcefully demonstrated. Various types of electronic music had not only come of age but had, apparently, settled into a comfortable niche of respectability.

OTHER DEVELOPMENTS: MUSICA ELETTRONICA VIVA, ONCE, AND THE PERFORMER.

It should be obvious from the events thus far related that the three prongs of the avant-garde following World War II—total serialism, chance or aleatoric procedures, and electronic tape explorations—were not mutually exclusive, and that, indeed, from time to time thay came together in an invigorating interchange. It is unfortunate that the number of personalities who were involved with and contributed to this ferment is so large that it is impossible to deal with each in a meaningful fashion.

There are several groups, nonetheless, that must be reviewed collectively because of their sizeable impact on developments of the time. Musica Elettronica Viva (MEV), formed during the mid-1960s in Rome by a group of American composer-performers, indicated their all-encompassing purview in the following statement:

> Tapes, complex electronics—Moog synthesizer, brainwave amplifiers, photocell mixers for movement of sound in space—are combined with traditional instruments, everyday objects and the environment itself, amplified by means of contact mikes, or not. Sounds may originate both inside and outside the performing-listening space and may move freely within and around it. Jazz, rock, primitive and Oriental musics, Western classical tradition, verbal and organic sound both individual and collective may all be present.[13]

Clearly, the relationship of such a view to the idea of the "happening," to a developing loosely structured music-theater, both electronic and nonelectronic, and to the experience of Cage, Stockhausen, and the Beatles, among others, is apparent. The idea of music as a performance art, relying heavily on improvisatory means under the watchful eye of the (collective) composer-conductor-performer mirrors the work of Riley, Reich, Stockhausen and, to an extent, Boulez.

The idea of audience participation, as in *Free Soup* (1968) by Frederic Rzewski, a charter member of MEV, was mirrored in a different way in certain works by the ONCE group, formed in Ann Arbor, Michigan in 1961. Gordon Mumma, one of its founders, became notably involved in the use of specially constructed "cybersonic" equipment to be worn by the performer in a work like *Hornpipe* (1967), which reacts to and responds to the sounds made by a French horn. His *Cybersonic Cantilevers* (1973) picks up on the idea of audience participation through the invitation to bring sounds to his electronic circuitry for on-the-spot transformation.

The beginnings of the Ann Arbor ONCE group are to be found in the collaboration of Mumma and Robert Ashley (b. 1930) with the visual artist Milton Cohen in what was called a "Space Theater" (1957–64), involving light projections, dance, and various visual-sonic combinations. The two composers soon cofounded the Cooperative Studio for Electronic Music (1958–66), which led to the inauguration of the ONCE Festivals (1961–68) and a large touring ensemble devoted to the performance of electronic theater-pieces from 1965 to

1969. The spinoff from this group was enormously influential for the 1960s, Mumma leaving for New York in 1966, where he formed with Ashley the Sonic Arts Union devoted to the performance of live electronic music. Ashley ultimately settled at Mills College in California, and another member of ONCE, Roger Reynolds (b. 1934), following a period in Japan and Europe, left to head up the Project for Music Experiment at the University of California, San Diego.

It may appear perfunctory to recall that Ashley had been a pupil of Riegger, Bassett, and Gerhard; or that Reynolds, also a pupil of Gerhard and Finney, readily acknowledges his lineage in Ives, Varèse, and Cage. Yet for all of the iconoclasm of much of their music of the 1960s, the distortions of vocal sound due to electronic feedback in a work like Ashley's *Wolfman* (1964) and the use of ring modulators in conjunction with conventional instruments in Reynold's *Ping* (1968; fl, pf, harmonium, bowed cymbal, tam-tam, electronic sound, film, slides; after Beckett) indicated that they were alive to the developments of others. Virtually all of the members of ONCE, however, made their own distinctive contribution with respect to the notion of live electronic performance in the context of an expanding definition of music-theater, often with social overtones.

The force of live electonic performance involving transformations of sound during the 1960s naturally encouraged varying degrees of performer-oriented, nonnarrative music theater: Stockhausen's *Mikrophonie I* (1964) is a good example involving tam-tam, microphones, filters, and potentiometers, while Jakob Druckman's *Animus III* (1969) transcends the idea of his *Animus I* (1966, for trombone and tape) in a work for clarinet and tape, with feedback for the soloist that creates unpredictable on-the-spot distortions. Both *Animus III* and the nonelectronic *Valentine* for solo contrabass written in the same year (1969) focus, by the composer's admission, "on the mindlessness, the driven quality of virtuosity." They also speak to the importance of the human factor in live performance: *Valentine* can be preceded by the only electronic work Druckman ever wrote, a work entitled *Synapse*, played to an empty stage with a spotlight on the double-bass's chair; the houselights fall and rise to see the chair occupied and *Valentine* (solo) ensues. Such discrete juxtapositions as well as the simultaneous alliance in *Animus III* reflect the frustration of Druckman, and many other composer's as well, over the spectacle of two loudspeakers that typically dominate the all-electronic concert.

Among the most notable electronic works involved with the transformation of vocal materials of the period were two works by the American Steve Reich (*Come Out*, 1966) and Milton Babbitt (*Philomel*, 1964). Babbitt's work to a poem by John Hollander utilizes a live singer who delivers the text against a tape of recorded voice intoning fragments of the text modified with electronically produced percussions, noises, and quasiorchestral simulations, in what many felt achieved a new level of communication well beyond *Vision and Prayer* (1961) of a few years before. Reich's title was taken from the phrase "Come out to show them" inspired by a black man who, having suffered police brutality during the Harlem riots of the summer of 1964, said before receiving hospital treatment, "I had to, like, open the bruise up and let the bruise blood come out to show them." Stated unaltered three times at the work's inception, the final phrase is then subjected to a series of repetitions through a modified tape loop. Recorded on two channels that begin together in unison, they gradually separate into two, four, and finally eight voices, creating a quasicanonic phase music related to Reich's nonelectronic minimalisms. The capacity of the electronic medium to begin with a comprehensible text and transform it into a sonic abstraction, however, brings another dimension to the work analogous to the narrative-dramatic use of echo in Babbitt's *Philomel.*

The exploration of instruments with tape or the electronic modification of traditional instruments in live performance continued at a vigorous rate throughout the 1960s and 1970s, and secured the notion through the variety of examples put forward that no sytlistic premise was involved in such investigations. Davidovsky's several *Synchronisms* (1962–74) throughout that period treated the solo instrument in a more-or-less traditional fashion in conjunction with a tape accompaniment, an idea first expounded by Bruno Maderna in his *Musica su due dimensioni* for flute and tape and Henk Badings's *Capriccio for Violin and 2 Sound-Tracks,* both of 1952. Similar but highly effective juxtapositions occur in Gerhard's *Symphony No. 3* (subtitled "Collages") for orchestra and tape of 1960; Kirchner's *Quartet No. 3 for Strings and Electronic Tape* of 1967; Bassett's *Collect* for SATB chorus and tape of 1969; Albright's *Organ Book II* and Krenek's *Orga-nastro* both for organ and tape from 1971; Henze's *Tristan* for piano, orchestra, and tape of 1973; and Reynold's *". . . the serpent-snapping eye"* (1978) for trumpet, percussion, piano, and four-channel tape.

More recent works that indicate the continuing fascination for the variable opportunities afforded by electronic developments include the work of the Polish Culture Quartet (1963–73), which was reformed in 1983 as the New Culture Quartet. Originally composed of only four trombones, the newly restructured group has focused on a variety of multimedia components (tape, electronics, lights, and movement) in a piece such as *The Ship of Fools,* collectively composed and presented at the Warsaw Autumn '84 Concerts.[14] At the same festival, Leo Küpper's *Aérosons* (1982) for stereo, mezzo-soprano, computer, and voice synthesis was performed together with his *Amkéa* (1984) for four-track tape, mezzo, and space performer. His position was described as an experimental composer aiming at a special kind of computer music where

> there is feedback between the computer and the public: in a hall fitted out with a great number of loudspeakers, the vocal and phonetic impulses sent out by the public are translated into digital code and processed mathematically. They in turn stimulate highly sensitive cell oscillators . . . at the same time sound operations are being transmitted to the speakers.[15]

Similarly, Tod Machover's *Soft Morning, City!* (1980), written for the soprano Jane Manning and double bassist Barry Guy, includes computer parts realized at IRCAM in Paris. Utilizing the final monologue of Joyce's *Finnigan's Wake,* whose "polyphonic verbal richness and inherent sonic structure" the composer found ideal for a musical setting, Machover has composed an aria for soprano with support and commentary from the bass, with both subject to direct transformation by the PDP-10 computer whose ultimate function is to promote fusion between the two.

While the appearance of many of these works in the record catalogues provides the opportunity to hear and judge their effect, many of the music-theater pieces, for which there is an important visual-dramatic component, were not well served by their recordings and helped to create a false or, at best, an incomplete impression. Contrarily, recordings of abstract pieces composed directly for tape, sometimes commissioned expressly by the record companies, were final, even "ultimate" performances of the pieces in question. In sum, the difficulties this music has had in settling into the mind of the potentially interested listener have been compounded in many cases by the lack of a communal public experience. With the advent of the videocassette, however, the possibility for another dimension of reinforcement seems to be upon us.

REPERTOIRE

Electronic and Concrète Sounds

Babbitt, *Composition for Synthesizer* (1961), four-track tape
Berio, *Momenti* (1960), four-track tape
Cage, *Williams Mix* (1952)
Cage, *Fontana Mix* (1958)
Carlos, *Switched-on Bach* (1968)
Davidovsky, *Electronic Study No. 2* (1962)
Dodge, *Earth's Magnetic Field* (1970)
Gaburo, *Lemon Drops* (1964–65)
Kagel, *Transición I* (1958–60)
Ligeti, *Artikulation* (1958), four-track tape
Mumma, *Music for the Venezia Space Theatre* (1964)
Oliveros, *Bye Bye Butterfly* (1965)
Pousseur, *Scambi* (1958)
Randall, *Quartersines* (1969)
Schaeffer, *Étude aux casseroles* (1948)
Schaeffer, *Étude aux chemins de fer* (1948)
Stockhausen, *Hymnen* (1966–67)
Stockhausen, *Kontakte* (tape version, 1959–60)
Stockhausen, *Elektronische Studie I* (1953)
Stockhausen, *Elektronische Studie II* (1954)
Stockhausen, *Telemusik* (1966), four-track tape
Subotnick, *Silver Apples of the Moon* (1966)
Subotnick, *The Wild Bull* (1967), two-track tape
Luening and Ussachevsky, *Suite from King Lear* (1956; 1966)
Varèse, *Poème électronique* (1958)
Wuorinen, *Time's Encomium* (1969)
Xenakis, *Concret P-H* (1958)
Xenakis, *Bohor I* (1962), four-track tape

Transformations from Voice and Instruments

Berio, *Omaggio à Joyce* (1958), modified voice
Henry, *Symphonie pour un homme seul* (1950)
Luening, *Fantasy in Space* (1952), modified flute sounds
Henry, *Vocalise* (1952)
Reich, *Come Out* (1966), two-track tape
Schaeffer, *Variations sur une flûte mexicaine* (1949)
Takemitsu, *Vocalism A-i* (1956)
Ussachevsky, *Sonic Contours* (1952), modified piano sounds

Combinations for Voice, Instruments, and Tape

Albright, *Organ Book II* (1971), org, tape
Ashley, *The Wolfman* (1964)
Babbitt, *Philomel* (1964), S, four-track tape

Babbitt, *Vision and Prayer* (1961), S, four-track tape
Babbitt, *Phonemena* (1974), S, tape
Badings, *Capriccio for Violin and 2 Sound-Tracks* (1952)
Bassett, *Collect* (1969), SATB chorus, tape
Maderna, *Musica su due dimensioni* (1952), fl, tape
Beatles, *Sergeant Pepper's Lonely Hearts Club Band* (1967)
Brown, *Times Five* (1963), fl, trbn, harp, vn, vc, four-track tape
Cage, *Cartridge Music* (1960), amplified sounds
Cage and Hiller, *HPSCHD* (1969), one to 7 harpsichords, one to 51 computer generated
        tapes
Davidovsky, *Synchronisms No. 1* (1962), fl, tape
Davidovsky, *Syncrhonisms No. 5* (1969), perc, tape
Davidovsky, *Syncrhonisms No. 6* (1970), pf, tape
Davidovsky, *Synchronisms No. 8* (1974), wind qnt, tape
Davis, *Bitches Brew* (1970), elec amp melody instr
Druckman, *Animus I* (1966), trbn, tape
Druckman, *Animus III* (1969), cl, tape, feedback
Foss, *Echoi* (1961–63), cl, vc, perc, pf, tape
Gaburo, *Antiphony III* (1962), cham chorus
Gerhard, *Symphony No. 3* ("Collages," 1960), orch, tape
Erb, *In No Strange Land* (1968), trbn, db, tape
Henze, *Tristan* (1974), pf, orch, tape
Kagel, *Transición II* (1958–59), pf, perc, 2 tapes
Kirchner, *Quartet No. 3 for Strings and Electronic Tape* (1966)
Krenek, *Orga-nostro* (1971), org, tape
Luening, *Gargoyles* (1960), vn, tape
Luening and Ussachevsky, *A Poem in Cycles and Bells* (1954), orch, tape
Machover, *Soft Morning, City* (1980), S, db, tape, PDP-10 computer
Mumma, *Hornpipe* (1967), cybersonic horn
Oliveros, *Double-Basses at Twenty Paces* (1968), 2 db, tape, slides, cond & referee, 2
        pfmrs
Reich, *Violin Phase* (1967), vn, 3-track tape/four vn
Reynolds, *Ping* (1969), fl, pf, harmon, bowed cymb, tam-tam, slides, tape
Salzman, *The Nude Paper Sermon* (1968–69), actor, chorus, Renaissance ensemble, elec-
        tronics, tape
Schwartz, *Echo Music I* (1973), cl, va, tape
Stockhausen, *Mantra* (1969–70), 2 pf, ring modulators
Stockhausen, *Mikrophonie I* (1964), tam-tam, 2 micro, 2 filters, potentiometers
Stockhausen, *Mixtur* (1964), 5 orch groups, sine-wave generators, 4 ring modulators
Stockhausen, *Kurzwellen* (1968), 4 instr, mics, filters, potentiometers, 4 shortwave
Stockhausen, *Kurzwellen mit Beethoven* (1969) = *Stockhoven-Beethausen Opus 1970*)
Stockhausen, *Kontakte* (with piano and perc, 1959–60)
Ussachevsky, *A Piece for Tape Recorder* (1956), instr, elec generated sound
Varèse, *Déserts* (1950–54), 14 winds, pf, five perc, 2-track tape
Zappa, *The Perfect Stranger* (1984)

READING

Pierre Schaeffer, *A la recherche d'un musique concrète* (Paris, 1952).
Charles Edouard Jeanneret-Gris, *Le poème électronique/Le Corbusier* (Paris, 1958).
Chou Wen-Chung, "Varèse: A Sketch of the Man and His Music," *Musical Quarterly*, lii
        (1966), 151–170.
Elliott Schwartz, *Electronic Music: A Listener's Guide* (New York, 1973).
Michael Nyman, *Experimental Music: Cage and Beyond* (New York, 1974).
Pierre Boulez, "Technology and the Composer" in *Orientations* (Cambrdige, Mass., 1986),
        486–94. Originally in *The Times Literary Supplement*, May 6, 1977.
David Ernst, *The Evolution of Electronic Music* (1977).

Paul Griffiths, *A Guide to Electronic Music* (1979).

Richard James, *Expansion of Sound Resources in France, 1913–1940, and its Relationship to Electronic Music* (PhD dissertation, University of Michigan, 1981).

David Cope, *New Directions in Music*, 4th ed. (Dubuque, 1984), Chapters V and VI.

Andrew Mead, "Recent Developments in the Music of Milton Babbitt," *Musical Quarterly*, lxx (1984), 310.

CHAPTER 29

THE NEW VIRTUOSITY

Alongside technical and formalistic developments in the areas of serialism, chance, and electronics in the period following World War II was a virtuosic strain involving the performer that quickly began to reflect not only the new demands of the composer but the artist's response and frequently his collaboration. This took place along the whole front of soloist and ensemble literature, leaving virtually no corner unexplored.

THE "NEW VOCALISM"

BACKGROUNDS.   In an article entitled "Music and Speech" that appeared in *Die Reihe* (1960),[1] Stockhausen undertook an analysis of three works completed in the period 1954–56: the author's *Gesang der Jünglinge*, Boulez' *Le marteau sans maître*, and Nono's *Il canto sospeso*. He discussed the ways in which words in variable degrees of comprehensibility could be made to serve the composer as a compositional variable. Numerous composers since that time have offered a kaleidoscopic array of evidence, which indicates the fascination such questions pose. The intricacy of analytical techniques that have been invoked to promote an analogy between textual ingredient and musical form can only be described as formidable. A hint of the multiplicity of underlying philosophies can be gleaned from numerous additional statements by Boulez, Berio, Babbitt, Lutosławski, and Crumb.

Implicit in all such discussion was a renewed interest in the potential of the human voice both as a carrier of a text and as an instrument of inherent flexibility with an enormous power for expression even without a text. In addition to a consideration of numerous literary and psychological theories of perception, cognition, and meaning, fascination in the sheer exuberance of abstract voice-play could be traced to Russolo's catalogue of vocal sounds (1913); to Milhaud's use of a textless vocal quartet in *L'homme et son désir* (1918); to the Dadaist Kurt Schwitters' *Sonata in Urlauten* (Sonata in primitive sounds), a phonetic text for voice; and even to the speaking chorus of Toch's "Geographical Fugue," a tour de force of place names from his *Gesprochene Musik* of 1930.

From a more purely musical background, any number of events helped to promote further exploration after 1950. Initially, the fervor with which the athleticism of Webern's vocal style was attacked and assimilated by numerous singers during the 1960s helped to encourage the composer to believe in the possibility of an extended interval technique formerly thought to be instrumental. While isolated instances in Mozart, Wagner, and Schoenberg were known to connoisseurs, such a persistent emphasis on large or difficult intervals without Puccini-like instrumental doubling had theretofore been considered at the limits of the unattainable, and then supposedly only by singers with perfect pitch. Concurrently, the flexibility of several generations of popular singers from Ella Fitzgerald to Sarah Vaughan and ultimately Cleo Laine gave proof of technical access to a whole range of acrobatics and vocal colorings. In an age that also saw the revival of the *bel canto* style of Bellini and Donizetti in a movement begun by the legendary Maria Callas, a wave of interest in reexploring the voice from the ground up could have hardly been forestalled, though not without periodic warnings from numerous vocal pedagogues. It was also a time that saw the American premiere of the incomplete version of *Lulu* (Santa Fe, 1963) and a successful search for a completed one (Paris, 1979). *Lulu*, which already contains the continuum from speech through *Sprechstimme* and song in its Prologue, exhibits one of the most elaborate and difficult coloratura roles in all operatic literature, but also one that, it is well to understand, was ripe for final consummation in the 1970s. It may also be added that the New Vocalism was predominately, if not exclusively, female.

Numerous works of the 1960s and 1970s by Berio, Crumb, and Babbitt, for example, were frequently associated with a principal singer (Cathy Berbarian, Jan de Gaetani, and Bethany Beardslee, respectively) who encouraged the composer to believe in the potential for expressive extensions in the human voice. Not only whispering, groaning, clicking of the tongue, but especially the projection of isolated words and syllables (Boulez, *Pli selon pli*, 1957–62; Berio, *Circles*, 1960, and *Visage*, 1961; Crumb, *Ancient Voices of Children*, 1970) brought a challenge to the human voice that disclosed more than a casual affinity with the experiments of the Futurists. In *Vision and Prayer* (1961), Babbitt associated the vowels of Dylan Thomas with specific timbres, while in *Phonemena* (1974) nonsense phonemes are subjected to dodecaphonic formalizations that "create" a text, a notion prefigured in part by the Canadian Harry Somers in his *Voiceplay* (1971) for Cathy Berbarian.

BERIO: *CIRCLES, VISAGE, RECITAL I, SINFONIA.*   It was Berbarian who also led her then husband, Luciano Berio, to his most important dicoveries in this field. Following his electronically manipulated *Omaggio à Joyce* (1958), he then composed *Circles* for live performers calling for a new level of interplay between the voice and its accompanying forces of harp and two percussion. The work is based on three poems of e. e. cummings (A B C) that are arranged in diminishing levels of comprehensibility and formally subjected to palindromic reversal in a plan ABCB'A'. This is matched by corresponding degrees of rhythmic and timbral freedom, the middle section being the freest. The voice, however, begins in a highly ornate manner that becomes progressively simpler through syllabic and finally speech modes in section C, but then, rather than reversing its style to conform to the beginning, increasingly approximates the manner of the instrumentalists through the close. Such a systematic investigation of the voice in relation to its surroundings had its next consequences in *Visage* (1961), a work for magnetic tape, based on the voice of Cathy Berbarian and electronic sounds. Berio has called the work a purely radio-program work not intended for the concert hall, and has provided the following orientation for the listener:

> *Visage* can be heard also as a metaphor of vocal behavior: it means discourse mainly at the onomatopoeic level. Thus *Visage* does not present meaningful speech but the semblance of it. Only a single word is pronounced and repeated: the word 'parole,' meaning 'words' in Italian. The vocal events from inarticulated or articulated 'speech,' from laughter to crying and to singing, from patterns of inflections modeled upon specific languages to 'aphasia,' etc., are constantly related to electrically produced sounds . . . For me, *Visage* also constitutes a tribute to the radio as the most widespread disseminator of useless words.[2]

Berio's New Vocalism, a term frequently restricted to nonelectronic compositions, has appeared attached to works of literary merit (e.e. cummings, Joyce, Garcia Lorca, Levi-Strauss, Beckett) as well as in association with the performances and tunes of popular groups such as the Swingle Singers. Berio has discussed the textual element of his *Sinfonia* (1968) as follows:

> The title *Sinfonia* bears no relationship to the classical form—rather it must be understood in its etymological sense, of "sounding together" of eight voices and instruments or, in a larger sense, of "sounding together" of different things, situations, meanings, references . . . the musical development of *Sinfonia* is always conditioned by the research for a continuity and an identity between text and music, between spoken and sung words and between the different harmonic stages of the work. Often the text is not immediately perceivable as such. The words and their components undergo an "analysis" which is integral to the total musical structure of the voices and instruments together. It is precisely because the varying degree of perceptibility of the text at different moments is part of the musical structure, that the experience of "not quite hearing", then, is to be conceived as essential to the nature of the musical process.
>
> I. The text of the first part consists of a series of short fragments from *Le cru et le cuit* by C. Levi-Strauss, in particular from those sections of the book where the French anthropologist analyzes the structure and symbology of Brazilian myths about the origins of water and related myths characterized by similar structure.
>
> II. The second part of *Sinfonia* is a tribute to the memory of Dr. Martin Luther King. The eight voices exchange among themselves the sounds constituting the name of the black martyr until the point when his name is clearly enunciated ("O Martin Luther King").
>
> III. The main text for the third section is formed by excerpts from S. Beckett's *The Unnamable*, which, in turn, generate a large number of "daily life" references and quotations . . .
>
> IV. The text of the fourth part, after a brief reference to the beginning words of the fourth movement of Mahler's Second Symphony, is based on a very short selection of the text used in the three preceding parts.
>
> V. Finally, the text for the fifth part recapitulates, develops and completes the texts of the preceding parts, giving narrative substance and continuity to those fragments (from *Le cru et le cuit*) that in the first part had been enunciated as snatches of imaginary stories . . . The five parts of *Sinfonia* are, apparently, very different, one from the other. However, it is the role of the fifth part to annul that difference, bringing to light and developing the latent unity of the preceding parts. In this fifth part, in fact, the discourse begun and left suspended in the first part, finds its conclusion: all other parts flow into it, either as fragments (third and fourth parts) or in its complete form (second part). This fifth part can thus be

considered as a true analysis of *Sinfonia* conducted with the "language" of the composition itself.[3]

The value and force of Berio's "not quite hearing" the text was also obviously understood by Salvitore Martirano in his mixed-media, *L's GA* of the same year (1968).

> Lincoln's Gettysburg *Address* for actor, tape, and film, using a helium 'bomb' which the actor breathes from at the end of the piece so that his voice goes up a couple of octaves . . . all you need to do is catch a few words now and then to understand what the meaning is. You hear 'government' and you hear 'people'. And thus I would hope that the person watching would create the framework of specific and exact meaning according to how he sees things. Because I'm not forcing him to catch on to a sequence of events in which each one has to be understood for the next one to make sense. It's almost kind of throwing it in all different places and gradually, I would hope, the conception is built up in the audience.[4]

An anti-war diatribe which projects Lincoln's words in a heavy German accent in one section, the work's tangled symbolism produces a harrowing effect.

Clearly, the capacity for multiple understandings in such multimedia works is not considered a hazard but rather the heart of the matter. As such, multiple interpretations carrying numerous social and aesthetic messages were not only possible but inevitable, meshing alternatively with Dadaist negation, Stockhausen's nonsequential moment, or modish themes of the day as in *Zeitoper*.

Such developments have led naturally to the theater piece, involving mixed media and/or many of the technical innovations cited above. While it is possible to claim an ancestry in this century that reaches back to *Histoire du soldat* and *Pierrot lunaire* (Sprechstimme; the ad hoc instrumental ensemble), *Die glückliche Hand* and *Prometheus* (the light-sound show), or Satie's *Relâche* (film), of necessity pieces like Cage's *Music Walk* (1958) and *Theater Piece* (1960) served not so much as an explicit model as a point of departure. Cage's notion expressed in *Silence* that "Theater takes place all the time, wherever one is, and art simply facilitates persuading one this is the case," helped to promote a new sense of spectacle—one that may have lacked a linear sense of narrative but which, in its endorsement of the indeterminate with respect to composition and performance, was free to pursue a seeming chaos and its unsuspected fruits through inference. A physical action, spontaneously introduced, could alternately substitute for an indeterminate sound, and together they could create a theater whose message the audience was left to divine. Chance and indeterminacy had now conspired to create a "happening."

In his *La testa d'Adriane* of 1976, R. Murray Schafer has an accordionist bring back to life the head of Adriane (or Ariadne), who in a previous act had been cut to pieces by a magician.

> The head sings, screams, laughs, sobs as the accordionist directs but at the end falls back into the sleep from which she came at the beginning.[5]

Part of a larger music-theater piece entitled *The Greatest Show on Earth*, the composer advises that when completed it

> will consist of one hundred small pieces to be performed in countless tents and booths outdoors as a village fair. The audience will be free to walk about and choose the entertainments which please them.[6]

Recollections of *musique d'ameublement* (see p. 000) or the Dadaist's scissors (see p. 000)?

Works such as R. Murray Schafer's *Requiems for the Party-Girl* (1966), Peter Maxwell Davies' *Eight Songs for a Mad King* (1969), or Berio's *Recital for Cathy I* (1972) have introduced an updated social theme that is more psychological-personal than political. The latter by Berio, a portrayal of the breakdown of a singer in concert, had been preceded by Cathy Berbarian's *Stripsody* (1966), a divertimento-collage of onomatopoeic words that appear in comic strips.

> Within this collage, short scenes have been inserted: either quotations from well known strips such as "Peanuts" or "Superman" or else sequences that could be brief movie bits, such as a murder scene, or a girl waiting for her boy friend (*Erwartung!*), or a cat-and-dog fight, or a cowboy and Indian show. In the performance, these short interpolated scenes are indicated by a double hand gesture to one side to signal the beginning, and the same sharp gesture to the other side when the scene has been finished. The physical gestures in the rest of the piece are just as inseparable from the vocal gestures—one could say that the action is irresistably bound to the production of the sound . . . *Stripsody* is in line with the recent re-evaluation of comic strips as a significant mirror of contemporary society with its phobias and problems.[7]

Other composers have been more interested in addressing moral and political issues. Even the work of social protest still persists as a genre in compositions such as Nono's *Intolleranza* (1960/70, two versions) or Rzewski's Minimalist extravaganzas, *Coming Together* and *Attica*, written in 1972 following prison riots in upstate New York. No composer, however, tuned his music so directly to such themes as Henze.

HENZE: *BEING BEAUTEOUS* AND *VOICES*. Hans Werner Henze (b. 1926), obsessively holding to the promotion of an underlying social message beginning in the 1960s, has understandably not employed the voice as an agent for the projection of phonemes or of textual obfuscation and has frequently endorsed its capacity for lyricism. While Stravinskian Neoclassicism and an intuitive application of Schoenbergian chromaticism combined to fashion Henze's early musical personality, his later claim in a variety of styles to a particular concern with melody is exemplified in his *Five Neapolitan Songs* (1956) for baritone and orchestra. A more rarified illustration of his lyric gifts is found in the cantata, *Being Beauteous* (1963), set to a Symbolist prose-poem from Rimbaud's *Illuminations* (tapped earlier by Britten for a vocal cycle). Written following a visit to Harlem by night, it speaks both of menace and beauty in a dark world. Its New Vocalism is marked by an eerie, fine spun vocal line with an elaborate coloratura inspired by the soprano Eda Moser. More allied to Schoenberg's *Herzgewächse* than to Boulez' *Le marteau sans maître*, the piece is a spiritual cousin of both. It is accompanied by four cellos and harp, which also punctuate Rimbaud's stanzas and clarify their structure.

Devant une neige, un Être de Beauté de haute taille. Des sifflements de mort et des cercles de musique sourde font monter, s'élargir et trembler comme un spectre ce corps adoré.

Against the snow a Beauteous Being of high stature. Whistlings of death and circles of faint music cause this adored body to rise up, stretch itself and tremble like a ghost.

Le couleurs propres de la vie se foncent, dansent, et se dégagent autour de la Vision, sur le chantier. Des blessure écarlates et noires éclatent dans les chairs superbes.	The colors proper to life deepen, dance, and detach themselves around the Vision as it forms. Scarlet and black wounds flash in the proud flesh.
Et les frissons s'élèvant et grondent, et la saveur forcenée de ces effets se chargeant avec les sifflements mortels et les rauques musiques que le mond, loin derrière nous, lance sur notre mère de beauté,—elle recule, elle se dresse. Oh! nos os sont revêtus d'un nouveau corps amoureux.	And shivers rise and snarl, and the mad flavor of these effects is filled with the mortal whistlings and the raucous music which the world, far behind us, hurls at our mother beauty,—she recoils, she rears up. Oh! our bones are recloaked with a new and amorous body.
O la face cendrée, l'écusson de crin, les bras de cristal! le canon sur lequel je dois m'abattre à travers la mêlée des arbres et de l'air léger!	O the ashen face, the escutcheon of horsehair, the crystal arms. The cannon on which I must throw myself through the conflict of the trees and the light air!

Rimbaud

In later works such as *Das Floss der "Medusa"* (1968), a requiem for Che Guevara inspired by Géricault's painting of the same name, Henze, without sacrificing the importance of his text, has set aside some of his earlier lyricism and intermingled a range of vocal sonorities with more traditional means. The same may be said of *Voices* (1973) for mezzo-soprano, tenor, electronics, and fifteen instrumentalists playing some seventy different instruments from around the world. In a cycle of twenty-two songs, which may be performed independently or in any combination, Henze has created a vast music-theater collage of widely differing styles, resources and languages (English, German, Spanish, and Italian as well as translations from Greek and Vietnamese). From the electronic background and spoken declamation à la Berio of "The Leg Irons" (Ho Chi Minh) to the tango rhythms à la Weill's *Petroleum Song* of "Keiner oder Alle" (Brecht) to the haunting duet of the concluding "Carnival of Flowers," Henze pursues his Marxist message in various tongues concerning the plight of the worker, the miseries of war, and the inevitability of revolution. Regardless of one's political leanings, the effect is chilling and the eclecticism powerful. The work as a whole, however, carries less the effect of a grab-bag of vocal tricks and stylistic adventures than the product of a composer with a keen ear for instrumental color and a powerful lyricism traceable to his works of the 1950s.

DAVIES, *EIGHT SONGS OF A MAD KING.*   In an article in *The Score* of March 1956, Peter Maxwell Davies (b. 1934) signaled his future stance by chiding British conservatism and lack of technique as well as insisting on the importance of a knowledge of early music. Something of all these beliefs was given testimony in a series of works written in 1961–62, all of which by the composer's admission had their starting point in a study of Monteverdi's Vespers of 1610. More important for the range of expression that was to appear in *Eight Songs of a Mad King* (1969), however, was *Revelation and Fall* (1966) for voice and sixteen players on a poem of Trakl.

Together with Harrison Birtwistle, Davies had formed the Pierrot Players in 1967. Using the basic ensemble of Schoenberg's piece with the addition of percussion, the music theater aspect of the group was prominent from its inception, though it was reformed independent of Birtwistle and renamed the

Fires of London in 1970. The extraordinary vocalism and histrionic abilities of the group's soprano, Mary Thomas, was apparent from early performances of *Pierrot* as well as in later works that Davies wrote especially for her (*Donnithorne's Maggot*, 1974, and *The Medium*, 1981). The infatuation with a freely exhuberant vocal style became the cornerstone of *Eight Songs of a Mad King* as well, a work wherein the composer recaptured the manic qualities of Schoenberg's score through a male singer of extended range portraying King George III. The instrumentalists, once again corresponding to the *Pierrot* ensemble, are kept in birdcages and portray both the bullfinches the King was teaching to sing as well as the reflections in his mind of the various persons and subjects touched on in his monologues. Thus in the seventh song when the King "snatches the violin through the bars of the player's cage and breaks it," it is "not just the killing of a bullfinch—it is a giving-in to insanity, and a ritual murder by the King of a part of himself, after which, at the beginning of No. 8, he can announce his own death."[8]

For sheer madness, there are few scores to compare with Davies' cycle. The psychological factor in Schoenberg's *Erwartung*, for example, is more of Freud's dream world, and the text of *Pierrot* fails to secure a mounting dementia through a constant shifting between the first and third person. The King's monologues, however, are his own, and the bedlam of his mind is mirrored in a vocal style not unlike the abstractions and vocal acrobatics of Berio's *Visage* or Druckman's *Animus II*, a textless theater piece of 1967–68 for soprano, percussion, and tape. The instrumental contortions, on the other hand, are only vaguely related to contemporaneous electronic collaborations. Thus, the extravagant clarinet part seems less a companion to Druckman's *Animus III* for clarinet, tape, and electronic feedback of the same year than a psychological wreck cast adrift from a life exhausted in playing the *Symphonie fantastique, Til Eulenspiegel*, and *Pierrot lunaire*.

Parallels between *Pierrot* and *Eight Songs* with respect to instrumental resource, exaggerated vocalism, and rotational combinations, including the use of voice and flute in No. 3, should not cloud the immediate prehistory of exploration with regard to the new vocalism or obscure the non-Schoenbergian stylistic variety of the work. Davies has remarked on these two qualities:

> The vocal writing calls for extremes of register and a virtuoso acting ability; my intention was, with this, and the mixture of styles in the music together with the look of the cages, suggesting prison or hospital beds, to leave open the question, is the persecuted protagonist Mad George III, or somebody who *thinks* he is George?[9]

Straight parody of Handel, appropriate eighteenth-century allusion, occurs in No. 6, which in No. 7, the climax of the work, becomes outright distortion through the transformation of familiar material from *Messiah* into a foxtrot. The latter dance has been used in numerous works by Davies as a symbol of 1920s decadence and is utilized here as an outrageous music for his "Country Dance" in a double stylistic incongruity.

After 1970, Davies became increasingly concerned with historical proto-types (e.g., *Tenebrae pro Gesualdo*, 1972; see p. 642), larger formal issues, isorhythmic processes, and magic squares (an arrangement of numbers in which all horizontal and vertical rows add up to the same number). Use of the latter in *Ave Maris Stella* (1975) as a means of determining various parameters tended to

Figure 29.1. Peter Maxwell Davies at home in the Orkney Islands.
Photo by Gunnie Moberg.

lead him away from the edge of such a sinister mockery clothed in the extravagant gesture and look forward to the large-scale symphonies which were to follow. In *The No. 11 Bus* (1984), however, Davies forsook the Scottish and Orkney Island references of many of the works of the preceding period (Figure 29.1), and relocating in the city (contemporary London) resumed his biting parody in a work for six virtuosi (*The Fires of London*), together with three singers, two dancers, and a mime on an allegorical journey.

Nonetheless, it was *Eight Songs* that forced the recognition of a major musical and theatrical talent, which had already written by that time the as yet unproduced opera *Taverner* (1962–68; premiered 1972). Birtwistle's *Punch and Judy* (1966–67) had also preceded it, but few products by an Englishman had previously captured the wit and bemused worldliness of this inimitable score. With it the promise of an English avant-garde, momentarily hinted at in 1921 with the appearance of Walton's *Façade*, was finally fulfilled.

Eight Songs for a Mad King:

6. THE COUNTERFEIT *(LE CONTREFAITE)*

The text is taken from one of the King's own monologues, recorded by Queen Charlotte's eavesdropper, Fanny Burney.

I am nervous. I am not ill
but I am nervous.
If you would know what is the matter
with me
I am nervous.
But I love you both very well;
if you would tell me the truth.
I love Doctor Heberden best:
for he has not told me a lie.
Sir George has told me a lie: 1
a white lie, he says
but I hate a white lie!
2   If you tell me a lie,
    let it be a black lie!

7. COUNTRY DANCE *(Scotch Bonnett)*

The King imagines the people of Windsor (of whom he once said, weeping: "These good people are fond of Me") engaged in country merrymaking. He encourages them with one of the quotations from Handel which punctuated his conversation. He recalls a piece of local knowledge with which he once startled his grooms. Then (as in his famous interview with Fanny Burney at Kew) he becomes suddenly agitated about the evils of the age. (The Kew interview was terminated by the doctors after the King had cried: "When once I get away, I shall rule with a rod of iron!")

(Piano Intro.: 4)

3   Comfort ye, comfort ye, my people
4   with singing and with dancing,
    with milk and with apples.
    The landlord of the Three Tuns
    makes the best purl in Windsor.
    Sin! Sin! Sin!
    black vice, intolerable vileness
    in lanes, by ricks, at Courts.[5]
    It is night on the world.
    Even I, your King, have contemplated
    evil.
6   I shall rule with a rod of iron.
7   Comfort ye.

[1] *V vs. I chord;* [2] *Flamenco style;* [3] *Handel quotation;* [4] *Foxtrot;* [5] *Handel chords and clusters;* [6] *Recitative;* [7] *Falsetto quotation.*

CRUMB, *ANCIENT VOICES OF CHILDREN.* Among American composers who came to the fore in the 1960s and whose reputation was strongly connected with the "new vocalism" in conjunction with a similar investigation of instrumental virtuosity, none found a more immediate and appreciative audience than George Crumb (b. 1929). His almost obsessive interest in setting texts by Garcia Lorca promoted not only an obvious continuity but also helped to determine the quality of much of his music, including strictly instrumental pieces. Emphasis on sonority—from the macabre to the delicate, from the dance ostinato to the mysterious sounds of the night—confirmed his acknowledged indebtedness to Debussy, Mahler, and Bartók. The attendant theatricality of both his texted (e.g., *Ancient Voices of Children*, 1970) and untexted pieces (e.g., *Vox balanae*, 1971) reflects the vivid state of affairs common in diverse quarters during the period. Yet where hysteria or nonsense antics may have ruled in the works of his American avant-garde contemporaries, Crumb found a haunting vocal style that was at once plastic, non-Western in orientation, and enormously evocative of his chosen texts. Stylistic unity achieved from a careful blend of seemingly disparate materials, including quotation, eerie echoes (the singer vocalizing into the piano with the damper pedal depressed or the use of electronic amplification), and a battery of unusual percussion instruments, led to a drama that found a wide appeal.

A work for soprano, boy soprano, oboe, mandolin, harp, electric piano, and percussion (including tam-tams, claves, maracas, Tibetan prayer stones, and Japanese temple bells), *Ancient Voices of Children* is remarkable not only for the elegant calligraphy of its score but for a notation that is as functional as it is symbolic. In five movements, it is punctuated by three dances: "Dances of the Ancient Earth" following the first movement; "Ghost Dance" preceding the last movement; and "Dance of the Sacred Life-Cycle" performed in conjunction with the central movement. The latter, formed over an ostinato in "tempo di bolero" is notated in a circle, and calls to mind both the circular score of Baude Cordier in the late fourteenth century as well as the more immediate appeal of circular forms for Berg, Berio, and Stockhausen or even Ravel's *Bolero* or the "Tango (perpétuel)" of Satie's *Sports et Divertissements*. The emphasis on the elements of life, death, and "the spirit of the earth" naturally point to Mahler, and the oboe refrain with tam-tam in the fifth movement marked "timidly, with a sense of loneliness" is a tender borrowing from the closing movement of *Das Lied von der Erde*. The net effect of this and other allusions discussed by Crumb in the following passage in no way prevents a stylistic congruity and, while reflective of a fashion of the seventies, holds little hint of pastiche or bifocal uneasiness.

The coloristic instrumental resource marked by a prominent use of unusual percussion with a decidedly Oriental patina cojoined to a vocalism that proclaims Lorca and non-Lorcan phonemes in alternating moods of exuberance and quiet furnish an immediate and lasting impact. The work was dedicated to Jan De Gaetani, who through this work joined other American singers such as Bethany Beardsley and Cathy Berbarian as a formidable collaborator in the cause of defining a new and expressive style—here indebted as much to Oriental vocalises as to Bellini.

The composer has spoken openly and articulately about the multiple forces at work in his *Ancient Voices of Children*, a work that like Davies' *Eight Songs of a Mad King* sealed his relation to a wider public.

> In *Ancient Voices of Children*, as in my earlier Lorca settings, I have sought musical images that enhance and reinforce the powerful, yet strangely haunting imagery of Lorca's poetry. I feel that the essential meaning of this poetry is concerned with the most primary things: life, death, love, the smell of the earth, the sounds of the wind and the sea. These 'ur-concepts' are embodied in a language which is primitive and stark, but which is capable of infinitely subtle nuance. In a

lecture entitled *Theory and Function of the 'Duende'*, Lorca has, in fact, identified the essential characteristic of his own poetry. *Duende* (untranslatable, but roughly: passion, elan, bravura in its deepest, most artistic sense) is for Lorca "all that has dark sounds . . . This 'mysterious power that everyone feels but no philosopher has explained' is in fact the spirit of the earth . . . All one knows is that it burns the blood like powdered glass, that it exhausts, that it rejects all the sweet geometry one has learned . . . "

The text of *Ancient Voices* are fragments of longer poems which I have grouped into a sequence that seemed to suggest a "larger rhythm" in terms of musical continuity. The two purely instrumental movements—"Dances of the Ancient Earth" and "Ghost Dances"—are dance-interludes rather than commentaries on the texts. These two pieces, together with the third song, subtitled "Dance of the Sacred Life-Cycle" (which contains a rising-falling *ostinato* bolero rhythm in the drums), can be performed by a solo dancer.

The vocal style in the cycle ranges from the virtuosic to the intimately lyrical, and in my conception of the work I very much had in mind Jan DeGaetani's enormous technical and timbral flexibility. Perhaps the most characteristic vocal effect in *Ancient Voices* is produced by the mezzo soprano singing a kind of fantastic vocalise (based on purely phonetic sounds) into an amplified piano, thereby producing a shimmering aura of echoes. The inclusion of a part for boy soprano seemed the best solution for those passages in the text where Lorca clearly implies a child's voice. The boy soprano is heard offstage until the very last page of the work, at which point he joins the mezzo-soprano onstage for the closing vocalise.

The instruments employed in *Ancient Voices* were chosen for their particular timbral potentialities. The pianist also plays toy piano (in the fourth song), the mandolinist musical saw (second song) and the oboist harmonica (fourth song). Certain special instrumental effects are used to heighten the "expressive intensity"—e.g., "bending" the pitch of the piano by application of a chisel to the strings (second song); use of a paper-threaded harp (in "Dances of the Ancient Earth"); the frequent 'pitch-bending' of the oboe, harp, and mandolin. The mandolin has one set of strings tuned a quarter-tone low in order to give a special pungency to its tone. The three percussionists command a wide range of instruments, including Tibetan prayer stone, Japanese temple bells, and tuned tom-toms. The instrumentalists are frequently called upon to sing, shout, and whisper.

In composing *Ancient Voices of Children* I was conscious of an urge to fuse various unrelated stylistic elements. I was intrigued with the idea of juxtaposing the seemingly incongruous: a suggestion of Flamenco with a Baroque quotation (*Bist du bei mir*, from the Notebook of Anna Magdalena Bach), or a reminiscence of Mahler with a breath of the Orient. It later occurred to me that both Bach and Mahler drew upon many disparate sources in their own music without sacrificing 'stylistic purity'.

It is sometimes of interest to a composer to recall the original impulse—the 'creative germ'—of a compositional project. In the case of *Ancient Voices* I felt this impulse to be the climactic final words of the last song: ". . . and I will go very far . . . to ask Christ the Lord to give me back my ancient soul of a child."

Notes to Nonesuch Record H-71255. Reprinted by permission.

Example 29.1. Crumb, *Ancient Voices of Children* Mvt. 4.

IV. Todas las tardes en Granada, todas las tardes se muere un niño
[Each afternoon in Granada, a child dies each afternoon]

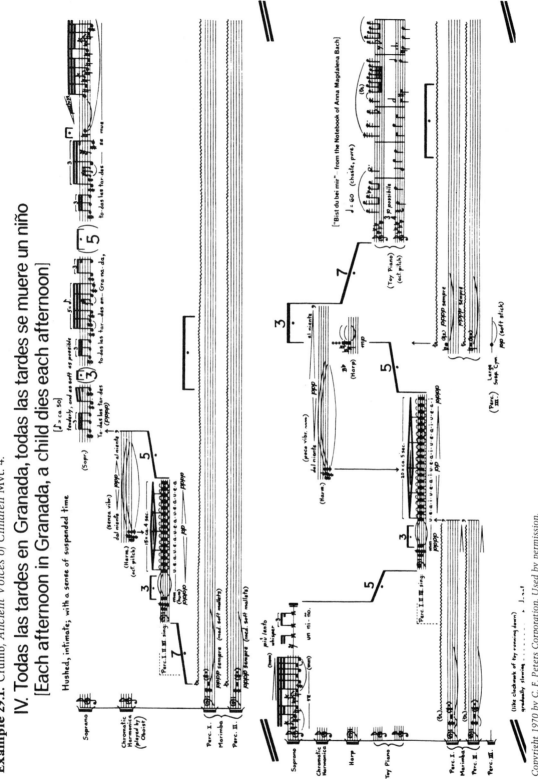

Ancient Voices of Children

I

El niño busca su voz.
(La tenía el rey de los grillos.)
En una gota de agua
buscaba su voz el niño.

No la quiero para hablar;
me haré con ella un anillo
que llevará mi silencio
en su dedo pequeñito.

The little boy was looking for his voice.
(The king of the crickets had it.)
In a drop of water
the little boy was looking for his voice.

I do not want it for speaking with;
I will make a ring of it
so that he may wear my silence
on his little finger.

II   ("Dances of the Ancient Earth")

Me he perdido muchas veces por el mar
con el oído lleno de flores recién cortadas,
con la lengua llena de amor y de agonía.
Muchas veces me he perdido por el mar,
como me pierdo en el corazón de algunos
    niños.

I have lost myself in the sea many times
with my ear full of freshly cut flowers,
with my tongue full of love and agony.
I have lost myself in the sea many times
as I lose myself in the heart of certain
    children.

III   "Dance of the Sacred Life-Cycle"

¿ De dónde vienes, amor, mi niño?
De la cresta del duro frío.
¿ Qué necesitas, amor, mi niño?
La tibia tela de tu vestido.
¡Que se agiten las ramas al sol
y salten las fuentes alrededor!
En el patio ladra el perro,
en los árboles canta el viento.
Los bueyes mugen al boyero
y la luna me riza los cabellos.
¿ Qué pides, niño, desde tan
    lejos?
Los blancos montes que hay en tu pecho.
¡Que se agiten las ramas al sol
y salten las fuentes alrededor!
Te diré, niño mío, que sí,
tronchada y rota soy para ti.
¡Cómo me duele esta cintura
donde tendrás primera cuna!
¿Cuando, mi niño, vas a venir?
Cuando tu carne huela a jazmín.
¡Que se agiten las ramas al sol
y salten las fuentes alrededor!

From where do you come, my love, my child?
From the ridge of hard frost.
What do you need, my love, my child?
The warm cloth of your dress.
Let the branches ruffle in the sun
and the fountains leap all around!
In the courtyard a dog barks,
in the trees the wind sings.
The oxen low to the ox-herd
and the moon curls my hair.
What do you ask for, my child, from so far
    away?
The white mountains of your breast.
Let the branches ruffle in the sun
and the fountains leap all around!
I'll tell you, my child, yes,
I am torn and broken for you.
How painful is this waist
where you will have your first cradle!
When, my child, will you come?
When your flesh smells of jasmine-flowers.
Let the branches ruffle in the sun
and the fountains leap all around!

IV

Todas las tardes en Granada,
todas las tardes se muere un niño.

Each afternoon in Granada,
a child dies each afternoon.

V   ("Ghost Dance")

Se ha llenado de luces
mi corazón de seda,
de campanas perdidas,
de lirios y de abejas.
Y yo me iré muy lejos,
más allá de esas sierras,

My heart of silk
is filled with lights,
with lost bells,
with lilies, and with bees,
and I will go very far,
farther than those hills,

más allá de los mares,	farther than the seas,
cerca de las estrellas,	close to the stars,
para pedirle a Cristo	to ask Christ the Lord
Señor que me devuelva	to give me back
mi alma antigua de niño.	my ancient soul of a child.

English Translations by W. S. Merwin (I), Stephen Spender and J. L. Gili (II), J. L. Gili (III and V), and Edwin Honig (IV).

LUTOSŁAWSKI, *TROIS POÈMES D'HENRI MICHAUX.* In the early part of the century, the single internationally important Polish composer had been Karol Szymanowski (1882–1937), and between the wars two groups loosely allied with the German-Russian axis and with Boulanger's Neoclassicism were held as the most prominent. In 1948, coincidental with the appearance of the Soviet Communist Party Central Committee's resolution condemning Western formalisms and decadent avantgardism, a burgeoning Socialist government in Poland began to impose guidelines for the composition of an "official" Polish music. As in Russia, works with a nationalist program and using native, preferably folk, materials were to be favored. As Stefan Jarocinski wrote,

> The proposition of composing music inspired by folklore was neither new nor harmless in itself but it was growing absurd when it was married with the demand of returning to functional harmony and to the major-minor system . . .[10]

While Witold Lutosławski (b. 1913) had been active as a composer since the 1930s, his first postwar success was the *Symphony No. 1* (1941–48), premiered in 1948. The work was now condemned as formalist, and though many composers followed the Soviet line, Lutosławski fell silent except for the writing of children's pieces, which he considered utilitarian as opposed to capitulatory. Though the use of folk tunes was typical for these and other works of the period such as *Bucolics* for piano of 1952, the composer gradually worked his way out of what Stucky[11] has called "the dark years: 1949–54" in the writing of a *Concerto for Orchestra* (1951–54). Combining a catalogue of Polish folk tunes with Neoclassic designations (the third movement is a Passacaglia, Toccata, and Chorale), Lutosławski unleashed a voice only modestly indebted to Bartók in a Poland, following the death of Stalin in 1953, that gradually experienced a liberating cultural thaw. With the serialist procedures of *Funeral Music* of 1954–58), intended as a commemoration of the tenth anniversary of Bartók's death (1955)—Lutosławski did not so much effect a rapprochement with Schoenberg as recognize in its two constituent intervals—alternating tritone and minor second (F-B, B♭-E, E♭-A, A♭-D, D♭-G, G♭-C)—a predisposition of longstanding that he shared with Bartók. With the "controlled" aleatoricism of his *Venetian Games* (1961), Lutosławski launched the style of his full maturity, but once again his devotion to such techniques was only mildly improvisatory, not philosophically Cageian. In the works ahead, neither dodecaphonism nor chance was to predominate, though both would color a language that had been thirty years in the making.

The amalgamation of many of these same ingredients into a forceful expression among other composers such as Kazmierz Serocki (b. 1922) and

Tadeusz Baird (b. 1928) soon brought the recognition of a so-called "Polish School." But what these composers and others of a younger generation that included Penderecki (b. 1933) and Gorecki (b. 1933) shared was not so much a style as a common enthusiasm and talent for taking a fresh look at the accretions to musical expression of the early postwar years. Their collective contribution, served up annually in the Warsaw Autumn Festivals beginning in 1956, was in a nondoctrinaire exploration of sound that produced many remarkable scores.

1962 brought Lutosławski on a visit to the United States at the invitation of Aaron Copland. Here he met numerous composers including Lukas Foss, Leon Kirchner, Irving Fine, and Arthur Berger at Tanglewood, and this was followed by visits to the Columbia-Princeton Electronic Music Center and the electronic studio at the University of Illinois. Although neither serialism nor electronics was destined to play a role in his music in the immediate years ahead, with the *Trois poèmes d'Henri Michaux* of 1961–63, a work for chorus and orchestra, Lutosławski created a piece of such originality and undeniable force that his name was immediately entered among the ranks of the avantgarde. Effective in its first hearings, like Britten's *War Requiem* and Crumb's *Ancient Voices of Children*, it has had to survive its initial popularity. That it was a thoughtful rethinking of the choral medium and involved a significant contribution to the portrayal of words as meaning as well as sonic resource has since been confirmed.

Among various unusual features of the score, the call for two conductors arises from rhythmic and temporal complexities that proceed independently. An ad libitum rhythmic freedom is promoted in the choral writing where durational values are clearly marked by horizontal lines according to the general equation: 2.5 cm = 1 sec. The pitch component is explicit in the first and third movements, including a full twelve-tone complement as the opening sonority of the work in the orchestra. But to the relative sense of time, he adds a nonspecific pitch dimension in the second movement that is relative to the general tessitura of a given voice part (Ex. 29.2).

The composer has noted his choice of Michaux as poet by pointing to his rhythmic and formal variety. For example, in the following two lines from the first poem,

> Qui glissez en nous, entre nous, loin de nous,
> Loin de nous éclairer, loin de rien pénétrer;

Lutosławski noted how the first of these created both a diminuendo and ritenuto through successive uses of the pronoun "nous," a prolongation and thinning down that was mirrored in the succeeding line as a variation of the same formal ideal. It was this extraordinary sense of musicality inherent in Michaux's verses, involving both a plan of sonority and a manner of organizing time, that appealed to the composer.[12]

Lutosławski's concern for textual intelligibility was also paramount, but he realized that

> the same phrases are sometimes repeated, and it is not necessary that the repetitions be intelligible, especially in certain moments of *Grand Combat* where different phrases are shouted at the same time. It is useless at such moments to require a comprehension of the text, since it has already been heard ... This

Example 29.2. Lutosławski, *Trois poèmes d'Henri Michaux:* "Le Grand Combat," nos. 42–45.

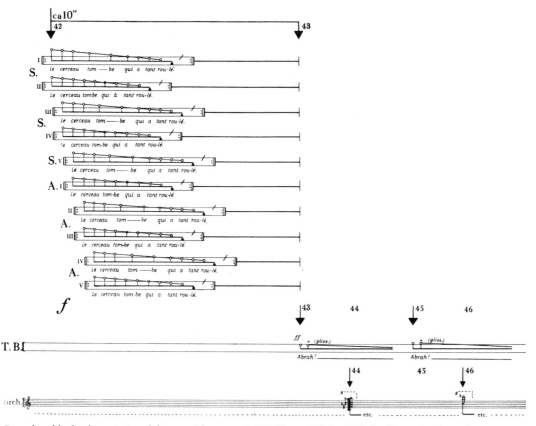

having been said, I understand only too well that a composer may not always have this same preoccupation, and he may see above all in the text, outside its collective meaning, a succession of syllables which he utilizes as sonorous elements of his music.

This also interests me in a certain sense. For example, in the *Grand Combat* I have utilised a manner of shouting as nearly natural as possible. And even the notation, which is only approximate since it is not determined by the exact pitch of the sound but only the register—this notation of registers, of rhythms, of accents came to me as an inspiration through the most natural manner of speaking the text with a certain emotional character. It is a furious crowd which comments upon the action by cries and this results in a grand sonic disorder.[13]

Thus Lutosławski's aim was not only to induce chaos but to control his means through a notation that was sufficiently precise yet free, and, as he put it, "to restore thereby the pleasure which the performer should feel with the performance of a work."[14]

Witold Lutosławski, Trois poèmes d'Henri Michaux (1963)

Three Poems by Henri Michaux

PENSEES

Penser, vivre, mer peu distincte;
Moi—ça—tremble,
Infini incessamment qui tressaille.

Ombres de mondes infimes,
ombres d'ombres,
cendres d'ailes.

Pensées à la nage merveilleuse,
qui glissez en nous, entre nous, loin de nous,

loin de nous éclairer, loin de rien pénétrer;

étrangères en nos maisons,
toujours à colporter,
poussières pour nous distraire et nous
    éparpiller la vie.

LE GRAND COMBAT

Il l'emparouille et l'endosque contre terre;
Il le rague et le roupète jusqu'à son drâle;
Il le pratèle et le libucque et lui barufle les
    ouillais;
Il le tocarde et le marmine,
Le manage rape à ri et ripe à ra.

Enfin il l'écorcobalisse.
L'autre hésite s'espudrine, se défaisse, se torse
    et se ruine.
C'en sera bientôt fini de lui;
Il se reprise et s'emmargine...
    mais en vain
Le cerceau tombe qui a tant roulé.
Abrah! Abrah! Abrah!
Le pied a failli!
Le bras a cassé!
Le sang a coulé!
Fouille, fouille, fouille,
Dans la marmite de son ventre est un grand
    secret
Mégères alentour qui pleurez dans vos
    mouchoirs;
On s'étonne, on s'étonne, on s'étonne
Et vous regarde
On cherche aussi, nous autres, le Grand
    Secret.

REPOS DANS LE MALHEUR

Le Malheur, mon grand laboureur,
Le Malheur, assois-toi,
Repose-toi,
Reposons-nous un peu, toi et moi,

THOUGHTS

To think, to live, sea barely distinct;
I—it—trembles
Infinity which incessantly cracks.

Shadows of tiny words
shadows of shadows,
cinders of wings.

Thoughts of marvelous waves
Which glide quietly in us, among us, far from
    us,
far from enlightening us, far from affecting
    anything.

strangers in our homes,
always on the prowl,
dusts which disturb us and squander away
    life.

THE GREAT BATTLE

He grabs him and throws him to the ground;
He galls him and shakes him to the marrow;
He punches him and teases him and boxes
    his ears.
He strikes him and bombards him.
The house grinds and scrapes from side to
    side.
Finally he flays him to the quick.
The other hesitates, retreats, undoes himself,
    contorts and ruins himself.
It will soon be the end for him;
He pulls himself together for a new start . . .
    but in vain
The hoop which had rolled so long falls.
Abrah! Abrah! Abrah!
The foot has failed!
The arm has shattered!
The blood has flowed!
Dig, dig, dig,
In the pot of his belly is a great secret.

Shrews all about who cry in their
    handkerchiefs;
One is amazed, amazed, amazed
And looks at you.
They also search, the rest of us, for The
    Great Secret.

REST IN MISFORTUNE

Misfortune, my noble laborer,
Misfortune, sit down,
Rest,
Let us rest a moment, you and I,

Repose,	Rest,
Tu me trouves, tu m'éprouves, tu me le prouves.	You find me, you test me, you prove it to me.
Je suis ta ruine.	I am your ruin.
Mon grand théâtre, mon havre, mon âtre,	My grand theater, my haven, my hearth
Ma cave d'or,	My vault of gold,
Mon avenir, ma vraie mère, mon horizon,	My future, my true mother, my horizon,
Dans ta lumière, dans ton ampleur, dans ton horreur,	In your light, in your abundance, in your horrow,
Je m'abandonne.	I surrender myself.

Texts by Henri Michaux: "Le grand combat" from "Qui je fus" in L'espace du dedans; *"Pensées" and "Repos dans le malheur" from* Plume. *Copyright by Editions Gallimard, 1928 (no. 2), 1938 (Nos. 1 & 3). Reprinted by permission.*

INSTRUMENTS: NEW SONORITIES AND TECHNIQUES, ANCIENT AND EXOTIC

KEYBOARD.   From the timbral and figural nuances, including the exploration of articulation, pedaling, and register, in the keyboard works of Debussy and Ravel at the turn of the century to the aggressive primitivisms of Bartók, Stravinsky, and Prokofiev, a review of the sonic potential of the piano had been undertaken. The early use of harmonics in Schoenberg's op. 11, no. 1 (1909)—perhaps an act of homage to Schumann's *Carnaval*—and Cowell's explorations in *The Tides of Manaunaun* (?1912), *The Aeolian Harp* (1923), and *The Banshee* (1925) were further indications of a new and developing sensibility toward the piano. Following Cage's pieces for prepared piano whose classic expression was made in the *Three Dances* (1944–45) and the *Sonatas and Interludes* (1948), the use of metal, wood, glass, and rubber to mute or otherwise modify the sound of the piano, the activation of the strings by the human hand rather than by the piano hammer, and electronic amplification all became commonplace options in the period after 1960. Some of the most notable recent piano music relying on such a legacy is to be found in *Makrokosmos*, Books I, II, and III (1972–74) by George Crumb.

The influence of the Minimalists has also led to distinctive keyboard sonics in a work like Ligeti's *Continuum* for harpsichord of 1968, whose perpetual motion, limited pitch content, virtuosic speed, and audible transformational processes point to a cross between Claude Debussy's "Feux d'artifice," Steve Reich's *Six Pianos*, and a piece for electronic tape. *Volumina* (1961–62) for organ had followed hard on the heels of Ligeti's *Atmosphères* (1961), an orchestral work written for the highly successful film *2001*, and like its orchestral predecessor removed melody, harmony, and rhythm as propelling agents in a chromatic field of dense clusters where stasis and curtains of sound move quietly and almost imperceptibly.

Other elements of a keyboard style frequently allied to the need for a new brand of digital dexterity prompted by patterns not directly traceable to eighteenth- and nineteenth-century repertoires can be laid directly at the doorstep of works such as Schoenberg's op. 11, no. 3 (1909) and especially Webern's *Concerto for Nine Instruments*, op. 24 (1934) and *Variations*, op. 27 (1936) for solo piano–all of which became widely known through recordings for the first time from the period of the late 1950s and early 1960s.

To this was cojoined a delayed knowledge, through similar auspices, of a large catalogue of works for both piano and organ by Olivier Messiaen that displayed a new level of keyboard pyrotechniques. Both Messiaen himself and the pianist Yvonne Loriod became the electrifying protagonists in this literature, which calls not only for fleet fingers in the passages involving ornithological flight or dense harmonic clusters but also a newly refined rhythmic sense that demands that the performer count religiously in practice until the patterns become second nature. From the time of *Vision de l'Amen* (1943), two pf, and *Vingt regards sur l'Enfant-Jésus* (1944) through *Cantéyodjayâ* (1949), *Quatre études de rythme* (1949–50), *Catalogue d'oiseaux* (1956–58), and *La fauvette des jardins* (1970), Messiaen created a vast output not only of solo piano works but ensemble pieces (*Turangalila-symphonie*, 1946–48; *Réveil des oiseaux*, 1953; *Oiseaux exotique*, 1956; *Sept haikai*, 1962; *Couleurs de la cité céleste*, 1963; *Des canyons aux étoiles*, 1971–74) that featured the piano in a prominent fashion. The same may be said with respect to technical extensions on the organ—Messiaen's personal instrument—in his *Messe de la Pentecôte* (1950), *Livre d'orgue* (1951), *Méditations sur le mystère de la Sainte Trinité* (1969), and in his longest and technically all-encompassing *Livre du Saint Sacrement* (1986).

Other works written in the wake of Messiaen's *Mode de valeurs* (1949) that demanded new levels of performer concentration included Boulez's *Structures I* (1951) and *Second* (1947–48) and *Third Piano Sonatas* (1956–58) as well as Stockhausen's various *Klavierstücke* (I–V, 1952; V–X, 1954–5; XI, 1956)—all of which took off in some degree from Webern's and Messiaen's rarified world.

Early evidence of the general appeal of a pianistic pointillism, even among musicians with a well-defined personality, came in Stravinsky's *Movements* for piano and orchestra of 1959 (Ex. 26.3) and may be said to have lasted to the extended, complex, and virtuoso *Night Fantasies* of Elliott Carter written in 1983. Both scores bring their composer's language to its most intricate rhythmic pitch in a series of lean keyboard acrobatics not far distant from the nonrepetitive paroxysms of Boulez's *Second Sonata*—Stravinsky in a brief work of under ten minutes duration whose piano filigree is placed alongside a flattering instrumental component; Carter in a lengthy and fitfull Expressionist dream that continuously borders on chaos. For this and a vast spiritually and technically related literature there emerged a cadre of exceptional pianists including Charles Rosen, Paul Jacobs, Gilbert Kalish, Ursala Oppens, David Burge, Robert Miller, Stephen Pruslin, Idil Biret, and Robert Conway, who appeared willing and eminently able to handle any challenge, both technical and expressive, the composer might offer.

A consolidation of numerous techniques began to emerge in the 1980s in a variety of works for the organ, an instrument pointedly neglected by most twentieth-century composers who were not themselves performers of the instrument. A revival of interest in the best surviving European instruments of the eighteenth century (e.g., Silbermann, Schnitger) prompted in the 1950s by E. Power Biggs and Robert Noehren among others in the United States, had led not only to a reconsideration of the organ's resource and character but the rediscovery of many of its tonal and timbral qualities. While Messiaen almost alone showed the way toward an extended idiom among the composers of his generation, other younger composers such as William Albright and William Bolcom readdressed the instrument with a keen ear and remarkable fervor. In addition to their common affection for ragtime that predictably appeared in some of their organ pieces of the 1960s, a subtle metamorphosis of the best of the Minimalist movement appeared in Albright's *Chasm* (1986), while jubilant rhythms, high spirit, and an abiding spirituality marked Bolcom's *Gospel Hymns* of 1984. Traditional audiences at first performances of these pieces may have felt an initial surprise at such an unfamiliar alliance of expression and instrument, but most agreed that the organ had been put to a new and compelling account.

The New Virtuosity also periodically clasped hands with some of the older keyboard virtues in the 1970s and 1980s. Numerous works by Ned Rorem illustrate an understanding of the flexibility of the instrument in question without resorting to avant-garde techniques, and force us to consider the role of persistent conservative values throughout the twentieth century. Thus the New Romanticism, while most clearly defined by careers such as George Rochberg that involved a radical stylistic reorientation, must be seen to have received an enormous impetus (acknowledged or not) from residual values practiced by composers like Rorem all along. While not patently Romantic in expression, his organ cycles *A Quaker Reader* (1976) and *Views from the Oldest House* (1981) reflected, among other values, a knowledge of the French organ school of the first half of the century and the home-spun style of Virgil Thomson. Together with works such as his two sets for flute, *Romeo and Juliet* (1977; with guitar), and *Book of Hours* (1975; with harp), Rorem provided ample evidence of the power of such a relaxed attitude, which embraces technical challenge and progressive options alongside more traditional communicative values. The grounding of most of these instrumental pieces in a literary base recalls his important contributions to the world of song as well as his skills as a writer.

That numerous organists had throughout the century shown a greater interest and willingness to explore the literature of today than their pianist counterparts can in part be explained by an unarguably leaner nineteenth-century repertoire from which to choose. But whatever the reason, the role of such figures as Marilyn Mason (who was the only person to have played Schoenberg's *Variations on a Recitative,* op. 40, for the composer and who commissioned many dozens of works over a period of more than forty years), William Albright, and others in different ways served a highly important and catalytic role in the development of a new technique and expression for their instrument.

PERCUSSION. Post-World War II investigations into the world of percussion had a natural foundation in the works of the Futurists as well as Stravinsky (*Histoire du soldat, Renard, Les noces*); Milhaud (*Les Choéphores,* 1915); *L'homme et son désir,* 1918); Shostakovich (*The Nose,* percussion interlude in Act I, 1927); Varèse (*Intégrales,* 1926; *Ionisation,* 1929–31), and Bartók (*Piano Concerto No. 1,* 1926; *Music for Strings, Percussion and Celesta,* 1936; *Sonata for Two Pianos and Percussion,* 1937). Explorations since then have encompassed the use of exotic instruments (Oriental, South American, primitive) and unusual per-formance techniques (different types of mallets, attacks, cymbals gradually submerged in water, electronic amplification, etc.). John Cage's interest in the percussive nuances of the prepared piano was paralleled by an interest in percussion ensembles at an early date: In his *First Construction (in Metal)* of

1939, six percussionists play orchestral bells, thundersheets, piano, sleigh bells, oxen bells, brake drums, cowbells, Japanese temple gongs, Turkish cymbals, anvils, water gongs, and tam-tams.

A special case among American composers was Harry Partch (1901–1976), whose investigations into various tunings and interest in percussion ensembles paralleled those of Lou Harrison. But the instruments he constructed for the performance of his music added a new dimension to the rethinking of instrumental sound. Although beginning with extensions of existing instruments that were called "adapted viola" and "adapted guitar," he proceeded to the invention of original instruments in virtually every category: chordophones, idiophones, aerophones. It was his idiophones (all tuned), however, that were visually the most striking, and a stage set up with his cloud-chamber bowls (glass), cone gongs (metal), diamond marimba (wood), and gourd tree invariably created a dramatic impression (Figure 29.2). His performing group, dubbed the Gate 5 ensemble, traditionally played from memory a music that placed small emphasis on harmony but rather on melody and timbre. His *Delusion of the Fury* (1969) brought a belated recognition late in life, while his *Genesis of a Music* (1949) remains a text concerning his theories of tuning and aesthetics.

In more recent years, the exploration of percussion ensembles, both

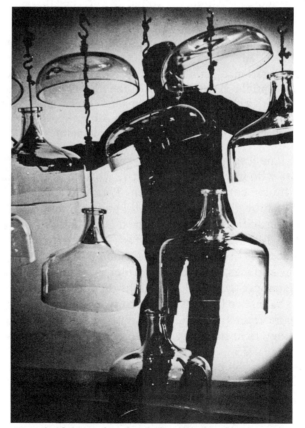

Figure 29.2. Harry Partch playing the cloud-chamber bowls.
Photo by Danlee Mitchell.

traditional and exotic, has led to such a range of instruments and variety of techniques as to defy summary. In 1959, Stockhausen composed two works for percussion alone. *Zyklus*, written as a test piece for Darmstadt in a spiral-bound score for a performer whose instruments are arranged in a circle about him; and *Refrain*, for pf + woodblocks, cel + crotales, vib + cowbells + glock, and vocalizing instrumentalists whose score contains a movable plastic strip containing the refrain. In Stockhausen's *Mikrophonie I* (1964), as noted earlier, the tam-tam provided the source for sonic exploration with the aid of microphones and filters and effected one of the notable early marriages between electronics and percussion.

Among composers of the Polish school, Kazmimierz Serocki (b. 1922), one of the founders of the Warsaw Autumn concerts, has placed a spotlight on percussion as few others of his compatriots. His *Episodes* (1959), for fifty strings and thirty-four percussion instruments in three groups, was followed by the shorter but more frequently performed *Segmenti* (1961) for twelve wind instruments, five strings and percussion; the *Symphonic Frescoes* (1964), for orchestra and fifty-eight percussion instruments; and climaxing in *Continuum* (1965–66) for six percussionists on 123 instruments, considered by many as one of his most accomplished works.

Serocki's countryman Henryk Gorecki (b. 1933), a composer himself of numerous scores with an ear tuned to the reevaluation of musical sound, has remarked:

> If today one utilizes a greater measure of percussion and noise-makers, that is the reality of our day—the mechinization, the marvels of electronics, great human agglomerations—permitting us to remark upon that which was only yesterday imperceptible. Have you noticed the marvelous sonic phenomenon of a stadium filled with a crowd of 100,000 persons? The resounding roar of 100,000 throats? Of dolorous sighs? Music is not only F♯-A-B♭, but also, as Debussy said, "the noise of the forest and the water." For me art is a manifestation of life.[15]

The Japanese percussionist Stomu Yamash'ta is typical of a group of specialists who have entered into the world of "performance art" as well as the realm of music composed for them. Toru Takemitsu's *Seasons* (1970), for tape plus one or four players on specially constructed metal instruments plus glass trombone, is indicative of the Partch-Cage legacy once removed. On the other hand Peter Maxwell Davies' *Turris Campanarum Sonantium* (Bell-Tower) of 1970 reflects his fascination for a kind of ritualistic magic. It is written for bells and metal surfaces, and the performer is confronted with a five-pitch set, six shaped Japanese gongs (kim), eight handbells, and a variety of gongs and cymbals that are to be activated according to certain permutations over a drone of the performer's choice. Highly ritualistic in content, its constructive methodology is in harmony with his attraction to the Magic Square, as in *Ave Maris Stella* (1975).

In America we have already noted Feldman's search for a notationally pure and performance freeing score in his *King of Denmark* (1964; see p. 570). Beginning only slightly later, Wuorinen's devotion to serial and electronic procedures did not prevent him from writing extended statements for percussion in his *Janissary Music* (1967), *Ringing Changes* (1971), and a *Percussion Symphony* (1976). Similarly, George Crumb's *Makrokosmos III* (1974) openly identifies with Bartók in its employment of two pianos and percussion. Michael Colgrass's *Déjà vu* (1977), winner of the Pulitzer Prize for 1978, is for four percussion soloists and orchestra and freely mixes jazz elements with other stylistic references. Christopher Rouse has championed the cause for percussion with a range of solo and ensemble pieces (*Ogoun Badagris, Ku-Ka-Ilimoku*) and larger orchestra pieces (*Thor, Gorgone, The Infernal Machine*) and places the spotlight on the battery with such frequency that he appears, at least in part, to have championed the combined legacies of Orff and Varèse.

The range of expression of the modern percussion ensemble is perhaps the largest with respect to dynamics and timbre of any instrumental grouping, a fact that helps to explain the multiple functions it has served in the twentieth century, from the hushed quietude of some of Crumb's magical nocturnes to the ear-splitting climaxes of pieces too numerous to mention. Fascination for its potential shows no sign of abating.

STRINGED INSTRUMENTS.   As with vocal and keyboard techniques, in the arena of string writing the example of the Viennese earlier in the century proved to be a powerful stimulus in the post-War years. The range of pizzicato, spiccato, glissando, *col legno*, and *sul ponticello* techniques in the string quartets of Schoenberg, Berg, Webern, and Bartók proved to be an intriguing resource as their music increasingly entered the repertoire of established performing groups. Berg's *Lyric Suite*, in particular, along with Webern's *Five Movements for String Quartet*, op. 5 (1909), his *Bagatelles* for string quartet, op. (1913), and the last three quartets of Bartók played host to a healthy number of composer-visitors.

The revival of interest in the string quartet in the postwar period among such composers as Cage, Druckman, Lutosławski, Penderecki, Feldman, Wolpe, Brown, Ligeti, Basset, C. Rouse, and Carter speaks less, however, of any commitment to the New Virtuosity than the realization of the challenge inherent in addressing a compact ensemble with such a venerable heritage. While Carter's *Second* (1959) and *Third* (1971) *Quartets* have achieved a considerable vogue and stand in the eyes of many as his most noble achievements, they can best be discussed in light of their constructive and formal premises (see pp. 000–00) in spite of a notable degree of challenge to the performer. Exploring new directions from the standpoint of a sonic surface in addition to questions of design are works like Crumb's *Black Angels* (1970) for electronically amplified string quartet and Leon Kirchner's *Quartet No. 3 for String Quartet and Electronic Tape* (1966), while Lejaren Hiller's *String Quartet No. 5 (In Quarter-Tones)* of 1962 mirrored the earlier work of Hába and the later interest of Ligeti.

Some have seen in Panufnik's *Lullaby* (1947, rev. 1955) for twenty-nine strings and one or two harps a possible prefiguration of Penderecki's *Threnody*. The work is "based on simple, almost pentatonic folk melody, repeated in the manner of a passacaglia; around and over this is woven a mobile fabric of quarter-tone harmonies played by a large number of solo strings, often giving the effect of mass glissandos and anticipating the music of Xenaxis."[16] But no post-World War II work among the larger string ensembles more dramatically demonstrated the capacity of conventional string instruments to transcend their traditional role than Penderecki's *Threnody for the Victims of Hiroshima* (1960) for fifty-two string players. In an ingenious rethinking of his sonic resource, the composer has evoked the psychological nightmare of the first nuclear holocaust in a gripping manner that sounds more like a piece for tape than one by Tartini. The notation of the score (see p. 000) is a direct mirror and measure of its conception.

Many of the solo string concerti written during the 1970s and 1980s, such as those for violin written by Rochberg and Penderecki, have overtly returned to a more classic stance and endorsed a Neoromantic expression. But the range of string sonorities that had been so enlarged and enriched throughout the century had also come to be known by heart and selectively employed by virtually every composer, regardless of his aesthetic orientation. The reader interested in witnessing the extent of such developments will not want to miss Ton de Leeuw's (b. 1920) *Music for Strings* (1970), written for the Solisti di Zagreb, a work that may stand as a virtual catalogue of string techniques and sonorities to the present time.

WIND INSTRUMENTS.   Among wind instruments, perhaps none has been more systematically explored in our century than the flute. Beginning with Debussy's *Syrinx* (1912) and Schoenberg's *Pierrot lunaire* (No. 7, 1912) and continuing through Varèse's *Density 21.5* (1935), the natural flexibility and range of the instrument has been noted and addressed. The unusual effect of fluttertonguing, already known from the late symphonies of Mahler (Nos. 7 and 9), was extended to the slapping of the keys to create a percussive echo by Varèse. In recent years, Berio (*Sequenza I*, 1958), Westergaard (*Divertimento*, 1967), Wuorinen (*Variations I & II*, 1963/68), and Reynolds (*Ambages*, 1965) have suggested that the potential of the flute through various fingerings and multiphonics (multiple sounds) has just begun to be realized. George Crumb, for example, described the opening "Vocalise" of his *Voice of the Whale* (1971) as "a kind of cadenza for the flutist, who simultaneously plays his instrument and sings into it. This combination of instrumental and vocal sound produces an eerie, surreal timbre, not unlike the sounds of the humpback whale."[17]

Although the use of flutter-tonguing and echo-tone in Berg's *Four Pieces*, op. 5 (1913), brought Schoenberg's charges of excessive novelty, they clearly pointed to the possibility of a similar rethinking of the clarinet. While the use of quarter-tones and glissandi common to jazz musicians found a memorable signature at the opening of Gershwin's *Rhapsody in Blue*, the period of the 1920s, when the idiom was being regularly tapped by the composer, saw little development in this regard. The obvious imitation of Gershwin's glissando (actually introduced by the clarinetist of Paul Whiteman's band in the first rehearsals of the work) at the palindromic center of Berg's concert aria, *Der Wein*, went virtually unnoticed (and unperformed in most recordings). Just as both Schoenberg (*Pierrot lunaire*, *Serenade*) and Stravinsky (*Berceuses du chat*, *Three Pieces for Clarinet*, *Histoire du soldat*, *Ebony Concerto*) exploited the sonority and flexibility of the instrument, Nielsen's *Clarinet Concerto* (1928); Bartók's *Contrasts* (1938) for piano, violin, and clarinet; Messiaen's *Quartet for the End of Time* (1940–41) for piano, violin, cello, and clarinet; and Hindemith's *Concerto* (1947) brought modest if artistically successful extensions to the instrument.

A probe beyond the traditional limits of the instrument occurred first, however, in the post-World War II period. It was then that the personality of a new breed of performer began to surface with artists such as Alan Hacker, for

Example 29.3. Penderecki, *Threnody "To the Victims of Hiroshima"* (1961), for fifty-two string players. No. 10.

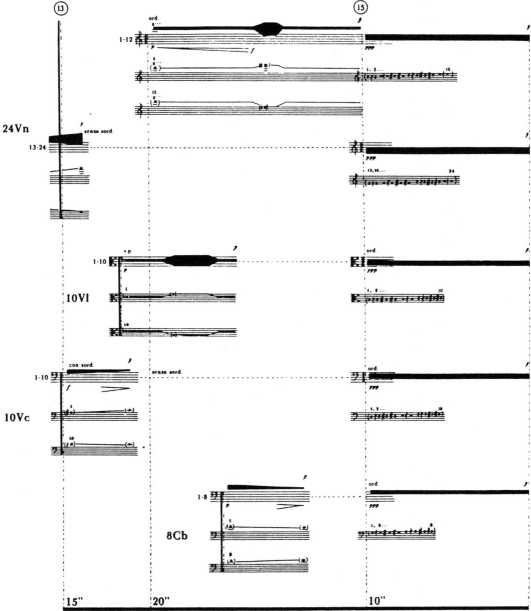

whom Peter Maxwell Davies created *Stedman Doubles* (1955; rev. 1968) for clarinet and percussion; *Hymnos* (1967), for clarinet and piano; and the showy clarinet antics of *Eight Songs for a Mad King* and other scores. Although Hacker has led the way in the research and codification of a range of multiphonics for wind instruments, because of their difficulty and unreliability they have been sparingly used by most composers and harnessed by even fewer performers. Yet their potential for creating a mawkish coloration has been amply proven in the woodwind multiphonics of Henze's *Heliogabulus imperator* (1971–72). And in George Perle's memorable *Sonata quasi una fantasia* (1972) for clarinet and piano, use of multiphonics, mutes, and flutter-tonguing combine with a gentle reference to "d" as a pitch center in a reflection and extension of the world of Berg's clarinet pieces, op. 5, more than that of Beethoven, which the title would seem to infer.

Beginning in the 1970s the transcendental virtuosity of Susanne Stevens on a range of clarinets has been showcased in a group of works by Stockhausen, and has forced all who have heard her to reconsider the potential of the instrument. The cojoining of an impish theater with new performance levels in a work like Stockhausen's *Harlekin* (1975), however, dramatizes the degree to which the long-playing record no longer well serves the composer, and argues that the age of the videocassette has arrived just in time. A work of forty-minutes duration for solo clarinet, it bears little resemblance to its precursors, escaping into a formula-based choreographed theater. Others of Stockhausen's musical household who have developed her coloristic range and technical prowess, including "circular breathing," are Kathinka Pesveer, flute, and Marcus Stockhausen, trumpet, and the best of their playing together, as in a version of *Tierkreis* for clarinet, flute and trumpet, vies with the excitement of a first-class jazz ensemble.

Additional contributions to this fresh new look at the clarinet have been made by Arthur Bloom, who worked with Jacob Druckman on his *Animus III* (1969) and who has premiered well over 100 compositions, many of which were written especially for him. And even the more classically oriented principal clarinetist of the New York Philharmonic, Stanley Druckman, performed Boulez' quasi-theater piece, *Domaines*, in the Philharmonic *Horizons '84* concerts, which included two evenings devoted to The New Virtuosity on the trombone (Stuart Dempster), contrabass (Jon Deak), voice (Diamánda Galás and Joan La Barbara), and flute (Robert Dick).

Perhaps no single composer has more systematically addressed the idea of the New Virtuosity in the instrumental domain than Luciano Berio. His interest in the vocal world has already been detailed, but in addition he has contributed one of the most ordered investigations of a list of instruments for which he has written a series of pieces already perceived as classics of their kind. All published under the title *Sequenza* followed by a Roman numeral, they are for: I, flute (1958); II, harp (1963); III, female voice (1965); IV, piano (1966); V, trombone (1966); VI, viola (1967); VII, oboe (1969); VIII, violin (1975–77); IX, clarinet (1980), arr. saxophone (1981); X, trumpet (1985).

Berio's belief that the true virtuoso is one capable of performing within a wide historical spectrum and his knowledge that most instruments have changed very little in the past 200 years or more led him to a consideration of how the performer's technique could be extended without resort to the invention of new instruments. Berio has stated that all of his *Sequenzas* for solo instruments were intended as melodic developments of essentially harmonic ideas and to prompt thereby a polyphonic type of listening to a "latent, implicit counterpoint" whose ideal model is found in the "polyphonic melodies" of Bach. He explains:

An inaccessible ideal, naturally, because what implicitly guided polyphonic listening in a Bach melody was nothing less than the history of baroque musical language, whereas in a "non-linguistic" melody like my *Sequenza* for flute, history provided no protection, and everything had to be planned out explicitly. But although it was a bit utopian, the experience was extremely useful to me . . . in pursuing my ideal of implicit polyphony, I discovered melody's heterophonic possibilities. The title was meant to underline that the piece was built from a sequence of harmonic fields (as indeed are almost all the *Sequenzas*) from which the other, strongly characterized musical functions were derived.[18]

In an attempt to create a polyphonic illusion with the flute in *Sequenza I*, Berio regulated the temporal, dynamic, pitch, and morphological dimensions according to predefined notions of maximum, medium, and minimum levels. In the temporal realm, for example, the maximum level is achieved by moments of maximum speed in articulation and moments of maximum duration of sounds; the medium level by more neutral sets of articulation and durations; and the minimum level through silence or a tendency to silence. In the morphological dimension he achieved maximum tension through transformations of its persona by more drastic alterations including flutter tones (the furthest extension of rapid articulation), key clicks (the furthest extension of a progressive move toward noise), and double stops (multiphonics), which represent his "desperate search for polyphony with the most monodic instrument in history."[19]

Berio's reliance on the knowledge and skill of individual artists (I, Gazzelloni; III, Berbarian; V, Globokar; VII, Holliger) appeared to make each a natural expression and extension of the conventional instrument involved. The theatrical inclinations and experience of the dedicatees for numbers III, V, and VII, however, led Berio to fashion pieces that were as much dramatic vehicles as musical ones.

Among the preceding names, Heinz Holliger (b. 1939) is both an oboist and a composer, whose exploitation of harmonics, double trills, glissandos, chords, and microphone alteration have become legendary both in works written by him (*Siebengesang*, for oboe, female voices, orchestra, and electronics, 1966–7) and for him by Berio, Henze, Krenek, Martin, Penderecki, Pousseur, and Stockhausen. The importance of biological factors in performance (breathing, heartbeat, etc.) have been exploited by Holliger in his own *Pneuma* (1970) for thirty-six winds, four radios, organ, and percussion and *Cardiophonie* (1971) for one wind and three tape recorders, which in both instances leads to a kind of theater of the absurd.

In a complementary manner, Vinko Globokar (b. 1934), Yugoslav composer and trombonist, has explored his personal instrument. Attracted to his easy virtuoso style and innate sense of theater, Stockhausen (*Solo*, trombone version, 1966), Berio (*Sequenza V*, 1966), and Kagel (*Der Atem*, 1970) have all written pieces for him. The "simultaneous and controlled use of the singing voice and the sound of the instrument" in both Berio's *Sequenza V* and Globokar's *Discours II* creates "a kind of 'beat' or oscillation"[20] that prefigures Crumb's use of the flute in *Voice of the Whale* (1971). In addition, a jazz plunger mute is also used by Globokar to help reproduce the complete range of vowels and consonants that the composer then uses to construct a "speech" that discusses the communality of verbal communication and trombone playing. Globokar has written numerous works that exploit his wide knowledge of wind instruments, such as *Atemstudie* (1971)—a piece written for Holliger requiring continuous circular breathing; or that exhibit a sure knowledge of the drama of ensemble playing, as in the series of *Discours* (II, five trombones or trombone and tape, 1967–68; III, five oboes, 1969; IV, three clarinets, 1974).

Two similar series, which reflect his experience with Berio's cycles, have been written by Bernard Rands (b. 1935). One, entitled *Memos*, is addressed to individual instrumental soloists (I, db, 1971; II, trbn, 1973; III, vc, 1974; IV, org, 1975; V, pf, 1975) and another, *Ballads*, involves vocal forces (I, Mez, 5 insts, 1970: II, v, pf, 1970; III, S, tape, 1973; IV, 8 solo vv, 21 insts).

While extensions of playing techniques have been explored on virtually every wind instrument, perhaps no work for the trumpet provided a more complete catalogue of the possible and the impossible (except for its dedicatee, Gerard Schwarz) than the tour de force *Space is A Diamond* (1970) by Lucia Dlugoszewski (b. 1931). In addition, the range of trumpets available to the contemporary trumpeter through recourse to instruments both ancient and modern is given perhaps its most brilliant forum in *Kryl* (1977), a work for soloist utilizing thirteen trumpets by Robert Erickson (b. 1917).

Reactions to the New Virtuosity that carried either a note of playful sarcasm or a negativism that reduced the whole to a performance fiction can be seen in works by Kagel and Xenakis. In Kagel's *Match* (1964) for two cellos and percussion, the extraordinary difficulty of the score—a welter of instructions and special effects—leads to a performance duel between the two cellists dressed as table tennis players refereed by the percussionist. The effect of the piece is, therefore, as much visual as aural, and the ultimate recording, as with *Ludwig van*, is possible only on film, of which the composer has directed a version. With Xenakis' *Evryali* (1973), a piano work impossible to execute by virtue of the simultaneous placement of notes through the whole range of the instrument, we are faced with an imaginary music for an imaginary performer,[21] which beyond its "conceptual" allure expresses with Tom Johnson's *Celestial Music for Imaginary Trumpets* (1974; see p. 571) the final frustration of a strained virtuosity.

ORIENTAL, EXOTIC, HISTORIC.   While the commitment of the performer to working in tandem with the composer has proven salutary for the development of technique and expression, the seemingly endless search for new sound sources has not stopped with the extension of standard instruments or newly invented machines but has also encompassed adaptations from exotic cultures. This has already been made apparent in discussions on Cage, Cowell, Lous Harrison, and Steve Reich, whose interest in the Orient and Africa was apparent almost from the beginning of their careers. Boulez' early *L'marteau sans maître* (1954), a work that inspired many imitations, was noted to reveal an undisguised fascination for the subtle tracery of the Javanese gamelan so beloved of Debussy a half century and more before. The continuation of such an interest is observable in Ton de Leeuw's *Gending* (1975), which he called "a Western homage to the musicians of the gamelan,"[22] while Rochberg's *Slow Fires of Autumn* (1979) for modern flute and harp, according to the composer owes "The Japanese flavor of the music . . . principally from my use of an old Japanese folk-tune which appears in its simplest form in the last section of the work."[23]

That World War II brought many Westerners in contact with the Orient for the first time no doubt accounts for a heightened awareness of things Japanese for the first time since the first decade of the twentieth century. Obvious examples of this attraction include Messiaen's *Seven Haikai* (1962), Ton de Leeuw's *Haiku II* (1968), Crumb's *Ancient Voices of Children* (1970), and Stockhausen's *Inori* (1972). Until the postwar period, however, no Oriental composer, with a Western audience in mind, attempted to put his native musical culture to account. Chou Wen-chung (b. 1923), Chinese by birth, came to the United States in 1946, and mirrored his native culture in a musical language clearly wedded to his intimate knowledge of Varèse (he completed the latter's unfinished *Nocturnal* and edited numerous other works). Toru Takemitsu (b. 1930), a Japanese composer of wide interest encompassing Western systems and electronic means, has been successful in writing works for native Japanese instruments, including the biwa (a kind of lute) and shakuhachi (a kind of flute) in *Eclipse* (1966) and together with orchestra in the highly successful *November Steps*, commissioned by the New York Philharmonic Orchestra in 1967, and *Aki* (Autumn) for the same forces of 1973. In a trip to Japan in 1959, Igor Stravinsky also expressed admiration for Takemitsu's *Requiem* for strings of 1957. In a different fashion, another Japanese composer, Ryo Noda, has adapted the techniques of the shakuhachi (microtonal pitch bending, variable vibrato, portamenti) as well as the formal norms of its literature in a work for saxophone, *Improvisation I* (1970), which seeks less to contrast East and West than to blend them.

On another front, Mauricio Kagel's rethinking of traditional instruments of the orchestra is dramatized in his *Heterophonies* (1959–61) for forty-two soloists divided into ensembles with their own music rejoined in a collage of variegated instrumental sonorities. But his *Exotica* (1971–72) for six players on exotic instruments has made no attempt, like Takemitsu, to marry East and West but only to press explorations backward in time and outward geographically in search for a new sonority from whatever source. In the same frame of mind, Kagel's *Music for Renaissance Instruments* (1965–66) is written for an ensemble of twenty-three musicians playing on instruments represented in Michael Praetorius' *Syntagma Musicum* of 1619. Though dedicated to the memory of Claudio Monteverdi, it eschews both quotation and allusion to early music except through a revitalization of the sonic potential of instruments originally associated with it, and stands in direct contrast to such pieces as Wuorinen's *Glogauer Liederbuch* (1962) and Peter Maxwell Davies's arrangement of sixteenth-century Scottish dances (1973), both of which preserve the music but project it on modern instruments.

Many of the above mentioned works may be seen, however, as explorations beyond the sonic domain, involving extensions outward to other cultures and backwards in time. Such maneuvering built in part on the virtuosic challenges of the serial avant-garde of the 1950s, but also in part on a reaction against it with the thought, as Lutosławski phrased it, of putting a little joy back into the act of performing. In the resulting virtuosic extensions, composers everywhere seemed less concerned with dogma than with the freedom to choose, and the performer less interested in tests of skill than challenges of expression. To the extent that some of these explorations occurred on early instruments or involved a confrontation with earlier repertoires, it signaled that other sensibilities had also been pricked. The idea of synthesis, both stylistic and formal, increasingly proved its attractiveness to composer and performer alike.

REPERTOIRE (The New Vocalism)

Babbitt, *Vision and Prayer* (1961), S, 4-track tape
Babbitt, *Philomel* (1964), S, 4-track tape
Babbitt, *Phonemena* (1974), S, tape/S, piano
Berbarian, *Stripsody* (1966)
Berio, *Omaggio à Joyce* (1958)
Berio, *Circles* (1960), female voice, 2 harps, percussion
Berio, *Epifanie* (1959–61; rev. 1965), voice, orchestra
Berio, *Visage* (1961), based on the voice of Cathy Berbarian and electronic sounds
Berio, *Sinfonia* (1968; fifth mvt. added 1969), soloists, orchestra
Berio, *Recital for Cathy (I)* (1972)
Bussotti, *"O"—Atti Vocali* (from *La Passion selon Sade,* 1965)
Boulez, *Le marteau sans maître* (1954), A, a fl, gui, vib, xylorimba, perc, va
Boulez, *Pli selon pli* (1957–62), S, orch
Crumb, *Songs, Drones, and Refrains of Death* (1968), Bar, elec gui, elec db, elec pf +
    elec hpd, 2 perc
Crumb, *Ancient Voices of Children* (1970), S, Tr, ob, mand, harp, elec pf, perc
Davies, *Eight Songs For a Mad King* (1969), male v, pic + fl, kbds, cl, perc, vn, vc
Druckman, *Animus II* (1967–68), S, perc, tape
Henze, *Five Neapolitan Songs* (1956), Bar, orch
Henze, *Being Beauteous* (1963), S, harp, 4 vc
Henze, *Das Floss der "Medusa"* (1968)
Henze, *Voices* (1973), Mez, T, 15 insts
Lutosławski, *Trois poèmes d'Henri Michaux* (1963), chorus, orch
Lutosławski, *Paroles tissées* (1965), T, chamb orch
Lutosławski, *Les espaces du sommeil* (1975), Bar, orch
Martirano, *L's GA* (1968)
Nono, *Il canto sospeso* (1955–56), S, Mez, T, chorus, orch
Pousseur, *Phonèmes pour Cathy* (1966), 1 v
Schafer, *Requiems for a Party-Girl* (1966)
Somers, *Voiceplay* (1971), singer-actor
Stockhausen, *Gesang der Jünglinge* (1955–56), 4-track tape
de Vries, *Areas* (1980), orch, chorus

READING (The New Vocalism)

Pierre Boulez, "Sound, Word, Synthesis" in *Orientations* (1986), 177–82. First part of two
    initially published as "Son, verbe, synthèse" in German in *Melos,* xxv.10 (1958),
    310–13. Complete text first published in French in *Points de repère* (1985).
Pierre Boulez, "Poetry—Centre and Absence—Music" in *Orientations* (1986), 183–198.
    Originally given as a lecture, "Poésie—centre et absence—musique" at Donaue-
    schingen in 1962; published in German in *Melos,* xxx.2 (1963), 33–40.
Karl H. Wörner, *Karlheinz Stockhausen* (Rodenkirchen, 1963; Eng. trans. 1973).
Karlheinz Stockhausen, "Music and Speech," *Die Reihe* (1964), no. 6, 40.
Stefan Jarocinski, "Witold Lutosławski," *Polish Music* (1965), 191.
Jonathan Cott, ed. *Stockhausen: Conversations with the Composer* (New York, 1973).
Jonathan Harvey, *The Music of Stockhausen: an Introduction* (London, 1975).
Robin Maconie, *The Works of Karlheinz Stockhausen* (London, 1976).
Paul Griffiths, *Peter Maxwell Davies* (London, 1981).
Jean-Paul Couchoud, *La musique polonaise et Witold Lutasławski* (Paris, 1981).
Steven Stucky, *Lutosławski and His Music* (Cambridge, 1981).
"Roger Reynolds" in Cole Gagne and Tracy Caras, *Soundpieces: Interviews With Ameri-
    can Composers* (Metuchen, NY, 1982), 333–35.

Luciano Berio, *Two Interviews* (Rome, 1981; Eng. trans. New York, 1985), 141–56.
David Osmond-Smith, *Playing on Words: A Guide to Luciano Berio's* Sinfonia (London, 1985).

REPERTOIRE (The New Virtuosity: Keyboard)

Albright, *Five Chromatic Dances* (1979), pf
Albright, *Chasm* (1986), org
Albright, *Sphaera* (1985), pf, tape
Babbitt, *Reflections* (1974), pf, tape
Berio, *Sequenza IV* (1966), pf
Bolcom, *Gospel Hymns*, Book IV (1984), org
Boulez, *Second Piano Sonata* (1948)
Boulez, *Third Piano Sonata* (1955–7)
Bussotti, *La vergine ispirata* (1982), hpd
Carter, *Night Fantasies* (1983), pf
Crumb, *Makrokosmos*, Book I (1972), amp pf
Crumb, *Makrokosmos*, Book II (1973), amp pf
Crumb, *Makrokosmos*, Book III (1974), 2 amp pf, 2 perc
Davidovsky, *Synchronisms No. 6* (1970), pf, tape
Kagel, *Phantasie für Orgel mit obbligati* (1967), org, assistants, 2 tape rec
Kagel, *Tactil* (1970), 3 pf, plucked str inst
Ligeti, *Continuum* (1968), hpd
Ligeti, *Volumina* (1961–62), org
Mâche, *Anaphores* (1982), hpd, perc
Messiaen, *Visions de l'amen* (1943), 2 pf
Messiaen, *Vingt regards sur l'enfant Jésus* (1944), pf
Messiaen, *Cantéyodjayâ* (1949), pf
Messiaen, *Quatre études de rhythme:* "IIe de feu," I & II; "Mode de valeurs et d'intensités" "Neumes rhythmiques" (1949–50), pf
Messiaen, *Messe de la Pentecôte* (1950), org
Messiaen, *Livre d'orgue* (1951), org
Messiaen, *Catalogue d'oiseaux* (1956–58), pf
Messiaen, *Méditations sur le mystère de la Sainte Trinité* (1969), org
Messiaen, *La fauvette des jardins* (1970), pf
Messiaen, *Livre du Saint Sacrement* (1986), org
Meyer, *Sonata for Harpsichord* (1973)
Rorem, *A Quaker Reader* (1976), org
Rorem, *Views from the Oldest House* (1981), org
Sessions, *Third Piano Sonata* (1965), pf
Sola, *Pièce pour clavecin et percussion* (1982)
Penderecki, *Partita* (1972), hpd, cham ens
Stockhausen, *Klavierstücke I–IV* (1952–53), pf
Stockhausen, *Klavierstücke V–X* (1954–55), pf
Stockhausen, *Klavierstücke XI* (1956), pf
Stockhausen, *Klavierstücke XIII* (1981), pf, elec, B
Stravinsky, *Movements* (1959), pf, orch
Xenakis, *Evryali* (1973), pf

REPERTOIRE (Percussion)

Albright, *Take That* (1972), 4 drummers
Colgrass, *Déjà vu* (1977), 4 perc, orch
Crumb, *Makrokosmos III* (1974), 2 pf, perc
Davidovsky, *Synchronisms No. 5* (1969), perc, tape
Davies, *Turris Campanarum Sonantium* (Bell Tower) (1970)
Erb, *Concerto for Percussion and Orchestra* (1966)
Feldman, *The King of Denmark* (1964)
Husa, *Concerto for Percussion and Wind Ensemble* (1970–71)

Partch, *Delusion of the Fury* (1969)
C. Rouse, *Ogoun Badagris* (1976)
C. Rouse, *Ku-Ka-Ilimoku* (1978)
Serocki, *Episodes* (1959), 50 str, 34 perc inst
Serocki, *Segmenti* (1951), 12 winds, 5 str, perc
Serocki, *Symphonic Frescoes* (1964), orch, 58 perc inst
Serocki, *Continuum* (1965–66), 6 perf, 123 perc inst
Stockhausen, *Refrain* (1959)
Stockhausen, *Zyklus* (1959)
Stockhausen, *Mikrophonie I* (1964), tam-tam, micro, filters
Takemitsu, *Seasons* (1970), 4 metal instr, glass trbn, tape
Udow, *Bog Music* (1976)
Wuorinen, *Janissary Music* (1967)
Wuorinen, *Ringing Changes* (1971)
Wuorinen, *Percussion Symphony* (1976)

READING (Percussion)

Danlee Mitchell, "Percussion in the Orchestra of Harry Partch," *Percussionist*, 34 (1966),
   37.
Reginald Brindle, *Contemporary Percussion* (London, 1970).
Harry Partch, *Genesis of a Music*, 2nd ed. (New York, 1974).
B. Johnson, "The Corporealism of Harry Partch," *Perspectives of New Music*, xiii.2
   (1975), 85.
M. Wisckol, "Harry Partch's Ensemble: Jazz Festival in San Diego," *Downbeat*, 1
   (December 1983), 58.
Michael Udow, "An Interview with Karlheinz Stockhausen," *Percussive Notes*, xxiii.6
   (September 1985), 6–47. A discussion of the role of percussion in Stockhausen's
   works.

REPERTOIRE (Strings, Winds)

Strings

Berio, *Sequenza VI* (1967), viola
Boulez, *Messagesquisse* (1977), 7 vc
Crumb, *Black Angels* (1970), elec str quartet
Druckman, *Valentine* (1969), contrabass
Henze, *Double Bass Concerto* (1966)
Hiller, *String Quartet No. 5 (In Quarter-Tones)* (1962)
T. de Leeuw, *Music for Strings* (1970)
Kagel, *Match* (1964), 2 vc, perc; film version (1966)
Kirchner, *Quartet No. 3 for String Quartet and Electronic Tape* (1966)
Panufnik, *Lullaby* (1947, rev. 1955), 29 str
Penderecki, *Threnody for the Victims of Hiroshima* (1960), 52 str

Flute

Badings, *Sonata* (1957), recorder, hpd
Badings, *Dialogues* (1967), fl, org
Berio, *Serenata I* (1957), fl, 14 instr
Berio, *Sequenza I* (1958), fl
Boulez, *Sonatine* (1946), fl, pf
Crumb, *Voice of the Whale* (1971), elec fl, elec pf, elec vc
Davidovsky, *Synchronisms No. 1* (1962), fl, tape
Dick, *Afterlight* (1973), fl
Fortner, *Sonata* (1947), fl, pf
Fortner, *New-Delhi Music* (1959), fl, vn, vc, hpd
Fortner, *Inventionen und ein Anhang* (1976), 2 fl

Heiss, *Four Lyric Pieces* (1962), fl
Heiss, *Five Pieces for Flute and Cello* (1963)
Hovhaness, *Sonata* (1967), fl
Luening, *Lyric Scene* (1958), fl, orch
Luening, *Sonority Canon* (1962), 2-37 fl
Leuning, *Trio* (1967), 3 fl
Maderna, *Musica su due dimensioni* (1952; rev. 1963), fl, tape
Maderna, *Honeyrêves* (1961), fl, pf
Messiaen, *Le merle noir* (1951), fl, pf
Perle, *Monody I* (1960), fl
Sollberger, *Riding the Wind II, III, IV* (1974), fl
Stockhausen, "Katinka's Gesang" (1983), fl, 6 perc (*Samstag aus Licht*, scene 2)
Westergaard, *Divertimento* (1967), fl, pf
Wuorinen, *Variations I & II* (1963/68), fl

Clarinet

Barraqué, *Concerto* (1968), clar, vibr, instr trios
Berio, *Sequenza IX* (1980), cl
Boulez, *Domaines* (1961-9), clar solo or with 6 instr
Davies, *Stedman Doubles* (1955; rev. 1968), clar, perc.
Davies, *Hymnos* (1967), clar, pf
Davies, *Eight Songs for a Mad King* (1969)
Denisov, *Sonata* (1972), cl
Druckman, *Animus III* (1969), clar, tape
Martino, *Triple Concerto* (1978), clar, bass clar, contrab clar, 16 instr
Perle, *Sonata quasi una fantasia* (1972), cl, pf
Stockhausen, *Harlekin* (1975), clar
Stockhausen, *Sirius* (1975-77), S, B, tpt, b cl, elec
Stockhausen, *Amour* (1976), clar
Smith, W. O., *Fancies for Clarinet Alone* (1969)
Tower, *Wings* (1981), cl

Other Winds

Albright, *Heater* (1977), sax, instr ens
Bassett, *Music for Saxophone and Piano* (1968)
Berio, *Sequenza V* (1966), trombone
Berio, *Sequenza VII* (1969), oboe
Davidovsky, *Synchronisms No. 8* (1974), wind quintet, tape
Denisov, *Sonata* (1970), a sax, pf
Dlugoszewski, *Space is A Diamond* (1970), trumpet
Druckman, *Animus I* (1966), trombone, tape
Erickson, *Kryl* (1977), soloist, 13 trumpets
Globokar, *Discours II* (1967-8), 5 tromb or tromb/tape
Globokar, *Discours III* (1969), 5 oboes
Globokar, *Discours IV* (1974), 3 clar
Globokar, *Atemstudie* (1971), oboe
Gompper, *Anon* (1984), oboe, pf
Henze, *Double Concerto* (1966), oboe, harp, str
Holliger, *Siebegesang* (1966-67), oboe, fem vv, orch, elec
Holliger, *Pneuma* (1970), 36 winds, 4 radios, organ, perc
Holliger, *Cardiophonie* (1971), 1 wind, tape rec
Henze, *Heliogabulus imperator* (1971-72), orch
Husa, *Music for Prague* (1968), wind ens
Husa, *Apotheosis of This Earth* (1970), wind ens
Husa, *Concerto for Trumpet and Winds* (1973)
Kagel, *Der Atem* (1970), 1 wind, tape rec

Kagel, *Heterophonies* (1959–61), 42 solo instr
Ligeti, *Double Concerto* (1972), ob, fl, orch
Ligeti, *Trio* (1982), pf, vln, French hn
Noda, *Improvisation I* (1972), sax
S. Rouse, *Crosswinds* (1984), org, 12 instr
S. Rouse, *Flash Point* (1984), woodwind quartet
Stanton, *Cantos* (1987), fl, alto sax, hpd
Stockhausen, "Lucifer's Dance" (1983), 80 winds (*Samstag aus Licht*, scene 3)
Stockhausen, *Solo* (1966), melody inst, tape rec

Exotic and Early Instruments

Cope, *The Way* (1981), for orig instr
Harrison, *Concerto in Slendro* (1961), vn, celesta, perc
Harrison, *Pacifika Rondo* (1963), cham orch of Western and Asian inst
Kagel, *Music for Renaissance Instruments* (1965–66)
Kagel, *Exotica* (1971–72), six players, exotic instr
Partch, *Delusion of the Fury* (1969), orig instr
Salzman, *The Nude Paper Sermon* (1969), Renaissance Consort, chor, elec
Takemitsu, *Eclipse* (1966), biwa, shakuhachi
Takemitsu, *November Steps* (1967), biwa, shakuhachi, orch

READING (Strings, Winds)

John C. Heiss, "Some Multiple Sonorities for Flute, Oboe, Clarinet and Bassoon," *Perspectives of New Music*, vii.1 (1968), 1.

William Brooks, "Instrumental and Vocal Resources" in John Vinton, ed., *Dictionary of Contemporary Music* (New York, 1974).

Thomas Howell, *The Avant-Garde Flute* (Berkeley, 1974).

Bertram Turetzky, *The Contemporary Contrabass* (Berkeley, 1974).

Robert Dick, *The Other Flute* (London, 1975)

Robert Erickson, *Sound Structure in Music* (Berkeley, 1975).

Phillip Rehfeldt, *New Directions for Clarinet* (Berkeley, 1977).

Stuart Dempster, *The Modern Trombone: A Definition of its Idiom* (Berkeley, 1980).

Paul Griffiths, *Modern Music* (London, 1981), 223–237.

Bruno Bartolozzi, *New Sounds for Woodwind*, 2nd ed. (New York, 1982).

David Cope, *New Directions in Music*, 4th ed. (Dubuque, 1984), Chapter IV, "Instrument Exploration," 87–140.

New York Philharmonic Horizons '84, a commemorative magazine: Programs for June 1 and 5 were labeled "The New Virtuosity" and included the following pieces: Stuart Dempster, *Standing Waves* and Robert Erickson, *General Speech* performed by Stuart Dempster, trombone; Kenneth Gaburo, *Inside* and Jon Deak, *Readings from "Steppenwolf"* performed by Jon Deak, contrabass; Diamánda Galás, *Solowork 1984* and *Tragouthia apo to Aima Exoun Fonos* performed by Diamánda Galás, soprano; George Lewis, *Rainbow Family* for four musicians and realtime computer system; Dean Drummond, *Columbus* performed by Newband; Joan La Barbara, *Silent Scroll: An Image of Entropy* performed by Joan La Barbara, soprano, with Newband; Dean Drummond, *Mysteries*, Newband; Joan La Barbara, *October Music: Star Showers*; and *Extraterrestrials; After Obervogelsang* performed by Joan La Barbara; Robert Dick, *Piece in Gamelan Style, T C, Glimpse from the Blimpse*; Martin Bresnick, *Conspiracies* performed by Robert Dick, flute; Salvatore Martirano, *Improvisation with Sal-Mar Construction.*

PART IX

PAST IMPERFECT— FUTURE SUBJUNCTIVE

Praise be to *amnesia*!"

—Pierre Boulez (1971)

"Music can be renewed by regaining contact with the tradition and means of the past . . . "

—George Rochberg (1972)

CHAPTER 30

USES OF THE PAST:
A SYNTHESIS

In *Music Ho!* (1934), Constant Lambert wrote a scathing denunciation of Stravinsky's turn toward Neoclassicism and accused him of "time-traveling." He was not alone in his assessment, as we have noted in our discussions on Schoenberg. It is somewhat paradoxical to note that in the closing years of the twentieth century, brands of "time-traveling" and serialism have both survived and that, at least for the moment, the former would seem to be the somewhat more vigorous of the two.

While the diversity in current uses of the past strikes a pose as far removed from 1920s Neoclassicism as current Serialism stands from the 1920s variety, the wide chronological range of models is not unrelatable to Stravinsky's endorsement of composers from Machaut to Webern over the long arch of his career. The present wave of interest in early music prompted by musicologist and performer alike has spawned numerous groups throughout the world devoted to "authentic performances on authentic instruments" and has seen the canonization of the expression "performance practice." But the editions of Medieval, Renaissance, and Baroque music that began pouring from the presses following the end of World War II whetted the appetite not only of the performer (resulting in a flood of recordings that radically changed our view of much early music) but also of the composer, who was frequently the first to take the bait.

BACH AND BEFORE

Thus in 1960, on the 400th anniversary of the birth of Gesualdo (c. 1560–1613) and shortly after his second visit to the composer's castle (Figure 30.1), Stravinsky wrote his *Monumentum pro Gesualdo ad CD annum*. While the surface effect may be that of an orchestration, Stravinsky clearly marked his intention on the title page with the claim "recomposed for instruments." The recomposition is, in fact, to be discovered on several levels: harmonic-melodic coloring with added dissonances not found in the original ("Asciugate i begli oochi"); octave displacements in "Ma tu, cagion"; and timbral, including *Klangfarben*, techniques at the beginning of the third madrigal, "Beltà poi che t'assenti." Thus, the composer's earlier antiquarian interests are reviewed and updated in light of issues current in the late 1950s. Other evidence of an

Figure 30.1. Igor Stravinsky and Robert Craft in the courtyard of Gesualdo's castle, October 16, 1959.

Photo courtesy of Columbia Records.

attraction to Gesualdo's music came with Vlijmen's *Omaggio à Gesualdo* (1971) for violin and six instrumental groups also on material from "Beltà poi"; Lalo Shifrin's *Variations on a Theme of Gesualdo* (1965) based on the madrigal "Io pur respiro"; and Ton de Leeuw's *Lamento pacis* (1969), whose first and third sections are labeled as homages to Gesualdo and Ockeghem respectively, the latter through a quotation from his *Missa Mi-Mi.*

Gesualdo's personal biography is sufficiently rich not only in the splendours of Renaissance courtly life but also in intrigue, jealousy, and murder that it would seem a natural for an opera or a Ken Russell movie. Indeed, several composers in the past have toyed with the idea, including David Diamond and especially William Walton, whose lengthy correspondence with Cecil Gray in the 1940s provides evidence of how far the project had developed.[1] Since then *Moro lasso* (1963/1972) by Peter Eötvös (b. 1944), although labelled a "madrigal comedy," makes use of the Renaissance prince's most notorious madrigal text in such a tenuous manner that oblique satire, totally lacking in narrative propulsion, results. An even further remove from the text, but a closer approximation to the musical values of the original, is to be found in Bruce Adolphe's *Variations on a Madrigal by Gesualdo* ("Moro lasso") for piano solo (1984).

While Stravinsky had originally looked at Gesualdo's *Responses for Holy Week* of 1611, newly published in an edition of 1959 by the present author, he found that the composer's madrigals were best suited to his announced purpose of attempting a definition of "'instrumental' as distinct from 'vocal.'" For a *Tenebrae super Gesualdo* (1972), however, Peter Maxwell Davies chose one of the darkest of these responses, "O vos omnes" ("All ye that pass by, attend and see if there be any sorrow like unto my sorrow"), for a work that contrasts a series of four instrumental meditations with three interludes for voice and guitar. Using a modified *Pierrot* ensemble with the addition of percussion, the meditations are transfigurative elaborations that emphasize the dark colors of the alto flute and bass clarinet coupled with the low registers of the strings, harpsichord, chamber organ and marimba and only occasionally highlighted by the sound of the violin, celesta, and glockenspiel. Beginning with a meditation, the alternating interludes that follow gradually accumulate Gesualdo's original music through the course of the piece. Technical matters aside, however, Davies' Gesualdo setting may be held as indicative of the composer's thorough-going interest in early music held from the beginning of his career.

Already in his *String Quartet, Leopardi Fragments,* and *Sinfonia,* all of 1961, Davies had adopted the formal solutions of Monteverdi's "Sonata sopra Sancta Maria" from the Vespers of 1610. This idea of a cantus-firmus technique working across the double bar was a treatment that was to appear again in his *Hymn to St. Magnus* of 1972. There, too, his use of a twelfth-century Orcadian hymn confirmed a predisposition already in evidence in his *Worldes Blis* of 1966–69, a motet for orchestra based on a Medieval monody. Elsewhere, an infatuation with plainsong, isorhythmic designs, and Magic Squares (*Seven In Nomine,* 1963–64; *Ave Maris Stella,* 1975) and the music of Dunstable, Taverner, Purcell, and Bach provided evidence that such adoptions were not mere occasional flirtations but representative of a fundamental orientation. It is a characteristic that, to a lesser extent, is also observable in his English compatriot, Harrison Birtwistle, who has made arrangements of Machaut (*Hoquetus David*) and Ockeghem (*Ut heremita olus*), both of 1969.

Something of this direct approach to early source material can also be found in works by Charles Wuorinen, whose role among American serialists has already been reviewed. His 1962 setting for modern instruments of pieces from the *Glogauer Liederbuch* (c. 1480) is not unlike Davies' *Renaissance Scottish Dances* (1973). But in his *Percussion Symphony* of 1976, his "integrated juxtaposition" of two settings of Dufay's "Vergina bella" (c. 1430) as "Entr'actes" between the movements of a fast-slow-fast scheme not only caters to his "hobby" of reworking old music, but provides an unsuspected compatibility as well as contrast to the main business of the work. The last movement, which is infused to a degree with reminiscences of the preceding interlude, is a disarming finale that, for all its dodecaphonic base, sounds like a fusion of early Cage, a Broadway Babbitt, and the George Shearing Quintet.

Even more surprising in this context is the name Alexei Volkonsky, a student of Dinu Lipatti and Nadia Boulanger before returning to the Soviet Union in 1947. Expelled from the Moscow Conservatory for insubordination, he quickly became a familiar name on the official party's blacklist before his defection to Western Europe in 1973. As early as 1956, however, he began to nourish his avant-garde activities privately, while becoming publicly engaged in the promotion of early music as a harpsichordist and organizer of a group called "Madrigal." His own *Quodlibit* of 1978, similarly based on pieces from the *Glogauer Liederbuch*—the original manuscript was lost in World War II, but a modern edition had existed from 1936–37—is an intriguing confirmation of the duality of his creative bias.

Numerous seventeenth-century composers began to achieve cult status in the 1960s and 1970s, and increasing familiarity with their music brought with it an air of discovery on the part of performer and audience. In addition to the operas of Monteverdi, those of his compatriot Cavalli began to appear on the boards of international houses in editions by Raymond Leppard during this period, and several works by Jacob Druckman are coincidental to this development. Three works (*Delizie contente che l'alme beate* of 1973 for wind quintet and tape; *Lamia* of 1975 for soprano and orchestra; and *Prism* of 1980 for orchestra) all quote from Cavalli's *Il Giasone.*

The appeal of such a giant figure as Bach would not wait until the Tricentennial of his birth in 1985, although when the final lists are in there will undoubtedly be a healthy tally of musical tributes. Bach's power to attract the twentieth-century composer, notably demonstrated in the decades of the 1920s and 1930s (see p. 318), was seen again in the 1950s and 1960s. But where Stravinsky's *Variations on "Vom Himmel Hoch"* of 1955 involved subtle glosses of timbre and mildly dissonant counterpoint with respect to Bach's generally unfamiliar treatment of a well-known chorale, Lukas Foss's *Baroque Variations* of 1967 presented a familiar work of Bach in his third variation while subjecting it to distortions through a process the composer has described as follows:

> Variations III: On the Prelude from Bach's Partita in E major for solo violin. The submerging into and emerging out of inaudibility is rendered more hazardous for the players because it is executed at moments varying with each performance. Though the conductor cues the various instruments in and out, he himself cannot keep track of the point at which an instrument will have arrived in its inaudible rendition when he calls upon it to emerge. As in Variation I, where only Handel's notes are used, Variation III's are entirely made out of Bach's violin solo. Even the glissandi are Bach-derived. What I wanted can perhaps best be described as "torrents of Baroque sixteenth-notes, washed ashore by ocean waves, sucked in again, returning"—a Bach dream—abruptly changing situations, some humorous (two flutes racing each other—xylophone spelling out JOHANN SEBASTIAN BACH in Morse code, etc.), some frightening (as the organ-percussion duel at the end).[2]

Not a member of the avant-garde of the 1950s, Bernd Alois Zimmermann (1918–1970) emerged as one of Germany's leading composers in the 1960s, drawing on an enlarged historical consciousness, both musical and literary. Though his exposure to the sounds of the Baroque organ at a monastery school as a boy was fundamental to his choice of profession and later to his sense of color, he never wrote for the instrument. In his *Monologe* for two pianos (1960–64), however, his knowledge and affection for its literature is revealed in a kind of double vision that simultaneously presents quotations from two organ works, Bach's "Wachet auf, rufet uns die Stimme" and Messiaen's "Alleluias sereins d'une âme désire le ciel" (*L'Ascension*).[3] His use of quotations from Bach and other composers in his contemporaneous *Die Soldaten*, an opera strongly indebted to *Wozzeck* as a model, reveals that, as in *Monologe*, juxtaposition, not integration, is his aim. Zimmermann's citation of a Messiaen "Alleluia" (Ex. 31.3) coincidentally forces recognition of the importance of plainchant to Messiaen's music from the beginning of his career to the present day. It is a claim that can be similarly made with respect to Peter Maxwell Davies and John Tavener (b. 1944).

BEETHOVEN'S BICENTENNIAL

> Beethoven
> a name   —the name
>   the least discussed
>   most accepted and acknowledged symbol of *our* musical culture
> Beethoven—from the philosophic essay to the comic strip
>   —from psychoanalytical study to *biographie romancée*
> Today   —the cult
>   or parody of the cult
>   —between Bach and Wagner
>   less austere than the former
>   less hysterical than the latter
>   —in any case: respected, loved
>   (we must not forget; more serious than Haydn
>   more profound than Mozart
>   less boring than Brahms
>   +, −, +, −, . . .)
> And yet the story had a strange beginning.
>   Delacroix: "This is the work of a madman or a genius.
>   In doubt, I plump for 'genius.'"
>
> *—Pierre Boulez.*[4]

So wrote Boulez in a lengthy critique published on Beethoven's 200th birthday. In such an atmosphere as the 1960s promoted, it is little surprise that the bicentennial of Beethoven's birth in 1970 found composers of numerous aesthetic persuasions seemingly clamoring to write an homage in their own distinct fashion. While the centennial of his death in 1927 had brought a somewhat more restrained reaction, composers now perhaps hoped to clarify questions of stylistic continuity that for some had by that time become troublesome. In many instances, however, the response can be viewed as no more than a reflection of the intensified historical awareness of today's composer and perhaps a wistful reflection on a master who lived at a time when such stylistic pluralism was less of a problem.

Among the various Beethoven-inspired pieces the listener may alternately sense a lack of compositional focus or open pleasure at the recognition of a familiar passage, and his reactions may vary on repeated hearings. Stockhausen's *Opus 1970 (Stockhoven-Beethausen)*, previously discussed, combines the subjectivity of spontaneous production with the objectivity of its model in what ultimately sounds like Beethoven heard sporadically as though by shortwave from a distant planet. Ginastera, on the other hand, in the first movement of his *Piano Concerto No. 2* of 1972 fashioned a set of thirty-two variations (an allusion to the piano variations in C minor) on the fourth movement polychord (F-A-D-C♯-E-G-B♭) of Beethoven's *Ninth Symphony*, while Tippett takes the *Schreckensfanfare* from the same movement and transforms it into a soprano blues solo in his *Third Symphony* of the same year. In his opus ultimum, a *Sonata for Viola and Piano* of 1975, Shostakovich's commentary on the "Moonlight Sonata" reflected a more integrated use of materials than the brief citations of Rossini and Wagner in his *Symphony No. 15* of 1971. George Rochberg's highly Romantic *Rocordanza* for cello and piano (1972) has carried such an attitude a step further, utilizing Beethoven's C major *Cello Sonata*, op. 102, as a model in an apparent attempt to recapture the style of a bygone era and abandon the concept of originality altogether.

The world of Beethoven's string literature is further explored by André Boucourechliev in his *Ombres* for string orchestra of 1970, where Beethoven's string quartets are appropriated as a source for fragmentation, quotation, and integration into a personal style. Ralph Shapey (b. 1921) approached the Beethoven question somewhat more obliquely in his *String Quartet No. 7* (1972). A work in four movements (I. Interludes and Fantasies; II. Scherzando; III. Song; IV. Passacaglia), Shapey eschewed quotation while holding to a classical formal structure. "Although I did not set out to imitate or paraphrase the past," Shapey has said, "I wrote it in response to my deep love for Beethoven's last quartets."[5]

Mauricio Kagel's presentation of a catalogue of Beethoven works in a chamber orchestra version of *Ludwig van* (1969) leads to an entirely different message in which the tonal element is compromised principally through temporal adjustments in the reassemblage of what he has called a "meta-collage".[6] In the process a whole range of questions concerning syntax, fidelity to the work, electronic distortion, open form, and the "work-in-progress" are reconsidered. The composer's point of view in this instance is clarified by his film of the same title (Figure 30.2) wherein Beethoven revisits his birthplace on the event of his bicentennial. What transpires is a fantasy exploration of the myth that led to his artistic canonization in the nineteenth and twentieth centuries and a consideration of its effect on contemporary man's approach to the original.

Thus, in the choice of Beethoven as an object of commentary by numerous composers of the 1970s, his bicentennial was not only celebrated but the continuing vitality of the notion of a Beethoven Succession, extensively explored at the beginning of this book, was alternately rejected as an impossibility or endorsed as a kind of nostalgic hope.

NINETEENTH-CENTURY MODELS AND THE "NEW ROMANTICISM"

The adaptation of music from Bach and Beethoven had occurred, as readers of this book know, with considerable vigor earlier in the century. If the interest of composers of the 1960s and 1970s had been restricted to music of the eighteenth century and before, it might have been easier to promote a parallel with the Neoclassic movement of the 1920s. In fact, however, the appeal of quotation, collage, and transformation has seen the composer rifling the pages of the nineteenth century as well, and the wholesale recovery of tonality and the triad in combination with a newly released expressivity has led to the recognition of a lively trend that has, appropriately or not, been dubbed the New Romanticism.

Figure 30.2. Kagel on the set for his film *Ludwig van* (1969), a critique and homage to Beethoven.

Photo courtesy of Universal Edition Ltd.

Again, as with the application of all labels, caution has been stressed and distinctions sought. In the Horizons '83 and '84 concerts sponsored by the New York Philharmonic, its artistic director Jacob Druckman noted this need, and in a commemorative magazine published for the 1984 performances between May 30 and June 8 brought together a series of articles by William Schuman, Milton Babbitt, Gregory Sandow, and Paul Griffiths on the subject "The New Romanticism—A Broader View." The struggle to identify the term and then to loosen it sufficiently for use was apparent. Druckman pointed to the presence of a new Dionysian sensibility, present in much music since 1970, that seemed to stem directly from a reaction to the Apollonian objectivity of the period of the 1950s and 1960s. Babbitt's reaction predictably argued the need to hold the course and offered words of encouragement to "those composers who dare to presume to attempt to make music as much as it can be rather than the minimum with which one obviously can get away with music's being"; Schuman posited the notion that to be a composer was by definition to be a Romantic, an artist-hero, defended expression and lamented the writing of "music by constraint" typically nourished in the academic environment during the height of the serial vogue. The arguments were familiar and had been around for a long time.

What did seem to emerge, however, was a sense that the composer, having weathered the rites of passage involved in the scientific inquiry of the difficult decades immediately following World War II, was now in a position to breathe a new expression backed by an enlarged technique. If ever there had been a time ripe for synthesis, this appeared to be it. The need to argue the point stemmed from such a recognition. This provides a quite different slant to the notion of New Romanticism than one that might imply the use of specific nineteenth century models, the negation of serial techniques, the reconstitution of a timid tonality, or the resurrection of schmalz.

Certainly the triads and tonal fields of many of the Minimalists must not be considered neoromantic any more than numerous pieces that have taken their orientation from nineteenth-century repertoires. The proposition can be tested by noting in Stravinsky's Tchaikovsky-based *The Fairy's Kiss* of 1928 an objectivity that is missing in Shchedrin's *Anna Karenina*, an emotionally more urgent ballet of 1972 openly indebted to the composer of the *Pathétique* symphony by one of the Soviet Union's leading composers.

For many, the music of George Rochberg (b. 1918) written during the early 1970s provided the first real crisis with the idea of the New Romanticism. Having espoused Schoenbergian dodecaphony throughout the 1950s, he began in the 1960s to endorse a brand of assemblage that in *Contra mortem et tempus* (1965) saw the juxtaposition of quotations from Boulez, Berio, Varèse, and Ives. This approach continued in *Music for the Magic Theater* (1965) for fifteen instruments, wherein music by Mozart, Beethoven, Mahler, Webern, Varèse, Stockhausen, and Rochberg himself were brought together in a tonal collage. Using Beethoven's *Cello Sonata* op. 102 as a model, Rochberg passed beyond quotation and assemblage to the recapture of a style based on it in his *Ricordanza* of 1972. The clear tonal language of this work coupled to a highly expressive, appoggiatura-laden melodic style came at the same time as his *Third String Quartet*, a period that followed by a decade the composition of his last serial work, a trio for violin, cello, and piano of 1963. Rochberg has described his personal story tellingly:

> My Third Quartet, composed between December 1971 and February 1972, is the first major work to emerge from what I have come to think of as "the time of turning." Every artist needs a way of viewing his situation in terms of where he's been, where he is now, and where he must go. The pursuit of art is much more than achieving technical mastery of means or even a personal style; it is a spiritual journey toward the transcendence of art and of the artist's ego. In my "time of turning," I have had to abandon the notion of "originality," in which the personal style of the artist and his ego are the supreme values; the pursuit of the one-idea, uni-dimensional work and gesture which seems to have dominated the esthetics of art in the 20th century; and the received idea that it is necessary to divorce oneself from the past, to eschew the taint of association with those great masters who not only preceded us but (let it not be forgotten) created the art of music itself. In these ways I am turning away from what I consider the cultural pathology of my own time toward what can only be called a *possibility:* that music can be renewed by regaining contact with the tradition and means of the past, to re-emerge as a spiritual force with reactivated powers of melodic thought, rhythmic pulse, and large-scale structure.
>
> As I see it, these things are only possible with tonality; the inclusion of tonality in a multi-gestural music such as the Third Quartet makes possible the

combination and juxtaposition of a variety of means which denies neither the past nor the present. In this quartet, I draw heavily on the melodic-harmonic language of the 19th century (even more specifically on the "styles" of Beethoven and Mahler), but in this open ambience tonal and atonal can live side by side—the decision of which to use depends entirely on the character and essence of the musical gesture. In this way, the inner spectrum of the music is enlarged and expanded; many musical languages are spoken in order to make the larger statement convincing.[7]

The *Quartet* begins with a "fantasia-like introduction" that juxtaposes tonal and atonal ideas, and a pair of marches of contrasting moods with a brief quotation at one point from Schoenberg's *Verklärte Nacht*. This is followed by a set of variations on an original theme whose unabashed Romanticism, clear tonality, and first violin part soaring high above the ensemble in a fashion reminiscent of late Beethoven left many first-time audiences ecstatic and others wondering if it was still possible to write such music. The work's Finale is composed out of a five-part alternation of two elements with a healthy Viennese tradition, Scherzo and Serenade. In the *String Quartets Nos. 4–6* (1977–78) that followed, Rochberg's fascination with the legacy of Haydn, Mozart, Schubert, and Beethoven continued to hold sway alongside occasional colorings derived from Mahler, Schoenberg, Berg, and Bartók. And in his essay "Reflections on the Renewal of Music," Rochberg, colliding head-on with the practitioners of his serial past, claimed openly that "There is no virtue in starting all over again. The past refuses to be erased. Unlike Boulez, I will not praise amnesia."[8] What this could mean, however, was soon evident in his *String Quartet No. 7* (1980), with baritone voice, where a return to acrid dissonances and melodies lacking any sense of tonal urgency seemed to provide a new meaning to his assertions concerning erasure.

Rochberg's journey to a newly found language based on the total recapture of a previous historical style left many bewildered, others gratified. Coming at the time of David Del Tredici's numerous "Alice in Wonderland" pieces, whose unashamed embrace of Strauss and Wagner pleased audiences and startled specialists, it confirmed that the seeds of a controversy had now been planted. The twentieth century's unflagging sponsorship of the Romantic Age in its concert halls and on recording had, to a large extent, allowed the general public to skirt the issue of "modern music." But numerous composers of the 1970s, it appeared, had also been harboring a nostalgia for the tonal past, and like Schoenberg, who suffered similar pangs, now began to give into the urge to employ many of its expressive gestures.

Having traversed an even more heterogenous path (serial, electronic, aleatoric, spoken text as exclusive sound material), it is not surprising that Berio was more open than most to the reintroduction of tonality in the late 1960s. For, in addition to the question of vocalism and textual meanings discussed earlier with respect to his *Sinfonia* (1968; see p. 607), Luciano Berio also addressed the questions of quotation and neoromanticism in the third section of that work. Denying any desire "to destroy Mahler," "to play out a private complex about post-Romantic music," or "to spin some enormous musical anecdote," he explained his intention in detail. His angle in the reuse of materials can be readily distinguished from Rochberg's, but his confession regarding "the weight of the entire history of music" is revealing both with regard to the work at hand and the period in general:

> It [Section III] is perhaps the most "experimental" music I have ever written. It is an homage to Gustav Mahler (whose work seems to bear the weight of the entire history of music of the last two centuries) and in particular to the third movement—the *Scherzo* of his Second Symphony (*Resurrection*). Mahler is to the totality of the music of the third part of my *Sinfonia* as Beckett is to the totality of the text. The result is a kind of "voyage to Cythera" made on board the third movement of Mahler's Second Symphony. The Mahler movement is treated like a container—rather, a generator—within whose framework a large number of musical references and characters is proliferated; they go from Bach to Schoenberg, from Beethoven to Strauss, from Brahms to Stravinsky, from Berg to Boulez, etc.[9] The different musical "characters" are always integrated into the flowing harmonic structure of Mahler's *Scherzo;* actually, they are signalling and commenting upon the events and transformations. Therefore, the references do not constitute a collage but, rather, illustrate an harmonic process.

> Besides, these well known "characters" are interacting and transform themselves—as it happens with those familiar objects or familiar faces that, placed in a different light or in a new context, suddenly acquire a different meaning. The combining and the unifying of different and even estranged musical "characters" may be the main motivation for this third part of my *Sinfonia*, for this meditation on a Mahlerian "objet trouvé." If I were to describe the presence of Mahler's *Scherzo* in *Sinfonia*, the image which comes most spontaneously to my mind is that of a river flowing through a constantly changing landscape, sometimes going underground and emerging in another altogether different place, sometimes disappearing completely, present either as a fully recognizable form or as small details lost in the surrounding host of musical presences.[10]

With such a range of aesthetic excuses to return to the tonal, Romantic past, the number of composers who in the 1970s and early 1980s opted at least momentarily to do so is not surprising. Some of the nineteenth-century masters who were tapped in variable fashion include Schumann (Schafer, Holloway), Wagner (Shostakovich, Henze, Holloway, Del Tredici), Strauss (Berio, Schafer, Del Tredici), Mahler (Crumb, Berio, Rochberg, Seegerstam), and Brahms (Kagel). Yet neither Ligeti's *Trio* (1982) for piano, horn, and violin (whose instrumentation obviously recalls Brahms) nor Henze's *Tristan* (1973), in spite of the title and the composer's general expressive inclination, would truly qualify as neoromantic in a manner that is analogous to the works of Berio or Rochberg discussed earlier. *Tristan* began as a set of piano preludes, whose style is not too distant from the piano part of Berg's *Chamber Concerto* or the composer's own *Piano Concerto No. 2* of 1967—that is to say, tonally ambiguous, virtuosic, and only mildly pointillistic. To that Henze has added an intricate and important tape part based on filtered strains of *Tristan* (rarely audible as such), a fourteenth century "Lamento di Tristano," and other materials. The work is expressive-dissonant, but not openly Romantic in feeling except for three intrusions on progressively less distinct levels of the opening of Brahms's *First Symphony* and a clear citation of the *Tristan* music common to the *Wesendoncklied*, "Im Treibhaus." The latter appears near the end against a human heartbeat on tape and the voice of a child reciting the following lines from Gottfried von Strassburg's renowned Tristan legend (c. 1210):

> She takes him in her arms, and then, lying out full length, she kisses his face and
> lips and clasps him tightly to her. Then straining body to body, mouth to mouth,
> she at once gives up her spirit and of sorrow for her lover dies thus at his side.

A work of forty-five minutes' duration, subtitled prelude for piano, tapes, and
orchestra, its collage technique for the most part rarely indulges in such
emblematic quotation and shares more with the numerous elusive and fleeting
recollections of Druckman's *Windows* (Pulitzer Prize, 1970) than with Berio's
Sinfonia (many such recognizable quotations) or Rochberg's *Ricordanza* (the
overt recapture of an earlier style based on a specific work).

It is often the most verbal composer who becomes charged with the
responsibility of securing the aims of a new aesthetic. But other composers who
have argued the point only through their music have made equally forceful,
though individual, statements regarding Rochberg's premise. As early as his *St.
Luke's Passion* (1963–65), Penderecki had introduced a newly expressive
conservatism that seemed far removed from the sonorous masses, string
glissandi, and other effects of his renowned *Threnody for the Victims of
Hiroshima* written only shortly before. An overt sense of return to the
nineteenth century was apparent in his orchestral *The Dream of Jacob,* and with
the virtuoso rhetoric of his *Violin Concerto* of 1976 a stylistic turn was clearly
apparent. It was still observable in his *Polish Requiem* (1982–84) where, for
example, the tonal orientation and conservative choral writing of the "Agnus
Dei," for all its beauty, can only be viewed as a throwback. Similarly, his
compatriot Tadeusz Baird has in his late works placed a high premium on an
intense lyricism whose roots are openly Romantic in a series of works for voice,
typically on contemporary Polish texts.

As with any reuse of the past, the nature of the "new" is almost always more
varied and difficult to categorize than the primary aesthetic that is being acted
upon, and among the above examples the range of expression is considerable.
Rochberg of the 1970s may be held as an extreme on the one hand, Kagel on the
other, with Berio occupying a kind of middle ground. Kagel's *Variationen ohne
Fuge* (1971–72) uses Brahms' *Variations on a Theme of Handel* as the source for
a kind of "meta-collage" previously discussed with respect to his *Ludwig van*—a
point of view that shares little with the special cases of Rochberg, Berio, and
Henze in the appropriation of nineteenth-century materials.

As the New Romanticism developed, then, it was more readily identified
by its devotion to expression than to quotation and only incidentally to the
invocation of specific models. It would be well to recall once again, however, the
healthy strain of Romanticism that had flourished everywhere and in virtually
every decade of the twentieth century. Thus the sense of revival for most
audiences of the 1970s was of necessity weak because their musical culture had
supported such values right along: Even two such popular staples as Rachmaninov's *Symphonic Dances* and Strauss's *Four Last Songs* had premiered as
late as 1940 and 1950, respectively. The revival was strongest and most
discernible among composers who had spent much of the preceding decade in
different waters and for whom such a mode of expression constituted a turn.

Seen against the backdrop of Penderecki's *Threnody for the Victims of
Hiroshima* of 1960 or Rochberg's serial *Piano Trio* of 1963, their violin concerti,
written in 1976 and 1975 respectively, could perhaps not have been predicted.

But there was little to startle most audiences already familiar with the popular twentieth-century violin concertos of Berg (1935), Prokofiev (No. 2, 1935), and Walton (1939)—a strain that continued in concerti for that instrument by Barber (1940), Gerhard (1945), Henze (No. 1, 1948), Menotti (1952), and Shostakovich (No. 2, 1967). For the average concertgoer the latter music was as much or more a part of the musical fabric of the time as the music of the avant-garde. To many, Rochberg and Penderecki seemed now only to have returned to more familiar terrain.

In retrospect it is also possible to note with greater clarity how some composers of the avant-garde seem never to have totally escaped the Romantic condition. Schoenberg would be a good example, and in spite of the difficulties of his *Violin Concerto* (1936) for both performer and listener, its base in a broadly gestured, antecedent-consequent phraseology now appears much closer to the manners of Berg's work than formerly. That Berg's music had frequently been treated with suspicion by the post-Webernites of the late 1940s and early 1950s is evident from Boulez's article of 1948.[11] Having attacked Berg's Romantic impulses at that time in an attempt to press the cause of Webern, Boulez became in the period of the late 1960s and 1970s one of Berg's most ardent champions through numerous performances and recordings. His older feelings about Schoenberg, Stravinsky, and Webern remained intact; but his new embrace of Berg was more than a realignment of personal sensibilities, it was symtomatic of the age—a time that also witnessed the wholesale rediscovery of Zemlinsky (see p. 356).

COMPOSITE AND CONTEMPORARY: ART AND POPULAR MODELS

Cage's emphasis on silence and chance and his endorsement of Cocteau's and Satie's antagonism to the idea of the masterpiece carried with it a natural opposition to the recognition of models, past or present. But in a lecture as early as 1948, Cage cited Webern (e.g., *Three Cello Pieces*, op. 11) and Satie (e.g., *Chose à droite et à gauche*), claiming that they had been responsible for "the one new idea since Beethoven," namely, the reconsideration of duration—both sound and silence. The possibility of using a specifically known work—which by definition honors the idea of the masterpiece and runs counter to the idea of the *objet trouvé*—was explored by Cage in *Cheap Imitation* of 1969, wherein Satie's *Socrate* is taken as a source for "subtraction." While retaining the rhythmical phraseology of the original intact, Cage, true to form, chose his pitches anew according to the principles of *I Ching*. Similar operations were performed in *Some of "The Harmony of Maine" (William Billings) Rewritten* (1978) and *Apartment House 1776* (1976). The inherent implication, gentle as it may have been, of a rapprochement with Western traditions (see *"Retro" Music or "Music of the Future"* at the end of this section) was a surprise to many followers of the contemporary scene and of Cage's career in particular.

On another level, something of the truth of Ravel's 1928 assessment regarding the compatibility of popular music with art music was testable beginning in the 1950s with Rolf Liebermann's *Concerto* for jazz band and symphony orchestra (1954)—a confrontation even more significantly tested shortly thereafter by Gunther Schuller who promoted the idea of combining jazz elements with Western art music in what he called a "Third Stream." In his *Concerto for Jazz Quartet & Orchestra* (1959), echoes of Berg may be heard near the beginning, just as flashes of Stravinsky and Varèse may be spotted elsewhere. A lively composer whose music traverses a number of moods and styles in a personal and inimitable fashion, his devotion to the premise of jazz as serious expression has perhaps been unequalled in our time.

The compatability of jazz with new art techniques, however, was also made tellingly clear by Zimmerman in discussing its use in his opera *Die Soldaten* (1958–60; rev. 1963–64):

> If there ever has been an auspicious time for the meeting between jazz and art music as it has been understood till now, that time is now. In the so-called post-serialistic phase of the "New Music", techniques have been worked out (or, if you wish, have been revived) which give improvisation or the aleatoric that room which jazz undeniably needs in order to be itself. And therefore, it seems possible to essentially deepen the form and area of expression in jazz, and to introduce aspects to it which have heretofore been reserved only for art music.[12]

It is an attitude to which Lukas Foss had made substantial contributions in writing his *Time Cycle* (1960) where improvised instrumental (nonjazz) interludes separate and distinguish the several movements.

In America, too, the rediscovery of classical ragtime in the late 1960s led not only to recordings of the works of Scott Joplin by Joshua Rifkin and others but to newly composed pieces essentially in homage of Joplin by William Albright (*Grand Sonata in Rag*, pf, 1968; *The Dream Rags*, pf, 1970) and William Bolcom, who also tapped the spirit of the cabaret in two operas for actors, *Dynamite Tonite* (1963) and *Greatshot* (1969). Perhaps ever more unexpectedly, Michael Tippet's juxtaposition of boogie-woogie with quotations from Wagner and Mussorgsky (*Songs for Dov*, 1969–70) and of the blues with Beethoven (*Third Symphony*, 1970–72) has demonstrated together with works like Peter Maxwell Davies' *St. Thomas Wake: Foxtrot for Orchestra on a Pavan by John Bull* (1969) the continuing appeal of sounds of American origins for Western European composers.

Among the various musical personalities in the contemporary musical scene, few have had such a broad influence on current taste as Leonard Bernstein (b. 1918), and his eclecticism may fairly be seen as a reflection of the values under consideration. Conductor of the New York Philharmonic Orchestra from 1957–69, Bernstein has been one of the most energetic and respected figures in American music since the mid-1940s. His reputation in the popular imagination stems from his association with Broadway in works like *On the Town* (1944), *Candide* (1956), and especially *West Side Story* (1957). His nondramatic works, however, typically have a philosophical or spiritual base, as witness the subtitles of his three symphonies: *Symphony No. 1* ("Jeremiah") with mezzo-soprano (1943); *Symphony No. 2* ("The Age of Anxiety" after Auden) with piano (1949); *Symphony No. 3* ("Kaddish") with voice and chorus (1961–63). Bernstein blended these two seemingly discrete sides of his personality in his religious theater piece *Mass*, commissioned for the inauguration of the Kennedy Center in Washington, D.C. in 1971. Here his continuing reflections on what he calls "the crisis in faith" are summed up in a work that tropes the text of the Roman Mass with ballade tunes, chorales, blues singers, Ivesian brass bands,

Medieval conductus, and a Mahlerian sense of resolution in the finale. While the concept of the juxtaposition of liturgical text and secular verse shares something with Britten's *War Requiem*, here the idea of musical theater as contemporary social commentary is less reminiscent of *Zeitoper* than reflective of the age of *Godspell* and *Jesus Christ Superstar* and a belief in the compatibility of "show biz" with spiritual messages. At the same time it affirms Bernstein's longstanding bipartisan commitment to Broadway and the Scriptures. The same may be said of the more recent *Requiem* (1984) for tenor, soprano, chorus, and orchestra by Andrew Lloyd Webber, a composer previously known for his Broadway hits *Evita* and *Cats*.

Further evidence of the appeal of this brand of pastiche, which could reasonably be argued to be a kind of mirror of the multiple values of contemporary life, can be seen in the works of a composer like William Bolcom (b. 1938). In his *Songs of Innocence and Experience by William Blake* (1983–84), the current taste for the mixed media, multiple-style theater piece is served up in the context of the traditional oratorio for orchestra, chorus, children's choir, madrigal group, boy soprano, soloists, and rock ensemble in a work of three-hours' duration. Stylistic references abound and encompass popular moods including folk and rock. As with Bernstein's work, the multiplicity of musical viewpoints searches not so much for an integrated vision or authentic Blakeian allusions (not even historically in the madrigal) as for a reflection of the contemporary values in our musical life and the option to communicate anew with a larger public.

Another composer with a similar disposition but different musical personality is Michael Colgrass (b. 1932), whose *As Quiet As* (1966) takes a simple Beethoven sonatina and serves it up à la Haydn, Stravinsky, Webern, and Count Basie. His later *Best Wishes, U.S.A.* (1976), a centennial piece for two choruses, jazz band, and orchestra "pays homage to a variety of indigenous American musical idioms,"[13] while his 1978 Pulitzer Prize-winning *Déjà vu* (1977) for four percussion soloists and orchestra, freely mixes jazz elements with other stylistic references. On another front, John Adams' *Harmonielehre* (1985) attempted a composite view through the juxtaposition of his minimalist style, familiar from his *Grand Pianola* (1982), with the neoromantic impulses explored by numerous composers in the preceding decade.

Further indications that polystylistic juxtaposition was not deemed antithetical to the idea of originality nor its appeal geographically localized could be seen in the music of composers from the Soviet Union. The music of Alfred Shnitke[14] (b. 1934; see p. 664), along with Rodion Shchedrin[15] (b. 1932; see pp. 550, 647), offers clear evidence of the attraction of such stylistic pluralism outside the West. Having made several approaches to strict serialism as early as 1964 (*Musik* for chamber orchestra; *Music* for piano and chamber orchestra), Shnitke quickly began to explore the possibilities of constructing a sonata idea through the juxtaposition of tonal and atonal, free and serial materials (recall Berg and Rochberg) in what he termed a "stylistic kaleidoscope." In works like *pianissimo . . .* (1968) for orchestra, and the *Serenade* for five musicians (1968), he created a polystylistic collage of compatible materials. In the *Symphony No. 1* (1969–72) he carried the principal further through citations from Beethoven, Chopin, Strauss, Grieg, Tchaikowsky, the "Dies irae," and Haydn, juxtaposed against his own previously written theater and film music. The following short list of Shnitke's compositions after 1970 provides numerous touchstones with ideas that have surfaced periodically throughout this book and suggests that numerous contemporary values in the West have been integrated and interpreted within the framework of present-day Soviet culture:

1. *Canon in memoriam Igor Stravinsky* (1971), string quartet.
2. *Der gelbe Klang* (1973), scenic composition after Wassily Kandinsky (*Der blaue Reiter*) for mime, 9 musicians, chorus (or tape), and light-projector.
3. *Hymnus I* (1974), vc, harp, timpani; *Klangfarben*-variations on Russian folksongs.
4. *Präludium in memoriam Dmitri Shostakovitch* (1975), 2 vns or vn and tape.
5. *Moz-Art* (1976), 2 vns.
6. *Moz-Art à la Haydn* (1977), 2 vns, 11 strings
7. *Concerto grosso* (1976–77), 2 vns, pf, prepared pf, 21 strings: freely tonal themes; quasiserial episodes; neoclassic toccata à la Vivaldi-Corelli; tango and folksong-like music—all bound by a common intervallic content.
8. *Hommage à Stravinsky, Prokofiev and Shostakovitch* (1978), pf, six-hnds.
9. *Symphonie No. 3* (1981), written for Kurt Masur and the Gewandhaus orchestra; a probe of the overtone series and tempered systems via a four movement structure (I. Introduction; II. Sonata movement; III. Scherzo; IV. Adagio-Finale) whose pitch material was drawn from the monograms of more than thirty German composers beginning with Bach, Handel, and Mozart and concluding with Schönberg, Berg, Webern, Eisler, Weill, Stockhausen, Zimmermann, and Henze.

It was frequently stated, following the death of Stravinsky in 1971, that the last of the "great modern masters" was gone. The need to pay homage was natural enough, as the sampling of the typically canonic offerings listed on p. 682 attests. But his passing forced other composers to a consideration not only of the paths traversed in the twentieth century but also of the possibilities for synthesis and discovery in the future.

Henri Pousseur's *Stravinsky au futur* (1971) and *L'effacement du Prince Igor* (1971) differ from the numerous canonic homages written following Stravinsky's death through the double allusion inherent in the use of the pitch series of Webern's *Variations for Orchestra* op. 31—a series that had served as a point of departure for the "Pas-de-deux" in Stravinsky's *Agon* (1953–57). From a different angle, Mauricio Kagel's *Prince Igor Stravinsky* (1982) for bass and instruments, was commissioned for the Venice Biennale in 1982, the 100th anniversary of Stravinsky's birth. Attracted to an aria from the second act of Borodin's *Prince Igor*, Kagel's music plays on the ambiguities of the text and the multidimensional qualities of Russian poetry and their relationship to Stravinsky's own music.[16] Implicit in both Pousseur's and Kagel's titles was the sense of loss felt by many composers at the passing of the last of the musical giants of the early twentieth century.

In speaking of the contemporary scene in 1966, Bernstein had remarked on how old-fashioned the notion of electronics, serialism, and chance appeared, and concluded with the observation "And tonal music lies in abeyance, dormant."[17] In 1976, ten years later, he observed that everything had changed, and noted that tonal music had now been received back into the world of the avant-garde.

But how did this come to be? First of all, the disappearance of Stravinsky from the creative scene, the loss of the Colossal Dad, as Auden said, made a whole new crisis, yet a third crisis of the 20th century. Now both Schoenberg and Stravinsky were gone; where was a younger composer to turn for guidance and inspiration? To himself, of course; composers were suddenly thrown back on their own resources. And what they found there, naturally, was their innate and long-denied sense of tonality. And they could now be re-nourished by it. So the crisis turns out after all to be a solution, ironically enough, just as the earlier crisis of the mid-fifties can now be seen in retrospect to have been an occasion for synthesis, the merging of the two previously hostile camps.[18]

Significantly, in his attempt to clarify a personal aesthetic position, the composer today has frequently proclaimed an awareness of trends tangential to his own direction. Indeed, the most recent "isms" are once again the confection of the composers, not the musicologists. In fact, it may be fairly judged that a considerable amount of the bias of music history in the making has always been due to the composer pleading his own special case, from Wagner and Brahms to Schoenberg and Stravinsky, Boulez and Stockhausen, and Babbitt and Rochberg.

A creative bias, however, provides nothing more nor less than a starting point for the composer. In the pronouncement and formulation of such biases today's composer has exhibited a knowledge of the music of the past and present without parallel in the history of the art, and at the same time has demonstrated the potential for renewal through such an awareness. Charges that such historicization of art signals a decadent sensibility on the eve of its own exhaustion seem premature. The variety of tapped sources has, as indicated, led to anything but a uniformity of style or intention, and both approach and result must be considered on virtually a work-by-work basis. The composer's unusual willingness to discuss his aims is undoubtedly indicative of his awareness of the potential for misunderstanding.

"RETRO" MUSIC OR "MUSIC OF THE FUTURE"

The stylistic pluralism, as reviewed in the last section, may collectively tend to suggest a simple pent-up nostalgia for the past, and as such potentially regarded as a temporary indulgence before getting on with more important investigations. The dilemma as well as the attendant slogans are familiar ones: Wagner's *Zukunftmusik* ("Music of the Future") was in its time opposed to the more classically oriented (backward looking or "retrospective" implying "retrograde") music of Brahms; Schoenberg, aping Wagner, spoke of his own solutions as the only possible wave of the future, and chided Stravinsky for wanting simply to write "music of today",[19] warning that in his "back to . . . " approach, he and others like him risked finding themselves farther back than they might imagine.

The feeling that the search for the "new" ought to be free of entangling alliances with the past can similarly be spotted in the momentary fever of many serialists of the 1950s who expressed a fundamental alignment with numerous pronouncements of Boulez. He openly charged that, following the "brilliant fireworks display" of the period 1909–1912, the creative energies of both Schoenberg and Stravinsky had ossified in the compulsive search for order based on absolute models. Haunted by history, they lost their instinct for the "wild" discovery and settled into sterile manipulation.[20] Such a point of view was frequently forwarded in proposing a new brand of serialism that would differ from Schoenberg's not only in eschewing the classical forms, but also in avoiding musical surfaces with stylistic reminiscences.

The pressure to avoid any reference to past models led to a confusion on the part of many listeners who felt at sea in a music that not only avoided tonality and the triad but frequently eschewed any reference to antecedent-consequent phraseological structures that had always been part of their listening grammar. Regardless of the reaction, it is well to remember that the priming action of this new musical language had derived from classical principles of organization including cellular manipulation and transformation.

In the 1950s, however, the problem was further compounded on another front. Cage's open war on the idea of music—which encompassed a collection of twentieth-century ideologies largely anchored in the other arts cojoined to those of oriental philosophies—not only introduced chance, along with rigor, in the confection of musical systems, but successively the notion of "indeterminacy," the negation of choice in filling a time space (4' 33"), and ultimately the possibility of the negation of time itself (0' 00"), the primary dimension of music.

Even if later there were to be positive consequences, in such radical prunings the sense of an inherited tradition had been broken down. What had been promoted in the name of total freedom or total control had narrowed the composer's responses to the point of a fundamental denial. It is a charge that could not readily be made against most music written before 1950. Music's renewed interest in its own past, beginning in the late 1960s and continuing to the present, has thus been promoted by circumstances somewhat different from yet equal in complexity to those that promoted Neoclassicism earlier in the century. More important than the traditions of the gloss, the variation, and simple stylistic allusion was the revival of the concept of composition as a continuing criticism. While its origins are in the origins of polyphony itself, a moment of extraordinary vitality is observable in the Renaissance, when the best painters and composers acknowledged that their art was premised on cultural memory and a shared system of artistic and intellectual conventions. Authority was to be found in tradition and the development of an inexhaustible memory; originality was discoverable through "imitatio" and "emulatio," through a critique that involved not only homage but the struggle to surpass a venerable model.[21]

In such a critique, Renaissance artists like Michelangelo and Josquin des Prez took pains to introduce the concept of "difficulty" (not to be confused with "complexity"). In his setting of "Des tous biens playne" (included in the earliest printed collection of polyphonic music, the *Odhecaton* of 1501), for example, Josquin dramatically demonstrated his willingness to accept the challenge of originality by borrowing the upper two voices of a slightly earlier three-voice setting of the same text by Hayne van Ghizeghem while introducing a newly composed faster paced two-voice canon below. In such a fashion, and other more subtle as well as more involved ways, the constant quest for the new was repeatedly worked out in reference to the old. One hundred years later, with the waning of the Renaissance and the birth of the Baroque, an Italian madrigalist, Carlo Gesualdo, was probably the first composer in history to make the charge of "plagiarism" when confronted with the appropriation of features of his most advanced style in the works of his contemporaries.[22]

Boulez' exclamation "What a delight it would be for once to discover a work without knowing *anything* about it . . . Shall we ever make up our minds to disregard contexts and to forget the time factors so relentlessly insisted upon by the history books"[23] was, however, a complementary but different side of the coin, as was Cage's feeling that the Renaissance notion of art (the model/masterpiece mentality) was heretical to the basic creative impulse (see p. 564). In spite of Boulez's warnings to the composer against musical history, his understanding of it is paradoxically acute and could lead to pronouncements like the folowing: "In principle all instruction should be based on historical evolution; there should be no obligation to make a specialized study of musicology, but a knowledge of texts of the past, recent or remote, should form a foundation."[24] There can be little doubt that his fundamental view of his own music comes from such an orientation—indeed, could have come only from an intense exposure and study born of a curiosity not only of what had been accomplished in the past and what therefore might be a legitimate challenge for the present, but of how his own music might fit into any telling of history in the future. In this he is not so different from most of his contemporaries, except that he has verbalized an ongoing polemic regarding the issue.

The appeal of searching out the consequences of a lengthy tradition and all of its implications as opposed to the appropriation of an iconoclastic aesthetic of brief tenure and recent vintage had conspicuously surfaced in various "uses of the past" in the period 1965–85. But the flight was not only from Cage. For in addition, Schoenberg's method, which had also claimed a role as an evolutionary step in the history of Western music, had also proved, for many, patently too restrictive and nonreferential. Though all keen observers of the contemporary scene realized the unquestionable importance of both of these men in extending the philosophical boundaries and constructive premises of music, their differing brands of negativism had left a scar. The renewed appeal of the multiple functions and range of stylistic allusion, extending far beyond the idea of brief symbolic quotation, now served in the recapture of one of music's richest premises. Paradoxically it quickly embraced the possibility of adopting both serial and aleatory techniques in its zeal to promote the complex of man's musical heritage. The resultant reintegration was thus born less of nostalgia for a particular style than from a desire to resuscitate one of the most venerable and enduring approaches to the act of creation in the history of Western music. As with all aesthetic turns, the possibilities for perceived abuse were abundant.

REPERTOIRE (Uses of the Past: A Synthesis)

Bach and Before

Berio, *Fantasia* (1977), orch, after Gabrieli
Berio, *Toccata* (1977), orch, after Frescobaldi
Birtwistle, *Hoquetus David* (1969), fl + pic, E♭ cl, glock, bells, vn, vc, after Machaut
Birtwistle, *Ut heremita solus* (1969), fl + a fl + pic, cl + b cl, pf, glock, va, vc, after Ockeghem
Brouwer, *Sonata pian'e forte* (1973), ens, after Gabrieli, quotations also from Beethoven, Skriabian, and Szymanowski
Bussotti, *Cinque frammenti all'Italia* (1967–68), voc ens, Renaissance madrigal
Carter, *A Fantasy on Purcell's Fantasia on One Note* (1974), brass qnt
Crumb, *Ancient Voices of Children* (1970), quotations from Bach, Mahler

Crumb, *Makrokosmos III: "Music for a Summer Evening"* (1974), 2 pf, perc, quotation from Bach's *W.T.C.*; ensemble after Bartók

Davies, *Ave Maris Stella* (1975), fl + a fl, cl/basset cl, mar, pf, va, vc, plainsong, Magic Square of the Moon

Davies, *Also hat Gott die Welt geliebet* (1971), S, fl, keyb, vn, vc, after Buxtehude

Davies, *Eight Songs for a Mad King* (1969), male v, pic + fl, cl, kbds, perc, vn, v, quotations from Handel

Davies, *Fantasia on a Ground and Two Pavans* (1968), fl, clar, kybds, perc, vn, vc, v ad lib, after Purcell

Davies, *Four Quartets* (1972), T.S. Eliot incidental music, fl, cl, pf, perc, vn, vc, after Machaut's "Ma fin est mon commencement"

Davies, *Hoquetus David* (1969), after Machaut

Davies, *Hymn to St. Magnus* (1972), S, fl, basset cl, pf + hpd + cel, perc, va, vc, after twelfth-century Orcadian hymn

Davies, *Missa super l'homme armé* (1971), popular song + completions of incomplete fifteenth-century setting

Davies, *Seven In Nomine* (1963–64), Wind gnt, harp, str gt, after Taverner, Bull, Blitheman

Davies, *String Quartet* (1963–64); *Leopardi Fragments* (1961), *Sinfonia* (1961); Monteverdi's *Vespers* of 1610 used as formal model

Davies, *Prelude and Fugue in c♯ minor* (1972), fl, cl, vib, pf, va, vc after J.S. Bach, *Das wohltemperirte Klavier*, Bk. I.

Davies, *Prelude and Fugue in C♯ Major* (1974), fl, basset cl, mar, hpd, va vc, after J.S. Bach, *Das wohltemperirte Klavier*, Bk. I.

Davies, *Renaissance Scottish Dances* (1973), fl, cl, kbds, per, vn, vc

Davies, *Taverner* (1962–70), opera, after sixteenth-century documents and music of Taverner

Davies, *Tenebrae super Gesualdo* (1972), Mez, gui, fl, cl, hpd, perc, va, vc, after Gesualdo Tenebrae response, "O vos omnes"

Davies, *Worldes Blis* (1966–69), motet for orch based on medieval monody

Druckman, *Delizie contente che l'alme beate* (1973), wind qnt, tape, quotes from Cavalli's *Il Giasone*

Druckman, *Lamia* (1975), S, orch, quotes from Cavalli's *Il Giasone*

Druckman, *Prism* (1980), quotes from Cavalli's *Il Giasone* and two other Medea operas by Charpentier and Cherubini

Foss, *Baroque Variations* (1967), orch, after Handel, Scarlatti, Bach

Henze, *Telemanniana* (1967), orch

Henze, *Jepthe* (1976), orch, after Carissimi

Henze, *Il Vitalino raddoppiato* (1977), vn, cham orch

de Leeuw, T., *Lamento pacis* (1969), chor, instr.: I. Homage to Gesualdo di Venosa; III. Homage to Ockeghem

de Leeuw, T., *Sweelinck variaties* (1972–73), organ

Ligeti, *Musica ricercata* (1951–3), eleven pieces for pf; No. 11: "Omaggio a Frescobaldi," arr. org (1953)

Maderna, Adaptations of Josquin des Pres, G. Gabrieli, Monteverdi, Viadana, Vivaldi

Rands, *Madrigali* (1977), orch

Rochberg, *String Quartet No. 6* (1978), 3rd mvt., variations on Pachelbel's "Canon"

Shapero, *On Green Mountain* (1957), thirteen inst. jazz ensemble, chaconne after Monteverdi

Shifrin, L., *Variations on a Theme of Gesualdo* (1965), wind ens

Stravinsky, *Vom Himmel Hoch Variations* (1955), unison chorus, orch, after Bach canonic variations for organ

Stravinsky, *Monumentum pro Gesualdo* (1960), orch, three madrigals "recomposed for instruments": "Asciugati i begli occhi," "Ma tu cagion," "Beltà poi che t'assenti"

Vlijman, *Omaggio à Gesualdo* (1971), vn, 6 instr groups, after Gesualdo's "Beltà poi che t'assenti"

Volkonsky, *Quodlibet* (1978), after pieces in the *Glogauer Liederbuch*

Wuorinen, *Bearbeitung über der Glogauer Liederbuch* (1962), fl, cl, vn, db

Wuorinen, *Percussion Symphony* (1976), includes two settings of Dufay's "Vergina bella" as interludes

"Classical" Models and the Beethoven Centennial

Boucourechliev, *Ombres* ("Homage à Beethoven) (1970), str orch
Chavez, *Piano Sonata No. 6* (1961), pf, a genuine classical replica
Colgrass, *As Quiet As* (1966), orch, after a Beethoven sonatina
Ginastera, *Piano Concerto No. 2* (1972), Beethoven chord, 32 variations
Kagel, *Ludwig van* (1968–70), meta-collage of Beethoven material
Perle, *Sonata quasi una fantasia* (1971), cl, pf
Rochberg, *Ricordanza* (1972), vc, pf, after Beethoven, op. 102
Rochberg, *String Quartet No. 3* (1972), Beethoven as one of models
Rochberg, *String Quartets Nos. 4–6* (1977–78)
Schwartz, *Music for Napoleon and Beethoven, on their 200th birthdays* (1971), tpt, pf, 2 tapes
Shapey, *String Quartet No. 7* (1972), Beethoven as model
Shostakovich, *Sonata for Viola and Piano* (1975), material from Beethoven's "Moonlight Sonata"
Stockhausen, *Stockhoven-Beethausen: Opus 1970* (1969)
Strauss, *Metamorphosen* (1947), after Beethoven, *Symphony No. 3*, funeral march

Nineteenth-Century Models

Berio, *Sinfonia* (1968), orch, 3rd mvt. after scherzo of Mahler's *Symphony No. 2* with other quotations from Strauss, Ravel, etc.
Castiglioni, *Omaggio a Edvard Grieg*, (1982), 2 pf
Catilglioni, *Morceaux lyriques* (1983), ob, orch, quotes Bach's "Fugue in g minor" from *Well-Tempered Clavier*, Book II, with shades of Haydn and Grieg
Druckman, *Animus IV* (1977), T, instr ens, tape, on excerpts from art songs by Chabrier and Liszt
Grudzien, *Tristaniana* (1984), pf
Henze, *Tristan* (1973), piano, tapes, orch: Wagner, *Tristan;* Lamento di Tristano" (fourteenth century); Brahms, *Symphony No. 1;* Chopin, "Funeral March" from Sonata in B♭ minor
Holloway, *Scenes from Schumann* (1969–70)
Holloway, *Fantasy-Pieces* (on *Liederkreis*) (1970–71), 13 insts
Kagel, *Variationen ohne Fuge* (1971–72), after Brahms' *Handel Variations*
Schafer, *Son of Ein Heldenleben* (1968), orch, tape
Schafer, *Adieu, Robert Schumann* (1976), A, orch
Schnebel, *Wagner-Idyll* (1980), cham ens after Schoenberg's *Herzgewächse* and Boulez's *Le marteau sans maître*, reworking of "Great Friday Miracle" from Wagner's *Parsifal*
Shchedrin, *Anna Karenina* (1972), ballet, use of Tchaikowsky materials
Shostakovich, *Symphony No. 15* (1971), quotations from Rossini's "William Tell" Overture and Wagner's *Ring* ("Fate" motif)

Composite and Contemporary

Berio, *Recital I (for Cathy)* (1972), S, pf, snatches of Monteverdi, Purcell, Poulenc, Berio, etc.
Bernstein, *Mass* (1971), rock, blues, Mahler, Bernstein, etc.
Bolcom, *Illuminations on Songs of Innocence and Experience* (1983–84), blues, rock, folk, Britten, Mahler, Ives, Vaughan-Williams, Bolcom, etc.
Colgrass, *As Quiet As* (1966), Beethoven sonatina in the style of Haydn, Stravinsky, Webern, Count Basie
Colgrass, *Concertmasters* (1975), 3 vns, orch, concerto styles of eighteenth, nineteenth, twentieth centuries

Colgrass, *Flashbacks* (1978), brass qnt, autobiographical references to both Western and Oriental music

Kagel, *Prince Igor Stravinsky* (1982), B, instrs

de Leeuw, R. *Hymns and Chorals* (1970), quotation from Satie's *Messe des pauvres* and Mozart

de Leeuw, T. *Symphonies of Winds* (1963), based on a chord of Stravinsky

Liebermann, *Concerto* (1954), jazz band, orch

Pousseur, *L'effacement du Prince Igor* (1971), orch

Pousseur, *Stravinsky au futur* (1971), v, solo inst, ens, elec

Schnebel, *Bearbeitungen* (1973-74), a cycle to update important works of the past (*Bach-Contrapuncti, Schubert-Phantasie, Wagner-Idyll, Webern-Variationen*)

Schnebel, *Tradition* (1974), a cycle reflecting his attitude toward the music of previous times

Tippet, *Symphony No. 3* (1970-72), Mussorgsky, Beethoven, blues

Wuorinen, *A Reliquary for Igor Stravinsky* (1978), orch, incorporating an incomplete orch work of Stravinsky

READING

Pierre Boulez, "Beethoven: Tell Me" in *Orientations* (1986), 205–211. Originally published in German in *Die Welt*, 12 December 1970, for the bicentenary of Beethoven's birth.

George Rochberg, "Reflections on the Renewal of Music," *Current Musicology*, xiii (1972), 75–82.

Paul Griffiths, "Quotation, Integration" in *Modern Music: The Avant-Garde Since 1945* (London, 1981), 188–222.

New York Philharmonic Horizons '84, a commemorative magazine for the series of concerts May–June 8, 1984, including the following articles on: *The New Romanticism—A Broader View:* Zubin Mehta, "A Message from the Music Director"; Jacob Druckman, "A Message from the Artistic Director"; Linda Sanders, "Romanticism: Coming to Terms"; Linda Sanders, "An Interview with William Schuman"; Milton Babbitt, "The More Than the Sounds of Music"; Gregory Sandow, "Alternative Classical Music"; Paul Griffiths, "New Romanticism/Romanticized Newness' A European View."

CHAPTER 31

USES OF THE PAST: THE GENERIC REVIVALS

In the 1970s Berio wrote a series of works with generic titles such as *Opera* (1969–70), *Recital I (for Cathy)* (1972), and *Coro* (1975–76). But just as the five sections of his *Sinfonia* were "not to be taken as movements analogous to those of the classical symphony" but understood only as a "sounding together", so these other works reconsider the genre as a potential transmitter with a new message. In *Recital*, through a barrage of quotations from Monteverdi to Berio with Purcell (Dido's "Lament"), Poulenc ("Hôtel"), and many others stitched in along the way, the composer portrays the gradual mental disintegration of the singer, while in *Questo vuol dire che* he reviews and interprets the natural performing styles of various folk musics. The idea of received repertoires also appears in Stockhausen's *Hymnen*, with sections dedicated to Berio and Cage. Here material is offered for the assemblage of a composition rather than a final choice of material in a fixed order. The two-hour version which Stockhausen has prepared for a recording recalls the shortwave interference and variable clarity of snippets of Beethoven in *Opus 1970*, here replaced by fragments from national anthems around the world in a work which the composer intended as an expression of universal brotherhood.

Collectively, Berio's use of generic titles hinted that they were not to be taken as examples of a type but rather as a critique. If the momentary unfashionableness of such genres, in the wake of the ad hoc ensemble in the period immediately following the end of World War II, was insufficiently protracted to allow a later sense of genuine revival, numerous composers from the mid-1960s to the present have, nonetheless, vigorously pursued not only the titles but their various formal implications with a thought to review and extension.

STRING QUARTET

The premieres of Schoenberg's fourth and last *String Quartet* (1936) and Bartók's final *String Quartets No. 5* (1934) and *No. 6* (1939) were followed by a healthy number of other works devoted to the premises of Neoclassicism and Serialism alike through the period around 1950. Beginning with the latter date, however, the death of the former aesthetic and the extension of the latter in an intense search for new laws of total serialism demanded that the procrustean forms of a previous age be at least momentarily set aside. The opinion was also loudly voiced in some quarters at this time that Schoenberg had been in error in tying his serial discoveries to the received classical forms, and that indeed new constructive principles would largely obviate the need for them. Such an attitude was clearly reminiscent of views held during the first decade of the century when reductive creative approaches (Skriabin's "mystic" chord; Webern's aphorisms; Debussy's and Schoenberg's motivic but nonrecapitulatory designs) signaled, along with the increasing abandonment of tonality as a formal propellant, the possibility of rejecting the inherited classical forms altogether.[1]

Although the appeal of the string quartet, symphony, and concerto may have faded in the 1950s in the wake of a pronounced optimism for the generative qualities of total serialism and aleatoric procedures, beginning in the 1960s and continuing to the present day the opinion has resurfaced that there were things that could best be said through an economical chamber group whose traditions encompassed an uninterrupted span of over 200 years and whose resilience to variable new modes of expression seemed almost limitless.

Not surprisingly, one premise or another, already considered in this book, tended to dominate any reconsideration of this venerable ensemble. In addition to the reinterpretation of sonatas, rondos, variations, marches, passacaglias, chaconnes, serenades, and waltzes, other questions reflecting more recent developments were also addressed. In the world of the string quartet, for example, Penderecki's *String Quartet No. 2* (1966) was primarily concerned with questions of sonic material (quarter-tones; bowing on the string holder; drumming on the strings or body of the instrument with the hand, fingernails, or the frog of the bow; glissandi; variously controlled vibrati, etc.) that could have been properly discussed alongside his *Threnody* for fifty-two strings. From a different angle, Crumb's *Black Angels* (1971) addressed the sonic potential of an "electric string quartet" put in the service of a three-part, thirteen-section palindromic form heavily weighted with numerology and a program. Rochberg's *String Quartets Nos. 3–7* (1972–80) have already been reviewed from the standpoint of larger stylistic currents (pp. 647–48), and Carter's *String Quartet No. 3* (1971) has also been drawn on earlier to discuss his approach to the simultaneous use of opposing instrumental groups and linear metric progress (pp. 538).

But beneath the trendy surfaces and novel approaches to the medium with respect to sonority, technique, and form, there was ample evidence of a healthy interest in and powerful readdress of more traditional values in the period 1970–80 with such works as Bassett's memorable *String Quartet No. 4* (1979); a group of eight (Nos. 5–12) by the Finnish composer Leif Segerstam (b. 1944), whose *String Quartet No. 6* (1974) ends with an enormous adagio "in spirto di Gustav Mahler"; and the final three *String Quartets Nos. 13–15* (1970, 1973, 1974) of Dmitri Shostakovich, parallelling his final three contributions to the symphony, Nos. 13–15 (1962, 1967, 1971). Even Britten, who had spent a career tuning his music to the subtleties of poetry and drama, in 1974 unearthed a pre-opus 1 *String Quartet* of 1931 and provided it with a new companion which was first performed posthumously. And Feldman's five-hour minimalist extravaganza for string quartet (1983) confirmed that not only those given to neoromanticism, indeterminacy, and serialism had an interest in undertaking a reconsideration of the formal component.

The lengthy, though partial, list of string quartets written since 1960 that appears at the end of this chapter provides dramatic testimony to the interest composers have shown in revitalizing the medium. It must be added that such a state of affairs has in no small part been encouraged by the numerous quartets devoted to the performance of this literature, among which the Concord, Fine Arts, Julliard, and La Salle have been especially important in the United States. More recently San Francisco's Kronos String Quartet has forced a reconsideration of the string quartet through the literature which it has appropriated. Alongside works of Anton Webern and Conlon Nancarrow, they have programmed music written for jazz piano trio, rock guitar quartet, mandolin, and percussion ensemble as well as rhythm and blues and have transformed it into music for string quartet. Heralded as the "next wave" in some circles, their blend of classical and popular repertoires has suggested a virtual redefinition of the idea of the string quartet.

SYMPHONY AND CONCERTO

Recent creations openly carrying the title of symphony have also appeared in surprising quantity and by some of the more familiar names. Peter Maxwell Davies' *Symphony No. 1* (1970) and *Symphony No. 2* (1980), on a commission for the Boston Symphony Orchestra's Centenary, was followed by a third symphony in 1984, for the BBC Orchestra on its fiftieth anniversary, with a fourth promised for 1989. Other notable contributions included Carter's *A Symphony of Three Orchestras* (1976), a U.S.A. bicentennial commission from the New York Philharmonic; Lutoslawski's *Symphony No. 3* (1983), premiered by the Chicago Symphony Orchestra; and two by Penderecki (1973, 1980). In each instance the expressive gestures and formalistic concerns (including cantus-firmus, aleatoric, or multiple ensemble relationship) familiar from a given composer's other works invariably surfaced in their symphonies. Collectively they confirmed that the resurrection of the idea of the symphony was not intended solely as an exhumation of sonata form, variation, and rondo, even as traces of all three were periodically in evidence.

The layout of Davies three symphonies all shared a traditional four-movement design, with the following tempo designations: No. 1 (Presto; Lento; Adagio; Presto); No. 2 (Allegro molto; Adagio; Allegro molto; Adagio-allegro); No. 3 (Lento-allegro al breve; Scherzo I-Allegro; Scherzo II-Allegro vivace; Lento). The first two symphonies shared a similar orchestra, with audible emphasis on tuned percussion actively engaged in building up a series of Orkney Island seascapes.

That new formal principles could be tested under the symphonic banner was made clear in the title of Carter's symphony even as the consequences of its spatial plan and layered form were found in the works of other composers without claim to a symphonic pedigree. Thus, Lutosławski's *Chain I* (1983) for chamber orchestra utilizes a structure previously found in the passacaglia of his *Concerto for Orchestra* (1954), which Lutosławski identified as follows:

> In a work composed in chain-form the music is divided into two strands. Particular sections do not begin at the same moment in each strand, nor do they end together. In other words, in the middle of a section in one strand a new section begins in the other.[2]

But in addition to the retrieval of generic titles or the formalization of new internal organizing procedures was the implication of a renewed interest on the part of many of the major symphony orchestras of the world in showcasing a vital contemporary musical culture. Commissions, in a word, once again gave the composer the courage, which he was unlikely to have without the promise of performance, to write for the large orchestral ensemble. Examples of such commissions among younger composers are the second of David Gompper's two powerful and articulate chamber symphonies (No. 1, 1979; No. 2, 1987) and Nicholas Thorne's luminously attractive *Symphony No. 2* ("Symphony of Light," 1984) which gave evidence that symphonic rhetoric was compatible with the arena of reduced means as well as an extended Bergian resource, respectively.

Outside the West, the *Symphony No. 2* ("St. Florian") of 1980 by Alfred Shnitke (b. 1934), one of the Soviet Union's more progressive composers, put aside the pseudo-Baroque and Beethoven quotations of his *Symphony No. 1* (1969–72) and combined the idea of the Mass with the symphony in what some listeners took to be an "unquestionably subversive message" concerning the "sureness in the power of prayer".[3] Whatever the political overtones, the full flowering of multiple means and messages, available through the use of electronic resources with traditional instruments and the mixing of sacred and secular materials, now appears to be at least a temporary reality in the Soviet Union.

The tendency of the concerto of the 1960s to exploit instrumental techniques developed by the new breed of virtuoso performers mirrors the state of affairs discussed under "The New Virtuosity" (p. 605), of which Henze's *Double Concerto* (1966) for Heinz and Ursala Holliger (oboe and harp) and *Concerto per Contrabasso* of the same year for Gary Karr may be held as representative. Here glissandi, extended ranges, multiphonics, double stops, and harmonics join the traditional patterning and lyric capacity of the oboe and contrabass to help shape designs of a generally familiar cast.

More recently, the idea of the concerto has continued to flourish in such works as Leslie Bassett's virtuoso *Concerto Grosso* for winds (1982), William Bolcom's polystylistic *Concerto for Piano and Orchestra* (1975–6), Steven Rouse's crackling *Crosswinds* (1984) for organ and twelve players, and Peter Lieberson's several additions to the form—e.g., the *Concerto for Four Groups of Instruments* (c. 1973), *Cello Concerto* (c. 1974), and more recently the *Piano Concerto* (1983), commissioned by the Boston Symphony Orchestra.

Shchedrin, the most prominent official composer of the U.S.S.R., has also written several concerti of considerable impact on Western audiences. Following his *Piano Concerto No. 2* of 1966, an attractive updated version of Prokofiev with an unexpected but virile use of jazz in its finale, Shchedrin increasingly explored the serial and aleatoric world in his *Concerto Grosso No. 2*, written for the 125th anniversary of the New York Philharmonic. In his *Third Piano Concerto* (1976), a surprising use of clusters and a range of timbral designs propelled a work that could well have been mistaken for the best of the so-called Polish School of its decade. The view of the sheltered Soviet composer, innocent of recent developments outside his own country, is not only in need of emendation but must be placed against the advent of an increasing conservatism in the West. Rochberg's *Violin Concerto* (1975) of the preceding year, for example, comes closer to the concertos for that instrument written by Walton and Prokofiev, with a hint of Bartók perhaps, than to those by Schoenberg and Berg. Bartókian energies are also observable to a degree in Harbison's *Piano Concerto* of 1978. Contrarily, Henze's *Violin Concerto No. 2* of 1971 escapes the conventional concerto format by coupling to a concertante violin part a tape and voices proclaiming Enzenberger's "Hommage à Gödel" in a work that is, according to the composer, "very nearly a stage piece, but not quite."[4]

ORCHESTRAL AND ENSEMBLE SONG

Just as Penderecki has promoted the idea of a traditional association between orchestra, chorus, and soloists in his recent *Polish Requiem* (1980–84), so the idea of the orchestral and ensemble song has continued to flourish in numerous guises, including the popular series that includes *Finale Alice* (1976) by David Del Tredici (b. 1937), whose abundant stylistic references and opulent recapture of Strauss and Wagner contributed to the sense of neoromantic revival. Its extreme stylistic posture predictably caused concern in numerous composers' quarters and led many to wonder if the question of "originality" should not once again be exhumed. Unexpected signs of a realignment were already apparent in the distended vocal angularity and absence of bitter-sweet harmonies of Rochberg's *String Quartet No. 7* (1980) with baritone solo, but whether or not this was to constitute a new trend was impossible to divine. Carter's *A Mirror on which to Dwell* (1975), an abstract meditation on texts of Elizabeth Bishop, and *Syringa* (1978), which juxtaposed ancient Greek texts with contemporary verses of John Ashbery, both argued, however, for an affirmative answer.

Of a different breed from either of these two extremes and reinforcing the earlier example of Henze and Crumb, to the degree that they adopted an expressive but virtuoso vocal part balanced by a carefully nuanced instrumental component, were two vocal cycles by Joseph Schwantner (b. 1943): *Sparrows* (1979) for soprano and chamber ensemble, and *Magabunda* (1982) for soprano and orchestra. The affective setting of alternating texts in Spanish and English in the latter cycle is supported by a masterful instrumental sense already known from the composer's *And the Mountains Rising Nowhere* for winds of 1977 and the orchestral *Aftertones of Infinity*, for which he won a Pulitzer Prize in 1979. Further evidence that the orchestral song was alive and well was provided by Bernard Rands' *Canti lunatici* and *Canti del sole*, of which the latter captured the Pulitzer Prize for 1984; and by the English composer Robin Holloway, whose *Sea Surface Full of Clouds* (1974–5) for S, A, Ct, T, chorus, and chamber orchestra calls for a soprano capable of singing *Herzgewächse* in a work of extraordinary vocal luminosity and instrumental power in its interludes.

Among works written for voice and chamber ensemble, few have carried the elemental magic of *Six Turkish Folkpoems* (1977) by the Dutch composer Theo Loevendie (b. 1930). Scored for soprano, flute, clarinet, violin, cello, harp, percussion, and piano, the texts are left untranslated from their original Turkish, whose sonorities contribute notably to the cycle. The odd-numbered songs search out the melancholy note, while the even ones are energized by primitive rhythms projected by piano and percussion. Variable instrumental combinations provide interludes between the pieces, the brevity of whose texts are akin to the Haiku. The total effect combines the senuousness of Ravel's *Chansons madécasses* (1927) and the propelling rhythms of the first of Cage's *Three Pieces*

(1945) for two prepared pianos. The composer has stated it differently, suggesting that his work "deploys 'foreign' techniques like polyrhythm (Africa) and isorhythm (Guillaume de Machaut) but in such a way that they are not recognisable as 'alien' because they are a component of my musical language."[5]

OPERA

In the period of the 1960s and 1970s—a time that saw the ascendency of the theater piece and when seemingly every work, texted or untexted, had a theatrical potential—it was not infrequently argued that the idea of traditional opera was irrelevant. In light of the expense involved with the production of opera and the general conservatism of most opera houses, Elliott Carter's declaration that "The whole idea of opera in America is insane"[6] was understandable. Yet it is noteworthy that Penderecki's substantial *Paradise Lost* was premiered by the Chicago Lyric Opera in 1978, and that Philip Glass's four-hour *Einstein on the Beach*, following its premiere at the Opéra Comique in Paris (1976), was performed shortly thereafter at the Metropolitan Opera House in New York under private sponsorship. The need of a visual component to counteract the threatening monotony of maximal doses of Minimalism can be tested by an enforced listening of the complete *Einstein on the Beach* on a phonograph recording. Yet many who have experienced live or video performances of Glass's *Satyagraha* have professed easy capitulation to the combined experience of a multidimensional music-theater. By the time of *Akhnaten* (1984)—the third of the trilogy concerning a scientist (Einstein), a politician (Gandhi), and a king (Akhnaten) as a reformer—some were reminded of the recycling spectacle of Orff, whose career was devoted to the cause of joining music to a dramatic action. What the future may hold for Glass's technique and point of view, only time will tell. Its cult status among teenage idolizers of pop culture had already been secured by the early 1980s.

No fair discussion of opera in America would imply, however, that Glass's solution is representative or typical. Indeed, America's most successful opera composer, Gian Carlo Menotti (b. 1911), did not stop writing in the genre following his first enormous successes (*Amelia Goes to the Ball*, 1936; *The Old Maid and the Thief*, 1939–41; *The Medium*, 1945; *The Telephone*, 1946; *The Consul*, 1949; *Amahl and the Night Visitors*, 1951; *The Saints of Bleecker Street*, 1954), but has continued its propagation to the present day (*Help, Help, the Globolinks!*, 1968; *Tamu-Tamu*, 1973; *The Boy Who Grew Too Fast*, 1982). The argument that Menotti's art belongs more to Broadway than to the Metropolitan says nothing except where he found his audience. *La Locca*, written for Beverly Sills, and *Goya* (1986), an opera on the life of the Spanish painter written especially for the tenor Placido Domingo, suggest, however, the degree to which these values currently appeal to opera stars of international rank.

Bernstein, too, whose sensibilities to music-theater were not far distant from Menotti, has also recently returned to bona-fide opera in composing *A Quiet Place* (a sequel to *Trouble in Tahiti*), which was unveiled initially in Houston in 1983 and in an integrated version of the two at La Scala in 1984. That American opera houses other than the New York City Opera—the sponsor of operas by Lee Hoiby and a few other Americans over the years—might be catching up either to their responsibilities or a public call for something besides

Mozart, Verdi, and Puccini, has been hinted at by the enterprising rosters of the Santa Fe Opera, which produced Rochberg's *The Confidence Man* in 1982, and the Chicago Lyric, which has announced an artist-in-residence program. William Neill, the first recipient of Chicago's new venture, also returned to traditional narrative music theater in *The Guilt of Lillian Sloan* (1986), an account of the Bywater-Thompson murder trial of 1923.

In Europe, it will be recalled that Henze also produced a series of genuine operas throughout the 1960s and 1970s, including *Elegy for Young Lovers* (1959–61), *The Young Lord* (1964), *The Bassarids* (1965), and *We Come to the River* (1974–76), while Britten also penned his last contributions to the genre in his *A Midsummer Night's Dream* (1960), *Owen Wingrave* (1970), and *Death in Venice* (1973). At the same time, a younger compatriot, Peter Maxwell Davies, gave us *Taverner* (1962–68, premiered 1972) and *The Martyrdom of St. Magnus* (1977), with the promise of another full-scale effort under the title of *Resurrection.*

None of this sounds very much like opera had been interred, no matter how irrelevant it may have been deemed by Pousseur, Berio, and Kagel. All three wrote works about the same time (1969–71) that appeared to critique opera as an exhausted form ripe for parody. Pousseur's pastiche, *Votre Faust* (1969), mirrors the capitulation of its author, a selling of his soul to the Devil in the very act of writing an opera that encompasses the whole of its traditions through allusion and quotation subject to audience control of certain variables. Berio's *Opera* (1971), on the other hand, spelled the three-pronged decline of opera, Western society, and the sinking of the *Titanic.* Beginning each of its acts with a song to a text from Striggio's libretto for *Orfeo,* which Monteverdi had used in his first opera at the dawn of the form, Berio brings the story full circle to its extinction. Kagel was even more irreverent in his *Staatstheater,* also of 1971, where all the trappings of a modern opera house (premiered by the Hamburg State Opera) are paraded forth only with the object of parody and mockery in mind.

That this trinitarian consensus, supported by Ligeti's *Le grand macabre* (1974–77), proved to be ill-founded with respect to the future of the genre had already been made dramatically evident by the early 1980s. Olivier Messiaen's five-hour plus *St. Francis d'Assisi* scored a triumph at the Paris Opera in 1983, and Stockhausen's monumental opera sequence *Licht* ("Light: The Seven Days of the Week"), designed to be performed on seven successive nights, was launched with the presentation at La Scala of the first two, *Donnerstag* in 1981 and *Samstag* in 1984, with *Montag* scheduled for production in 1988.

Not only the gigantism of Stockhausen's plan—a project that is slated to occupy the composer to the year 2000—but the unifying effect of shared material from one opera to the next through a series of melodic formulae virtually demands the recognition of a parallel with Wagner's music-drama. Add to that the composer's role in devising his own scenario, libretto, costumes, lighting, and dance as well as music, and the idea of a later twentieth-century *Gesamtkunstwerk* is inescapable. Yet, Stockhausen has undoubtedly been attracted to writing for the opera house not because of any pent-up desire to write a traditional opera but because of, as Ligeti put it, "the facilities an opera house offers".[7] *Samstag,* for example, has a relatively low degree of narrative and continuity, and places the main musical and theatrical burden on wind instruments and elaborate theatrical trappings, while utilizing the vaulted spaces and energizing volumes of a sports palace and a church to annul a sense of time and space. In what can only be seen as an allegory—as near in conception to Cavalieri's *Rappresentatione di Anima, et di Corpo* (1600) as to Wagner's *Ring*—Stockhausen has nonetheless left the smaller theater-piece (e.g., *Harlekin* and *Musik im Bauch*, both of 1975) behind and has brought the grandeur of his largest theatrical rituals (e.g., *Inori*, 1972) into the opera house while continuing to espouse a "formula"-laden structure common to both.

While the appearance in 1984 of Davies' *The No. 11 Bus* signaled the continuing viability of the theater piece that had surfaced in the 1960s, among Englishmen Oliver Knussen (*Where the Wild Things Are*, 1979–83) and Harrison Birtwistle (*Mask of Orpheus*, premiered 1986) also gave impetus to an invigorating species of lyric theater in the 1980s that is properly dubbed opera. Knussen's popular *Where the Wild Things Are* was (note the similarity of language to Kagel and Ligeti) "conceived for the resources of an opera house—six singers, dancers, an orchestra of forty-eight players, and extensive scenic requirements."[8] Labeled a fantasy opera by the composer, it was openly promoted as belonging to the tradition of Humperdinck's *Hänsel und Gretel*, Stravinsky's *Le Rossignol*, and Ravel's *L'enfant et les sortilèges*. While its general language and effect was decidedly closest to the last of these, the citation and development of musical material from Mussorgsky's *Boris Godunov* and Debussy's *La boîte à joujoux* approximate some of the more stylish currents of the 1970s and 1980s. Wedded to "a large mosaic of some twenty-six interdependent microforms"—including pantomimes, interludes, a rag, a waltz-mazurka, and a procession on a double ground—various stylistic and formal manners redolent of the 1920s (Hindemith, Berg, Ravel) were also recalled. In spite of the difficulties and expense of production, clearly "opera," in all of its guises, had by the 1980s once again become a mainstream partner and mirror of contemporary musical culture.

RITUALS

As early as 1922, Stravinsky had written what he called "an austere ritual" in the *Symphonies of Wind Instruments*. Dedicated to the memory of Claude Debussy, it was a type of piece that was to appear frequently in works of brief dimension in his old age as friends (T.S. Eliot, Aldous Huxley), collaborators (Dylan Thomas), and martyred politicians (John F. Kennedy) departed the scene. It seemed only just that there should have been an outpouring of similar works written in honor of Stravinsky in his old age and in his memory shortly after his death in 1971. Canons, string quartets, and other less time-honored forms and genres were invoked by Eimert, Krenek, Davies, Carter, Copland, Sessions, Denisov, Shnitke, Pousseur, and Milhaud. Even Boulez' . . . *explosant-fixe* . . . began as a memorial tribute to Stravinsky, and the soprano melody for Feldman's *Rothko Chapel* was, by the composer's admission, written on the day of Stravinsky's funeral service in New York.

But beyond the immediate circumstances that prompted or coincided with the writing of many of these pieces lay a pronouncedly increasing desire on the part of numerous composers to address spiritual matters—a desire that was more than marginally redolent of the period between the two World Wars (see Chapter 24). While the 1960s saw several elder statesmen turning from the specter of war to the Scriptures and liturgies in valedictory works, such as Poulenc's *Sept répons de ténèbres* (1961), Hindemith's *Mass* (1963), and Stravinsky's *Requiem Canticles* (1966), the younger generation of post-World War II composers typically sought out contemporary statements in poetry, painting, or architecture to serve as a backdrop to abstract instrumental works with a spiritual or contemplative cast.

BERIO AND FELDMAN. For Berio, his *Nones* (1953–54) was, as he put it, his first exorcism from the influence of Darmstadt. Initially planned as a vast secular oratorio for soloists, chorus, and orchestra based on a text of W. H. Auden, the length and complexity of the poem dissuaded him, and he ultimately conserved from his unfinished project five orchestral episodes. A reading of Auden's verses (unrecited in the work) is as essential to its comprehension as an awareness of the M–m third clusters of his thirteen-tone series (B,D,B♭/G,E,E♭/ /A♭/ /D♭, C,A/F♯,D,F) or the proportions based on nine that predominate throughout. These properties are organized so as to produce a set of extremes: texture (condensations and rarefications), harmony (from the octave to noise), and movement (speed and stasis).[9] Auden's transfiguration of "the passion of Christ into a lucid and burning inquiry about the agony of man chained to the enigma of a sudden, final moment"[10] is matched by what Berio termed "fatalistic" serial procedures. It suggests, with Messiaen, the momentary usefulness of such highly rational, though personally defined, ritualistic controls in dealing with the ultimate, unresolvable questions, here left unspoken and suggested only by a title:

What we know to be not possible
Though time after time foretold
. . . comes to pass
Before we realize it: we are surprised
At the ease and speed of our deed
And uneasy: it is barely three,
Mid afternoon, yet the blood
Of our sacrifice is already
Dry on the grass; we are not prepared
For silence so sudden and so soon . . . .

W.H. Auden (from "Nones", *Horae Canonica*, ed. Edward Mendelson in *W.H. Auden: Collected Poems.* Copyright Random House, New York, 1976).

In Feldman's serene and contemplative ritual, *Rothko Chapel* (1971), a sense of the surroundings that led to its commission is fundamental to the listening experience. Intended as an environmental soundscape for the fourteen huge canvases of the Rothko Chapel in Houston, Texas, the work's blend of declamation, lyricism, and delicate color (soprano, chorus, viola, tympani, chimes, and vibraphones) releases a quiet grandeur that gives rise to a new connotation to the word Minimalism (see p. 572). The attendant simplicity, solemnity, and stasis were not newly found, however, but had been refined over a career.

RITUAL THEATER: STOCKHAUSEN, BRITTEN, AND PARTCH.   The power of ritual and nonsectarian musical prayer has perhaps nowhere been more uncompromisingly and effectively projected than in Stockhausen's *Inori* (Japanese for "prayers" or "adorations") of 1973–74 for orchestra and one or two solists (melody instrument or mimed-dancers) wherein acts of worship from various cultures are composed as part of the music. In the composer's form-scheme (Fig. 31.1), the primacy of the melodic *formel* is apparent, and its expanding pitch wedge outward in both directions from G to D is not only notationally visible but audible in performance. However, it was the harmonic aura of the work, whose richness recalled Messiaen, that frequently left the most lasting impression for many. A massive work of seventy minutes duration, its large scale encourages deep breathing and a slowed pulse, and admirably serves John Cage's dictum that the function of music is to quieten the soul and render it susceptible to divine influence. Here, as with Berio's *Nones* and Feldman's *Rothko Chapel*, unspoken verse, image, and gesture have replaced the scriptures but inspired a work with a deeply spiritual base.

Another aspect of Stockhausen's devotion to the melodic formula can be seen in the *Zodiac (Tierkreis)* melodies (1975–76) which have been manufactured as a set of 12 music boxes. Their capacity for reincarnation in various guises can be studied in works like *Musik im Bauch* (1975) and *Sirius* (1975–77) devoted to the ritualistic portrayal of mankind and the seasons. The melodies are stretched and compressed, slowed down, speeded up, intervallically expanded and contracted, and subjected to rhythmic transformations from one

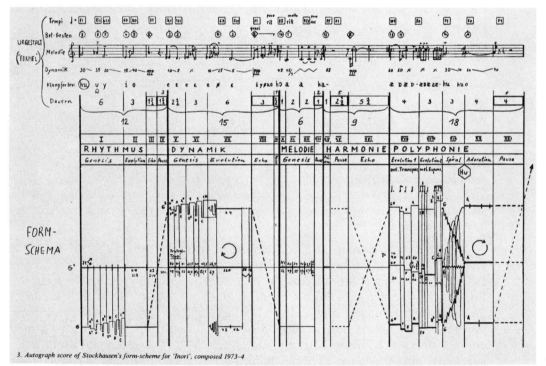

3. *Autograph score of Stockhausen's form-scheme for 'Inori', composed 1973–4*

Figure 31.1. Stockhausen. Autograph of Stockhausen's form-scheme for *Inori*:
Courtesy of the composer.

to another in an ongoing process. Fascination with the seasons and the signs of the Zodiac can be spotted from Rimsky-Korsakov (see p. 198) to George Crumb (*Makrokosmos*, Book I). But Stockhausen's idea of process, which the composer holds to be fundamental to all of his music, should not be confused with that of the Minimalists and requires that the listener remember these melodies from work to work so that he can trace their metamorphosis. Their memorability, due to their highly organic nature, can readily be tested in the "Capricorn" melody (Ex. 30.1). While the character of many of these melodies is traceable to his *Formel* of 1951, Stockhausen has denied any indebtedness to the plainsong elaborations of Messiaen (Ex. 31.1), and has protested that his individual melodic gifts were already observable in his *Drei Lieder, Sonatine,* and *Choral* which antedated his journey to Paris.

Example 31.1. Stockhausen, *Tierkreis* [Zodiac]: "Capricorn" (1975).

Used by permission of the composer.

The several acts of Stockhausen's *Samstag aus Licht* (1983) may also be seen, and even performed, as individual rituals. Carrying the subtitles "Lucifer's Dream," "Lucifer's Requiem," "Lucifer's Dance," and "Lucifer's Farewell," each is a self-contained piece working its own magic through a series of incantations on a melodic formula. The last of these, for a chorus of monks, seven trombones, organ, and church bells, reinforces our knowledge of Stockhausen's instinct for prayer demonstrated in *Inori* (1972). In his choice of "Lodi delle virtù" of St. Francis of Assisi as his text as well as in the musical stasis that seems to suspend time, he has also followed his early mentor, Messiaen, though with a personalized stamp that could not be mistaken for another.

In *Licht's* investigation of birth, life, and death as a natural destiny and its call on instrumentalists, mimers, and dancers as carriers of an elaborate action, Stockhausen approximated qualities not only of the earlier *sacre rappresentatione* but also of the Japanese Noh drama. The compatibility of Noh drama with a telling of a Christian parable had already been discovered by Britten as early as *Curlew River* (1964) and later in his *The Burning Fiery Furnace* (1966) and *The Prodigal Son* (1968). Here the use of masks, costume, and stylized gesture confirm once again the complementary natures of East and West.

In light of the longstanding fascination with the Orient on the part of numerous West Coast composers in America, a similar adoption of ingredients by Harry Partch in his *The Delusion of the Fury* (1969) should have come as no surprise. In a lifetime devoted to an investigation of musical tuning systems and the invention of his own instruments, Partch brought the total force of his vision to bear in this work. In a sonic universe that periodically recalls the timbres and rhythms of Cowell, Cage (*Three Dances*), Harrison, Orff, and Varèse, Partch confects a distinctive admixture whose most immediately identifiable features are the variety of percussion (including kitharas, marimbas, gourd tree, and cone gong) and the nontempered tunings that are especially notable among a group of resonating (cloud-chamber bowls) and sustaining (chromelodeons) instruments. A vast ceremonial theater piece that uses ingredients of Noh drama in its Part I ("On a Japanese Theme"), an instrumental "Sanctus" as an "Entr'acte," and choral-voice sounds from the instrumentalists in Part II ("On an African Theme"), *The Delusion of the Fury* integrates mime, dance, and music in the telling of a tragedy and a comedy without libretto. Vocal, instrumental, and corporeal elements combine in a "full, ritualistic expression . . . of the reconciliation by the living both with death and with life."[11] It is a point of view Partch had explored in his earlier dance-satire *The Bewitched* (1952–55), a work the composer identified as "in the tradition of world-wide ritual theatre" and in which "the complementary character, the strange affinity, of seeming opposites" in both the human and musical spheres are explored.

BOULEZ AND MESSIAEN.   With the announcement of Boulez's plans for a new opera on a libretto by Genet to open the new quarters of the Paris Opera designed by the architect Carlos Ott, the list of converts to a lyric musical theater amongst yesterday's "bad boys of music" would now appear to be virtually complete. While it was perhaps unpredictable that the composers of *Kreuzspiel* (1951) or *Structures*, Book I (1952) would ever write operas for international establishment houses, Boulez, like Stockhausen, had already by the mid-1970s produced scores with a more composed exterior and compelling argument. With Boulez this was due in large measure to an increased attention to what he calls the "pitch envelope,"[12] promoting control over the harmonic resource and assisting in the capture of a *grand ligne* to which the frenetic vocalizations of *Le marteau sans maître* are attached only as a coloristic ornament. Such discoveries have frequently taken place in works of a patently ritualistic content.

Boulez's *Rituel in memoriam Maderna* (1974) is a work of alternating quietude and majesty that could hardly have been predicted twenty years before. Based on a fourteen-note, seven pitch melody, it is a call from beyond the Abyss of awesome grandeur and enormous individuality and power, directly linkable both to the wind sonorities and ritual drumming of Messiaen's *Et exspecto resurrectionem mortuorum* (1964) and the quiet simmering of the Introduction to Stravinsky's *Rite of Spring*. Eight groups (one oboe, two clarinets, three flutes, four violins, wind quintet, string sextet, woodwind septet, and fourteen brass) perform alternatingly synchronized and unsynchronized verse and refrain, respectively. Continuing a formal trend that may be said to derive from Messiaen and observable in his own work at least from the time of his *Third Sonata*, Boulez builds on the principle of opposition and juxtaposition not only through synchronized and unsynchronized properties but in matters of texture (homophony, heterophony), tempo (Trés lent; Modéré), and resonance (a pronounced antimony between resonators and nonresonators). In these latter qualities, too, his stylistic roots are clearly visible in the music of Debussy and Messiaen.

The material of the first verse, which is the material of the piece through extension and transformation, reveals a persistent thirty-second-note upbeat and an accompanimental drumming reminiscent of Stravinsky's *Introitus T.S. Eliot* (1965). The expressive interval succession (M3, Tr, P4, m9, M7, Tr, M6), of which only a symmetrically positioned tritone is repeated (Ex. 31.2), invites comparison with the recent tritone-rich melodies of Stockhausen (Ex. 31.1) and those of Messiaen (Ex. 31.3) as early as the plainsong elaboration of "Serene Allelulias" (*L'Ascension*, 1933).

Example 31.2. Boulez, *Rituel in memoriam Maderna* (1974), monophonic opening (8 mm.).

Example 31.3. Messiaen, *L'Ascension:* "Alleluias sereins d'une âme qui désire le ciel" (1933).

Boulez' upbeat becomes increasingly ornamental and extended in the even number sections—mirroring Messiaen's ornithological fantasies more than his plainsong alleluias—while in the odd-numbered sections this development is extended to a collection of suffixes to each of the intervals. Working through and across this elaborate plan, the sonority of ritual drumming is gradually modified by a systematic accretion of a variety of percussion instruments through each of the first fourteen sections that exit palindromically in the fifteenth, the final and largest of all. The primacy of melody and its all encompassing role in an extended work complements Stockhausen's recent preoccupation not only in his operas but in the pieces based on the melodies of his magical "Zodiac" music boxes. Both may fairly stand as current representatives of a new brand of serialism that would hardly be recognized as such were it not for the insistence of the protagonists.

If Messiaen's five-hour opera *St. Francis of Assisi* seemed to vie with Stockhausen both in dimension and in its insistent probe of spiritual questions, his *Livre du saint sacrement (Book of the Blessed Sacrement)* of 1986 recalled the alliance of Christian mysticism with the organ that initially brought Messiaen before the public in the 1930s. A vast cycle of eighteen pieces of slightly less than two hours duration, the work recalls the themes of Ascension, Nativity, Eucharist, Tenebrae, and Resurrection, climaxing in an "Offrande et Alléluia final." More a source book than an integral ritual intended for complete performance, it reinforced once again the composer's lifelong claims to being a true believer. As with other composers of the 1970s and 1980s who seemed preoccupied with exploring musical canvases of larger dimensions, Messiaen's cycle seemed to protest that there is much to believe, and that the composer need not fear repeating himself in such matters.

BIRTWISTLE AND TAVENER.   Harrison Birtwistle (b. 1934), one of the most important English composers of his generation, has frequently been preoccupied with the mesmerizing on-rush of time and its repetitive qualities. *Chronometer* (1971) for eight-track tape, for example, exploits a montage of clocks and bells whose ticks and chimes speak less of a Futurist fantasy than the inexorable procession of the pendulum. Putting aside his earlier interest in refrain forms, his more mature output frequently has partaken of an incontestable element of ritual. His *The Fields of Sorrow* (1971) for two sopranos, chorus, and ensemble was preparatory to his more developed work, *The Triumph of Time* of 1972 for orchestra alone, and the abiding stasis of both develops a mood that can only be heard as a processional. The latter work reinforces the message of Brueghel's painting of the same name that though man perishes, life returns and repeats. It is a quality that is to be mirrored in another theme dear to Birtwistle, the Orpheus legend. His attraction to the ritualistic reenactment of this story, and especially of Orpheus's turning again and again as in the moment when he last saw Eurydice, has appeared in several works over a period of years: *Nenia on the Death of Orpheus* (1971), S, b cl + cl, two b cl, pf + damped pf, crotales; and two operas, *Orpheus* (1974–77) and *The Mask of Orpheus* (premiered 1986). In these works, Birtwistle has developed a serious and highly recognizable profile that commands increasing respect and anticipation of each new work.

Evidence of the direct legacy of Stravinsky's brand of ritualism, especially as preached in the late sacred works of the 1960s, can be heard in the works of another Englishman, John Tavener (b. 1944). Pieces in honor of Stravinsky's eighty-fifth birthday (*Birthday Bells*, pf, 1967) and to commemorate his passing (*In memoriam Igor Stravinsky*, two a fl, org, bells, 1971) betray his admiration and prepare the listener for an orientation that, however, proves in the final analysis to be more expansive than Stravinsky. Less ascetic, occasionally more ecstatic, and for all its reliance on plainsong-like monophony, harmonically frequently more opulent as well, Tavener has shown his preference for the ritualistic in numerous works: *Introit for the Feast of St. John Damascene,* 1967–68; *Celtic Requiem,* 1969; *Ultimos ritos* (St. John of the Cross, Crucifixus from Nicene creed, 1969–72); and especially in his *Requiem for Father Malachy* (1972). The latter work, based on a seven-note cell (A'-B♭'-C"-D"-C♯"-G'-E'), is scored for six male singers and chamber ensemble (tpt, trbn, chamber org, perc, pf, str), and relies heavily on monophonic singing in octaves and the stark power of the percussion (piano with tam-tam; tympani) to propel its message. If the "Introit" and concluding "In Paradisum" capture a stasis appropriate to their respective texts, the "Dies irae" eschews virtually all models from Berlioz to Britten and Stravinsky by invoking a rhythmic energy more akin to the composer's own setting of Spanish *cantigas* in his *Canciones Españolas* of 1971. The continuing appeal of such lengthy texts as the entire Office of the Dead is indicative not only of the interest in larger statements by many of today's composers but of their natural turn to the age-old liturgies in search for an expression of their concern for modern man's predicament.

PENDERECKI.   In a similar fashion, the blend of more resonant harmonies with a heightened interest in melody is also manifest in Penderecki's *Polish Requiem* of 1980–84. Here the conservative, if luxurious, choral writing in the "Agnus Dei" is combined with the fiery vocalisms of the principal soloists in several of the other movements. While in the main the work reinforces the stylistic tendencies of its composer audible from the time of his *St. Luke's Passion* (1965) and *Utrenia* (1970), his overt allusions to Verdi's *Manzoni Requiem* force a reconsideration of its message. Just as Verdi's work became a rallying point in the 1870s for the Italian nationalist movement, so Penderecki's references to Verdi in the opening "Requiem in aeternam," the "Dies irae," and the "Libera me" suggest a political as well as a musical *double entendre,* which is underscored in the "Recordare" through the quotation of a popular Polish nineteenth-century hymn together with its Polish text. The several movements having been written variously for the 1982 funeral of Stefan Cardinal Wyszynski ("Agnus Dei"), the victims of the Katyn Forest massacre of 1940 ("Libera me"), or commissioned by Lech Walesa to mark the tenth anniversary of the 1970 Gdansk uprising ("Lacrimosa"), the message is clear and readily earns for the work its title of "Polish Requiem." The current appeal of liturgies of extended scope is thus confirmed and extended with respect to its potential function.

DAVIES, ROUSE, SCHAFER, BASSETT, WERNICK AND HYKES.   Further instances of the contemporary recognition of the force of the liturgies as well as their potential organizing powers can be seen in Peter Maxwell Davies' *From Stone to Thorn* (1971) and Christopher Rouse's *Rotae Passionis* (1982), both of which have used the fourteen Stations of the Cross as a basic formal structure: the former in a setting of fourteen two-line poems by the Orkney Island poet, George Mackay Brown, for mezzo, harpsichord, guitar and percussion; the latter in a series of twenty-second flashes located as the central panel of a three-part instrumental work without text.

Reflective of man's journeys into space and his first landing on the moon on July 20, 1969 are Leslie Bassett's *Moon Canticle* (1969) and *Celebration: In praise of Earth* (1970), works that are representative of the composer's alluring successes in writing for choral ensembles. His impressive capacity to register music's power for prayer is perhaps nowhere better exemplified than in his frequently performed *Collect* (1969) for chorus and tape.

Though purportedly a sequel to his *Haiku of Bashō*, Richard Wernick's *Moonsongs from the Japanese* (1969) for voice and tape were also inspired as much by the news of the astronauts' journey as the composer's interest in Oriental literature. R. Murray Schafer's *Epitaph for Moonlight* (1968) similarly signals a recognition of man's new realignment with the planet nearest his own earth. Sharing something of Cage's, Dallapicolla's and Stockhausen's celestial orientation (see discussion on pp. 490, 571), together with Feldman's stasis and the calmer dimension of Lutosławski's choral virtuosity that places a premium on sonority and its gradual transformation, it is accompanied by a delicate ensemble of bells that glistens with cosmological energy. Clearly the mystery of the moon has remained in spite of earthly visitations. Music's capacity to suggest man's wonderment of such eternal things is here made especially poignant by delivering its message without resort to a text.

Related but distant cousins are the ritualistic pronouncements of David Hykes' Harmonic Choir, which seem less the result of composition than improvisation. Elements of the New Vocalism and Minimalism are typically cojoined to a textless search for harmonic resonances in a live acoustical space such as St. John the Divine in New York City. The interaction of volumes and gradually shifting simple intervals in extended registers create the mystery of a choir of Tibetan monks whose chantings proclaim the end of time in a blended but subtly shifting ectasy.

In many of these works the reflection on the human condition frequently betrays a characteristic lack of need to preach according to a particular creed. The recognition that music can be a powerful ally in establishing the proper conditions for prayer and the thoughtful consideration of contemporary man's dilemma, which is now no less than survival, has once again surfaced.

REPERTOIRE (The Generic Revivals)

String Quartet (since 1960)

Bassett, *String Quartet No. 2* (1962)
Bassett, *String Quartet No. 4* (1980)
Babbitt, *String Quartet No. 3* (1969)
Babbitt, *String Quartet No. 4* (1970)
Berry, *String Quartet No. 2* (1964)
Berry, *String Quartet No. 3* (1966)
Blacher, *String Quartet No. 5* (1967)
Brown, *String Quartet* (1965)
Britten, *String Quartet No. 3* (1975)
Bussotti, *Quartetto Gramsci* (1971)
Carter, *String Quartet No. 3* (1971)
Cooper, *String Quartet No. 2* (1963)
Crumb, *Black Angels* (1970), elec str qt
Davies, *String Quartet* (1961)

Feldman, *String Quartet No. 2* (1983)
Ferneyhough, *Sonatas* for str qt (1968)
Ferneyhough, *String Quartet No. 2* (1980)
Gerhard, *String Quartet No. 2* (1961)
Goehr, *String Quartet No. 2* (1967)
Goehr, *String Quartet No. 3* (1976)
Hába, *String Quartet No. 12* (1960)
Hába, *String Quartet No. 13* (1961)
Hába, *String Quartet No. 14* (1963)
Hába, *String Quartet No. 15* (1964)
Hába, *String Quartet No. 16* (1967)
Holliger, *String Quartet* (1973)
Holmboe, *String Quartet No. 11* (1972)
Holmboe, *String Quartet No. 12* (1973)
Holmboe, *String Quartet No. 13* (1975)
Holmboe, *String Quartet No. 14* (1975)
Holmboe, *String Quartet No. 15* (1977)
Kagel, *String Quartet* (1967)
Kirchner, *Quartet No. 3* (1967), str qt, tape
Lerdahl, *String Quartet No. 2* (1980–82)
Lutosławski, *String Quartet* (1964)
Maconchy, *String Quartet No. 10* (1972)
Maconchy, *String Quartet No. 11* (1977)
Maconchy, *String Quartet No. 12* (1979)
Martin, *String Quartet* (1967)
Nono, *Fragmente-Stille, an Diotima* (1980)
Penderecki, *String Quartet No. 2* (1968)
Perle, *String Quartet No. 5* (1960)
Perle, *String Quartet No. 6* (1969)
Perle, *String Quartet No. 7* (1973)
Rochberg, *String Quartet No. 3* (1972)
Rochberg, *String Quartet No. 4* (1977)
Rochberg, *String Quartet No. 5* (1978)
Rochberg, *String Quartet No. 6* (1978)
Rochberg, *String Quartet No. 7* (1980)
C. Rouse, *String Quartet* (1982)
Rubbra, *String Quartet No. 4* (1977)
Schuller, *String Quartet No. 2* (1966)
Segerstam, *String Quartet Nos. 1–12* (1962–77)
Schafer, *String Quartet No. 2* (1976)
Shapey, *String Quartet No. 7* (1972)
Shnitke, *String Quartet* (1966)
Shostakovich, *String Quartet Nos. 7–8* (1960)
Shostakovich *String Quartet Nos. 9–10* (1964)
Shostakovich, *String Quartet No. 11* (1966)
Shostakovich *String Quartet No. 12* (1968)
Shostakovich, *String Quartet No. 13* (1970)
Shostakovich, *String Quartet No. 14* (1973)
Shostakovich, *String Quartet No. 15* (1974)
Tippett, *String Quartet No. 4* (1979)
Wellesz, *String Quartet No. 9* (1966)
Wuorinen, *String Quartet* (1971)
Xenakis, *ST/4* (1962)

Symphony

Carter, *A Symphony of Three Orchestras* (1976)
Davies, *Symphony No. 1* (1975–76)

Davies, *Symphony No. 2* (1980)
Davies, *Symphony No. 3* (1984)
Davies, *Symphony No. 4* (1989)
Gompper, *Chamber Symphony No. 1* (1979)
Gompper, *Chamber Symphony No. 2* (1987)
Henze, *Symphony No. 6* (1968), 2 chamb orch
Lutosławski, *Symphony No. 2* (1966–67)
Lutosławski, *Symphony No. 3* (1983)
Mead, *Chamber Symphony* (1986)
Penderecki, *Symphony No. 1* (1973)
Penderecki, *Symphony No. 2* (1980)
C. Rouse, *Symphony No. 2* (1987)
Shnitke, *Symphony No. 1* (1972)
Shnitke, *Symphony No. 2* ("St. Florian") (1980)
Shostakovich, *Symphony No. 14* (1967)
Shostakovich, *Symphony No. 15* (1971)
Thorne, *Symphony No. 2* ("A Symphony of Light") (1984)

Concerto

Babbitt, *Piano Concerto* (1985)
Bassett, *Concerto Grosso* (1982), winds
Bolcom, *Concerto for Piano and Orchestra* (1975–76)
Carter, *Concerto for Orchestra* (1969)
Carter, *Double Concerto* (1961), hpd, pf, 2 chamb orch
Carter, *Piano Concerto* (1964–65)
Corigliano, *Clarinet Concerto* (1977)
Davies, *Violin Concerto* (1986)
Davies, *Trumpet Concerto* (1987)
Denisov, *Cello Concerto* (1972)
Denisov, *Piano Concerto* (1974)
Harbison, *Piano Concerto* (1978)
Harbison, *Violin concerto* (1980)
Harrison, *Piano Concerto* (1985)
Henze, *Concerto per Contrabbasso* (1966)
Henze, *Double concerto* (1966), oboe, harp, str
Henze, *Piano Concerto No. 2* (1967)
Henze, *Violin Concerto No. 2* (1976), vln, tape, vv, 33 instrs
Kirchner, *Piano Concerto No. 2* (1963)
Lieberson, *Cello Concerto* (1974)
Lieberson, *Piano Concerto* (1974)
Ligeti, *Cello Concerto* (1966)
Ligeti, *Chamber Concerto* (1969–70), 13 instrs
Ligeti, *Double Concerto* (1972), fl, ob, orch
Lutosławski, *Cello Concerto* (1970)
Lutosławski, *Double Concerto*, ob, harp, chamb orch
Maderna, *Violin Concerto* (1969)
Maderna, *Oboe Concerto No. 3* (1973)
Martino, *Triple Concerto* (1978), clar, bass clar, contrab clar, 16 inst
Meyer, *Chamber Concerto* (1972), oboe, perc, str
Moevs, *Concerto Grosso* (1968), pf, perc, orch
Penderecki, *Cello Concerto No. 1* (1972)
Penderecki, *Violin Concerto* (1976)
Penderecki, *Cello Concerto No. 2* (1981–82)
Penderecki, *Viola Concerto* (1982–83)
Petrassi, *Concerto for Orchestra No. 8* (1970–72)
Rochberg, *Violin Concerto* (1975)
Rorem, *Organ Concerto* (1985)
Shchedrin, *Piano Concerto No. 2* (1966)

Shchedrin, *Piano Concerto No. 3* (1976)
B. Schaeffer, *Concerto* (1980), sax qrt
B. Schaeffer, *Guitar Concerto* (1984)
B. Schaeffer, *Concerto for Organ and Orchestra (B-A-C-H)* (1984)

Orchestral and Ensemble Song

Baird, *Voices from Afar* (1982), Bar, orch
Carter, *A Mirror On Which to Dwell* (1975), S, fl + pic + a fl, ob + eng hn, cl + E♭ cl +
    b cl, perc, pf, vn, va, vc db
Carter, *Syringa* (1978), Mez/Bar, 11 insts
Clayton, *Cree Songs to the Newborn* (1978), S, cham ens
Del Tredici, *Final Alice* (1976), S, orch
Del Tredici, *Child Alice* (1977–81), S, orch
Denisov, *Chant d'automne* (1971), S, orch
Druckman, *Lamia* (1976), S, orch
Gompper, *Ladies* (1980), T, pf, xyl, vn, vc, hn, gui (texts by Ezra Pound)
Holloway, *Sea Surface Full of Clouds* (1974–75), S, Con, T, Ct, chor, cham orch
Lerdahl, *Beyond the Realm of Bird* (1981–84), S, cham orch (texts by Emily Dickinson)
Louvandie, *Six Turkish Folk Poems* (1977), S, fl, cl, vn, va, vc perc, pf
Lutosławski, *Paroles tissées* (1965), T, cham orch
Lutosławski, *Les espaces du sommeil* (1975), Bar, orch
Neill, *A Play of Poems* (1985), S, Bar, orch
Rands, *Canti lunatici* (1980), S, orch
Rands, *Canti del sole* (1982), T, orch
Rorem, *Last Poems of Wallace Stevens* (1972), S, pf, vc
C. Rouse, *Nuits d'ivresse* (1981), Mez, Bar, pf, ob d'amour
Schwantner, *Sparrows* (1978), S, cham ens
Schwantner, *Magabunda* (1983), S, orch

REPERTOIRE (Opera Since c. 1960)

America

Argento, *The Masque of Angels* (1964)
Argento, *Postcard from Morocco* (1971)
Argento, *The Voyage of Edgar Allan Poe* (1974–76)
Barber, *Vanessa* (1958)
Barber, *Antony and Cleopatra* (1966)
Bernstein, *A Quiet Place* (1983); rev. *A Quiet Place and Trouble in Tahiti* (1984)
Floyd, *Susannah* (1955)
Floyd *Bilby's Doll* (1976)
Floyd, *Of Mice and Men* (1965)
Glass, *Einstein on the Beach* (1976)
Glass, *Satyagraha* (1981)
Glass, *Akhnaten* (1984)
Hoiby, *Natalia Petrovna* (1964)
Hoiby, *Summer and Smoke* (1971)
Levy, *Mourning Becomes Electra* (1967)
Menotti, *The Last Savage* (1963)
Menotti, *Help, Help, the Globolinks!* (1968)
Menotti, *The Most Important Man* (1971)
Menotti, *Tamu-Tamu* (1973)
Menotti, *La Loca* (1979)
Menotti, *The Boy Who Grew Too Fast* (1982)
Menotti, *Goya* (1986)
Kirchner, *Lily* (1977)
Neill, *The Guilt of Lillian Sloan* (1986)
Pasatieri, *The Seagull* (1974)

Rochberg, *The Confidence Man* (1982)
Sessions, *Montezuma* (1964)
Silverman, *Elephant Steps* (1968)
Thomson, *Lord Byron* (1972)
Weisgall, *Six Characters in Search of an Author* (1960)

England

Bennet, *Victory* (1970)
Birtwhistle, *Punch and Judy* (1968)
Birtwhistle, *The Mask of Orpheus* (1985)
Britten, *A Midsummer Night's Dream* (1960)
Britten, *Owen Wingrave* (1970)
Britten, *Death in Venice* (1973)
Crosse, *Purgatory* (1966)
Crosse, *The Grace of Todd* (1968)
Crosse, *The Story of Vasco* (1968–73)
Crosse, *Potter Thompson* (1972–73)
Davies, *Taverner* (1962–68)
Davies, *The Martyrdom of St. Magnus* (1977)
Davies, *Resurrection* (in preparation)
Maw, *The Rising Moon* (1970)
Tippett, *The Midsummer Marriage* (1955)
Tippett, *King Priam* (1962)
Tippett, *The Knot Garden* (1970)

France

Daniel-Lesur, *Andrea del Sarto* (1961–68)
Messiaen, *Saint Francis d'Assisi* (1983)
Milhaud, *La mère coupable* (1966)
Poulenc, *Dialogues des Carmelites* (1957)
Poulenc, *La vois humaine* (1959)
Pousseur, *Votre Faust* (1969)

Germany

Dessau, *Lanzelot* (1967–69)
Dessau, *Einstein* (1971–73)
Fortner, *Die Bluthochzeit* (1957)
Fortner, *In seinem Garten liebt Don Perlimplin Belisa* (1962)
Fortner, *Elizabeth Tudor* (1972)
Henze, *Der König Hirsch* (1952–55)
Henze, *Der Prinz von Homburg* (1958)
Henze, *Elegy for Young Lovers* (1959–61)
Henze, *Der junge Lord* (1964)
Henze, *The Bassarids* (1965)
Henze, *We Come to the River* (1974–76)
Kagel, *Staatstheater* (1967–70)
Krenek, *Der goldene Bock* (1963)
Krenek, *Der Zauberspiegel* (1966)
Krenek, *Sardakai* (1967–69)
Ligeti, *Le grand macabre* (1974–77)
Ligeti, *The Tempest* (in progress)
Orff, *Oedipus der Tyran* (1959)
Orff, *Prometheus* (1968)
Orff, *De Temporum Fine Comoedia* (1973)
Reimann, *Melusine* (1971)
Stockhausen, *Donnerstag aus "Licht"* (1980)
Stockhausen, *Samstag aus "Licht"* (1983)

von Einem, *Der Besuch der alten Dame* (1971)
Weishappel, *König Nicolo* (1972)
Zimmermann, *Die Soldaten* (1958–64)

Italy

Berio, *Opera* (1971)
Dallapiccola, *Ulisse* (1967)
Malipiero, *Le Metamorfosi di Bonaventura* (1966)
Malipiero, *Gli Eroi di Bonaventura* (1969)
Negri, *Giovanni Sebastiano* (1970)
Pizzetti, *Assassinio nella cattedrale* (1957)
Pizzetti, *Clitennestra* (1964)

Poland

Penderecki, *Paradise Lost* (1978)
Penderecki, *Ubu roi* (in preparation)

REPERTOIRE (Rituals)

Babbitt, *A Solo Requiem* (1976–77)
Bassett, *Collect* (1969), SATB, tape
Bassett, *Moon Canticle* (1969), amp narrator, SATB, vc
Bassett, *Celebration: In praise of Earth* (1970), amp narrator, SATB, orch
Birtwistle, *The Fields of Sorrow* (Ausonius, trans. Waddell, 1971), 2S, chorus, ens
Birtwistle, *The Triumph of Time* (1972), orch
Boulez, *Rituel in memoriam Maderna* (1974)
Cage, *Atlantis eclipticalis* (1961), any ens from 86 insts
Cage, *Étude australe* (1974–75), 32 pieces, pf
Dallapicolla, *Sicut umbra* (1970), mezzo, 12 instrs
Davies, *Versalii Icones* (1969), vc, va, fl, basset cl, pf, perc, dancer
Davies, *From Stone to Thorn* (1971), Mezzo, hpd, guit, perc
Denisov, *Plachi* ("Laments") (1966), S, pf, 3 perc
Feldman, *Rothko Chapel* (1972)
Messiaen, *Et exspecto resurrectionem mortuorum* (1964), 18 ww, 16 brass, 3 perc
Messiaen, *La Transfiguration de Notre Seigneur Jésus-Christ* (1969), SSMez AATTBarBB
     (100 vv), pf, vc, fl, cl, vib, mar, xylorimba, orch
Messiaen, *Méditations sur le mystère de la Sainte Trinité* (1969), org
Messiaen, *Des canyons aux étoiles* (1971–74), pf, hn, orch
Messiaen, *Livre du Saint Sacrement* (1986), org
Penderecki, *St. Luke's Passion* (1963–65), solo vv, narrator, boys' chorus, chorus, orch
Penderecki, *Utrenia* (1970–71), solo vv, two choruses, orch
Penderecki, *Polish Requiem* (1980–84), soloists, chorus, orch
Rorem, *A Quaker Reader* (1976), org
A. Rossi, *Ancestral Rites of a Forgotten Culture* (1983)
C. Rouse, *Rotae Passionis* ("Passion Wheels") (1983): I. Circular Lament—Agony in the
     Garden; II. Passion Wheels (Fourteen Stations of the Cross); III. Parallel Wheel—
     Christ Asleep
Schafer, *Epitaph for Moonlight* (1968), youth SATB, bells
Shapey, *Rituals* (1959), orch
Stockhausen, *Sternklang* (1971)
Stockhausen, *Inori* (1972)
Stockhausen, *Lucifer's Farewell* (aus *Samstag*, 1982)
Stockhausen, *Lucifer's Requiem* (aus *Samstag*, 1982)
Stravinsky, *A Sermon, A Narrative and a Prayer* (1961)
Stravinsky, *Introitus* (1965)
Stravinsky, *Requiem Canticles* (1966)
Tavener, *The Whale* (1969)

Tavener, *Introit for the Feast of St. John Damascene* (1967–68)
Tavener, *Celtic Requiem* (1969)
Tavener, *Ultimos ritos* (St. John of the Cross, Crucifixus from Nicene creed) (1969–72)
Tavener, *Requiem for Father Malachy* (1972)
Tavener, *Akhmatova: rekviem* (1979–80), S, B, ens

(In honor and memory of Igor Stravinsky)

Berio, *Autre fois: berceuse canonique pour I. Stravinsky* (1971), fl, cl, harp
Birtwistle, *Tombeau: in memoriam Igor Stravinsky* (1972), fl, cl, harp, str qt
Carter, *Canon for 3: in memoriam Igor Stravinsky* (1971)
Copland, *Threnody I: Igor Stravinsky, in memoriam* (1971)
Davies, *Canon ad honorem I.S.* (1967)
Davies, *Canon in memoriam I.S.* (1971)
Denisov, *Canon in memoriam Stravinsky* (1971)
Eimert, *Zu Ehren von Igor Stravinsky* (1957), tape
Kagel, *Prince Igor Stravinsky* (1982), Bass, instrs
Krenek, *Canon for Stravinsky's 80th Birthday* (1962)
Milhaud, *Hommage à Igor Stravinsky* (1971), str qrt
Pousseur, *Stravinsky au futur* (1971), v, inst ens, elec
Pousseur, *L'effacement du Prince Igor* (1971), orch
Sessions, *Canons in memory of I. S.* (1971), str qrt
Shnitke, *Canon in memory of Stravinsky* (1971), str qrt
Taverner, *In memoriam I.S.* (1971)
Wuorinen, *A Reliquary for Igor Stravinsky* (1978), orch

READING (String Quartet, Opera, Rituals)

Paul Griffiths, *Modern Music* (1981): "Opera, Music Theatre," pp. 248–270;
    "Series, Melody," pp. 271–293.
Paul Griffiths, *The String Quartet* (1983), pp. 169–227.
Ethan Morden, *Opera in the Twenthieth Century* (1978), pp. 211–321.

CHAPTER 32

ENVOI

I should prefer this note not be read or, if skimmed, that it should be forgotten. [Mallarmé, Preface to "Un coup de dés" (1897)]

We present for the first time, under the supervision of MM. Erik Satie and Darius Milhaud . . . 'furnishing music' (*musique d'ameublement*) to be played during the entr'actes. We beg you to take no notice of it and to behave during the entr'actes as if the music did not exist. This music . . . claims to make its contribution to life in the same way as a private conversation, a picture, or the chair on which you may or may not be seated. [Pierre Bertin, Introduction to a play by Max Jacob with *musique d'ameublement* by Erik Satie (1920)]

I can't recognize *Cartridge Music* from one performance to the next. Somewhere I tell that story of going into a house . . . and the hostess to be nice had put *Cartridge Music* on in another room . . . I turned to her and asked, "What is that music?" And she said, "You can't be serious." I said, "It's very interesting; what is it?" And then she told me. I was pleased that I couldn't recognize it . . . I don't hear it, you see. I performed it . . . with David Tudor, and we made a recording when Earle Brown was in charge of Time Records. Earle asked David and me if . . . we wanted to hear the end result. Neither one of us wanted to hear it. [David Cope, "An Interview with John Cage" (1980)]

Where are the new frontiers? Who is there? What is being composed and what is it like? The questions were asked yesterday and will be restated tomorrow, and by the time the answers come conditions will already have changed. Even a brief search for contemporary interest in recurrent trends of the past quickly proves the elusiveness of fixing the present. The anti-art pose, for example—periodically observable throughout the past century from Mallarmé to Satie and Cage seems to have receded notably in recent years. On the other hand there are signs that the anti-masterpiece mentality is alive and well. Equally ambivalent is the recasting of an acknowledged masterpiece of the past as modern day *musique d'ameublement*. Though capable of being interpreted as a trivialization, the appropriation of Ravel's *Gaspard de la nuit* of 1908 for a building graphic (Figure 32.1)—instead of Ligeti's appealing *Artikulation* of 1970 (Figure 28.6), for example—can also be said to constitute a kind of canonization, a nostalgic recognition of early twentieth-century values which seemingly elude our contemporary grasp.

Figure 32.1. Outdoor mural excerpt of "Scarbo" from Ravel's *Gaspard de la nuit. Musique d'ameublement* for today? Schmitt Music Center, Minneapolis, Minnesota.
Photo courtesy of Schmitt Music Center.

It is a paradox, too, that even as composers generally decry categorization, they tend to group themselves in identifiable clusters and encourage the recognition of new trends. In any attempt to sense the current musical scene, the important centers and institutions can hardly be ignored. But are all of the most significant personalities in attendance? Boulez's Institute for Resarch and Coordination of Acoustics/Music (IRCAM) at the Pompidou Center in Paris, open since 1977, is purportedly designed to cover the whole range of musical inquiry, and a performance there of the initial version of his projected hour-long work-in-progress *Répons* (1981–   ) in the "Espace de projection" (Figure 32.2) led some to claim yet another breakthrough for this energetic musician in the domain of electronics—a resource he had previously tended to skirt.[1] His insistence, however, upon pursuing innovation in the service of a "Music of the Future" (recalling Wagner and Schoenberg) and an unyielding disdain for what he labels "retro" music (read Brahms and the neoclassic Stravinsky) has sounded not only familiar but, to many, old-fashioned. Yet more recently he has clarified that he is not disturbed by the variety inherent in the new stylistic pluralism, only by the seeming "lack of real adventure" in "rediscovering the past but without any meaning."[2] Berio's assessment of Boulez sums it up:

It is remarkable that, even in his writings, he has succeeded in putting ascetic parentheses around history, and in pursuing *l'être absolument moderne*, though without the dry blood of a season in hell on his face.[3]

Tellingly, Boulez's *Répons*, for all of its use of the 4X processor and associated computer hardware, continues to explore the relationships of live performers (an instrumental ensemble of twenty-four musicians and a group of six soloists) with the latest technologies: The ensemble (woodwinds, brass, strings) is placed in the center of the hall, the soloists (piano, organ, cymbalum, xylophone, harp, vibraphone) around the perimeter; the sounds of the soloists are transformed electronically and broadcast through a network of six large loudspeakers; furthermore each soloist is connected to a tape recorder, and during the piece the soloists' performance activates a tape of synthesized music heard on six small loudspeakers placed behind each of the players. Boulez has revealingly declared, however, that the antiphonal interplay between ensemble and soloists in *Répons* ("response") is merely the latest instance of an on-going interest in Medieval procedures reflected earlier in the "Trope" of his *Third Piano Sonata*. The Boulezian paradox continues, and old and new are once again endorsed as potential coexistors.

Few would deny the importance of both Boulez and Babbitt, who happily perform the work of the composer-scientist-scholar, or the potential usefulness of investigations carried out in their laboratories. But it is interesting to note

Figure 32.2."Espace de Projection," Institut de Recherche et Coordination Acoustique/Musique, Centre Georges Pompidou, Paris.

Photo by Jean-Pierre Armand courtesy of IRCAM.

that, in spite of ongoing verbal polemics, their most recent music sounds less insistently new and their former amnesia appears now less complete. The composers' threatened withdrawal from society to a circle of cognoscenti, implicit in Schoenberg's Society for Private Performances (1918) and again in a prevailing attitude amongst many university campuses in the late 1950s and 1960s, no longer appears to shine as an attractive option. While most would defend the continuing need to probe both empirically and theoretically the infinity of possibilities in the domain of sound—whether in Paris or Princeton, the need to find and connect with an audience has come to be an increasingly expressed concern.

Meanwhile, many composers, including some of the most communicative of the day, are presently less involved with extending the boundaries of sound and organization than with mining the consequences of ideas already received. For many the dilemma appears to be not in any poverty of invention but in the proliferation of materials and stylistic options as well as in the identification of an appropriate audience. Obviously the technology (radio, television, stereo LP, compact disc, audio cassette, videocassette) is in place as never before for the ready dissemination of any and all music for an interested public. Not only such specialty labels as CRI, New World, and Nonesuch but RCA, Philips, Columbia, and DGG have continued to place a vast recorded catalogue at the disposal of a public that can no longer claim ignorance of contemporary repertories because of the lack of live performances. Television's potential, especially for music with a theatrical or visual component, has hardly been tapped, although there have been a few notable attempts such as a 1984 PBS series, entitled "Soundings", focused upon the music of Michael Colgrass, Joan Tower, Lukas Foss, Ivanna Themmen, and Ralph Shapey.

Significantly, however, the number of ensembles devoted to the live performance of contemporary music has steadily increased from the time of Schoenberg's Society for Private Musical Performances formed in 1918. The Donaueschingen Festival was inaugurated shortly thereafter in 1921 under the patronage of Max Egon zu Fürstenberg, and although it disbanded in 1930, it revived again in 1950 and has been responsible for the premieres of such important scores as Stockhausen's *Mantra* (1970) and *Inori* (1974), and Boulez's *Pli selon pli* (1962) and *Répons* (1981). During the period 1954–73 Boulez was extremely active promoting the music of the avant-garde through the performances of his Domaine Musical, and since 1976 he has joined with Peter Eötvös in directing new repertoires with the chamber orchestra Ensemble InterContemporain. Beginning with Harvey Sollberger's Group for Contemporary Music founded in 1962 at Columbia University, numerous groups—such as The Contemporary Chamber Ensemble and Speculum Musicae; The American Composer's Orchestra and the Louisville Orchestra; the Fromm Foundation, the summer symposia at Tanglewood and Aspen; the Horizons Concerts of the New York Philharmonic as well as the composer-in-residence programs of several American orchestras; and the Contemporary Directions ensembles and programs at a few American universities (from San Diego to Chicago, Ann Arbor, and New York)—have continued to ferret out a reasonably wide spectrum of contemporary music without which it would undoubtedly have gone unheard.

Though commissions for ensembles, orchestras and opera companies may be said to continue in a small trickle, the Fromm Foundation has been especially vigorous in its support of the new music scene. The removal of the Fromm Week of New Music from Tanglewood to Aspen in 1985 emphasized the sustained importance of supporting stylistic diversity as reflected in Fromm's keynote address "Musical Pluralism in the 1980s." Judging from the musical wares displayed, pluralism does not necessarily imply the anxious and continuing search for a "cutting edge" any more than it rejects the notion of a single stylistic modus for a given composer, and the unveiling of works such as Berio's arrangement of Boccherini's *Night Music of Madrid* or Alvin Lucier's *Serenade for Thirteen Winds and Pure Wave Oscillators* (premised on the division of the interval of the half-step into eight discrete gradations) promoted the notion that both "time-travelling" (Berio) and the "anti-masterpiece mentality" (openly discussed by Lucier) are both still vigorously at large. In addition, however, the range of Fromm Foundation commissions in 1984 from Susan Blaustein, Todd Brief, Oliver Marshall, Stephen Mosko, David Myska, Eugene O'Brien, Bernard Rands, Steve Reich, Morton Subotnick, James Tenney, and Joan Tower mirrors the catholicity of its approach. The recognition elsewhere of Laura Clayton's critically acclaimed *Cree Songs to the Newborn* (1978) also demands that we note the increasing number of women on such lists.

But the lists are long, and the task of keeping up is increasingly difficult, rendering any single person's view of the contemporary music scene partial and necessarily given to a compounding bias. One could quickly conclude that the world has a superfluity of composers with respect to consumer needs, if only because, unlike the visual arts, there is no demand for an original in every home. Yet the amount of music which is consumed (used and then discarded) in our society today is astonishing, and in many instances music is the fleeting variable, the performer the constant member of the equation and today's music hero. It is small wonder, then, that the notion of "performance art," combining the creative and re-creative roles, should at least momentarily be exercising such a significant appeal, or that composers have become increasingly visible figures in their own productions, either as ensemble directors or mandatory production consultants. This is hardly a new phenomenon, however, as the names of Mozart, Beethoven, Brahms, Wagner, Liszt, and Mahler will readily attest. But the role of singers like Joan La Barbara, Diamanda Gallas, and the poet-percussionist Charles Amirkhanian (the latter of whose investigations, such as *Mental Radio*, are largely restricted to text-sound compositions not unallied to Reich's *Come Out* of 1966) clearly reinforces a trend well known from more recent composer-performer careers: Harry Partch (specially constructed instruments, specially trained performers, an emphasis on the "corporeal" aspect of music); Robert Ashley (who, resisting the idea of the intermediary, was from the beginning fundamentally involved in the production of his own music); Steve Reich (a standing ensemble to promote his works); and Karlheinz Stockhausen (a less exclusive yet notable reliance on extended relationships with certain performers).

In spite of the promotion of the American composer's music by the American Music Center (a vast repository of scores and tapes available on loan), one often hears the American composer complain that his music is little known and seldom performed in Europe, though it is a complaint that could easily be made in reverse. Toward this end the Composers' Forum in New York has recently become active not in clarifying the "Uptown-Downtown" distinctions of the Serialists and Minimalists of the 1960s and 1970s but, under the direction of Joel Chadabe, in promoting a better understanding of lesser known works by contemporary composers in Europe.[4]

Perhaps such improvements in communication will soon bring to this country the likes of *Jonon et Avos*, the Soviet Union's first rock opera. A two-hour blend of religious chant, punk rock, and Russian folk melodies, it was brought to Paris for its debut in December 1983 by the fashion designer Pierre Cardin with "a loud and colorful clash of synthesizers, amplifiers and laser lights."[5] Increasingly, urban critics and some musicologists have pressed for the serious consideration of the whole spectrum of popular music. Among others, the New York critic John Rockwell has promoted the cause by devoting half the contents of a book entitled *All-American Music: Composition in the Late Twentieth Century* (1983) to such figures as Laurie Anderson, Keith Jarrett, Ornett Coleman, Eddie Palmer, Stephen Sondheim, and Neil Young in the company of such names as Ernst Krenek, Milton Babbitt, Elliott Carter, and John Cage. In an age of diversity in every phase of human existence, caught in a time that emphasizes the concept of one world, the urge to see the complete picture is natural. But it is undoubtedly beyond our grasp either to synthesize or to predict. As in the concept of "moment" form, attention to any new perspective is almost always purchased at the expense of some of the older ones.

It would appear in retrospect that, following a mid-century crisis that seemingly demanded that a choice be made between Serialism and Neoclassicism, we have come to the point where we are comfortable with the wealth of our various alternatives, and an "anything goes" attitude prevails. Pitch series and rhythmic modulation (Babbitt, Carter, Wuorinen), raga and ragtime (Messiaen, Cage; Albright, Bolcom), triadic formation and pentatonic wash (Rochberg and Crumb), quotation and collage (Berio, Stockhausen; Davies, Kagel), stochastics, cybernetics and computers (Xenakis, Mumma, Hiller)—all remain possible and vital options for the composer. We are even occasionally reminded that the composer can still lead us to spiritual reflection and prayer (Penderecki, Feldman, Bassett, Messiaen and, perhaps unexpectedly, Stockhausen and Boulez). Computer music, mixed media, improvisation, indeterminacy, theater music, Minimalism, New Romanticism, happening, biomusic, danger music, soundscape, and performance art have come and in some instances departed from our vocabulary, leaving terms such as "Post-Avant-Garde" or "Post-Modern" with a hollow ring. Yet the latter two expressions may be important indicators that many composers are currently less interested in insistently probing those frontiers that appear to point to some unknown, unconceivable and perhaps glorious future than in surveying and synthesizing the vast sonic terrain of human cultures past and present.

An interest in bridging the gap between audience and composer (paradoxically at the heart of Babbitt's widely misunderstood "Who Cares if You Listen?") now appears to be growing in all quarters. The sense of isolation felt by both parties stands in need of a cure that demands capitulation from neither side. The profusion of composerly polemics, however, seems to have momentarily abated, and the idea that a music capable of seducing audiences or at least provoking their attention may also require the best of the composer's craft has once more gained respectability.

The accusation that no period in history except our own has spent its primary energies performing the music of the past—turning the music of the eighteenth and nineteenth centuries in the process into our standard fare—is one that has been voiced repeatedly. In an open letter to the International Music Council of November 21, 1984, Karlheinz Stockhausen spoke passionately:

> What can be done: Shake up the leading interpreters in the world, ask them to refuse to serve any longer the machinery of composer stripping, financial exploitation of dead composers through established gangs of cultural manipulation and "music marketing"; insist that they serve musical evolution: help vulnerable new musical organisms rather than living from a 300 year-old bank account of musical literature; spend at least 50% of their time rehearsing and performing new works; fight for progress and refuse to continue this ugly game of idolizing the past.[6]

His injunction, for all its ardor, mirrors concerns shared by numerous musicians other than composers. Stravinsky's willing and correct observation that the contemporary composer's wares have been disseminated through recording in a quantity and with a speed unimaginable in any previous age must be kept in mind, however, as a partial redress.[7] Yet in a century, now closing, in which many of the landmarks of the first two decades are still little known to the concert-going public, the prospect of catching up while remaining *au courant* is formidable.

In addition, the problem is compounded through our increasing interest in the music of the twelfth through the eighteenth centuries, much of which is being unearthed, edited, and performed for the first time since its birth. New musical museums are opening every day, and excitement runs high in many quarters. Furthermore, the technologies which allow the speedy dissemination of twentieth-century repertoires have also served this older and expanding literature, which now competes keenly for the music lover's attention. It is a dilemma which is new to the twentieth century, the composer having never been previously asked to share his potential audience with music of a prior age to any appreciable extent. Now music is being confronted for the first time with its own history in the concert hall, and it has proven to be a heady and unusually challenging experience. Hopefully, there will be enough energy, talent, and good-will to accommodate it all. If, in the act of time-sharing with a bygone era, the music of our own age is, by a previous definition, short-changed, it will not be due solely to a nostalgia for the past, but also because, as in literature and the visual arts, there is a sense of discovery to be enjoyed there as well.[8]

READING

Pierre Boulez, "Orchestras, Concert Halls, Repertory, Audiences" in *Orientations* (Cambridge, Mass., 1986), 467–70, based upon an interview of March, 1970.

Pierre Boulez, "What's New?" in *Orientations* (Cambridge, Mass., 1986), 477–80. Originally in *Celebration of Contemporary Music*, program of a week of contemporary music at the Julliard School of Music (March ,1976).

Pierre Boulez, "Technology and the Composer" in *Orientations* (Cambridge Mass., 1986), 486–94. Originally in *The Times Literary Supplement*, May 6, 1977.

G. S. Bourdain, "The Electronic World of Pierre Boulez," *Saturday Review* (February 1982), 43–45.

Andrew Gerzso, "Reflections on *Répons*," *Contemporary Music Review*, i.1 (1984).

Dominique Jameux, "Boulez and the 'Machine'," *Contemporary Music Review*, i.1 (1984).

Todd Machover, "A View of Music at IRCAM," *Contemporary Music Review*, i.1 (1984).

Karlheinz Stockhausen, "Open Letter to the International Musical Council," November 21, 1984.

Luciano Berio, *Two Interviews* (1985), 34.

David Gable, "Ramifying Connections: an Interview with Pierre Boulez," *Journal of Musicology*, iv.1 (Winter 1985–86), 106.

Imogene Horsley, "Has Musicology Destroyed the Historical Process?" in *Essays on Music for Charles Warren Fox* (Eastman School of Music Press, 1979), 126–31.

NOTES

PREFACE

1. Carl Dahlhaus, "Analyse und Werturteil, Musikpädagogik," *Forschung und Lehre*, viii, ed. S. Abel-Struth (1970).
2. Carl Dahlhaus, *Between Romanticism and Modernism* (1980), 3.
3. Cf. Robert P. Morgan, "Rewriting Music History: Second Thoughts on Ives and Varèse," *Musical Newsletter*, iii.1 (1973), 3–12; iii.2 (1973), 15–23, 28.

CHAPTER 1

1. W. Schuh, ed., *Richard Strauss: Betrachtungen und Erinnerungen* (1949; Eng. trans., 1953) as quoted in *New Grove Dictionary of Music*, vol. 18, 279. See R. Kaplan, "Sonata Form in the Orchestral Works of Liszt: The Revolutionary Reconsidered," *19th Century Music*, viii.2 (1984), 142–52, for an appraisal that confirms the presence of abstract formal principles in conjunction with narrative considerations.
2. Eduard Hanslick, "Richard Strauss's *Don Juan*," in *Vienna's Golden Years of Music. 1850–1900*, ed., trans. Henry Pleasants (New York: Simon & Schuster, 1950), 308–9.
3. Walter B. Bailey, *Programmatic Elements in the Works of Schoenberg* (1984).
4. G. Mahler, *Selected Letters*, ed. Knud Martner (New York: Farrar, Straus, 1979; London: Faber and Faber), No. 205 dated February 17, 1897, 212.
5. Cf. Wagner's "Beethoven" in *Music in the Western World: A History in Documents*, ed. P. Weiss and R. Taruskin (New York: Schirmer Books, 1984), 377–80.
6. Cf. Piero Weiss, ed., *Letters of Composers Through Six Centuries* (Philadelphia: Chilton Books, 1967), 392–94, for a letter of March 26, 1896, which discusses the Symphony No. 2; also in Weiss-Taruskin, eds., *op. cit.*, 413–14.
7. I am grateful to Timothy Taylor who brought this to my attention.
8. Henry-Louis de La Grange, *Mahler* (Garden City, NY: Doubleday, 1973), 785.
9. Cf. *Richard Wagner's Prose Works*, trans. William Ashton Ellis, (London, 1985), vol. 1, 123–26; also Weiss-Taruskin, *op. cit.*, 377–80.
10. N. Bauer-Lechner, *Errinerungen* (Vienna, 1923), 30, as translated in W. J. McGrath, "The Metamusical Cosmos of Gustav Mahler" in *Dionysian Art and Populist Politics in Austria* (New Haven: Yale University Press, 1974), 120–162. Copyright © 1974 by Yale University Press.
11. Willi Reich, *Schoenberg: A Critical Biography*, trans. Leo Black (London: Longman, 1971), 130.
12. Arnold Schoenberg, *Style and Idea*, ed. Leonard Stein, trans. Leo Black (New York: St. Martin's Press, 1975), 141.
13. Pierre Boulez, "Gustav Mahler: Our Contemporary?" Preface to *Gustav Mahler et Vienne* by Bruno Walter (Paris, 1979). English translation in *Orientations* (Cambridge, Mass.: Harvard University Press, 1986), 298.
14. I am grateful to Christopher Rouse for bringing this to my attention.
15. Pierre Boulez, "Mahler: Our Contemporary?" Preface to Bruno Walter, *Gustav Mahler et Vienne* (Paris, 1979). English translation in *Orientations* (Cambridge, Mass.: Harvard University Press, 1986), 296.

CHAPTER 2

1. Arnold Schoenberg, "National Music (2)" (1931), *Style and Idea*, ed. Leonard Stein (New York: St. Martin's Press, 1975), 173–4. Copyright © 1975 Belmont Music Publishers. Reprinted by permission of the copyright holders.
2. Arnold Schoenberg, "My Evolution" (1949), *ibid.*, 79–92.
3. Arnold Schoenberg, "National Music (2)," *ibid.*, 172–3.
4. Arnold Schoenberg, "My Technique and Style" (1950), *ibid.*, 110. The *Two Ballades*, which also include "Jane Grey," were written on required texts for a competition also entered by Zemlinsky. Neither composer won.
5. Glenn Watkins, "Schoenberg Re-Cycled" in *Essays on Music for Charles Warren Fox* (1979), 72.
6. See William Austin, *Music in the 20th Century* (New York: W.W. Norton, 1966), 204–05.
7. The relationship of motifs a and b to the opening trumpet motif (d-f-a-c♯) of Mahler's *Third Symphony* (1895–96) can hardly go unrecognized.
8. Perhaps relatable to Beethoven's *String Quartet*, op. 95, about whose identical motivic content Schoenberg spoke at length in his article "Brahms the Progressive," (1947); cf. Arnold Schoenberg, *Style and Idea*, ed. L. Stein (1975), 423–24.
9. *Ibid.*, 485.
10. Arnold Schoenberg, *Harmonielehre* (1911), Eng. trans. Roy Carter (Berkeley: University of California Press, 1978), 421.
11. Josef Rufer, *The Works of Arnold Schoenberg*, Eng. trans. Dika Newlin (London: Faber & Faber, 1962), 34.

CHAPTER 3

1. Hans Moldenhauer in collaboration with Rosaleen Moldenhauer, *Anton von Webern* (New York: Knopf, 1979), 51.
2. *Ibid.*, 55.
3. *Ibid.*, 72.
4. Anton Webern, *The Path to the New Music*, Eng. trans. Leo Black (Bryn Mawr, PA: Theodore Presser, 1963), 48.
5. Walter Kolneder, *Anton Webern*, Eng. trans. Humphrey Searle (Berkeley: University of California Press, 1968), 36.
6. Hans Moldenhauer, *ibid.*, 113.
7. Walter Kolneder, *ibid.*, 68–9.

CHAPTER 4

1. *Alban Berg, Letters to his Wife*, ed., trans., and annotated by Bernard Grun (New York: St. Martin's Press, 1971), 132–3.
2. The identical progression, also at the same pitch level, appears in Debussy's "Pour le danseuse aux crotales" from *Six Epigraph Antiques* (1915). While much of this music was based on Debussy's earlier *Chansons de Bilitis* (1900–01), the passage in question is new to the 1915 version. See Ex. 7.1.
3. For the poster announcing this event see Moldenhauer, *Anton von Webern* (1978), 230.
4. Hans Redlich, *Alban Berg* (London: John Calder, 1957), 231.
5. *Alban Berg's Letters to His Wife*, ed. Bernard Grun (New York: St. Martin's Press, 1971), 147.
6. George Perle, "Alban Berg," *The New Grove Dictionary of Music and Musicians* (1980), II, 527.
7. Mark DeVoto, "Alban Berg's 'Marche Macabre'," *Perspectives of New Music*, xxii/1–2 (1983–84), 386–447, is a highly detailed study of the thematics of the last movement of Berg's op. 6.
8. Connoiseurs of Puccini's *Tosca* will recognize the rhythm to be identical to the one repeated in a mounting crescendo by the snare drums in Scarpia's discourse of the fate of Cavaradossi immediately preceding "Vissi d'arte" in Act II. Though *Tosca* was

not in Mahler's repertoire as a conductor, his admiration for *La Boheme* is well documented. *Tosca* was first performed in 1900; Mahler's Sixth Symphony dates from 1903-04.

9. Hans Redlich, *Alban Berg* (1957), 70. See also Douglas Jarman, *The Music of Alban Berg* (1979), 151-2.

10. George Perle, *The Operas of Alban Berg: Volume I, Wozzeck* (Berkeley: University of California Press, 1980), 18. Reprinted by permission of the publisher. See also pp. 193-94, this book.

11. Igor Stravinsky and Robert Craft, *Conversations* (Garden City, NY: Doubleday, 1959), 79-80.

CHAPTER 5

1. R. Brussel, "Claude Debussy et Paul Dukas," *La Revue musicale*, vii (1926), 101.

2. Set also by Chabrier in 1870 and by Charpentier in 1895.

3. Debussy was to borrow the third line of this poem, "Les sons et les parfums tournent dans l'air du soir," for the title of one of his *Préludes*, Book I.

4. Robin Holloway, *Debussy and Wagner* (London: Eulenburg Books, 1979), 235.

5. Jean Cocteau, "Fragments d'un conférence sur Erik Satie," *Revue musicale*, 5 (1924), 217-23; Nigel Wilkins, trans. and ed., *The Writings of Erik Satie* (London: Eulenburg Books, 1980), 110.

6. Alan Gilmore, "Erik Satie and the Concept of the Avant-Garde," *Musical Quarterly* (Winter 1983), 109-10.

7. J. Cocteau, *op. cit.*

8. J. Morland, "Enquete sur l'influence allemande: VI. Musique," *Mercure de France*, xlv (January, 1903), 89-110. Trans. Scott Messing.

9. William Austin, "The History of the Poem and the Music" in his critical edition of *Prélude à L'aprés-midi d'un faune* (New York: W.W. Norton, 1970), 13-14.

10. Arthur Wenk, *Claude Debussy and the Poets* (1976), 148-170.

11. E. Lockspeiser, *Debussy: His Life and Mind*, vol. 1, 206. Copyright © Edward Lockspeiser 1962. Reproduced by permission of Curtis Brown Ltd.

12. Trans. W. Austin, *op. cit.*, 14.

13. Notes to CBS Record 32 11 0056.

14. J. Hepokoski, "Formulaic Openings in Debussy," *19th Century Music*, viii.1 (1984), 45.

15. *Ibid.*, 51.

16. Stéphane Mallarmè, *Oeuvres complètes*, ed. H. Mondor and G. Jean-Aubrey (1965), 1465.

17. Notes to CBS Record 32 11 0056.

18. Carolyn Abbate, "*Tristan* in the Composition of *Pelléas*," *19th Century Music*, ii (1981), 128-140.

19. Edward Lockspeiser, *Debussy His Life and Mind*, vol. 1, 206-7. Copyright © Edward Lockspeiser 1962. Reproduced by permission of Curtis Brown Ltd.

20. Kurt von Fisher, "Claude Debussy and das Klima des Art Nouveau: Bermerkungen zur Äesthetik Debussys and James McNeill Whistlers" in *Art Nouveau, Jugenstil und Musik*, ed. Jürg Stenzl (1980), 31-46.

21. *Etude compariée des harmonique de Fauré et de Debussy*, special numbers 272-3, *La Revue musicale* (1971), vol. 1, 41. See also Roy Howat, *Debussy in Proportion* (Cambridge, England: Cambridge University Press, 1983), 48-9.

22. R. Howat, *Debussy in Proportion*, 64-135.

23. Annie Joly-Ségalen, ed., *Ségalen et Debussy* (1962), 107. Interview of December 17, 1908. Trans. in Jarockinski, *Debussy, Impressionism and Symbolism* (London: Eulenburg Books, 1976).

24. Herbert Eimert, "Debussy's Jeux," *Die Reihe*, no. 5 (1959; Eng. trans. 1961), 3.

25. See Jean Barraqué, *Debussy* (1962), 166, 169; J. Pasler, "Debussy, *Jeux*: Playing with Time and Form," *19th Century Music*, vi.1 (1982), 60; Herbert Eimert, *op. cit.*, 29.

26. In addition to Eimert's article, Boulez's recording of *Jeux*, CBS 32 11 0056, helped to promote this view, which was clearly expressed by E. Salzman in *Twentieth-Century Music: An Introduction* (2nd ed., 1974), 29.

27. *Alban Berg: Letters to His Wife*, ed. and trans. by B. Grun (New York: St. Martin's, 1971), 168-9.

CHAPTER 6

1. Roland-Manuel, "Une Esquisse autobiographie de Maurice Ravel," *La Revue musicale* (Dec. 1938), 17-23, as trans. in A. Orenstein, *Ravel* (New York: Columbia University Press), 181.
2. Arbie Ornstein, *Ravel* (1975), 181. See Ned Rorem's notes to the complete recording of Ravel's songs on CBS Record M 39023.
3. Wallace Fowlie, *Mallarmé* (Chicago: University of Chicago Press, 1953), 51.
4. John Smith, *The Arts Betrayed* (London: Herbert Press, 1978), 11, 96.

CHAPTER 7

1. Edward Lockspieser, *Debussy: His life and mind* (London: Curtis Brown, 1962), 185.
2. B. Newbould, "Ravel's Pantoum," *Music and Letters* (1975), 228-31.

CHAPTER 8

1. Carl Schorske, *Fin-de-siècle Vienna* (New York: Alfred A. Knopf, 1980), xix: "In what seemed like ubiquitous fragmentation–Nietzsche and the Marxists agreed in calling it 'decadence'–European high culture entered a whirl of infinite innovation, with each field proclaiming independence of the whole, each part in turn falling into parts."
2. Philippe Julian, *Dreamers of Decadence* (Paris, 1969), Eng. trans. R. Baldick (New York: Holt, Rinehart and Winston, 1971), 33.
3. Joris-Karl Huysmans, *Against Nature*, Eng. trans. Robin Baldick (New York: 1959), 63-70. Copyright © the Estate of Robin Baldick, 1959. Reproduced by permission of Penguin Books Ltd.
4. Quoted in P. Julian, *op. cit.*, 183.
5. Cf. P. Weiss and R. Taruskin, eds., *Music in the Western World* (New York: Schirmer Books, 1984), 415.
6. Egon Wellesz, "Schönberg und die Anfänge der Wiener Schule," *Oesterreichisches Musikzeitung*, xv.5 (May 1960), 237. Eng. trans. G. Watkins.
7. Jan Pasler, "Stravinsky and the Apaches," *The Musical Times* (June 1982), 406.
8. Robert Craft and Vera Stravinsky, *Stravinsky in Pictures and Documents* (New York, 1978), 82.
9. Halsey Stevens, *The Life and Music of Béla Bartók* (London: Oxford University Press, 1953, rev. 1964), 30.
10. Béla Bartók, "Harvard Lectures (No. IV)" (1943) in *Béla Bartók Essays*, ed. Benjamin Suchoff (London: Faber and Faber, 1976), 386.

CHAPTER 9

1. Timbre: percussion, black; strings, blue; flute, white; brasses, red. Keys: F, white; C, blue; G, red; D, yellow; A, green; F♯, black; A♭, purple. Vowels: e, clear blue; a, red; u, cream; o, gray, etc. See Michael Murray, *Marcel Dupré* (Boston: Northeastern University Press, 1985), 92, fn. 18.
2. Joris-Karl Huysmans, *Against Nature*, Eng. trans. Robin Baldick (New York, 1959), 58-9. Copyright © the Estate of Robin Baldick, 1959. Reproduced by permission of Penguin Books Ltd.
3. Arthur Gold and Robert Fizdale, *Misia* (New York: Knopf, 1980), 105. Reprinted by permission.
4. Kandinsky wrote several other plays with the same central premise, although they were never published: *The Green Sound* (1909), *Black and White* (1909), and *Violet* (1911).
5. Wassily Kandinsky, *Der gelbe Klang* (1909), Eng. trans. V. Miesel in *Voices of German Expressionism*, 137ff. Copyright © 1970 Prentice Hall, Englewood Cliffs, NJ. Reprinted by permission of the publisher.

6. David Johnson, notes to Columbia Records M2S 679.
7. Jelena Hahl-Koch, ed., *Arnold Schoenberg/Wassily Kandinsky: Letters, Pictures and Documents* (1980), Eng. trans. J.C. Crawford (London: Faber & Faber, 1984), 142.
8. Text by Arnold Schoenberg reprinted by permission of Belmont Music Publishers. English trans. G. Watkins.
9. Malcolm Brown, "Skriabin and Russian 'Mystic' Symbolism," *19th-Century Music*, iii.1 (1979), 42–51.
10. Jay Reise, "Late Skriabin: Some Principles Behind the Style," *19th-Century Music*, vi.3 (1983), 220–31.

CHAPTER 10

1. See Victor Miesel, *German Voices of Expressionism* (1970), 6.
2. A. Strindberg, *Plays*, trans. Edwin Björkman (New York: C. Scribners, 1912). See also A. Strindberg, *Five Plays*, trans. H.G. Carlson (1983).
3. Cf. John C. Crawford, "Schoenberg's Artistic Development to 1911," in J. Hahl-Koch, ed., *Schoenberg/Kandinsky*, Eng. trans. J. Crawford (1984), 185.
4. Cf. Robert Craft, "*Erwartung*: Notes on the Dramatic Structure" in notes to Columbia Record 2S 679.
5. Philip Friedheim, "Wagner and the Aesthetics of the Scream," *19th Century Music*, vii (Summer 1983), 63–79. Friedheim traces a lineage from Wagner through Strauss's *Elektra* to Schoenberg's *Pierrot lunaire* without mentioning, however, Exs. 10.2 and 10.3.
6. Charles Rosen, *Arnold Schoenberg* (1975), 39, fn 8.
7. Pierre Boulez, "Speaking, Playing Singing: *Pierrot lunaire* and *Le Marteau sans maître*" in *Orientations* (1986), 335–36.
8. Willi Reich, *Schoenberg: a critical biography* (1969); Eng. trans. Leo Black (New York: Praeger, 1971), 76.
9. Reich, *op. cit.*, 77–8.
10. See *La Revue musicale* (December, 1938), 70–1. Trans. in Orenstein, *Ravel: Man and Musician*, 74. Copyright © 1975, Columbia University Press. By permission.
11. Donald Harris, "Ravel Visits the *Verein*: Alban Berg's Report," *Journal of the Arnold Schoenberg Institute*, iii (March 1978), 75–82.
12. Maurice Ravel, "Contemporary Music," *Rice Institute Pamphlets*, xv (1928), 141. Reprinted by permission of *Rice University Studies*. See also Ravel, "Une Conférence de Maurice Ravel à Houston (1928)" with an introduction by Bohdan Pilarski, *Revue de musicologie*, 1 (1964), 218.

CHAPTER 11

1. Igor Stravinsky and Robert Craft, *Expositions and Developments* (Garden City, NY: Doubleday, 1962), 163.
2. See Richard Taruskin, "How the Acorn Took Root: A Tale of Russia," *19th Century Music*, vi.3 (1983), 189–212.
3. Collections of Russian folkmusic had appeared as early as L'vov and Prach's edition of 1790, but in the nineteenth century their number becomes legion. Balakirev's anthology dates from 1866; others are by Tchaikovsky, 1869–77; Istomin and Liaponov, 1893; Juskiewicz, 1900. Lyadov began collecting officially in 1897 and published numerous melodies and arrangements.
4. N. Rimsky-Korsakov, *My Musical Life* (3rd ed., trans. Judah A. Joffe, ed. Carl Van Vechten, New York: Alfred A. Knopf, 1942), 208. Reprinted by permission.
5. Gerald Abraham, "Rimsky-Korsakov," *New Grove Dictionary of Music and Musicians* (London: Macmillan, 1980), XVI, 29.
6. Rimsky-Korsakov, *op. cit.*, 201. Reprinted by permission.
7. Richard Taruskin, "From Subject to Style: Stravinsky and the Painters," *Confronting Stravinsky*, ed. J. Pasler (1986), 27.
8. Camilla Gray, *The Great Experiment: Russian Art, 1863-1922* (London: Thames and Hudson, 1962), 48–9.
9. Quoted from Eric Walter White, *Stravinsky: The Composer and His Music* (Berkeley: University of California Press, 1966), 158–9, which combines the 1911 synopsis and a general note printed in the score.

10. Based on Frederick W. Sternfeld, "Some Russian Folk Songs in Stravinsky's *Petrouchka,*" *Music Library Association Notes,* ii (1945), 98–104; reprinted in Norton Critical Score of *Petrushka* (1967), ed. Charles Hamm, 203–215.
11. Simon Karlinsky, "Stravinsky and Russian Pre-Literate Theater," *19th Century Music,* vi.3 (1983), 232–40.
12. See Vera Stravinsky and Robert Craft, *Stravinsky in Pictures and Documents* (1978), Plate 2, for a facsimile.
13. Karlinsky, *loc. cit.*
14. The four scenarios are given in Vera Stravinsky and Robert Craft, *Stravinsky in Pictures and Documents* (New York: Simon and Schuster, 1978), 75, 77, 92. For an examination of Roerich's contributions to *The Rite of Spring,* see Richard Taruskin, "*The Rite* Revisited: The Idea and Sources of the Scenario," *Music and Civilization: Essays in Honor of Paul Henry Lang,* ed. Maria Rika Maniates and Edmond Strainchamps (New York, 1984), 183–202.
15. Reprinted in Igor Stravinsky and Robert Craft, *Expositions and Developments* (1962), 159–69.
16. R. Taruskin, "From Subject to Style: Stravinsky and the Painters," *Confronting Stravinsky,* ed. J. Pasler (Berkeley, Calif.,: University of California Press, 1986), 28.
17. Elmer Schönberger and Louis Andriessen, "The Utopian Unison," *Confronting Stravinsky,* ed. J. Pasler (1986), 207.
18. Stravinsky's claim that the only folktune quotation in *The Rite* was the opening bassoon melody was never challenged until after his death. Two studies by Lawrence Morton (1979) and Richard Taruskin (1980) permanently changed this view. See *Readings* at the end of this chapter (p. 231).
19. For a discussion, see van den Toorn, *The Music of Igor Stravinsky* (1983), 151, 161. For a demonstration of diatonic-octatonic linkage in *Les noces,* see the present volume, pp. 228–29.
20. Pierre Boulez, "Stravinsky Remains," *Notes of an Apprenticeship* (1968), 72–145; see especially 125–7.
21. Vera Stravinsky and Robert Craft, *Stravinsky in Pictures and Documents* (New York: Simon and Schuster, 1978), 65.
22. Pierre Boulez, "Stravinsky: *The Rite of Spring*" in *Orientations* (Cambridge, Mass.: Harvard University Press, 1986), 363. English translation by Felix Aprahamian.
23. All musical examples and sources based upon Lawrence Morton, "Footnotes to Stravinsky Studies: 'Le Sacre du Printemps,'" *Tempo,* cxxviii (1979), 9–16.
24. Igor Stravinsky and Robert Craft, *Expositions and Developments* (Garden City, NY: Doubleday, 1962), 137–8.
25. See V. Stravinsky and R. Craft, *op. cit.,* 107, for a facsimile of the sketch.
26. I. Stravinsky, *An Autobiography* (New York, 1936), 45. For a consideration of the original Japanese texts and the background for these songs, see Takashi Funayama, "*Three Japanese Lyrics* and Japonisme," *Confronting Stravinsky,* ed. J. Pasler (1986), 273.
27. A term introduced by Nicholas Slonimsky (*Music Since 1900,* 1937, xxii) to connote a style based on diatonic materials without the support of functional harmony. An emphasis on counterpoint and rhythm is frequently a direct result.
28. Peter van den Toorn, *The Music of Igor Stravinsky* (1983), 155–77.

CHAPTER 12

1. Filippo T. Marinetti, *The Founding and Manifesto of Futurism* (1909) as translated in *Marinetti: Selected Writings,* ed. R. W. Flint, trans. R. W. Flint and A. Coppotelli (New York: Farrar, Straus and Giroux, 1971), 42.
2. *Ibid.,* 69–70.
3. Umbro Apollonio, ed., *Futurist Manifestos* (London: Thames and Hudson, 1973), 74, 88. Trans. by Caroline Tisdall. Reprinted by permission. Of the three excerpts presented here, only the first and third appear as in Apollonio. The second is rephrased.
4. Caroline Tisdall and Angelo Bozzolo, *Futurism* (London: Thames and Hudson, 1977), 118. Reprinted by permission.

5. *Ibid.*, 119.
6. For examples see pages 568, 570, 590, 591, 616, 620, 629.
7. C. Gray, *The Great Experiment: Russian Art, 1863–1922* (1962), 124.
8. For a detailed discussion by Stravinsky of his relation with Futurist personalities Boccioni, Russolo, Carrà, Marinetti and Pratella see I. Stravinsky and R. Craft, *Conversations* (Garden City, NY: Doubleday, 1959), 103–105.
9. Nigel Wilkins, ed., *The Writings of Erik Satie* (London: Eulenburg Books, 1980), 96.
10. *The New York Times* (Nov. 20, 1983), 21, 24.
11. Victor Seroff, *Sergei Prokofiev* (New York: Funk and Wagnalls, 1968), 133.
12. Henry Cowell, *New Musical Resources* (1930). For excerpts see Weiss-Taruskin, eds., *Music in the Western World* (1984), 483–87.
13. See Rita Mead, *Henry Cowell's New Music 1925–36: The Society, the Music Editions, and the Recordings* (1981).

CHAPTER 13

1. Arbie Orenstein, *Ravel, Man and Musician* (New York: Columbia University Press, 1975), 162–5.
2. It is worth remembering when considering Stravinsky's and Satie's reductive keyboard style that Florent Schmitt also wrote a group of piano pieces in 1907 entitled *Sur cinq notes* and that the opening work of Debussy's set of twelve *Etudes* of 1915 is entitled "Pour les cinq doigts."
3. Erik Satie, *Sports et Divertissements* (Paris: Lucien Vogel, c. 1925; reprinted New York: Dover Publications, Inc., 1982, with English trans. by Stanley Appelbaum).
4. Margaret Crosland, ed. and trans., *Cocteau's World: An Anthology of Writings by Jean Cocteau*, (New York: Dodd, Mead, 1972), 309.
5. Frederick Brown, *An Impersonation of Angels: A Biography of Jean Cocteau* (New York: Viking Press, 1968), 128–9.
6. Igor Stravinsky and Robert Craft, *Expositions and Developments* (Garden City, NY: Doubleday, 1962), 103–4.
7. Nigel Wilkins, ed., *The Writings of Erik Satie* (London: Eulenburg Books, 1980), 84.
8. Because of its great height a telegraph antenna had been installed on the Eiffel Tower.
9. Jean Cocteau, *The Infernal Machine and other plays* (1963), 165–7. Copyright © 1963 by New Directions Publishing Corporation. Reprinted by permission.
10. *Ibid.*, 155.
11. F. Brown, *An Impersonation of Angels* (1968), 205.
12. Trans. in Robert Hughes, *The Shock of the New* (New York: Alfred A. Knopf, 1980), 38. Reprinted by permission.
13. A. Knight, *Encyclopedia Brittanica* (1968), XX, 221.
14. Francis Poulenc, *Moi et mes amis* (1963), Eng. trans. J. Harding, *My Friends and Myself* (London: Dennis Dobson, 1978), 31.
15. Darius Milhaud, *Notes Without Music*, trans. Donald Evans, ed. Rollo H. Myers (New York: Alfred A. Knopf, 1953), 101–3. Reprinted by permission.
16. See Jean Wiéner, *Allegro Appasionato* (1978), 44.
17. Published in *L'Esprit Nouveau*, 25 (1924), n.p.
18. Maurice Ravel, "Contemporary Music," *Rice Institute Pamphlets*, xv (1928), 140. Reprinted by permission of *Rice University Studies*.
19. *Ibid.*, 138.
20. See N. Wilkins, *op. cit.*, 66, for a reproduction.

CHAPTER 14

1. See Susan Cook, *Weimar Opera During the Third Repubic: Ernst Krenek, Kurt Weill, Paul Hindemith and Zeitoper* (PhD dissertation, University of Michigan, 1985), Chapter IV, "The Social and Musical Influence of Jazz," 107–187.
2. Virgil Thomson, *A Virgil Thomson Reader*, 15–18. Copyright © 1981 by Virgil Thomson. Reprinted by permission of Houghton Mifflin Company.
3. Darius Milhaud, *Notes Without Music* (New York: Alfred A. Knopf, 1953), 136.

4. Adolphe Weissman, "La jeune musique Allemande et Paul Hindemith," *L'Esprit Nouveau*, nos. 20, 22 (1925), n.p., cited and trans. in S. Cook, *op. cit.*, 347.
5. S. Cook, *op. cit.*, 344.
6. For a comprehensive treatment of *Jonny spielt auf*, see S. Cook, *op. cit.*, Chapter V, 188–267.
7. Ernst Krenek, *Horizons Circled* (Berkeley: University of California Press, 1974), 26.
8. The English translation is by Krenek except for the bracketed expressions, which the composer leaves untranslated from the French in his English version.
9. Olin Downes, "The Generation of Krenek," *The New York Times*, February 28, 1929.
10. For the Weill-Schoenberg relationship, see the Editor's Preface to Alan Chapman's "Crossing the Cusp: The Schoenberg Connection" in *A New Orpheus: Essays on Kurt Weill*, ed. Kim H. Kowalke (1986), 103–06.
11. Stephen Hinton, "Weill: *Neue Sachlichkeit*, Surrealism, and *Gebrauchsmusik*" in *A New Orpheus: Essays on Kurt Weill*, fn. 32, 76.
12. Alexander L. Ringer, "*Kleinkunst* and *Küchenlied* in the Socio-Musical World of Kurt Weill" in *A New Orpheus: Essays on Kurt Weill*, 39.
13. Douglas Jarman, *Kurt Weill* (1982), 36.
14. Susan C. Cook, "*Der Zar lässt sich photographieren:* Weill and Comic Opera" in *A New Orpheus: Essay on Kurt Weill*, 83–101.
15. Douglas Jarman, *Kurt Weill* (Bloomington: Indiana University Press, 1982), 109.
16. Stephen Hinton, "Weill: *Neue Sachlichkeit*, Surrealism, and *Gebrauchsmusik*" in *A New Orpheus: Essays on Kurt Weill*, 61–82.
17. *Ibid.*, 108–09.
18. See *Alban Berg: Letters to His Wife*, ed., trans., and annotated by B. Grun (1971), 363.

CHAPTER 15

1. Jean Moréas, *Les Syrtes* (1892), 53–4. Trans. by Scott Messing in *Neo-Classicism: The Origins of the Term and its Use in the Schoenberg/Stravinsky Polemic in the 1920's* (PhD dissertation, University of Michigan, 1986), 22.
2. The movement was summed up on Dénis's *Théories: Du symbolisme et de Gaugin vers un nouvel ordre classique* of 1912.
3. Alexandre Benois, *Reminiscences of the Russian Ballet*, trans. M. Britnieva (1977), 349.
4. Eric Walter White, *Stravinsky* (Berkeley: University of California Press, 1979), 588.
5. Guillaume Apollinaire, "L'esprit nouveau et les poets" in *Mercure de France*, December 1, 1918.
6. Igor Stravinsky, *Autobiography* (New York: Simon and Schuster, 1936), 93.
7. Igor Stravinsky and Robert Craft, *Expositions and Developments* (Garden City, NY: Doubleday, 1962), 128–9.
8. Egon Wellesz, "Die jüngste Entwicklung der neufranzösischen Musik," *Der Merker*, ii.6 (May, 1911), 656–65.
9. E. Wellesz, "Maurice Ravel,"*Anbruch*, October, 1920, as translated and discussed in S. Messing, *Neo-Classicism: The Origins of the Term and its Use in the Schoenberg/Stravinsky Polemic in the 1920's* (PhD dissertation, University of Michigan, 1986), 164.
10. Michel Georges-Michel, *Ballets Russes: Histoires Anecdotique* (1923), 8, as trans. in Messing, *op. cit.*, 183.
11. Igor Stravinsky, *Selected Correspondence*, vol. I, ed. Robert Craft (1982), 160.
12. Boris de Schloezer, "La musique" in *Revue contemporaine* (February 1, 1923), 257. See Messing, *op. cit.*, 1–2.
13. Landowska's "How to Interpret Bach's Inventions" had appeared in *Le monde musical* in July, 1921, and in an enlarged version in September, 1922.
14. Igor Stravinsky and Robert Craft, *Conversations* (Garden City, NY: Doubleday, 1959), 18.
15. Igor Stravinsky and Robert Craft, *Memories and Commentaries* (Garden City, NY: Doubleday, 1960), 145.
16. *Ibid.*, 148.

17. Igor Stravinsky and Robert Craft, *Expositions and Developments* (Garden City, NY: Doubleday, 1962), 88.

18. Glenn Watkins, "The Canon and Stravinsky's Late Style" in *Confronting Stravinsky: Man, Musician and Modernist*, ed. J. Pasler (Berkeley: University of California Press, 1986), 241–43.

19. Igor Stravinsky and Robert Craft, *Conversations* (Garden City, NY: Doubleday, 1959), 142.

20. See Messing, *op. cit.*, 35–37, and the pertinent criticisms of Wolf. 1881; R. Roland, 1902, 1908; Dukas, 1904; and d'Indy, 1902.

21. Preface to *Three Satires*, op. 28. Used by permission Belmont Music Publishers. English translation in Willi Reich, *Schoenberg: a critical biography*, trans. Leo Black (London: Longman Group, 1971), 153–54.

22. Arnold Schoenberg, "My Evolution" in *Style and Idea*, ed. Leonard Stein (New York: St. Martin's Press, 1975), 88.

23. Ernst Krenek, *Horizons Circled* (Berkeley: University of California Press, 1974), 29.

24. Glenn Watkins, "Schoenberg and the Organ" in *Perspectives on Schoenberg and Stravinsky* (Princeton: Princeton University Press, 1968), 100–104.

25. Arnold Schoenberg, "Variations for Orchestra, op. 31," *The Score* (July, 1960), 33.

26. In the performances directed by Kandinsky of Musorgsky's *Pictures at an Exhibition* in 1928, the images for some of the sets which he designed were built up gradually by assembling the component parts. The final scene, *The Great Gate of Kiev* (Figure 15.4), "began with side elements and twelve props representing abstract figures, to which were added successively the arch, the towered Russian city and the back drop, each lowered slowly from above. At the end these were raised, the lighting became a strong red and was then extinguished. . . " See Clark V. Poling, introductory essay to *Kandinsky: Russian and Bauhaus Years, 1915-1933* (New York: The Solomon R. Guggenheim Museum, 1983), 72. For earlier parallels between Schoenberg and Kandinsky, see pp. 159–60, 170–72.

27. Pierre Boulez, *Conversations with Célestin Deliège* (London: Eulenburg Books, 1976), 31.

28. Charles Rosen, *Arnold Schoenberg* (1975), 70–105. But see also A. Lessem, "Schoenberg, Stravinsky, and Neo-Classicism: The Issues Reexamined," *Musical Quarterly*, lxvii.4 (1982), 527–42.

29. See Schoenberg Archives, Rufer II.D.34 and II.C.100, and Messing, *op. cit.*, 322.

30. Arnold Schoenberg, "How One Becomes Lonely" in *Style and Idea*, ed. Leonard Stein (New York: St. Martin's Press, 1975), 52.

31. Milton Babbitt, *Perspectives of New Music*, ix.2 and x.1 (1971), 106–7.

32. Igor Stravinsky and Robert Craft, *Memories and Commentaries* (Garden City, NY: Doubleday, 1960), 117–18.

33. Geoffrey Skelton, *Paul Hindemith* (London: Victor Gollancz, 1975), 120–1.

34. Skelton, *op. cit.*, 235–6.

35. See Hindemith's discussion of "Atonality and Polytonality" in *The Craft of Musical Composition*, trans. Arthur Mendel (1942), 152–6.

CHAPTER 17

1. Hans Redlich, *Alban Berg: The Man and His Music* (London: John Calder, 1957), 271.

2. Willi Reich, "Ein unbekannten Briefen von Alban Berg an Anton Webern," *Schweizerische Musikzeitung*, xciii.2 (February, 1953), 50, as trans. in G. Perle, *The Operas of Alban Berg*, vol. I: *Wozzeck* (Berkeley: University of California Press, 1980), 20.

3. Willi Reich, "A Guide to Wozzeck," *Musical Quarterly*, xxxviii (January, 1952), 1–21.

4. The names of the leitmotifs are those used by George Perle in his study, *The Operas of Alban Berg*, vol. I: *Wozzeck* (Berkeley: University of California Press, 1980).

5. See Douglas Jarman, *The Music of Alban Berg* (Berkeley: University of California Press, 1979), 184, for an amplification of this diagram.

6. The following discussion was developed by the author and distributed in print to students as early as 1981. Jarman's article, "The Secret Program of the Violin

Concerto" (1982, see Reading List at end of Chapter) was the earliest published discussion and includes one refinement incorporated here concerning the nickname of Berg's Carinthian girlfriend. Jarman also presents an elaborate discussion of numerology with far-reaching implications beyond the Violin Concerto.

7. Hans Redlich, *Alban Berg* (1957), 203–214.
8. Herwig Knaus, "Berg's Carinthian Folk Tune," Eng. trans. Mosco Carner in *Musical Times*, cxvii (June 1976), 487.
9. Karen Monson, *Alban Berg* (1979), 17–18.
10. See Kirk Varnedoe, "Dreams and Sexuality" in pamphlet for *Vienna 1900: Art, Architecture and Design* (The Museum of Modern Art, New York, July 31–October 21, 1986), 10.
11. Alma Mahler, *And the Bridge is Love* (New York: Harcourt Brace Jovanovich, 1958), 135. Author's italics.
12. For the complete text with an English translation by Susan Davies see Douglas Jarman, *The Music of Alban Berg* (Berkeley: University of California Press, 1979), 245–8.

CHAPTER 18

1. Anton Webern, *The Path to Twelve-Note Composition*, ed. Willi Reich, Eng. trans. Leo Black (Bryn Mawr: Theodore Presser, 1963), 60.
2. Igor Stravinsky and Robert Craft, *Memories and Commentaries* (Garden City, NY: Doubleday, 1960), 98.

CHAPTER 19

1. E. Lendvai, *Béla Bartók: an Analysis of his Music* (1971).
2. *Documenta Bartókiana*, Vol. 5, 100, in French; Eng. trans. by author.
3. E. von der Nüll, *Béla Bartók: ein Beitrag zur Morphologie der neuen Musik* (1930), 108.
4. Benjamin Suchoff, ed., *Béla Bartók Essays* (London: Faber and Faber, 1976), 346.
5. As quoted in F. Bónis, "Quotations in Bartók's Music," *Studia musicologia Academiae scientiarum hungaricae*, v (1963), 355.

CHAPTER 20

1. The complete text is printed in Nicolas Slonimsky, ed., *Music Since 1900*, 4th ed. (1971), 1353–57.
2. For the complete text of the letter, see N. Slonimsky, ed., *op. cit.*, 1373–74.
3. Royal S. Brown, "The Three Faces of Lady Macbeth" in *Russian and Soviet Music: Essays for Boris Scwarz* (1984), 246.
4. Boris Schwarz, *Music and Musical Life in Soviet Russia, 1917–1981* (Bloomington: Indiana University Press, 1983), 171.
5. Notes to Columbia/Melodyia M 34507.

CHAPTER 21

1. Ralph Vaughan Williams, *National Music and Other Essays* (Oxford: Oxford University Press, 1963).
2. *Ibid.*, 190.
3. William P. Malm, "The Noh Play *Sumidagawa* and Benjamin Britten's *Curlew River*— One Story in Two Musical Worlds" in *Six Hidden Views of Japanese Music* (Berkeley, 1986), 151.

CHAPTER 22

1. Quoted in Henry and Sidney Cowell, *Charles Ives and His Music* (New York: Oxford University Press, 1955), 114n.
2. Quoted in John Kirpatrick's preface to the published score (New York: Associated Music Publishers, 1965), viii; also includes quotations for following movements.

3. Quotation of hymn tunes in original keys, not as found in Ives.

4. Charles Ives, *Essays Before a Sonata and Other Writings*, ed. by Howard Boatwright (New York: W. W. Norton, 1962), 47–48.

5. See Rita Mead, *Henry Cowell's New Music, 1925–1936: The Society, the Music Editions, and the Recordings* (1981).

6. Aaron Copland and Vivian Perlis, *Copland, 1900 through 1942* (New York: St. Martin's/Marek, 1984), 32.

7. *Ibid.*, 44.

8. *Ibid.*, 104.

9. Aaron Copland, "Jazz Structure and Influence," *Modern Music*, iv.2 (January–February 1927), 9–14.

10. For a complete listing of the Copland-Sessions Concerts programs see Carol Oja, "The Copland-Sessions Concerts and Their Reception in the Contemporary Press," *Musical Quarterly*, lxv.2 (April 1979), 227–9.

11. Copland-Perlis, *op. cit.*, 182. Copyright 1984 by St. Martin's/Marek.

12. Copland-Perlis, *op. cit.*, 201. Copyright 1984 by St. Martin's/Marek.

13. *Ibid.*, "Interlude III," 207–230, contains especially right information concerning this issue.

14. *Ibid.*, 357–362, for de Mille's account.

15. Brinnin, *The Third Rose* (New York: Little, Brown, 1959), 240.

16. Virgil Thomson, *Virgil Thomson* (New York: Alfred A. Knopf, 1966), 95. Reprinted by permission of the publisher.

17. M. Raymond, *From Baudelaire to Surrealism* (1950), 271.

18. John Cage and Kathleen Hoover, *Virgil Thomson* (1959), 157.

19. Virgil Thomson, "French Music Here," in *A Virgil Thomson Reader*, 207–210. Copyright 1981 by Virgil Thomson. Reprinted by permission of Houghton Mifflin Company.

20. Virgil Thomson, "On Being American," in *A Virgil Thomson Reader*, 304–306.

21. Virgil Thomson, "Modernism Today," in *Music Reviewed 1940–1954* (1967), 23–33.

22. Notes to Columbia Records ML 5843.

23. George Antheil, *Bad Boy of Music* (Garden City, NY: Doubleday, 1945), 61.

CHAPTER 23

1. Arbie Orenstein, *Ravel, Man and Musician*, 73. Copyright 1975, Columbia University Press. By permission.

2. *Alban Berg: Letters to his Wife*, ed., trans. B. Grun (New York: St. Martin's Press, 1971), 170.

3. *Stravinsky: Selected Correspondence*, vol. I, ed. R. Craft (1982), 99–100.

4. Vera Stravinsky and Robert Craft, *Stravinsky in Pictures and Documents* (1978), 222, reprints the letter and contains a discussion of the point in question.

5. Eric Walter White, *Stravinsky* (Berkeley: University of California Press, 1979), 328.

6. Roger Nichols, *Messiaen* (London: Oxford University Press, 1975), 8.

7. R. S. Johnson, *Messiaen* (Berkeley: University of California Press, 1975), 14.

8. Based on descriptions in Harry Halbreich, *Olivier Messiaen* (Paris: Fayard, Foundation SACEM, 1980), 139–140.

9. Arnold Schoenberg, *Letters*, ed. E. Stein (1958); Eng. trans. Leo Black (London: Faber and Faber, 1964), no. 153.

10. Willi Reich, *Schoenberg: a critical biography* (1968; Eng. trans. L. Black, London: Longman, 1971), 189–190.

11. Oliver Neighbour, "Arnold Schoenberg" in *The New Grove Dictionary of Music and Musicians*, vol. 16, 706–8.

12. Arnold Schoenberg, "On revient toujours," *Style and Idea*, ed. L. Stein (New York: St. Martin's Press, 1975), 109.

13. Luigi Dallapiccola, "The Genesis of the *Canti di prigionia* and *Il prigioniero*," *Musical Quarterly*, xxxix (1953), 355.

14. *Ibid.*

15. Ursula Vaughan Williams, *R.V.W.: A Biography of Ralph Vaughan Williams* (1964), 29. For a general discussion of Vaughan Williams's nationalist tendencies, see p. 424ff of the present book.

16. Igor Stravinsky and Robert Craft, *Dialogues and a Diary* (Garden City, NY: Doubleday, 1968), 50–52.
17. Notes to Columbia Record CBS 32 11 CC48.
18. Notes to Columbia Record MA 7315.
19. Open letter "To the International Music Council," November 21, 1984.

CHAPTER 24

1. Pierre Boulez, "Propositions" in *Polyphonie* (1948); reprinted as "Proposals" in *Notes of an Apprenticeship* (1968), 66–71.
2. Pierre Boulez, "Schoenberg is Dead," *The Score* (May 1952), 18–22; reprinted in *Relevés d'apprenti* (Paris: Editions du Seuil, 1966), and *Notes of an Apprenticeship* (1968), Eng. trans. Herbert Weinstock. Copyright by Editions du Seuil, 1966. Reprinted by permission.
3. See Ligeti's analysis, *Die Reihe* (Eng. trans. 1960), vol. 4, p. 38, for the double matrix, which is here combined into one.
4. Lev Koblyakov, "P. Boulez, 'Le Marteau sans maître,' Analysis of Pitch Structure," *Zeitschrift für Musiktheorie*, vii.1 (1977), 24–39.
5. See especially Fred Lerdahl, "Cognitive Constraints on Compositional Systems" in John Sloboda, ed., *Generative Processes in Music* (New York: Oxford University Press, 1987) for a consideration of the constraints of both a compositional and a listening grammar utilized by Boulez in writing *Le marteau sans maître*.
6. Pierre Boulez, "Speaking, Playing, Singing: *Pierrot lunaire* and *Le marteau sans maître*" in *Orientations* (Cambridge, Mass.: Harvard University Press, 1986), 341. Originally published as "Dire, jouer, chanter," *Cahiers Renaud-Barrault*, xli (1963), 300–21.
7. Communication from the composer. The *New Grove Dictionary of Music* incorrectly states that "timbre stands outside the scope of serial organization" in *Kreuzspiel*.
8. See J. Harvey, *The Music of Stockhausen* (1975), 59–61, for a discussion of this work.
9. See Ian D. Bent, "Analysis" in *New Groves Dictionary of Music and Musicians* (1980) for a highly informative overview.
10. Luciano Berio, *Two Interviews* (1985), 18–19.
11. *Ibid.*, 77.
12. David Gable, "Ramifying Connections: An Interview with Pierre Boulez, *Journal of Musicology*, iv.1 (Winter 1985–86), 111.
13. Pierre Boulez, *Conversations with Célestin Deliège* (1975; Eng. trans. 1976), 62.
14. Leonard B. Meyer, *Music, The Arts, and Ideas* (1967).
15. C. Lévi-Strauss, *Le cru et le cuit* (1964; Eng. trans., 1970), 31ff.
16. N. Ruwet, "Contradictions du langage sérial," *Revue belge de musicologie*, xiii (1959), 83.

CHAPTER 25

1. Jacob Druckman in C. Gagne and T. Caras, *Soundpieces: Interviews with American Composers* (Metuchen, NY: Scarecrow Press, 1982), 156.
2. George Perle has made an extensive analysis of the work in *Serial Composition and Atonality* (1962, 4th ed. 1978), 99–101, 135–6, 139–41.
3. See Peter Westergaard, "Some Problems Raised by the Rhythmic Serialism in Milton Babbitt's Composition for Twelve Instruments," *Perspectives of New Music*, iv.1 (1965), 109–188.
4. *The Score*, xii (June 1955), 54–61.
5. M. Babbitt, "Who Cares if You Listen?", *High Fidelity*, viii.2 (February 1958), 38–40, 126–7; reprinted in *Contemporary Composers on Contemporary Music*, ed. E. Schwartz and B. Childs, eds. (1967), and *Music in the Western World*, P. Weiss and R. Taruskin, eds. (1984), 529–34. It should be noted that the provocative sounding title was not by Babbitt, who had originally submitted the article as "The Composer as Specialist." See the interview with Babbitt in C. Gagne and T. Caras, *Soundpieces* (1982), 36–38.
6. For a "Statement of Aims of the Society" see N. Slonimsky, ed., *Music Since 1900*, 4th ed. (1971), 1307–8.

7. Milton Babbitt, "On Relata I" in *The Orchestral Composer's Point of View: Essays on Twentieth-Century Music by Those Who Wrote it* (1970), 22, ed. Robert S. Hines, with an Introduction by William Schuman. Copyright 1970 by the University of Oklahoma Press.
8. Roger Sessions, "Music in Crisis: Some Notes on Recent Musical History," *Modern Music*, x (1932–33), 63–78.
9. *Musical Quarterly*, xlvi (1960), 159–71.
10. Notes to Columbia Record MS 7431.
11. Notes to Columbia Record M 32737.
12. Aaron Copland and Vivian Perlis, *Copland, 1900 through 1942* (New York: St. Martin's/Marek, 1984), 209.
13. Notes to Nonesuch Record H-71283.
14. Notes to Nonesuch Record H-71319. Used by permission.
15. Notes to Columbia Record M 32738.
16. *Ibid.*
17. Allen Edwards, *Flawed Words and Stubborn Sounds: A Conversation with Elliott Carter* (New York: W. W. Norton, 1971), 90–94.

CHAPTER 26

1. Conversation with the author, Fontainbleau, Summer 1956.
2. Luciano Berio, *Two Interviews* (with Rossana Dalmonte and Bálint András Varga), trans. and ed. David Osmond-Smith (New York: Marion Boyars, 1985), 65.
3. Glenn Watkins, "The Canon and Stravinsky's Late Style" in *Confronting Stravinsky: Man, Musician and Modernist*, ed. J. Pasler (Berkeley: University of California Press, 1986), 217.
4. Igor Stravinsky and Robert Craft, *Memories and Commentaries* (Garden City, NY: Doubleday, 1960), 100–101.
5. "Khruschev on Culture," *Encounter*, Pamphlet No. 9, 29–30, quoted in Boris Schwarz, *Music and Musical Life in Soviet Russia, 1917–1981* (Bloomington: Indiana University Press, 1983), 418.
6. *Current Digest of the Soviet Press*, XX, no. 20, p. 21; original in *Pravda*. 18 May 1968. Translation copyright 1968 by *The Current Digest of the Soviet Press*, Columbus, Ohio. Reprinted by permission of *The Current Digest*.
7. An interview with Natalia Lagina in *Yunost*, May 5, 1968; condensed English translation in *Current Digest of the Soviet Press*, XX, no. 24, p. 16. Translation Copyright 1968 by *The Current Digest of the Soviet Press*, Columbus, Ohio. Reprinted by permission of *The Current Digest*.

CHAPTER 27

1. Charles Baudelaire, "Exposition universelle, 1855, Beaux-arts: I. Méthode de critique. De l'idée moderne du progrès appliquée aux beaux-arts," *Oeuvres complètes* (Paris: Éditions Gallimard, 1976), 577–78.
2. Pierre Boulez, "Sonate, que me veux-tu?" (1960), reprinted in *Orientations* Cambridge, Mass.: Harvard University Press, 1986), 144–45.
3. Pierre Boulez, *Boulez on Music Today* (Paris, 1963; Eng. trans. 1971), 26. Copyright 1971, Harvard University Press. Reprinted by permission of the publisher.
4. John Cage, *Silence*, 274. Copyright © 1961. Reprinted from *Silence* by permission of Wesleyan University Press.
5. *Ibid.*, 76.
6. Originally in *Revue musicale*, 1952; Eng. trans in *Notes of an Apprenticeship* (New York: Knopf, 1968), 175. Copyright 1966 by Les Editions du Seuil, S.A.
7. Pierre Boulez, "Aléa," *Nouvelle Revue Française*, no. 59, November 1, 1957; Eng. trans. in *Perspectives of New Music*, iii.1 (1964), 42–53, and in *Notes of an Apprenticeship* (New York: Knopf, 1968), 35–51. Copyright 1966 by Les Editions du Seuil, S. A.
8. John Cage, *Silence*, 36. Copyright © 1961. Reprinted from *Silence* by permission of Wesleyan University Press.
9. Pierre Boulez, "Aléa," *loc. cit.* Copyright 1966 by Les Editions du Seuil, S.A.

10. Robin Maconie, *The Works of Karlheinz Stockhausen* (London: Oxford University Press, 1976), 97.
11. Ekbert Faas, "Interview with Karlheinz Stockhausen Held August 11, 1976," *Interface,* vi (1977), 191.
12. Antoine Goléa, *Recontres avec Pierre Boulez* (1958), 229.
13. See Anne Trenkamp, "The Concept of 'Aléa' in Boulez's *Constellation-Miroir*," *Music and Letters,* lvii.1 (January 1976), 1–10; and P. Boulez, "Sonate, que me veux-tu?," trans. D. Noakes and P. Jacobs in *Perspectives of New Music,* 1/2 (1963), 32–94.
14. John Cage, *Silence* (Weslyan University Press, 1961), 39.
15. Pierre Boulez, *Conversations with Célestin Deliège* (London: Eulenburg Books, 1976), 105.
16. K. H. Wörner, *Stockhausen: His Life and Work,* trans. and ed. Bill Hopkins (Berkeley: University of California Press, 1973), 110. See also Stockhausen's "Momentform" in *Texte,* i (1963), 189–210.
17. A. Edwards, *Flawed Words and Stubborn Sounds: A Conversation With Elliott Carter* (New York: W.W. Norton, 1971), 94.
18. Communication to the author concerning corrections to the *New Grove Dictionary of Music* (1980).
19. John Cage, notes to Nonesuch Record H-71202.
20. John Cage, *Silence* (Weslyan University Press, 1961), 7–8. Reprinted by permission of the publisher.
21. Notes from Deutsche Grammophon Record DGG 2530 255.
22. Notes from Deutsche Grammophon Record DGG 2707 123.
23. "Ars Polona," Warsaw. From notes to Philips Record PHS 900-159.
24. Notes to Columbia Record MH 7178.
25. Notes to Angel Record S 36059.
26. Steve Reich, "Music As a Gradual Process" (1968) in *Writings About Music* (University of Nova Scotia Press, 1974), 9–11. Reprinted by permission of the publisher.
27. Notes to Decca, HEAD-12.

CHAPTER 28

1. Glenn Watkins, "Schoenberg and the Organ," *Perspectives on Schoenberg and Stravinsky* (Princeton University Press, 1968), 93.
2. For a "Chronological List of Pre-1948 Events Related to Electronic Music," see D. Ernst, *The Evolution of Electronic Music* (1977), xxxvii-xl.
3. See Richard James, *Expansion of Sound Resources in France, 1913–1940, and its Relationship to Electronic Music* (PhD dissertation, University of Michigan, 1981), 107–111.
4. David Cope, *New Directions in Music* (1980), 140–141.
5. Gunther Schuller, "Conversation with Varèse," *Perspectives of New Music,* iii.2 (Spring-Summer 1965), 36–7. By permission of the publisher and author.
6. David Ernst, *The Evolution of Electronic Music* (1977), 42. See also E. Varèse, "Spatial Music," 204–07, and "The Electronic Medium," 207–08, in *Contemporary Composers on Contemporary Music,* ed. E. Schwartz and B. Childs (1967).
7. C. E. Jeanneret-Gris, *Le poème électronique/Le Corbusier* (Editions de Minuit, 1958).
8. *Gravesander Blätter,* no. 1 (1955), 2.
9. Communication to the author regarding corrections to the article on Stockhausen in the *New Grove Dictionary.*
10. See note 9.
11. See note 9.
12. Richard Kostelanetz, ed., *John Cage* (New York: Praeger, 1970), 19.
13. Michael Nyman, *Experimental Music: Cage and Beyond* (New York: Schirmer Books, 1974), 110, By permission of the publisher.
14. Warsaw Autumn '84 Booklet: 27th International Festival of Contemporary Music, Warsaw (September 20-28, 1984), 21.
15. *Ibid.,* 95.

CHAPTER 29

1. English trans., *Die Reihe,* no. 6 (1964), 40.
2. Notes to Turnabout Record TV 34046 S. Reprinted courtesy of the Moss Music Group, Inc.
3. Commentary reprinted courtesy of the composer. The original version of *Sinfonia* (1968), commissioned by the New York Philharmonic on the occasion of its 125th anniversary, was in four parts (recorded on Columbia); the extension to five parts was made in 1969 and first performed in 1970 by the Philharmonic under the direction of Leonard Bernstein (later recorded on Erato by Pierre Boulez).
4. *ASUC Proceedings 3* (1968), 43. See also Roger Reynolds, *Mind Models* (1975), 211-15.
5. Warsaw Autumn '84 Booklet, 114.
6. *Loc. cit.*
7. Notes to Wergo Records, WER 60054.
8. Notes to Nonesuch Record H-71285. Used by permission.
9. *Ibid.*
10. S. Jarocinski, ed., *Polish Music* (1965), 182-3.
11. Steven Stucky, *Lutosławski and His Music* (Cambridge University Press, 1981), 34-59.
12. Jean-Paul Couchoud, *La musique polonaise et Witold Lutosławski* (Paris: Stock Plus, 1981), 109-117; Eng. trans. G. Watkins.
13. *Ibid.*
14. Notes to Wergo Record 60019.
15. J-P. Couchoud, *op. cit.,* 47-8.
16. B. Schäffer, "A. Panufnik" in *The New Grove Dictionary of Music* (1980), XIV, 164.
17. Notes to Columbia Record M 32729.
18. Luciano Berio, *Two Interviews,* with R. Dalmonte and B.A. Varga, trans. D. Osmond-Smith (New York: Marion Boyars, 1985), 97.
19. *Ibid.,* 98.
20. Notes to Deutsche Grammophon Record DGG 137 005.
21. Paul Griffiths, *Modern Music* (1981), Ex. 63 for a sample of *Match;* Ex. 64 for an excerpt from *Evryali.*
22. Notes to Composer's Voice Record 7273-4.
23. Notes to CRI Record SD 436.

CHAPTER 30

1. Housed in the Manuscript Collection of the British Library, London.
2. Notes to Nonesuch Record H-71202. Used by permission.
3. See Paul Griffiths, *Modern Music* (1981), 204-5, for a reproduction of the passage in question.
4. Written for the bicentenary of Beethoven's birth and published in German in *Die Welt,* December 12, 1970. Complete text, "Beethoven: Tell Me," in Pierre Boulez, *Orientations* (Cambridge: Harvard University Press, 1986), 205-211.
5. Notes to CRI recording of *String Quartet No. 7.*
6. See the notes to Deutsche Grammophon Record DGG 2530 014 for an extensive and informative interview with the composer about this work.
7. Notes to Nonesuch Record H-71283. Used by permission.
8. George Rochberg, "Reflections on the Renewal of Music," *Current Musicology,* 13 (New York: Dept. of Music, Columbia University, 1972), 76. The reference is to Boulez's article, "Stravinsky: Style or Idea?—In Praise of Amnesia" of 1971, English translation in *Orientations* (1986), 349-59.
9. In the original note on Columbia Record MS 7268 Berio acknowledged the following additional references: Debussy, Ravel, Berlioz, Hindemith, Wagner, Stockhausen, Globokar, Pousseur, Ives and Berio.
10. Commentary courtesy of the composer.
11. Pierre Boulez, "Incidence actuelles de Berg" (1948), reprinted in *Notes of an Apprenticeship* (Eng. trans. 1968), as "Present-Day Encounters with Berg," 235-41. For

Boulez's more recent thoughts on Berg see *Conservations with Célestin Deliège* (Eng. trans. 1976), 17–18, 21, 23–26, 73.
12. Notes to Wergo Record 2549 005.
13. Notes to New World Record 318.
14. See "Alfred Garrijewitsch Schnittke" in *Fünfzig sowjetische Komponisten,* ed. Hannelore Gerlach (Leipzig: Edition Peters, 1984), 360–371.
15. *Ibid.,* 383–407.
16. See the booklet for the Warsaw Autumn '84 Concerts, 188–9, for a further discussion by the composer.
17. Leonard Bernstein, Preface to *The Infinite Variety of Music* (1966).
18. Leonard Bernstein, *The Unanswered Question* (Cambridge, Mass.: Harvard University Press, 1976), 421. Reprinted by permission of the publisher.
19. A. Schoenberg, "Stravinsky: Der Restaurateur" (1926) in L. Stein, ed., *Style and Idea* (1975), 481.
20. Pierre Boulez, "Stravinsky: Style or Idea?—In Praise of Amnesia," *Musique en jeu,* iv (1971); Eng. trans. in *Orientations* (1986), 349–59.
21. Glenn Watkins and Thomasin La May, "*Imitatio* and *Emulatio* in the Madrigals of Gesualdo and Monteverdi in the 1590s" in *Festschrift for Rheinhold Hammerstein* (1986), 453–88.
22. Glenn Watkins, *Gesualdo* (London: Oxford University Press, 1973), 165–68.
23. Pierre Boulez, "The Ring," *Orientations* (Cambrdige, Mass.: Harvard University Press, 1986), 261. Originally published as "Le Temps re-cherché" in the 1976 Bayreuth Festival program book for *Das Rheingold,* 1–17, 76–80.
24. Pierre Boulez, "The Teacher's Task" in *Orientations* (Cambridge, Mass.: Harvard University Press, 1986), 119. Originally a lecture "Discipline et communication" given at Darmstadt in 1961.

CHAPTER 31

1. See Robert P. Morgan, "Secret Languages: The Roots of Musical Modernism," *Critical Inquiry,* x.3 (March 1984), 442–61.
2. Warsaw Autumn '84 program booklet, 132.
3. Paul Griffiths, *Musical Times,* June 1980, 394.
4. Notes to Deutsche Grammophon Record DGG SLPM 139 382.
5. Notes to Composer's Voice Record CV 7802.
6. L. Schwartz, "Elliott Carter and the Conflict of Chaos and Order," *Harvard Magazine,* Nov.–Dec. 1983, 60.
7. Paul Griffiths, *Modern Music* (1981), 248.
8. Oliver Knussen in notes to Arabesque Record Z6535-L
9. Luciano Berio, *Two Interviews* (1985), 62.
10. Notes to RCA ARL 1-1674.
11. Notes to Columbia Record M2-30576.
12. See David Gable, "Ramifying Connections: An Interview with Pierre Boulez," *Journal of Musicology,* iv.1 (Winter 1985–86), 105–13; 111.

CHAPTER 32

1. See G. S. Bourdain, "The Electronic World of Pierre Boulez," *Saturday Review* (February 1982), 43–45, and especially *Contemporary Music Review,* i.1 (1984) devoted to "Musical Thought at IRCAM," including: Tod Machover, "A view of music at IRCAM"; Dominique Jameux, "Boulez and the 'Machine'"; and Andrew Gerzso, "Reflections on *Répons.*"
2. David Gable, "Ramifying Connections: An Interview with Pierre Boulez," *Journal of Musicology,* iv.1 (Winter 1985–86), 106.
3. Luciano Berio, *Two Interviews,* trans. and ed. by David Osmond-Smith (New York: Marion Boyars, 1985), 34.
4. See "Composers' Forum is International Now" in *New York Times,* October 30, 1983.
5. Associated Press story of December 12, 1983.

6. Karlheinz Stockhausen, open letter "To the International Music Council," November 21, 1984.
7. Igor Stravinsky and Robert Craft, *Conversations* (Garden City, NY: Doubleday, 1959), 139.
8. See Imogene Horsley, "Has Musicology Destroyed the Historical Process?" in *Essays on Music for Charles Warren Fox* (Eastman School of Music Press, 1979), 126–131.

INDEX